The Major Poets

THE
MAJOR POETS:
English and American
second edition

Charles M. Coffin

Revised and edited by

Gerrit Hubbard Roelofs

Kenyon College

HB HARCOURT, BRACE & WORLD, INC.

New York / Chicago / San Francisco / Atlanta

COPYRIGHTS AND ACKNOWLEDGEMENTS

The author thanks the following publishers and copyright holders for their permission to use the selections reprinted in this book:

THE CLARENDON PRESS for Sonnets 1, 4, 14, 15, 20, 24, 31, 39, 41, 59, 71, 108 from "Astrophil and Stella"; "Leave me, ô love, which reachest but to dust," and "The Nightingale as soon as Aprill bringeth" from "Certaine Sonets"; "My true love hath my heart, and I have his" from "Arcadia," Book III; all from *The Poems of Sir Philip Sidney*, edited by W. A. Ringler, Jr., 1962. For "To the Reader," "To my Book," "To J. D. (Who shall doubt)," "On My First Son" from "Epigrammes"; "To Penshurst" from "The Forrest"; "Her Triumph," "To the immortall memorie, and friendship of that noble paire, Sir Lucius Cary, and Sir H. Morison" from "The Under-wood"; "Come, my Celia, let us prove," "Still to be neat, still to be drest," "Slow, slow, fresh fount," "The Hymne to Cynthia," "To the memory of my beloved, The Author Mr. William Shakespeare: And what he hath left us"; all from *Ben Johnson*, edited by C. H. Herford and P. and E. Simpson, 1947. For "Song [Goe and catche a falling starre]," "Song [Sweetest love, I do not goe]," "A Valediction: forbidding Mourning," "The Good-morrow," "The Sunne Rising," "The Canonization," "Loves Infiniteness," "A Nocturnall upon S. Lucies Day, being the shortest day" from "Songs and Sonnets"; "Satire III"; all from *The Elegies and the Songs and Sonnets of John Donne*, edited by H. Gardner, 1965. For "Thou hast made me, And shall thy work decay?," "I am a little world made cunningly," "At the round earths imagin'd corners, blow," "Death be not proud, though some have called thee," "What if this present were the worlds last night?," "Batter my heart, three-person'd God," "Since she whome I lovd hath payd her last debt" from "Holy Sonnets"; "Hymne to God my God, in my sicknesse"; all from *The Divine Poems of John Donne*, edited by H. Gardner, 1964. For "The Fifth Ode of Horace, Lib. I," "At a Solemn Musick," "L'Allegro," "Il Penseroso," "Arcades," "Lycidas," "On the Detraction Which Follow'd upon My Writing Certain Treatises," "On the Late Massacher in Piemont," "When I consider how my light is spent," "Methought I saw my late espousèd saint"; "The Invocation to Light," "The Garden," "Epithalamion" from "Paradise Lost"; all from *Milton's Poetical Works*, edited by H. Darbishire, 1952. For excerpts from "Absalom and Achitophel"; "Mac Flecknoe," "Epilogue from Tyrannick Love," "To the Memory of Mr. Oldham," "A Song for St. Cecilia's Day, 1687," "The Secular Masque" all from *The Poems of John Dryden*, edited by J. Kinsley, 1958. All reprinted by permission of the publishers.

J. M. DENT AND SONS, LIMITED for "The force that through the green fuse drives the flower," "Especially when the October wind," "In the beginning," "And death shall have no dominion," "When all my five and country senses see," "A Refusal to Mourn the Death, by Fire, of a Child in London," "Poem in October," "Do not go gentle into that good night," "In my craft or sullen art," "Fern Hill" from *Collected Poems* by Dylan Thomas. Reprinted by permission of the publishers and the Literary Executors of the Dylan Thomas Estate.

FABER AND FABER, LIMITED for Canadian rights to "Musée des Beaux Arts," "In Memory of W. B. Yeats," "The Unknown Citizen," "As I walked out one evening," "Lullaby," "On This Island" from *Collected Shorter Poems 1927–1957* by W. H. Auden. Reprinted by permission of Faber and Faber, Ltd. For "Matthew Arnold," "September 1, 1939" from *Collected Shorter Poems 1930–1944* by W. H. Auden. Reprinted by permission of Faber and Faber, Ltd.

FARRAR, STRAUS & GIROUX, INC. for "Skunk Hour," "Man and Wife," "To Speak of Woe That Is in Marriage" from *Life Studies* by Robert Lowell, copyright © 1958 by Robert Lowell. Reprinted by permission of Farrar, Straus & Giroux, Inc. For "Jonathan Edwards in Western Massachusetts," "Tenth Muse," "For the Union Dead" from *For the Union Dead* by Robert Lowell, copyright © 1960, 1962, 1964 by Robert Lowell. Reprinted by permission of Farrar, Straus & Giroux, Inc.

HARCOURT, BRACE & WORLD, INC. for "The Love Song of J. Alfred Prufrock," "La Figlia che Piange," "Gerontion," "Sweeney Among the Nightingales," "Journey of the Magi"; IV and V from "Five Finger Exercises"; all from *Collected Poems 1909–1962* by T. S. Eliot, copyright 1936 by Harcourt, Brace & World, Inc.; copyright © 1963, 1964 by T. S. Eliot. Reprinted by permission of Harcourt, Brace & World, Inc. For "The Dry Salvages" from

TO THE MEN OF KENYON COLLEGE

Contents

x

xvi

To the Reader

When *The Major Poets: English and American* first appeared in 1954, it differed markedly from other anthologies. The late editor, Charles Coffin, described his book as one that "represents poetry in English from Chaucer to the present with a generous selection from a limited number of our best poets." It was neither a sampler of familiar poems from the works of all the poets nor a series of subcollections arranged according to genres, themes, and verse forms. It was an anthology organized according to historical chronology, with the authors limited to those who are considered "major" poets and the selections designed, wherever possible within the limits of the book, to represent the different phases of each poet's career. Furthermore, it provided the student with a generous number of notes to enable him to master on his own these poems, their historical contexts, their traditions, and their particular allusions. The anthology was given a coherent structural purpose by a clearly defined principle of literary education: that the nature and value of poetry are "better learned at first from a concentration upon the work of a few authors, such as we have here, rather than from scattering our attention over many isolated texts."

In revising *The Major Poets*, I have kept the main features of the original conception of the book as well as Professor Coffin's canon of major poets. Two new poets have been added: Wallace Stevens and Robert Lowell. The experience of instructors who have used the first edition of this book, the response of their students, and my own experience have indicated that the representation of the modern period should be increased to give the book greater variety, better balance, and sharper historical pertinence. There are, therefore, thirty more poems for the period beginning with Emily Dickinson. The changes in the modern period have necessarily reduced the number of lines available for the earlier periods, but I have tried to balance out the legitimate demands of all just claimants for space according to a criterion that can conveniently be called "taste" as well as by practical experience of the classroom—my own and, above all, that of my colleagues at home and elsewhere. I have always tried to choose poems that "work" in the classroom, not simply poems that are "good." Wit, gaiety, and dramatic verve are virtues that work to special advantage in the classroom, and sometimes the "important" poem is a dud. For this reason too, I have increased the space given to Jonson, Marvell, and Dryden.

In general, the book reflects a preference for shorter rather than longer poems, partly because few modern poets write the long narrative and argumentative discourses common a hundred years ago and earlier, and partly because teaching long and complex poems, particularly those that require considerable historical explanation, presents more problems than can be easily solved in the time available in first- and second-year courses in literature. Moreover, with the restrictions upon space in a book of this sort, long poems invariably become fragments, and fragments inevitably produce either tedious explanations or absolute disregard. Ignorance of bits and pieces is a happier condition than boredom or frustration. Hence, wherever possible, I have printed only whole and complete poems. There are certain notable exceptions, however. The historical and esthetic importance of Milton, Dryden, Wordsworth, Byron, and Tennyson depends in large part upon poems that are obviously too long to be reprinted in full, but from which it is possible to choose passages that have independent status and structural and thematic unity.

One aim of this edition has been to give richer representation to a particular form—the sonnet—and to a particular theme—the art and craft of poetry and the responsibilities of the calling of the poet. Seven sonnets from Spenser's "Amoretti," a sequence entirely different in tone, form, and theme from other Elizabethan sequences, have been added, as well as a scattering of sonnets from other poets, and lyrics other than the sonnet that make use of the conceits, situations, and themes of the Petrarchan sonneteer. In choosing the sonnets, I have also tried to represent the narrative line and tonal quality of the whole of each sonnet sequence and thus to provide the instructor and student with adequate materials for comparison and contrast. (Similarly, Milton's "Arcades" has been introduced to give the reader another example of the masque-like "entertainment," so that Dryden's splendid "Secular Masque" would not stand in isolation.) The theme of the art and craft of poetry is a particularly effective device for giving unity to the study of poems from a variety of periods. What these poets considered to be their responsibilities as poets, what effect they hoped to have upon their readers, what they valued or rejected in each other, and what modes and occasions they used to express their convictions, attitudes, and feelings can give students powerful insights into the major work of the poets they read. The varieties of pastoral elegies and memorial verses printed here can also show how the great poets are able to work within the same general tradition while still shaping their expression of it in entirely different and individual styles. Poems like "The Invocation to Light" from Book III of *Paradise Lost*, Dryden's "To the Memory of Mr. Oldham," Arnold's "Memorial Verses," Dickinson's "This was a Poet—It is That (No. 448)," Yeats's "The Circus Animals' Desertion," Stevens' "Of Modern Poetry," Auden's "Matthew Arnold," and Thomas' "In my craft and sullen art" give varied representation of this theme. A poet is never more revealing than when he addresses himself to the passions, difficulties, doubts, and exaltations of his vocation.

For a number of poets, notably Sidney, Spenser, Jonson, Donne, Milton, and Dryden, standard modern texts have been substituted for those in the first edition of this book. If the student is curious about the language, spelling, and punctuation of the texts printed here, he can more easily discover the whole range of possible readings of the celebrated cruxes by referring to these basic and valuable editions than by referring to manuscripts and first editions, particularly since there is not room in this book to provide textual notes to explain them all. The texts of the modern poets under copyright follow the authors' text without alteration. In particular the text of the poems of Emily Dickinson follows the Johnson edition, which reproduces the poet's punctuation and sometimes whole lines and stanzas that differ from what was printed in the first edition of *The Major*

Poets. In Pope's "Rape of the Lock" and "Epistle II" the eighteenth-century style of capitalization has been retained for two reasons: First, the capitalization almost invariably falls on the stressed syllable, and the eye thus can more readily support the ear by seeing the position of the stress and of the caesural pause; second, the capitalization alerts the mind to the way Pope uses general and abstract terms as if they were concrete entities.

In making these changes, I have tried to encourage the student, as Professor Coffin did, to read these poems with the intonation and emphasis originally indicated by the poets, so that the sound and movement of the lines effectively support their meaning. Poetry must be read aloud, must be heard in performance as well as seen, and to be read well it should be read with some awareness of the linguistic and metrical contexts in which it was written. For example, modern poetry is less clearly and regularly cadenced than the earlier poetry, and if one tries to read the poetry of Pope as if it were Auden's, then he will misread both; for even at his most informal, Pope's brisk irony depends upon the reader's awareness of the subtleties of his strict iambic pentameter line, and Auden's upon the awareness of subtleties of a line that is just as strictly controlled but by means quite different from the judicious precision of the heroic couplet. These subtleties must be heard before they can be truly felt and understood. Students should be encouraged to hear—not just see—these poems, to measure, weigh, and balance on their tongues the intonation (that is, the stress, pitch, and juncture) of each line they read, and to listen with the mind's ear to the meaningfulness of the assonance and consonance of the poet's words.

The notes in this book fall into several groups: information about and meanings of difficult words (archaic, obsolete, rare, and obscure) not readily available in a standard student's dictionary like the Funk & Wagnalls *Standard College Dictionary;* meanings of words that can be found in the dictionary but that are used in a special way or could easily be misinterpreted or ignored; explanation of allusions to the Bible, the Book of Common Prayer, Homer, Hesiod, Sophocles, Ovid, Virgil, *The Bestiary*, Dante, classical and folk myths, and other writings that have public objectivity as the commonplaces of literary education; identification of allusions to historical events and to the careers and achievements of famous and remarkable persons (but usually not to the private acquaintances of the poets); inferences to be drawn from certain allusions, indicating how they function in the poem; references to other poems for comparison or corroboration; and, occasionally, commentary in the light of literary tradition and history. In each instance I have endeavored to make the poem immediately and quickly available to the student, intelligible and meaningful in a literary fashion. Since few readers will begin with Chaucer and work their way steadily through the book to Robert Lowell, some information is repeated in the footnotes; the student who has been assigned Keats's "On Sitting Down to Read *King Lear* Again," for example, will not necessarily have read Donne's "Canonization." I have also glossed words and allusions that experienced readers of poetry would know without being told, but I have learned from editing this book that we all tend to think we know more than we actually do.

No poems, including those of our own generation, can be read with full appreciation by a mind and sensibility innocent of a considerable amount of general information and experience, both physical and intellectual. The commonplaces of one generation are the archeological treasures of the next. Allusions made in 1939 to the Second World War today produce only vague recollections at second hand. A city boy who has never climbed a tree can quite possibly have real difficulty with Frost's "Birches." Proper footnoting should be able to alert the mind and imagination to the presence of the extraordinary in the ordinary, but there is a limit to what can be explained. I cannot tell the city boy to go climb a tree and be a swinger of birches, but I can suggest to all readers that the Epistle and Gospel for the Feast of the Epiphany are relevant to Eliot's "Journey of the Magi" and that this information allows them to see more clearly how the poem "works." I have endeavored to provide the reader with references to books, information, and explanations wherever in my experience in teaching these poems I have found that a conscientious and careful reader has difficulties in understanding meaning, usage, situation, tradition, and allusion.

It is not to be feared that I have left nothing for the student to do or the instructor to say. There is a great deal more to reading poetry than hunting through a dictionary or a concordance to the Bible, and there is a great deal more to teaching than finding out what the student does not know and giving him the true word. Digital dexterity with an index is no substitute for the creative power of the imagination, and drudgery often blasts the first bloom of the young imagination. Teacher and student must together create an excited and imaginative awareness of the meaning of the poem, an awareness that must be experienced as well as understood. Having the necessary information at hand, I have found, can make this experience much more happy and rewarding.

Some notes contain commentary as well as information, but no readings should be regarded as all-inclusive and final. No one editor can exhaust the meaning of a poem, for the poem can make more meanings and responses than any one man can capture; nor can any one set of notes ever say more than a fraction of what there is to say. Moreover, even the rawest bit of information (for example, couch grass is quack grass) is "interpretive" just by virtue of being placed in apposition with the poem. The critic may be mistaken and arbitrary, but even if he is right, he cannot say everything. I have taken these risks in the hope that what I have to say will help the student to be more at ease with the poem and to seek with greater confidence the reality that the poem embodies. The student, however, must see for himself. I hope that my notes will help him see with clearer eyes, even if I might have intruded occasionally upon his prerogatives.

I have tried to avoid giving the reader trivial and irrelevant bits of information about biography, sources, or dates, but rather to concentrate upon the specific linguistic, literary, and historical problems of each poem. What should or should not be glossed is sometimes a matter of personal choice. One man's note is another man's nit, but I would rather be accused of dictating a meaning than of teasing a reader with odds and ends. With the ever increasing ratio of students to teachers, the instructor has to rely more and more upon independent study by his students. Furthermore, he is obliged to do so, even if he has a small class, because there is always more to read and discuss than anyone can do properly in the hours assigned for class discussion. Obviously the student has to do a great deal of hard reading on his own, without the help of the instructor. It is here that an editor should lend a hand.

The reader will discover that I have provided him with many references to the Bible, some of which are quoted (and unless otherwise stated, I refer to the Authorized Version) so that the specific words of the Bible that the poet knew can be seen and heard against the text of the poem. The English Bible and liturgical expression in response to the Biblical narratives are the commonplaces of human experience to which poets, orthodox and unorthodox alike, seemingly never weary of alluding. These allusions—to which the modern audience is generally not very alert—function directly or ironically to particularize and to give universal significance to the specific vision expressed in the poem; they should not be interpreted as proving or disproving the "truth" of the Bible or dramatizing the subtleties of the writer's personal belief or nonbelief.

Allusions present other problems. In many anthologies they are treated simply as sources, and identifying notes seem to announce that the poet ran out of ideas and images and silently stole "what 'e thought 'e might require," as Kipling says he and Homer have done. But allusions almost invariably frame and give added dimension to the poet's images. Brilliant and all-inclusive allusions, such as those in Arnold's "Dover Beach," have an almost unlimited power to invest the particular time and situation of the poem with a relevancy and poignancy that is universal and fabulous. The attention given to allusions here is intended to suggest that they are not mere sources but wellsprings of life and power; and the inferences some-times drawn from them are made not to show that these are the only ones possible, but to suggest what is available if one allows his imagination, like the sun, to warm and bring to life and bloom the seed that the poet has planted in his poem. Allusions function organically within the body of the poem, and the excitement of seeing them unfold is one of the great pleasures of reading poetry.

To read a poem is, or can be, more than the gratification of our natural hunger for pleasure in the exercise of our feelings. It is an act through which we focus all our capacities to see with passionate intensity what is neither our own experience nor really the poet's, but a realm of experience that only the poem embodies and that can never be ours until we have been possessed by the poem. If we read a poem only to watch our feelings at play, only to indulge ourselves, then we are reading not the poem but our ordinary selves, and since our feelings are never constant, it is quite possible to lose ourselves in a phantasmagoria of erratic feelings. Unless we ourselves are a true poem, as Milton would say, the value of reading ourselves is usually inferior to that of reading the poem. Too few of us are true poems. But the written poem is always "there," constant in form and attitude, resonant, secure, complete, always holding up for us a vision that stretches as far as the eye of the imagination can see, inexhaustible in its capacity to inspirit us if only we will listen.

The civilizing power of great poetry is that it always enables us to see, and if we see with passionate intensity, we can discover our true identity in relation to the poem, know what it is we truly feel. Because we see and feel with knowledge, we can act with purpose and hope. If we read a poem with objective intensity, we can escape from our egocentric concern for what we alone feel, from our sense of security in our supposed individualism, and enter into the fellowship of the manhood of all ages. Otherwise, we are the prisoners of our own concerns, preoccupied with our sensibilities, and the victim of our ignorance of ourselves, of our past, present, and future.

In writing these notes I have asked myself and the readers of this book to look steadily at each poem, at the traditions in which the poem is established, at its form, design, and metaphoric structure. In "Lycidas," for example, the notes direct the reader's attention to the several pastoral traditions that Milton transforms into one coherent utterance and to the tone and rhythms of the different styles; to the accurate description of the savage violation of the order of nature in the lines "Or frost to flowers . . . When first the White-thorn blows"; to the speaker's awareness of the terrible discrepancy between the "false surmise" of the wishful symbolism of the "flowrets of a thousand hues" and the fearful truth, which no man wishes to face, of the "whelming tide," a truth that requires heroic faith if a man is ever to accept honestly his fate and destiny. Whatever else the poem means, it seems to me that the critic must incorporate into his reading these and other indestructible landmarks of the poem's landscape. To ignore them is to lose one's way, and lost, one has little chance to accompany the pastoral speaker to the "fresh woods, and pastures new."

In annotating these poems I have incurred many debts of gratitude, more than I can properly acknowledge. My first debt is to the late Professor Charles Coffin, whom I have known only through his book and for whose concept of what it ought to be and the basic choice of texts I have nothing but admiration. Since this book is a classroom text and not a variorum edition, I have not been able to acknowledge at every point the help I have received from the many men and women who have also studied these poems. As Professor Coffin remarked, no one annotates even one poem, let alone this many, independently. I am happy to acknowledge my debt of gratitude to all scholars and lovers of poetry, particularly my own teachers, who have contributed to my awareness and understanding of these poems and the historical contexts in which they were written. Wherever possible I have tried to acknowledge my direct use of their specific learning, and in stating my gratitude to them I also acknowledge my debt to all others who have indirectly helped me.

I have relied constantly upon the *Oxford English Dictionary*, the *American Century Dictionary*, the Funk & Wagnalls *Dictionary of Folk Lore*, the *Oxford Classical Dictionary*, Young's *Analytical Concordance to the Bible*, and many other reference books, mythologies, and concordances. No anthology of this sort could be possible without these books, and I am very grateful to their compilers.

My colleagues at Kenyon College have loyally supported and encouraged me and, what is more, patiently endured my interruptions of their study, withstood my questions, and tolerated my preoccupation with my own concerns. Their good humor, honest answers, and clear delight in my excitement in "discovering" something I should have known have cheered me immensely. Robert Daniel, Patrick Cruttwell, Galbraith Crump, Alan Donovan, Anthony Bing, Philip Church, Michael Mott, and William Heath in the English Department have been my friends and alert critics in this enterprise. I am grateful also to Joseph and Patricia Slate, who have generously given me advice about art and religious symbolism. My debt to William McCulloh is considerable and very specific: He has alerted me to and searched out for me allusions to classical literature and mythology and has translated passages, corrected my interpretations, and encouraged me always to "press the text." His help to me has been indispensable. In addition the presence and kindness of John Crowe Ransom have enabled me to work and teach in a literary atmosphere that has always been very exciting and rewarding. Finally, no one who has studied or taught at Kenyon since the Second World War will soon forget the devotion, enterprise, and intensity of concern that the late Denham Sutcliffe brought to the teaching of poetry and the literary concerns of the College. These and many others have assisted me, corrected my errors, and shown me what I had overlooked. I am, however, alone responsible for all errors of fact, mistakes of judgment, and sins of omission and commission.

My wife Janet has been a "help meet for" me. She has clarified my style, corrected proof, compiled the index, and saved me from many embarrassments.

It was to the students of Kenyon College that Professor Coffin dedicated his book. It is to them also that I dedicate this Second Edition. They have always taught me at least as much as I have taught them. In particular, Harley Henry, James and Thomas Carr, and Edward Hallowell have given me specific assistance in the preparation of this edition. The pleasure of reading poetry with students will always remain one of the best rewards that a man may possess.

G. H. R.

NOTE ON READING CHAUCER'S ENGLISH:

Chaucer's language (Middle English, South East Midlands, the dialect of educated Londoners in the last half of the fourteenth century), like our own, is not fixed and uniform. For example, while most of the regular inflectional endings of Old English (e.g., the *-es* of the genitive) had been lost by 1385, Chaucer uses some of them whenever his line require it. Moreover, the intonation of his words is not always consistent. Hence it is not possible to give a succinct, unqualified description of his language along with a few uniformly applicable rules that would quickly enable the student to read his poetry aloud easily and accurately (and his poetry should be read aloud if its full force, sweetness, humor, and humanity are to be experienced). The following generalizations are offered as preliminary aids to a first reading. Flexibly applied, they are satisfactory.

1. Pronounce all the syllables in a word, using the meter as a guide to when and where elisions occur. Note that the final *-e*, silent in Modern English, is regularly pronounced except when it is followed by a word beginning with a vowel or silent *h* when it is regularly elided. Note also that the suffix *-ion* is regularly disyllabic.

2. Pronounce the vowels according to their Continental value, e.g., that of modern French, German, and Italian. Long vowels are often (but not always) indicated by doubling. The long vowels *e* and *i* are either *close* (i.e., pronounced with a partial closing of the lips or a contraction of the oral cavity) or *open* (i.e., pronounced with the mouth and oral cavity open). After the "great vowel shift" in the late fifteenth century, these vowels were raised to become diphthongs: e.g., Chaucer's *I* (first person pronoun), pronounced like the *i* in *machine,* is now pronounced like the *i* in *ice*.

CHAUCER'S SPELLING	MIDDLE ENGLISH EXAMPLE	SOUND	PRONOUNCE LIKE
a, aa	b*a*thed	ā	*a* in *father*
a	wh*a*n, wh*a*t	ă	*a* in German *Mann*, and *what*
e, ee	sw*ee*te	ē (close)	ē in *they*, or *a* in *mate*
e, ee	h*ee*th	ē (open)	e in *where*
e	t*e*ndre	ĕ	*e* in *let*
e	soot*e*	ə	*a* in *quota*
i, y	r*y*de	ī	*i* in *machine*
i, y	h*i*s	ĭ	*i* in *sit*
o, oo	r*oo*te	ō (close)	*o* in *vote*
o, oo	g*oo*n	ō (open)	*oa* in *broad*
o	*o*n	ŏ	*o* in *hot*
ou, ow, ogh	h*ou*s, f*ow*eles	ū	*oo* in *toot*
u, o	y*o*nge	ŭ	*u* in *full*
u, eu, ew	vert*u*	iū	*u* in *mute*
au, aw	str*au*nge	au	*ou* in *mouse*

3. Pronounce *all* consonants, except the *h* in French words like *honour* and *g* in French *gn* (e.g., *resigne*), using Modern English as a guide. Note that some consonants that are silent in Modern English are pronounced: e.g., *k* and *g* in *knyght, knowe, gnawe;* the *gh* (pronounced like the spirant *ch* in the German *ich* or *Bach*) in *droghte*. Pronounce *ch* as in *chirp; ng* (when stressed, e.g., *singen*) as in *finger*, but not in the unstressed *-ing*. Finally, pronounce *l* before *f, k, m:* e.g., *folk*. As best you can, roll or trill the *r*.

4. Chaucer's syntax is similar to that of Modern English; but he sometimes shifts construction, changes tense abruptly, and neglects to provide pronouns with antecedents or to have subjects and predicates agree.

5. Chaucer's meter is for the most part regular, but he allows for the normal variations from the iambic pattern (his usual measure) for rhetorical and dramatic emphasis (e.g., inversion of the initial foot, substitution of a trochee for an iamb, introduction of an extra unstressed syllable in any foot, elimination of the first unstressed syllable of a line as in *Whán|that Á|prill wíth|his shoú|res sootë*). Downright irregularities, however, are exceptional if all syllables are pronounced and if the regular elision (of final, lightly stressed *-e* with the initial

GEOFFREY CHAUCER
c. 1340–1400

Gentilesse

MORAL BALADE OF CHAUCIER

The firste stok, fader of gentilesse—
'What man that claymeth gentil for to be
Must folowe his trace, and alle his wittes dresse
Vertu to sewe, and vyces for to flee.
For unto vertu longeth dignitee,   5
And noght the revers, saufly dar I deme
Al were he mytre, croune, or diademe.

This firste stok was ful of rightwisnesse,
Trewe of his word, sobre, pitous, and free,
Clene of his gost, and loved besinesse,   10
Ayeinst the vyce of slouthe, in honestee;
And, but his heir love vertu, as dide he,
He is noght gentil, thogh he riche seme,
Al were he mytre, croune, or diademe.

Vyce may wel be heir to old richesse;   15
But ther may no man, as men may wel see,
Bequethe his heir his vertuous noblesse,
(That is appropred unto no degree,
But to the firste fader in magestee,
That maketh hem his heyres that him queme),   20
Al were he mytre, croune, or diademe.

GENTILESSE. 1 *stok:* origin. *fader of gentilesse:* I.e., Christ is the only source and true model of this virtue of virtues, the preeminent Chaucerian virtue and the *sine qua non* for all other virtues. See *The Wife of Bath's Tale*, ll. 1109–64. 3 *trace:* course, footsteps. 3–4 *alle . . . sewe:* prepare all his faculties to follow virtue. 5 *longeth:* belongs. 6 *saufly . . . deme:* I dare safely suppose. 7 *Al . . . diademe:* although he wear miter, crown, or diadem. 8 *rightwisnesse:* righteousness. 9 *pitous:* merciful. 10 *Clene . . . besinesse:* pure of spirit, and loved diligence. 11 *Ayeinst:* against. *slouthe:* sloth. 12 *his heir:* i.e., each and every man. 15 *Vyce . . . richesse:* To be sure, vice may inherit ancient wealth. 18 *appropred unto:* made the peculiar property of. *degree:* rank. 20 *queme:* please.

---

vowel or silent *h-* of the following word) is respected. If in doubt, hammer out a five-stress line and then introduce variations according to dramatic intonation, shift in the position of the caesural pause, and the demands of run-on lines. Remember that the stress pattern of many of Chaucer's words is not always that of Modern English: e.g., *colóur, coráge, cotáge, phisýk, plesaúnce, solémpnely,* and *suffisaúnce* (not as in cólor, coúrage, cóttage, phýsic, pléasure, sólemnly, suffíciency).

2

from *The General Prologue*

Whan that Aprill with his shoures soote
The droghte of March hath perced to the roote
And bathed every veyne in swich licour
Of which vertu engendred is the flour,
Whan Zephirus eek with his sweete breeth   5
Inspired hath in every holt and heeth
The tendre croppes, and the yonge sonne
Hath in the Ram his halve cours y-ronne,
And smale foweles maken melodye
That slepen al the nyght with open eye,   10
So priketh hem Nature in hir corages,
Than longen folk to goon on pilgrymages,
And palmeres for to seken straunge strondes,
To ferne halwes kouthe in sondry londes.
And specially, from every shires ende   15
Of Engelond, to Caunterbury they wende,
The holy, blisful martir for to seke

THE CANTERBURY TALES: THE GENERAL PROLOGUE.   The first eighteen lines of
the Prologue form a standard trope, a kind of *chronographia* that describes the
time appropriate for the action of the poem, that is, spring, the analogue of the
original creation of the world and man, the beginning of the solar year, the
time shortly after Lady Day (March 25) when men celebrate the annunciation
of the promised redemption.   The pilgrimage is a celebration of the renewal of
life, of the body and of the spirit.   The theme of the whole poem—the frame
tale and the tales—is the simultaneousness of creation and redemption.
   The opening scene of the Prologue is the Tabard Inn at Southwark, opposite
London on the south bank of the Thames, the initial point of the sixty-mile
journey to the shrine of St. Thomas Becket at Canterbury.   Here the pilgrims
agree to entertain themselves on the road under the direction of the Host,
Harry Bailly, by telling tales in competition with each other.   They are each to
tell two tales *to Caunterburyward* and two on the return journey.   The pilgrim
who *bereth hym best of alle*, telling tales of *best sentence* [wisdom] *and moost
solaas* [delight] will be rewarded with a supper at general expense when all
return to the Tabard.   The Host agrees to serve as judge and critic, and the
pilgrims agree to be under his rule, telling their tales when he requires them to
do so.
   1 *Whan that:* when.   *soote:* sweet.   3 *veyne:* vein, sap-vessel.   *swich licour:*
such liquid.   4 *Of which vertu:* by power of which.   5 *Zephirus:* the west wind,
traditionally associated with spring.   See the figure on far right in Botticelli's
Primavera.   *eek:* also.   6 *holt:* wood.   *heeth:* heath.   7 *croppes:* shoots.
7–8 *yonge . . . y-ronne:* the young sun of spring has run its second half-course
through the zodiacal sign of the Ram (April 11).   9 *foweles:* birds.   11 *So
. . . corages:* Nature [goddess and creatrix] so stirs them in their hearts.
12 *Than longen:* then long.   *goon:* go.   13 *palmeres:* pilgrims.   *seken:* seek.
strondes: shores.   14 *ferne halwes kouthe:* distant shrines known.   17 *martir:*
i.e., Thomas Becket, Archbishop of Canterbury, martyred 1170.

That hem hath holpen whan that they were seeke.
   Bifel that in that seson on a day
In Southwerk at the Tabard, as I lay   20
Redy to wenden on my pilgrymage
To Caunterbury with full devout corage,
At nyght was come into that hostelrye
Wel nyne-and-twenty in a compaignye
Of sondry folk by aventure y-falle   25
In felaweshipe, and pilgrims were they alle
That toward Caunterbury wolden ryde.
The chambres and the stables weren wyde,
And wel we weren esed atte beste.
And shortly, whan the sonne was to reste,   30
So hadde I spoken with hem everichon
That I was of hir felawshipe anon;
And made forward erly for to ryse
To take oure wey ther-as I yow devyse.

The Portrait of the Prioresse

   Ther was also a nonne, a PRIORESSE,
That of hir smylyng was ful symple and coy.
Hir gretteste ooth was but "By Seint Loy!"
And she was cleped Madame Eglentyne.
   Ful wel she soong the servyce dyvyne,   5
Entuned in hir nose ful semely,
And Frenssh she spak ful faire and fetisly

---

18 *holpen:* helped.   *seeke:* sick.   19 *Bifel:* it befell.   25 *by aventure y-falle:*
fallen by chance.   27 *wolden:* intended to.   28 *wyde:* spacious.   29 *esed atte
beste:* entertained in the best way.   31 *everichon:* every one.   32 *hir:* their.
33 *made forward:* [we] agreed.   34 *devyse:* tell.

THE PORTRAIT OF THE PRIORESSE. In the Prologue, Chaucer presents the
pilgrims both as fourteenth-century English men and women and also as the
fully human, wholly appropriate, and varied tellers of the best tales Chaucer
has heard and read.   Almost every portrait is ironic in some way or other.
The pilgrims' human follies and vanities, as well as their native virtues and
superlative capacity to know how to do excellently the duties of their offices,
give added depth and dramatic power to their tales.   Thus each tale is told by
just the right teller at just the right moment and in a language and a style wholly
appropriate to the teller and to the dramatic situation.   Since the pilgrims are
in competition with each other, the tales are often told at the expense of a rival
pilgrim and his tale.
   2 *symple and coy:* naive and quiet.   3 *ooth:* oath.   *Seint Loy:* a courtly
seventh-century French goldsmith, later a bishop, who was supposedly averse
to swearing.   4 *cleped:* called.   *Eglentyne:* sweetbriar, a name commonly
given to heroines of sentimental romances.   6 *entuned:* intoned.   *semely:*
properly, i.e., in the latest fashion.   7 *fetisly:* elegantly.

After the scole of Stratford atte Bowe,
For Frenssh of Parys was to hire unknowe.
   At mete wel y-taught was she with alle;   10
She leet no morsel from hir lippes falle,
Ne wette hir fyngres in hir sauce depe;
Wel koude she carie a morsel, and wel kepe
That no drope ne fille upon hir brest.
In curteisie was set ful muchel hir lest.   15
Hir over lippe wyped she so clene
That in hir coppe ther was no ferthyng sene
Of grece whan she dronken hadde hir draughte
Ful semely after hir mete she raughte,
And sikerly she was of greet desport,   20
And ful plesaunt and amyable of port,
And peyned hire to countrefete cheere
Of court, and to been estatlich of manere,
And to been holden digne of reverence.
   But for to speken of hir conscience,   25
She was so charitable and so pitous,
She wolde wepe if that she sawe a mous
Caught in a trappe, if it were deed or bledde.
Of smale houndes hadde she that she fedde
With rosted flessh, or mylk and wastel breed;   30
But soore wepte she if oon of hem were deed,
Or if men smoot it with a yerde smerte.
And al was conscience and tendre herte.
   Ful semely hir wympel pynched was,
Hir nose tretys, hir eyen greye as glas,   35
Hir mouth ful smal, and there-to softe and reed,
But sikerly she hadde a fair forheed;
It was almoost a spanne brood, I trowe,
For hardily she was nat undergrowe.
Ful fetys was hir cloke, as I was war;   40
Of smal coral aboute hir arm she bar

---

8 *Stratford atte Bowe:* Stratford at the Bow, about two miles outside London where presumably there was a kind of finishing school for girls; i.e., she speaks French with a schoolgirl accent. 9 *unknowe:* unknown. 10 *mete:* food. 11 *leet:* allowed. 13 *Wel koude she:* she well knew how to. *kepe:* take care. 14 *fille :* fell. 15 *muchel:* much. *lest :* concern. 17 *ferthyng :* particle. 19 *raughte:* reached. 20 *sikerly:* certainly. *desport:* fun. 21 *port:* deportment. 22 *peyned . . . cheere:* strove to imitate the appearance. 23 *estatlich:* stately. 24 *holden digne :* considered worthy. 26 *pitous :* sympathetic. 30 *wastel:* expensive, fine white bread. 32 *men:* someone. *yerde:* stick. *smerte:* severely. 34 *semely:* gracefully. *wympel:* linen headdress. *pynched:* pleated. 35 *tretys:* shapely, well proportioned. *eyen:* eyes. *greye:* blue. 38 *spanne brood:* handspan wide, i.e., beautiful. *trowe:* believe. 39 *hardily:* undeniably. 40 *fetys:* graceful. *war:* aware. 41 *bar:* carried.

A peyre of bedes, gauded al with grene,
And ther-on heng a brooch of gold ful shene,
On which ther was first writen a crowned A,
And after *Amor vincit omnia.*   45

The Nun's Priest's Tale

A poure widwe, somdel stape in age,
Was whilom dwellyng in a narwe cotage
Biside a grove, stondyng in a dale.
This widwe of which I telle yow my tale,
Syn thilke day that she was last a wyf,   5
In pacience ladde a ful symple lyf,
For litel was hir catel and hir rente.
By housbondrye of swich as God hir sente
She foond hirself and eek hir doghtren two.
Thre large sowes hadde she and namo,   10
Thre kyn, and eek a sheep that highte Malle.
Ful sooty was hir bour and eek hir halle,
In which she eet ful many a sklendre meel.
Of poynaunt sauce hir neded never a deel.

---

42 *A . . . grene:* a set of (rosary) beads with every gaud (large bead among smaller beads) colored green.   43 *shene:* bright.   45 *Amor . . . omnia:* Love conquers all.

THE NUN'S PRIEST'S TALE. The Nun's Priest is, presumably, the prioress' chaplain, or administrative assistant, or simply her appropriate ecclesiastical bodyguard, for she really was not supposed to take part in a public pilgrimage. When the Nun's Priest is asked to tell his tale, the Monk has just been stopped by the Knight from telling a seemingly endless series of dull tragedies about the "sudden fall" of great men from high estate.   He says that it is distressing to hear of such accidents, but that the contrary—the rise from fallen and poor estate to riches and high estate—brings *joye and greet solas.* When the Host agrees, saying that the Monk's *talkyng is not worth a boterflye,* the haughty Monk falls into anger and refuses to continue. The Nun's Priest is then asked to tell his tale. Unlike most of the other tellers, the Priest is not described in "The General Prologue," so we know nothing of him. His tale is thus accompanied by no personal bias, at least directly. Since Madame Eglentyne, his "superior," is seemingly addicted to the worldly ways of sentimental and courtly romance, however, and since earlier Chaucer's own parody of a romance, "Sir Thopas," had also been stopped by the Host for being dull and worthless, we can see in "The Tale of Chauntecleer and Pertelote" a satire on the style and argument of standard tragedies and romances and their silly readers. "The Nun's Priest's Tale" is simultaneously a mock tragedy and a mock heroic and courtly romance, as well as a beast-fable.

1 *widwe:* widow. *somdel stape:* somewhat advanced. 2 *whilom:* once. *narwe:* small. 5 *Syn thilke:* since that same. 6 *ladde:* led. 7 *catel:* goods, property. *rente:* income. 8 *swich:* such. 9 *foond:* supported. *doghtren:* daughters. 10 *namo:* no more. 11 *kyn:* cows. *highte:* was called. 12 *bour:* bedroom. 13 *sklendre:* slender. 14 *poynaunt:* pungent. *hir neded:* she needed. *deel:* bit.

6

No deyntee morsel passed thurgh hir throte;   15
Hir diete was acordant to hir cote.
Repleccioun ne made hir never syk;
Attempree diete was al hir phisyk,
And excercise, and hertes suffisaunce.
The goute lette hir nothyng for to daunce,   20
N'apoplexie shente nat hir heed.
No wyn ne drank she, neither whit ne reed.
Hir bord was served moost with whit and blak,
Milk and broun breed, in which she foond no lak,
Seynd bacoun, and som tyme an ey or tweye,   25
For she was, as it were, a maner deye.
   A yeerd she hadde, enclosed al aboute
With stikkes, and a drye dych withoute,
In which she hadde a cok hight Chauntecleer.
In al the land of crowyng nas his peer.   30
His voys was murier than the murie orgon
On massedayes that in the chirche gon.
Wel sikerer was his crowyng in his logge
Than is a clokke or an abbey orlogge.
By nature he knew ech ascensioun   35
Of the equinoxial in thilke toun,
For whan degrees fiftene were ascended,
Thanne crew he that it myghte nat ben amended.
His comb was redder than the fyn coral
And batailled as it were a castel wal.   40
His byle was blak, and as the jeet it shoon.
Lyk asure were his legges and his toon,
Hise nayles whitter than the lylye flour,
And lyk the burned gold was his colour.
This gentil cok hadde in his governaunce   45
Sevene hennes for to doon al his plesaunce,

---

16 *cote:* means. 17 *Repleccioun:* over-eating. 18 *Attempree:* temperate.
19 *suffisaunce:* sufficiency. 20 *lette:* hindered. *nothyng:* in no way.
21 *N'apoplexie . . . heed:* Nor did apoplexy trouble her head. 22 *whit:* white.
reed: red. 23 *bord:* table. 25 *Seynd:* broiled. *ey or tweye:* egg or two.
26 *maner deye:* sort of dairy-woman. 28 *dych:* ditch. 30 *nas:* [there] was
not. 31 *murier:* merrier. 32 *gon:* (pl.) go, i.e., plays; *orgon* (l. 31) is often
plural. 33 *Wel sikerer:* much more accurate. *logge:* lodge, where *crowyng*
may have a double meaning. 34 *orlogge:* clock. 35–36 *ascensioun . . .
equinoxial:* In the old astronomy, the heavens were thought to make a
complete revolution around the equator—through a counter-clockwise motion
called "ascension"—every twenty-four hours. When fifteen degrees were
"ascended," an hour had passed. 36 *in thilke toun:* Since time in this sense
varies with the geographical location of the observer, his time-keeping is
precisely accurate with respect to this farmstead (*toun*). 38 *that . . . amended:*
that the accuracy of his crowing couldn't be improved upon. 40 *batailled
as:* battlemented as if. 41 *byle:* bill. *jeet:* jet. 42 *toon:* toes. 44 *burned:*
burnished. 46 *doon:* do.

Whiche were his sustres and his paramours,
And wonder lyk to hym as of colours,
Of whiche the faireste hewed on hir throte
Was cleped faire damoysele Pertelote.   50
Curteys she was, discreet, and debonaire,
And compaignable, and bar hirself so faire
Syn thilke day that she was seven nyght oold
That, trewely, she hath the herte in hoold
Of Chauntecleer, loken in every lith.   55
He loved hir so that wel was hym therwith.
But swich a joye was it to here hem synge,
Whan that the brighte sonne gan to sprynge,
In swete acord "My leef is faren in londe."
For thilke tyme, as I have understonde,   60
Beestes and briddes koude speke and synge.
    And so bifel that in a dawenynge,
As Chauntecleer among his wyves alle
Sat on his perche, that was in the halle,
And next hym sat this faire Pertelote,   65
This Chauntecleer gan gronen in his throte
As man that in his dreem is drecched soore.
    And whan that Pertelote thus herde hym rore,
She was agast and seyde, "Herte deere,
What eyleth yow to grone in this manere?   70
Ye ben a verray sleper. Fy, for shame!"
    And he answerde and seyde thus: "Madame,
I pray yow that ye take it nat agrief.
By God, me mette I was in swich meschief
Right now, that yet myn herte is soore afright.   75
Now God," quod he, "my swevene recche aright,
And keep my body out of foul prisoun!
Me mette how that I romed up and doun
Withinne our yeerd, where as I saugh a beest,
Was lyk an hound and wolde han maad areest   80
Upon my body and wolde han had me deed.
His colour was bitwixe yelow and reed,
And tipped was his tayl and bothe his erys
With blak, unlik the remenaunt of his herys,

47 *sustres:* sisters. 48 *wonder:* wonderfully. 50 *cleped:* called. 52 *bar:* carried. 55 *loken:* locked. *lith:* limb. 56 *wel . . . therwith:* He was well contented. 57 *hem:* them. 58 *sprynge:* rise. 59 *My . . . londe:* My sweetheart has gone to the country. 61 *briddes:* birds. 62 *in a dawenynge:* early one morning. 67 *drecched:* tormented. 71 *verray:* sound. 73 *agrief:* ill. 74 *me mette:* I dreamed. 76 *quod:* said. *my . . . aright:* May God make my dream turn out favorably. 79 *saugh:* saw. 80 *han maad areest:* have seized. 81 *han . . . deed:* have killed me. 83 *erys:* ears. 84 *remenaunt:* rest. *herys:* hair.

His snowte smal, with glowyng eyen tweye. 85
Yet of his look for fere almoost I deye.
This caused me my gronyng, doutelees."
   "Avoy!" quod she. "Fy on yow, hertelees!
Allas," quod she, "for, by that God above,
Now han ye lost myn herte and al my love. 90
I kan nat love a coward, by my feith!
For, certes, what so any womman seith,
We alle desiren, if it myghte be,
To han housbondes hardy, wise, and fre,
And secree, and no nygard, ne no fool, 95
Ne hym that is agast of every tool,
Ne noon avauntour, by that God above.
How dorste ye seyn, for shame, unto youre love
That any thyng myghte make yow aferd?
Have ye no mannes herte, and han a berd? 100
   "Allas, and konne ye ben agast of swevenys.
Nothyng, God woot, but vanytee in swevene is.
Swevenes engendren of replexions,
And ofte of fume and of complexions,
Whan humours ben to habundant in a wight. 105
   "Certes, this dreem which ye han met to-nyght
Cometh of the grete superfluytee
Of youre rede colera, pardee,
Which causeth folk to dreden in hir dremes
Of arwes, and of fyr with rede lemes, 110
Of rede bestes that they wol hem byte,
Of contek, and of whelpes grete and lyte;
Right as the humour of malencolie
Causeth ful many a man in sleep to crie
For fere of blake beres or boles blake, 115
Or elles blake develes, wol hem take.
Of othere humours koude I telle also
That werken many a man in sleep ful wo,
But I wol passe as lightly as I kan.

---

88 *Avoy:* shame. 92 *certes:* certainly. *what so:* whatever. 94 *fre:* generous.
95 *secree:* discreet. 96 *tool:* weapon. 97 *avauntour:* boaster. 98 *dorste:*
dared. 101 *ben . . . swevenys:* be afraid of dreams. 102 *woot:* knows.
103 *engendren of replexions:* are brought on by repletion, i.e., over-eating.
104 *fume:* vapor. *complexions:* temperaments. 105 *humours . . . wight:*
humors are too abundant in a person. A superabundance of any one of the
four humors—yellow bile, black bile, phlegm, or blood—was thought to affect
temperament, making one choleric, melancholy, phlegmatic, or sanguine.
106 *han met to-nyght:* have dreamed this night. 108 *rede colera:* red
choler. *pardee :* certainly. 109 *to dreden :* be frightened. *hir :* their.
110 *arwes :* arrows. *lemes:* flames. 112 *contek:* strife. 113 *Right :* just.
115 *beres:* bears. *boles:* bulls. 116 *hem:* them. 118 *werken:* make. *ful
wo:* woeful.

Lo Catoun, which that was so wys a man,   120
Seyde he nat thus: 'Ne do no fors of dremes'?
   "Now sire," quod she, "whan we fle fro the bemes,
For Goddes love, as taak som laxatif.
Up peril of my soule and of my lif,
I conseille yow the beste, I wol nat lye,   125
That bothe of colere and of malencolye
Ye purge yow. And, for ye shal nat tarye,
Thogh in this toun is noon apothecarye,
I shal myself to herbes techen yow
That shul ben for youre heele and for your prow.   130
And in oure yerd tho herbes shal I fynde
The whiche han of hir propretee by kynde
To purge yow bynethe and eek above.
Foryet nat this, for Goddes owene love:
Ye ben ful colerik of complexioun.   135
Ware the sonne in his ascensioun
Ne fynde yow nat repleet of humours hote,
And, if it do, I dar wel leye a grote
That ye shul have a fevere terciane
Or an agu that may be youre bane.   140
A day or two ye shul have digestyves
Of wormes er ye take your laxatyves
Of lauriol, centaure, and fumetere,
Or elles of ellebor that groweth there,
Of katapuce, or of gaitrys beryis,   145
Of herbe yve growyng in oure yerd, ther merye is.
Pekke hem up right as they growe, and ete hem in.
Be myrie, housbond, for your fader kyn!
Dredeth no dreem. I kan sey yow namoore."
   "Madame," quod he, "graunt mercy of your loore.   150
But nathelees, as touchyng daun Catoun,
That hath of wisdom swich a gret renoun,
Thogh that he bad no dremes for to drede,
By God, men may in olde bokes rede
Of many a man moore of auctoritee   155

120 *Catoun:* Dionysius Cato, supposed author of a well known collection of
Latin maxims.   121 *Ne . . . of:* pay no attention to.   122 *fle fro:* fly down
from.   123 *as taak:* take.   124 *Up:* upon.   127 *for:* so; in order that.   129
techen: direct.   130 *heele:* cure.   *prow:* benefit.   131 *tho:* those.   132 *kynde:*
nature.   134 *Foryet:* forget.   136 *Ware:* beware that.   138 *grote:* groat
(fourpence).   139 *fevere terciane:* tertian fever (a fever every third day).
140 *bane:* death.   142 *er:* before.   143–45 *lauriol, centaure,* etc.: all medicinal herbs, some nauseous, some laxative; see l. 133.   144 *elles:* else.   146
herbe yve: ground ivy.   *ther merye is:* where it is pleasant.   148 *fader kyn:*
father's kin, i.e., family honor. Ironic; cf. l. 475 where it is revealed that his
father also was fooled by the fox.   150 *graunt . . . loore:* thanks for your
instruction.   151 *daun:* sir.

10

Than ever Catoun was, so mote I thee,
That al the revers seyn of his sentence
And han wel founden by experience
That dremes ben significaciouns
As wel of joye as of tribulaciouns   160
That folk enduren in this lyf present.
Ther nedeth make of this noon argument;
The verray preeve sheweth it in dede.
      "Oon of the gretteste auctor that men rede
Seith thus, that whilom two felawes wente   165
On pilgrimage in a ful good entente,
And happed so they coomen in a toun
Where as ther was swich congregacioun
Of peple, and eek so streit of herbergage
That they ne founde as muche as a cotage   170
In which they bothe myghte y-logged be.
Wherefore they mosten of necessitee,
As for that nyght, departen compaignye,
And ech of hem gooth to his hostelrye
And took his loggyng as it wolde falle.   175
That oon of hem was logged in a stalle,
Fer in a yeerd, with oxen of the plow.
That oother man was logged wel ynow
As was his aventure or his fortune,
That us governeth alle as in commune.   180
      "And so bifel that, longe er it were day,
This man mette in his bed ther as he lay
How that his felawe gan upon hym calle
And seyde, 'Allas, for in oxes stalle
This nyght I shal be mordred ther I lye.   185
Now help me, deere brother, or I dye.
In alle haste com to me,' he sayde.
      "This man out of his sleep for feere abrayde,
But whan that he was wakned of his sleep,
He turned hym and took of this no keep.   190
Hym thoughte his dreem nas but a vanytee.
Thus twies in his slepyng dremed he,
And atte thridde tyme yet his felawe

156 *so . . . thee:* so may I thrive, prosper.   157 *revers:* contrary.   *sentence:*
opinion.   159 *ben:* are.   162 *Ther nedeth:* there is [no] need to.   163 *preeve:*
proof.   164 *Oon:* one.   *auctor:* author(s).   165 *felawes:* companions.   167
happed: it happened.   169 *streit of herbergage:* short of lodgings.
171 *y-logged:* lodged.   172 *mosten:* must.   173 *As for:* for.   *departen:* part.
177 *Fer . . . yeerd:* far off in a courtyard.   178 *ynow:* enough.   179 *aventure:*
lot.   180 *commune:* common.   182 *ther as:* where.   185 *mordred ther:*
murdered where.   188 *abrayde:* started up.   190 *keep:* heed.   191 *nas
but:* was only.   193 *thridde:* third.

Cam, as hym thoughte, and seyde, 'I am now slawe.
Bihoold my blody woundes, depe and wyde.   195
Arys up erly in the morwe tyde,
And at the west gate of the toun,' quod he,
'A carte ful of dong ther shaltow se,
In which my body is hid ful prively.
Do thilke carte aresten boldely.   200
My gold caused my mordre, sooth to seyn';
And tolde hym every point how he was slayn
With a ful pitous face pale of hewe.
And truste wel his dreem he fond ful trewe,
For on the morwe, as soone as it was day,   205
To his felawes in he took the way,
And whan that he cam to this oxes stalle,
After his felawe he bigan to calle.
    "The hostiler answerde hym anon
And seyde, 'Sire, your felawe is agon.   210
As soone as day he wente out of the toun.'
    "This man gan fallen in suspecioun,
Remembrynge on his dremes that he mette,
And forth he gooth, no lenger wolde he lette,
Unto the west gate of the toun and fond   215
A dong carte, wente as it were to donge lond,
That was arrayed in the same wise
As ye han herd the dede man devyse,
And with an hardy herte he gan to crye
Vengeaunce and justice of this felonye.   220
'My felawe mordred is this same nyght,
And in this carte he lyth gapyng upright.
I crye out on the ministres,' quod he,
'That sholden kepe and reulen this citee.
Harrow, allas! Heer lyth my felawe slayn!'   225
What sholde I moore unto this tale sayn?
The peple out sterte and caste the cart to grounde,
And in the myddel of the dong they founde
The dede man, that mordred was al newe.
    "O blisful God, that art so just and trewe,   230
Lo, how that thow biwreyest mordre alway!
Mordre wol out, that se we day by day.
Mordre is so wlatsom and abhomynable

---

194 *slawe:* slain. 196 *Arys:* rise. *morwe tyde:* morning. 198 *dong:* dung.
shaltow se: you will see. 199 *ful prively:* very secretly. 200 *aresten:* stop.
201 *sooth to seyn:* truth to tell. 206 *in:* inn. 214 *lette:* stay. 216 *to donge:*
to manure. 218 *devyse:* describe, tell. 222 *lyth:* lies. *upright:* face-
upward. 225 *Harrow:* help. 229 *al newe:* just recently. 231 *biwreyest:*
make known. 232 *se:* see. 233 *wlatsom:* foul.

To God, that is so just and resonable,
That he ne wol nat suffre it heled be,   235
Thogh it abyde a yeer, or two, or thre.
Mordre wol out, this is my conclusioun.
And right anon ministres of that toun
Han hent the cartere and so soore hym pyned
And eek the hostiler so soore engyned   240
That they biknewe hir wikkednesse anon
And were an-hanged by the nekke bon.
    "Heere may men seen that dremes ben to drede.
And, certes, in the same book I rede,
Right in the nexte chapitre after this—   245
I gabbe nat, so have I joye or blys—
Two men that wolde han passed over see
For certeyn cause into a fer contree,
If that the wynd ne hadde ben contrarie,
That made hem in a citee for to tarie,   250
That stood ful myrie upon an haven syde.
But on a day, agayn the even tyde,
The wynd gan chaunge and blew right as hem leste.
Jolif and glad they wente unto hir reste
And casten hem ful erly for to saille.   255
    "But herkneth! To that o man fil a greet mervaille,
That oon of hem, in slepyng as he lay,
Hym mette a wonder dreem agayn the day.
Hym thoughte a man stood by his beddes syde,
And hym comanded that he sholde abyde,   260
And seyde hym thus: 'If thow tomorwe wende,
Thow shalt be dreynt. My tale is at an ende.'
He wook, and tolde his felawe what he mette,
And preyde hym his viage for to lette.
As for that day, he preyde hym to abyde.   265
His felawe, that lay by his beddes syde,
Gan for to laughe, and scorned hym ful faste.
'No dreem,' quod he, 'may so myn herte agaste
That I wol lette for to do my thynges.
I sette nat a straw by thy dremynges,   270
For swevenes ben but vanytees and japes.

---

235 *ne . . . be:* will not let it be hidden.   239 *hent:* seized.   *pyned:* examined
[him] by torture.   240 *engyned:* racked.   241 *biknewe hir:* confessed their.
242 *bon:* bone.   246 *gabbe:* exaggerate.   *so have I:* may I have.   247 *han . . .
see:* have crossed the sea.   251 *myrie:* pleasant.   *haven:* harbor.   252
agayn . . . tyde: toward evening.   253 *hem leste:* they wished.   254 *Jolif:*
jolly.   255 *casten hem:* they decided.   256 *o:* one.   *fil:* befell.   258 *wonder:*
wonderful.   262 *dreynt:* drowned.   263 *wook:* awoke.   264 *viage . . . lette:*
to delay his voyage.   268 *agaste:* frighten.   269 *lette . . . thynges:* stop
my activities.   271 *japes:* tricks.

Men dreme alday of owles and of apes
And eek of many a maze therwithal;
Men dreme of thyng that never was ne shal.
But, sith I see that thow wolt here abyde,   275
And thus forslewthen wilfully thy tyde,
God woot, it reweth me, and have good day!'
And thus he took his leve and wente his way.
But er that he hadde half his cours y-seyled,
Noot I nat why ne what mischaunce it eyled,   280
But casuelly the shippes botme rente,
And ship and man under the water wente
In sighte of othere shippes it bisyde
That with hem seyled at the same tyde.
And therfor, faire Pertelote so deere,   285
By swiche ensamples olde maystow leere
That no man sholde been to recchelees
Of dremes, for I sey thee, doutelees,
That many a dreem ful soore is for to drede.
    "Lo, in the lyf of Seint Kenelm I rede,   290
That was Kenulphus sone, the noble kyng
Of Mercenrike, how Kenelm mette a thyng.
A lite er he was mordred on a day,
His mordre in his avysioun he say.
His norice hym expowned every del   295
His swevene, and bad hym for to kepe hym wel
For traisoun, but he nas but seven yeer old,
And therfore litel tale hath he told
Of any dreem, so holy was his herte.
By God, I hadde levere than my sherte   300
That ye had rad his legende as have I.
Dame Pertelote, I sey yow trewely,
Macrobeus, that writ the avysioun
In Affrike of the worthy Cipioun,
Affermeth dremes and seith that they been   305
Warnynge of thynges that men after seen.
And forthermoore, I pray yow, looketh wel

272 *alday:* every day.   273 *maze:* wonder.   274 *shal:* shall [be].   275 *sith:* since.   276 *forslewthen:* waste.   *tyde:* time.   277 *it reweth me:* I rue it.   279 *y-seyled:* sailed.   280 *Noot I:* I don't know.   *ne:* nor.   *eyled:* ailed [it].   281 *casuelly:* by chance.   283 *bisyde:* beside.   286 *maystow leere:* you may learn.   287 *to recchelees:* too reckless.   288 *sey:* tell.   289 *for to drede:* to be dreaded.   291 *Kenulphus:* Cenwulf's.   292 *Mercenrike:* Mercia.   293 *lite:* little.   294 *avysioun:* vision.   *say:* saw.   295 *norice:* nurse.   *expowned every del:* expounded fully.   296 *for . . . hym:* to take care of himself.   297 *For:* for fear of.   298 *tale:* heed.   *told:* paid.   300–01 *I . . . rad:* I.e., I'd have given my shirt if you had read.   303 *Macrobeus:* Cicero's *Somnium Scipionis* (Scipio Africanus Minor) with the Latin commentary of Macrobius was considered a standard authority on dreams.

In the Olde Testament, of Daniel,
If he heeld dremes any vanytee.
Rede eek of Joseph, and there shul ye see   310
Wher dremes by somtyme, I sey nat alle,
Warnynge of thynges that shul after falle.
Looke of Egipt the kyng, daun Pharao,
His bakere, and his butiller also,
Wher they ne felte noon effect in dremes.   315
Who-so wol seken actes of sondry remes
May rede of dremes many a wonder thyng.
Lo Cresus, which that was of Lyde kyng,
Mette he nat that he sat upon a tree,
Which signified he sholde an-hanged be?   320
Lo heere Andromacha, Ectores wyf,
That day that Ector sholde lese his lyf,
She dremed on the same nyght biforn
How that the lyf of Ector sholde be lorn
If thilke day he wente in to bataille.   325
She warned hym, but it myghte nat availle;
He wente for to fighte, nathelees.
But he was slayn anon of Achilles.
But thilke tale is al to long to telle,
And eek it is ny day, I may nat dwelle.   330
    "Shortly I seye, as for conclusioun,
That I shal han of this avysioun
Adversitee, and I seye forthermoor,
That I ne telle of laxatyves no stoor,
For they ben venymes, I woot it wel.   335
I hem deffye! I love hem never a del.
    "Now lat us speke of myrthe and stynte al this.
Madame Pertelote, so have I blis,
Of o thyng God hath sent me large grace,
For whan I se the beautee of youre face,   340
Ye ben so scarlet reed aboute youre eyen,
It maketh al my drede for to dyen,
For, also siker as *In principio*,

---

308 *Olde Testament:* See Dan. 7; Gen. 37, 40, 41. 311 *Wher:* whether.
316 *remes:* realms. 318 *Cresus:* Croesus of Lydia. The Nun's Priest perhaps
here glances satirically at the Monk, for it was at the tragedy of Croesus
that the Knight stopped him. 319 *tree:* gallows tree. 321 *Andromacha:*
Andromache, Hector's wife. 322 *lese:* lose. 324 *lorn:* lost. 327 *natheless:*
nevertheless. 328 *of:* by. 330 *ny:* near. 334 *ne . . . stoor:* set no store by
laxatives. 335 *venymes:* venomous. 336 *never a del:* not at all. 337 *stynte:*
stop. 338 *so have I:* may I have. 341 *reed:* For a chicken this is accurate
but, in the context of the courtly language he is using, hilariously
inappropriate. 343 *also . . . principio:* as surely as "in the beginning" (John
1:1); i.e., "Gospel truth."

'*Mulier est hominis confusio.*'
    "Madame, the sentence of this Latyn is,   345
'Womman is mannes joye and al his blis.'
For whan I feele a-nyght your softe syde,
Al be it that I may nat on yow ryde
For that our perche is maad so narwe, allas,
I am so ful of joye and of solas   350
That I deffye bothe swevene and dreem."
    And with that word he fley doun fro the beem,
For it was day, and eek hise hennes alle.
And with a chuk he gan hem for to calle,
For he had founde a corn, lay in the yerd.   355
Real he was; he was na moore aferd.
He fethered Pertelote twenty tyme
And trad as ofte, er that it was pryme.
He looketh as it were a grym leoun,
And on his toos he rometh up and doun.   360
Hym deyned nat to sette his foot to grounde.
He chukketh whan he hath a corn y-founde,
And to hym rennen thanne his wyves alle.
Thus real as a prince is in his halle
Leve I this Chauntecleer in his pasture,   365
And after wol I telle his aventure.
   Whan that the monthe in which the world bigan,
That highte March, whan God first maked man,
Was complet, and passed were also,
Syn March bigan, thritty dayes and two,   370
Bifel that Chauntecleer in al his pryde,
His seven wyves walkyng hym bisyde,
Caste up hise eyen to the brighte sonne,
That in the signe of Taurus hadde y-ronne
Twenty degrees and oon, and somwhat moore,   375
And knew by kynde and by noon oother loore
That it was pryme, and krew with blisful stevene.
"The sonne," he seyde, "is clomben up on hevene
Fourty degrees and oon, and moore ywis.

---

344 *Mulier . . . confusio:* Woman is man's ruin. This is carefully mis-
translated by Chauntecleer in l. 346. 345 *sentence:* meaning. 349 *For
that:* because. 351 *swevene:* vision. 355 *corn:* grain [of corn]. *lay:*
[which] lay. 356 *Real:* regal. *aferd:* afraid. 357 *fethered:* covered with
outspread feathers, i.e., copulated with. 358 *trad:* trod, covered [her].
pryme: prime; period from 6 A.M. to 9 A.M. 359 *leoun:* lion. 361 *Hym
deyned:* he deigned. 363 *rennen thanne:* then run. 368 It was believed in
medieval times that God created the world and man in March. 370 *Syn:*
since; i.e., it was May 3, a day traditionally unlucky for lovers. See *Troilus
and Criseyde,* II, 56, and "The Knight's Tale," l. 1462. 376 *kynde:* nature.
377 *stevene:* voice. 378 *is clomben:* has climbed. 379 *ywis:* indeed.

16

Madame Pertelote, my worldes blis,   380
Herkneth thise blisful briddes, how they synge,
And se the fresshe floures how they sprynge.
Ful is myn herte of revel and solas."
But sodeynly hym fil a sorweful cas,
For ever the latter ende of joye is wo.   385
God woot that worldly joye is soone ago,
And if a rethor koude faire endite,
He in a cronycle saufly myghte it write
As for a sovereyn notabilitee.
Now every wys man, lat hym herkne me;   390
This storie is also trewe, I undertake,
As is the book of *Launcelot de Lake*,
That wommen holde in ful gret reverence.
Now wol I torne agayn to my sentence.
    A colfox ful of sly iniquitee,   395
That in the grove hadde woned yeres three,
By heigh ymaginacioun forncast,
The same nyght thurgh-out the hegges brast
Into the yerd ther Chauntecleer the faire
Was wont, and eek his wyves, to repaire,   400
And in a bed of wortes stille he lay
Til it was passed undren of the day,
Waitynge his tyme on Chauntecleer to falle,
As gladly doon thise homycides alle
That in await liggen to mordre men.   405
O false mordrour, lurkynge in thy den,
O newe Scariot, newe Genyloun,
False dissimilour, O Greek Synoun,
That broghtest Troye al outrely to sorwe!
O Chauntecleer, acursed be that morwe   410
That thou into the yerd flaugh fro the bemes.
Thou were ful wel y-warned by thy dremes

381 *Herkneth:* listen to. 384 *hym fil:* befell him. *cas:* mishap. 386 *ago:* gone. 387 *rethor:* rhetorician. *endite:* compose. 388 *saufly:* safely. 389 *As . . . notabilitee:* as a most notable fact. 391 *also:* as. *undertake:* vow. 392 *Launcelot de Lake:* a romance relating the love of Lancelot for Guinevere, King Arthur's queen, perhaps one of the favorite "true romances" of the Prioress: in other words, not true but wholly fictitious. 394 *sentence:* subject. 395 *colfox:* coal fox, one with much black hair. 396 *woned:* lived. 397 *By . . . forncast:* perhaps "foreseen by the prophetic vision." The exact meaning is uncertain; *ymaginacioun* probably refers to Chauntecleer's dream. 398 *hegges:* hedges. *brast:* burst. 401 *wortes:* herbs. 402 *undren:* mid-morning. 404 *gladly:* usually. *homycides:* murderers. 405 *liggen:* lie. 407 *Scariot:* Judas Iscariot, who betrayed Christ. *Genyloun:* Ganelon, who betrayed Roland, Charlemagne's nephew, and thus caused the defeat at Roncesvalles. 408 *dissimilour:* deceiver. *Synoun:* Sinon, who persuaded the Trojans to take the Greeks' wooden horse into Troy. 409 *al outrely:* utterly. *sorwe:* grief. 411 *flaugh:* flew.

That thilke day was perilous to thee.
But what that God forwoot moot nedes be
After the opynyoun of certeyn clerkis.   415
Witnesse on hym that any parfit clerk is,
That in scole is greet altercacioun
In this matere, and greet disputisoun,
And hath ben of an hundred thousand men.
But I ne kan nat bulte it to the bren   420
As kan the holy doctour Augustyn
Or Boece, or the Bisshop Bradwardyn,
Wheither that Goddes worthy forewityng
Streyneth me nedely for to doon a thyng—
"Nedely" clepe I symple necessitee—   425
Or ellis, if free choys be graunted me
To do that same thyng, or do it noght,
Though God forwoot it er that it was wroght;
Or if his wityng streyneth never a del
But by necessitee condicionel.   430
I wol nat han to do of swich matere.
My tale is of a cok, as ye may heere,
That took his conseil of his wyf, with sorwe,
To walken in the yerd upon that morwe
That he had met the dreem that I yow tolde.   435
Wommennes conseils ben ful ofte colde.
Wommannes conseil broghte us first to wo
And made Adam fro Paradys to go,
Ther as he was ful myrie and wel at ese.
But, for I noot to whom it myghte displese   440
If I conseil of wommen wolde blame,
Passe over, for I seyde it in my game.
Rede auctours wher they trete of swich matere,
And what they seyn of wommen ye may heere.
Thise ben the cokkes wordes and nat myne;   445

414 *forwoot . . . be:* foreknows must needs be. 415 *clerkis:* scholars. 418 *disputisoun:* disputation. 420 *I . . . bren:* I can't sift it to the bran; i.e., I can't reach certainty in this much-disputed theological problem. (If God foreknows the future, to what extent does man have free will?) 421 *Augustyn:* St. Augustine of Hippo, who discussed the likelihood that man has "free choice" (l. 426) of action despite the infallibility of God's foreknowledge of future events. 422 *Boece :* Boethius, sixth-century philosopher, whose *Consolation of Philosophy* Chaucer translated. He was also an authority on music; see l. 474. Boethius distinguished between "simple" (l. 425) and "conditional" (l. 430) necessity of man's action. *Bradwardyn:* Thomas Bradwardine (Archbishop of Canterbury, d. 1349) lectured at Oxford on God's foreknowledge. 423 *forewityng:* foreknowing. 424 *Streyneth:* constrains. *nedely:* necessarily. 425 *clepe:* call. 429 *wityng . . . del:* knowing constrains not at all. 431 *han:* have [anything]. *of:* with. 436 *colde:* fatal. 440 *for I noot:* since I don't know. 442 *game:* jest. 444 *seyn:* say.

I kan noon harm of no womman devyne.
   Faire in the sond to bathe hir myrily
Lith Pertelote, and alle hir sustres by,
Agayn the sonne; and Chauntecleer so free
Song myrier than the mermayde in the see,   450
For Phisiologus seith sikerly
How that they syngen wel and myrily.
   And so bifel that, as he caste his eye
Among the wortes on a boterflye,
He was war of this fox that lay ful lowe.   455
No thyng ne liste hym thanne for to crowe,
But cryde anon "Cok! cok!" and up he sterte
As man that was affrayed in his herte,
For naturelly a beest desireth flee
Fro his contrarie, if he may it see,   460
Though he never erst had syn it with his eye.
   This Chauntecleer, whan he gan hym espye,
He wolde han fled but that the fox anon
Seyde, "Gentil sire, allas! Wher wol ye gon?
Be ye affrayed of me that am your freend?   465
Now, certes, I were worse than a feend
If I to yow wolde harm or vileynye.
I am nat come your conseil for t' espye,
But trewely the cause of my comynge
Was oonly for to herkne how that ye synge,   470
For trewely ye have as myrie a stevene
As any aungel hath that is in hevene.
Therwith ye han in musyk moore feelynge
Than hadde Boece, or any that kan synge.
My lord, your fader—God his soule blesse!—   475
And eek your moder, of hir gentillesse,
Han in myn hous y-ben to my greet ese.
And, certes, sire, ful fayn wolde I yow plese.
   "But, for men speke of syngynge, I wol seye—
So mote I brouke wel myne eyen tweye!—   480
Save yow, I herde nevere man so synge
As dide youre fader in the morwenynge.

---

446 *devyne:* imagine. 447 *sond:* sand. 448 *Lith:* lies. 449 *Agayn:* in. 450
Song: sang. 451 *Phisiologus seith sikerly:* Physiologus says certainly. He was
reputed to be the author of the first *Bestiary*, a compendium of fictitious,
pseudoscientific information about natural and supernatural creatures, including mermaids, and their allegorical interpretations. 455 *war:* aware. 456
No ... thanne: he did not at all then wish. 458 *As man:* like someone. 459
flee: to flee. 460 *contrarie:* opposite; i.e., enemy. 461 *erst:* before. *syn:*
seen. 462 *gan hym espye:* noticed him. 467 *wolde:* intended. 468 *conseil ...
espye:* secret to discover. 471 *stevene:* voice. 477 *y-ben:* been. *ese:* satisfaction. 478 *fayn:* gladly. 479 *for:* in spite of what. 480 *So ... tweye:* So
may I enjoy [the use of] my two eyes. 482 *morwenynge:* early morning.

Certes, it was of herte, al that he song.
And for to make his voys the moore strong,
He wolde so peyne hym that with bothe his eyen   485
He moste wynke, so loude he wolde cryen,
And stonden on his tiptoon ther-with-al,
And strecche forth his nekke long and smal.
And eek he was of swich discrecioun
That ther nas no man in no regioun   490
That hym in song or wisdom myghte passe.
I have wel rad in *Daun Burnel the Asse*,
Among his vers, how that ther was a cok,
For a preestes sone yaf hym a knok
Upon his leg, whil he was yong and nyce,   495
He made hym for to lese his benefice.
But, certeyn, ther nys no comparisoun
Bitwix the wisdom and discrecioun
Of youre fader and of his subtiltee.
Now syngeth, sire, for seinte charitee!   500
Lat se, konne ye your fader countrefete?''
    This Chauntecleer his wynges gan to bete
As man that koude his traysoun nat espie,
So was he ravysshed with his flaterie.
    Allas, ye lordes, many a fals flatour   505
Is in your courtes, and many a losengeour,
That plesen yow wel moore, by my feith,
Than he that soothfastnesse unto yow seith.
Redeth Ecclesiaste of flaterye.
Beth war, ye lordes, of hir trecherye.   510
This Chauntecleer stood hye upon his toos,
Strecchynge his nekke, and heeld his eyen cloos,
And gan to crowe loude for the nones.
And daun Russell the fox stirte up atones,
And by the gargat hente Chauntecleer,   515
And on his bak toward the wode hym beer,
For yet ne was ther no man that hym sewed.
    O destynee, that mayst nat ben eschewed!

---

483 *of herte:* from his heart. 485 *peyne hym:* strive. 486 *moste wynke:* must shut [his eyes]. 492 *Daun . . . Asse: Burnellus the Ass,* a twelfth-century Latin poem by Nigel Wireker. 495 *he:* the priest's son. *nyce:* foolish. 496 *lese:* lose [his benefice, according to the story, because the cock failed to crow to awaken Gundulf, the priest's son, in time for him to attend his ordination and receive appointment to his living]. 500 *seinte:* holy. 501 *Lat se:* Let's see [if]. *countrefete:* imitate. 505 *flatour:* flatterer. 506 *losengeour:* deceiver. 507 *plesen:* please. 508 *soothfastnesse:* truth. 509 *Ecclesiaste of:* Ecclesiasticus on. A book in the Apocrypha; see 12:10–18; cf. Prov. 29:5. 510 *Beth ware:* beware. 512 *cloos:* closed. 513 *nones:* occasion. 514 *stirte up atones:* sprang up at once. 515 *gargat:* throat. *hente:* seized. 516 *beer:* carried. 517 *sewed:* pursued. 518 *eschewed:* avoided.

Allas, that Chauntecleer fleigh fro the bemes!
Allas, his wif ne roghte nat of dremes!   520
And on a Friday fil al this meschaunce.
   O Venus, that art goddesse of plesaunce,
Syn that thy servant was this Chauntecleer,
And in thy servyce dide al his power
Moore for delit than world to multiplie,   525
Why woldestow suffre hym on thy day to dye?
   O Gaufred, deere maister soverayn,
That whan thy worthy kyng Richard was slayn
With shot, compleynedest his deth so soore,
Why ne hadde I now thy sentence and thy loore   530
The Friday for to chide, as diden ye?
For on a Friday, soothly, slayn was he.
Than wolde I shewe yow how that I koude pleyne
For Chauntecleres drede and for his peyne.
   Certes, swich cry ne lamentacioun   535
Was nevere of ladyes maad whan Ylioun
Was wonne, and Pirrus with his streite swerd
Whan he hadde hent kyng Priam by the berd
And slayn hym, as seith us *Eneydos*,
As maden alle the hennes in the cloos   540
Whan they had seyn of Chauntecleer the sighte.
But sovereynly dame Pertelote shrighte
Ful louder than dide Hasdrubales wyf
Whan that hir housbonde hadde lost his lyf
And that the Romayns hadden brend Cartage.   545
She was so ful of torment and of rage
That wilfully into the fyr she sterte
And brende hirselven with a stedefast herte.
   O woful hennes, right so cryden ye
As, whan that Nero brende the citee   550
Of Rome, cryden senatours wyves
For that hir housbondes losten alle hir lyves.

---

519 *fleigh:* flew.   520 *ne . . . nat:* took no heed.   525 *Moore . . . multiplie:*
More for pleasure than to [be fruitful and] multiply [and replenish] the earth.
See Genesis 1:29, which to the strictly orthodox was the sole justification for
sexual activity. In serving Venus, Chauntecleer is a heretic.   526 *woldestow:*
would you.   527 *Gaufred:* Geoffrey de Vin Sauf, twelfth-century author of a
Latin treatise on poetics. Chaucer alludes to his "lamentation" on King
Richard I, famous as a courtly lover and mortally wounded on a Friday.
529 *compleynedest:* lamented.   530 *sentence:* erudition.   *loore:* learning.
535 *ne:* nor.   536 *Ylioun:* Ilium (Troy).   537 *Pirrus:* Achilles' son.   *streite
swerd:* drawn sword.   539 *seith us Eneydos:* [the] Aeneid tells us (II, 469–553).
540 *cloos:* enclosure.   542 *sovereynly:* especially.   *shrighte:* shrieked.   543
Hasdrubales: Hasdrubal, general and defender of Carthage against the Romans
under Scipio (146 B.C.).   545 *brend:* burned.   547 *wilfully:* voluntarily.
sterte: leaped.

Withouten gilt this Nero hath hem slayn.
Now wol I turne to my tale agayn.
   The sely widwe and eek hir doghtres two   555
Herden thise hennes crye and maken wo,
And out at dores stirten they anon,
And syen the fox toward the grove gon,
And bar upon his bak the cok away,
And criden "Out! Harrow!" and "Weilaway!   560
Ha, ha, the fox!" And after hym they ran,
And eek with staves many another man.
Ran Colle our dogge, and Talbot, and Gerland,
And Malkyn, with a distaf in hir hand.
Ran cow, and calf, and eek the verray hogges,   565
So fered for the berkyng of the dogges
And shoutyng of the men and wommen eek.
They ronne so, hem thoughte hir herte breek.
They yelleden as fendes doon in helle.
The dokes cryden as men wolde hem quelle.   570
The gees for feere flowen over the trees.
Out of the hyve cam the swarm of bees.
So hydous was the noyse, A, *benedicitee !*
Certes, he Jakke Straw and his meynee
Ne made never shoutes half so shrille   575
Whan that they wolden any Flemyng kille
As thilke day was maad upon the fox.
Of bras they broghten bemes, and of box,
Of horn, of boon, in whiche they blewe and powped,
And ther-with-al they skryked, and they howped. 580
It semed as that heven sholde falle.
Now goode men, I pray yow, herkneth alle.
   Lo, how Fortune turneth sodeynly
The hope and pryde eek of hire enemy.
This cok that lay upon the foxes bak   585
In al his drede unto the fox he spak
And seyde, "Sire, if that I were as ye,

---

553 *Withouten gilt:* modifies (*t*)*hem.* 555 *sely :* poor. 558 *syen :* saw.
560 *Weilaway:* alas. 564 *Malkyn:* name for a country girl. 566 *fered
for:* frightened by. 568 *They . . . breek:* They ran so [hard], they thought
their heart(s) would break. 569 *fendes doon:* fiends do. 570 *dokes:*
ducks. *as:* as if. *quelle:* kill. 573 *hydous:* hideous. *A:* ah. *benedicitee:*
bless ye. 574 *Jakke . . . meynee:* During the Peasants' Revolt (1381), Jack
Straw led a company (*meynee*) of Kentish rebels into London, where they
murdered a number of clothmakers from Flanders who had kept their tech-
nique secret from the native workers. 578 *broghten bemes:* brought trumpets
(made of brass, box[wood], horn, and bone). 579 *powped:* puffed. 580
skryked: shrieked. *howped:* whooped.

Yet sholde I seyn, as wys God helpe me,
'Turneth agayn, ye proude cherles alle.
A verray pestilence upon yow falle! 590
Now I am come unto this wodes syde,
Maugree youre heed, the cok shal here abyde.
I wol hym ete, in feith, and that anon.' "
   The fox answerde, "In feith, it shal be don."
And as he spak that word, al sodeynly 595
This cok brak from his mouth delyverly,
And hye upon a tree he fley anon.
And whan the fox say that he was gon,
"Allas," quod he, "O Chauntecleer, allas!
I have to yow," quod he, "y-doon trespas 600
In as muche as I maked yow aferd
Whan I yow hente and broghte out of the yerd.
But, sire, I dide it in no wikke entente.
Com doun, and I shal telle yow what I mente.
I shal seye sooth to yow, God help me so." 605
   "Nay thanne," quod he, "I shrewe us bothe two.
And first I shrewe myself, bothe blood and bones,
If thou bigile me ofter than ones.
Thou shalt namoore thurgh thy flaterye
Do me to synge and wynke with myn eye, 610
For he that wynketh, whan he sholde see,
Al wilfully, God lat hym nevere thee."
   "Nay," quod the fox, "but God yeve hym meschaunce
That is so undiscreet of governaunce
That jangleth whan he sholde holde his pees." 615
   Lo, swich it is for to be recchelees,
And necligent, and truste on flaterye.
   But ye that holden this tale a folye
As of a fox, or of a cok and hen,
Taketh the moralitee, good men. 620

---

588 *seyn:* say. *wys:* wise. 589 *agayn:* back. *cherles:* churls. 591 *wodes:* wood's. 592 *Maugree youre heed:* despite all you can do. 596 *delyverly:* nimbly. 597 *fley:* flew. The Knight asked for a "tragedy" that showed not only how the man of high estate falls but also how he recovers from his "fall" and regains his high estate. The Nun's Priest here obliges. 598 *say:* saw. 600 *trespas:* offense. 603 *wikke:* evil. 606 *shrewe:* curse. 608 *bigile:* beguile. *ofter:* more often. 609 *thurgh:* through. 610 *Do:* persuade. *wynke with:* close. 612 *God . . . thee:* God let him never prosper. 613 *yeve:* give. 614 *governaunce:* self-control. 615 *jangleth:* chatters. *pees:* peace. 618 *a folye:* foolishness.

For seint Paul seith that al that writen is,
To oure doctryne it is y-write, ywis.
Taketh the fruyt, and lat the chaf be stille.
Now goode God, if that it be thy wille,
As seith my lord, so make us alle goode men,   625
And brynge us to his heye blisse. Amen.

621–22 *al . . . ywis:* All that is written is surely written for our instruction.
See I Cor. 10:11.   626 *heye:* high.

SIR THOMAS WYATT
1503–1542

My galley charged with forgetfulness

My galley charged with forgetfulness
   Thorough sharp seas in winter nights doth pass
   'Tween rock and rock; and eke mine enemy, alas,
   That is my lord, steereth with cruelness;
And every oar a thought in readiness,   5
   As though that death were light in such a case.
   An endless wind doth tear the sail apace
   Of forced sighs and trusty fearfulness.
A rain of tears, a cloud of dark disdain,
   Hath done the wearied cords great hinderance: 10
   Wreathed with error and eke with ignorance.
The stars be hid that led me to this pain,
   Drowned is reason that should me comfort,
   And I remain despairing of the port.

They flee from me that sometime did me seek

They flee from me that sometime did me seek
   With naked foot stalking in my chamber.
I have seen them gentle tame and meek
   That now are wild and do not remember
   That sometime they put themselves in danger   5
To take bread at my hand; and now they range
Busily seeking with a continual change.

MY GALLEY. *My . . . forgetfulness:* adapted from Petrarch's sonnet, *In vita*, CLVI (Bohn tr.). Wyatt develops what became a standard Renaissance conceit in which the lover compares his state to that of a ship tossed on the stormy seas of desire.
  1 *charged with forgetfulness:* overloaded with forgetfulness; i.e., he is so burdened by the demands of love that he forgets all but his troubled state. 3 *eke:* also. 3, 4 *enemy, lord:* I.e., his love, his lady. In courtly love, the lady was conventionally described as both the lover's "sweet foe" and his feudal *lord* who had absolute sovereignty over him. 5–6 *every . . . case:* I.e., my wretchedness in her service is such that everything I do makes me think that the pain of death would be insignificant compared to my present misery. 8 *trusty fearfulness:* He trusts and fears simultaneously (a standard oxymoron). 10 *hinderance:* damage. 11 *wreathed:* fouled, entangled. 13 *me comfort:* console and guide me and not expose me to arbitrary violence.

THEY FLEE FROM ME. 5 *put . . . danger:* put themselves in my power and protection, i.e., trusted that I would protect them from scandal attached to the relationship. 7 *seeking:* paying obsequious court to others. Cf. the animal connotations of ll. 4–6.

24

Thank'd be fortune, it hath been otherwise
    Twenty times better; but once in special,
In thin array after a pleasant guise,   10
    When her loose gown from her shoulders did fall,
    And she me caught in her arms long and small,
Therewith all sweetly did me kiss,
And softly said, *Dear heart, how like you this?*

It was no dream: I lay broad waking.   15
    But all is turned thorough my gentleness
Into a strange fashion of forsaking;
    And I have leave to go of her goodness,
    And she also to use new-fangleness.
But since that I so kindely am served,   20
I would fain know what she hath deserved.

In eternum I was once determed

In eternum I was once determed
For to have loved, and my mind affirmed
That with my heart it should be confirmed,
        In eternum.

Forthwith I found the thing that I might like   5
And sought with love to warm her heart alike,
For, as methought, I should not see the like
        In eternum.

To trace this dance I put myself in press;
Vain hope did lead and bade I should not cease   10
To serve, to suffer, and still to hold my peace
        In eternum.

With this first rule I ford'red me apace,
That, as methought, my truth had taken place
With full assurance to stand in her grace   15
        In eternum.

9 *in special:* (trisyllabic) especially.   10 *after . . . guise:* in a delightful style.
17 *forsaking:* i.e., lightly giving up lovers, merrily playing false.   18 *goodness:*
generosity (sarcastic).   19 *new-fangleness:* new fashions, i.e., fickleness.   20
kindely: (trisyllabic) generously, naturally (again sarcastic).

IN ETERNUM.   1 *In eternum:* everlastingly.   2–3 *mind . . . confirmed:* My
mind decided that my heart should agree that I love.   9 *put . . . press:* I
exerted myself, undertook.   13 *ford'red me apace:* I furthered, helped myself
forward, quickly.   14 *truth . . . place:* faithfulness had won a place [in her].

It was not long or I by proof had found
That feeble building is on feeble ground;
For in her heart this word did never sound,
    "In eternum."   20

In eternum then from my heart I kest
That I had first determin'd for the best;
Now in the place another thought doth rest,
    In eternum.

You that in love find luck and abundance

You that in love find luck and abundance
    And live in lust and joyful jollity,
    Arise for shame! Do away your sluggardy!
    Arise, I say, do May some observance!
Let me in bed lie dreaming in mischance;   5
    Let me remember the haps most unhappy
    That me betide in May most commonly,
    As one whom love list little to advance.
Sephame said true that my nativity
    Mischanc'd was with the ruler of the May: 10
    He guessed, I prove, of that the verity.
In May my wealth and eke my life, I say,
    Have stood so oft in such perplexity:
    Rejoice! Let me dream of your felicity.

My lute awake!

My lute awake! perform the last
Labor that thou and I shall waste,
    And end that I have now begun;
For when this song is sung and past,
    My lute be still, for I have done.   5

---

17 *or:* ere.   18 *feeble building is:* one builds feebly.   21 *kest:* cast out.

YOU THAT IN LOVE.   2 *lust:* pleasure (no perjorative connotation).   4 *do
. . . observance:* do homage to May.   5 *mischance:* unlucky state.   9 *Sephame:* some astrologer who cast the poet's horoscope.   10 *Mischanc'd:* was
come to ill luck.   *ruler:* dominant planetary influence.

MY LUTE AWAKE.   3 *that:* what.

As to be heard where ear is none,
As lead to grave in marble stone,
   My song may pierce her heart as soon;
Should we then sigh, or sing, or moan?
    No, no, my lute, for I have done.   10

The rocks do not so cruelly
Repulse the waves continually,
   As she my suit and affection,
So that I am past remedy:
    Whereby my lute and I have done.   15

Proud of the spoil that thou hast got
Of simple hearts thorough love's shot,
   By whom, unkind, thou hast them won,
Think not he hath his bow forgot,
    Although my lute and I have done.   20

Vengeance shall fall on thy disdain,
That mak'st but game on earnest pain;
   Think not alone under the sun
Unquit to cause thy lovers plain,
    Although my lute and I have done.   25

Perchance thee lie withered and old,
The winter nights that are so cold,
   Plaining in vain unto the moon;
Thy wishes then dare not be told;
    Care then who list, for I have done.   30

And then may chance thee to repent
The time that thou hast lost and spent
   To cause thy lovers sigh and swoon;
Then shalt thou know beauty but lent,
    And wish and want as I have done.   35

Now cease, my lute: this is the last
Labor that thou and I shall waste,
   And ended is that we begun;
Now is this song both sung and past:
    My lute be still, for I have done.   40

---

7 *As . . . marble:* as lead (an extremely soft metal) to carve in marble.
17 *love's shot:* Cupid's arrow.   18 *unkind:* cruel, unnatural lady.   19 *Think
. . .forgot:* I.e., Cupid can cause me to love another.   22 *mak'st . . . pain:*
laughs at, makes sport of a lover's real suffering.   24 *Unquit to cause:* go
unpunished for having caused.   *plain:* to lament, mourn.   30 *list:* wishes.

Blame not my lute

Blame not my lute for he must sound
   Of this or that as liketh me;
For lack of wit the lute is bound
   To give such tunes as pleaseth me:
Though my songs be somewhat strange,   5
And speak such words as touch thy change,
     Blame not my lute.

My lute, alas, doth not offend
   Though that perforce he must agree
To sound such tunes as I intend   10
   To sing to them that heareth me;
Then though my songs be somewhat plain,
And toucheth some that use to feign,
     Blame not my lute.

My lute and strings may not deny,   15
   But as I strike they must obey;
Break not them then so wrongfully,
   But wreak thyself some wiser way:
And though the songs which I indite
Do quit thy change with rightful spite,   20
     Blame not my lute.

Spite asketh spite and changing change,
   And falsëd faith must needs be known;
The fault so great, the case so strange,
   Of right it must abroad be blown: 25
Then sins that by thine own desert
My songs do tell how true thou art,
     Blame not my lute.

Blame but thyself that hast misdone
   And well deserved to have blame;   30
Change thou thy way, so evil begone,
   And then my lute shall sound the same:
But if til then my fingers play
By thy desert their wonted way,
     Blame not my lute.   35

BLAME NOT MY LUTE. 2 *liketh me:* as it pleases me. 6 *change:* change in love. 18 *wreak:* revenge.

Farewell, unknown, for though thou break
  My strings in spite with great disdain,
Yet have I found out for thy sake
  Strings for to string my lute again;
And if perchance this foolish rhyme   40
Do make thee blush at any time,
    Blame not my lute.

Tangled I was in lovës snare

Tangled I was in lovës snare,
Oppressed with pain, torment with care,
Of grief right sure, of joy full bare,
  Clean in despair by cruelty,—
  But ha! ha! ha! full well is me,   5
  For I am now at liberty.

The woeful day so full of pain,
The weary night all spent in vain,
The labor lost for so small gain,
  To write them all it will not be.   10
  But ha! ha! ha! full well is me,
  For I am now at liberty.

Everything that fair doth show,
When proof is made it proveth not so,
But turneth mirth to bitter woe;   15
  Which in this case full well I see.
  But ha! ha! ha! full well is me,
  For I am now at liberty.

Too great desire was my guide
And wanton will went by my side;   20
Hope ruled still, and made me bide
  Of lovës craft th' extremity.
  But ha! ha! ha! full well is me,
  For I am now at liberty.

With feigned words which were but wind   25
To long delays I was assigned;
Her wily looks my wits did blind;
  Thus as she would I did agree.
  But ha! ha! ha! full well is me,
  For I am now at liberty.   30

TANGLED I WAS.   1 *lovës:* (dissyllabic) love's.

30

Was never bird tangled in lime
That brake away in better time
Than I, that rotten boughs did climb,
 And had no hurt, but scapèd free.
 Now ha! ha! ha! full well is me,   35
 For I am now at liberty.

And if an eye may save or slay

And if an eye may save or slay
 And strike more deep than weapon long,
And if an eye by subtle play
 May move one more than any tongue,
 How can ye say that I do wrong   5
Thus to suspect without desert?
For the eye is traitor of the heart.

To frame all well I am content
 That it were done unwittingly;
But yet I say, who will assent,   10
 To do but well, do no thing why
 That men should deem the contrary.
For it is said by men expert
That the eye is traitor of the heart.

But yet, alas, that look all soul   15
 That I do claim of right to have,
Should not, methinks, go seek the school
 To please all folk; for who can crave
 Friendlier thing than heart witsave?
By look to give in friendly part;   20
For the eye is traitor of the heart.

And my suspect is without blame,
 For, as ye say, not only I
But other more have deemed the same;
 Then is it not jealousy   25
 But subtle look of reckless eye
Did range too far to make me smart,
For the eye is traitor of the heart.

---

31 *lime:* birdlime, a sticky substance smeared on branches to catch small birds. 32 *brake:* broke.

AND IF AN EYE. 1 *eye:* the eye of the lady from which the beam of beauty streams to pierce the eye of the lover and thence to wound his heart. 7 *traitor:* I.e., the eye of the lover, smitten by beauty, betrays the heart and persuades it to love. 19 *witsave:* vouchsafe.

But I your friend shall take it thus,
 Since you will so, as stroke of chance;   30
And leave further for to discuss
 Whether the stroke did stick or glance;
 But 'scuse who can, let him advance
Dissembled looks; but for my part
My eye must still betray my heart.   35

And of this grief ye shall be quit
 In helping truth steadfast to go;
The time is long that doth sit
 Feeble and weak and suffers woe.
 Cherish him well, continue so,   40
Let him not from your heart astart;
Then fears not the eye to show the heart.

36 *quit:* excused, relieved. 41 *astart:* escape.

SIR PHILIP SIDNEY
1554–1586

1

Loving in truth, and faine in verse my love to show,
That the deare She might take some pleasure of my paine:
Pleasure might cause her reade, reading might make her know,
Knowledge might pitie winne, and pitie grace obtaine,
    I sought fit words to paint the blackest face of woe,   5
Studying inventions fine, her wits to entertaine:
Oft turning others' leaves, to see if thence would flow
Some fresh and fruitfull showers upon my sunne-burn'd braine.
    But words came halting forth, wanting Invention's stay,
Invention, Nature's child, fled step-dame Studie's blowes,   10
And others' feete still seem'd but strangers in my way.
Thus great with child to speake, and helplesse in my throwes,
    Biting my trewand pen, beating my selfe for spite,
    'Foole,' said my Muse to me, 'looke in thy heart and write.'

4

    Vertue alas, now let me take some rest,
    Thou setst a bate betweene my will and wit,
    If vaine love have my simple soule opprest,
    Leave what thou likest not, deale not thou with it.
        Thy scepter use in some old *Catoe's* brest;   5
    Churches or schooles are for thy seate more fit:
    I do confesse, pardon a fault confest,
    My mouth too tender is for thy hard bit.

SIDNEY. The text of Sidney's poems is that established by W. A. Ringler, Jr. (Oxford, at the Clarendon Press, 1962).

ASTROPHIL AND STELLA. A sonnet sequence celebrating the love of the "star lover" (Astrophil, which is also a pun on Philip) for his "star" (Stella).

[1] 1 *faine:* desirous. 6 *inventions:* ideas, devices, arguments. *Invention,* a term from classical rhetoric, is the art of discovering and selecting the topics to be treated: it also means the method of treatment. 7 *leaves:* pages. 8 *sunne-burn'd:* burned by beams streaming from the lady's sun-like eyes (a standard conceit). Cf. sonnet 20, and Shakespeare's sonnet 130. 9 *stay:* support. 10 *Nature's child:* I.e., a good poet is born with the gift of Invention. 11 *feete:* i.e., lines of poetry. 13 *trewand:* truant, rebellious, idle.

[4] 2 *bate:* debate. *will and wit:* desire and reason. 5 *Catoe:* i.e., some old stoic moralist like Cato (the Younger). 8 *bit:* the metal mouthpiece of a bridle. A horse that has a "tender" mouth ought to be treated gently.

But if that needs thou wilt usurping be,
The litle reason that is left in me,   10
And still th'effect of thy perswasions prove:
I sweare, my heart such one shall shew to thee,
That shrines in flesh so true a Deitie,
That *Vertue*, thou thy selfe shalt be in love.

14

Alas have I not paine enough my friend,
Upon whose breast a fiercer Gripe doth tire
Then did on him who first stale downe the fire,
While *Love* on me doth all his quiver spend,
But with your Rubarb words yow must contend   5
To grieve me worse, in saying that Desire
Doth plunge my wel-form'd soule even in the mire
Of sinfull thoughts, which do in ruine end?
If that be sinne which doth the maners frame,
Well staid with truth in word and faith of deed,   10
Readie of wit and fearing nought but shame:
If that be sinne which in fixt hearts doth breed
A loathing of all loose unchastitie,
Then Love is sinne, and let me sinfull be.

15

You that do search for everie purling spring,
Which from the ribs of old *Parnassus* flowes,
And everie floure, not sweet perhaps, which growes
Neare therabout, into your Poesie wring;
You that do Dictionarie's methode bring   5
Into your rimes, running in ratling rowes:
You that poore *Petrarch's* long deceased woes,
With new-borne sighes and denisend wit do sing;
You take wrong waies, those far-fet helpes be such,
As do bewray a want of inward tuch: 10

[14]   2 *Gripe doth tire:* vulture does tear (more than the one that ripped the vitals of Prometheus; cf. l. 3).   5 *Rubarb:* a bitter purgative.   9 *maners:* the outward sign of inward moral character.   10 *staid:* braced, propped.

[15]   1 *purling:* rippling.   2 *Parnassus:* Greek mountain sacred to Apollo and the Muses.   8 *denisend:* naturalized, i.e., imported from abroad.   9 *far-fet:* farfetched.   10 *inward tuch:* natural emotion.

And sure at length stolne goods do come to light.
  But if (both for your love and skill) your name
  You seeke to nurse at fullest breasts of Fame,
Stella behold, and then begin to endite.

20

Flie, fly, my friends, I have my death wound; fly,
See there that boy, that murthring boy I say,
Who like a theefe, hid in darke bush doth ly,
Till bloudie bullet get him wrongfull pray.
  So Tyran he no fitter place could spie,   5
Nor so faire levell in so secret stay,
As that sweete blacke which vailes the heav'nly eye:
There himselfe with his shot he close doth lay.
  Poore passenger, passe now thereby I did,
And staid pleasd with the prospect of the place,   10
While that blacke hue from me the bad guest hid:
But straight I saw motions of lightning' grace,
  And then descried the glistring of his dart:
  But ere I could flie thence, it pierc'd my heart.

24

Rich fooles there be, whose base and filthy hart
Lies hatching still the goods wherein they flow:
And damning their owne selves to *Tantal's* smart,
Wealth breeding want, more blist, more wretched grow.
  Yet to those fooles heav'n such wit doth impart,   5
As what their hands do hold, their heads do know,
And knowing, love, and loving, lay apart
As sacred things, far from all daunger's show.
  But that rich foole, who by blind Fortune's lot
The richest gemme of Love and life enjoyes,   10
And can with foule abuse such beauties blot;
Let him, deprived of sweet but unfelt joyes,
  (Exil'd for ay from those high treasures, which
  He knowes not) grow in only follie rich.

[20] 2 *boy:* Cupid. 4 *pray:* prey. 5 *Tyran:* tyrant. 6 *levell:* aim.
stay: place, station, i.e., ambush. 7 *blacke:* I.e., Stella's eyes are black.
9 *passenger:* traveller. *thereby:* near that place.

[24] 1 *Rich fooles:* presumably Robert, Lord Rich, Penelope Devereux's
(Stella's) husband. 3 *Tantal's smart:* Tantalus' punishment, i.e., never being
able to feast on the food and drink surrounding him. 4 *blist:* blest.

31

With how sad steps, ô Moone, thou climb'st the skies,
  How silently, and with how wanne a face,
  What, may it be that even in heav'nly place
That busie archer his sharpe arrowes tries?
Sure, if that long with *Love* acquainted eyes   5
  Can judge of *Love*, thou feel'st a Lover's case;
  I reade it in thy lookes, thy languisht grace,
To me that feele the like, thy state descries.
  Then ev'n of fellowship, ô Moone, tell me
Is constant *Love* deem'd there but want of wit?   10
Are Beauties there as proud as here they be?
Do they above love to be lov'd, and yet
  Those Lovers scorne whom that *Love* doth possesse?
  Do they call *Vertue* there ungratefulnesse?

39

Come sleepe, ô sleepe, the certaine knot of peace,
The baiting place of wit, the balme of woe,
The poore man's wealth, the prisoner's release,
Th'indifferent Judge betweene the high and low;
  With shield of proofe shield me from out the prease   5
Of those fierce darts, dispaire at me doth throw:
O make in me those civill warres to cease;
I will good tribute pay if thou do so.
  Take thou of me smooth pillowes, sweetest bed,
A chamber deafe to noise, and blind to light: 10
A rosie garland, and a wearie hed:
And if these things, as being thine by right,
  Move not thy heavy grace, thou shalt in me,
  Livelier then else-where, *Stella's* image see.

[31] 6 *case:* condition, situation. 14 *Do . . . ungratefulness:* I.e., do they call ingratitude a virtue there?

[39] 1 *knot:* bond of union. 2 *baiting place:* place for rest and refreshment on a journey. 5 *prease:* crowd. 11 *rosie garland:* garland of silence; cf. *sub rosa* (under the rose), secretly. 7 *civill warres:* i.e., wars between reason and passion within his soul.

41

Having this day my horse, my hand, my launce
  Guided so well, that I obtain'd the prize,
  Both by the judgement of the English eyes,
And of some sent from that sweet enemie *Fraunce;*
Horsemen my skill in horsmanship advaunce;   5
  Towne-folkes my strength; a daintier judge applies
  His praise to sleight, which from good use doth rise;
Some luckie wits impute it but to chaunce;
  Others, because of both sides I do take
My bloud from them, who did excell in this,   10
Thinke Nature me a man of armes did make.
How farre they shoote awrie! the true cause is,
  Stella lookt on, and from her heavenly face
  Sent forth the beames, which made so faire my race.

59

Deare, why make you more of a dog then me?
  If he do love, I burne, I burne in love:
  If he waite well, I never thence would move:
If he be faire, yet but a dog can be.
Litle he is, so litle worth is he: 5
  He barks, my songs thine owne voyce oft doth prove:
  Bid'n, perhaps he fetcheth thee a glove,
But I unbid, fetch even my soule to thee.
  Yet while I languish, him that bosome clips,
That lap doth lap, nay lets, in spite of spite,   10
This sowre-breath'd mate tast of those sugred lips.
Alas, if you graunt only such delight
  To witlesse things, then *Love* I hope (since wit
  Becomes a clog) will soone ease me of it.

[41] 5 *advaunce:* praise. 6 *daintier:* more discerning.

[59] 3 *waite:* attend. 6 *prove:* approve. 9 *clips:* embraces. 10 *That lap doth lap:* that lap [yours] does infold.

71

Who will in fairest booke of Nature know,
   How Vertue may best lodg'd in beautie be,
   Let him but learne of *Love* to reade in thee,
Stella, those faire lines, which true goodnesse show.
There shall he find all vices' overthrow,   5
   Not by rude force, but sweetest soveraigntie
   Of reason, from whose light those night-birds flie;
That inward sunne in thine eyes shineth so.
   And not content to be Perfection's heire
Thy selfe, doest strive all minds that way to move,   10
Who marke in thee what is in thee most faire.
So while thy beautie drawes the heart to love,
   As fast thy Vertue bends that love to good:
   'But ah,' Desire still cries, 'give me some food.'

108

When sorrow (using mine owne fier's might)
   Melts downe his lead into my boyling brest,
   Through that darke fornace to my hart opprest,
There shines a joy from thee my only light;
But soone as thought of thee breeds my delight,   5
   And my yong soule flutters to thee his nest,
   Most rude dispaire my daily unbidden guest,
Clips streight my wings, streight wraps me in his night,
   And makes me then bow downe my head, and say,
Ah what doth *Phœbus'* gold that wretch availe,   10
Whom iron doores do keepe from use of day?
So strangely (alas) thy works in me prevaile,
   That in my woes for thee thou art my joy,
   And in my joyes for thee my only annoy.

[71]   1 *booke of Nature:* the whole realm of created nature.   7 *night-birds:* i.e., owls, often used to represent such vices as sloth and avarice.

[108]   The last sonnet of the sequence. The lover in darkness laments the loss of the light of his lady's presence—often the conventional conclusion of a courtly love affair.   8 *clips:* cuts the feathers so that flight is impossible. 9 *Phoebus' gold:* sunlight.   11 *iron doores:* i.e., the darkness of enforced [by duty?] separation.

Leave me, ô Love, which reachest but to dust

Leave me, ô Love, which reachest but to dust,
And thou, my mind, aspire to higher things:
Grow rich in that which never taketh rust:
Whatever fades, but fading pleasure brings.

Draw in thy beames, and humble all thy might,   5
To that sweet yoke, where lasting freedomes be:
Which breakes the clowdes and opens forth the light,
That doth both shine and give us sight to see.

O take fast hold, let that light be thy guide,
In this small course which birth drawes out to death,   10
And thinke how evill becommeth him to slide,
Who seeketh heav'n, and comes of heav'nly breath.
   Then farewell world, thy uttermost I see,
   Eternal Love maintaine thy life in me.

Splendidis longum valedico nugis.

The Nightingale as soon as Aprill bringeth

The Nightingale as soon as Aprill bringeth
Unto her rested sense a perfect waking,
While late bare earth, proud of new clothing springeth,
Sings out her woes, a thorne her song-booke making:
   And mournfully bewailing,   5
   Her thoate in tunes expresseth
   What grief her breast oppresseth,

LEAVE ME, Ô LOVE. The conventional "renunciation" sonnet in which the lover forsakes earthly for heavenly love. Cf. Shakespeare's sonnet 146. 1–3 *dust . . . rust:* Cf. Matt. 6:19–21. 5 *beames:* i.e., the light of the eye, so as to avoid temptation. Cf. Matt. 6:22–23. 6 *yoke:* symbol of obedience. Cf. Matt. 11:29–30. 7 *light:* the light of the world. Cf. John 8:12. 10 *course:* i.e., the race prescribed for men to run. Cf. II Tim. 4:7. 11 *evill:* ill. *slide:* slide back, to be stubborn, to err, and thence to fall victim to the vengeance of God. Cf. Deut. 32:35; Hos. 4:16; Psa. 26:1. 12 *breath:* breath of life from God. Cf. Gen. 2:7. 14 *life:* everlasting life. Cf. John 3:16. *Splendidis . . . nugis:* I bid farewell forever to the splendid trifles [of the world].

THE NIGHTINGALE. 2 *rested sense:* i.e., after her winter's silence. 4 *thorne:* simultaneously the thorn of the hawthorn tree against which the bird presses her breast, thus making her song more ravishing, and remembered sorrow, which pricks the bird into plaintive song.

For *Thereus'* force on her chaste will prevailing.
  O *Philomela* faire, ô take some gladnesse,
  That here is juster cause of plaintfull sadnesse: 10
  Thine earth now springs, mine fadeth,
  Thy thorne without, my thorne my heart invadeth.

Alas, she hath no other cause of anguish
But *Thereus'* love, on her by strong hand wrokne,
Wherein she suffring all her spirits' languish,   15
Full womanlike complaines her will was brokne.
  But I who dayly craving,
  Cannot have to content me,
  Have more cause to lament me,
Since wanting is more woe then too much having.   20
  O *Philomela* faire, ô take some gladnesse,
  That here is juster cause of plaintful sadnesse:
  Thine earth now springs, mine fadeth:
  Thy thorne without, my thorne my heart invadeth.

from ARCADIA (THIRD BOOK)

My true love hath my hart, and I have his

[Charita's Song to Dametas]

My true love hath my hart, and I have his,
By just exchange, one for the other giv'ne.
I hold his deare, and myne he cannot misse:
There never was a better bargaine driv'ne.

His hart in me, keepes me and him in one,   5
My hart in him, his thoughtes and senses guides:
He loves my hart, for once it was his owne:
I cherish his, because in me it bides.

8–9 *For . . . faire:* Tereus, a Thracian king (see Ovid, *Metamorphoses*, VI, ll. 424–678), ravished Philomela, the sister of Procne, his wife, and then cut out her tongue to keep her from telling of his brutality and infidelity. Philomela managed to weave her story into a web, which was taken to Procne. The sisters then joined in a horrible revenge: Itys, Tereus' son by Procne, was slain and served to the father. When Tereus discovered what had taken place, he tried to kill the sisters, but they were saved by being transformed into birds— Philomela into a nightingale, Procne into a swallow.   14 *wrokne:* wreaked, inflicted.   18 *have:* have anything.

His hart his wound receaved from my sight:
My hart was wounded with his wounded hart,   10
For as from me, on him his hurt did light,
So still me thought in me his hurt did smart:
   Both equal hurt, in this change sought our blisse:
   My true love hath my hart and I have his.

EDMUND SPENSER
c. 1552–1599

November

AEGLOGA UNDECIMA

Argument

In this xi. Aeglogue he bewayleth the death of some mayden of greate bloud, whom he calleth Dido. The personage is secrete, and to me altogether unknowne, albe of him selfe I often required the same. This Aeglogue is made in imitation of Marot his song, which he made upon the death of Loys the frenche Queene. But farre passing his reache, and in myne opinion all other the Eglogues of this booke.

THENOT

Colin my deare, when shall it please thee sing,
As thou were wont songs of some jouisaunce?
Thy Muse to long slombreth in sorrowing,

THE SHEPHEARDES CALENDER. Revolutionary when it was first published anonymously in 1579, this poem comprises twelve pastoral eclogues, one for each month of the year. Spenser used this form to experiment with a wide variety of meters, styles, themes, and with different kinds of poetic diction, deliberately reviving "old and unwonted words." The eclogue for November is a "complaint," more popularly known as a "pastoral elegy"; it makes systematic use of the conventions developed in the pastoral tradition from Theocritus (third century B.C. Greek poet) to Virgil (first century B.C. Roman poet) to Spenser's more immediate Italian and French predecessors—such as Petrarch, Mantuan, and Marot—and also to the English poet Skelton. As Milton did later in "Lycidas," Spenser brought to the poem the whole of the pastoral tradition he inherited and by experimenting in language, form, and style gave to the poets of his day a model of a thoroughly modern English yet classical poem.

The pastoral is essentially a mask behind which the anonymous poet comments upon his world and upon the literary, spiritual, and political frustrations of the life of the poet himself. The rural scene is not literal or realistic but conventional and allegorical in meaning. Behind the obvious yet graceful artifices of this "complaint" is the harsh reality from which men generally try to hide. The notes and glosses (many of which are those of the still unidentified E.K. who supposedly edited the first edition) aim at elucidating the now unfamiliar conventions of the pastoral elegy and the old and difficult words Spenser revived in his experiment with poetic diction.

Aeglogue: (eclogue) i.e., a selection, a term usually associated with the pastoral. *Thenot:* an old shepherd friend of Colin Cloute (Spenser's pseudonym). In the pastoral, shepherds often meet and invite each other to engage in singing contests or in a solo performance. The semidramatic rural frame here sets off the elegance and sophistication of the stylized lament.

2 *were wont:* used to do. *jouisaunce:* "myrth" (E.K.).

Lulled a sleepe through loves misgoveraunce.
Now somewhat sing, whose endles sovenaunce,   5
Emong the shepeheards swaines may aye remaine,
Whether thee list thy loved lasse advaunce,
Or honor *Pan* with hymnes of higher vaine.

COLIN

Thenot, now nis the time of merimake.
Nor *Pan* to herye, nor with love to playe: 10
Sike myrth in May is meetest for to make,
Or summer shade under the cocked haye.
But nowe sadde Winter welked hath the day,
And *Phoebus* weary of his yerely taske,
Ystabled hath his steedes in lowlye laye,   15
And taken up his ynne in *Fishes* haske.
Thilke sollein season sadder plight doth aske:
And loatheth sike delightes, as thou doest prayse:
The mornefull Muse in myrth now list ne maske,
As shee was wont in youngth and sommer dayes.   20
But if thou algate lust light virelayes,
And looser songs of love to underfong
Who but thy selfe deserves sike Poetes prayse?
Relieve thy Oaten pypes, that sleepen long.

THENOT

The Nightingale is sovereigne of song,   25
Before him sits the Titmose silent bee:
And I unfitte to thrust in skilfull thronge,
Should *Colin* make judge of my fooleree.
Nay, better learne of hem, that learned bee,
And han be watered at the Muses well: 30
The kindlye dewe drops from the higher tree,

---

4 *misgovernaunce:* misgovernment. 5 *sovenaunce:* "remembrance" (E.K.). 7
list: wish. *advaunce:* praise. 8 *Pan:* god of the fields, of shepherds, and also,
perhaps, Christ, the Greater Pan for whom *hymnes of higher vaine* [vein] are
appropriate. 9 *nis:* is not. 10 *herye:* praise. 11 *Sike:* such. *meetest:* most
suitable. *make:* write verses. 13 *welked:* "shortned or empayred" (E.K.).
14 *Phoebus:* Apollo, the sun god who drives his chariot across the heavens.
yerely taske: annual revolution. 15 *laye:* place, field. 16 *ynne:* inn, abode.
Fishes haske: "a wicker pad, wherein they use to carry fish" (E.K.). The sign of
Pisces corresponds, however, to the position of the sun in February, not in
November. 17 *Thilke sollein:* this gloomy. 19 *mornefull Muse:* Melpomene,
Muse of Tragedy. *list ne maske:* is not inclined to take part in a pageant or a
disguising. 21 *algate:* nevertheless. *lust:* desire. *virelayes:* "a light kind of
song" (E.K.). 22 *underfong:* undertake. 24 *Relieve:* take up again. *Oaten
pypes:* shepherds' pipes. 27 *thronge:* i.e., of singers. 30 *han . . . well:* have
drunk of the waters of Helicon, over which the Muses preside.

And wets the little plants that lowly dwell.
But if sadde winters wrathe and season chill,
Accorde not with thy Muses meriment:
To sadder times thou mayst attune thy quill,   35
And sing of sorrowe and deathes dreeriment.
For deade is Dido, dead alas and drent,
Dido the greate shepehearde his daughter sheene:
The fayrest may she was that ever went,
Her like shee has not left behinde I weene.   40
And if thou wilt bewayle my wofull tene:
I shall thee give yond Cosset for thy payne:
And if thy rymes as rownd and rufull bene,
As those that did thy *Rosalind* complayne,
Much greater gyfts for guerdon thou shalt gayne,   45
Then Kidde or Cosset, which I thee bynempt:
Then up I say, thou jolly shepeheard swayne,
Let not my small demaund be so contempt.

COLIN

Thenot to that I choose, thou doest me tempt,
But ah to well I wote my humble vaine,   50
And howe my rymes bene rugged and unkempt:
Yet as I conne, my conning I will strayne.

Up then *Melpomene* thou mournefulst Muse of nyne,
Such cause of mourning never hadst afore:
Up grieslie ghostes and up my rufull ryme,   55
Matter of myrth now shalt thou have no more.
For dead shee is, that myrth thee made of yore.
　　Dido my deare alas is dead,
　　　Dead and lyeth wrapt in lead:
　　　　O heavie herse,   60
Let streaming teares be poured out in store:
　　　　O carefull verse.

---

35 *quill:* shepherd's pipe. 36 *dreeriment:* anguish. 37 *drent:* drowned. 38
sheene: fair. 39 *may:* "mayde" (E.K.). 40 *weene:* think. 41 *tene:* sorrow.
42 *Cosset:* lamb reared by hand, apart from its mother. 43 *rownd:* perfect.
44 *Rosalind:* maiden whom Colin has unsuccessfully wooed; her refusal has
prevented him from writing poetry. *complayne:* lament. 45 *guerdon:* reward.
46 *bynempt:* promised. 48 *contempt:* viewed with contempt. 50 *wote:* know.
51 *rugged and unkempt:* the singer of the complaint traditionally claims that
he is inadequate, that his song is rough and harsh. Cf. Milton's "forc'd fingers
rude" in "Lycidas," l. 4. 52 *conne:* am able. 53 *nyne:* the nine Muses. 59
lead: lead coffin. 60 *herse:* "the solemn obsequy [burial rites] in funerals"
(E.K.). 62 *carefull:* full of care.

Shepheards, that by your flocks on Kentish downes abyde,
Waile ye this wofull waste of natures warke:
Waile we the wight, whose presence was our pryde: 65
Waile we the wight, whose absence is our carke.
The sonne of all the world is dimme and darke:
   The earth now lacks her wonted light,
   And all we dwell in deadly night,
     O heavie herse.   70
Breake we our pypes, that shrild as lowde as Larke,
     O carefull verse.

Why doe we longer live (ah why live we so long)
Whose better dayes death hath shut up in woe?
The fayrest floure our gyrlond all emong,   75
Is faded quite and into dust ygoe.
Sing now ye shepheards daughters, sing no moe
   The songs that *Colin* made in her prayse,
   But into weeping turne your wanton layes,
     O heavie herse,   80
Now is time to dye. Nay time was long ygoe,
     O carefull verse.

Whence is it, that the flouret of the field doth fade,
And lyeth buryed long in Winters bale:
Yet soone as spring his mantle hath displayd,   85
It floureth fresh, as it should never fayle?
But thing on earth that is of most availe,
   As vertues braunch and beauties budde,
   Reliven not for any good.
     O heavie herse,   90
The braunch once dead, the budde eke needes must quaile,
     O carefull verse.

She while she was (that was, a woful word to sayne)
For beauties prayse and plesaunce had no pere:
So well she couth the shepherds entertayne,   95
With cakes and cracknells and such country chere.
Ne would she scorne the simple shepheards swaine,

63 *Shepheardes:* conventionally, the whole pastoral world must mourn.
64 *warke:* work. 65 *wight:* person. 66 *carke:* care. 75 *gyrlond:* garland.
76 *ygoe:* gone. 77 *moe:* more. 79 *wanton:* merry. *layes:* songs. 83
Whence . . . : the conventional question, the "riddle of this painful earth," that
challenges faith: Why is it that the flowers revive, but man does not? 84 *bale:*
misery. 89 *Reliven not:* come not to life again. 91 *eke:* also. *quaile:* perish.
93 *She . . . :* conventional recollection of the pastoral life together. *sayne:*
say. 94 *plesaunce:* pleasing behavior. *pere:* peer. 95 *couth:* knew how
[to]. 96 *cracknells:* crisp, curved biscuits.

For she would cal hem often heame
And give hem curds and clouted Creame.
    O heavie herse,   100
Als *Colin Cloute* she would not once disdayne.
    O carefull verse.

But nowe sike happy cheere is turnd to heavie chaunce,
Such pleasaunce now displast by dolors dint:
All musick sleepes, where death doth leade the daunce,   105
And shepherds wonted solace is extinct.
The blew in black, the greene in gray is tinct,
    The gaudie girlonds deck her grave,
    The faded flowres her corse embrave.
    O heavie herse,   110
Morne nowe my Muse, now morne with teares besprint.
    O carefull verse.

O thou greate shepheard *Lobbin*, how great is thy griefe,
Where bene the nosegayes that she dight for thee:
The coloured chaplets wrought with a chiefe,   115
The knotted rushrings, and gilte Rosemaree?
For shee deemed nothing too deere for thee.
    Ah they bene all yclad in clay,
    One bitter blast blewe all away.
    O heavie herse,   120
Thereof nought remaynes but the memoree.
    O carefull verse.

Ay me that dreerie death should strike so mortall stroke,
That can undoe Dame natures kindly course:
The faded lockes fall from the loftie oke,   125
The flouds do gaspe, for dryed is theyr sourse,
And flouds of teares flowe in theyr stead perforse.
    The mantled medowes mourne,
    Theyr sondry colours tourne.
    O heavie herse,   130
The heavens doe melt in teares without remorse.
    O carefull verse.

---

98 *heame:* home.   99 *clouted:* clotted.   103 *heavie chaunce:* misfortune, the conventional unlucky event that destroys life.   104 *dint:* stroke.   107 *The blew . . . tinct:* The blue is stained black; the green, gray.   109 *corse:* corpse. *embrave:* beautify.   111 *besprint:* sprinkled.   113 *Lobbin:* Dido's lover. 114 *nosegayes:* bunch of sweet-smelling flowers or herbs.   *dight:* made.   115 *chaplets . . . chiefe:* probably, garlands woven to make a special feature of some flower.   116 *gilte:* golden.   118 *yclad in clay:* i.e., dead.   123 *Ay me . . . :* All nature mourns, the conventional pathetic fallacy.   126 *flouds:* rivers.

The feeble flocks in field refuse their former foode,
And hang theyr heads, as they would learne to weepe:
The beastes in forest wayle as they were woode,   135
Except the Wolves, that chase the wandring sheepe:
Now she is gon that safely did hem keepe.
　　The Turtle on the bared braunch,
　　Laments the wound, that death did launch.
　　　O heavie herse,   140
And *Philomele* her song with teares doth steepe.
　　　O carefull verse.

The water Nymphs, that wont with her to sing and daunce,
And for her girlond Olive braunches beare,
Now balefull boughes of Cypres doen advaunce: 145
The Muses, that were wont greene bayes to weare,
Now bringen bitter Eldre braunches seare:
　　The fatall sisters eke repent,
　　Her vitall threde so soone was spent.
　　　O heavie herse,   150
Morne now my Muse, now morne with heavie cheare.
　　　O carefull verse.

O trustlesse state of earthly things, and slipper hope
Of mortal men, that swincke and sweate for nought,
And shooting wide, doe misse the marked scope: 155
Now have I learnd (a lesson derely bought)
That nys on earth assuraunce to be sought:
　　For what might be in earthlie mould,
　　That did her buried body hould.
　　　O heavie herse,   160
Yet saw I on the beare when it was brought,
　　　O carefull verse.

But maugre death, and dreaded sisters deadly spight,
And gates of hel, and fyrie furies forse:
She hath the bonds broke of eternall night,   165
Her soule unbodied of the burdenous corpse.

---

135 *woode:* mad.　　138 *Turtle:* turtledove.　　141 *Philomele:* nightingale.
Cf. Sidney, p. 39.　143 *The water . . . :* the traditional procession of
mourners.　145 *Cypres:* "sign of all sorrow" (E.K.).　148 *fatall sisters:* the
Fates.　149 *vitall threde:* i.e., of life, as spun, measured, and cut by the Fates.
Cf. Milton, "Lycidas," ll. 75–76.　153 *slipper:* slippery.　154 *swincke:* toil.
155 *scope:* target.　161 *beare:* bier.　163 *But maugre death . . . :* But in spite of
death . . . . The apotheosis, conventional since Virgil.　*dreaded sisters:* the
Fates.

Why then weepes Lobbin so without remorse?
  O Lobb, thy losse no longer lament,
  Dido nis dead, but into heaven hent.
    O happye herse,   170
Cease now my Muse, now cease thy sorrowes sourse,
    O joyfull verse.

Why wayle we then? why weary we the Gods with playnts,
As if some evill were to her betight?
She raignes a goddesse now emong the saintes,   175
That whilome was the saynt of shepheards light:
And is enstalled nowe in heavens hight.
  I see thee blessed soule, I see,
  Walke in *Elisian* fieldes so free.
    O happy herse,   180
Might I once come to thee (O that I might)
    O joyfull verse.

Unwise and wretched men to weete whats good or ill,
We deeme of Death as doome of ill desert:
But knewe we fooles, what it us bringes until,   185
Dye would we dayly, once it to expert.
No daunger there the shepheard can astert:
  Fayre fieldes and pleasaunt layes there bene,
  The fieldes ay fresh, the grasse ay greene:
    O happy herse,   190
Make hast ye shepheards, thether to revert,
    O joyfull verse.

Dido is gone afore (whose turne shall be the next?)
There lives shee with the blessed Gods in blisse,
There drincks she *Nectar* with *Ambrosia* mixt,   195
And joyes enjoyes, that mortall men doe misse.
The honor now of highest gods she is,
  That whilome was poore shepheards pryde,
  While here on earth she did abyde.
    O happy herse,   200
Ceasse now my song, my woe now wasted is.
    O joyfull verse.

---

169 *hent:* caught [up].   173 *playnts:* lamentations.   174 *betight:* betide.
175 *saintes:* See Rev. 7:9–17. See also "Collect for All Saints' Day"
(November 1) in *Book of Common Prayer.*   176 *whilome:* once.   183 *weete:*
know.   184 *deeme:* think.   186 *expert:* experience.   187 *astert:* disturb.
189 *ay:* always.   191 *revert:* return.   201 *wasted:* spent.

THENOT

Ay francke shepheard, how bene thy verses meint
With doolful pleasaunce, so as I ne wotte,
Whether rejoyce or weepe for great constrainte?   205
Thyne be the cossette, well hast thow it gotte.
Up *Colin* up, ynough thou morned hast,
Now gynnes to mizzle, hye we homeward fast.

COLINS EMBLEME

La mort ny mord.

Prothalamion

1

Calme was the day, and through the trembling ayre,
Sweete breathing *Zephyrus* did softly play
A gentle spirit, that lightly did delay
Hot *Titans* beames, which then did glyster fayre:
When I whom sullein care,   5
Through discontent of my long fruitlesse stay
In Princes Court, and expectation vayne
Of idle hopes, which still doe fly away,
Like empty shaddowes, did aflict my brayne,
Walkt forth to ease my payne   10
Along the shoare of silver streaming *Themmes*,
Whose rutty Bancke, the which his River hemmes,
Was paynted all with variable flowers,
And all the meades adornd with daintie gemmes,
Fit to decke maydens bowres,   15
And crowne their Paramours,
Against the Brydale day, which is not long:
    Sweete *Themmes* runne softly, till I end my Song.

2

There, in a Meadow, by the Rivers side,
A Flocke of *Nymphes* I chaunced to espy,   20
All lovely Daughters of the Flood thereby,

203 *francke:* honest.   *meint:* mingled. 208 *gynnes to mizzle:* begins to drizzle.
La mort ny mord: ". . . death biteth not" (E.K.).

PROTHALAMION.   A "marriage song," honoring the double marriage of the
Ladies Elizabeth and Katherine Somerset. 2 *Zephyrus:* the west wind.   4
Titans: the sun's. 12 *rutty:* full of ruts. 21 *Flood:* River [Thames].

With goodly greenish locks all loose untyde,
As each had bene a Bryde,
And each one had a little wicker basket,
Made of fine twigs entrayled curiously,   25
In which they gathered flowers to fill their flasket:
And with fine Fingers, cropt full feateously
The tender stalkes on hye.
Of every sort, which in that Meadow grew,
They gathered some; the Violet pallid blew,   30
The little Dazie, that at evening closes,
The virgin Lillie, and the Primrose trew,
With store of vermeil Roses,
To decke their Bridegromes posies,
Against the Brydale day, which was not long: 35
    Sweete *Themmes* runne softly, till I end my Song.

3

With that I saw two Swannes of goodly hewe,
Come softly swimming downe along the Lee;
Two fairer Birds I yet did never see:
The snow which doth the top of *Pindus* strew,   40
Did never whiter shew,
Nor Jove himselfe when he a Swan would be
For love of *Leda*, whiter did appeare:
Yet *Leda* was they say as white as he,
Yet not so white as these, nor nothing neare;   45
So purely white they were,
That even the gentle streame, the which them bare,
Seem'd foule to them, and bad his billowes spare
To wet their silken feathers, least they might
Soyle their fayre plumes with water not so fayre,   50
And marre their beauties bright,
That shone as heavens light,
Against their Brydale day, which was not long:
    Sweete *Themmes* runne softly, till I end my Song.

---

22 *greenish:* traditional color of the hair of mermaids and water nymphs.   23
As: As if.   25 *entrayled:* entwined.   26 *flasket:* shallow basket.   27 *feateously:*
deftly.   33 *vermeil:* bright red.   38 *Lee:* the stream, and perhaps the Lea, a
river that flows into the Thames at Greenwich.   40 *Pindus:* mountain in
Thessaly.   42–43 *Jove . . . Leda:* a mortal wooed by Jove (Zeus) in the form
of a swan. Among their offspring were Castor and Pollux (l. 173) and Helen of
Troy. Cf. Yeats, "Leda and the Swan, " p. 470.   55 *Eftsoones:* at once.

4

Eftsoones the *Nymphes*, which now had Flowers their fill,   55
Ran all in haste, to see that silver brood,
As they came floating on the Christal Flood,
Whom when they sawe, they stood amazed still,
Their wondring eyes to fill.
Them seem'd they never saw a sight so fayre,   60
Of Fowles so lovely, that they sure did deeme
Them heavenly borne, or to be that same payre
Which through the Skie draw *Venus* silver Teeme,
For sure they did not seeme
To be begot of any earthly Seede,   65
But rather Angels or of Angels breede:
Yet were they bred of *Somers-heat* they say,
In sweetest Season, when each Flower and weede
The earth did fresh aray,
So fresh they seem'd as day,   70
Even as their Brydale day, which was not long:
   Sweete *Themmes* runne softly, till I end my Song.

5

Then forth they all out of their baskets drew
Great store of Flowers, the honour of the field,
That to the sense did fragrant odours yield,   75
All which upon those goodly Birds they threw,
And all the Waves did strew,
That like old *Peneus* Waters they did seeme,
When downe along by pleasant *Tempes* shore
Scattred with Flowres, through *Thessaly* they streeme,   80
That they appeare through Lillies plenteous store,
Like a Brydes Chamber flore:
Two of those *Nymphes*, meane while, two Garlands bound,
Of freshest Flowres which in that Mead they found,
The which presenting all in trim Array,   85
Their snowie Foreheads therewithall they crownd,
Whil'st one did sing this Lay,
Prepar'd against that Day,
Against their Brydale day, which was not long:
   Sweete *Themmes* runne softly, till I end my Song.   90

---

63 *Venus silver Teeme:* Venus is associated with swans. 67 *Somers-heat:*
pun on Somerset, surname of the two brides whose marriages are being
celebrated. 78 *Peneus:* river in Thessaly, rising in Mt. Pindus (l. 40) and
flowing through the Vale of Tempe.

6

Ye gentle Birdes, the worlds faire ornament,
And heavens glorie, whom this happie hower
Doth leade unto your lovers blisfull bower,
Joy may you have and gentle hearts content
Of your loves couplement: 95
And let faire *Venus*, that is Queene of love,
With her heart-quelling Sonne upon you smile,
Whose smile they say, hath vertue to remove
All Loves dislike, and friendships faultie guile
For ever to assoile.   100
Let endlesse Peace your steadfast hearts accord,
And blessed Plentie wait upon your bord,
And let your bed with pleasures chast abound,
That fruitfull issue may to you afford,
Which may your foes confound,   105
And make your joyes redound,
Upon your Brydale day, which is not long:
   Sweete *Themmes* run softly, till I end my Song.

7

So ended she; and all the rest around
To her redoubled that her undersong,   110
Which said, their bridale daye should not be long.
And gentle Eccho from the neighbour ground,
Their accents did resound.
So forth those joyous Birdes did passe along,
Adowne the Lee, that to them murmurde low,   115
As he would speake, but that he lackt a tong,
Yet did by signes his glad affection show,
Making his streame run slow.
And all the foule which in his flood did dwell
Gan flock about these twaine, that did excell   120
The rest, so far, as *Cynthia* doth shend
The lesser starres. So they enranged well,
Did on those two attend,
And their best service lend,
Against their wedding day, which was not long: 125
   Sweete *Themmes* run softly, till I end my Song.

---

97 *Sonne:* i.e., Cupid. 100 *assoile:* absolve. 110 *redoubled . . . undersong:*
repeated the refrain of the "lay." See l. 87. 112 *Eccho:* nymph of woods
and hills. 121 *Cynthia:* goddess of the moon; also an allusion to Queen
Elizabeth. *shend:* outshine. 122 *enranged:* arranged.

52

8

At length they all to mery *London* came,
To mery London, my most kyndly Nurse,
That to me gave this Lifes first native sourse:
Though from another place I take my name,   130
An house of auncient fame.
There when they came, whereas those bricky towres,
The which on *Themmes* brode aged backe doe ryde,
Where now the studious Lawyers have their bowers,
There whylome wont the Templer Knights to byde,   135
Till they decayd through pride:
Next whereunto there standes a stately place,
Where oft I gayned giftes and goodly grace
Of that great Lord, which therein wont to dwell,
Whose want too well, now feeles my freendles case: 140
But Ah here fits not well
Olde woes but joyes to tell
Against the bridale daye, which is not long:
    Sweete *Themmes* runne softly, till I end my Song.

9

Yet therein now doth lodge a noble Peer,   145
Great *Englands* glory and the Worlds wide wonder,
Whose dreadfull name, late through all *Spaine* did thunder,
And *Hercules* two pillors standing neere,
Did make to quake and feare:
Faire branch of Honor, flower of Chevalrie,   150
That fillest *England* with thy triumphes fame,
Joy have thou of thy noble victorie,
And endlesse happinesse of thine owne name
That promiseth the same:
That through thy prowesse and victorious armes,   155
Thy country may be freed from forraine harmes:
And great *Elisaes* glorious name may ring
Through al the world, fil'd with thy wide Alarmes,
Which some brave muse may sing

128 *my:* i.e., Spenser's. 130 *place . . . name:* possibly from the Spencers of Althorpe (Northamptonshire). 132–35 *bricky . . . byde:* The Temple (Inner Temple, Middle Temple); from its former occupation by the Knights Templars. After the suppression of their order in the fourteenth century, their house was turned over to law students for their use and became known as the Inns of Court. 136 *they:* the Knights Templars. 137 *stately place:* probably the house of the Earl of Essex, formerly the home of the Earl of Leicester, at one time Spenser's patron. 145 *Peer:* Earl of Essex; in 1596 Essex returned from the capture of Cadiz. 148 *Hercules two pillors:* the Strait of Gibraltar. 157 *Elisaes:* Queen Elizabeth's.

To ages following,   160
Upon the Brydale day, which is not long:
   Sweete *Themmes* runne softly, till I end my Song.

10

From those high Towers, this noble Lord issuing,
Like Radiant *Hesper* when his golden hayre
In th'*Ocean* billowes he hath Bathed fayre,   165
Descended to the Rivers open vewing,
With a great traine ensuing.
Above the rest were goodly to bee seene
Two gentle Knights of lovely face and feature
Beseeming well the bower of anie Queene,   170
With gifts of wit and ornaments of nature,
Fit for so goodly stature:
That like the twins of *Joue* they seem'd in sight,
Which decke the Bauldricke of the Heavens bright.
They two forth pacing to the Rivers side,   175
Received those two faire Brides, their Loves delight,
Which at th'appointed tyde,
Each one did make his Bryde,
Against their Brydale day, which is not long:
   Sweete *Themmes* runne softly, till I end my Song.   180

from AMORETTI

1

Happy ye leaves when as those lilly hands,
   which hold my life in their dead doing might
   shall handle you and hold in love's soft bands,
   lyke captives trembling at the victor's sight.

---

164 *Hesper:* the Evening Star.   173 *twins:* Castor and Pollux, the constellation Gemini. See ll. 42–43.   174 *Bauldricke . . . Heavens:* i.e., the belt
of the Zodiac, of which Gemini is the third sign.

AMORETTI.   An unusual sonnet sequence in that it celebrates, presumably,
Spenser's courtship of Elizabeth Boyle, whom he married in 1594. The standard
courtly themes are often crossed with domestic and entirely licit matrimonial
desires. Although the sequence ends (with No. 89) in the traditional darkness
that follows the lover's forced separation from his beloved, Spenser breaks with
tradition by publishing the "Epithalamion," a rapturous marriage song,
instead of the traditional "renunciation" sonnet at the conclusion of the
Amoretti, thus transforming darkness into eternal light.

  [1]   1 *leaves:* pages of the manuscript that the poet presents to his beloved.

And happy lines, on which with starry light,   5
   those lamping eyes will deigne sometimes to look
   and reade the sorrowes of my dying spright,
   written with teares in hart's close bleeding book.
And happy rymes, bath'd in the sacred brooke,
   of *Helicon* whence she derived is,   10
   when ye behold that Angel's blessed looke,
   my soule's long lacked foode, my heaven's blis.
Leaves, lines, and rymes, seeke her to please alone,
   whom if ye please, I care for other none.

19

The merry Cuckow, messenger of Spring,
   his trompet shrill hath thrise already sounded:
   that warnes al lovers wayt upon their king,
   who now is comming forth with girland crouned.
With noyse whereof the quyre of Birds resounded   5
   their anthemes sweet devized of love's prayse,
   that all the woods their ecchoes back rebounded,
   as if they knew the meaning of their layes.
But 'mongst them all, which did Love's honor rayse
   no word was heard of her that most it ought,   10
   but she his precept proudly disobayes,
   and doth his idle message set at nought.
Therefore O love, unlesse she turne to thee
   ere Cuckow end, let her a rebell be.

34

Lyke as a ship that through the Ocean wide,
   by conduct of some star doth make her way,
   whenas a storme hath dim'd her trusty guyde,
   out of her course doth wander far astray.
So I whose star, that wont with her bright ray   5
   me to direct, with cloudes is overcast,
   doe wander now in darknesse and dismay,
   through hidden perils round about me plast.
Yet hope I well that when this storme is past
   my *Helice* the lodestar of my lyfe   10

6 *lamping:* shining. 10 *Helicon:* fountain near Mt. Parnassus, sacred to Apollo and the Muses.

[19] 5 *Birds:* Cf. Song of Sol. 2:12.

[34] 10 *Helice:* the constellation *Ursa Minor* (the Little Dipper), of which the outermost star is the pole star (*lodestar*).

will shine again, and looke on me at last,
with lovely light to cleare my cloudy grief.
Till then I wander carefull comfortlesse,
in secret sorrow and sad pensivenesse.

68

Most glorious Lord of lyfe that on this day,
    did'st make thy triumph over death and sin:
    and having harrowd hell did'st bring away
    captivity thence captive us to win:
This joyous day, deare Lord, with joy begin,   5
    and grant that we for whom thou diddest dye
    being with thy deare blood clene washt from sin,
    may live for ever in felicity.
And that thy love we weighing worthily,
    may likewise love thee for the same againe: 10
    and for thy sake that all like deare did'st buy,
    with love may one another entertayne.
So let us love, deare love, lyke as we ought,
    love is the lesson which the Lord us taught.

71

I joy to see how in your drawen work,
    your selfe unto the Bee ye doe compare;
    and me unto the Spyder that doth lurke,
    in close await to catch her unaware.
Right so your selfe were caught in cunning snare   5
    of a deare foe, and thralled to his love:
    in whose streight bands ye now captived are
    so firmely, that ye never may remove.
But as your worke is woven all above,
    with woodbynd flowers and fragrant Eglantine: 10
    so sweet your prison you in time shall prove,
    with many deare delights bedecked fyne.
And all thensforth eternall peace shall see,
    betweene the Spyder and the gentle Bee.

---

[68]   2 *triumph:* i.e., Easter Day.   3 *harrowd:* raided. Between Good Friday and Easter Sunday, Christ "harrowd" Hell and freed from damnation the captive righteous—those worthy of salvation but who, until the Resurrection, were ineligible.

[71]   1 *drawen work:* embroidery.

75

One day I wrote her name upon the strand,
    but came the waves and washed it away:
    agayne I wrote it with a second hand,
    but came the tide, and made my paines his pray.
Vayne man, said she, that doest in vaine assay,   5
    a mortall thing so to immortalize,
    for I my selve shall lyke to this decay,
    and eek my name bee wiped out lykewize.
Not so, (quod I) let baser things devize
    to dy in dust, but you shall live by fame: 10
    my verse your vertues rare shall eternize
    and in the hevens wryte your glorious name.
Where whenas death shall all the world subdew,
    our love shall live, and later life renew.

89

Lyke as the Culver on the bared bough,
    sits mourning for the absence of her mate:
    and in her songs sends many a wishfull vow,
    for his returne that seemes to linger late.
So I alone now left disconsolate,
    mourne to my selfe the absence of my love:
    and wandring here and there all desolate,
    seek with my playnts to match that mournful dove:
Ne joy of ought that under heaven doth hove,
    can comfort me, but her owne joyous sight: 10
    whose sweet aspect both God and man can move,
    in her unspotted pleasauns to delight.
Dark is my day, whyles her faire light I mis,
    and dead my life that wants such lively blis.

Epithalamion

Ye learned sisters which have oftentimes
Beene to me ayding, others to adorne:
Whom ye thought worthy of your gracefull rymes,

[75] In the tradition of *Ars longa, vita brevis est* (Art is long, life is short): i.e., because we love, your beauty, ordinarily mortal, shall be eternal in art (this poem).

[89] 1 *Culver:* mourning dove. 9 *hove:* rise. 12 *pleasauns:* pleasing behavior; also, a secluded garden with walks and ornamental pools. The lady's face was often described as a garden.

EPITHALAMION. 1 *sisters:* the nine Muses who inspire artists.

That even the greatest did not greatly scorne
To heare theyr names sung in your simple layes,   5
But joyed in theyr prayse.
And when ye list your owne mishaps to mourne,
Which death, or love, or fortunes wreck did rayse,
Your string could soone to sadder tenor turne,
And teach the woods and waters to lament   10
Your dolefull dreriment.
Now lay those sorrowfull complaints aside,
And having all your heads with girland crownd,
Helpe me mine owne love's prayses to resound,
Ne let the same of any be envide: 15
So Orpheus did for his owne bride,
So I unto my selfe alone will sing,
The woods shall to me answer and my Eccho ring.

Early before the worlds light giving lampe,
His golden beame upon the hils doth spred,   20
Having disperst the night's unchearful dampe,
Doe ye awake, and with fresh lusty hed
Go to the bowre of my beloved love,
My truest turtle dove,
Bid her awake; for Hymen is awake,   25
And long since ready forth his maske to move,
With his bright Tead that flames with many a flake,
And many a bachelor to waite on him,
In theyr fresh garments trim.
Bid her awake therefore and soone her dight,   30
For lo the wished day is come at last,
That shall for al the paynes and sorrowes past,
Pay to her usury of long delight:
And whylest she doth her dight,
Doe ye to her of joy and solace sing,   35
That all the woods may answer and your eccho ring.

---

9 *tenor:* the particular quality, character, and nature of the mood of the music.   16 *Orpheus:* mythological poet-musician who so charmed the warring elements of all creation (animal, vegetable, mineral) with his song that they were in harmony with each other; he regained his wife, Eurydice, when she had been taken to Hell by Pluto, only to lose her when, against instructions, he looked back at her as they left the underworld. As the Orphic poet and lover, Spenser also charms nature (see refrain) and happily wins his bride without fear of loss.   24 *turtle dove:* As in many Renaissance love lyrics, the imagery here is derived largely from the "Song of Solomon," here particularly 2:12.   25 *Hymen:* Roman god of marriage.   27 *Tead:* torch carried by Hymen. *flake:* spark.   32 *paynes . . . past:* the traditional torments the lover has suffered at the hands of his lady.   34 *dight:* adorn, dress.

Bring with you all the Nymphes that you can heare
Both of the rivers and the forrests greene:
And of the sea that neighbours to her neare,
Al with gay girlands goodly wel beseene.   40
And let them also with them bring in hand,
Another gay girland
For my fayre love of lillyes and of roses,
Bound true love wize with a blew silke riband.
And let them make great store of bridale poses,   45
And let them eeke bring store of other flowers
To deck the bridale bowers.
And let the ground whereas her foot shall tread,
For feare the stones her tender foot should wrong
Be strewed with fragrant flowers all along,   50
And diapred lyke the discolored mead.
Which done, doe at her chamber dore awayt,
For she will waken strayt,
The whiles doe ye this song unto her sing,
The woods shall to you answer and your Eccho ring.   55

Ye Nymphes of Mulla which with carefull heed,
The silver scaly trouts doe tend full well,
And greedy pikes which use therin to feed,
(Those trouts and pikes all others doo excell)
And ye likewise which keepe the rushy lake,   60
Where none doo fishes take,
Bynd up the locks the which hang scatterd light,
And in his waters which your mirror make,
Behold your faces as the christall bright,
That when you come whereas my love doth lie,   65
No blemish she may spie.
And eke ye lightfoot mayds which keepe the deere,
That on the hoary mountayne use to towre,
And the wylde wolves which seeke them to devoure,
With your steele darts doo chace from comming neer   70
Be also present heere,
To helpe to decke her and to help to sing,
That all the woods may answer and your eccho ring.

---

40 *beseene:* adorned.   43 *lillyes . . . roses:* Cf. Song of Sol. 2:1.   44 *true
. . . riband:* a bowknot, blue to indicate faith.   45 *poses:* posies.   51 *diapred:*
diamond patterned.   *discolored mead:* many-colored field.   53 *strayt:* immediately.   56 *Mulla:* Spenser's name for the river Awbeg in Ireland, near
his manor, Kilcolman.

Wake, now my love, awake; for it is time,
The Rosy Morne long since left Tithonès bed,   75
All ready to her silver coche to clyme,
And Phœbus gins to shew his glorious hed.
Hark how the cheerefull birds do chaunt theyr laies
And carroll of love's praise.
The merry Larke hir mattins sings aloft,   80
The thrush replyes, the Mavis descant playes,
The Ouzell shrills, the Ruddock warbles soft,
So goodly all agree with sweet consent,
To this daye's merriment.
Ah my deere love why doe ye sleepe thus long,   85
When meeter were that ye should now awake,
T'awayt the comming of your joyous make,
And hearken to the birds' love-learned song,
The deawy leaves among.
For they of joy and pleasance to you sing,   90
That all the woods them answer and theyr eccho ring.

My love is now awake out of her dreame,
And her fayre eyes like stars that dimmed were
With darksome cloud, now shew theyr goodly beams
More bright then Hesperus his head doth rere.   95
Come now ye damzels, daughters of delight,
Helpe quickly her to dight,
But first come ye fayre houres which were begot
In Jove's sweet paradice, of Day and Night,
Which doe the seasons of the yeare allot,   100
And al that euer in this world is fayre
Doe make and still repayre.
And ye three handmayds of the Cyprian Queene,
The which doe still adorne her beauties pride,
Helpe to addorne my beautifullest bride: 105
And as ye her array, still throw betweene
Some graces to be seene,
And as ye use to Venus, to her sing,
The whiles the woods shal answer and your eccho ring.

75 *Tithone:* Tithonus, husband of Aurora, who is the goddess of the dawn.
76 *coche:* coach.   80 *mattins:* service of morning prayer.   81 *Mavis:* thrush.
descant: melodious accompaniment to the plainsong sung or extemporized
above it. 82 *Ouzell:* blackbird. *Ruddock:* robin. 86 *meeter:* more fit.
87 *make:* mate. 95 *Hesperus:* Venus, the evening star. 98 *houres:* the
Horae—to Hesiod, daughters of Zeus and Themis—Eunomiā (Good Order),
Dikē (Justice), Eirēnē (Peace)—goddesses of order in nature who cause the
seasons to change and all things to blossom and ripen at their appointed time,
guardians of the gates of Olympus and the fields of men. 103 *handmayds
. . . Queene:* the Graces who attend Venus. 108 *use:* are accustomed.

Now is my love all ready forth to come,   110
Let all the virgins therefore well awayt,
And ye fresh boyes that tend upon her groome
Prepare your selves; for he is comming strayt.
Set all your things in seemely good aray
Fit for so joyfull day,   115
The joyfulst day that ever sunne did see.
Faire Sun, shew forth thy favorable ray,
And let thy lifull heat not fervent be
For feare of burning her sunshyny face,
Her beauty to disgrace.   120
O fayrest Phœbus, father of the Muse,
If ever I did honour thee aright,
Or sing the thing, that mote thy mind delight,
Doe not thy servants simple boone refuse,
But let this day, let this one day be myne,   125
Let all the rest be thine.
Then I thy soverayne prayses loud wil sing,
That all the woods shal answer and theyr eccho ring.

Harke how the Minstrels gin to shrill aloud
Their merry Musick that resounds from far,   130
The pipe, the tabor, and the trembling Croud,
That well agree withouten breach or jar.
But most of all the Damzels doe delite,
When they their tymbrels smyte,
And thereunto doe daunce and carrol sweet,   135
That all the sences they doe ravish quite,
The whyles the boyes run up and downe the street,
Crying aloud with strong confused noyce,
As if it were one voyce.
"Hymen iö Hymen, Hymen" they do shout,   140
That even to the heavens theyr shouting shrill
Doth reach, and all the firmament doth fill,
To which the people standing all about,
As in approvance doe thereto applaud
And loud advaunce her laud,   145
And evermore they "Hymen, Hymen" sing,
That all the woods them answer and theyr eccho ring.

119 *sunshyny:* The brightness of the beauty from her face rivals that of the sun's rays. 131 *tabor:* drum. *Croud:* fiddle. 132 *breach:* pause. *jar:* discord. 140 *iö:* hail (pronounced "yo").

Loe where she comes along with portly pace
Lyke Phœbe from her chamber of the East,
Arysing forth to run her mighty race,   150
Clad all in white, that seemes a virgin best.
So well it her beseemes that ye would weene
Some angell she had beene.
Her long loose yellow locks lyke golden wyre,
Sprinckled with perle, and perling flowres atweene,   155
Doe lyke a golden mantle her attyre,
And being crowned with a girland greene,
Seeme lyke some mayden Queene.
Her modest eyes abashed to behold
So many gazers, as on her do stare,   160
Upon the lowly ground affixed are.
Ne dare lift up her countenance too bold,
But blush to heare her prayses sung so loud,
So farre from being proud.
Nathlesse doe ye still loud her prayses sing.   165
That all the woods may answer and your eccho ring.

Tell me ye merchants' daughters did ye see
So fayre a creature in your towne before,
So sweet, so lovely, and so mild as she,
Adornd with beautye's grace and vertue's store,   170
Her goodly eyes lyke Saphyres shining bright,
Her forehead yvory white,
Her cheekes lyke apples which the sun hath rudded,
Her lips lyke cherryes charming men to byte,
Her brest like to a bowle of creame uncrudded,   175
Her paps lyke lyllies budded,
Her snowie necke lyke to a marble towre,
And all her body like a pallace fayre,
Ascending uppe with many a stately stayre,
To honor's seat and chastitie's sweet bowre.   180
Why stand ye still ye virgins in amaze,
Upon her so to gaze,
Whiles ye forget your former lay to sing,
To which the woods did answer and your eccho ring.

---

148 *portly:* stately. 149 *Phœbe:* goddess of the moon. 151 *seemes:* becomes.
154 *wyre:* a standard simile for hair. 155 *perling:* spiraling. 165 *Nathlesse:*
nevertheless. 173 *rudded:* made ruddy. 174 *cherryes:* a standard comparison. 175 *uncrudded:* uncurdled. 176–77 *paps . . . towre:* Cf. Song of Sol.
4:4–5. 178 *pallace:* palace, a standard comparison between the body and
a goodly castle, i.e., the castle of health.

But if ye saw that which no eyes can see,   185
The inward beauty of her lively spright,
Garnisht with heavenly guifts of high degree,
Much more then would ye wonder at that sight,
And stand astonisht lyke to those which red
Medusae's mazeful hed.   190
There dwels sweet love and constant chastity,
Unspotted fayth and comely womanhood,
Regard of honour and mild modesty,
There vertue raynes as Queene in royal throne,
And giveth lawes alone.   195
The which the base affections doe obay,
And yeeld theyr services unto her will,
Ne thought of thing uncomely ever may
Thereto approch to tempt her mind to ill.
Had ye once seene these her celestial threasures,   200
And unrevealed pleasures,
Then would ye wonder and her prayses sing,
That al the woods should answer and your echo ring.

Open the temple gates unto my love,
Open them wide that she may enter in,   205
And all the postes adorne as doth behove,
And all the pillours deck with girlands trim,
For to recyve this Saynt with honour dew,
That commeth in to you.
With trembling steps and humble reverence,   210
She commeth in, before th'almighties vew,
Of her ye virgins learne obedience,
When so ye come into those holy places,
To humble your proud faces:
Bring her up to th'high altar, that she may   215
The sacred ceremonies there partake,
The which do endlesse matrimony make,
And let the roring Organs loudly play
The praises of the Lord in lively notes,
The whiles with hollow throates   220
The Choristers the joyous Antheme sing,
That al the woods may answere and their eccho ring.

---

186 *spright:* spirit. 189 *red:* perceived. 190 *Medusae's mazeful hed:* Medusa's confounding head. According to Greek myth, whoever looked at Medusa's "hair" of snakes was frozen into stone by horror. 196 *affections:* emotions. 198 *Ne:* nor. 206 *doth behove:* is fitting.

Behold whiles she before the altar stands
Hearing the holy priest that to her speakes
And blesseth her with his two happy hands,   225
How the red roses flush up in her cheekes,
And the pure snow with goodly vermill stayne,
Like crimsin dyde in grayne,
That even th'Angels which continually,
About the sacred Altare doe remaine,   230
Forget their service and about her fly,
Ofte peeping in her face that seemes more fayre,
The more they on it stare.
But her sad eyes still fastened on the ground,
Are governed with goodly modesty,   235
That suffers not one looke to glaunce awry,
Which may let in a little thought unsownd.
Why blush ye love to give to me your hand,
The pledge of all our band?
Sing ye sweet Angels, Alleluya sing,   240
That all the woods may answere and your eccho ring.

Now al is done; bring home the bride againe,
Bring home the triumph of our victory,
Bring home with you the glory of her gaine,
With joyance bring her and with jollity.   245
Never had man more joyfull day then this,
Whom heaven would heape with blis.
Make feast therefore now all this live long day,
This day for ever to me holy is,
Poure out the wine without restraint or stay,   250
Poure not by cups, but by the belly full,
Poure out to all that wull,
And sprinkle all the postes and wals with wine,
That they may sweat, and drunken be withall.
Crowne ye God Bacchus with a coronall,   255
And Hymen also crowne with wreathes of vine,
And let the Graces daunce unto the rest;
For they can doo it best:
The whiles the maydens doe theyr carroll sing,
To which the woods shal answer and theyr eccho ring.   260

---

227 *vermill:* vermilion, brilliant red.   228 *dyde in grayne:* i.e., a fast dye.
234 *sad:* serious.   239 *band:* the matrimonial bond.   244 *of her gaine:* of
having gained her.   252 *wull:* will.   255 *Bacchus:* god of wine.   259 *carroll:*
a dance as well as a song.

64

Ring ye the bels, ye yong men of the towne,
And leave your wonted labors for this day:
This day is holy; doe ye write it downe,
That ye for ever it remember may.
This day the sunne is in his chiefest hight,   265
With Barnaby the bright,
From whence declining daily by degrees,
He somewhat loseth of his heat and light,
When once the Crab behind his back he sees.
But for this time it ill ordained was,   270
To chose the longest day in all the yeare,
And shortest night, when longest fitter weare:
Yet never day so long, but late would passe.
Ring ye the bels, to make it weare away,
And bonefiers make all day,   275
And daunce about them, and about them sing:
That all the woods may answer, and your eccho ring.

Ah when will this long weary day have end,
And lende me leave to come unto my love?
How slowly do the houres theyr numbers spend?   280
How slowly does sad Time his feathers move?
Hast thee O fayrest Planet to thy home
Within the Westerne fome:
Thy tyred steedes long since have need of rest.
Long though it be, at last I see it gloome,   285
And the bright evening star with golden creast
Appeare out of the East.
Fayre childe of beauty, glorious lampe of love
That all the host of heaven in rankes doost lead,
And guydest lovers through the nightès dread,   290
How chearefully thou lookest from above,
And seemst to laugh atweene thy twinkling light
As joying in the sight
Of these glad many which for joy doe sing,
That all the woods them answer and their echo ring.   295

Now ceasse ye damsels your delights forepast;
Enough is it, that all the day was youres:
Now day is doen, and night is nighing fast:
Now bring the Bryde into the brydall boures.

266 *Barnaby:* St. Barnabas' day, June 11, which under the old calendar coincided
with the summer solstice (now June 22).   269 *Crab:* Cancer, which the sun
leaves in mid-June to enter the sign of Leo.   275 *bonefiers:* bonfires, a symbol
of public joy.   281 *feathers:* i.e., the wings of time.   282 *Planet:* the sun.
286 *evening star:* Hesperus, i.e., Venus.   *creast:* crest.   292 *laugh:* the
standard Homeric epithet for Aphrodite (Venus) is "laughter loving."

Now night is come, now soone her disaray,   300
And in her bed her lay;
Lay her in lillies and in violets,
And silken courteins over her display,
And odourd sheets, and Arras coverlets.
Behold how goodly my faire love does ly   305
In proud humility;
Like unto Maia, when as Jove her tooke,
In Tempe, lying on the flowry gras,
Twixt sleepe and wake, after she weary was,
With bathing in the Acidalian brooke.   310
Now it is night, ye damsels may be gon,
And leave my love alone,
And leave likewise your former lay to sing:
The woods no more shal answere, nor your echo ring.

Now welcome night, thou night so long expected,   315
That long daies labour doest at last defray,
And all my cares, which cruell love collected,
Hast sumd in one, and cancelled for aye:
Spread thy broad wing over my love and me,
That no man may us see,   320
And in thy sable mantle us enwrap,
From feare of perrill and foule horror free.
Let no false treason seeke us to entrap,
Nor any dread disquiet once annoy
The safety of our joy: 325
But let the night be calme and quietsome,
Without tempestuous storms or sad afray:
Lyke as when Jove with fayre Alcmena lay,
When he begot the great Tirynthian groome:
Or lyke as when he with thy selfe did lie,   330
And begot Majesty.
And let the mayds and yongmen cease to sing:
Ne let the woods them answer, nor theyr eccho ring.

---

300 *disaray:* disrobe. 303 *courteins:* curtains. 304 *Arras:* city in France
famous for tapestry making. 307 *Maia:* daughter of Atlas, on whom Jove
begot Mercury. 323 *treason:* the peril of disclosure that lovers in the courtly
tradition of secret love always feared. Spenser here underscores the difference
between lawful and unlawful lovemaking. 328 *Jove . . . lay:* When Jove lay
with Alcmene, begetting Hercules, he ordered Mercury to increase the length
of the night to that of three and Sleep to make men so drowsy that they would
not notice, because the procreation of such a hero could not be accomplished
in haste. Spenser's wedding night was the shortest night of the year (see l. 266
and note), and Ireland in 1594 was torn by civil unrest and anarchy. 329
Tirynthian groome: Hercules, born at Tiryus, who cleaned the stables of King
Augeas. 331 *Majesty:* This myth is Spenser's invention.

Let no lamenting cryes, nor dolefull teares,
Be heard all night within nor yet without: 335
Ne let false whispers, breeding hidden feares,
Breake gentle sleepe with misconceived dout.
Let no deluding dreames, nor dreadful sights
Make sudden sad affrights;
Ne let housefyres, nor lightnings helpelesse harmes,   340
Ne let the Pouke, nor other evill sprights,
Ne let mischivous witches with theyr charmes,
Ne let hob Goblins, names whose sence we see not,
Fray us with things that be not.
Let not the shriech Oule, nor the Storke be heard: 345
Nor the night Raven that still deadly yels,
Nor damned ghosts cald up with mighty spels,
Nor griesly vultures make us once affeard:
Ne let th'unpleasant Quyre of Frogs still croking
Make us to wish theyr choking.   350
Let none of these theyr drery accents sing;
Ne let the woods them answer, nor theyr eccho ring.

But let stil Silence trew night watches keepe,
That sacred peace may in assurance rayne,
And tymely sleep, when it is tyme to sleepe,   355
May poure his limbs forth on your pleasant playne,
The whiles an hundred little winged loves,
Like divers fethered doves,
Shall fly and flutter round about your bed,
And in the secret darke, that none reproves,   360
Their prety stealthes shal worke, and snares shal spread
To filch away sweet snatches of delight,
Conceald through covert night.
Ye sonnes of Venus, play your sports at will,
For greedy pleasure, carelesse of your toyes,   365
Thinks more upon her paradise of joyes,
Then what ye do, albe it good or ill.
All night therefore attend your merry play,
For it will soone be day:
Now none doth hinder you, that say or sing,   370
Ne will the woods now answer, nor your Eccho ring.

---

341 *Pouke:* Puck, a mischievous folk spirit.   344 *Fray:* frighten.   345 *Oule:*
owl, predictor of death.   *Storke:* traditionally the "wreckere of avouterye"
(avenger of adultery); see Chaucer, *Parlement of Foules*, l. 361, and also ll.
337–64 for the significance of birds.   346 *night Raven:* bringer of bad luck.
364 *sonnes of Venus:* i.e., paranymphs, attendants and friends of the bridal
pair sitting in the outer room, singing encouraging songs, telling wanton jokes,
and cracking nuts. See George Puttenham's discussion of the "epithalamion"
in his *Art of English Poetry* (1589).   365 *toyes:* trifles.

Who is the same, which at my window peepes?
Or whose is that faire face, that shines so bright,
Is it not Cinthia, she that never sleepes,
But walkes about high heaven al the night? 375
O fayrest goddesse, do thou not envy
My love with me to spy:
For thou likewise didst love, though now unthought,
And for a fleece of woll, which privily,
The Latmian shephard once unto thee brought, 380
His pleasures with thee wrought.
Therefore to us be favorable now;
And sith of wemens labours thou hast charge,
And generation goodly dost enlarge,
Encline thy will t'effect our wishfull vow, 385
And the chast wombe informe with timely seed,
That may our comfort breed:
Till which we cease our hopefull hap to sing,
Ne let the woods us answere, nor our Eccho ring.

And thou great Juno, which with awful might 390
The lawes of wedlock still dost patronize,
And the religion of the faith first plight
With sacred rites hast taught to solemnize:
And eeke for comfort often called art
Of women in their smart, 395
Eternally bind thou this lovely band,
And all thy blessings unto us impart.
And thou glad Genius, in whose gentle hand,
The bridale bowre and geniall bed remaine,
Without blemish or staine, 400
And the sweet pleasures of theyr love's delight
With secret ayde doest succour and supply,
Till they bring forth the fruitfull progeny,
Send us the timely fruit of this same night.

374 *Cinthia:* Diana, goddess of the moon. 378 *though now unthought:* though
no one would believe it. 379–81 *fleece . . . wrought:* Spenser alludes to the
legend of Endymion, shepherd of Mount Latmos, beloved by the moon
goddess. 383 *charge:* Diana, although goddess of chastity, is also the patroness
of women in childbirth. 384 *enlarge:* bring to birth. Cf. Gen. 1:28: "Be
fruitful, and multiply, and replenish the earth, and subdue it." 385 *vow:*
In the marriage service in *Queen Elizabeth's Prayer Book* (1558) is the prayer
that "these two persones . . . may both be fruitefull in procreation of
children," which the marriage vow implies. 388 *hap:* chance, lot. 395
smart: labor pains. 398 *Genius:* the indwelling spirit of a man that gives
him the power to reproduce; hence the god of the marriage-bed. 399 *geniall:*
nuptial. 400 *without . . . staine:* Cf. courtly love, which was illicit and often
adulterous; moreover, offspring from such a union was a blemish and an
unhoped-for embarrassment.

And thou fayre Hebe, and thou Hymen free,   405
Grant that it may so be.
Til which we cease your further prayse to sing,
Ne any woods shal answer, nor your Eccho ring.

And ye high heavens, the temple of the gods,
In which a thousand torches flaming bright   410
Doe burne, that to us wretched earthly clods,
In dreadful darknesse lend desired light;
And all ye powers which in the same remayne,
More then we men can fayne,
Poure out your blessing on us plentiously,   415
And happy influence upon us raine,
That we may raise a large posterity,
Which from the earth, which they may long possesse,
With lasting happinesse,
Up to your haughty pallaces may mount,   420
And for the guerdon of theyr glorious merit
May heavenly tabernacles there inherit,
Of blessed Saints for to increase the count.
So let us rest, sweet love, in hope of this,
And cease till then our tymely joyes to sing,   425
The woods no more us answer, nor our eccho ring.

Song made in lieu of many ornaments,
With which my love should duly have bene dect,
Which cutting off through hasty accidents,
Ye would not stay your dew time to expect,   430
But promist both to recompens,
Be unto her a goodly ornament,
And for short time an endlesse moniment.

405 *Hebe:* goddess of youth. *free:* generous, noble. 414 *fayne:* imagine. 416 *influence:* originally the ethereal fluid (hence *Poure* and *raine*) that flows from the stars, affecting men's lives. 420–23 *Up . . . count:* Through marriage the race of man is increased and multiplied (Gen. 1:28), and through salvation man's posterity will increase the count of saints who inherit the tabernacles of heaven left vacant by the fall of Satan and his followers. 427–31 *Song . . . recompens:* Apparently, because of accident and perhaps haste, the bride was not decked with appropriate ornaments; the poem is thus the poet's best gift to his bride. 433 *endlesse moniment:* eternal memorial in this mutable world. Cf. *Amoretti,* No. 75 and note.

WILLIAM SHAKESPEARE
1564–1616

from SONNETS

18

Shall I compare thee to a summer's day?
Thou art more lovely and more temperate:
Rough winds do shake the darling buds of May,
And summer's lease hath all too short a date:
Sometime too hot the eye of heaven shines,   5
And often is his gold complexion dimm'd;
And every fair from fair sometime declines,
By chance, or nature's changing course untrimm'd:
But thy eternal summer shall not fade,
Nor lose possession of that fair thou ow'st;   10
Nor shall Death brag thou wand'rest in his shade,
When in eternal lines to time thou grow'st:
   So long as men can breathe or eyes can see,
   So long lives this, and this gives life to thee.

29

When in disgrace with Fortune and men's eyes,
I all alone beweep my outcast state,
And trouble deaf heaven with my bootless cries,
And look upon myself and curse my fate,

SONNETS. Although many of Shakespeare's sonnets had been written and praised at least as early as 1598, they were not published until 1609 and then most probably in an unauthorized edition. Whether or not they form a unified sequence, like *Astrophil and Stella*, is still disputed, as is whether the traditional order of the sonnets is what Shakespeare planned or is the order in which he wrote them. It is clear, however, that they incorporate many traditional Petrarchan themes and conventions and that some are more in the form of epistles on various occasions than links in a narrative sequence. There is a strong presumption that the first 126 are addressed to a man in the Renaissance tradition of platonic friendship and that the remaining ones are addressed to a dark-haired woman and describe a relationship that is not particularly platonic. These selections are treated in the notes more as splendid performances making expert use of tradition and convention than as lyrically expressed crucial moments in a genuinely personal dramatic narrative.

[18]   4 *lease:* term (as of a lease). 5 *eye of heaven:* the sun. 7 *every fair:* every beautiful thing. 8 *untrimm'd:* stripped [of beauty]. 10 *ow'st:* own. 12 *to . . . grow'st:* i.e., you live for all time.

[29]   3 *bootless:* profitless.

Wishing me like to one more rich in hope,   5
Featur'd like him, like him with friends possess'd,
Desiring this man's art, and that man's scope,
With what I most enjoy contented least;
Yet in these thoughts myself almost despising,
Haply I think on thee, and then my state,   10
Like to the lark at break of day arising
From sullen earth, sings hymns at heaven's gate;
    For thy sweet love rememb'red such wealth brings,
    That then I scorn to change my state with kings.

30

When to the sessions of sweet silent thought
I summon up remembrance of things past,
I sigh the lack of many a thing I sought,
And with old woes new wail my dear time's waste:
Then can I drown an eye, unus'd to flow,   5
For precious friends hid in death's dateless night,
And weep afresh love's long since cancell'd woe,
And moan th' expense of many a vanish'd sight.
Then can I grieve at grievances foregone,
And heavily from woe to woe tell o'er   10
The sad account of fore-bemoaned moan,
Which I new pay as if not paid before.
    But if the while I think on thee, dear friend,
    All losses are restor'd, and sorrows end.

55

Not marble, nor the gilded monuments
Of princes, shall outlive this powerful rhyme;
But you shall shine more bright in these contents
Than unswept stone besmear'd with sluttish time.
When wasteful war shall statues overturn,   5
And broils root out the work of masonry,

6 *Featur'd:* well shaped in face and body.   7 *art:* skill.   *scope:* opportunity, range of powers.   12 *sullen:* dark, dull.

[30]   1 *sessions:* Cf. the sitting of a court of justice.   8 *expense:* loss. 9 *foregone:* past.   10 *tell:* count.

[55]   3 *contents:* of these poems that praise you.   4 *unswept stone:* i.e., illegible gravestones and monuments overgrown with moss and tarnished by corrosion.   *sluttish time:* i.e., as if time were a slovenly maid servant.   6 *broils:* brawls.   *root:* dig under and topple.

Nor Mars his sword nor war's quick fire shall burn
The living record of your memory.
'Gainst death and all-oblivious enmity
Shall you pace forth; your praise shall still find room   10
Even in the eyes of all posterity
That wear this world out to the ending doom.
   So, till the judgment that yourself arise,
   You live in this, and dwell in lovers' eyes.

65

Since brass, nor stone, nor earth, nor boundless sea,
But sad mortality o'ersways their power,
How with this rage shall beauty hold a plea,
Whose action is no stronger than a flower?
O how shall summer's honey breath hold out   5
Against the wrackful siege of batt'ring days,
When rocks impregnable are not so stout,
Nor gates of steel so strong but Time decays?
O fearful meditation, where alack,
Shall Time's best jewel from Time's chest lie hid?   10
Or what strong hand can hold his swift foot back,
Or how his spoil of beauty can forbid?
   O none, unless this miracle have might,
   That in black ink my love may still shine bright.

73

That time of year thou mayst in me behold,
When yellow leaves, or none, or few, do hang
Upon those boughs which shake against the cold,
Bare ruin'd choirs, where late the sweet birds sang.
In me thou see'st the twilight of such day,   5
As after sunset fadeth in the west,

---

7 *quick:* living, burning briskly.   13 *judgment:* the decree at doomsday (when the dead shall arise).

  [65]   1–2 *Since . . . power:* i.e., since nothing, from *brass* (the hardest, most concentrated of materials) to the *sea* (unlimited in volume and size) can exist without time and death destroying it.   2 *sad:* (multiple meanings) steadfast, strong, regular, mournful, violent, heavy (*OED*).   *mortality:* condition of being mortal; death; power to kill.   3 *rage:* violence.   *hold a plea:* submit its case to trial.   4 *action:* legal action.   10 *best jewel:* i.e., beauty.   *chest:* (pun) both jewel casket and coffin.

  [73]   4 *choirs:* that part of a church between the nave and the apse reserved for those who sing the responses during divine services.

72

Which by and by black night doth take away,
Death's second self, that seals up all in rest.
In me thou see'st the glowing of such fire
That on the ashes of his youth doth lie,   10
As the death-bed whereon it must expire,
Consum'd with that which it was nourish'd by.
  This thou perceiv'st, which makes thy love more strong,
  To love that well, which thou must leave ere long.

90

Then hate me when thou wilt; if ever, now,
Now while the world is bent my deeds to cross,
Join with the spite of fortune, make me bow,
And do not drop in for an after-loss:
Ah, do not, when my heart hath 'scap'd this sorrow,   5
Come in the rearward of a conquer'd woe;
Give not a windy night a rainy morrow,
To linger out a purpos'd overthrow.
If thou wilt leave me, do not leave me last,
When other petty griefs have done their spite,   10
But in the onset come: so shall I taste
At first the very worst of fortune's might,
  And other strains of woe, which now seem woe,
  Compar'd with loss of thee will not seem so.

104

To me, fair friend, you never can be old,
For as you were when first your eye I eyed,
Such seems your beauty still. Three winters cold
Have from the forests shook three summers' pride,
Three beauteous springs to yellow autumn turn'd   5
In process of the seasons have I seen,
Three April perfumes in three hot Junes burn'd,
Since first I saw you fresh, which yet are green.
Ah! yet doth beauty, like a dial-hand,
Steal from his figure and no pace perceived;   10

12 *Consum'd:* destroyed, reduced to ashes. *that:* (paradox) the flames of the fire that burns itself out.

[90] 2 *cross:* thwart. 4 *for an after-loss:* as a further misfortune. 8 *linger out:* prolong. 13 *strains:* kinds, as well as high-pitched feelings, and perhaps tunes.

[104] 4 *pride:* i.e., beauty (of leaf and blossom). 9 *dial-hand:* hand of a clock or shadow on a sundial.

So your sweet hue, which methinks still doth stand,
Hath motion and mine eye may be deceived,—
    For fear of which, hear this, thou age unbred:
    Ere you were born was beauty's summer dead.

106

When in the chronicle of wasted time,
I see descriptions of the fairest wights,
And beauty making beautiful old rhyme,
In praise of ladies dead and lovely knights,
Then, in the blazon of sweet beauty's best,   5
Of hand, of foot, of lip, of eye, of brow,
I see their antique pen would have express'd
Even such a beauty as you master now.
So all their praises are but prophecies
Of this our time, all you prefiguring;   10
And, for they look'd but with divining eyes,
They had not skill enough your worth to sing:
    For we which now behold these present days,
    Have eyes to wonder, but lack tongues to praise.

107

Not mine own fears, nor the prophetic soul
Of the wide world dreaming of things to come,
Can yet the lease of my true love control,
Suppos'd as forfeit to a confin'd doom.
The mortal moon hath her eclipse endur'd,   5
And the sad augurs mock their own presage;
Incertainties now crown themselves assur'd,
And peace proclaims olives of endless age.
Now with the drops of this most balmy time,
My love looks fresh, and Death to me subscribes,   10
Since, spite of him, I'll live in this poor rhyme,
While he insults o'er dull and speechless tribes:

[106] 2 *wights:* persons.   5 *blazon:* heraldic description, i.e., glorification.
11 *for:* because.   *divining:* conjecturing.

[107] 3 *lease:* duration.   4 *Suppos'd . . . doom:* the lease assumed
(wrongly) to be doomed to be forfeited to death.   6 *sad augurs:* gloomy
prophets of doom.   *presage:* predictions.   8 *olives:* branches of olives, symbol
of peace.   10 *subscribes:* yields.   12 *insults:* triumphs.

And thou in this shalt find thy monument,
When tyrants' crests and tombs of brass are spent.

121

'Tis better to be vile than vile esteemed,
When not to be, receives reproach of being,
And the just pleasure lost, which is so deemed,
Not by our feeling, but by others' seeing.
For why should others' false adulterate eyes   5
Give salutation to my sportive blood?
Or on my frailties why are frailer spies,
Which in their wills count bad what I think good?
No, I am that I am, and they that level
At my abuses, reckon up their own: 10
I may be straight though they themselves be bevel;
By their rank thoughts my deeds must not be shown;
   Unless this general evil they maintain,
   All men are bad, and in their badness reign.

129

Th' expense of spirit in a waste of shame
Is lust in action; and till action, lust
Is perjur'd, murd'rous, bloody, full of blame,
Savage, extreme, rude, cruel, not to trust,
Enjoy'd no sooner but despised straight,   5
Past reason hunted, and no sooner had,
Past reason hated as a swallowed bait,
On purpose laid to make the taker mad:
Mad in pursuit, and in possession so,
Had, having, and in quest to have, extreme,   10
A bliss in proof, and prov'd, a very woe,
Before, a joy propos'd, behind, a dream.
   All this the world well knows; yet none knows well
   To shun the heaven that leads men to this hell.

14 *crests:* trophies.

[121]   6 *Give salutation:* affect.   *sportive:* wanton, amorous.   7 *on . . . spies:* spies frailer than I am, spying on my frailties.   9 *level:* aim.   11 *bevel:* oblique, slant.

[129]   1 *expense:* expenditure of the "spirit generative" in the sexual act.   11 *proof:* trial, experiment.   *prov'd:* experienced.

130

My mistress' eyes are nothing like the sun;
Coral is far more red than her lips' red;
If snow be white, why then her breasts are dun;
If hairs be wires, black wires grow on her head.
I have seen roses damask'd, red and white,   5
But no such roses see I in her cheeks;
And in some perfumes is there more delight
Than in the breath that from my mistress reeks.
I love to hear her speak, yet well I know
That music hath a far more pleasing sound;   10
I grant I never saw a goddess go;
My mistress, when she walks, treads on the ground.
    And yet, by Heaven, I think my love as rare
    As any she belied with false compare.

136

If thy soul check thee that I come so near,
Swear to thy blind soul that I was thy *Will*,
And will, thy soul knows, is admitted there.
Thus far for love, my love-suit, sweet, fulfill.
Will will fulfill the treasure of thy love—   5
Aye, fill it full with wills, and my will one.
In things of great receipt with ease we prove
Among a number one is reckoned none.
Then in the number let me pass untold,
Though in thy store's account I one must be,   10
For nothing hold me, so it please thee hold
That nothing me, a something sweet to thee.
    Make but my name thy love, and love that still,
    And then thou lov'st me, for my name is *Will*.

[130] 1 *eyes . . . sun:* Here, and in following lines, Shakespeare plays on many of the conventional Petrarchan similes. 5 *damask'd:* ornamented in a wavy pattern. 8 *reeks:* is exhaled, emanates.

[136] 1 *check:* restrain, chide. 2 *Swear:* i.e., lie. *blind soul:* the soul must rely upon the senses to identify external objects. *Will:* passion, desire, appetitive reason (the soul was believed to be comprised of Reason, Will, and Appetite), and also the name Will(iam). 3 *will . . . there:* i.e., your soul knows that passion is dominant there. 7 *receipt:* capacity. 8 *one . . . none:* i.e., one is no number. 9 *number:* i.e., of your lovers. 12 *nothing, something:* i.e., no thing, some thing, which Elizabethan pronunciation and intonation support.

146

Poor soul, the center of my sinful earth,
[Thrall to] these rebel pow'rs that thee array,
Why dost thou pine within and suffer dearth,
Painting thy outward walls so costly gay?
Why so large cost, having so short a lease,   5
Dost thou upon thy fading mansion spend?
Shall worms, inheritors of this excess,
Eat up thy charge? Is this thy body's end?
Then, soul, live thou upon thy servant's loss,
And let that pine to aggravate thy store;   10
Buy terms divine in selling hours of dross;
Within be fed, without be rich no more:
   So shalt thou feed on Death, that feeds on men,
   And Death once dead, there's no more dying then.

SONGS FROM THE PLAYS

Spring: When daisies pied and violets blue

[By Holofernes, Moth, Costard, and Others]

When daisies pied and violets blue,
And lady-smocks of silver white,
And cuckoo-buds of yellow hue,
Do paint the meadows with delight,
The cuckoo then on every tree,   5
Mocks married men, for thus sings he,
Cuckoo.
Cuckoo, cuckoo: O word of fear,
Unpleasing to a married ear.

When shepherds pipe on oaten straws,   10
And merry larks are ploughmen's clocks,
When turtles tread, and rooks and daws,
And maidens bleach their summer smocks,

---

[146] 1 *earth:* body. 2 *Thrall to:* anonymous conjecture, accepted by many editors, for the typographical blunder in the 1609 edition that repeats the last phrase of the first line. Other emendations suggested by various editors are, Rebuke; Fool'd by; Foil'd by. 8 *charge:* i.e., the body entrusted to your care, and also that on which you have lavished such great expense. 11 *terms divine:* eternal time (cf. limited terms of *lease* in l. 5).

WHEN DAISIES PIED. 6 *Mocks:* the name of the bird (which lays its eggs in other birds' nests) and its call suggest cuckold(ry). 12 *turtles tread:* turtle doves copulate.

The cuckoo then on every tree,
Mocks married men, for thus sings he,   15
Cuckoo.
Cuckoo, cuckoo: O word of fear,
Unpleasing to a married ear.

[*Love's Labor's Lost*, V, ii]

Winter: When icicles hang by the wall

[By Holofernes, Moth, Costard, and Others]

When icicles hang by the wall,
And Dick the shepherd blows his nail,
And Tom bears logs into the hall,
And milk comes frozen home in pail;
When blood is nipp'd, and ways be foul,   5
Then nightly sings the staring owl,
Tu-whit, to-who:
    A merry note,
    While greasy Joan doth keel the pot.

When all aloud the wind doth blow,   10
And coughing drowns the parson's saw,
And birds sit brooding in the snow,
And Marian's nose looks red and raw;
When roasted crabs hiss in the bowl,
Then nightly sings the staring owl,   15
Tu-whit, to-who:
    A merry note,
    While greasy Joan doth keel the pot.

[*Love's Labor's Lost*, V, ii]

O mistress mine, where are you roaming

[Feste]

O mistress mine, where are you roaming?
O, stay and hear; your true love's coming,
    That can sing both high and low.

WHEN ICICLES. 2 *nail:* fingernail; i.e., he warms his fingers by blowing on them. 9 *keel:* cool; prevent the pot from boiling over by skimming. 11 *saw:* moral maxim, sermon. 12 *brooding:* sitting or hovering with outspread, cherishing wings. 14 *crabs:* crab apples (added to mulled ale).

Trip no further, pretty sweeting;
Journeys end in lovers meeting,   5
    Every wise man's son doth know.

What is love? 'Tis not hereafter;
Present mirth hath present laughter;
    What's to come is still unsure:
In delay there lies no plenty;   10
Then come kiss me, sweet and twenty!
    Youth's a stuff will not endure.

                                        [*Twelfth Night*, II, ii]

Fear no more the heat o' th' sun

[Dirge: Sung by Guiderius and Arviragus]

GUI.   Fear no more the heat o' th' sun,
       Nor the furious winter's rages,
       Thou thy worldly task hast done,
       Home art gone, and ta'en thy wages.
       Golden lads, and girls all must,   5
       As chimney-sweepers, come to dust.

ARV.   Fear no more the frown o' th' great,
       Thou art past the tyrant's stroke;
       Care no more to clothe and eat;
       To thee the reed is as the oak: 10
          The scepter, learning, physic, must,
          All follow this and come to dust.

GUI.   Fear no more the lightning flash.
ARV.   Nor th' all-dreaded thunderstone.
GUI.   Fear not slander, censure rash.   15
ARV.   Thou hast finish'd joy and moan.
BOTH All lovers young, all lovers must,
       Consign to thee, and come to dust.

GUI.   No exorciser harm thee,
ARV.   Nor no witchcraft charm thee.   20
GUI.   Ghost unlaid forbear thee.
ARV.   Nothing ill come near thee,

FEAR NO MORE. 14 *thunderstone:* thunderbolt. 18 *Consign:* Submit to the
same terms.

BOTH   Quiet consummation have,
        And renowned by thy grave.

                              [*Cymbeline*, IV, ii]

Come unto these yellow sands

[Ariel]

Come unto these yellow sands,
        And then take hands:
Courtsied when you have and kiss'd
        The wild waves whist,
Foot it featly here and there;   5
And, sweet sprites, the burthen bear.
              Burthen: Hark, hark!
                              Bow-wow.
        The watch-dogs bark:
                              Bow-wow.   10

Hark, hark! I hear
The strain of strutting chanticleer
Cry, Cock-a-diddle-dow.

                              [*The Tempest*, I, ii]

Full fadom five thy father lies

[Ariel]

Full fadom five thy father lies.
Of his bones are coral made;
Those are pearls that were his eyes:
Nothing of him that doth fade,
But doth suffer a sea-change   5
Into something rich and strange.
Sea nymphs hourly ring his knell.
              Burthen: Ding dong.
Hark! now I hear them, ding-dong bell.

                              [*The Tempest*, I, ii]

COME UNTO.   3 *Courtsied . . . kiss'd:* i.e., the ceremonial salutation before
the dance.   4 *whist:* quiet.   5 *featly:* nimbly.   6 *burthen:* droning undersong
in the bass; here, *Bow wow.*

Where the bee sucks, there suck I

[Ariel]

Where the bee sucks, there suck I:
In a cowslip's bell I lie;
There I couch when owls do cry.
On the bat's back I do fly
After summer merrily.   5
Merrily, merrily shall I live now
Under the blossom that hangs on the bough.

[*The Tempest*, V, i]

BEN JONSON
1573?–1637

I

TO THE READER

Pray thee, take care, that tak'st my booke in hand,
　To reade it well: that is, to understand.

II

TO MY BOOKE

It will be look'd for, booke, when some but see
　Thy title, *Epigrammes*, and nam'd of mee,
Thou should'st be bold, licentious, full of gall,
　Wormewood, and sulphure, sharpe, and tooth'd withall;
Become a petulant thing, hurle inke, and wit,　　　　5
　As mad-men stones: not caring whom they hit.
Deceive their malice, who could wish it so.
　And by thy wiser temper, let men know
Thou are not covetous of least selfe-fame,
　Made from the hazard of anothers shame:　　　　10
Much lesse with lewd, prophane, and beastly phrase,
　To catch the worlds loose laughter, or vaine gaze.
He that departs with his owne honesty
　For vulgar praise, doth it too dearely buy.

　The text of these poems is based on that established by Herford and Simpson, *Ben Jonson*, Vol. VIII (Oxford, at the Clarendon Press, 1947). It is referred to in the notes as (H & S). The spelling has been slightly normalized: *u* is changed to *v*, *v* to *u*, and *i* to *j*.

EPIGRAMMES.　Epigram: a terse, witty, often satiric poem of praise or dispraise, modeled after those of the Latin poet Martial.

　[II]　10 *hazard:* i.e., the chance of exposing.

XLV

ON MY FIRST SONNE

Farewell, thou child of my right hand, and joy;
    My sinne was too much hope of thee, lov'd boy,
Seven yeeres tho'wert lent to me, and I thee pay,
    Exacted by thy fate, on the just day.
O, could I loose all father, now. For why   5
    Will man lament the state he should envie?
To have so soone scap'd worlds, and fleshes rage,
    And, if no other miserie, yet age?
Rest in soft peace, and, ask'd, say here doth lye
    BEN. JONSON his best piece of *poetrie*.   10
For whose sake, hence-forth, all his vowes be such,
    As what he loves may never like too much.

XCVI

TO JOHN DONNE

Who shall doubt, DONNE, where I a *Poet* bee,
    When I dare send my *Epigrammes* to thee?
That so alone canst judge, so'alone dost make:
    And, in thy censures, evenly, dost take
As free simplicitie, to dis-avow,   5
    As thou hast best authoritie, t[o]'allow.
Reade all I send: and, if I find but one
    Mark'd by thy hand, and with the better stone,
My title's seal'd. Those that for claps doe write,
    Let pui'nees, porters, players praise delight,   10
And, till they burst, their backs, like asses load:
    A man should seeke great glorie, and not broad.

[XLV] 1 *child:* died of the plague in 1603. *right hand:* the Hebrew signification of Benjamin, name given by Jacob to his youngest son. See Gen. 35:18. 5 *father:* i.e., sense of being a father. 10 *poetrie:* i.e., something made, for the poet is a maker.

[XCVI] 8 *better stone:* Cf. Horace, Odes I, 36, l. 10. In ancient Rome, especially happy days were recorded with a white stone, "*cressa . . . nota.*" 9 *claps:* applause. 10 *pui'ness:* inferiors.

from THE FORREST

To Penshurst

Thou art not, PENSHURST, built to envious show,
    Of touch, or marble; nor canst boast a row
Of polish'd pillars, or a roofe of gold:
    Thou hast no lantherne, whereof tales are told;
Or stayre, or courts; but stand'st an ancient pile,   5
    And these grudg'd at, art reverenc'd the while.
Thou joy'st in better markes, of soyle, of ayre,
    Of wood, of water: therein thou art faire.
Thou hast thy walkes for health, as well as sport:
    Thy *Mount*, to which the *Dryads* doe resort,   10
Where PAN, and BACCHUS their high feasts have made,
    Beneath the broad beech, and the chest-nut shade;
That taller tree, which of a nut was set,
    At his great birth, where all the *Muses* met.
There, in the writhed barke, are cut the names   15
    Of many a SYLVANE, taken with his flames.
And thence, the ruddy *Satyres* oft provoke
    The lighter *Faunes*, to reach thy *Ladies oke*.
Thy copp's, too, nam'd of GAMAGE, thou hast there,
    That never failes to serve thee season'd deere,   20
When thou would'st feast, or exercise thy friends.
    The lower land, that to the river bends,
Thy sheepe, thy bullocks, kine, and calves doe feed:
    The middle grounds thy mares, and horses breed.
Each banke doth yeeld thee coneyes; and the topps   25
    Fertile of wood, ASHORE, and SYDNEY's copp's,
To crowne thy open table, doth provide
    The purpled pheasant, with the speckled side:
The painted partrich lyes in every field,
    And, for thy messe, is willing to be kill'd.   30

THE FORREST. Cf. *Silvae* of Statius. The word *silva* meant an *ex tempore* occasional poem. Thus Jonson describes his book as being a miscellany of poems in a variety of forms on various themes, many of which are genuinely experimental and unique.

TO PENSHURST. A topographical poem, the first in English. 1 *Penshurst:* home of the Sidney family in Kent. 2 *touch:* very durable stone suitable for preserving inscriptions or fine monumental work; also black jasper. 4 *lantherne:* a skylight with vertical walls on the roof of a building, often a spectacular object of attention on a Gothic tower. 14 *his:* Sir Philip Sidney's. 15 *writhed:* thick and contorted. 16 *Sylvane . . . flames:* rustics overcome by love. 19 *copp:* thicket of small trees periodically cut for economic purposes. *Gamage:* after Barbara Gamage, wife of Lord Robert Sidney, who fed deer there (H & S). 25 *coneyes:* rabbits. 30 *messe:* food, or a course of food.

And if the high-swolne *Medway* faile thy dish,
   Thou hast thy ponds, that pay thee tribute fish,
Fat, aged carps, that runne into thy net.
   And pikes, now weary their owne kinde to eat,
As loth, the second draught, or cast to stay,   35
   Officiously, at first, themselves betray.
Bright eeles, that emulate them, and leape on land,
   Before the fisher, or into his hand.
Then hath thy orchard fruit, thy garden flowers,
   Fresh as the ayre, and new as are the houres.   40
The earely cherry, with the later plum,
   Fig, grape, and quince, each in his time doth come:
The blushing apricot, and woolly peach
   Hang on thy walls, that every child may reach.
And though thy walls be of the countrey stone,   45
   They'are rear'd with no mans ruine, no mans grone,
There's none, that dwell about them, wish them downe;
   But all come in, the farmer, and the clowne:
And no one empty-handed, to salute
   Thy lord, and lady, though they have no sute.   50
Some bring a capon, some a rurall cake,
   Some nuts, some apples; some that thinke they make
The better cheeses, bring 'hem; or else send
   By their ripe daughters, whom they would commend
This way to husbands; and whose baskets beare   55
   An embleme of themselves, in plum, or peare.
But what can this (more then expresse their love)
   Adde to thy free provisions, farre above
The neede of such? whose liberall boord doth flow,
   With all, that hospitalitie doth know!   60
Where comes no guest, but is allow'd to eate,
   Without his feare, and of thy lords owne meate:
Where the same beere, and bread, and selfe-same wine,
   That is his Lordships, shall be also mine.
And I not faine to sit (as some, this day,   65
   At great mens tables) and yet dine away.
Here no man tells my cups; nor, standing by,
   A waiter, doth my gluttony envy:
But gives me what I call, and lets me eate,
   He knowes, below, he shall finde plentie of meate,   70
Thy tables hoord not up for the next day,
   Nor, when I take my lodging, need I pray

---

31 *Medway:* river bordering the estate.   35 *draught:* a pulling in of fish.
36 *Officiously:* dutifully.   44 *walls:* The fruit trees are trained on the walls,
i.e., espaliered.   50 *sute:* formal request.   58 *free:* generous.   67 *tells:* counts.
72 *lodging:* i.e., bedroom.

For fire, or lights, or livorie: all is there;
    As if thou, then, wert mine, or I raign'd here:
There's nothing I can wish, for which I stay.   75
    That found King JAMES, when hunting late, this way,
With his brave sonne, the Prince, they saw thy fires
    Shine bright on every harth as the desires
Of thy *Penates* had beene set on flame,
    To entertayne them; or the countrey came,   80
With all their zeale, to warme their welcome here.
    What (great, I will not say, but) sodayne cheare
Did'st thou, then, make 'hem! and what praise was heap'd
    On thy good lady, then! who, therein, reap'd
The just reward of her high huswifery;   85
    To have her linnen, plate, and all things nigh,
When shee was farre: and not a roome, but drest,
    As if it had expected such a guest!
These, PENSHURST, are thy praise, and yet not all.
    Thy lady's noble, fruitfull, chaste withall.   90
His children thy great lord may call his owne:
    A fortune, in this age, but rarely knowne.
They are, and have beene taught religion: Thence
    Their gentler spirits have suck'd innocence.
Each morne, and even, they are taught to pray,   95
    With the whole houshold, and may, every day,
Reade, in their vertuous parents noble parts,
    The mysteries of manners, armes, and arts.
Now, PENSHURST, they that will proportion thee
    With other edifices, when they see   100
Those proud, ambitious heaps, and nothing else,
    May say, their lords have built, but thy lord dwells.

from THE UNDER-WOOD

Her Triumph

See the Chariot at hand here of Love,
    Wherein my Lady rideth!
Each that drawes, is a Swan, or a Dove,
    And well the Carre Love guideth.

73 *fire . . . livorie:* fire for his room, candles to light his way, and service from a liveried servant. 79 *Penates:* household gods. 99 *proportion:* compare.

THE UNDER-WOOD. In his prefatory note, Jonson says that he uses this title by analogy with "The Forrest," since these occasional poems are a kind of "second growth" of trees lesser than the *silvae* that stand in his first book.

HER TRIUMPH. Ceremonial procession celebrating Charis (no one knows who she was or even if she was a real person).

As she goes, all hearts doe duty   5
       Unto her beauty;
And enamour'd, doe wish, so they might
       But enjoy such a sight,
That they still were to run by her side,
Th[o]rough Swords, th[o]rough Seas, whether she would ride.   10

Doe but looke on her eyes, they doe light
  All that Loves world compriseth!
Doe but looke on her Haire, it is bright
  As Loves starre when it riseth!
Doe but marke, her forehead's smoother   15
       Then words that sooth her!
And from her arched browes, such a grace
       Sheds it selfe through the face,
  As alone there triumphs to the life
All the Gaine, all the Good, of the Elements strife.   20

Have you seene but a bright Lillie grow,
  Before rude hands have touch'd it?
Have you mark'd but the fall o'the Snow
  Before the soyle hath smutch'd it?
Have you felt the wooll o' the Bever?   25
       Or Swans Downe ever?
Or have smelt o'the bud o'the Brier?
       Or the Nard i' the fire?
  Or have tasted the bag o'the Bee?
O so white! O so soft! O so sweet is she!   30

[from *A Celebration of Charis*]

To the immortall memorie, and friendship of that noble paire, Sir Lucius Cary, and Sir H. Morison

THE TURNE

Brave Infant of *Saguntum*, cleare
Thy comming forth in that great yeare,

10 *Th[o]rough:* through, pronounced in two syllables. *whether:* whither.
20 *Elements:* The four elements—earth, air, fire, water—traditionally are in warring conflict, but through the power of love their strife becomes the harmony of creation. 25 *wooll:* fur. 28 *Nard:* aromatic plant, spikenard.

TO THE IMMORTALL MEMORIE. A Pindaric ode. Jonson uses English terms for the strophe (turne), antistrophe (counter-turne), epode (stand). Morison died in 1629, aged 20, when Cary (who died in 1643, aged 33) was 19. 1 *Infant of Saguntum:* According to Pliny (*Nat. Hist.* VIII, 3), a child born during Hannibal's terrible sack of Saguntum, a city of Spain, took one look at the destruction and returned to the womb (H & S).

When the Prodigious *Hannibal* did crowne
His rage, with razing your immortall Towne.
Thou, looking then about,   5
E're thou wert halfe got out,
Wise child, did'st hastily returne,
And mad'st thy Mothers wombe thine urne.
How summ'd a circle didst thou leave man-kind
Of deepest lore, could we the Center find!   10

THE COUNTER-TURNE

Did wiser Nature draw thee back,
From out the horrour of that sack?
Where shame, faith, honour, and regard of right
Lay trampled on; the deeds of death, and night,
Urg'd, hurried forth, and horld   15
Upon th'affrighted world:
Sword, fire, and famine, with fell fury met;
And all on utmost ruine set;
As, could they but lifes miseries fore-see,
No doubt all Infants would returne like thee.   20

THE STAND

For, what is life, if measur'd by the space,
Not by the act?
Or masked man, if valu'd by his face,
Above his fact?
Here's one out-liv'd his Peeres,   25
And told forth fourescore yeares;
He vexed time, and busied the whole State;
Troubled both foes, and friends;
But ever to no ends:
What did this Stirrer, but die late?   30
How well at twentie had he falne, or stood!
For three of his foure-score, he did no good.

THE TURNE

Hee entred well, by vertuous parts,
Got up and thriv'd with honest arts:
He purchas'd friends, and fame, and honours then,   35
And had his noble name advanc'd with men:
But weary of that flight,
Hee stoop'd in all mens sight

---

3 *Prodigious:* i.e., ominous, portentous. Hannibal began the second Punic
War by destroying Saguntum.   24 *fact:* deeds.

To sordid flatteries, acts of strife,
And sunke in that dead sea of life   40
So deep, as he did then death's waters sup;
But that the Corke of Title boy'd him up.

THE COUNTER-TURNE

Alas, but *Morison* fell young:
Hee never fell, thou fall'st, my tongue.
Hee stood, a Souldier to the last right end,   45
A perfect Patriot, and a noble friend,
But most, a vertuous Sonne.
All Offices were done
By him, so ample, full, and round,
In weight, in measure, number, sound,   50
As though his age imperfect might appeare,
His life was of Humanitie the Spheare.

THE STAND

Goe now, and tell out dayes summ'd up with feares,
And make them yeares;
Produce thy masse of miseries on the Stage,   55
To swell thine age;
Repeat of things a throng,
To shew thou hast beene long,
Not liv'd; for Life doth her great actions spell,
By what was done and wrought   60
In season, and so brought
To light: her measures are, how well
Each syllab'e answer'd, and was form'd, how faire;
These make the lines of life, and that's her ayre.

THE TURNE

It is not growing like a tree   65
In bulke, doth make man better bee;
Or standing long an Oake, three hundred yeare,
To fall a logge at last, dry, bald, and seare:
A Lillie of a Day,
Is fairer farre, in May,   70
Although it fall, and die that night;
It was the Plant, and flowre of light.
In small proportions, we just beautie see:
And in short measures, life may perfect bee.

---

48 *Offices:* duties.   52 *Spheare:* perfect whole.   64 *lines:* i.e., of a heroic
poem.   *ayre:* manner, style; perhaps inspiration.

THE COUNTER-TURNE

Call, noble *Lucius*, then for Wine,   75
And let thy lookes with gladnesse shine:
Accept this garland, plant it on thy head,
And thinke, nay know, thy *Morison's* not dead.
Hee leap'd the present age,
Possest with holy rage,   80
To see that bright eternall Day:
Of which we *Priests*, and *Poëts* say
Such truths, as we expect for happy men,
And there he lives with memorie; and *Ben*

THE STAND

Jonson, who sung this of him, e're he went   85
Himselfe to rest,
Or taste a part of that full joy he meant
To have exprest,
In this bright *Asterisme:*
Where it were friendships schisme,   90
(Were not his *Lucius* long with us to tarry)
To separate these twi-
Lights, the *Dioscuri;*
And keepe the one halfe from his *Harry*.
But fate doth so alternate the designe,   95
Whilst that in heav'n, this light on earth must shine.

THE TURNE

And shine as you exalted are;
Two names of friendship, but one Starre:
Of hearts the union. And those not by chance
Made, or indentur'd, or leas'd out t[o]'advance   100
The profits for a time.
No pleasures vaine did chime,
Of rimes, or ryots, at your feasts,
Orgies of drinke, or fain'd protests:
But simple love of greatnesse, and of good;   105
That knits brave minds, and manners, more then blood.

THE COUNTER-TURNE

This made you first to know the Why
You lik'd, then after, to apply
That liking; and approach so one the tother,

89 *Asterisme:* a constellation.   93 *Dioscuri:* Castor and Pollux, twin sons of
Zeus and Leda.   109 *the tother:* to the other.

Till either grew a portion of the other: 110
Each stiled, by his end,
The Copie of his friend.
You liv'd to be the great surnames,
And titles, by which all made claimes
Unto the Vertue. Nothing perfect done,   115
But as a CARY, or a MORISON.

THE STAND

And such a force the faire example had,
As they that saw
The good, and durst not practise it, were glad
That such a Law   120
Was left yet to Man-kind;
Where they might read, and find
Friendship, in deed, was written, not in words:
And with the heart, not pen,
Of two so early men,   125
Whose lines her rowles were, and records.
Who, e're the first downe bloomed on the chin,
Had sow'd these fruits, and got the harvest in.

SONGS FROM THE PLAYS

Come, my Celia, let us prove

[Volpone's Song]

Come, my CELIA, let us prove,
While we can, the sports of love;
Time will not be ours, for ever,
He, at length, our good will sever;
Spend not then his gifts, in vaine.   5
Sunnes, that set, may rise againe:
But if, once, we lose this light,
'Tis with us perpetuall night.
Why should wee deferre our joyes?
Fame, and rumor are but toyes.   10
Cannot we delude the eyes
Of a few poore houshold-spies?

125 *early:* i.e., in time, with reference to future students of the *Law* of *Friendship*, as well as young.   126 *rowles:* rolls, i.e., records.

COME, MY CELIA. Cf. Catullus, fifth ode.   1 *prove:* to test, to find by experience.

Or his easier eares beguile,
Thus remooved, by our wile?
'Tis no sinne, loves fruits to steale;   15
But the sweet thefts to reveale:
To be taken, to be seene,
These have crimes accounted beene.

[*Volpone, or the Foxe*, III, vii]

Still to be neat, still to be drest

[Clerimont's Song]

Still to be neat, still to be drest,
As, you were going to a feast;
Still to be pou'dred, still perfum'd:
Lady, it is to be presum'd,
Though arts hid causes are not found,   5
All is not sweet, all is not sound.

Give me a looke, give me a face,
That makes simplicitie a grace;
Robes loosely flowing, haire as free:
Such sweet neglect more taketh me,   10
Then all th'adulteries of art.
They strike mine eyes, but not my heart.

[*Epicoene, or the Silent Woman*, I, i]

Slow, slow, fresh fount

[Echo's Song]

Slow, slow, fresh fount, keepe time with my salt teares;
Yet slower, yet, ô faintly gentle springs:
List to the heavy part the musique beares,
    "Woe weepes out her division, when shee sings.
        Droupe hearbs, and flowres;   5
        Fall griefe in showres;
        "Our beauties are not ours:

STILL TO BE NEAT.   1 *Still:* always, continually.   *neat:* elegant.   *drest:* i.e., in fashion.

SLOW, SLOW FRESH FOUNT.   3 *heavy:* somber, sorrowful.   4 *division:* in music, a florid, rapid melodic passage, sung at one breath; originally thought of as the division of each note in a series of long notes into an ornamental phrase (or run) of shorter notes.

       O, I could still
  (Like melting snow upon some craggie hill,)
     drop, drop, drop, drop,   10
  Since natures pride is, now, a wither'd daffodill.

           [Cynthia's Revels, I, ii]

The Hymne to Cynthia

  Queene, and *Huntresse*, chaste, and faire,
  Now the *Sunne* is laid to sleepe,
  Seated, in thy silver chaire,
  State in wonted manner keepe:
   Hesperus intreats thy light,   5
   Goddesse, excellently bright.

  Earth, let not thy envious shade
  Dare it selfe to interpose;
  Cynthias shining orbe was made
  Heaven to cleere, when day did close: 10
   Blesse us then with wished sight,
   Goddesse, excellently bright.

  Lay thy bow of pearle apart,
  And thy cristall-shining quiver;
  Give unto the flying hart   15
  Space to breathe, how short soever:
   Thou that mak'st a day of night,
   Goddesse, excellently bright.

           [Cynthia's Revels, V, vi]

To the memory of my beloved,

The AUTHOR

Mr. William Shakespeare:
And
what he hath left us

To draw no envy (*Shakespeare*) on thy name,
 Am I thus ample to thy Booke, and Fame:
While I confesse thy writings to be such,

the hymne to cynthia. 1 *Queene, and Huntresse:* Cynthia, epithet of Artemis/Diana, goddess of the moon, the hunt, and chastity. 5 *Hesperus:* the evening star.

to shakespeare. 2 *ample:* i.e., capable of treating your *Booke* and *Fame* at full length. *Booke:* the First Folio, 1623.

As neither *Man*, nor *Muse*, can praise too much.
'Tis true, and all mens suffrage. But these wayes   5
  Were not the paths I meant unto thy praise:
For seeliest Ignorance on these may light,
  Which, when it sounds at best, but eccho's right;
Or blinde Affection, which doth ne're advance
  The truth, but gropes, and urgeth all by chance;   10
Or crafty Malice, might pretend this praise,
  And thinke to ruine, where it seem'd to raise.
These are, as some infamous Baud, or Whore,
  Should praise a Matron. What could hurt her more?
But thou art proofe against them, and indeed   15
  Above th'ill fortune of them, or the need.
I, therefore will begin. Soule of the Age!
  The applause! delight! the wonder of our Stage!
My *Shakespeare*, rise; I will not lodge thee by
  Chaucer, or *Spenser*, or bid *Beaumont* lye   20
A little further, to make thee a roome:
  Thou art a Moniment, without a tombe,
And art alive still, while thy Booke doth live,
  And we have wits to read, and praise to give.
That I not mixe thee so, my braine excuses;   25
  I meane with great, but disproportion'd *Muses:*
For, if I thought my judgement were of yeeres,
  I should commit thee surely with thy peeres,
And tell, how farre thou didst our *Lily* out-shine,
  Or sporting *Kid*, or *Marlowes* mighty line.   30
And though thou hadst small *Latine*, and lesse *Greeke*,
  From thence to honour thee, I would not seeke
For names; but call forth thund'ring *Æschilus*,
  Euripides, and *Sophocles* to us,
Paccuvius, *Accius*, him of *Cordova* dead,   35
  To life againe, to heare thy Buskin tread,
And shake a Stage: Or, when thy Sockes were on,
  Leave thee alone, for the comparison
Of all, that insolent *Greece*, or haughtie *Rome*
  Sent forth, or since did from their ashes come.   40
Triúmph, my *Britaine*, thou hast one to showe,

---

5 *suffrage:* assent and testimony.   7 *seeliest:* most artless, simple.   13 *as:* as if.   19 *lodge thee:* i.e., in Westminster Abbey, where the three poets named were buried.   22 *Moniment:* monument, a memorial.   29–30 *Lily* [Lyly], *Kyd*, *Marlowe:* Shakespeare's predecessors in drama.   33–34 *Æschilus, Euripides, Sophocles:* principal writers of Greek tragedy.   35 *Paccuvius, Accius:* writers of Latin tragedy.   *him . . . dead:* Seneca, whose Latin tragedies influenced many Elizabethan dramatists.   36 *Buskin:* the high, thick-soled boot (*cothurnus*) worn by actors in Greek tragedy; hence, tragedy.   37 *Sockes:* the low, light shoe (*soccus*) worn by actors in Greek comedy; hence comedy.

94

To whom all Scenes of *Europe* homage owe.
He was not of an age, but for all time!
　And all the *Muses* still were in their prime,
When like *Apollo* he came forth to warme　　　　45
　Our eares, or like a *Mercury* to charme!
Nature her selfe was proud of his designes,
　And joy'd to weare the dressing of his lines!
Which were so richly spun, and woven so fit,
　As, since, she will vouchsafe no other Wit.　　50
The merry *Greeke*, tart *Aristophanes*,
　Neat *Terence*, witty *Plautus*, now not please;
But antiquated, and deserted lye
　As they were not of Natures family.
Yet must I not give Nature all: Thy Art,　　　　55
　My gentle *Shakespeare*, must enjoy a part.
For though the *Poets* matter, Nature be,
　His Art doth give the fashion. And, that he,
Who casts to write a living line, must sweat,
　(Such as thine are) and strike the second heat　　60
Upon the *Muses* anvile: turne the same,
　(And himselfe with it) that he thinkes to frame;
Or for the lawrell, he may gaine a scorne,
　For a good *Poet's* made, as well as borne.
And such wert thou. Looke how the fathers face　　65
　Lives in his issue, even so, the race
Of *Shakespeares* minde, and manners brightly shines
　In his well torned, and true-filed lines:
In each of which, he seemes to shake a Lance,
　As brandish't at the eyes of Ignorance.　　　　70
Sweet Swan of *Avon*! what a sight it were
　To see thee in our waters yet appeare,
And make those flights upon the bankes of *Thames*,
　That so did take *Eliza*, and our *James*!
But stay, I see thee in the *Hemisphere*　　　　75
　Advanc'd, and made a Constellation there!
Shine forth, thou Starre of *Poets*, and with rage,
　Or influence, chide, or cheere the drooping Stage;
Which, since thy flight from hence, hath mourn'd like night,
　And despaires day, but for thy Volumes light.　　80

BEN: JONSON.

42 *Scenes:* theaters.　45 *Apollo:* god of the sun and poetry.　*warme:* please. 46 *Mercury:* god of eloquence.　51–52 *Aristophanes, Terence, Plautus:* Greek and Latin writers of comedy.　57 *matter:* subject.　59 *casts:* proposes.　60 *strike . . . heat:* i.e., to temper by revision (metal is tempered by being heated and hammered twice).　74 *Eliza*[beth I], *James* [I]: the monarchs reigning during Shakespeare's life.　63 *lawrell:* laurel, symbol of poetic excellence.　77 *rage:* poetic inspiration and enthusiasm.

JOHN DONNE
1572–1631

from SONGS AND SONNETS

Song

Goe, and catche a falling starre,
  Get with child a mandrake roote,
Tell me, where all past yeares are,
  Or who cleft the Divels foot,
Teach me to heare Mermaides singing,   5
Or to keep off envies stinging,
        And finde
        What winde
Serves to'advance an honest minde.

If thou beest borne to strange sights,   10
  Things invisible to see,
Ride ten thousand daies and nights,
  Till age snow white haires on thee,
Thou, when thou retorn'st, wilt tell mee
All strange wonders that befell thee,   15
        And sweare
        No where
Lives a woman true, and faire.

If thou findst one, let mee know,
  Such a Pilgrimage were sweet,   20
Yet doe not, I would not goe,
  Though at next doore wee might meet,
Though shee were true, when you met her,
And last, till your write your letter,
        Yet shee   25
        Will bee
False, ere I come, to two, or three.

SONGS AND SONNETS. The text is that established by Helen Gardner, *The Elegies and the Songs and Sonnets of John Donne* (Oxford, at the Clarendon Press, 1965). Notes specifically derived from this edition are marked (G).

SONG. 2 *mandrake:* a narcotic herb with a forked root, thought to resemble the human form. It supposedly shrieked when pulled out of the ground, its cry killing all humans who heard it; hence the impossibility of getting it with child. Ironically, its fruit when eaten by women was supposed to be an aid in conception. 10 *borne . . . sights:* gifted with powers of clairvoyance.

Song

Sweetest love, I do not goe,
   For wearinesse of thee,
Nor in hope the world can show
   A fitter Love for mee;
     But since that I   5
Must dye at last, 'tis best,
To use my selfe in jest
   Thus by fain'd deaths to dye.

Yesternight the Sunne went hence,
   And yet is here to day,   10
He hath no desire nor sense,
   Nor halfe so short a way:
     Then feare not mee,
But beleeve that I shall make
Speedier journeyes, since I take   15
   More wings and spurres then hee.

O how feeble is mans power,
   That if good fortune fall,
Cannot adde another houre,
   Nor a lost houre recall!   20
     But come bad chance,
And wee joyne to it our strength,
And wee teach it art and length,
   It selfe o'r us to'advance.

When thou sigh'st, thou sigh'st not winde,   25
   But sigh'st my soule away,
When thou weep'st, unkindly kinde,
   My lifes blood doth decay.
     It cannot bee
That thou lov'st mee, as thou say'st,   30
If in thine my life thou waste,
   Thou art the best of mee.

Let not thy divining heart
   Forethinke me any ill,
Destiny may take thy part,   35
   And may thy feares fulfill;

SONG. 25–26 *When . . . away:* based on the notion that a sigh is literally the expiration of the soul. 27 *unkindly kinde:* (oxymoron) literally, unnaturally natural; hence, cruelly loving. 33 *divining:* foreboding.

But thinke that wee
Are but turn'd aside to sleepe;
They who one another keepe
    Alive, ne'r parted bee.   40

A Valediction: forbidding Mourning

As virtuous men passe mildly'away,
    And whisper to their soules, to goe,
Whilst some of their sad friends doe say,
    The breath goes now, and some say, no:

So let us melt, and make no noise,   5
    No teare-floods, nor sigh-tempests move,
'Twere prophanation of our joyes
    To tell the layetie our love.

Moving of th'earth brings harmes and feares,
    Men reckon what it did and meant,   10
But trepidation of the spheares,
    Though greater farre, is innocent.

Dull sublunary lovers love
    (Whose soule is sense) cannot admit
Absence, because it doth remove   15
    Those things which elemented it.

But we by'a love, so much refin'd,
    That our selves know not what it is,
Inter-assured of the mind,
    Care lesse, eyes, lips, and hands to misse.   20

Our two soules therefore, which are one,
    Though I must goe, endure not yet
A breach, but an expansion,
    Like gold to ayery thinnesse beate.

A VALEDICTION. 5 *melt:* change by imperceptible degrees from one state to another; also, to suffer dissolution. The word implies change (and hence separation) and continued union. 8 *layetie:* the uninformed, those ignorant of love. 9 *Moving . . . earth:* i.e., earthquakes. 11 *trepidation . . . spheares:* "trembling" or fearful agitation; a condition observed in the perturbations in the supposedly regular motions of heavenly bodies. 13 *sublunary:* literally, below the moon; hence, earthly. All sublunar bodies are subject to mortal change. 15 *absence:* a pun. 16 *elemented:* constituted.

If they be two, they are two so   25
    As stiffe twin compasses are two,
Thy soule the fixt foot, makes no show
    To move, but doth, if the'other doe.

And though it in the center sit,
    Yet when the other far doth rome,   30
It leanes, and hearkens after it,
    And growes erect, as it comes home.

Such wilt thou be to mee, who must
    Like th'other foot, obliquely runne;
Thy firmnes makes my circle just,   35
    And makes me end, where I begunne.

The Good-morrow

I wonder by my troth, what thou, and I
    Did, till we lov'd? were we not wean'd till then?
But suck'd on countrey pleasures, childishly?
    Or snorted we i'the seaven sleepers den?
'Twas so; But this, all pleasures fancies bee.   5
If ever any beauty I did see,
Which I desir'd, and got, 'twas but a dreame of thee.

And now good morrow to our waking soules,
    Which watch not one another out of feare;
For love, all love of other sights controules,   10
    And makes one little roome, an every where.
Let sea-discoverers to new worlds have gone,
Let Maps to others, worlds on worlds have showne,
Let us possesse our world, each hath one, and is one.

My face in thine eye, thine in mine appeares,   15
    And true plaine hearts doe in the faces rest,

---

26 *compasses:* dividers, an instrument for describing true circles and also for determining distances on a seaman's chart.

THE GOOD-MORROW. A variation of the traditional *Aubade.* Cf. Chaucer, *Troilus and Criseyde,* III, 1415–1519. 4 *snorted:* snored. *seaven sleepers:* seven Christian youths who, to escape persecution, hid in a cave where they slept miraculously for two centuries. 12 *Let . . . gone:* let navigators who have gone to new worlds [possess what they have discovered—see l. 14]. 13 *Let . . . showne:* let maps [perhaps of the heavens as well as the earth], which have shown new worlds to other [passive?] seekers. 15 *face . . . eye:* i.e., reflected in your eye [a hemisphere].

Where can we finde two better hemispheares
  Without sharpe North, without declining West?
What ever dyes, was not mixt equally;
  If our two loves be one, or, thou and I   20
Love so alike, that none doe slacken, none can die.

The Sunne Rising

    Busie old foole, unruly Sunne,
      Why dost thou thus,
Through windowes, and through curtaines call on us?
Must to thy motions lovers seasons run? *S -F -N -S*
    Sawcy pedantique wretch, goe chide   5
    Late schoole boyes, and sowre prentices,
  Goe tell Court-huntsmen, that the King will ride,
  Call countrey ants to harvest offices;
Love, all alike, no season knowes, nor clyme,
Nor houres, dayes, months, which are the rags of time.   10

    Thy beames, so reverend, and strong
      Why shouldst thou thinke?
I could eclipse and cloud them with a winke,
But that I would not lose her sight so long:
    If her eyes have not blinded thine,   15
    Looke, and to morrow late, tell mee,
  Whether both the'India's of spice and Myne
Be where thou leftst them, or lie here with mee.
Aske for those Kings whom thou saw'st yesterday,
And thou shalt heare, All here in one bed lay.   20

    She'is all States, and all Princes, I,
      Nothing else is.
Princes doe but play us; compar'd to this,
All honor's mimique; All wealth alchimie.
    Thou sunne art halfe as happy'as wee,   25
    In that the world's contracted thus;
  Thine age askes ease, and since thy duties bee
  To warme the world, that's done in warming us.
Shine here to us, and thou art every where;
This bed thy center is, these walls, thy spheare.   30

---

18 *sharpe . . . West:* the coldness of the *North* and the declining sun in the *West* both symbolize death.

THE SUNNE RISING.   17 *both the'India's:* East Indies (spice) and West Indies (gold).

The Canonization

For Godsake hold your tongue, and let me love,
  Or chide my palsie, or my gout,
My five gray haires, or ruin'd fortune flout,
With wealth your state, your minde with Arts improve,
    Take you a course, get you a place,   5
    Observe his honour, or his grace,
And the Kings reall, or his stamped face
  Contemplate; what you will, approve,
    So you will let me love.

Alas, alas, who's injur'd by my love?   10
  What merchants ships have my sighs drown'd?
Who saies my teares have overflow'd his ground?
When did my colds a forward spring remove?
    When did the heats which my veines fill
    Adde one man to the plaguie Bill?   15
Soldiers finde warres, and Lawyers finde out still
  Litigious men, which quarrels move,
    Though she and I do love.

Call us what you will, wee'are made such by love;
  Call her one, mee another flye,   20
We'are Tapers too, and at our owne cost die,
And wee in us finde the'Eagle and the Dove;
    The Phœnix ridle hath more wit
    By us, we two being one, are it,
So, to one neutrall thing both sexes fit.   25
  Wee dye and rise the same, and prove
    Mysterious by this love.

THE CANONIZATION. The order of this poem is perhaps controlled by the *processus* of canonization of saints in the Roman Catholic Church as it existed before 1625. See John A. Clair, "Donne's 'The Canonization'," *PMLA*, LXXX, 1965, pp. 300–02. 7 *stamped face:* on coins. 11–14 *sighs . . . teares . . . colds . . . heats:* the conventional symptoms of acute love, which Donne ironically exaggerates. Cf. Wyatt, "My Galley," p. 24. 15 *plaguie Bill:* death list of plague victims, issued weekly. 20 *flye:* The (butter)fly, attracted to the candle's flame, is consumed. 22 *Eagle . . . Dove:* symbols of strength and constancy in love. Also, according to the *Bestiary*, the eagle renews its sight by flying directly into the sun and its vigor by plunging next into a fountain. 23 *Phœnix ridle:* the fabulous bird of the east that, when old, builds a pyre of spices, turns its body toward the rays of the sun, ignites itself, and rises renewed from its own ashes. 26 *dye . . . same:* consumed like the fly, taper, eagle, and phœnix, and like the eagle and phœnix, renewed. *Dye* also has a sexual signification: to become lifeless after the expenditure of the "spirit generative" in sexual intercourse.

Wee can dye by it, if not live by love,
    And if unfit for tombes or hearse
Our legend bee, it will be fit for verse;   30
And if no peece of Chronicle wee prove,
    We'll build in sonnets pretty roomes;
    As well a well wrought urne becomes
The greatest ashes, as halfe-acre tombes,
    And by these hymnes, all shall approve   35
      Us *Canoniz'd* for Love.

And thus invoke us; You whom reverend love
    Made one anothers hermitage;
You, to whom love was peace, that now is rage;
Who did the whole worlds soule extract, and drove   40
    Into the glasses of your eyes,
    So made such mirrors, and such spies,
That they did all to you epitomize,
    Countries, Townes, Courts: Beg from above
      A patterne of your love!   45

Loves Infiniteness

If yet I have not all thy love,
    Deare, I shall never have it all;
I cannot breath one other sigh, to move,
    Nor can intreat one other teare to fall.
All my treasure, which should purchase thee,   5
    Sighs, teares, and oathes, and letters I have spent,
Yet no more can be due to mee,
    Then at the bargaine made was ment.
If then thy gift of love were partiall,
That some to mee, some should to others fall,   10
    Deare, I shall never have Thee All.

Or if then thou gav'st mee all,
    All was but All, which thou hadst then,
But if in thy heart, since, there be or shall,
    New love created bee, by other men,   15
Which have their stocks intire, and can in teares,
    In sighs, in oathes, and letters outbid mee,

---

30 *legend:* specifically, the life history of a saint. 31 *Chronicle:* specifically, a history of times and events. 37 *You:* the lovers, who like saints are to *beg* (intercede) from the divine power *above* a *patterne* of love for earthbound lovers.

This new love may beget new feares,
  For, this love was not vowed by thee.
And yet it was, thy gift being generall,   20
The ground, thy heart is mine, what ever shall
  Grow there, deare, I should have it all.

Yet I would not have all yet,
  Hee that hath all can have no more,
And since my love doth every day admit   25
  New growth, thou shouldst have new rewards in store;
Thou canst not every day give me thy heart,
  If thou canst give it, then thou never gav'st it:
Loves riddles are, that though thy heart depart,
  It stayes at home, and thou with losing sav'st it: 30
But wee will have a way more liberall,
Then changing hearts, to joyne them, so wee shall
  Be one, and one anothers All.

A Nocturnall upon S. Lucies Day, being the shortest day

'Tis the yeares midnight, and it is the dayes,
Lucies, who scarce seaven houres herself unmaskes,
  The Sunne is spent, and now his flasks
  Send forth light squibs, no constant rayes;
    The world's whole sap is sunke: 5
The generall balme th'hydroptique earth hath drunk,
Whither, as to the beds-feet, life is shrunke,
Dead and enterr'd; yet all these seeme to laugh,
Compar'd with mee, who am their Epitaph.

LOVES INFINITENESS. 21 *ground:* Legally, in the sale of land, the crops growing on the land belonged to the new owner unless otherwise stipulated. The legal terminology and argument are conventional in love poetry at least since Andreas Cappellanus' *The Art of Courtly Love* (*ca.* 1200). Donne's use of them is characteristically realistic and yet tender.

A NOCTURNALL. 1–2 *dayes, Lucies:* December 13, under the old calendar the date of the winter solstice, the shortest day of the year (G). St. Lucy, a third-century virgin martyr, is the patronesss of the blind and is traditionally associated with light, especially in Germany and Scandinavia, where on this day maidens dressed in white and crowned with lighted candles commemorate the miraculous restoration of the eyes of St. Lucy and also pay homage to the rebirth of the sun. 3 *flasks:* the stars, which were thought to store up light from the sun (G). 4 *light squibs:* slight explosive rays, as from a small rocket. 5–6 *world's . . . drunk:* No life is left in the world, because its vital sap (medicinally preservative balm) has been drunk by the thirsty (*hydroptique*) earth. 7 *beds-feet:* foot of the bed, where the dying man slips down (G).

Study me then, you who shall lovers bee   10
At the next world, that is, at the next Spring:
  For I am every dead thing,
    In whom love wrought new Alchimie.
      For his art did expresse
A quintessence even from nothingnesse,   15
From dull privations, and leane emptinesse:
He ruin'd mee, and I am re-begot
Of absence, darknesse, death; things which are not.

All others, from all things, draw all that's good,
Life, soule, forme, spirit, whence they beeing have; 20
  I, by loves limbecke, am the grave
  Of all, that's nothing. Oft a flood
    Have wee two wept, and so
Drownd the whole world, us two; oft did we grow
To be two Chaosses, when we did show   25
Care to ought else; and often absences
Withdrew our soules, and made us carcasses.

But I am by her death, (which word wrongs her)
Of the first nothing, the Elixer grown;
  Were I a man, that I were one,   30
  I needs must know; I should preferre,
    If I were any beast,
Some ends, some means; Yea plants, yea stones detest,
And love; All, all some properties invest;
If I an ordinary nothing were,   35
As shadow,'a light, and body must be here.

But I am None; nor will my Sunne renew.
You lovers, for whose sake, the lesser Sunne
  At this time to the Goat is runne
  To fetch new lust, and give it you,   40
    Enjoy your summer all;

12–15 *For . . . nothingnesse:* Alchemy ordinarily tries to discover the elixir or quintessence for transmuting base metals into gold and for prolonging life. Here, in ironic reversal, the lover, already *every dead thing*, is reduced even further by love to a superlative degree of annihilation: the *quintessence* of nothingness.   17 *ruin'd:* probably an alchemical term meaning broken down into elements, as well as destroyed or made bankrupt.   21 *limbecke:* alembic, an apparatus used in alchemical distillation.   25 *Chaosses:* When fully preoccupied with their love, the lovers are one world; when they are separated, they are *Chaosses.*   29 *first nothing:* i.e., the "nothing" out of which the world was created. *Elixir:* Cf. ll. 12–15 and note.   34 *properties invest:* are endued with powers.   37 *Sunne:* his beloved, whose eyes (like the sun) illuminated his world.   39 *Goat:* Capricorn, the constellation into which the sun runs at the winter solstice, signalling his return or rebirth.

Since shee enjoyes her long nights festivall,
Let mee prepare towards her, and let mee call
This houre her Vigill, and her Eve, since this
Both the yeares, and the dayes deep midnight is.   45

Satire III

Kind pity chokes my spleen; brave scorn forbids
Those tears to issue which swell my eye-lids;
I must not laugh, nor weep sins, and be wise,
Can railing then cure these worn maladies?
Is not our Mistress fair Religion,   5
As worthy of all our soul's devotion,
As virtue was to the first blinded age?
Are not heaven's joys as valiant to assuage
Lusts, as earth's honor was to them? Alas,
As we do them in means, shall they surpass   10
Us in the end, and shall thy father's spirit
Meet blind philosophers in heaven, whose merit
Of strict life may be imputed faith, and hear
Thee, whom he taught so easy ways and near
To follow, damn'd? O if thou dar'st, fear this: 15
This fear great courage, and high valor is.
Dar'st thou aid mutinous Dutch, and dar'st thou lay
Thee in ships' wooden sepulchers, a prey
To leaders' rage, to storms, to shot, to dearth?
Dar'st thou dive seas, and dungeons of the earth?   20
Hast thou courageous fire to thaw the ice
Of frozen North discoveries? and thrice

42 *festivall:* the feast of a saint.   44 *Vigill:* the eve of the saint's day, which commemorates with a fast the earthly struggles of the saint, while the day celebrates her heavenly victory with a feast.

SATIRE III.   1 *spleen:* In the old physiology, the seat of indignation, ill humor, and melancholy, and also of laughter: feelings and actions appropriate for a satire; hence appropriate for a poem in which prevalent vices and follies are seriously denounced and energetically ridiculed.   7-9 *As . . . them:* The pre-Christian pagan world had *virtue* inasmuch as it was instructed by reason and the "light of Nature"; yet it was *blinded* because it lacked Christian revelation. For the pagans the greatest good was *earth's honor;* for Christians, *heaven's joy.*   10 *means:* our religion.   12 *blind philosophers:* Plato, Socrates, *et al.,* who did not know Christianity.   14 *so easy ways:* Cf. Matt. 11:30, "For my yoke is easy, and my burden is light."   17–28 *Dar'st . . . straw:* The hazards man endures for gain require *courage of straw* compared to the *high valor* required for living a Christian life. Note the paradoxical relation to *easy ways,* l. 14.   22 *frozen North discoveries:* i.e., attempts, such as those by Cabot and Frobisher, to discover the northwest passage.

Colder than salamanders, like divine
Children in th' oven, fires of Spain, and the line,
Whose countries limbecs to our bodies be,   25
Canst thou for gain bear? and must every he
Which cries not, "Goddess," to thy Mistress, draw,
Or eat thy poisonous words? courage of straw!
O desperate coward, wilt thou seem bold, and
To thy foes and his (who made thee to stand   30
Sentinel in his world's garrison) thus yield,
And for forbidden wars, leave th' appointed field?
Know thy foes: the foul Devil h' is (whom thou
Striv'st to please), for hate, not love, would allow
Thee fain, his whole realm to be quit; and as   35
The world's all parts wither away and pass,
So the world's self, thy other lov'd foe, is
In her decrepit wane, and thou loving this
Dost love a withered and worn strumpet; last,
Flesh (it self's death) and joys which flesh can taste,   40
Thou lovest; and thy fair goodly soul, which doth
Give this flesh power to taste joy, thou dost loathe.
    Seek true religion. O where? Mirreus
Thinking her unhous'd here, and fled from us,
Seeks her at Rome; there, because he doth know   45
That she was there a thousand years ago,
He loves her rags so, as we here obey
The statecloth where the Prince sat yesterday.
Crantz to such brave loves will not be inthrall'd,

23–24 *Colder . . . line:* as if they were salamanders (supposed to be able to live in fire). Like Meshach, Shadrach, and Abed-nego, who survived the fiery furnace into which they had been placed for refusing to fall down and worship the golden image (Dan. 3:19–27), men will endure for gain the torments of the Spanish climate and equatorial heat, and perhaps the tortures of the Spanish Inquisition. 25 *limbecs:* see above, NOCTURNALL, l. 21. In this climate our bodies, like *limbecs,* distill sweat. 33 *thy foes:* the Devil, the world, and the flesh. 43 *Mirreus:* The five proper names following (Mirreus, Crantz, Graius, Phrygius, Graccus) apparently have no immediate historical significance but seem to suggest characteristic types of men who have abandoned their obligation to strive to reach *Truth. Mirreus* (derived from Murrheus: yellowish, annointed with myrrh, an ingredient of incense) suggests the type who surrenders merely to the incense, richness of vestments, and outward show of Roman Catholic ceremony. *Mirreus* and *Crantz* probably refer to religious ceremony and ornament, the others to doctrine and discipline. 44 *unhous'd here:* i.e., thrown out of English churches by the Reformers and by practices of the Elizabethan Establishment. 48 *statecloth:* canopy over a throne. 49 *Crantz:* i.e., any Dutch Calvinist or Scottish Presbyterian, one sternly opposed to ornate rituals and vestments. Crants (a spelling supported by some mss.), a word of Dutch origin then in common use, is a garland, wreath, or chaplet; thus, a plain and natural ornament compared with the elaborate (*brave*) *rags* of Rome. Cf. *Hamlet,* V, i, 226: the "virgin crants" of Ophelia means not only the garlands of white papers customary for a young girl's funeral but also rites.

But loves her only, who at Geneva is call'd   50
Religion, plain, simple, sullen, young,
Contemptuous, yet unhandsome; as among
Lecherous humors, there is one that judges
No wenches wholesome, but coarse country drudges.
Graius stays still at home here, and because   55
Some preachers, vile ambitious bawds, and laws
Still new like fashions, bid him think that she
Which dwells with us, is only perfect, he
Embraceth her, whom his godfathers will
Tender to him, being tender, as wards still   60
Take such wives as their guardians offer, or
Pay values. Careless Phrygius doth abhor
All, because all cannot be good, as one
Knowing some women whores, dares marry none.
Graccus loves all as one, and thinks that so   65
As women do in divers countries go
In divers habits, yet are still one kind;
So doth, so is Religion; and this blind-
ness too much light breeds; but unmoved thou
Of force must one, and forc'd but one allow;   70

53 *Lecherous humors:* lecherous men. 55 *Graius:* i.e., the Greek. Cf. Virgil, *Aeneid* III, 588–692 (see particularly l. 594, where this usage occurs), and the story of Achaemenides, the desperate Greek castaway, left behind among the Cyclops when Ulysses escaped from Polyphemus, whose suffering and willingness to take risks contrast ironically with the lazy Englishman who believes just what he is told. 59–60 *will/Tender . . . tender:* (pun) his godfathers (spiritual *guardians*) at baptism will present formally (*tender*) their acceptance of the Articles of Religion for the *tender* infant. 62 *Pay values:* i.e., pay fines. Cf. to pay the "valour of Mariage": a ward who refused to accept the marriage arranged by his guardian was required to pay a fine that would allow his "lord" to recover the "value of the mariage" (see *OED, valour*). Likewise Elizabethan law fined a man if he refused to accept the "marriage" with the Anglican Church arranged by his sponsors. *Careless Phrygius:* i.e. (in contrast with *Graius*) the Trojan; ironic because Aeneas (the "Phrygian King," *Aeneid* XII, 75) deliberately risked all in single combat with Turnus for the hand of Lavinia; *Careless,* because in non-poetic usage in classical literature, the Phrygians were noted for their indolence, stupidity, and effeminacy, as well as for their skill in embroidering with gold, which in this context would suggest stupid fastidiousness. In Greek music, the Phrygian was the religious mode, exciting and emotional. The term also refers to a heretical, severely ascetic Christian sect of the second century, founded by Montanus and two women whose prophetic utterances were characterized by esctasy and "uncontrollable madness." 65 *Graccus:* i.e. (in contrast with *Graius* and *Phrygius*) the Roman, ironically modeled after Tiberius and Caius Graccus, Roman patriots who were carefully educated by their mother, Cornelia, to exemplify the ideals of Roman piety and virtue, and whose eloquent and vehement attachment to the interests of the people led to acts of sedition, riots, and their deaths. Here *Graccus'* democratic ideals consist only of his inability to make any distinctions among *women,* a failure that may conclude in disaster. 70 *Of force:* by necessity. *forc'd:* i.e., when compelled actually to make a choice.

And the right; ask thy father which is she,
Let him ask his; though truth and falsehood be
Near twins, yet truth a little elder is;
Be busy to seek her, believe me this,
He's not of none, nor worst, that seeks the best.   75
To adore, or scorn an image, or protest,
May all be bad; doubt wisely; in strange way
To stand inquiring right, is not to stray;
To sleep, or run wrong, is. On a huge hill,
Cragged, and steep, Truth stands, and he that will   80
Reach her, about must, and about must go;
And what the hill's suddenness resists, win so;
Yet strive so, that before age, death's twilight,
Thy soul rest, for none can work in that night.
To will, implies delay, therefore now do: 85
Hard deeds, the body's pains; hard knowledge too
The mind's endeavors reach, and mysteries
Are like the sun, dazzling, yet plain to all eyes.
Keep the truth which thou hast found; men do not stand
In so ill case here, that God hath with his hand   90
Sign'd kings' blank-charters to kill whom they hate,
Nor are they vicars, but hangmen to Fate.
Fool and wretch, wilt thou let thy soul be tied
To man's laws, by which she shall not be tried
At the last day? Oh, will it then boot thee   95
To say a Philip, or a Gregory,
A Harry, or a Martin taught thee this?
Is not this excuse for mere contraries,
Equally strong? cannot both sides say so?
That thou mayest rightly obey power, her bounds know;   100
Those past, her nature, and name is chang'd; to be
Then humble to her is idolatry.
As streams are, power is; those blest flowers that dwell

71 *ask thy father:* Cf. Moses' song, Deut. 32:7, "Remember the days of old, consider the years of many generations: ask thy father, and he will show thee; thy elders, and they will tell thee"; i.e., go to the true prophets of old, not to the modern mothers (churches) of easy virtue. 82 *suddenness:* steepness. 83–84 *death's . . . night:* Cf. John 9:4. 86–88 *Hard . . . eyes:* Hard deeds are achieved by toil; hard knowledge by mind's effort; but mysteries, *dazzling* like the sun, blind the understanding, and yet their truth is plain to all. 90 *case:* condition. 91 *blank-charters:* i.e., documents like those "given to agents of the crown in Richard II's reign with power to fill it up as they pleased" (*OED, blank*, 10). See also Shakespeare, *Richard II*, I, iv, 48. 92 *hangmen to Fate:* executors of Fate's orders. 95 *boot:* profit. 96–97 *Philip . . . Martin:* Symbolic of various recognized churches: Philip II of Spain (Roman Catholic), or Philipp Melanchthon (Lutheran); Popes Gregory XIII and XIV; Henry VIII (Anglican); Luther. 98 *mere:* absolute, sheer, perfect. 101 *Those past:* (once) past the bounds.

At the rough stream's calm head, thrive and do well,
But having left their roots, and themselves given   105
To the stream's tyrannous rage, alas are driven
Through mills, and rocks, and woods, and at last, almost
Consum'd in going, in the sea are lost:
So perish souls, which more choose men's unjust
Power from God claim'd, than God himself to trust.   110

from HOLY SONNETS
(1633)

Divine Meditations

4

At the round earths imagin'd corners, blow
Your trumpets, Angells, and arise, arise
From death, you numberlesse infinities
Of soules, and to your scattred bodies goe,
All whom the flood did, and fire shall o'erthrow,   5
All whom warre, dearth, age, agues, tyrannies,
Despaire, law, chance, hath slaine, and you whose eyes,
Shall behold God, and never tast deaths woe.
But let them sleepe, Lord, and mee mourne a space,
For, if above all these, my sinnes abound,   10
'Tis late to aske abundance of thy grace,
When wee are there; here on this lowly ground,
Teach mee how to repent; for that's as good
As if thou'hadst seal'd my pardon, with thy blood.   (VII)

6

Death be not proud, though some have called thee
Mighty and dreadfull, for, thou art not soe,
For, those, whom thou think'st, thou dost overthrow,
Die not, poore death, nor yet canst thou kill mee;
From rest and sleepe, which but thy pictures bee,   5
Much pleasure, then from thee, much more must flow,
And soonest our best men with thee doe goe,

HOLY SONNETS. The text and the numbering of the "Holy Sonnets" is that established by Helen Gardner, *The Divine Poems of John Donne* (Oxford, at the Clarendon Press, 1952). The Roman numerals in parentheses refer to the traditional numbering of the sonnets.

[4]   1 *corners:* Cf. Rev. 7:1, "I saw four angels standing on the four corners of the earth . . . ."   4 *scattred bodies:* At the last Judgment, the souls are to rejoin their bodies wherever they may have been scattered, whole or in pieces.

Rest of their bones, and soules deliverie.
Thou art slave to Fate, chance, kings, and desperate men,
And dost with poyson, warre, and sicknesse dwell,   10
And poppie, or charmes can make us sleepe as well,
And better then thy stroake; why swell'st thou then?
One short sleepe past, wee wake eternally,
And death shall be no more, Death thou shalt die.   (X)

9

What if this present were the worlds last night?
Marke in my heart, O Soule, where thou dost dwell,
The picture of Christ crucified, and tell
Whether that countenance can thee affright,
Teares in his eyes quench the amasing light,   5
Blood fills his frownes, which from his pierc'd head fell,
And can that tongue adjudge thee unto hell,
Which pray'd forgivenesse for his foes fierce spight?
No, no; but as in my idolatrie
I said to all my profane mistresses,   10
Beauty, of pitty, foulnesse onely is
A signe of rigour: so I say to thee,
To wicked spirits are horrid shapes assign'd,
This beauteous forme assures a pitious minde.   (XIII)

Know this as a metaphor   *Father, Son, H. Ghost*

10

Batter my heart, three person'd God; for, you
As yet but knocke, breathe, shine, and seeke to mend;   *Metaphor*
That I may rise, and stand, o'erthrow mee,'and bend   *Body to a Town*
Your force, to breake, blowe, burn and make me new.
I, like an usurpt towne, to'another due,   *Pleading for his heart*
Labour to'admit you, but Oh, to no end,
Reason your viceroy in mee, mee should defend,   *Vice / Royalty*
But is captiv'd, and proves weake or untrue,
Yet dearely'I love you, and would be lov'd faine,
But am betroth'd unto your enemie. *Devil*   10
Divorce mee,'untie, or breake that knot againe,
Take mee to you, imprison mee, for I   *Freed from physical life*
Except you'enthrall mee, never shall be free,   *and take or heavenly concerns*
Nor ever chast, except you ravish mee.   (XIV)

Metaphor maiden — God makes Queen —

[6] 12 *swell'st:* i.e., with pride.

[9] 5 *amasing:* amazing, i.e., terrifying. 8 *forgivenesse . . . spight:* Cf.
Luke 23:34, "Father, forgive them; for they know not what they do." 11
Beauty . . . pitty: beauty is a sign of pity, as ugliness is of rigour.

[10] 4 *breake . . . new:* i.e., violent intensifications of *knocke . . . mend* (l. 2).

from HOLY SONNETS
(ADDED IN 1635)

Divine Meditations

1

Thou hast made me, And shall thy worke decay?
Repaire me now, for now mine end doth haste,
I runne to death, and death meets me as fast,
And all my pleasures are like yesterday,
I dare not move my dimme eyes any way,   5
Despaire behind, and death before doth cast
Such terrour, and my feebled flesh doth waste
By sinne in it, which it t'wards hell doth weigh;
Onely thou art above, and when towards thee
By thy leave I can looke, I rise againe;   10
But our old subtle foe so tempteth me,
That not one houre I can my selfe sustaine;
Thy Grace may wing me to prevent his art
And thou like Adamant draw mine iron heart.   (I)

2

I am a little world made cunningly
Of Elements, and an Angelike spright,
But black sinne hath betraid to endlesse night
My worlds both parts, and (oh) both parts must die.
You which beyond that heaven which was most high   5
Have found new sphears, and of new lands can write,
Powre new seas in mine eyes, that so I might
Drowne my world with my weeping earnestly,
Or wash it, if it must be drown'd no more:
But oh it must be burnt; alas the fire   10
Of lust and envie have burnt it heretofore,
And made it fouler; Let their flames retire,
And burne me ô Lord, with a fiery zeale
Of thee and thy house, which doth in eating heale.   (V)

HOLY SONNETS (ADDED IN 1635). [1] 8 *weigh:* carry; also, to bear down, as on a balance scale. 11 *subtle foe:* Satan. 13 *wing:* give me wings to escape hell and to *sustaine* me. *prevent:* to come before, i.e., by grace, which "maye alwayes prevente and followe us" to frustrate. Cf. Collect for Seventeenth Sunday after Trinity in *Book of Common Prayer.* 14 *Adamant:* magnet.

[2] 5 *was most high:* a reference, perhaps, to the new astronomy, which destroyed the sense that heaven was just beyond the stars. 7–10 *Powre . . . Drowne . . . wash . . . burnt:* microcosmic enactment of Biblical and apocalyptic history: the Flood (cf. Gen. 9:11), Baptism, Last Judgment. 13–14 Cf. Psalm 69:9.

from HOLY SONNETS
(FROM THE WESTMORELAND MS.)

1

Since she whome I lovd, hath payd her last debt
To Nature, and to hers, and my good is dead,
And her soule early into heaven ravished,
Wholy in heavenly things my mind is sett.
Here the admyring her my mind did whett   5
To seeke thee God; so streames do shew the head,
But though I have found thee, and thou my thirst hast fed,
A holy thirsty dropsy melts mee yett.
But why should I begg more love, when as thou
Dost wooe my soule, for hers offring all thine: 10
And dost not only feare least I allow
My love to saints and Angels, things divine,
But in thy tender jealosy dost doubt
Least the World, fleshe, yea Devill putt thee out.   (XVII)

Hymne to God my God, in my sicknesse

Since I am comming to that Holy roome,
    Where, with thy Quire of Saints for evermore,
I shall be made thy Musique; As I come
    I tune the Instrument here at the dore,
    And what I must doe then, thinke now before.   5

Whilst my Physitians by their love are growne
    Cosmographers, and I their Mapp, who lie
Flat on this bed, that by them may be showne
    That this is my South-west discoverie
    Per fretum febris, by these streights to die,   10

I joy, that in these straits, I see my West;
    For, though theire currants yeeld returne to none,
What shall my West hurt me? As West and East
    In all flatt Maps (and I am one) are one,
    So death doth touch the Resurrection.   15

HOLY SONNETS (FROM THE WESTMORELAND MS.). [1] Cf. "renunciation"
sonnets of Sidney and Shakespeare. 6 *head:* source. 8 *dropsy:* Those
afflicted with this disease are always thirsty.

HYMNE TO GOD. 7 *Cosmographers:* geographers of the universe. *Mapp.*
On flat (Mercator projection) maps, the shortest distance between two points
is a straight line. 9 *South-west discoverie:* South accords with fever, West with
death. 10 *Per fretum febris:* means through both "raging heat of fever" and
"strait of fever." 11 *straits:* (pun) narrow passages, distressed circumstances.

Is the Pacifique Sea my home? Or are
  The Easterne riches? Is *Jerusalem?*
Anyan, and *Magellan,* and *Gibraltare,*
  All streights, and none but streights, are wayes to them,
  Whether where *Japhet* dwelt, or *Cham,* or *Sem.*   20

We thinke that *Paradise* and *Calvarie,*
  Christs Crosse, and *Adams* tree, stood in one place;
Looke Lord, and finde both *Adams* met in me;
  As the first *Adams* sweat surrounds my face,
  May the last *Adams* blood my soule embrace.   25

So, in his purple wrapp'd receive mee Lord,
  By these his thornes give me his other Crowne;
And as to others soules I preach'd thy word,
  Be this my Text, my Sermon to mine owne,
  Therfore that he may raise the Lord throws down.   30

17 *Jerusalem:* the East and hence life. 18 *Anyan:* Bering Strait. 20 *where
. . . Sem:* sons of Noah, whose descendants populated the earth. 21 *Paradise
and Calvarie:* place of man's original sin and of the atonement for it. 22
Crosse . . . tree: both trees, for it was thought that the wood for the cross
came from a descendant of the Tree of Knowledge of Good and Evil. 23 *both
Adams:* Cf. Rom. 5:14, where Adam "is the figure of him that was to come
[Christ]." Cf. also 1 Cor. 15:22, 45. 24–25 *sweat . . . blood:* Cf. Gen 3:19
and Luke 22:44.

ROBERT HERRICK
1591–1674

from HESPERIDES

Delight in Disorder

A sweet disorder in the dress
Kindles in clothes a wantonness:
A lawn about the shoulders thrown
Into a fine distraction:
An erring lace, which here and there   5
Enthralls the crimson stomacher:
A cuff neglectful, and thereby
Ribbands to flow confusedly:
A winning wave (deserving note)
In the tempestuous petticoat: 10
A careless shoe-string, in whose tie
I see a wild civility:
Do more bewitch me, than when art
Is too precise in every part.

Corinna's Going a Maying

Get up, get up for shame, the blooming morn
Upon her wings presents the god unshorn.
    See how Aurora throws her fair
    Fresh-quilted colors through the air:
    Get up, sweet-slug-a-bed, and see   5
    The dew-bespangling herb and tree.
Each flower has wept, and bow'd toward the east,
Above an hour since; yet you not drest,
    Nay! not so much as out of bed?
    When all the birds have matins said,   10
    And sung their thankful hymns: 'tis sin,
    Nay, profanation to keep in,

DELIGHT IN DISORDER. 2 *wantonness:* sportive and playful behavior, innocent but erotic. 3 *lawn:* fine linen scarf. 6 *stomacher:* often bejewelled, ornamented covering for the bosom and abdomen worn under the bodice.

CORINNA'S. 2 *god unshorn:* Apollo, the god of light, music, and youth, often represented with hair flowing down his neck. 3 *Aurora:* goddess of the dawn. 10 *matins:* earliest of the seven canonical hours of daily prayer; less strictly, service of Morning Prayer, usually sung.

113

When as a thousand virgins on this day,
Spring, sooner than the lark, to fetch in May.

Rise; and put on your foliage, and be seen   15
To come forth, like the springtime, fresh and green;
    And sweet as Flora. Take no care
    For jewels for your gown, or hair:
    Fear not; the leaves will strew
    Gems in abundance upon you: 20
Besides, the childhood of the day has kept,
Against you come, some orient pearls unwept:
    Come, and receive them while the light
    Hangs on the dew-locks of the night:
    And Titan on the eastern hill   25
    Retires himself, or else stands still
Till you come forth. Wash, dress, be brief in praying:
Few beads are best, when once we go a Maying.

Come, my Corinna, come; and coming, mark
How each field turns a street; each street a park   30
    Made green, and trimm'd with trees: see how
    Devotion gives each house a bough,
    Or branch: each porch, each door, ere this,
    An ark a tabernacle is
Made up of white-thorn neatly interwove;   35
As if here were those cooler shades of love.
    Can such delights be in the street,
    And open fields, and we not see 't?
    Come, we'll abroad; and let's obey
    The proclamation made for May: 40
And sin no more, as we have done, by staying;
But my Corinna, come, let's go a Maying.

There's not a budding boy, or girl, this day,
But is got up, and gone to bring in May.
    A deal of youth, ere this, is come   45
    Back, and with white-thorn laden home.

---

14 *fetch in May:* the folk custom, rooted in pagan fertility celebrations, of
bringing in flowers on May Day, particularly the white hawthorn (often called
"May"), with which to decorate the doors of houses.   17 *Flora:* goddess of
fertility and flowers.   22 *Against:* in expectation of the time when. *orient pearls
unwept:* i.e., dewdrops; the tears of Eos (Aurora) for her son Memnon were
shed in the form of dew.   25 *Titan:* Helios, the sun in its annual and daily
course. He is usually represented as a charioteer climbing the vault of heaven.
28 *beads:* of the rosary; prayers.   34 *ark a tabernacle:* In Biblical
phraseology, the first is a portable sacred repository, the second a portable
temporary sanctuary; hence, a shrine consecrated to the transitory joys of
youth and beauty.

Some have dispatcht their cakes and cream,
    Before that we have left to dream:
And some have wept, and woo'd, and plighted troth,
And chose their priest, ere we can cast off sloth: 50
        Many a green gown has been given;
        Many a kiss, both odd and even:
        Many a glance too has been sent
        From out the eye, Love's firmament:
Many a jest told of the keys betraying   55
This night, and locks pickt, yet w' are not a Maying.

Come, let us go, while we are in our prime;
And take the harmless folly of the time.
        We shall grow old apace, and die
        Before we know our liberty.   60
        Our life is short; and our days run
        As fast away as does the sun:
And as a vapor, or a drop of rain
Once lost, can ne'er be found again:
        So when or you or I are made   65
        A fable, song, or fleeting shade;
        All love, all liking, all delight
        Lies drown'd with us in endless night.
Then while time serves, and we are but decaying;
Come, my Corinna, come, let's go a Maying.   70

To the Virgins, to Make Much of Time

        Gather ye rose-buds while ye may,
            Old Time is still a flying:
        And this same flower that smiles today,
            Tomorrow will be dying.

        The glorious lamp of heaven, the sun,   5
            The higher he's a getting;
        The sooner will his race be run,
            And nearer he's to setting.

48 *left to dream:* left off dreaming.   51 *Many . . . given:* I.e., many a girl has
had her gown stained green by rolling on the grass with her lover.   54 *Love's
firmament:* i.e., the heavens from which streams the light of beauty.   58 *take
. . . time:* i.e., *carpe diem,* "seize the day," the theme of this poem and "To
the Virgins," below. Cf. also Jonson, "Come, my Celia," and Marvell, "To
His Coy Mistress."

116

That age is best, which is the first,
   When youth and blood are warmer;   10
But being spent, the worse, and worst
   Times, still succeed the former.

Then be not coy, but use your time;
   And while ye may, go marry:
For having lost but once your prime,   15
   You may forever tarry.

To Daffodils

Fair daffodils, we weep to see
   You haste away so soon:
As yet the early-rising sun
   Has not attain'd his noon.
      Stay, stay,   5
    Until the hasting day
      Has run
    But to the Even-song;
And, having pray'd together, we
    Will go with you along.   10

We have short time to stay, as you,
   We have as short a spring;
As quick a growth to meet decay,
   As you, or any thing.
      We die,   15
   As your hours do, and dry
      Away,
   Like to the summer's rain;
Or as the pearls of morning's dew
    Ne'er to be found again.   20

The Night-Piece, to Julia

Her eyes the glow-worm lend thee,
The shooting stars attend thee,
   And the elves also,
   Whose little eyes glow,
Like the sparks of fire, befriend thee.   5

TO DAFFODILS. 8 *Even-song:* the service of Evening Prayer.

No will-o'-th'-wisp mis-light thee;
Nor snake, or slow-worm bite thee;
    But on, on thy way
    Not making a stay,
Since ghost there's none to affright thee.   10

Let not the dark thee cumber;
What though the moon does slumber?
    The stars of the night
    Will lend thee their light,
Like tapers clear without number.   15

Then Julia let me woo thee,
Thus, thus to come unto me:
    And when I shall meet
    Thy silv'ry feet,
My soul I'll pour into thee.   20

Upon Julia's Clothes

Whenas in silks my Julia goes,
Then, then (methinks) how sweetly flows
That liquefaction of her clothes.

Next, when I cast mine eyes and see
That brave vibration each way free;
O how that glittering taketh me!

Dean-bourn, a Rude River in Devon, by which Sometimes He Lived

Dean-bourn, farewell; I never look to see
Dean, or thy warty incivility.
Thy rocky bottom that doth tear thy streams
And makes them frantic, ev'n to all extremes,
To my content I never should behold,   5
Were thy streams silver, or thy rocks all gold.
Rocky thou art, and rocky we discover
Thy men, and rocky are thy ways all over.
O men, O manners, now and ever known
To be a rocky generatïon!   10

THE NIGHT-PIECE. 7 *slow-worm:* originally slāwyrm, i.e., slay-worm, the blindworm, a small, pretty lizard whose bite is harmless. 11 *cumber:* hinder, perplex.

118

A people currish, churlish as the seas,
And rude, almost, as rudest savages,
With whom I did, and may re-sojourn, when
Rocks turn to rivers, rivers turn to men.

His Return to London

From the dull confines of the drooping west
To see the day spring from the pregnant east,
Ravished in spirit, I come, nay more, I fly
To thee, blest place of my nativity!
Thus, thus with hallowed foot I touch the ground   5
With thousand blessings by thy fortune crowned.
O fruitful genius! that bestowest here
An everlasting plenty, year by year.
O place! O people! Manners framed to please
All nations, customs, kindreds, languages!   10
I am a free-born Roman, suffer then
That I amongst you live a citizen.
London my home is, though by hard fate sent
Into a long and irksome banishment;
Yet since called back, henceforward let me be,   15
O native country, repossessed by thee!
For rather than I'll to the west return,
I'll beg of thee first here to have mine urn.
Weak I am grown, and must in short time fall;
Give thou my sacred relics burial.   20

His Prayer to Ben Jonson

When I a verse shall make,
Know I have prayed thee,
For old religion's sake,
Saint Ben, to aid me.

Make the way smooth for me,   5
When I, thy Herrick,
Honoring thee, on my knee
Offer my lyric.

Candles I'll give to thee,
And a new altar;   10
And thou, Saint Ben, shalt be
Writ in my psalter.

HIS RETURN.   1 *west:* Devon, where he had been living, is west of London.

To Live Merrily, and to Trust to Good Verses

Now is the time for mirth,
  Nor cheek or tongue be dumb;
For with the flow'ry earth
  The golden pomp is come.

The golden pomp is come;   5
  For now each tree does wear,
Made of her pap and gum,
  Rich beads of amber here.

Now reigns the rose, and now
  Th' Arabian dew besmears   10
My uncontrollëd brow
  And my retorted hairs.

Homer, this health to thee,
  In sack of such a kind
That it would make thee see   15
  Though thou wert ne'er so blind.

Next, Virgil I'll call forth
  To pledge this second health
In wine, whose each cup's worth
  An Indian commonwealth.   20

A goblet next I'll drink
  To Ovid, and suppose,
Made he the pledge, he'd think
  The world had all one nose.

Then this immensive cup   25
  Of aromatic wine,
Catullus, I quaff up
  To that terse muse of thine.

TO LIVE MERRILY.   7 *pap:* pulp. 10 *Arabian dew:* i.e., perfumed gums and oils.
12 *retorted:* twisted back. 20 *Indian commonwealth:* i.e. Virgil's *Aeneid,*
which celebrates the founding of the Eternal City and the Empire of the
Caesars, is still worth the price of the richest and most exotic political realm
of the modern world of the seventeenth century.   24 *nose:* the cognomen of
Ovid, by which he usually referred to himself.

Wild I am now with heat;
   O Bacchus! cool thy rays!   30
Or frantic, I shall eat
   Thy thyrse, and bite the bays.

Round, round the roof does run;
   And being ravished thus,
Come, I will drink a tun   35
   To my Propertïus.

Now, to Tibullus, next,
   This flood I drink to thee;
But stay, I see a text
   That this presents to me.   40

Behold, Tibullus lies
   Here burnt, whose small return
Of ashes scarce suffice
   To fill a little urn.

Trust to good verses then;   45
   They only will aspire,
When pyramids, as men,
   Are lost i' th' funeral fire.

And when all bodies meet,
   In Lethe to be drowned,   50
Then only numbers sweet
   With endless life are crowned.

---

32 *thyrse:* staff, wrapped round with ivy (or bay?) leaves, carried by the bacchants when they celebrated their orgies.   39 *text:* Cf. Ovid, *Amores*, IX, an elegy for Tibullus, which laments that the dedication to "beautiful song" of the poet is no defense against death even though his life is supposedly sacred to the gods; but nevertheless, Tibullus perhaps will be "safe in Elysium's Vale" because he was a true poet and his bones will then be "safe in the embrace of the urn" (tr. by R. Humphries). 50 *Lethe:* the river of forgetfulness.   51 *numbers:* i.e., poetry. Life is short, but art is eternal.

GEORGE HERBERT
1593–1633

Affliction (1)

When first thou didst entice to thee my heart,
    I thought the service brave:
So many joys I writ down for my part,
    Besides what I might have
Out of my stock of natural delights,   5
Augmented with thy gracious benefits.

I looked on thy furniture so fine,
    And made it fine to me:
Thy glorious household-stuff did me entwine,
    And 'tice me unto thee.   10
Such stars I counted mine: both heav'n and earth
Paid me my wages in a world of mirth.

What pleasures could I want, whose King I served,
    Where joys my fellows were?
Thus argu'd into hopes, my thoughts reserved   15
    No place for grief or fear.
Therefore my sudden soul caught at the place,
And made her youth and fierceness seek thy face.

At first thou gav'st me milk and sweetnesses;
    I had my wish and way: 20
My days were straw'd with flow'rs and happiness;
    There was no month but May.
But with my years sorrow did twist and grow,
And made a party unawares for woe.

My flesh began unto my soul in pain,   25
    Sicknesses cleave my bones;
Consuming agues dwell in ev'ry vein,
    And tune my breath to groans.

AFFLICTION (I). Cf. Ps. 22, 38, 102. 2 *brave:* splendid. 17 *sudden:* impetuous, passionate. *caught at:* endeavored to possess. 21 *straw'd:* strewed. 24 *party:* partner, accomplice. 25 *began unto:* took the first action against, began to assail; "begin" literally means "to cut open." *Began* may also control *cleave, dwell,* and *tune* if they are treated as infinitives. 26 *cleave:* stick to, cling to.

Sorrow was all my soul; I scarce believed,
Till grief did tell me roundly, that I lived.   30

When I got health, thou took'st away my life,
              And more; for my friends die:
My mirth and edge was lost; a blunted knife
              Was of more use than I.
Thus thin and lean without a fence or friend,   35
I was blown through with ev'ry storm and wind.

Whereas my birth and spirit rather took
              The way that takes the town;
Thou didst betray me to a ling'ring book,
              And wrap me in a gown.   40
I was entangled in the world of strife,
Before I had the power to change my life.

Yet, for I threat'ned oft the siege to raise,
              Not simp'ring all mine age,
Thou often didst with academic praise   45
              Melt and dissolve my rage.
I took thy sweet'ned pill, till I came where
I could not go away, nor persevere.

Yet lest perchance I should too happy be
              In my unhappiness,   50
Turning my purge to food, thou throwest me
              Into more sicknesses.
Thus doth thy power cross-bias me, not making
Thine own gift good, yet me from my ways taking.

Now I am here, what thou wilt do with me   55
              None of my books will show:
I read, and sigh, and wish I were a tree;
              For sure then I should grow
To fruit or shade: at least some bird would trust
Her household to me, and I should be just.   60

---

30 *roundly:* plainly, unceremoniously. 35 *fence:* defence. 38 *way . . . town:*
pleasures of society. 39 *ling'ring book:* i.e., arduous study. 40 *gown:*
academic gown of a scholar. 44 *simp'ring:* smiling in an affected manner.
45 *academic praise:* praise of learned men (like that actually received by
Herbert when he was University Orator at Cambridge, 1619–28). 51
purge: sweet'ned pill: l. 47. 53 *cross-bias me:* cause me to go counter to my
natural inclination.

Yet, though thou troublest me, I must be meek;
    In weakness must be stout.
Well, I will change the service, and go seek
    Some other master out.
Ah my dear God! though I am clean forgot,   65
Let me not love thee, if I love thee not.

Prayer (I)

Prayer the Church's banquet, angels' age,
    God's breath in man returning to his birth,
    The soul in paraphrase, heart in pilgrimage,
The Christian plummet sounding heav'n and earth;
Engine against th' Almighty, sinner's tower,   5
    Reversed thunder, Christ-side-piercing spear,
    The six-days-world transposing in an hour,
A kind of tune, which all things hear and fear;
Softness, and peace, and joy, and love, and bliss,
    Exalted manna, gladness of the best,   10
    Heaven in ordinary, man well drest,
The milky way, the bird of paradise,
    Church-bells beyond the stars heard, the soul's blood,
    The land of spices; something understood.

Church-Monuments

While that my soul repairs to her devotion,
Here I entomb my flesh, that it betimes
May take acquaintance of this heap of dust;
To which the blast of death's incessant motion,
Fed with the exhalation of our crimes,   5
Drives all at last. Therefore I gladly trust

PRAYER (I). 1 *angels' age:* a long time, rather than man's "three score years and ten." See also Ps. 39:5–7. 2 *breath:* See Gen. 2:7. 3 *paraphrase:* clear, ample restatement. 4 *plummet:* a ball of lead attached to a line to ascertain depths. 5 *Engine . . . tower:* catapult or battering-ram and movable tower (medieval war machines) used to batter down and storm the walls of a fortified city—namely, God. Cf. Donne, Sonnet 10 (XIV). 7 *six-days-world:* the world created in six days. *transposing:* transforming. 11 *in ordinary:* in ordinary dress; also, a public meal regularly provided at a fixed price in a tavern.

CHURCH MONUMENTS. 1 *repairs:* goes, retires. 2 *Here:* i.e., in the church among the monuments (tombs) of the dead. 3 *dust:* See Service of Burial of the Dead: "We therefore commit his body to the ground; earth to earth, ashes to ashes, dust to dust; in sure and certain hope of resurrection to eternal life." See also Gen. 2:7, and Ps. 103:14–16.

My body to this school, that it may learn
To spell his elements, and find his birth
Written in dusty heraldry and lines;
Which dissolution sure doth best discern,   10
Comparing dust with dust, and earth with earth.
These laugh at jet and marble put for signs,

To sever the good fellowship of dust,
And spoil the meeting. What shall point out them,
When they shall bow, and kneel, and fall down flat   15
To kiss those heaps, which now they have in trust?
Dear flesh, while I do pray, learn here thy stem
And true descent; that when thou shalt grow fat,

And wanton in thy cravings, thou mayst know,
That flesh is but the glass, which holds the dust   20
That measures all our time; which also shall
Be crumbled into dust. Mark here below
How tame these ashes are, how free from lust,
That thou mayst fit thyself against thy fall.

The Windows

Lord, how can man preach thy eternal word?
        He is a brittle crazy glass:
Yet in thy temple thou dost him afford
        This glorious and transcendent place,
        To be a window, through thy grace.   5

But when thou dost anneal in glass thy story,
        Making thy life to shine within

---

8 *spell his elements:* literally, to name the ABC's of the origins of his body (i.e., *dust*) from the inscriptions (*heraldry and lines*) on the tombs. *Elements* here means both the letters of the alphabet and the simple substances (earth, air, fire, water) out of which his material body was made. 10 *dissolution:* (triple pun) separation of body and soul at death; separation of "dusts"; and "solution" to a problem in school. 12 *These:* i.e., *heraldry and lines.* 13 *sever . . . fellowship:* I.e., the marble monuments prevent the mingling of the dust of the body with that of the earth. 14 *them:* the monuments. 17–18 *stem . . . descent:* (puns) origin and stock (green and growing up from earth), lineage (movement downward to earth). 20 *glass:* hour-glass. 24 *fit:* prepare. *against:* in expectation of.

THE WINDOWS. 2 *crazy:* flawed by minute cracks caused by rapid cooling. 6 *anneal:* temper and toughen; to render the glass less brittle by heating to high temperature and cooling slowly; also, to fix by heat colors laid on glass.

The holy Preachers; then the light and glory
　　　More rev'rend grows, and more doth win:
　　　Which else shows wat'rish, bleak, and thin.　　10

Doctrine and life, colors and light, in one
　　　When they combine and mingle, bring
A strong regard and awe: but speech alone
　　　Doth vanish like a flaring thing,
　　　And in the ear, not conscience ring.　　15

Man

　　　My God, I heard this day,
That none doth build a stately habitation,
　　　But he that means to dwell therein.
　　　What house more stately hath there been,
Or can be, than is Man? to whose creation　　5
　　　All things are in decay.

　　　For Man is ev'ry thing,
And more: He is a tree, yet bears more fruit;
　　　A beast, yet is, or should be more:
　　　Reason and speech we only bring,　　10
Parrots may thank us, if they are not mute,
　　　They go upon the score.

　　　Man is all symmetry,
Full of proportions, one limb to another,
　　　And all to all the world besides:　　15
　　　Each part may call the furthest, brother:
For head with foot hath private amity,
　　　And both with moons and tides.

　　　Nothing hath got so far,
But Man hath caught and kept it, as his prey.　　20
　　　His eyes dismount the highest star:
　　　He is in little all the sphere.
Herbs gladly cure our flesh, because that they
　　　Find their acquaintance there.

MAN.　7 *ev'ry thing:* a microcosm, a little world.　10 *only:* alone.　12 *They . . . score:* They are in debt to man.　13–15 *Man . . . besides:* the standard "organic" analogy that the symmetrical body of man (the microcosm) corresponds item to item with the symmetrical order of the universe (the macrocosm).　21 *dismount:* bring down, by using the telescope.

The earth doth rest, heav'n move, and fountains flow.
    Nothing we see, but means our good,
    As our delight, or as our treasure:
The whole is, either our cupboard of food,
        Or cabinet of pleasure.   30

        The stars have us to bed;
Night draws the curtain, which the sun withdraws;
    Music and light attend our head.
    All things unto our flesh are kind
In their descent and being; to our mind   35
        In their ascent and cause.

        Each thing is full of duty:
Waters united are our navigation;
    Distinguished, our habitation;
    Below, our drink; above, our meat;   40
Both are our cleanliness. Hath one such beauty?
        Then how are all things neat?

        More servants wait on Man,
Than he'll take notice of: in ev'ry path
    He treads down that which doth befriend him,   45
    When sickness makes him pale and wan.
Oh mighty love! Man is one world, and hath
        Another to attend him.

        Since then, my God, thou hast
So brave a palace built; O dwell in it,   50
    That it may dwell with thee at last!
    Till then, afford us so much wit;
That, as the world serves us, we may serve thee,
        And both thy servants be.

---

31 *have:* lead.   34 *kind:* natural.   35 *their descent:* their origin and their
being placed here by their Creator. *being:* physical existence.   36 *In . . .
cause:* i.e., as they refer to their Creator who caused them.   38–39 *Waters
. . . habitation:* Cf. Gen. 1:9–10. The waters "gathered together" (*united*)
become the means of our *navigation*, and separated (*distinguished*) so that
the "dry land" may "appear," our *habitation.*   40 *above . . . meat:* i.e.,
the rains that make the earth productive, and also manna. See Ps. 78:24, "He
rained down manna also upon them for to eat . . . ."   41 *cleanliness:* bodily
and spiritual (as baptismal water). *one:* i.e., one element, water.   42 *neat:*
summarizes the stanza: clean, complete, well proportioned, and precisely
contrived.   50 *palace:* Cf. 1 Chron. 29:1; 1 Cor. 3:9–17; 6:19.

The Quip

The merry World did on a day
With his train-bands and mates agree
To meet together, where I lay,
And all in sport to jeer at me.

First, Beauty crept into a rose,   5
Which when I pluckt not, Sir, said she,
Tell me, I pray, whose hands are those?
But thou shalt answer, Lord, for me.

Then Money came, and chinking still,
What tune is this, poor man? said he: 10
I heard in music you had skill.
But thou shalt answer, Lord, for me.

Then came brave Glory puffing by
In silks that whistled, who but he?
He scarce allow'd me half an eye.   15
But thou shalt answer, Lord, for me.

Then came quick Wit and Conversation,
And he would needs a comfort be,
And to be short, make an oration.
But thou shalt answer, Lord, for me.   20

Yet when the hour of thy design
To answer these fine things shall come;
Speak not at large; say, I am thine:
And then they have their answer home.

The Collar

I struck the board, and cried, No more.
            I will abroad.
    What? shall I ever sigh and pine?
My lines and life are free; free as the road,
    Loose as the wind, as large as store.   5

THE QUIP. *Quip:* A short, witty saying, a verbal conceit. 2 *train-bands:*
citizen soldiery. 3 *lay:* was lodging. 13 *brave:* showy. *puffing:* sneering.
23 *at large:* diffusely, in a prolix fashion. 24 *home:* precisely, specifically.

THE COLLAR. Symbol of restraint, yet "service" that is "perfect freedom."
1 *board:* table spread with food. 4 *lines:* lot. 5 *as . . . store:* abundant.

Shall I be still in suit?
Have I no harvest but a thorn
To let me blood, and not restore
What I have lost with cordial fruit?
       Sure there was wine   10
Before my sighs did dry it: there was corn
      Before my tears did drown it.
   Is the year only lost to me?
      Have I no bays to crown it?
No flowers, no garlands gay? all blasted?   15
      All wasted?
   Not so, my heart: but there is fruit,
      And thou hast hands.
Recover all thy sigh-blown age
On double pleasures: leave thy cold dispute   20
Of what is fit, and not: forsake thy cage,
      Thy rope of sands,
Which petty thoughts have made, and made to thee
   Good cable, to enforce and draw,
       And be thy law,   25
   While thou didst wink and wouldst not see.
      Away! take heed.
      I will abroad.
Call in thy death's-head there: tie up thy fears.
      He that forbears   30
     To suit and serve his need,
      Deserves his load.
But as I rav'd and grew more fierce and wild
      At every word,
   Methought I heard one calling, *Child!*   35
     And I replied, *My Lord.*

Redemption

Having been tenant long to a rich Lord,
   Not thriving, I resolvëd to be bold,
   And make a suit unto him to afford
A new small-rented lease and cancel th' old.
In heaven at his manor I him sought.   5
   They told me there that he was lately gone
   About some land which he had dearly bought

---

6 *in suit:* in service to another. 9 *cordial:* restorative. 11 *corn:* wheat.
14 *bays:* bay leaves, symbol of success. 25 *law:* Cf. Rom. 7:19–23. 29
death's-head: skull, the traditional *memento mori* (i.e., remember that you have
to die). 31 *To suit:* to agree with.

Long since on earth, to take possessïon.
I straight returned, and knowing his great birth,
  Sought him accordingly in great resorts,   10
  In cities, theaters, gardens, parks, and courts.
At length I heard a ragged noise and mirth
  Of thieves and murderers; there I him espied,
  Who straight, Your suit is granted, said, and died.

Easter Wings

Lord, who created'st man in wealth and store,
  Though foolishly he lost the same,
    Decaying more and more
      Till he became
        Most poor;   5
      With thee
    Oh, let me rise
  As larks, harmoniously,
  And sing this day thy victories;
Then shall the fall further the flight in me.   10

My tender age in sorrow did begin;
  And still with sicknesses and shame
    Thou didst so punish sin,
      That I became
        Most thin.   15
      With thee
    Let me combine,
  And feel this day thy victory;
  For if I imp my wing on thine,
Affliction shall advance the flight in me.   20

Virtue

Sweet day, so cool, so calm, so bright,
The bridal of the earth and sky;
The dew shall weep thy fall to-night,
    For thou must die.

EASTER WINGS.   This poem belongs to the style of *technopaignia* (*poemata figurata*), in which the shape of the printed poem represents to the eye the main figure of the poem.

10 *fall:* the paradox of the *felix culpa* (the fortunate fall) that prompted (in Christ's Easter sacrifice) a greater revelation of Divine love than that shown in the earlier creation referred to in l. 1.   19 *imp:* in falconry, to mend a deficient wing by inserting a feather, thus restoring the power of flight.

Sweet rose, whose hue angry and brave   5
Bids the rash gazer wipe his eye;
Thy root is ever in its grave,
       And thou must die.

Sweet spring, full of sweet days and roses,
A box where sweets compacted lie;   10
My music shows ye have your closes,
       And all must die.

Only a sweet and virtuous soul,
Like seasoned timber, never gives;
But though the whole world turn to coal,   15
       Then chiefly lives.

Love (III)

Love bade me welcome: yet my soul drew back,
       Guilty of dust and sin.
But quick-ey'd Love, observing me grow slack
       From my first entrance in,
Drew nearer to me, sweetly questioning,   5
       If I lack'd any thing.

A guest, I answer'd, worthy to be here:
       Love said, You shall be he.
I the unkind, ungrateful? Ah my dear,
       I cannot look on thee.   10
Love took my hand, and smiling did reply,
       Who made the eyes but I?

Truth Lord, but I have marr'd them: let my shame
       Go where it doth deserve.
And know you not, says Love, who bore the blame?   15
       My dear, then I will serve.
You must sit down, says Love, and taste my meat:
       So I did sit and eat.

VIRTUE. 15 *coal:* i.e. the conflagration of the world at the Last Judgment.

LOVE (III). Cf. in *Book of Common Prayer* the prayer of "Humble Access" in the service of Holy Communion. 17 *my meat:* the Body of Christ administered in Holy Communion.

JOHN MILTON
1608–1674

The Fifth Ode of Horace. Lib. I

What slender Youth bedew'd with liquid odours
Courts thee on Roses in some pleasant Cave,
    Pyrrha for whom bind'st thou
    In wreaths thy golden Hair,
Plain in thy neatness; O how oft shall he   5
On Faith and changed Gods complain: and Seas
    Rough with black winds and storms
    Unwonted shall admire:
Who now enjoyes thee credulous, all Gold,
Who alwayes vacant, alwayes amiable   10
    Hopes thee; of flattering gales
    Unmindfull. Hapless they
To whom thou untry'd seem'st fair. Me in my vow'd
Picture the sacred wall declares t' have hung
    My dank and dropping weeds   15
    To the stern God of Sea.

At a Solemn Musick

Blest pair of *Sirens*, pledges of Heav'ns joy,
Sphear-born harmonious Sisters, Voice, and Vers,
Wed your divine sounds, and mixt power employ
Dead things with inbreath'd sense able to pierce,
And to our high-rais'd phantasie present,   5
That undisturbed Song of pure concent,
Ay sung before the saphire-colour'd throne
To him that sits theron

MILTON. The text of Milton's poems is that established by Helen Darbishire (Oxford, at the Clarendon Press, 1952). The spelling and punctuation are most probably what Milton intended and are essential to an understanding of the "sound, movement, and meaning of his lines." (See Miss Darbishire's introduction.)

FIFTH ODE. 13–16 *vow'd . . . Sea:* Roman sailors who had been shipwrecked and rescued often dedicated a votive picture to Neptune, placing it on the wall of the temple along with the clothes (*weeds*) they had worn at the time. The "shipwreck" and *storms* are part of the familiar figure of the lover tossed on the stormy seas of desire, always about to be shipwrecked by the lady who steers with cruelness. Cf. Wyatt, "My Galley."

AT A SOLEMN MUSICK. 5 *phantasie:* fancy, imagination. 6 *concent:* harmony. 7 *saphire-colour'd throne:* See Ezek. 1:26.

132

With Saintly shout, and solemn Jubily,
Where the bright Seraphim in burning row   10
Their loud up-lifted Angel trumpets blow,
And the Cherubick host in thousand quires
Touch their immortal Harps of golden wires,
With those just Spirits that wear victorious Palms,
Hymns devout and holy Psalms   15
Singing everlastingly;
That we on Earth with undiscording voice
May rightly answer that melodious noise;
As once we did, till disproportion'd sin
Jarr'd against natures chime, and with harsh din   20
Broke the fair musick that all creatures made
To their great Lord, whose love their motion sway'd
In perfet Diapason, whilst they stood
In first obedience, and their state of good.
O may we soon again renew that Song,   25
And keep in tune with Heav'n, till God ere long
To his celestial consort us unite,
To live with him, and sing in endles morn of light.

L'Allegro

Hence loathed Melancholy
    Of *Cerberus*, and blackest midnight born,
In *Stygian* Cave forlorn
    'Mongst horrid shapes, and shreiks, and sights unholy,
Find out som uncouth cell,   5
    Wher brooding darknes spreads his jealous wings,
And the night-Raven sings;
    There under *Ebon* shades, and low-brow'd Rocks,
As ragged as thy Locks,
    In dark *Cimmerian* desert ever dwell.   10

14 *just Spirits:* Cf. Rev. 7:9–17.   23 *Diapason:* harmony throughout the
whole scale of creation.   27 *consort:* company of musicians, orchestra.

L'ALLEGRO.   This poem and "Il Penseroso" are companion poems whose
meanings are derived from comparison and contrast of the two, not simply
from the reading of each individually. They mock as well as complement each
other. *Melancholy* here is significant not only in its denotation of "morbid
sobriety" but also as the foil for the effervescent gaiety of *Mirth*, and vice versa.
The opening ten lines of each poem attack their opposites in parallel and hyper-
bolic form—a common rhetorical device—and banish, as Rosemond Tuve says,
"the travesty of what is praised in the other." The whole meaning of each poem
is to be found in the combined reading of both poems as a single expression of a
unified sensibility.   2 *Cerberus:* the three-headed watchdog of Hades.   3
Stygian: on the Styx, the principal river of the underworld.   5 *uncouth:*
strange, wild.   10 *Cimmerian desert:* a place of mist and darkness; see
Odyssey, XI, 14–18.

But com thou Goddes fair and free,
In Heav'n ycleap'd *Euphrosyne*,
And by men, heart-easing Mirth,
Whom lovely *Venus* at a birth
With two sister Graces more   15
To Ivy-crowned *Bacchus* bore;
Or whether (as som Sager sing)
The frolick Wind that breathes the Spring,
Zephir with *Aurora* playing,
As he met her once a Maying,   20
There on Beds of Violets blew,
And fresh-blown Roses washt in dew,
Fill'd her with thee a daughter fair,
So bucksom, blith, and debonair.
Haste thee nymph, and bring with thee   25
Jest and youthful Jollity,
Quips and Cranks, and wanton Wiles,
Nods, and Becks, and Wreathed Smiles,
Such as hang on *Hebe's* cheek,
And love to live in dimple sleek;   30
Sport that wrincled Care derides,
And Laughter holding both his sides.
Com, and trip it as ye go
On the light fantastick toe,
And in thy right hand lead with thee,   35
The Mountain Nymph, sweet Liberty;
And if I give thee honour due,
Mirth, admit me of thy crue
To live with her, and live with thee,
In unreproved pleasures free;   40
To hear the Lark begin his flight,
And singing startle the dull night,
From his watch-towre in the skies,
Till the dappled dawn doth rise;
Then to com in spight of sorrow,   45
And at my window bid good morrow,
Through the Sweet-Briar, or the Vine,
Or the twisted Eglantine.

---

12 *ycleap'd:* called. *Euphrosyne:* Gladness, one of the three Graces. 16
Bacchus: god of wine. 17 *Sager:* wiser, i.e., Milton. This geneology of
Euphrosyne is unique with him and chaster than most. 19 *Zephir, Aurora:*
West Wind, Dawn. 24 *bucksom:* compliant, yielding. 27 *Quips and Cranks:*
sharp jests and witty turns of speech. 29 *Hebe:* goddess of youth, who
pours out nectar for the gods. 40 *unreproved:* innocent. 45 *to com:* parallel
with *To live* (l. 39), *To hear* (l. 41).

While the Cock with lively din,
Scatters the rear of darknes thin, 50
And to the stack, or the Barn dore,
Stoutly struts his Dames before,
Oft list'ning how the Hounds and horn,
Chearly rouse the slumbring morn,
From the side of som Hoar Hill, 55
Through the high wood echoing shrill.
Som time walking not unseen
By Hedge-row Elms, on Hillocks green,
Right against the Eastern gate,
Where the great Sun begins his state, 60
Rob'd in flames, and Amber light,
The clouds in thousand Liveries dight,
While the Plowman neer at hand,
Whistles ore the Furrow'd Land,
And the Milkmaid singeth blithe, 65
And the Mower whets his sithe,
And every Shepherd tells his tale
Under the Hawthorn in the dale.
Streit mine eye hath caught new pleasures
Whilst the Lantskip round it measures, 70
Russet Lawns, and Fallows Gray,
Where the nibling flocks do stray,
Mountains on whose barren brest
The labouring clouds do often rest:
Meadows trim with Daisies pide, 75
Shallow Brooks, and Rivers wide.
Towers, and Battlements it sees
Boosom'd high in tufted Trees,
Where perhaps som beauty lies,
The Cynosure of neighbouring eyes. 80
Hard by, Cottage chimney smokes,
From betwixt two aged Okes,
Where *Corydon* and *Thyrsis* met,
Are at their savory dinner set
Of Hearbs, and other Country Messes, 85
Which the neat-handed *Phillis* dresses;
And then in haste her Bowre she leaves,
With *Thestylis* to bind the Sheaves;

60 *state:* stately journey. 62 *dight:* dressed. 66 *whets his sithe:* sharpens his scythe with a ringing sound. 67 *tells his tale:* counts his sheep and sings of his love. 69 *Streit:* immediately. *Lantskip:* landscape. 74 *labouring:* heaving, rolling. 75 *pide:* particolored, variegated. 80 *Cynosure:* i.e., like the pole-star, hence the center of attraction of all would-be lovers. Cf. Astrophil's attitude toward Stella, p. 32. 83 *Corydon and Thyrsis* (also *Phillis,* l. 86, and *Thestylis,* l. 88): rustic names given to shepherds and shepherdesses in pastoral poetry from Theocritus on. 87 *Bowre:* cottage.

Or if the earlier season lead
To the tann'd Haycock in the Mead, 90
Som times with secure delight
The up-land Hamlets will invite,
When the merry Bells ring round,
And the jocond rebecks sound
To many a youth, and many a maid, 95
Dancing in the Chequer'd shade;
And young and old com forth to play
On a Sunshine Holyday,
Till the live-long day-light fail,
Then to the Spicy Nut-brown Ale, 100
With stories told of many a feat,
How *Faery Mab* the junkets eat,
She was pincht, and pull'd she sed,
And he by Friars Lanthorn led
Tells how the drudging *Goblin* swet, 105
To ern his Cream-bowle duly set,
When in one night, ere glimps of morn,
His shadowy Flale hath thresh'd the Corn
That ten day-labourers could not end,
Then lies him down the Lubbar Fend, 110
And stretch'd out all the Chimney's length,
Basks at the fire his hairy strength;
And Crop-full out of dores he flings,
Ere the first Cock his Mattin rings.
Thus don the Tales, to bed they creep, 115
By whispering Windes soon lull'd asleep.
Towred Cities please us then,
And the busie humm of men,
Where throngs of Knights and Barons bold,
In weeds of Peace high triumphs hold, 120
With store of Ladies, whose bright eies
Rain influence, and judge the prise
Of Wit, or Arms, while both contend
To win her Grace, whom all commend.
There let *Hymen* oft appear 125
In Saffron robe, with Taper clear,
And pomp, and feast, and revelry,

91 *secure:* carefree. 94 *rebecks:* archaic three-stringed fiddle. 102 *Faery Mab:* queen of the fairies. 104 *Friars Lanthorn:* will-o'-the-wisp. 105 *drudging Goblin:* beneficent household spirit, hobgoblin. 110 *Lubbar Fend:* i.e., Lob-lie-by-the-fire; a beneficent goblin who likes to lie down by the fire after doing his chores. 113 *Crop-full:* with his stomach full. 121 *bright eies:* like the stars, which *Rain influence,* i.e., rain down on men an ethereal fluid that was thought to flow from the stars, affecting the lives and fortunes of men in love and war. 125 *Hymen:* god of marriage. 126 *Saffron:* traditional color of Hymen.

136

With mask, and antique Pageantry,
Such sights as youthfull Poets dream
On Summer eeves by haunted stream.   130
Then to the well-trod stage anon,
If *Jonsons* learned Sock be on,
Or sweetest *Shakespear* fancies childe,
Warble his native Wood-notes wilde;
And ever against eating Cares,   135
Lap me in soft *Lydian* Aires,
Married to immortal verse
Such as the meeting soul may pierce
In notes, with many a winding bout
Of lincked sweetnes long drawn out,   140
With wanton heed, and giddy cunning,
The melting voice through mazes running;
Untwisting all the chains that ty
The hidden soul of harmony.
That *Orpheus* self may heave his head   145
From golden slumber on a bed
Of heapt *Elysian* flowres, and hear
Such streins as would have won the ear
Of *Pluto*, to have quite set free
His half regain'd *Eurydice*.   150
These delights, if thou canst give,
Mirth with thee, I mean to live.

Il Penseroso

Hence vain deluding joyes,
    The brood of folly without father bred,
How little you bested,
    Or fill the fixed mind with all your toyes;

128 *mask:* courtly entertainment, combining drama, song, and dance in an elaborate spectacle. 132 *Jonsons learned Sock:* Jonson's learned, satiric comedy. See Jonson, "To Shakespeare," l. 37 and note. 133 *fancies:* Fancy's, the imagination personified. 134 *native Wood-notes wilde:* original, intuitive (as opposed to "learned") comedy of love in the green woods. 136 *Lydian:* one of the modes (a form of scale) of classical Greek music, considered to be plaintive, pathetic, and soft. 138 *meeting:* welcoming, responsive. 139–40 *winding . . . out:* Cf. the contrapuntal melodic lines of madrigals. 141 *wanton . . . cunning:* (oxymorons) wild close attention and thoughtless ingenuity. 145 *Orpheus:* Thracian poet and musician, son of Apollo and Calliope (muse of heroic poetry), famous for his power to enthrall man and nature with his song so that rocks, trees, and even wild beasts were spellbound. When Eurydice, his wife, was killed by a snake, he descended into Hades and with his music persuaded Pluto to release her, on condition that he not look back at her as she followed him until they reached the upper air. He looked back too soon and lost her forever, hence *half regain'd*.

IL PENSEROSO. 3 *bested:* avail.

Dwell in som idle brain,   5
    And fancies fond with gaudy shapes possess,
As thick and numberless
    As the gay motes that people the Sun Beams,
Or likest hovering dreams
    The fickle Pensioners of *Morpheus* train.   10
But hail thou Goddes, sage and holy,
Hail divinest Melancholy,
Whose Saintly visage is too bright
To hit the Sense of human sight;
And therfore to our weaker view,   15
Ore laid with black staid Wisdoms hue,
Black, but such as in esteem,
Prince *Memnons* sister might beseem,
Or that Starr'd *Ethiope* Queen that strove
To set her beauties praise above   20
The Sea Nymphs, and their powers offended.
Yet thou art higher far descended,
Thee bright-hair'd *Vesta* long of yore,
To solitary *Saturn* bore;
His daughter she (in *Saturns* raign,   25
Such mixture was not held a stain)
Oft in glimmering Bowres, and glades
He met her, and in secret shades
Of woody *Ida's* inmost grove,
While yet there was no fear of *Jove*.   30
Com pensive Nun, devout and pure,
Sober, stedfast, and demure,
All in a robe of darkest grain,
Flowing with majestick train,
And sable stole of *Cipres* Lawn,   35
Over thy decent shoulders drawn.

6 *fond:* foolish. 9 *hovering:* fickle. 12 *Melancholy:* refers here to the wholly unmorbid, noble, intellectual virtues of the man under the aegis of Saturn, whose attributes are those essential to true genius and near divinity and whose mind ascends to the knowledge of future things. 18 *Memnons sister:* Hemera, sister of Memnon, son of Eos (Aurora) and Tithonus, Ethiopian prince and hero of Troy. 19 *Starr'd Ethiope Queen:* Cassiopeia, wife of Cepheus, the Ethiopian King of Joppa, boasted that she and her daughter, Andromeda, were more beautiful than the Sea Nymphs and was later punished by Poseidon, who transformed her into the unflattering constellation that bears her name. 23 *Vesta:* goddess of the blazing hearth, worshipped in every Roman household. 24 *solitary Saturn:* (Cronus) To the Renaissance Neo-Platonists, Saturn, highest of the planets and former ruler of the Olympians until dethroned and (some say) castrated and banished by his son, Jove, was the Cosmic Mind contemplating the highest and most secret things. The rule of Saturn was said to be a Golden Age on earth. 29 *Ida:* mountain in Crete where Jove, hiding from his father who would have devoured him, grew up among the shepherds. 35 *Cipres Lawn:* fine black linen fabric.

138

Com, but keep thy wonted state,
With eev'n step, and musing gate,
And looks commercing with the skies,
Thy rapt soul sitting in thine eyes: 40
There held in holy passion still,
Forget thy selfe to Marble, till
With a sad Leaden downward cast,
Thou fix them on the earth as fast.
And joyn with thee calm Peace, and Quiet,   45
Spare Fast, that oft with gods doth diet,
And hears the Muses in a ring,
Ay round about *Joves* Altar sing.
And adde to these retired Leasure,
That in trim Gardens takes his pleasure;   50
But first, and chiefest, with thee bring,
Him that yon soars on golden wing,
Guiding the fiery-wheeled throne,
The Cherub Contemplation,
And the mute Silence hist along,   55
 Less *Philomel* will daign a Song,
In her sweetest, saddest plight,
Smoothing the rugged brow of night,
While *Cynthia* checks her Dragon yoke,
Gently o're th'accustom'd Oke;   60
Sweet Bird that shunn'st the noise of folly,
Most musicall, most melancholy!
Thee Chauntrees oft the Woods among,
I woo to hear thy Eeven-Song;
And missing thee, I walk unseen   65
On the dry smooth-shaven Green,
To behold the wandring Moon,
Riding neer her highest noon,
Like one that had bin led astray
Through the Heav'ns wide pathles way;   70
And oft, as if her head she bow'd,
Stooping through a fleecy cloud.
Oft on a Plat of rising ground,

42 *Forget . . . Marble:* i.e., lose all sense of yourself and become as motionless as marble.   52–54 *Him . . . Contemplation:* i.e., one of the Cherubim, order of angels second only to the Seraphim, on whose wings the Lord flies (Ps. 18:10), who escort His sapphire throne, wheeled and carrying coals of fire (Ezek. 10:1–2), whose golden wings cover both sides of the mercy-seat and whose faces turn to contemplate the divine presence who dwells between (Exodus 25:17–20), and who symbolize fullness of knowledge as guardians of the Tree of Life (Gen. 3:24).   56 *Philomel:* See Sidney, "The Nightingale," p. 38.   59 *Cynthia:* goddess of the moon.   *Dragon yoke:* a pair of dragons yoked together to draw her chariot.   73 *Plat:* plot.

I hear the far-off *Curfeu* sound,
Over som wide-water'd shoar,   75
Swinging slow with sullen roar;
Or if the Ayr will not permit,
Som still removed place will fit,
Where glowing Embers through the room
Teach light to counterfeit a gloom,   80
Far from all resort of mirth,
Save the Cricket on the hearth,
Or the Belmans drousie charm,
To bless the dores from nightly harm:
Or let my Lamp at midnight hour,   85
Be seen in som high lonely Towr,
Where I may oft out-watch the *Bear*,
With thrice great *Hermes*, or unsphear
The spirit of *Plato* to unfold
What Worlds, or what vast Regions hold   90
The immortal mind that hath forsook
Her mansion in this fleshly nook:
And of those *Dæmons* that are found
In fire, air, flood, or under ground,
Whose power hath a true consent   95
With Planet, or with Element.
Som time let Gorgeous Tragedy
In Scepter'd Pall com sweeping by,
Presenting *Thebs*, or *Pelops* line,
Or the tale of *Troy* divine.   100
Or what (though rare) of later age,
Ennobled hath the Buskind stage.
But, O sad Virgin, that thy power
Might raise *Musæus* from his bower,

---

83 *Belmans drousie charm:* the rhythmic, sleep-inducing incantation of the night watchman who chants the hours.   87 *Bear:* constellation Ursa Major. Jove, as an infant, pursued by his father, Saturn, escaped by transforming himself into a serpent and his nurses into bears: thus the constellations Draco (the Serpent) and Ursa Major and Ursa Minor (Graves, *The Greek Myths*). To *out-watch the Bear* means to stay up all night watching Ursa Major, which never sets. 88 *Hermes:* Hermes Trismegistus, legendary Egyptian philosopher and scientist, esteemed with Moses as one of the first men of learning and wisdom. 93 *Dæmons:* attendant spirits.   95 *consent:* correspondence, harmony.   97–98 *Gorgeous . . . Pall:* Greek tragedy is royally clad (*Scepter'd Pall*) because its characters were of the royal houses of Thebes (e.g., Sophocles' *Oedipus*) or Troy (e.g., Euripides' *The Trojan Women*) or descendants of King Pelops (e.g., Aeschylus' trilogy of the Oresteia.) 102 *Buskind stage:* tragedy; see Jonson, "To Shakespeare," l. 36 and note.   104 *Musæus:* legendary Thracian poet said to be a pupil Orpheus; also the fifth-century A.D. author of a poem on Hero and Leander, the Latin translation of which was a major source for Marlowe's "Hero and Leander." Milton perhaps is alluding to l. 52 of that poem: "Whose tragedy divine Musæus sung."

Or bid the soul of *Orpheus* sing   105
Such notes as warbled to the string,
Drew Iron tears down *Pluto's* cheek,
And made Hell grant what Love did seek.
Or call up him that left half told
The story of *Cambuscan* bold,   110
Of *Camball*, and of *Algarsife*,
And who had *Canace* to wife,
That own'd the vertuous Ring and Glass,
And of the wondrous Hors of Brass,
On which the *Tartar* King did ride;   115
And if ought els, great *Bards* beside,
In sage and solemn tunes have sung,
Of Turneys and of Trophies hung;
Of Forests, and inchantments drear,
Where more is meant then meets the ear.   120
Thus Night oft see me in thy pale career,
Till civil-suited Morn appeer,
Not trickt and frounc't as she was wont,
With the Attick Boy to hunt,
But kerchef't in a comly Cloud,   125
While rocking Winds are Piping loud,
Or usher'd with a shower still,
When the gust hath blown his fill,
Ending on the russling Leaves,
With minute drops from off the Eaves.   130
And when the Sun begins to fling
His flaring beams, me Goddes bring
To arched walks of twilight groves,
And shadows brown that *Sylvan* loves
Of Pine, or monumental Oake,   135
Where the rude Ax with heaved stroke,
Was never heard the Nymphs to daunt,
Or fright them from their hallow'd haunt.
There in close covert by som Brook,
Where no profaner eye may look,   140

---

108 *seek:* Cf. "L'Allegro," l. 150. Note that the parallelism between the poems ceases here and that "Il Penseroso" continues in such a way as to suggest a synthesis of the two in the dedication of the speaker to the whole life and work of the poet.   109 *him:* i.e., Chaucer. In the *Canterbury Tales*, the "Squire's Tale" of *Cambuscan, Camball, Algarsife,* and *Canace* is left *half told.*   120 *more . . . ear:* i.e., the "darke conceit" of allegory, as in Spenser's *Faerie Queene.*   122 *civil-suited:* modestly dressed.   123 *trickt and frounc't:* gaudily decked out and adorned with frills.   *she:* Morn (Aurora).   124 *Attick Boy:* Cephalus. Aurora fell in love with him, causing discord between him and his wife, Procris, whom he eventually killed accidentally.   130 *minute:* (accent on the first syllable) repeated every minute.   134 *Sylvan:* god of the woods.

Hide me from Day's garish eie,
While the Bee with Honied thie,
That at her flowry work doth sing,
And the Waters murmuring
With such consort as they keep,   145
Entice the dewy-feather'd Sleep;
And let som strange mysterious dream,
Wave at his Wings in Airy stream,
Of lively portrature display'd,
Softly on my eye-lids laid.   150
And as I wake, sweet musick breath
Above, about, or underneath,
Sent by som spirit to mortals good,
Or th'unseen Genius of the Wood.
But let my due feet never fail,   155
To walk the studious Cloysters pale,
And love the high embowed Roof,
With antick Pillars massy proof,
And storied Windows richly dight,
Casting a dimm religious light.   160
There let the pealing Organ blow,
To the full voic'd Quire below,
In Service high, and Anthems cleer,
As may with sweetnes, through mine ear,
Dissolve me into extasies,   165
And bring all Heav'n before mine eyes.
And may at last my weary age
Find out the peacefull hermitage,
The Hairy Gown and Mossy Cell,
Where I may sit and rightly spell,   170
Of every Star that Heav'n doth shew,
And every Herb that sips the dew;
Till old experience do attain
To somthing like Prophetic strain.
These pleasures *Melancholy* give,   175
And I with thee will choose to live.

142 *thie:* thigh.   145 *consort:* harmony.   155 *due:* duty-bound.   156 *pale:* enclosure.   157 *embowed:* vaulted.   158 *antick:* grotesque, fantastic; refers to the incongruously combined figures of men, animals, foliage, and flowers often carved on the capitals of gothic pillars.   *massy proof:* of massive tested strength.   159 *storied Windows:* stained glass richly depicting Biblical stories.   170 *rightly spell:* correctly teach, disclose.

142

Arcades

1. SONG

Look Nymphs, and Shepherds look,
What sudden blaze of Majesty
Is that which we from hence descry
Too divine to be mistook:
    This this is she   5
To whom our vows and wishes bend,
Heer our solemn search hath end.

Fame that her high worth to raise,
Seem'd erst so lavish and profuse,
We may justly now accuse   10
Of detraction from her praise,
    Less then half we find exprest,
    Envy bid conceal the rest.

Mark what radiant state she spreds,
In circle round her shining throne,   15
Shooting her beams like silver threds,
This this is she alone,
    Sitting like a Goddes bright,
    In the center of her light.

ARCADES. "Part of an entertainment presented to the Countess Dowager of Darby at Harefield by some Noble persons of her Family, who appear on the Scene in pastoral habit, moving toward the seat of State, with this Song" [Milton's headnote]. Although this "entertainment" properly is classified as a sub-species of the literary genre of the *masque*, it has strong affinities with the pastoral panegyric, a celebration to honor the great patroness of poetry, much like Spenser's recreative April eclogue in *The Shepheardes Calender*. The Countess is Alice Spencer, to whom Spenser dedicated *The Teares of the Muses* and who is Amaryllis in his "Colin Clout's Come Home Again." She encouraged not only Spenser but also Shakespeare, Jonson, Donne, and many others. Milton's panegyric of her therefore commemorates the poetry of the age and its influence over the lives of men. 1 *Nymphs, Shepherds:* the "Arcades," inhabitants of Arcadia, a region much celebrated in legends, in the center of the Peloponnesus containing the mountains *Cyllene* (l. 98), *Erimanth[us]* (l. 100), and *Lycæus* (l. 98; according to one account, the birthplace of Zeus), and *Mænalus* (l. 102), sacred to the god Pan and frequented by shepherds. Through it run the rivers *Alpheus* (l. 30) and *Ladon* (l. 97), on whose sandy banks Pan caught the virgin nymph *Syrinx* (l. 106), who was immediately transformed into reeds from which Pan made and named his pipes. (See Ovid, *Met.*, I, 687–712.) Idealized by Virgil, Arcadia became the preeminent locale of pastoral poetry and romance, particularly in Sidney's *Arcadia.*

Might she the wise *Latona* be,   20
Or the towred *Cybele*,
Mother of a hunderd gods;
Juno dare's not give her odds;
   Who had thought this clime had held
   A deity so unparalel'd?   25

As they com forward, the Genius of the Wood appears, and
       turning toward them, speaks.

Gen. Stay gentle Swains, for though in this disguise,
I see bright honour sparkle through your eyes,
Of famous *Arcady* ye are, and sprung
Of that renowned flood, so often sung,
Divine *Alpheus*, who by secret sluse,   30
Stole under Seas to meet his *Arethuse;*
And ye the breathing Roses of the Wood,
Fair silver-buskind Nymphs as great and good,
I know this quest of yours, and free intent
Was all in honour and devotion ment   35
To the great Mistres of yon princely shrine,
Whom with low reverence I adore as mine,
And with all helpful service will comply
To furder this nights glad solemnity;
And lead ye where ye may more neer behold   40
What shallow-searching *Fame* hath left untold;
Which I full oft amidst these shades alone
Have sate to wonder at, and gaze upon:
For know by lot from *Jove* I am the powr
Of this fair Wood, and live in Oak'n bowr,   45
To nurse the Saplings tall, and curl the grove
With Ringlets quaint, and wanton windings wove.
And all my Plants I save from nightly ill,
Of noisom winds, and blasting vapours chill.
And from the Boughs brush off the evil dew,   50

20 *Latona:* Leto, beloved of Zeus, mother of Apollo and Artemis (Diana),
both strongly associated with poetry and prophecy. 21 *Cybele:* "The
Great Mother," identified with Rhea, mother of Zeus, Phrygian Aphrodite, goddess of the powers of nature, mother of the gods, and turret crowned
(see *Aeneid*, VI, 784–87) since she first taught men to fortify cities. 24 *clime:*
Milton believed that the cold northern latitudes were not conducive to writing
poetry; also, since the Titans, after Cronus was dethroned, were thought to
have been banished to the northern Celtic regions, including the British Isles
(see *Paradise Lost*, I, 519–21), this is the last place one would expect to find a
deity so unparalel'd.   30–31 *Alpheus . . . Arethuse:* The river god Alpheus fell
in love with the nymph Arethusa, who fled his embraces and later was transformed into the fountain in Ortygia in the harbor of Syracuse; Alpheus pursued
her under the sea and eventually mingled his waters with those of the fountain
(see Ovid, *Met.*, V, 572–641).   39 *furder:* further.

And heal the harms of thwarting thunder blew,
Or what the cross dire-looking Planet smites,
Or hurtfull Worm with canker'd venom bites.
When Eev'ning gray doth rise, I fetch my round
Over the mount, and all this hallow'd ground,   55
And early ere the odorous breath of morn
Awakes the slumbring leaves, or tasseld horn
Shakes the high thicket, haste I all about,
Number my ranks, and visit every sprout
With puissant words, and murmurs made to bless, 60
But els in deep of night when drowsines
Hath lockt up mortal sense, then listen I
To the celestial *Sirens* harmony,
That sit upon the nine enfolded Sphears,
And sing to those that hold the vital shears,   65
And turn the Adamantine spindle round,
On which the fate of gods and men is wound.
Such sweet compulsion doth in musick ly,
To lull the daughters of *Necessity*,
And keep unsteddy Nature to her law,   70
And the low world in measur'd motion draw
After the heavenly tune, which none can hear
Of human mould with grosse unpurged ear;
And yet such musick worthiest were to blaze
The peerles height of her immortal praise,   75
Whose lustre leads us, and for her most fit,
If my inferior hand or voice could hit
Inimitable sounds, yet as we go,
What ere the skill of lesser gods can show,
I will assay, her worth to celebrate,   80
And so attend ye toward her glittering state;
Where ye may all that are of noble stemm
Approach, and kiss her sacred vestures hemm.

2. SONG

O're the smooth enameld green
Where no print of step hath been,   85
 Follow me as I sing,
 And touch the warbled string.

---

51 *thunder blew:* blue, the color of the thunderbolt. 63 *celestial Sirens:* Cf. the Pythagorean and Platonic notion that the planets were set in transparent shells—hence spheres—and that as they moved an attendant angel on each gave forth a sound inaudible to all except the prophetic few, the true poets. Hence the *celestial Sirens* are beneficent, unlike Odysseus' evil sirens, and coax men to participate in the harmony of all creation. Cf. "At a Solemn Musick." 65 *those:* i.e., the Fates— Lachesis, who draws off the thread; Clotho, who holds the distaff; and Atropos, who cuts the thread short. 80 *assay:* try. 82 *stemm:* family line

Under the shady roof
Of branching Elm Star-proof,
   Follow me,   90
I will bring you where she sits,
Clad in splendor as befits
   Her deity.
Such a rural Queen
All *Arcadia* hath not seen.   95

3. SONG

Nymphs and Shepherds dance no more
   By sandy *Ladons* Lillied banks.
On old *Lycæus* or *Cyllene* hoar,
   Trip no more in twilight ranks,
Though *Erymanth* your loss deplore,   100
   A better soyl shall give ye thanks.
From the stony *Mænalus*,
Bring your Flocks, and live with us,
Here ye shall have greater grace,
To serve the Lady of this place.   105
   Though *Syrinx* your *Pans* Mistres were,
   Yet *Syrinx* well might wait on her.
     Such a rural Queen
   All *Arcadia* hath not seen.

Lycidas

Yet once more, O ye Laurels, and once more
Ye Myrtles brown, with Ivy never-sear,
I com to pluck your Berries harsh and crude,
And with forc'd fingers rude,

106 *Syrinx:* See l. 1 above and note. Pan here is chaste and benign in his relationship with Syrinx; together they suggest the music and verse of idealized pastoral poetry now deified in the *rural Queen.*

LYCIDAS. "In this Monody the Author bewails a learned Friend [Edward King, Milton's classmate at Cambridge], unfortunately drown'd in his Passage from Chester on the Irish Seas, 1637. And by occasion foretels the ruine of our corrupted Clergy then in their height" [Milton's headnote]. See Spenser's *Shepheardes Calender* and note. *Lycidas:* name of a shepherd in Virgil, Eclogue IX. 1–7 *Yet . . . due:* Milton uses the convention that the surviving, and still apprentice, poet is obliged, before he is ready, to write the polished master poem honoring the lost and better poet. That he does write the poem signifies that he has inherited the elder poet's pipe, that he accepts the responsibility of the office of pastor of the flock, and no longer needs the disguise of the pastoral, which has hitherto concealed his identity from the world. 1–2 *Laurels, Myrtles, Ivy:* all evergreens, symbols of poetic excellence and poetry itself. 3 *crude:* unripe.

Shatter your leaves before the mellowing year.   5
Bitter constraint, and sad occasion dear,
Compels me to disturb your season due:
For *Lycidas* is dead, dead ere his prime
Young *Lycidas*, and hath not left his peer:
Who would not sing for *Lycidas?* he well knew   10
Himself to sing, and build the lofty rhyme.
He must not flote upon his watry bear
Unwept, and welter to the parching wind,
Without the meed of som melodious tear.
  Begin then, Sisters of the sacred well,   15
That from beneath the seat of *Jove* doth spring,
Begin, and somwhat loudly sweep the string.
Hence with denial vain, and coy excuse,
So may som gentle Muse
With lucky words favour my destin'd Urn,   20
And as he passes turn,
And bid fair peace be to my sable shroud.
For we were nurst upon the self-same hill,
Fed the same flock, by fountain, shade, and rill.
  Together both, ere the high Lawns appear'd   25
Under the opening eye-lids of the morn,
We drove a field, and both together heard
What time the Gray-fly winds her sultry horn,
Batt'ning our flocks with the fresh dews of night,
Oft till the Star that rose, at Ev'ning, bright   30
Toward Heav'ns descent had slop'd his westering wheel.
Mean while the Rural ditties were not mute,
Temper'd to th'Oaten Flute,
Rough *Satyrs* danc'd, and *Fauns* with clov'n heel,
From the glad sound would not be absent long,   35
And old *Damœtas* lov'd to hear our song.
  But O the heavy change, now thou art gon,
Now thou art gon, and never must return!
Thee Shepherd, thee the Woods, and desert Caves,
With wilde Thyme and the gadding Vine o'regrown,   40

---

12 *bear:* bier, the framework on which the coffin or body is laid.   13 *welter:*
roll, toss about.   15 *Sisters:* the Muses, invoked as required by the pastoral
convention.   *sacred well:* Pierian Spring, at the foot of Mt. Olympus,
source of poetic inspiration.   23 *we were nurst:* the convention of
recalling the pastoral life lived together.   28 *Gray-Fly:* perhaps the common
black dung-beetle or dumble-dor that flies after sunset (*OED*).   *winds:* blows.
29 *Batt'ning:* fattening.   30 *Star:* Hesperus.   32 *Rural ditties:* i.e., pastoral
poetry, which in the Virgilian tradition is the first genre the young poet attempts.
36 *old Damœtas:* name of shepherd in Virgil, Eclogue III; possibly also a
tutor whom Milton and King both respected.   37–49 *But . . . ear:* the conventional pathetic fallacy that all nature mourns.   40 *gadding:* rambling.

And all their echoes mourn.
The Willows, and the Hazle Copses green,
Shall now no more be seen,
Fanning their joyous Leaves to thy soft layes.
As killing as the Canker to the Rose,   45
Or Taint-worm to the weanling Herds that graze,
Or Frost to Flowers, that their gay wardrop wear,
When first the White-thorn blows;
Such, *Lycidas*, thy loss to Shepherds ear.
   Where were ye Nymphs when the remorseless deep   50
Clos'd o're the head of your lov'd *Lycidas?*
For neither were ye playing on the steep,
Where your old *Bards*, the famous *Druids* ly,
Nor on the shaggy top of *Mona* high,
Nor yet where *Deva* spreads her wisard stream: 55
Ay me, I fondly dream!
Had ye bin there . . . for what could that have don?
What could the Muse her self that *Orpheus* bore,
The Muse her self, for her inchanting son
Whom Universal nature did lament,   60
When by the rout that made the hideous roar,
His goary visage down the stream was sent,
Down the swift *Hebrus* to the *Lesbian* shore.
   Alas! What boots it with uncessant care
To tend the homely slighted Shepherds trade,   65
And strictly meditate the thankles Muse,
Were it not better don as others use,
To sport with *Amaryllis* in the shade,
Or with the tangles of *Neæra's* hair?
Fame is the spur that the clear spirit doth raise   70

47–48 *Frost . . . blows:* [*as killing as*] the "killing" frost is to flowers in May,
long past the time when frost is expected. Cf. Herrick, "Corinna's," l. 14 and
note.   50 *Where were ye:* the conventional question to the guardian nymphs
who might have protected Lycidas. 53–55 *Bards, Druids, Mona, Deva:*
allusions to places near the site of the disaster, which naturalize the pastoral by
bringing its traditional classical, Sicilian, and Italian myths and symbols into
association with ancient and current English folklore and symbols. *Druids:*
order of poets and priests of ancient Celtic religion; *Mona:* Isle of Anglesey,
Wales; *Deva:* the river Dee, which empties into the Irish sea above Chester;
by observing the Dee, wise men could foretell future events, hence *wisard.*
56 *fondly:* foolishly. 61–63 *When . . . shore:* Orpheus was torn to pieces by
Thracian women, votaries of Dionysius, and his head, still singing, was thrown
into the Hebrus and floated down to the island of Lesbos, where it was buried.
63 *boots:* profits. Milton here shifts to the theme and style of both the complaint
(cf. Spenser's June and October eclogues) and the harsh moral eclogues reminis-
cent of the Psalms. 65 *Shepherds trade:* craft of poetry. 68–69 *To sport
. . . Amaryllis . . . Neæra:* i.e., to engage in the *ludus Veneris* (play or pastime
of Venus) with wanton Amaryllis and Neæra, traditionally frolicsome and willing shepherdesses. Also, figuratively, to write erotic, popular poetry to gain
immediate recognition.

(That last infirmity of Noble mind)
To scorn delights, and live laborious dayes;
But the fair Guerdon when we hope to find,
And think to burst out into sudden blaze,
Comes the blind *Fury* with th'abhorred shears,   75
And slits the thin-spun life. But not the praise,
Phœbus repli'd, and touch'd my trembling ears;
Fame is no plant that grows on mortal soil,
Nor in the glistering foil
Set off to th'world, nor in broad rumour lies,   80
But lives and spreds aloft by those pure eyes,
And perfet witnes of all-judging *Jove;*
As he pronounces lastly on each deed,
Of so much fame in Heav'n expect thy meed.

  O Fountain *Arethuse*, and thou honour'd floud,   85
Smooth-sliding *Mincius*, crown'd with vocall reeds,
That strain I heard was of a higher mood:
But now my Oate proceeds,
And listens to the Herald of the Sea
That came in *Neptune's* plea,   90
He ask'd the Waves, and ask'd the Fellon winds,
What hard mishap hath doom'd this gentle swain?
And question'd every gust of rugged wings
That blows from off each beaked Promontory;
They knew not of his story,   95
And sage *Hippotades* their answer brings,
That not a blast was from his dungeon stray'd,
The Ayr was calm, and on the level brine,
Sleek *Panope* with all her sisters play'd.

75 *Fury:* Fate; Atropos who cuts short the thread of life.   77 *Phœbus:* Apollo, god of wisdom, poetic inspiration, and music. *touch'd . . . ears:* Virgil, in Eclogue VI, ll. 3–4, says that Apollo warned him against the ambition of writing epic poetry before he was ready; in the Renaissance tradition, epic poetry would bring the poet fame, while pastoral poetry, being anonymous, would not.   79 *glistering foil:* leaf of bright metal used to set off an inferior stone; hence, the showy glitter of fraudulent fame.   82 *perfet:* perfect. *Jove:* God. Cf. *Paradise Regained,* III, 60–70. Only in God's eyes does man possess true fame. Milton here refers to the paradoxes of the Beatitudes (Matt. 5:3–12). True fame is one's power to accept the mystery of fate and to assume the burden of the inexplicable judgment of God. See also Ps. 73.   83 *lastly:* i.e., at Last Judgment, hence irrevocably.   85–87 *O . . . mood:* with the reference to *Arethuse* (Sicilian fountain of Theocritus; see "Arcades," ll. 30–31 and note) and *Mincius* (river near Virgil's birthplace), Milton signals a return from the *higher mood* (mode, style) of the moral eclogue to the sweetness of the Theocritan pastoral.   88 *Oate:* oaten flute of the pastoral. The conventional procession of the mourners begins here.   89 *Herald . . . Sea:* Triton, son of Neptune (god of the sea), calmer of storms, comes in defense of his father.   96 *Hippotades:* Aeolus, god of the winds. 99 *Panope:* a Nereid (sea nymph).

It was that fatall and perfidious Bark   100
Built in th'eclipse, and rigg'd with curses dark,
That sunk so low that sacred head of thine.
　　Next *Camus*, reverend Sire, went footing slow,
His Mantle hairy, and his Bonnet sedge,
Inwrought with figures dim, and on the edge   105
Like to that sanguine flower inscrib'd with woe.
Ah! Who hath reft (quoth he) my dearest pledge?
Last came, and last did go,
The Pilot of the *Galilean* lake,
Two massy Keyes he bore of metals twain,   110
(The Golden opes, the Iron shuts amain)
He shook his Miter'd locks, and stern bespake,
How well could I have spar'd for thee young swain,
Anow of such as for their bellies sake,
Creep and intrude, and climb into the fold?   115
Of other care they little reck'ning make,
Then how to scramble at the shearers feast,
And shove away the worthy bidden guest;
Blind mouthes! that scarce themselves know how to hold
A Sheep-hook, or have learn'd ought els the least   120
That to the faithfull Herdmans art belongs!
What recks it them? What need they? They are sped;
And when they list, their lean and flashy songs
Grate on their scrannel Pipes of wretched straw,
The hungry Sheep look up, and are not fed,   125
But swoln with wind, and the rank mist they draw,
Rot inwardly, and foul contagion spread:
Besides what the grim Woolf with privy paw
Daily devours apace, and nothing sed,

---

103 *Camus:* personification of the river Cam; thus a symbol of Cambridge University. 106 *sanguine . . . woe:* the purple hyacinth, whose markings (said to have been made by the blood of the young Hyacinth, accidentally slain by Apollo) were thought to spell the Greek words for *Woe! Woe!* 107 *pledge:* child. 109–112 *Pilot . . . locks:* St. Peter, fisherman of Galilee, keeper of the keys of heaven, first bishop of the Church (hence *Miter'd locks*), and thus the appropriate apostolic leader of all subsequent pastors (i.e., priests). 112 *stern bespake:* Milton again returns to the harsh style of the moral eclogue. See Ps. 94 and also Ezek. 34 for the *locus classicus* for attack on false shepherds. 113 *young swain:* young shepherd, i.e., pastor, priest. Edward King was an Anglican priest on his way to his first parish when he was drowned. 120 *Sheep-hook:* Cf. a bishop's crosier. 122 *What recks . . . sped:* What do they care? What do they need to worry about? They have prospered. 124 *scrannel:* thin, squeaking. 125 *fed:* See Ezek. 34:3–5. 126 *wind:* a disease of sheep, occurring immediately after shearing if they are not cared for; the intestines become inflamed and distended with air. 128 *Woolf:* literally, the traditional devourer of sheep; figuratively, the satanic destroyer of the flock. See John 10:12 and Acts 20:28–29.

But that two-handed engine at the door,   130
Stands ready to smite once, and smite no more.
    Return *Alpheus*, the dread voice is past,
That shrunk thy streams; Return *Sicilian* Muse,
And call the Vales, and bid them hither cast
Their Bels, and Flourets of a thousand hues.   135
Ye valleys low where the milde whispers use,
Of shades and wanton winds, and gushing brooks,
On whose fresh lap the swart Star sparely looks,
Throw hither all your quaint enameld eyes,
That on the green terf suck the honied showres,   140
And purple all the ground with vernal flowres.
Bring the rathe Primrose that forsaken dies,
The tufted Crow-toe, and pale Gessamine,
The white Pink, and the Pansie freakt with jeat,
The glowing Violet,   145
The Musk-rose, and the well-attir'd Woodbine,
With Cowslips wan that hang the pensive hed,
And every flower that sad embroidery wears:
Bid *Amaranthus* all his beauty shed,
And Daffadillies fill their cups with tears,   150
To strew the Laureat Herse where *Lycid* lies.
For so to interpose a little ease,
Let our frail thoughts dally with false surmise.
Ay me! Whilst thee the shores, and sounding Seas
Wash far away, where ere thy bones are hurld,   155
Whether beyond the stormy *Hebrides*,
Where thou perhaps under the whelming tide

---

130 *two-handed engine:* specifically, the *gladius Dei*, the sword of Divine vengeance. See Ezek. 21:3–15. In general, *engine* suggests any offensive instrument
of warfare, from a battering ram to a sword.   132–33 *Return . . . Muse:* again,
a return to the *Sicilian Muse* of Theocritus. See above, l. 85 and note.   138
swart Star: Sirius, the Dog Star, which in August is said to burn the flowers
black.   142 *rathe:* early.   144 *freakt:* streaked.   149 *Aramanthus:* imaginary
flower that when picked does not wither or die.   151 *Herse:* an open canopy,
set over a bier, used to support candles (here flowers) during a funeral ceremony.
153 *dally:* to play with without taking seriously; hence to defer facing the truth.
false surmise: false, because Lycidas is not on the bier. See above, l. 12.   154–
55 *Ay . . . hurld:* i.e., Alas! while the terrible truth [as opposed to *false surmise*]
is that the menacing and shallow waters (*shores*) and reverberating and deep
(*sounding*) seas wash you far away.   156–62 *Hebrides . . . hold:* Again (as in
ll. 53–55) the geographical allusions are connected with the area where Lycidas
was drowned: the *Hebrides*, west of northern Scotland, suggest a northern
limit; *Bellerus* (Land's End), a southern. St. Michael's *Mount*, the tip of Land's
End, according to the *fable* was *guarded* by the archangel, whose vigilant eye
looked southward toward Spain (*Namancos* and *Bayona's hold*) to "succor and
defend us in earth" (see Collect for St. Michael and All Angels in *Book of
Common Prayer*). He is also the conductor of the souls of the dead.

Visit'st the bottom of the monstrous world;
Or whether thou to our moist vows deny'd,
Sleep'st by the fable of *Bellerus* old,   160
Where the great vision of the guarded Mount
Looks toward *Namancos* and *Bayona's* hold;
Look homeward Angel now, and melt with ruth,
And, O ye *Dolphins*, waft the haples youth.
Weep no more, woful Shepherds weep no more,   165
For *Lycidas* your sorrow is not dead,
Sunk though he be beneath the watry floar,
So sinks the day-star in the Ocean bed,
And yet anon repairs his drooping head,
And tricks his beams, and with new spangled Ore,   170
Flames in the forehead of the morning sky:
So *Lycidas* sunk low, but mounted high,
Through the dear might of him that walk'd the waves;
Where other groves, and other streams along,
With *Nectar* pure his oozy Locks he laves,   175
And hears the unexpressive nuptiall Song,
In the blest Kingdoms meek of joy and love.
There entertain him all the Saints above,
In solemn troops, and sweet Societies
That sing, and singing in their glory move,   180
And wipe the tears for ever from his eyes.
Now *Lycidas* the Shepherds weep no more;
Henceforth thou art the Genius of the shore,
In thy large recompense, and shalt be good
To all that wander in that perilous flood.   185

---

158 *monstrous:* inhabited by sea monsters.   164 *Dolphins:* symbol of the Resurrection and salvation and long associated with poetry. Arion, who first converted the dithyramb to a literary composition and who invented the tragic mode in music, was rescued by dolphins after being thrown overboard.   165 *Weep no more:* the consolation, apotheosis, and heroic acceptance of the demands of faith begin here, and the styles of the idyllic pastoral, the complaint. and the harsh moral eclogue resolve into the style of the redeemed pastoral of Revelation 7:2–17.   168 *day-star:* the sun; also implied pun for *son.*   170 *tricks:* trims.   171 *Flames . . . sky:* "His eyes were as a flame of fire" (Rev. 19:12). Cf. also the resurrected Christ, "the bright and morning star" (Rev. 22:16).   173 *him:* Christ. See Matt. 14:25–26.   176 *unexpressive:* inexpressible.   *nuptiall song:* the marriage feast of the Lamb; see Rev. 19:7.   181 *And . . . eyes:* See ". . . God shall wipe away all tears from their eyes" (Rev. 7:17). Cf. Rev. 21:4; Isa. 25:8; and Collect, Epistle, and Gospel for All Saints Day (Nov. 1) in *Book of Common Prayer.* "Lycidas" was written near All Saints in November, 1637.   183 *Genius:* guardian spirit.

Thus sang the uncouth Swain to th'Okes and rills,
While the still morn went out with Sandals gray,
He touch'd the tender stops of various Quills,
With eager thought warbling his *Dorick* lay:
And now the Sun had stretch'd out all the hills,   190
And now was dropt into the Western bay;
At last he rose, and twitch'd his Mantle blew:
To morrow to fresh Woods, and Pastures new.

SONNETS

XII

I did but prompt the age to quit their cloggs
  By the known rules of antient libertie,
  When strait a barbarous noise environs me
  Of Owles and Cuckoes, Asses, Apes and Doggs.
As when those Hinds that were transform'd to Froggs   5
  Raild at *Latona's* twin-born progenie
  Which after held the Sun and Moon in fee.
But this is got by casting Pearl to Hoggs;
  That bawle for freedom in their senseless mood,
  And still revolt when truth would set them free.   10
  Licence they mean when they cry libertie;
For who loves that, must first be wise and good;
  But from that mark how far they roave we see
  For all this wast of wealth, and loss of blood.

186 *uncouth Swain:* unknown and unskilled shepherd, like Virgil and Spenser
in their pastoral verse.   188 *Quills:* reed pipes.   189 *Dorick:* the broad dialect
affected by the Greek pastoralists: Theocritus, Bion, and Moschus; hence
"pastoral."   192 *twitch'd:* fastened securely.   *blew:* blue, the color associated
with hope and constancy as well as the distinctive color of the dress of
servants and apprentices; hence, literally, the mantle of a real shepherd and,
figuratively, the mantle of the tested and faithful poet who can now proceed
to write the epic poem, i.e., to seek *Pastures new.*

  SONNETS. Milton did not write a sonnet sequence; all his sonnets are
"occasional." However, he uses freely, in a precise and condensed form,
previous traditions and conventions.

  [XII] 1 *I . . . cloggs:* Milton refers to his pamphlets in defense of personal,
political, and religious freedom.   5 *transform'd:* See Ovid, *Met.*, VI, 335–81,
where Latona transforms into frogs the Lycian peasants who refused to give
water to her and Apollo and Diana, her children.   7 *in fee:* in possession.
8 *Pearl:* See Matt. 7:6.

XVIII

On the Late Massacher in Piemont

Avenge O Lord thy slaughter'd Saints, whose bones
  Lie scatter'd on the Alpine mountains cold,
  Ev'n them who kept thy truth so pure of old
  When all our Fathers worship't Stocks and Stones,
Forget not: in thy book record their groanes   5
  Who were thy Sheep and in their antient Fold
  Slayn by the bloody *Piemontese* that roll'd
  Mother with Infant down the Rocks. Their moans
The Vales redoubl'd to the Hills, and they
  To Heav'n. Their martyr'd blood and ashes sow   10
  O're all th'*Italian* fields where still doth sway
The triple Tyrant: that from these may grow
  A hunderd-fold, who having learnt thy way
  Early may fly the *Babylonian* wo.

XIX

When I consider how my light is spent,
  Ere half my days, in this dark world and wide,
  And that one Talent which is death to hide,
  Lodg'd with me useless, though my Soul more bent
To serve therewith my Maker, and present   5
  My true account, least he returning chide,
  Doth God exact day-labour, light deny'd,
  I fondly ask; But patience to prevent
That murmur, soon replies, God doth not need
  Either man's work or his own gifts, who best   10
  Bear his milde yoak, they serve him best, his State
Is Kingly. Thousands at his bidding speed
  And post o're Land and Ocean without rest:
  They also serve who only stand and waite.

[xviii] 1 *slaughter'd Saints:* the Waldenses, a pre-Reformation Protestant sect (twelfth century) in northwestern Italy, in the realm of the Duke of Savoy, who had granted them freedom of worship yet authorized the massacre of April 24, 1655—"Piedmontese Easter." Indignation was nearly universal in Europe. Cromwell made an official protest (written by Milton as Secretary for Foreign Tongues). 12 *triple Tyrant:* the Pope (from his triple crown). 14 *Babylonian wo:* probably an allusion to Petrarch's comparison of the Papal Court at Avignon to Babylon (*In Vita*, CVII [Bohn tr.]).

[xix] 2 *Ere . . . days:* Milton became totally blind in March of 1651, when he was 42. 3 *one Talent:* See Matt. 25:24–30. 8 *fondly:* foolishly. *prevent:* forestall, anticipate. 11 *milde yoak:* See Matt. 11:30. 12 *Thousands:* of angels. 14 *They also:* angels other than the *Thousands*.

154

XXIII

Methought I saw my late espoused Saint
   Brought to me like *Alcestis* from the grave,
   Whom *Joves* great Son to her glad Husband gave,
   Rescu'd from death by force though pale and faint.
Mine as whom washt from spot of child-bed taint,   5
   Purification in the old Law did save,
   And such, as yet once more I trust to have
   Full sight of her in Heaven without restraint,
Came vested all in white, pure as her mind:
   Her face was vail'd, yet to my fancied sight,   10
   Love, sweetness, goodness, in her person shin'd
So clear, as in no face with more delight.
   But O as to embrace me she enclin'd,
   I wak'd, she fled, and day brought back my night.

from PARADISE LOST

[*The Invocation to Light*]

Hail holy Light, ofspring of Heav'n first-born,
Or of th' Eternal Coeternal beam
May I express thee unblam'd? since God is Light,
And never but in unapproached Light
Dwelt from Eternitie, dwelt then in thee,   5

[XXIII] 1 *Saint:* perhaps refers to Katherine Woodcock, Milton's second wife who died in not but three months following childbirth (1658), fifteen months after their marriage. W. R. Parker, however, argues that *Saint* refers to Mary Powell, Milton's first wife, who did die in childbirth. There is considerable controversy on this question. Milton, who never refers exclusively to himself but to a personal yet symbolic situation, here may be using standard images of the lover lamenting that he is deprived of the light of his lady's face, as well as those renouncing all earthly love, to universalize his particular fate and to express a vision of eternal bliss. Cf. Spenser, Sonnet 89, and Sidney, "Leave me ô Love." For the reverse situation, see *Paradise Lost*, VIII, 470–84. 2 *Alcestis:* wife of Admetus. She offered herself in place of her husband, who, about to die, was told by Apollo that he might live if a substitute were found. She was rescued by Hercules (*Joves great Son*) and brought back to the upper world. 5–6 *Mine . . . save:* Purified according to the old Levitical law regarding the ritualistic cleansing of women after childbirth. See Lev. 12. 10 *vail'd:* as was Alcestis' face in Euripides' *Alcestis*.

[INVOCATION] A sufficient account of Milton's theory of poetic inspiration and the responsibilities of the office of poet. 1 *ofspring . . . first-born:* i.e., light, the first physical creation (Gen. 1:3) of the Son, the first spiritual "creation" (John 1:1–5). 3 *May . . . unblam'd:* May I unblamed represent [by imitation] what you are? *Unblam'd* because of the Second Commandment, which forbids the making of "graven images."

Bright effluence of bright essence increate.
Or hear'st thou rather pure Ethereal stream,
Whose Fountain who shall tell? before the Sun,
Before the Heav'ns thou wert, and at the voice
Of God, as with a Mantle didst invest   10
The rising world of waters dark and deep,
Won from the void and formless infinite.
Thee I re-visit now with bolder wing,
Escap't the *Stygian* Pool, though long detaind
In that obscure sojourn, while in my flight   15
Through utter and through middle darkness borne
With other notes then to th' *Orphean* Lyre
I sung of *Chaos* and *Eternal Night*,
Taught by the heav'nly Muse to venture down
The dark descent, and up to reascend,   20
Though hard and rare: thee I revisit safe,
And feel thy sovran vital Lamp; but thou
Revisit'st not these eyes, that rowle in vain
To find thy piercing ray, and find no dawn:
So thick a drop serene hath quencht thir Orbs,   25
Or dim suffusion veild. Yet not the more
Cease I to wander where the Muses haunt
Cleer Spring, or shadie Grove, or Sunnie Hill,
Smit with the love of sacred Song; but chief
Thee *Sion* and the flowrie Brooks beneath   30
That wash thy hallowd feet, and warbling flow,
Nightly I visit: nor somtimes forget
Those other two equald with me in Fate,
So were I equald with them in renown,
Blind *Thamyris* and blind *Mæonides*,   35

6 *increate:* uncreated. The Invocation is based on the distinction between external, created light and internal, creative light (i.e., God).   8 *before the Sun:* See Gen. 1:1–8.   13 *re-visit:* i.e., I who descended to the depths of Hell [Bks. I and II] now return to the realms of light.   17 *then:* than.   20–21 *dark . . . rare:* Cf. *Aenid*, VI, 129: *Hoc opus, hic labor est*. The poet, taught by the Muse like the Sybil who taught Aeneas, has descended into darkness with relative ease but has now returned, a journey that is truly *hard and rare*. Cf. Satan's pompous forecast of his journey back to light, *Paradise Lost*, II, 432–33.   25 *quencht:* I.e., the poet is blind.   32 *Nightly:* Milton is said to have composed his poem at night; *Nightly* also refers to the darkness of his blindness.   35 *Thamyris:* legendary Thracian poet and musician, blinded by the Muses after he was vanquished by them in a trial of skill.   *Mæonides:* the epic poet, Homer, also blind.

And *Tiresias* and *Phineus* Prophets old:
Then feed on thoughts, that voluntarie move
Harmonious numbers; as the wakeful Bird
Sings darkling, and in shadiest Covert hid
Tunes her nocturnal Note. Thus with the Year   40
Seasons return, but not to mee returns
Day, or the sweet approach of Ev'n or Morn,
Or sight of vernal bloom, or Summers Rose,
Or flocks, or herds, or human face divine;
But cloud in stead, and ever-during dark   45
Surrounds me, from the chearful waies of men
Cut off, and for the Book of knowledg fair
Presented with a Universal blanc
Of Natures works to mee expung'd and ras'd,
And wisdom at one entrance quite shut out.   50
So much the rather thou Celestial Light
Shine inward, and the mind through all her powers
Irradiate, there plant eyes, all mist from thence
Purge and disperse, that I may see and tell
Of things invisible to mortal sight.   55

[Book III, ll. 1–55]

[*The Garden*]

Beneath him with new wonder now he views
To all delight of human sense expos'd
In narrow room Natures whole wealth, yea more,
A Heav'n on Earth: for blissful Paradise
Of God the Garden was, by him in the East   5
Of *Eden* planted; *Eden* stretchd her Line

36 *Tiresias:* celebrated prophet of Thebes (see Sophocles, *Oedipus Tyrannus*)
and infallible oracle to all Greece; blinded, some say, by Hera for deciding
against her in her dispute with Zeus about which sex received the greatest
pleasure in marriage, or by Athena because he had seen her bathing in the
fountain Hippocrene, sacred to the Muses. *Phineus:* king of Thrace and blind
prophet who directed the Argonauts to Colchis; blinded by the gods, some say,
for rashly foretelling men the future. By these allusions the speaker prays that
as his blindness is more dreadful and inexplicable (Milton says that he wore
his eyes out in the defence of his country) than that of his predecessors, so may
his prophetic inspiration and power of performance be greater, just as his
theme is more sublime ("Things unattempted yet in Prose or Rhime"), but
he asks for no more than equal *renown*. Cf. his Sonnet XIX. 38 *Bird:*
Philomel, the nightingale who sings only at night. 48 *blanc:* a white void.
49 *ras'd:* erased.

[THE GARDEN] 1 *him:* Satan, as he views the garden while perched on the
Tree of Life, the highest in the Garden.

From *Auran* Eastward to the Royal Towrs
Of great *Seleucia*, built by *Grecian* Kings,
Or where the Sons of *Eden* long before
Dwelt in *Telassar:* in this pleasant soile   10
His farr more pleasant Garden God ordaind;
Out of the fertil ground he caus'd to grow
All Trees of noblest kind for sight, smell, taste;
And all amid them stood the Tree of Life,
High eminent, blooming Ambrosial Fruit   15
Of vegetable Gold; and next to Life
Our Death the Tree of Knowledge grew fast by,
Knowledge of Good bought dear by knowing ill.
Southward through *Eden* went a River large,
Nor chang'd his course, but through the shaggie hill   20
Passd underneath ingulft, for God had thrown
That Mountain as his Garden mould high rais'd
Upon the rapid current, which through veins
Of porous Earth with kindly thirst up drawn,
Rose a fresh Fountain, and with many a rill   25
Waterd the Garden; thence united fell
Down the steep glade, and met the nether Flood,
Which from his darksom passage now appeers,
And now divided into four main Streams,
Runs divers, wandring many a famous Realme   30
And Country whereof here needs no account,
But rather to tell how, if Art could tell,
How from that Saphire Fount the crisped Brooks,
Rowling on Orient Pearl and sands of Gold,
With mazie error under pendant shades   35
Ran Nectar, visiting each plant, and fed
Flours worthy of Paradise, which not nice Art
In Beds and curious Knots, but Nature boon
Powrd forth profuse on Hill and Dale and Plaine,
Both where the morning Sun first warmly smote   40
The op'n field, and where the unpierc't shade
Imbround the noontide Bowrs: Thus was this place,
A happy rural seat of various view;
Groves whose rich Trees wept odorous Gumms and Balme,

7–10 *Auran . . . Telassar:* i.e., the western and eastern boundaries of Eden, from *Aurantis*, a region south of Damascus and east of the Jordan river, to *Seleucia*, an ancient city (now in ruins) founded by Alexander the Great's lieutenant Seleucus on the west bank of the Tigris about twenty miles south-southeast of Baghdad, or to *Thelasar*, a city and region thought to have been in Mesopotamia, inhabited by the children of Eden (see 2 Ki. 19:12). 35 *mazie error:* intricate wandering.   38 *curious Knots:* precise formal gardens with intersecting lines of flowers; parterres. *boon:* bounteous.   42 *Imbround:* Made dusky, dark.

Others whose fruit burnisht with Gold'n Rinde   45
Hung amiable, *Hesperian* Fables true,
If true, here onely, and of delicious taste:
Betwixt them Lawns, or level Downs, and Flocks
Grasing the tender herb, were interpos'd,
Or palmie hilloc, or the flourie lap   50
Of som irriguous Valley spred her store,
Flours of all hue, and without Thorn the Rose:
Another side, umbrageous Grots and Caves
Of coole recess, ore which the mantling Vine
Layes forth her purple Grape, and gently creeps   55
Luxuriant; mean while murmuring waters fall
Down the slope hills, disperst, or in a Lake,
That to the fringed Bank with Myrtle crownd,
Her crystal mirror holds, unite thir streams.
The Birds thir quire apply; aires, vernal aires,   60
Breathing the smell of field and grove, attune
The trembling leaves, while Universal *Pan*
Knit with the *Graces* and the *Hours* in dance
Led on th' Eternal Spring. Not that faire field
Of *Enna*, where *Proserpin* gathring flours   65
Her self a fairer Floure by gloomie *Dis*
Was gatherd, which cost *Ceres* all that pain
To seek her through the World; nor that sweet Grove
Of *Daphne* by *Orontes*, and th' inspir'd
Castalian Spring, might with this Paradise   70
Of *Eden* strive; nor that *Nyseian* Ile
Girt with the River *Triton*, where old *Cham*,
Whom Gentiles *Ammon* call and *Libyan Jove*,
Hid *Amalthea* and her Florid Son
Young *Bacchus* from his Stepdame *Rhea's* eye;   75
Nor where *Abassin* Kings thir issue Guard,
Mount *Amara*, though this by som suppos'd

---

46 *amiable:* exciting love and delight. *Hesperian Fables:* the irresistible golden apples of the Hesperides, which Venus gave to Hippomenes so that he could defeat Atalanta in a footrace and thus win her for his bride. See Ovid, *Met.*, X, 560–680. 62 *Universal Pan:* not the earthy Greek god of flocks and shepherds but the personification of pure, unfallen nature. 63 *Graces . . . Hours:* attendant goddesses in Greek mythology, the first personifying grace and loveliness, the latter the seasons. 64 *Eternal Spring:* Before the advent of death, Paradise was the garden of generation only. Cf. Gen. 1:28: "Be fruitful, and multiply, and replenish the earth." Cf. also Spenser, *Faerie Queene:* III, vi, 42, "The Garden of Adonis." 65–68 *Enna . . . Ceres:* See Ovid, *Met.*, V, 385–571, for the story of the rape of *Proserpine* by Pluto (Dis), god of the underworld, from another garden of eternal spring and *Ceres'* painful search for her lost daughter. The garden of *Enna*, Daphne, and all the others here mentioned by Milton are famous both for their beauty and for some sad event. None can compare with Paradise, however, either in beauty or in the sadness of the event that occurred there.

True Paradise under the *Ethiop* Line
By *Nilus* head, enclos'd with shining Rock,
A whole dayes journey high, but wide remote   80
From this *Assyrian* Garden, where the Fiend
Saw undelighted all delight, all kind
Of living Creatures new to sight and strange:
Two of farr nobler shape erect and tall,
Godlike erect, with native Honour clad   85
In naked Majestie seemd Lords of all,
And worthie seemd, for in thir looks Divine
The image of thir glorious Maker shon,
Truth, Wisdom, Sanctitude severe and pure,
Severe, but in true filial freedom plac't;   90
Whence true autoritie in men; though both
Not equal, as thir sex not equal seemd;
For contemplation hee and valour formd,
For softness shee and sweet attractive grace,
Hee for God onely, shee for God in him: 95
His fair large Front and Eye sublime declar'd
Absolute rule; and Hyacinthin Locks
Round from his parted forelock manly hung
Clustring, but not beneath his shoulders broad:
Shee as a vail down to the slender waste   100
Her unadorned gold'n tresses wore
Dissheveld, but in wanton ringlets wav'd
As the Vine curles her tendrils, which impli'd
Subjection, but requir'd with gentle sway,
And by her yeilded, by him best receivd,   105
Yeilded with coy submission, modest pride,
And sweet reluctant amorous delay.
Nor those mysterious parts were then conceald,
Then was not guiltie shame, dishonest shame
Of Natures works, honor dishonorable,   110
Sin-bred, how have ye troubl'd all mankind
With shews instead, meer shews of seeming pure,
And banisht from Mans life his happiest life,

---

90 *Severe . . . freedom:* characteristic oxymoron; Adam and Eve reveal simultaneously strictness of discipline and freedom from restraint. 91 *true autoritie:* to Milton and the Renaissance, all authority of men over men is derived from the Fifth Commandment, which is the earthly parallel of man's proper relationship with God; hence, *filial* freedom. 92 *Not equal:* they are equal as *Lords of all* but unequal in sex and capacities; but his *absolute rule* and her *subjection* so complement each other that when *hand in hand* both are invested with equal grace and authority. Apart, each is incomplete; together, whole. 106 *coy . . . pride:* oxymorons that express the paradoxical unity of unfallen man and woman in each other. The garden is an extended figure that corresponds with and reveals the splendor—and the potential ambiguities—of Adam and Eve.

Simplicitie and spotless innocence.
So passd they naked on, nor shunnd the sight   115
Of God or Angel, for they thought no ill:
So hand in hand they passd, the lovliest pair
That ever since in loves imbraces met,
Adam the goodliest man of men since borne
His Sons, the fairest of her Daughters *Eve*.   120

[Book IV, ll. 205–324]

[*Epithalamion*]

Haile wedded Love, mysterious Law, true sourse
Of human ofspring, sole proprietie
In Paradise of all things common else.
By thee adulterous lust was driv'n from men
Among the bestial herds to raunge, by thee   5
Founded in Reason, Loyal, Just, and Pure,
Relations dear, and all the Charities
Of Father, Son, and Brother first were known.
Farr be it, that I should write thee sin or blame,
Or think thee unbefitting holiest place,   10
Perpetual Fountain of Domestic sweets,
Whose Bed is undefil'd and chast pronounc't,
Present, or past, as Saints and Patriarchs us'd.
Here Love his gold'n shafts imploies, here lights
His constant Lamp, and waves his purple wings,   15
Reigns here and revels; not in the bought smile
Of Harlots, loveless, joyless, unindeard,
Casual fruition, nor in Court Amours,
Mixt Dance, or wanton Mask, or Midnight Ball,
Or Serenate, which the starv'd Lover sings   20
To his proud fair, best quitted with disdain.
These lulld by Nightingales imbraceing slept,
And on thir naked limbs the flourie roof
Showrd Roses, which the Morn repaird. Sleep on,
Blest pair; and O yet happiest if ye seek   25
No happier state, and know to know no more.

[Book IV, ll. 750–75]

[EPITHLAMION] 4 *adulterous lust:* In the marriage service in the *Book of Common Prayer*, matrimony is declared to have been introduced for the following causes: ". . . procreation of children . . . a remedy against sinne and to avoide fornication . . . for the mutual societie, helpe, and comfort . . . ." Cf. Spenser's "Epithalamion," particularly ll. 383–404 and notes. 20–21 *Serenate . . . disdain:* Cf. Wyatt, "My Lute Awake."

ANDREW MARVELL
1621–1678

To His Coy Mistress

Had we but world enough, and time,
This coyness lady were no crime.
We would sit down, and think which way
To walk, and pass our long love's day.
Thou by the Indian Ganges' side   5
Should'st rubies find: I by the tide
Of Humber would complain. I would
Love you ten years before the Flood:
And you should if you please refuse
Till the conversion of the Jews.   10
My vegetable love should grow
Vaster than empires, and more slow.
An hundred years should go to praise
Thine eyes, and on thy forehead gaze.
Two hundred to adore each breast: 15
But thirty thousand to the rest.
An age at least to every part,
And the last age should show your heart.
For lady you deserve this state;
Nor would I love at lower rate.   20
    But at my back I always hear
Time's winged chariot hurrying near:
And yonder all before us lie
Deserts of vast eternity.
Thy beauty shall no more be found;   25
Nor, in thy marble vault, shall sound
My echoing song: then worms shall try
That long preserv'd virginity:

TO HIS COY MISTRESS.   *Coy:* cf. *coy* in Chaucer, "Portrait of the Prioresse,"
l. 2; here a paradox: not only "quiet," "aloof," "disdainful," without any
affectation, but also, from the verb form, "coaxing" and "alluring," as in
decoy but without malice.   7 *Humber:* river flowing between Lincolnshire
and Marvell's native Yorkshire. *complain:* i.e., write love "complaints," a
technical term describing the song the lover sings of his hard-hearted, unre-
lenting mistress.   8 *Flood:* i.e., that of Noah, which concluded the first *age*
(l. 17) of the world.   10 *conversion . . . Jews:* i.e., the last age, for to Orthodox
Christian doctrine they will not be converted until just before the end of the
world, which means, of course, never.   11 *vegetable love:* capable of passive
growth only; cf. "rational," "animal," and "vegetable" divisions of the soul.
13–14 *praise Thine eyes:* ironic version of the standard catalogue of the lady's
beautiful parts. Cf. Spenser, "Epithalamion," ll. 167–82.

And your quaint honor turn to dust;
And into ashes all my lust.   30
The grave's a fine and private place,
But none I think do there embrace.
    Now therefore, while the youthful hue
Sits on thy skin like morning dew,
And while thy willing soul transpires   35
At every pore with instant fires,
Now let us sport us while we may;
And now, like am'rous birds of prey,
Rather at once our time devour,
Than languish in his slow-chapt pow'r.   40
Let us roll all our strength, and all
Our sweetness, up into one ball:
And tear our pleasures with rough strife,
Thorough the iron gates of life.
Thus, though we cannot make our sun   45
Stand still, yet we will make him run.

The Definition of Love

I

My love is of a birth as rare
As 'tis for object strange and high:
It was begotten by despair
Upon impossibility.

II

Magnanimous Despair alone   5
Could show me so divine a thing,
Where feeble Hope could ne'er have flown
But vainly flapt its tinsel wing.

III

And yet I quickly might arrive
Where my extended soul is fixt,   10

29 *quaint:* In this ironic context, *quaint* assumes the whole range of meanings of artful, ingenious, whimsical, fastidious, and prim; it is also a pun on *queynte* (pudendum). See Chaucer, "The Miller's Tale," ll. 3275–76 (ed. Robinson). 37 *sport:* generally, to enjoy ourselves, as well as to engage in the *ludus Veneris.* Cf. Milton, "Lycidas," ll. 68–69 and note. 40 *slow-chapt:* slowly devouring. 42 *ball:* image of unbreakable union and completeness, as in the union of two hemispheres in Donne's "Good Morrow" (ll. 15–18), or, as here, in the cannonball that pursues and destroys and yet remains intact. 44 *Thorough:* (disallabic) through. 45–46 *sun Stand still:* as Zeus did when he lay with Alcmene begetting Heracles.

But Fate does iron wedges drive,
And always crowds itself betwixt.

IV

For Fate with jealous eye does see
Two perfect loves; nor lets them close:
Their union would her ruin be,   15
And her tyrannic pow'r depose.

V

And therefore her decrees of steel
Us as the distant poles have plac'd,
(Though Love's whole world on us doth wheel)
Not by themselves to be embrac'd.   20

VI

Unless the giddy heaven fall,
And earth some new convulsion tear;
And, us to join, the world should all
Be cramp'd into a planisphere.

VII

As lines so loves *oblique* may well   25
Themselves in every angle greet:
But ours so truly *parallel*,
Though infinite can never meet.

VIII

Therefore the love which us doth bind,
But Fate so enviously debars,   30
Is the conjunction of the mind,
And opposition of the stars.

THE DEFINITION OF LOVE.   19 *Love's . . . wheel:* I.e., we are the axis on
which Love's world turns.   20 *Not . . . embrac'd:* The poles, at opposite ends
of the same axis, cannot touch one another.   24 *planisphere:* a polar projection
(map), here of both the heavens and the earth.   25 *oblique:* neither parallel
nor perpendicular.   26 *every angle:* i.e., in geometry, every angle except 180°
(parallel) or 90° (perpendicular, i.e., a right angle). Part of the effect is derived
not only from the precision of the geometric distinctions but also from the
implied distinctions between oblique lines (the indirect lines of ordinary love)
and "right" lines (straight, hence direct, true love—theirs).   31 *conjunction:*
in astrology, a favorable meeting; in astronomy, the meeting of two stars in
the same longitude.   32 *opposition:* in astrology, an unfavorable encounter;
in astronomy, said of stars whose longitude differs by 180° when seen from the
earth's surface.

An Horatian Ode upon Cromwell's Return from Ireland

The forward Youth that would appear
Must now forsake his Muses dear,
   Nor in the shadows sing
   His numbers languishing.
'Tis time to leave the books in dust,   5
And oil th' unused armor's rust:
   Removing from the wall
   The corslet of the hall.
So restless Cromwell could not cease
In the inglorious arts of peace,   10
   But through adventrous war
   Urged his active star.
And, like the three-fork'd lightning, first
Breaking the clouds where it was nurst,
   Did thorough his own side   15
   His fiery way divide.
For 'tis all one to courage high
The emulous or enemy;
   And with such, to inclose
   Is more than to oppose.   20
Then burning through the air he went,
And palaces and temples rent:
   And Caesar's head at last
   Did through his laurels blast.
'Tis madness to resist or blame   25
The force of angry Heaven's flame:
   And, if we would speak true,
   Much to the Man is due.
Who, from his private gardens, where
He liv'd reserved and austere,   30
   As if his highest plot
   To plant the bergamot,
Could by industrious valor climb
To ruin the great work of Time,
   And cast the kingdom old   35
   Into another mold.

AN HORATIAN ODE. *Cromwell's . . . Ireland:* at the end of May, 1650, to direct the Scottish campaign. 2 *forsake his Muses:* The humanistic ideal required that the poet be a public man of action as well as a private, contemplative man. 4 *numbers:* poetry. 12 *Urged . . . star:* encouraged his own destiny. 15 *thorough . . . side:* through the side of the cloud, and of the Parliamentary party, becoming the leader of the minority Independent forces in opposition to the Presbyterians. 18 *emulous:* jealous rival. 19 *inclose:* restrain. 23 *Caesar's:* Charles I, whom Cromwell and Parliament dethroned. 32 *bergamot:* pear tree.

Though Justice against Fate complain,
And plead the ancient rights in vain:
    But those do hold or break
    As men are strong or weak.   40
Nature that hateth emptiness,
Allows of penetration less:
    And therefore must make room
    Where greater spirits come.
What field of all the Civil Wars,   45
Where his were not the deepest scars?
    And Hampton shows what part
    He had of wiser art.
Where, twining subtle fears with hope,
He wove a net of such a scope,   50
    That Charles himself might chase
    To Carisbrook's narrow case.
That thence the Royal Actor born
The tragic scaffold might adorn:
    While round the armed bands   55
    Did clap their bloody hands.
He nothing common did or mean
Upon that memorable scene:
    But with his keener eye
    The axe's edge did try: 60
Nor call'd the gods with vulgar spite
To vindicate his helpless right,
    But bow'd his comely head,
    Down as upon a bed.
This was that memorable hour   65
Which first assur'd the forced pow'r.
    So when they did design
    The Capitol's first line,
A bleeding head where they begun,
Did fright the architects to run;   70
    And yet in that the State
    Foresaw its happy fate.
And now the Irish are asham'd
To see themselves in one year tam'd:

41–42 *Nature . . . less:* As much as Nature abhors a vacuum, it is more opposed to permitting two bodies to occupy the same space simultaneously. 47 *Hampton:* Hampton Court, from which Charles I fled November 11, 1647, to Carisbrooke Castle (l. 52). 50 *net:* Marvell believed that Cromwell instigated Charles' flight, a belief no longer accepted. 52 *narrow case:* small, confined, limited house. 54 *tragic scaffold:* Charles was beheaded on January 30, 1649. 57 *He:* Charles I. 66 *forced pow'r:* i.e., the Commonwealth. 68 *Capitol's:* Rome's. *line:* plan. 69 *bleeding . . . begun:* found when they were laying the foundation of the Temple of Jupiter.

So much one Man can do, 75
That does both act and know.
They can affirm his praises best,
And have, though overcome, confest
    How good he is, how just,
    And fit for highest trust: 80
Nor yet grown stiffer with command,
But still in the Republic's hand:
    How fit he is to sway
    That can so well obey.
He to the Commons' feet presents 85
A kingdom, for his first year's rents:
    And, what he may, forbears
    His fame to make it theirs:
And has his sword and spoils ungirt,
To lay them at the Public's skirt. 90
    So when the falcon high
    Falls heavy from the sky,
She, having kill'd, no more does search,
But on the next green bough to perch;
    Where, when he first does lure, 95
    The falconer has her sure.
What may not then our Isle presume
While victory his crest does plume!
    What may not others fear
    If thus he crown each year! 100
A Caesar he ere long to Gaul,
To Italy an Hannibal,
    And to all States not free
    Shall climacteric be.
The Pict no shelter now shall find 105
Within his party-color'd mind;
    But from this valor sad
    Shrink underneath the plad:
Happy if in the tufted brake
The English Hunter him mistake; 110
    Nor lay his hounds in near
    The Caledonian Deer.
But thou the Wars' and Fortune's Son

---

82 *in . . . hand:* acting under Commonwealth authority; Cromwell had not yet become the dictatorial Lord Protector. 86 *kingdom:* Ireland. 90 *skirt:* Cf. *to the Commons' feet* (l. 85). 95 *lure:* recall. 104 *climacteric:* the man identified with a critical period marked by a great change. 105 *Pict:* the Scot(s), who were divided between loyalty to the crown and zeal for their own national and religious interests; hence, *party-color'd mind* (l. 106). 107 *sad:* steadfast. 108 *plad:* plaid. 110 *mistake:* fail to identify. 111 *hounds:* i.e., troops. 112 *Caledonian Deer:* i.e., the Scots.

March indefatigably on;
   And for the last effect   115
   Still keep thy sword erect:
Besides the force it has to fright
The spirits of the shady night,
   The same arts that did gain
   A Pow'r must it maintain.   120

The Garden

I

How vainly men themselves amaze
To win the palm, the oak, or bays;
And their uncessant labors see
Crown'd from some single herb or tree,
Whose short and narrow verged shade   5
Does prudently their toils upbraid;
While all flow'rs and all trees do close
To weave the garlands of repose.

II

Fair quiet, have I found thee here,
And Innocence thy sister dear!   10
Mistaken long, I sought you then
In busy companies of men.
Your sacred plants, if here below,
Only among the plants will grow.
Society is all but rude,   15
To this delicious solitude.

III

No white nor red was ever seen
So am'rous as this lovely green.
Fond lovers, cruel as their flame,
Cut in these trees their mistress' name.   20
Little, alas, they know, or heed,
How far these beauties hers exceed!

---

117 *it:* the raised sword-hilt as the sign of the cross, which will *fright the spirits of the shady night.*

THE GARDEN. 1 *amaze:* perplex. 2 *palm . . . bays:* wreaths emblematic of victory in games, battle, and poetry contests. 3 *uncessant:* unceasing 5 *short:* I.e., the leaves of the wreath soon wither. 17 *white nor red:* i.e., of the lily and the rose, standard comparisons with the lady's beauty.

Fair trees! wheres'e'er your barks I wound,
No name shall but your own be found.

IV

When we have run our passions' heat,   25
Love hither makes his best retreat.
The gods, that mortal beauty chase,
Still in a tree did end their race.
Apollo hunted Daphne so,
Only that she might laurel grow.   30
And Pan did after Syrinx speed,
Not as a nymph, but for a reed.

V

What wond'rous life in this I lead!
Ripe apples drop about my head;
The luscious clusters of the vine   35
Upon my mouth do crush their wine;
The nectarine, and curious peach,
Into my hands themselves do reach;
Stumbling on melons, as I pass,
Insnar'd with flow'rs, I fall on grass.   40

VI

Meanwhile the mind, from pleasure less,
Withdraws into its happiness:
The mind, that ocean where each kind
Does straight its own resemblance find;
Yet it creates, transcending these,   45
Far other worlds, and other seas;
Annihilating all that's made
To a green thought in a green shade.

VII

Here at the fountain's sliding foot,
Or at some fruit-tree's mossy root,   50
Casting the body's vest aside,

29 *Daphne:* Pursued by enamoured Apollo, Daphne implored the gods to
save her, and they changed her into a laurel. Apollo crowned his head with
its leaves and ordered that the tree be forever sacred to his divinity. See Ovid,
Met. I, 452–567. 31 *Syrinx:* See Ovid, *Met.* I, 687–712. See above, Milton,
"Arcades," l. 1 and note. 43–44 *mind . . . find:* The microcosmic mind, like
the ocean (in which may be found the counterparts of every land creature),
is stocked with all possible ideas and images. 48 *green thought:* i.e., the
thought of thoughts, since the *green thought* is the reduction of the garden
(which contains all thoughts) into one thought. 51 *body's vest:* the flesh.

My soul into the boughs does glide:
There like a bird it sits, and sings,
Then whets, and combs its silver wings;
And, till prepar'd for longer flight,   55
Waves in its plumes the various light.

VIII

Such was that happy garden-state,
While man there walk'd without a mate:
After a place so pure, and sweet,
What other help could yet be meet!   60
But 'twas beyond a mortal's share
To wander solitary there:
Two paradises 'twere in one
To live in Paradise alone.

IX

How well the skilful gardner drew   65
Of flow'rs and herbs this dial new;
Where from above the milder sun
Does through a fragrant zodiac run;
And, as it works, th' industrious bee
Computes its time as well as we.   70
How could such sweet and wholesome hours
Be reckon'd but with herbs and flow'rs!

The Mower Against Gardens

Luxurious man, to bring his vice in use,
    Did after him the world seduce,
And from the fields the flowers and plants allure,
    Where nature was most plain and pure.
He first enclosed within the garden's square   5
    A dead and standing pool of air;
And a more luscious earth for them did knead,
    Which stupefied them while it fed.
The pink grew then as double as his mind;

---

54 *whets:* preens, trims.   57 *happy garden state:* Eden. Cf. Milton's account
of the Garden of Paradise (pp. 156–60).   58 *without a mate:* i.e., before Eve
was created.   60 *meet:* suitable; cf. Gen. 2:18 where Eve was proposed as
a "help meet for him [Adam]."   66, 68 *dial, zodiac:* flowers and herbs planted
to resemble a sundial complete with the signs of the zodiac.

THE MOWER AGAINST GARDENS.   1 *use:* common use.   9 *pink:* the *dianthus*,
a pink flower.

170

The nutriment did change the kind.   10
With strange perfumes he did the roses taint;
 And flowers themselves were taught to paint.
The tulip, white, did for complexion seek,
 And learned to interline its cheek;
Its onion root they then so high did hold   15
 That one was for a meadow sold.
Another world was searched, through oceans new,
 To find the marvel of Peru.
And yet these rarities might be allowed
 To man, that sov'reign thing and proud,   20
Had he not dealt between the bark and tree,
 Forbidden mixtures there to see.
No plant now knew the stock from which it came;
 He grafts upon the wild the tame,
That the uncertain and adult'rate fruit   25
 Might put the palate in dispute.
His green seraglio has its eunuchs too,
 Lest any tyrant him outdo;
And in the cherry he does nature vex,
 To procreate without a sex.   30
'Tis all enforced, the fountain and the grot,
 While the sweet fields do lie forgot,
Where willing nature does to all dispense
 A wild and fragrant innocence;
And fauns and fairies do the meadows till   35
 More by their presence than their skill.
Their statues, polished by some ancient hand,
 May to adorn the gardens stand;
But howsoe'er the figures do excel,
 The gods themselves with us do dwell.   40

On a Drop of Dew

 See how the orient dew,
 Shed from the bosom of the morn
  Into the blowing roses,
 Yet careless of its mansion new,
 For the clear region where 'twas born   5

18 *marvel of Peru:* plant, native of tropical America, of the genus *Mirabilis Jalapa*, whose red, white, and yellow flowers open only toward night; also called "afternoon-ladies." 21–22 *bark . . . see:* to join unnaturally by grafting different species.

ON A DROP OF DEW. 3 *blowing:* blooming. 4 *careless:* unmindful. 5 *For:* in the place of.

Round in itself incloses,
  And in its little globe's extent
Frames as it can its native element;
How it the purple flower does slight,
  Scarce touching where it lies,   10
But gazing back upon the skies,
    Shines with a mournful light
      Like its own tear,
Because so long divided from the sphere.
    Restless it rolls and unsecure,   15
      Trembling lest it grow impure,
    Till the warm sun pity its pain,
And to the skies exhale it back again.
      So the soul, that drop, that ray
Of the clear fountain of eternal day,   20
Could it within the human flower be seen,
      Rememb'ring still its former height,
      Shuns the sweet leaves and blossoms green;
      And recollecting its own light,
Does, in its pure and circling thoughts, express   25
The greater heaven in an heaven less.
      In how coy a figure wound,
      Every way it turns away;
      So the world excluding round,
      Yet receiving in the day;   30
      Dark beneath but bright above,
      Here disdaining, there in love;
      How loose and easy hence to go,
      How girt and ready to ascend;
      Moving but on a point below,   35
      It all about does upwards bend.
Such did the manna's sacred dew distil,
White and entire, though congealed and chill;
Congealed on earth, but does, dissolving, run
Into the glories of th' almighty sun.   40

---

14 *sphere:* i.e., of heaven from whence it came. 18 *exhale:* cause to be emitted as vapor. 24 *recollecting:* gathering together again. 27 *coy:* quiet, retiring. *wound:* turned this way and that. 29 *excluding round:* shutting out in every direction. 37 *manna's sacred dew:* See Exodus 16:13–21. *distil:* fall in drops. 38 *entire:* perfect, undivided. 39 *dissolving:* disunite (cf. *entire*), melt. 40 *glories:* circles of prismatic colors surrounding the sun. *sun:* (pun) sun and Son of God.

The Coronet

When for the thorns with which I long, too long,
   With many a piercing wound
   My Savior's head have crowned,
I seek with garlands to redress that wrong;
   Through every garden, every mead, 5
I gather flowers (my fruits are only flowers),
   Dismantling all the fragrant towers
That once adorned my shepherdess's head.
And now when I have summed up all my store,
   Thinking, so I myself deceive, 10
   So rich a chaplet thence to weave
As never yet the King of Glory wore,
   Alas, I find the serpent old
   That twining in his speckled breast
   About the flowers disguised does fold 15
   With wreaths of fame and interest.
Ah, foolish man, that wouldst debase with them
And mortal glory, heaven's diadem!
But thou who only couldst the serpent tame,
Either his slipp'ry knots at once untie 20
And disentangle all his winding snare,
Or shatter too with him my curious frame
And let these wither so that he may die,
Though set with skill and chosen out with care,
That they, while thou on both their spoils dost tread, 25
May crown thy feet, that could not crown thy head.

THE CORONET. 1 *thorns:* See John 19:2. 4 *garlands:* of flowers and figuratively, in the pastoral tradition, collections of poems. Cf. "posy," a bouquet of flowers, and also the accompanying verse. 20 *knots:* intertwining coils of the serpent parallel to the knots that bind the flowers into *garlands*. 22 *curious frame:* carefully wrought structure (i.e., *garlands* and also poems). 23 *these:* i.e., flowers. 25 *tread:* See Luke 10:18–19.

HENRY VAUGHAN
1621–1693

from SILEX SCINTILLANS

The Retreat

Happy those early days! when I
Shin'd in my Angel-infancy.
Before I understood this place
Appointed for my second race,
Or taught my soul to fancy ought   5
But a white, celestial thought,
When yet I had not walkt above
A mile, or two, from my first love,
And looking back (at that short space),
Could see a glimpse of his bright-face;   10
When on some gilded cloud, or flow'r
My gazing soul would dwell an hour,
And in those weaker glories spy
Some shadows of eternity;
Before I taught my tongue to wound   15
My conscience with a sinful sound,
Or had the black art to dispense
A sev'ral sin to ev'ry sense,
But felt through all this fleshy dress
Bright shoots of everlastingness.   20

O how I long to travel back
And tread again that ancient track!
That I might once more reach that plain,
Where first I left my glorious train,
From whence th' enlightened spirit sees   25
That shady City of Palm Trees;
But (ah!) my soul with too much stay
Is drunk, and staggers in the way.
Some men a forward motion love,
But I by backward steps would move,   30

SILEX SCINTILLANS. I.e., Sparks from the Flint.

THE RETREAT. 4 *second race:* implies a first race in heaven prior to birth. *Race* or "course" is the biblical expression for the circuit of one's life. See Heb. 21:1 and 2 Tim. 4:7. 17 *black art:* sorcery, black magic. 18 *sev'ral:* particular. 24 *train:* retinue of angels. 25–26 *From . . . Trees:* As Moses on Mt. Pisgah just before he died was permitted a vision of the land of Gilead and ". . . the plain of the valley of Jericho, the city of palm trees" (Deut. 34:1–3). 27 *stay:* stopping, continued sojourn.

174

And when this dust falls to the urn
In that state I came return.

The Morning-Watch

O joys! infinite sweetness! with what flow'rs,
And shoots of glory, my soul breaks, and buds!
    All the long hours
    Of night, and rest
    Through the still shrouds   5
    Of sleep, and clouds,
  This dew fell on my breast;
    O how it bloods,
And spirits all my earth! hark! In what rings,
And hymning circulations the quick world   10
    Awakes, and sings!
    The rising winds,
    And falling springs,
    Birds, beasts, all things
  Adore him in their kinds.   15
    Thus all is hurl'd
In sacred hymns, and order, the great chime
And symphony of Nature. Prayer is
    The world in tune,
    A spirit-voice,   20
    And vocal joys
  Whose echo is heav'n's bliss.
    O let me climb
When I lie down! The pious soul by night
Is like a clouded star, whose beams though said   25
    To shed their light
    Under some cloud,
    Yet are above,
    And shine, and move
  Beyond that misty shroud.   30
    So in my bed,

THE MORNING-WATCH. 2 *breaks:* puts forth new buds. 5 *shrouds:* Since sleep is "death's second self," *shroud*, the winding sheet of the dead, suggests the appropriate covering for the sleeping living. 7 *dew:* i.e., the regenerative water of grace. 8 *bloods:* literally, stains with blood; figuratively, excites, rouses, confirms. May also suggest the regenerative power of the Blood of Christ. 9 *spirits . . . earth:* both animates my body and animates the natural world. *rings:* peals (as of bells) as well as circular or spiral courses. 10 *quick:* living, animate. 15 *in their kinds:* according to their natures. 16 *hurl'd:* whirled.

That curtain'd grave, though sleep, like ashes, hide
My lamp, and life, both shall in Thee abide.

The World

1

I saw Eternity the other night
Like a great ring of pure and endless light,
    All calm, as it was bright,
And round beneath it, Time in hours, days, years
      Driv'n by the spheres   5
Like a vast shadow mov'd, in which the world
    And all her train were hurl'd;
The doting Lover in his quaintest strain
    Did there complain,
Near him, his lute, his fancy, and his flights,   10
    Wit's sour delights,
With gloves and knots, the silly snares of pleasure,
    Yet his dear treasure
All scatter'd lay, while he his eyes did pour
    Upon a flow'r.   15

2

The darksome Statesman hung with weights and woe
Like a thick midnight-fog mov'd there so slow
    He did not stay, nor go;
Condemning thoughts (like sad eclipses) scowl
    Upon his soul,   20
And clouds of crying witnesses without
    Pursued him with one shout.
Yet digg'd the Mole, and lest his ways be found
    Workt under ground,
Where he did clutch his prey, but one did see   25
    That policy,
Churches and altars fed him, perjuries
    Were gnats and flies,
It rain'd about him blood and tears, but he
    Drank them as free.   30

32 *curtain'd grave:* i.e., his canopied bed.

THE WORLD. 5 *spheres:* the concentric spheres of Ptolemaic astronomy.
7 *hurl'd:* whirled. 8 *quaintest:* most whimsical and ingenious. 10 *flights:*
i.e., affected, exaggerated poetry. 21 *clouds . . . witnesses:* See Heb. 12:1.
26 *policy:* i.e., Machiavellian duplicity and cunning stratagems. 28 *gnats and*
flies: i.e., perjuries were as inconsequential as *gnats and flies.* 30 *as free:* freely.

176

3

The fearful Miser on a heap of rust
Sat pining all his life there, did scarce trust
    His own hands with the dust,
Yet would not place one piece above, but lives
    In fear of thieves. 35
Thousands there were as frantic as himself
    And hugg'd each one his pelf,
The downright Epicure plac'd heav'n in sense
    And scorn'd pretense
While others slipt into a wide excess 40
    Said little less;
The weaker sort slight, trivial wares enslave
    Who think them brave,
And poor, despised Truth sat counting by
    Their victory. 45

4

Yet some, who all this while did weep and sing,
And sing, and weep, soar'd up into the ring,
    But most would use no wing.
O fools (said I), thus to prefer dark night
    Before true light, 50
To live in grots, and caves, and hate the day
    Because it shows the way,
The way which from this dead and dark abode
    Leads up to God,
A way where you might tread the sun, and be 55
    More bright than he.
But as I did their madness so discuss
    One whisper'd thus,
This ring the Bridegroom did for none provide
    But for his Bride. 60

All that is in the world, the lust of the flesh, the lust of the eyes, and the pride of life, is not of the Father, but is of the world.

And the world passeth away, and the lusts thereof, but he that doth the will of God abideth for ever.

[I John 2:16–17]

34 *place:* invest. *piece above:* Cf. "But lay up for yourselves treasures in heaven, where neither moth nor rust doth corrupt, and where thieves do not break through nor steal: For where your treasure is, there will your heart be also" (Matt. 6:20–21). 37 *pelf:* ill-gotten or stolen riches. 38 *downright:* absolute. *plac'd . . . sense:* found heaven in sensual indulgence. 43 *brave:* splendid. 44 *counting:* considerably. 59–60 *This . . . Bride:* reference to the marriage of Christ and the Church, the Bride of the Lamb. See Rev. 21:9.

They are all gone into the world of light

They are all gone into the world of light!
    And I alone sit ling'ring here;
Their very memory is fair and bright,
    And my sad thoughts doth clear.

It glows and glitters in my cloudy breast   5
    Like stars upon some gloomy grove,
Or those faint beams in which this hill is drest,
    After the Sun's remove.

I see them walking in an air of glory,
    Whose light doth trample on my days: 10
My days, which are at best but dull and hoary,
    Mere glimmering and decays.

O holy hope! and high humility,
    High as the Heavens above!
These are your walks, and you have shew'd them me   15
    To kindle my cold love,

Dear, beauteous death! the Jewel of the Just,
    Shining no where, but in the dark;
What mysteries do lie beyond thy dust;
    Could man outlook that mark!   20

He that hath found some fledg'd birds' nest, may know
    At first sight, if the bird be flown;
But what fair Well, or Grove he sings in now,
    That is to him unknown.

And yet, as Angels in some brighter dreams   25
    Call to the soul, when man doth sleep:
So some strange thoughts transcend our wonted themes,
    And into glory peep.

If a star were confin'd into a Tomb
    Her captive flames must needs burn there;   30
But when the hand that lockt her up, gives room,
    She'll shine through all the sphere.

THEY ARE ALL GONE. 4 *clear:* brighten. 5 *It:* i.e., *Their very memory,*
l. 3. 20 *mark:* boundary. 23 *Well:* spring or fountain. 31 *gives room:*
gives her opportunity.

178

O Father of eternal life, and all
   Created glories under thee!
Resume thy spirit from this world of thrall   35
   Into true liberty.

Either disperse these mists, which blot and fill
   My perspective (still) as they pass,
Or else remove me hence unto that hill,
    Where I shall need no glass.   40

Cock-Crowing

Father of lights! what sunny seed,
What glance of day hast thou confin'd
Into this bird? To all the breed
This busy ray thou hast assign'd;
        Their magnetism works all night,   5
        And dreams of paradise and light.

Their eyes watch for the morning hue,
Their little grain expelling night
So shines and sings, as if it knew
The path unto the house of light.   10
        It seems their candle, howe'er done,
        Was tinn'd and lighted at the sun.

If such a tincture, such a touch,
So firm a longing can impow'r

35 *Resume:* take back. *spirit:* i.e., the poet's, which belongs to God. 38 *perspective:* i.e., perspective glass, a telescope, as well as the view seen through it. 40 *Where . . . glass:* i.e., face to face. Cf. "Whom I shall see for myself, and mine eyes shall behold . . . ." (Job 19:27) and the opening sentences for the Order for the Burial of the Dead in the *Book of Common Prayer.* Cf. also I Cor. 13:12 (but "glass" there means "mirror"), and also 2 Cor. 3:18.

COCK-CROWING. According to the *Bestiary,* the crowing of the cock vivifies the spirit and restores faith, since Peter, after denying Christ thrice before cock crow (Matt. 26:34, 69–75) wept bitterly, and "by testifying devotedly after cock-crow . . . washed away the sin of the church" that he had incurred by denying Christ (tr. T. H. White). Also, Christian tradition has long associated the office of the cock with that of the priest. See also Don Cameron Allen, "Vaughan's 'Cock-Crowing' and the Tradition," *ELH* (1954), pp. 94–106. 1 *Father of lights:* See James 1:17: "Every good gift and every perfect gift is from above, and cometh from the Father of lights, with whom there is no variableness, neither shadow of turning." 5 *magnetism:* the mysterious power in the cock that draws him to the *light.* 8 *grain:* Cf. *seed,* l. 1; also a scarlet dye, cochineal, that produces a tincture (Cf. l. 13). *Seed* and *grain* may also suggest the elements (bread and wine) of the Holy Communion. 13 *tincture:* in alchemy, the spiritual *seed* mysteriously infused in the material bird. *touch:* touchstone, which tests and proves.

Shall thy own image think it much   15
To watch for thy appearing hour?
        If a mere blast so fill the sail,
        Shall not the breath of God prevail?

O thou immortal light and heat!
Whose hand so shines through all this frame,   20
That by the beauty of the seat,
We plainly see, who made the same.
        Seeing thy seed abides in me,
        Dwell thou in it, and I in thee.

To sleep without thee, is to die;   25
Yea, 'tis a death partakes of hell:
For where thou dost not close the eye
It never opens, I can tell.
        In such a dark, Egyptian border,
        The shades of death dwell and disorder.   30

If joys, and hopes, and earnest throws,
And hearts, whose pulse beats still for light,
Are given to birds; who, but thee, knows
A love-sick soul's exalted flight?
        Can souls be track'd by any eye   35
        But his, who gave them wings to fly?

15 *thy own image:* i.e., man.   20 *frame:* universe.   21 *seat:* the earth, man's dwelling place.   29 *Egyptian border:* darkness of the Egyptian land. See Exodus 10:21–23 for the "plague" of "thick darkness" that God caused there. 31 *throws:* throes, efforts.   37 *veil:* that which "divides between the holy place and the most holy" in which are placed the mercy seat and the ark of the testimony. See Exodus 26:33–34.   See also Matt. 27:51 for the rending of the veil, which symbolizes the full access to the presence and knowledge of God that had been denied by the veil and that was made possible by the sacrifice of Christ. See also 2 Cor. 3:12–18 for the "veil" that blinds the hearts and minds of men committed to the "reading of the old testament," and not to the "liberty" that the New gives to those who, by turning to the Lord, have the "veil" taken away so that they "with open face beholding as in a glass the glory of the Lord" may be changed "into the same image from glory to glory." See also Heb. 10:19–20 where *veil* is used figuratively as the "flesh" of Christ broken for man's salvation. *Veil* in this context may suggest both any curtain or covering, which separates man from sight of the divine light of God's eyes, and the Eucharist in the symbolism of the sacramental veils, which cover the chalice and elements, the Body of Christ broken for man; *fractions* (l. 42), as the liturgical act of breaking the eucharistic bread, may also suggest the latter (*fractions* also means deflected, refracted light). *Cock, seed,* and *grain* also have eucharistic connotations. In the Holy Communion men enter into the presence of the light of God sacramentally and symbolically, but, because they are men, imperfectly and incompletely. Only in the Resurrection will man see God.

Only this veil which thou hast broke,
And must be broken yet in me,
This veil, I say, is all the cloak
And cloud which shadows thee from me.   40
      This veil thy full-eyed love denies,
      And only gleams and fractions spies.

O take it off! make no delay,
But brush me with thy light, that I
May shine unto a perfect day,   45
And warm me at thy glorious eye!
      O take it off! or till it flee,
      Though with no lily, stay with me!

Quickness

False life! a foil and no more, when
      Wilt thou be gone?
Thou foul deception of all men
That would not have the true come on.

Thou art a moon-like toil; a blind   5
      Self-posing state;
A dark contest of waves and wind;
A mere tempestuous debate.

Life is a fix'd, discerning light,
      A knowing joy;   10
No chance, or fit: but ever bright,
And calm and full, yet doth not cloy.

---

48 *Through . . . me:* See Matt. 6:28–29 and Luke 12:27, where the *lily* is
"arrayed" (i.e., *brushed* by the light of the *glorious eye* of God, i.e., Christ) so
that it outshines "Solomon in all his glory." See also Song of Sol. 2:16 and
6:3, where in the mystical interpretation of Christ the Bridegroom's love for his
Church, he "feedeth his flock among the lilies," warming them with his glance
and bringing to his [the poet's] "Cold thoughts a lively sense of spring" (see
Vaughan's "Mount of Olives," l. 20). Although the poet is "unworthy" to be
called a *lily*, yet the *seed abides* (l. 23) in him; hence he can pray that God
may *stay* with him until he attains everlasting life.

  QUICKNESS. 1 *foil:* leaf of bright metal used to set off an inferior stone that
has no light of its own. 4 *true:* true life. 5 *moon-like toil:* (used with multiple
meanings) confusion; harassing labor, because the moon waxes and wanes,
causes the tides to ebb and flow, and signifies (by eclipses and rings) drastic
weather changes; also a snare (*toil*) because of its delusive beauty. Cf. *fix'd light*,
l. 9. 6 *Self-posing:* self-puzzling.

'Tis such a blissful thing, that still
                    Doth vivify,
And shine and smile, and hath the skill   15
To please without eternity.

Thou art a toilsome mole, or less
                    A moving mist.
But life is, what none can express,
A quickness, which my God hath kist.   20

The Queer

O tell me whence that joy doth spring
Whose diet is divine and fair,
Which wears heaven, like a bridal ring,
And tramples on doubts and despair?

Whose eastern traffic deals in bright   5
And boundless empyrean themes,
Mountains of spice, day-stars and light,
Green trees of life, and living streams?

Tell me, O tell who did thee bring
And here, without my knowledge, plac'd,   10
Till thou didst grow and get a wing,
A wing with eyes, and eyes that taste?

17 *Thou:* false life.   20 *quickness:* state of being alive, vivified by God's kiss;
also, rapidity of movement, as opposed to the *toilsome* effort of the *mole*.

THE QUEER.   Very probably *Queer* means simultaneously "odd," "whimsical," "eccentric"; and because *queer* is an obsolete spelling of *quire*, a "little
book" or "poem," possibly a reference to Revelation and the Song of Solomon,
the principal sources of imagery of the poem. Also, since the verb *quire* means
"inquire," it can mean "question" or "query." Note that the first three stanzas
are questions.   3 *ring:* Cf. "The World," ll. 59–60 and note.   5 *eastern
traffic:* i.e., the spice and jewel trade with India, a metaphor for the soul's
traffic with Christ and the Heavenly Jerusalem, also *eastern*.   6 *empyrean:* of
the region of pure light and fire of the highest heaven.   7 *spice:* See Song of
Sol. 4:15–16.   *day-stars:* the "bright and morning star" of Rev. 22:16–17.
8 *Green . . . streams:* See Rev. 22:1–2.   12 *wing . . . taste:* whimsical paradox, perhaps derived from the vision of heavenly creatures of Ezek. 1:6–14
and Rev. 4:6–8 and from the account in the *Bestiary* of the eagle, which renews
its strength and eyesight by flying directly into the sun and then by bathing in
the fountain.

Sure, holiness the magnet is,
And love the lure, that woos thee down;
Which makes the high transcendent bliss   15
Of knowing thee, so rarely known.

from THALIA REDIVIVA

The Revival

Unfold, unfold! take in his light,
Who makes thy cares more short than night.
The joys, which with his Day-star rise,
He deals to all, but drowsy eyes:
And what the men of this world miss,   5
Some drops and dews of future bliss.
    Hark! how his winds have chang'd their note,
And with warm whispers call thee out.
The frosts are past, the storms are gone:
And backward life at last comes on.   10
The lofty groves in express joys
Reply unto the turtle's voice,
And here in dust and dirt, O here
The lilies of his love appear!

13 *magnet:* Cf. "Cock-Crowing," l. 5.

THE REVIVAL. 3 *Day-star:* Christ. See "The Queer," l. 7. 4 *drowsy eyes:* of man addicted to the darkness of this world. 10 *backward:* Cf. "The Retreat," l. 30. 12 *turtle's:* turtledove's. See Song of Sol. 2:10–13. 14 *lilies:* Cf. "Cock-Crowing," l. 48 and note.

JOHN DRYDEN
1631–1700

from ABSALOM AND ACHITOPHEL

In pious times, e'r Priest-craft did begin,
Before *Polygamy* was made a sin;
When man, on many, multiply'd his kind,
E'r one to one was, cursedly, confind:
When Nature prompted, and no law deny'd   5
Promiscuous use of Concubine and Bride;
Then, *Israel's* Monarch, after Heaven's own heart,
His vigorous warmth did, variously, impart
To Wives and Slaves: And, wide as his Command,
Scatter'd his Maker's Image through the Land.   10
Michal, Of Royal blood, the Crown did wear,
A Soyl ungratefull to the Tiller's care:
Not so the rest; for several Mothers bore
To Godlike *David*, several Sons before.
But since like slaves his bed they did ascend,   15
No True Succession could their seed attend.
Of all this Numerous Progeny was none
So Beautifull, so brave as *Absolon:*

The text is that established by James Kinsley, *The Poems of John Dryden*, Oxford at the Clarendon Press, 1958.

ABSALOM AND ACHITOPHEL. In 1678 the perjurer Titus Oates fabricated the so-called Popish Plot, in which he claimed that the Jesuits were conniving to assassinate the King and his ministers, plotting the invasion of Ireland by the French, intriguing to offer the crown to the Duke of York, and conspiring to massacre the Protestants—allegations that created a violent uproar and were instrumental in causing the judicial murder of some thirty-five supposed conspirators. Two years later, the Whigs under the leadership of the Earl of Shaftesbury (*Achitophel*) tried to capitalize on public fear, religious bigotry, and unrest over the uncertainty of the royal succession by attempting to pass a bill that would exclude King Charles II's brother, James, the Duke of York and an avowed Roman Catholic, from succession to the throne, hoping to supplant him with the Duke of Monmouth (*Absalom*), the Protestant, popular, but illegitimate son of the King (*David*). Charles had no legitimate heirs by his wife, Queen Catharine (*Michal*), but many illegitimate children by his mistresses. The Exclusion Bill was voted down in the House of Lords, and the Earl of Shaftesbury was arrested on charges of treason. Dryden published his 1031-line poem anonymously in 1681 while charges of treason were being presented to the grand jury, obviously trying to encourage the jury to indict the Earl. A week later the grand jury refused to indict him, but the poem was an immediate success.

Dryden bases his political allegory on the Biblical story (2 Sam. 3:13–18) of the conspiracy and rebellion of Absalom against his father, David, thereby attempting to reveal the true characters of the scheming politicians. Political satire in Dryden's time was praised more for its brilliant, witty acrimony, its elegance and vigor of characterization, and its energy and variety of rhyme than for its fairness and accuracy.

Whether, inspir'd by some diviner Lust,
His Father got him with a greater Gust;   20
Or that his Conscious destiny made way
By manly beauty to Imperiall sway.
Early in Foreign fields he won Renown,
With Kings and States ally'd to *Israel's* Crown:
In Peace the thoughts of War he coud remove,   25
And seem'd as he were only born for love.
What e'r he did was done with so much ease,
In him alone, 'twas Natural to please.
His motions all accompanied with grace;
And *Paradise* was open'd in his face.   30
With secret Joy, indulgent *David* view'd
His Youthfull Image in his Son renew'd:
To all his wishes Nothing he deny'd,
And made the Charming *Annabel* his Bride.
What faults he had (for who from faults is free?)   35
His Father coud not, or he woud not see.
Some warm excesses, which the Law forbore,
Were constru'd Youth that purg'd by boyling o'r:
And *Amnon's* Murther, by a specious Name,
Was call'd a Just Revenge for injur'd Fame.   40
Thus Prais'd, and Lov'd, the Noble Youth remain'd,
While *David*, undisturb'd, in *Sion* raign'd.
But Life can never be sincerely blest:
Heaven punishes the bad, and proves the best.
The *Jews*, a Headstrong, Moody, Murmuring race,   45
As ever try'd th' extent and stretch of grace;
God's pamper'd people whom, debauch'd with ease,
No King could govern, nor no God could please;
(Gods they had tri'd of every shape and size
That God-smiths could produce, or Priests devise:)   50
These *Adam*-wits, too fortunately free,
Began to dream they wanted libertie;
And when no rule, no president was found
Of men, by Laws less circumscrib'd and bound,
They led their wild desires to Woods and Caves,   55
And thought that all but Savages were Slaves.

20 *Gust:* zest, enjoyment. 39 *Amnon's Murther:* See 2 Sam. 13:1–29. Amnon, another son of David, raped Tamar, Absalom's sister, and was later murdered at the instigation of Absalom. The allusion here is to some brutal attack that Monmouth's bullies had committed on his orders. 45 *Jews:* the English. 49–50 *Gods . . . devise:* reference to religious controversy and theological disputes from the time of Henry VIII to the end of the seventeenth century. 51 *Adam-wits:* fools, like Adam, who did not know a good thing when they had it. 52 *wanted:* lacked. 56 *Savages were Slaves:* reference to primitivistic theories about the noble savage uncorrupted by civilization.

They who when *Saul* was dead, without a blow,
Made foolish *Ishbosheth* the Crown forgo;
Who banisht *David* did from *Hebron* bring,
And, with a Generall Shout, proclaim'd him King: 60
Those very *Jewes*, who, at their very best,
Their Humour more than Loyalty exprest,
Now, wondred why, so long, they had obey'd
An Idoll Monarch which their hands had made:
Thought they might ruine him they could create;   65
Or melt him to that Golden Calf, a State.
But these were randome bolts: No form'd Design,
Nor Interest made the Factious Croud to joyn:
The sober part of *Israel*, free from stain,
Well knew the value of a peacefull raign: 70
And, looking backward with a wise afright,
Saw Seames of wounds, dishonest to the sight;
In contemplation of whose ugly Scars,
They Curst the memory of Civil Wars.
The moderate sort of Men, thus qualifi'd,   75
Inclin'd the Ballance to the better side:
And *David's* mildness manag'd it so well,
The Bad found no occasion to Rebell.
But, when to Sin our byast Nature leans,
The carefull Devil is still at hand with means;   80
And providently Pimps for ill desires:
The Good old Cause reviv'd, a Plot requires.
Plots, true or false, are necessary things,
To raise up Common-wealths, and ruin Kings.
    Th' inhabitants of old *Jerusalem*   85
Were *Jebusites:* the Town so call'd from them;
And their's the Native right—
But when the chosen people grew more strong,
The rightfull cause at length became the wrong:
And every loss the men of *Jebus* bore,   90
They still were thought God's enemies the more.
Thus, worn and weaken'd, well or ill content,
Submit they must to *David's* Government:

57 *Saul:* i.e., Oliver Cromwell.   58 *Ishbosheth:* i.e., Cromwell's ineffective
son, Richard.   59 *Hebron:* where David had been annointed king; refers here
to Scotland, where Charles had been crowned before his state coronation in
London.   62 *Humour:* peculiar whim.   66 *Golden Calf:* See Exodus 32:1–4.
67 *bolts:* shots.   68 *joyn:* pronounced *jine.*   74 *Civil Wars:* the wars between
Charles I and Parliament, 1642–46 and 1648–51, which cost Charles his head in
1649.   79 *byast:* biased.   80 *still:* always.   82 *Good old Cause:* i.e., that of
the Puritan Revolution.   85 *Jerusalem:* i.e., London.   86 *Jebusites:* descendants of a son of Canaan, son of Ham, who long withstood the Israelites, and
who were the original inhabitants of Jerusalem until dispossessed by David;
here, the Roman Catholics.   88 *chosen people:* the Jews, i.e., the Protestants.

186

Impoverisht, and depriv'd of all Command,
Their Taxes doubled as they lost their Land,   95
And, what was harder yet to flesh and blood,
Their Gods disgrac'd, and burnt like common wood.
This set the Heathen Priesthood in a flame;
For Priests of all Religions are the same:
Of whatsoe'r descent their Godhead be,   100
Stock, Stone, or other homely pedigree,
In his defence his Servants are as bold
As if he had been born of beaten gold.
The *Jewish Rabbins* thô their Enemies,
In this conclude them honest men and wise: 105
For 'twas their duty, all the Learned think,
T'espouse his Cause by whom they eat and drink.
From hence began that Plot, the Nation's Curse,
Bad in it self, but represented worse.
Rais'd in extremes, and in extremes decry'd;   110
With Oaths affirm'd, with dying Vows deny'd.
Not weigh'd, or winnow'd by the Multitude;
But swallow'd in the Mass, unchew'd and Crude.
Some Truth there was, but dash'd and brew'd with Lyes;
To please the Fools, and puzzle all the Wise.   115
Succeeding times did equal folly call,
Believing nothing, or believing all.
Th' *Egyptian* Rites the *Jebusites* imbrac'd;
Where Gods were recommended by their Tast.
Such savory Deities must needs be good,   120
As serv'd at once for Worship and for Food.
By force they could not Introduce these Gods;
For Ten to One, in former days was odds.
So Fraud was us'd, (the Sacrificers trade,)
Fools are more hard to Conquer than Perswade.   125
Their busie Teachers mingled with the *Jews;*
And rak'd, for Converts, even the Court and Stews:
Which *Hebrew* Priests the more unkindly took,
Because the Fleece accompanies the Flock.
Some thought they God's Anointed meant to Slay   130

104 *Rabbins:* Rabbis, i.e., the clergy of the Church of England. 108 *Plot:* the Popish Plot of 1678. 111 *dying Vows:* i.e., of those about to be executed for crimes they had not committed. 118 *Egyptian:* i.e., French. 121 *Food:* blasphemous reference to the Roman Catholic doctrine of Transubstantiation. 123 *Ten to One:* traditional odds that one Englishman can whip ten Frenchmen. 126 *Teachers:* the Jesuits, popularly thought to be crafty intriguers. 127 *Stews:* brothels. Some of Charles' mistresses were Catholics, said to be "planted" by the Jesuits to convert him. 128 *Hebrew Priests:* i.e., Anglican clergy. 129 *Fleece:* i.e., tithes. 130 *God's Anointed:* the King. Cf. I Sam. 16:1-13.

By Guns, invented since full many a day:
Our Authour swears it not; but who can know
How far the Devil and *Jebusites* may go?
This Plot, which fail'd for want of common Sense,
Had yet a deep and dangerous Consequence: 135
For, as when raging Fevers boyl the Blood,
The standing Lake soon floats into a Flood;
And every hostile Humour, which before
Slept quiet in its Channels, bubbles o'r:
So, several Factions from this first Ferment,   140
Work up to Foam, and threat the Government.
Some by their Friends, more by themselves thought wise,
Oppos'd the Power, to which they could not rise.
Some had in Courts been Great, and thrown from thence,
Like Feinds, were harden'd in Impenitence.   145
Some by their Monarch's fatal mercy grown,
From Pardon'd Rebels, Kinsmen to the Throne;
Were rais'd in Power and publick Office high:
Strong Bands, if Bands ungratefull men could tye.
   Of these the false *Achitophel* was first: 150
A Name to all succeeding Ages Curst.
For close Designs, and crooked Counsels fit;
Sagacious, Bold, and Turbulent of wit:
Restless, unfixt in Principles and Place;
In Power unpleas'd, impatient of Disgrace.   155
A fiery Soul, which working out its way,
Fretted the Pigmy Body to decay:
And o'r inform'd the Tenement of Clay.
A daring Pilot in extremity;
Pleas'd with the Danger, when the Waves went high   160
He sought the Storms; but for a Calm unfit,
Would Steer too nigh the Sands, to boast his Wit.
Great Wits are sure to Madness near ally'd;
And thin Partitions do their Bounds divide:
Else, why should he, with Wealth and Honour blest,   165
Refuse his Age the needful hours of Rest?
Punish a Body which he coud not please;
Bankrupt of Life, yet Prodigal of Ease?
And all to leave, what with his Toyl he won,
To that unfeather'd, two Leg'd thing, a Son.   170
Got, while his Soul did hudled Notions try;

138 *hostile Humour:* an overabundance of one of the four humours—yellow
bile, black bile, phlegm, and blood—was believed to upset the balance of bodily
fluids and produce an exaggerated psychological condition.   149 *Bands:*
bonds.   152 *close:* secret.   171 *Got . . . try:* begotten while Achitophal was
thinking about confused and disordered ideas (so that his son was as confused
as his conception).

And born a shapeless Lump, like Anarchy.
In Friendship False, Implacable in Hate:
Resolv'd to Ruine or to Rule the State.
To Compass this the Triple Bond he broke;   175
The Pillars of the publick Safety shook:
And fitted *Israel* for a Foreign Yoke.
Then, seiz'd with Fear, yet still affecting Fame,
Unsurp'd a Patriott's All-attoning Name.
So easie still it proves in Factious Times,   180
With publick Zeal to cancel private Crimes:
How safe is Treason, and how sacred ill,
Where none can sin against the Peoples Will:
Where Crouds can wink; and no offence be known,
Since in anothers guilt they find their own.   185
Yet, Fame deserv'd, no Enemy can grudge;
The Statesman we abhor, but praise the Judge.
In *Israels* Courts ne'r sat an *Abbethdin*
With more discerning Eyes, or Hands more clean:
Unbrib'd, unsought, the Wretched to redress;   190
Swift of Dispatch, and easie of Access.
Oh, had he been content to serve the Crown,
With vertues only proper to the Gown;
Or, had the rankness of the Soyl been freed
From Cockle, that opprest the Noble seed: 195
David, for him his tunefull Harp had strung,
And Heaven had wanted one Immortal song.
But wilde Ambition loves to slide, not stand;
And Fortunes Ice prefers to Vertues Land:
Achitophel, grown weary to possess   200
A lawfull Fame, and lazy Happiness;
Disdain'd the Golden fruit to gather free,
And lent the Croud his Arm to shake the Tree.
Now, manifest of Crimes, contriv'd long since,
He stood at bold Defiance with his Prince: 205
Held up the Buckler of the Peoples Cause,
Against the Crown; and sculk'd behind the Laws.
The wish'd occasion of the Plot he takes,
Some Circumstances finds, but more he makes.
By buzzing Emissaries, fills the ears   210

175 *Triple Bond:* the Triple Alliance of England, Holland, and Sweden against
France, made in 1668 and broken in 1670 with the war against Holland.
180 *Factious:* turbulent because of conflicting political factions.   183 *Peoples
Will:* i.e., that of the London mob, a potent factor in Restoration and
eighteenth-century English politics.   188 *Abbethdin:* an officer of the high
court of the Jews; Shaftesbury had been Lord Chancellor and as honest and
just as Dryden describes him.   193 *Gown:* i.e., office of the judge.   195 *Cockle:*
a weed common in grainfields.   197 *Immortal song:* i.e., a psalm.

Of listning Crowds, with Jealosies and Fears
Of Arbitrary Counsels brought to light,
And proves the King himself a *Jebusite:*
Weak Arguments! which yet he knew full well,
Were strong with People easie to Rebell.   215
For, govern'd by the *Moon*, the giddy *Jews*
Tread the same track when she the Prime renews:
And once in twenty Years, their Scribes Record,
By natural Instinct they change their Lord.
Achitophel still wants a Chief, and none   220
Was found so fit as Warlike *Absolon:*
Not, that he wish'd his Greatness to create,
(For Polititians neither love nor hate:)
But, for he knew, his Title not allow'd,
Would keep him still depending on the Crowd: 225
That Kingly power, thus ebbing out, might be
Drawn to the dregs of a Democracy.
Him he attempts, with studied Arts to please,
And sheds his Venome, in such words as these.
    Auspicious Prince! at whose Nativity   230
Some Royal Planet rul'd the Southern sky;
Thy longing Countries Darling and Desire;
Their cloudy Pillar, and their guardian Fire:
Their second *Moses*, whose extended Wand
Divides the Seas, and shews the promis'd Land: 235
Whose dawning Day, in every distant age,
Has exercis'd the Sacred Prophets rage:
The Peoples Prayer, the glad Deviners Theam,
The Young-mens Vision, and the Old mens Dream!
Thee, *Saviour*, Thee, the Nations Vows confess;   240
And, never satisfi'd with seeing, bless:
Swift, unbespoken Pomps, thy steps proclaim,
And stammerring Babes are taught to lisp thy Name.
How long wilt thou the general Joy detain;
Starve, and defraud the People of thy Reign?   245
Content ingloriously to pass thy days
Like one of Vertues Fools that feeds on Praise;
Till thy fresh Glories, which now shine so bright,
Grow Stale and Tarnish with our daily sight.
Believe me, Royal Youth, thy Fruit must be,   250
Or gather'd Ripe, or rot upon the Tree.
Heav'n, has to all allotted, soon or late,
Some lucky Revolution of their Fate:

224 *not allow'd:* because he was an illegitimate son.   233 *Pillar . . . Fire:*
See Exodus 13:21.   237 *rage:* ecstasy.   251 *Or:* Either.

Whose Motions, if we watch and guide with Skill,
(For humane Good depends on humane Will,)   255
Our Fortune rolls, as from a smooth Descent,
And, from the first Impression, takes the Bent:
But, if unseiz'd, she glides away like wind;
And leaves repenting Folly far behind.
Now, now she meets you, with a glorious prize,   260
And spreads her Locks before her as she flies.
Had thus Old *David*, from whose Loyns you spring,
Not dar'd, when Fortune call'd him, to be King,
At *Gath* an Exile he might still remain,
And heavens Anointing Oyle had been in vain.   265
Let his successfull Youth your hopes engage,
But shun th' example of Declining Age:
Behold him setting in his Western Skies,
The Shadows lengthning as the Vapours rise.
He is not now, as when on *Jordan's* Sand   270
The Joyfull People throng'd to see him Land,
Cov'ring the *Beach*, and blackning all the *Strand*:
But, like the Prince of Angels from his height,
Comes tumbling downward with diminish'd light;
Betray'd by one poor Plot to publick Scorn,   275
(Our only blessing since his Curst Return:)
Those heaps of People which one Sheaf did bind,
Blown off and scatter'd by a puff of Wind.
What strength can he to your Designs oppose,
Naked of Friends, and round beset with Foes?   280
If *Pharaoh's* doubtfull Succour he shoud use,
A Foreign Aid woud more Incense the *Jews*:
Proud *Egypt* woud dissembled Friendship bring;
Foment the War, but not support the King:
Nor woud the Royal Party e'r unite   285
With *Pharaoh's* Arms, t'assist the *Jebusite*;
Or if they shoud, their Interest soon woud break,
And with such odious Aid make *David* weak.
All sorts of men by my successfull Arts,
Abhorring Kings, estrange their alter'd Hearts   290
From *David's* Rule: And 'tis the general Cry,
Religion, Common-wealth, and Liberty.
If you as Champion of the publique Good,

261 *Locks:* the forelock by which one seizes Fortune. 264 *Gath:* i.e., Brussels, where Charles had in exile sought refuge, as David had found refuge among the Philistines. See 1 Sam. 27:1–3. 270–72 *He . . . strand:* reference to the landing of the youthful Charles at Dover, May 1, 1660. 273 *Prince of Angels:* Lucifer falling to become Satan. 281 *Pharaoh's doubtfull Succour:* aid from King Louis XIV of France.

Add to their Arms a Chief of Royal Blood;
What may not *Israel* hope, and what Applause   295
Might such a General gain by such a Cause?
Not barren Praise alone, that Gaudy Flower,
Fair only to the sight, but solid Power:
And Nobler is a limited Command,
Giv'n by the Love of all your Native Land,   300
Than a Successive Title, Long, and Dark,
Drawn from the Mouldy Rolls of *Noah's* Ark.
   What cannot Praise effect in Mighty Minds,
When Flattery Sooths, and when Ambition Blinds!
Desire of Power, on Earth a Vitious Weed,   305
Yet, sprung from High, is of Cælestial Seed:
In God 'tis Glory: And when men Aspire,
'Tis but a Spark too much of Heavenly Fire.
Th' Ambitious Youth, too Covetous of Fame,
Too full of Angells Metal in his Frame;   310
Unwarily was led from Vertues ways;
Made Drunk with Honour, and Debauch'd with Praise.
Half loath, and half consenting to the Ill,
(For Loyal Blood within him strugled still)
He thus reply'd—And what Pretence have I   315
To take up Arms for Publick Liberty?
My Father Governs with unquestion'd Right;
The Faiths Defender, and Mankinds Delight:
Good, Gracious, Just, observant of the Laws;   .
And Heav'n by Wonders has Espous'd his Cause.   320
Whom has he Wrong'd in all his Peaceful Reign?
Who sues for Justice to his Throne in Vain?
What Millions has he Pardon'd of his Foes,
Whom Just Revenge did to his Wrath expose?
Mild, Easy, Humble, Studious of our Good;   325
Enclin'd to Mercy, and averse from Blood.
If Mildness Ill with Stubborn *Israel* Suite,
His Crime is God's beloved Attribute.
What could he gain, his People to Betray,
Or change his Right, for Arbitrary Sway?   330
Let Haughty *Pharoah* Curse with such a Reign,
His Fruitfull *Nile*, and Yoak a Servile Train.
If *David's* Rule *Jerusalem* Displease,
The *Dog-star* heats their Brains to this Disease.

---

305 *Vitious:* vicious. 310 *Metal:* mettle, courage. 318 *Faiths Defender:*
Since the time of Henry VIII, Defender of the Faith has been one of the official
titles of the King of England. 334 *Dog-star:* Sirius, when in its zenith in
late August, was thought to burn vegetation black and bring madness and
pestilence.

Why then shoud I, Encouraging the Bad,   335
Turn Rebell, and run Popularly Mad?
Were he a Tyrant who, by Lawless Might,
Opprest the *Jews*, and Rais'd the *Jebusite*,
Well might I Mourn; but Natures Holy Bands
Woud Curb my Spirits, and Restrain my Hands: 340
The People might assert their Liberty;
But what was Right in them, were Crime in me.
His Favour leaves me nothing to require;
Prevents my Wishes, and outruns Desire.
What more can I expect while *David* lives,   345
All but his Kingly Diadem he gives;
And that: But there he Paus'd; then Sighing, said,
Is Justly Destin'd for a Worthier Head.
For when my Father from his Toyls shall Rest,
And late Augment the Number of the Blest: 350
His Lawfull Issue shall the Throne ascend,
Or the *Collateral* Line where that shall end.
His Brother, though Opprest with Vulgar Spight,
Yet Dauntless and Secure of Native Right,
Of every Royal Vertue stands possest;   355
Still Dear to all the Bravest, and the Best.
His Courage Foes, his Friends his Truth Proclaim;
His Loyalty the King, the World his Fame.
His Mercy even th' Offending Crowd will find,
For sure he comes of a Forgiving Kind.   360
Why shoud I then Repine at Heavens Decree;
Which gives me no Pretence to Royalty?
Yet oh that Fate Propitiously Enclind,
Had rais'd my Birth, or had debas'd my Mind;
To my large Soul, not all her Treasure lent,   365
And then Betray'd it to a mean Descent.
I find, I find my mounting Spirits Bold,
And *David's* Part disdains my Mothers Mold.
Why am I Scanted by a Niggard Birth?
My Soul Disclaims the Kindred of her Earth: 370
And made for Empire, Whispers me within;
Desire of Greatness is a Godlike Sin.

[from Part I]

339 *Bands:* the natural bond of obedience of child to father.   344 *Prevents:*
anticipates.   352 *Collateral Line:* descended in a parallel line from a common
ancestor, i.e., Charles I.   353 *Brother:* the Duke of York, later James II.

Mac Flecknoe

All humane things are subject to decay,
And, when Fate summons, Monarchs must obey:
This *Fleckno* found, who like *Augustus*, young
Was call'd to Empire, and had govern'd long:
In Prose and Verse, was own'd, without dispute   5
Through all the Realms of *Non-sense*, absolute.
This aged Prince now flourishing in Peace,
And blest with issue of a large increase,
Worn out with business, did at length debate
To settle the succession of the State: 10
And pond'ring which of all his Sons was fit
To Reign, and wage immortal War with Wit;
Cry'd, 'tis resolv'd; for Nature pleads that He
Should onely rule, who most resembles me:
Sh——alone my perfect image bears,   15
Mature in dullness from his tender years.
Sh——alone, of all my Sons, is he
Who stands confirm'd in full stupidity.
The rest to some faint meaning make pretence,
But *Sh*——never deviates into sense.   20
Some Beams of Wit on other souls may fall,
Strike through and make a lucid intervall;
But *Sh*——'s genuine night admits no ray,
His rising Fogs prevail upon the Day:
Besides his goodly Fabrick fills the eye,   25
And seems design'd for thoughtless Majesty:
Thoughtless as Monarch Oakes, that shade the plain,
And, spread in solemn state, supinely reign.
Heywood and *Shirley* were but Types of thee,
Thou last great Prophet of Tautology: 30
Even I, a dunce of more renown than they,
Was sent before but to prepare thy way;

MAC FLECKNOE. The subtitle of the first edition (1682) adds *Or A Satyr Upon The Trew-Blew-Protestant Poet T[homas] S[hadwell]*. MacFlecknoe means son of Flecknoe. Shadwell was a fellow dramatist and a better one than Dryden allows. If Dryden had a personal reason to satirize his rival, no one has discovered it. Earlier Marvell had roughly satirized the "hideous verse" of Richard Flecknoe (d. 1678), an Irish priest, poet, and musician who was prolific and dull, and Dryden continues the game with wit and relish. 3 *Augustus* [Caesar]: First Roman Emperor, who came to power at the age of thirty-two and ruled for more than forty years. 12 *Wit:* (a key word in eighteenth-century poetry) the keenness of the faculty of the imagination to discover connections between ideas that produce pleasure and amusement and the brilliance and aptness of the expression of those connections. 28 *supinely:* indolently, passively. 29 [Thomas] *Heywood and* [James] *Shirley:* Elizabethan dramatists, then considered dull.

And coursly clad in *Norwich* Drugget came
To teach the Nations in thy greater name.
My warbling Lute, the Lute I whilom strung   35
When to King *John* of *Portugal* I sung,
Was but the prelude to that glorious day,
When thou on silver *Thames* did'st cut thy way,
With well tim'd Oars before the Royal Barge,
Swell'd with the Pride of thy Celestial charge;   40
And big with Hymn, Commander of an Host,
The like was ne'er in *Epsom* Blankets tost.
Methinks I see the new *Arion* Sail,
The Lute still trembling underneath thy nail.
At thy well sharpned thumb from Shore to Shore   45
The Treble squeaks for fear, the Bases roar:
Echoes from *Pissing-Ally*, *Sh*——call,
And *Sh*——they resound from *A*——*Hall*.
About thy boat the little Fishes throng,
As at the Morning Toast, that Floats along.   50
Sometimes as Prince of thy Harmonious band
Thou weild'st thy Papers in thy threshing hand.
St. *Andre's* feet ne'er kept more equal time,
Not ev'n the feet of thy own *Psyche's* rhime:
Though they in number as in sense excell;   55
So just, so like tautology they fell,
That, pale with envy, *Singleton* forswore ⎫
The Lute and Sword which he in Triumph bore, ⎬
And vow'd he ne'er would act *Villerius* more. ⎭
Here stopt the good old *Syre;* and wept for joy   60
In silent raptures of the hopefull boy.
All arguments, but most his Plays, perswade,
That for anointed dullness he was made.
  Close to the Walls which fair *Augusta* bind,
(The fair *Augusta* much to fears inclin'd)   65

---

33 *Norwich Drugget:* a coarse woolen fabric.   34 *greater name:* i.e., as John
the Baptist proclaimed the *greater name* of Christ.   36 *When . . . sung:*
Flecknoe had visited Portugal and had exhibited his skill in music.   42 *in . . .
tost:* reference to Shadwell's plays, one of which was *Epsom Wells*.   43 *Arion:*
legendary Greek poet and musician who, after having sung his last song, was
thrown overboard by thieving sailors but was rescued by dolphins who had
been charmed by his music.   47 *Pissing-Alley:* Stow says, "a very proper name
for it" (*A Survey of London*, ed. John Strype, London, 1720, II, 4, 117).   48
A[ston] *Hall:* unidentified.   50 *Morning Toast:* i.e., sewage and garbage that
floats like toast on wine or other morning beverages.   53 *St. Andre:* a well-
known dancing-master.   54 *Psyche's rhime:* a reference to Shadwell's rhyming
verse opera *Psyche* (1675).   57 [John] *Singleton:* a famous musician.   59
Villerius: a leading role in D'Avenant's dramatic opera *The Siege of Rhodes*
(1656).   64 *fair Augusta:* London.

An ancient fabrick, rais'd t'inform the sight,
There stood of yore, and *Barbican* it hight:
A watch Tower once; but now, so Fate ordains,
Of all the Pile an empty name remains.
From its old Ruins Brothel-houses rise,   70
Scenes of lewd loves, and of polluted joys.
Where their vast Courts the Mother-Strumpets keep,
And, undisturb'd by Watch, in silence sleep.
Near these a Nursery erects its head,
Where Queens are form'd, and future Hero's bred;   75
Where unfledg'd Actors learn to laugh and cry,
Where infant Punks their tender Voices try,
And little *Maximins* the Gods defy.
Great *Fletcher* never treads in Buskins here,
Nor greater *Johnson* dates in Socks appear.   80
But gentle *Simkin* just reception finds
Amidst this Monument of vanisht minds:
Pure Clinches, the suburbian Muse affords;
And *Panton* waging harmless War with words.
Here *Fleckno*, as a place to Fame well known,   85
Ambitiously design'd his *Sh——*'s Throne.
For ancient *Decker* prophesi'd long since,
That in this Pile should Reign a mighty Prince,
Born for a scourge of Wit, and flayle of Sense:
To whom true dulness should some *Psyches* owe,   90
But Worlds of *Misers* from his pen should flow;
Humorists and *Hypocrites* it should produce,
Whole *Raymond* families, and Tribes of *Bruce*.
    Now Empress *Fame* had publisht the Renown
Of *Sh——*'s Coronation through the Town.   95
Rows'd by report of Fame, the Nations meet,
From near *Bun-Hill*, and distant *Watling-street*.
No *Persian* Carpets spread th' Imperial way,
But scatter'd Limbs of mangled Poets lay:
From dusty shops neglected Authors come,   100
Martyrs of Pies, and Reliques of the Bum.

---

67 *hight:* called.   74 *Nursery:* a school and theater for training young actors.
75 *Queens:* (pun) stage queens and *quean* meaning hussy, harlot.   77 *Punks:*
prostitutes.   78 *Maximins:* Maximin was the protagonist in Dryden's *Tyrannic
Love.*   79 [John] *Fletcher:* early seventeenth-century dramatist whose plays
were then as popular as Shakespeare's.   79, 80 *Buskins, Socks:* Cf. Jonson,
"To Shakespeare," ll. 36, 37 and notes.   81 *Simkin:* a contemporary clown.
83 *Clinches:* puns.   *suburbian Muse:* the muse of prostitutes, since the
"suburbs" were the places where the brothels flourished.   84 [Thomas]
Panton: a noted wit and punster.   87 [Thomas] *Decker:* Elizabethan dramatist.
90–93 *Psyches . . . Bruce:* sarcastic allusions to plays and their characters by
Shadwell.   101 *Martyrs . . . Bum:* leaves torn from the books of *neglected
authors* were used for lining pie pans and for toilet paper.

Much *Heywood, Shirly, Ogleby* there lay,
But loads of *Sh*——almost choakt the way.
Bilk't *Stationers* for Yeomen stood prepar'd,
And *H*——was Captain of the Guard.   105
The hoary Prince in Majesty appear'd,
High on a Throne of his own Labours rear'd.
At his right hand our young *Ascanius* sate
Rome's other hope, and pillar of the State.
His Brows thick fogs, instead of glories, grace,   110
And lambent dullness plaid arround his face.
As *Hannibal* did to the Altars come,
Sworn by his *Syre* a mortal Foe to *Rome;*
So *Sh*——swore, nor should his Vow bee vain,
That he till Death true dullness would maintain;   115
And in his father's Right, and Realms defence,
Ne'er to have peace with Wit, not truce with Sense.
The King himself the sacred Unction made,
As King by Office, and as Priest by Trade:
In his sinister hand, instead of Ball,   120
He plac'd a mighty Mug of potent Ale;
Love's Kingdom to his right he did convey,
At once his Sceptre and his rule of Sway;
Whose righteous Lore the Prince had practis'd young,
And from whose Loyns recorded *Psyche* sprung.   125
His Temples last with Poppies were o'erspread,
That nodding seem'd to consecrate his head:
Just at that point of time, if Fame not lye,
On his left hand twelve reverend *Owls* did fly.

---

102 [John] *Ogleby:* an inept translator of classics. 104 *Bilk't Stationers:*
Defrauded booksellers. *Yeomen:* household troops, the Beefeaters. 105
[Henry] *H*[erringman]: Dryden's first publisher, and a noted one.
107 *Throne:* Cf. the description of Satan's throne, *Paradise Lost*, II, ll. 1–2.
108 *Ascanius:* son of Aeneas in Virgil's *Aeneid*, hence, Shadwell, the
son and heir. 112 *Hannibal:* The Carthaginian general who nearly conquered
Rome was required by his father at the age of nine to swear never to make
peace with Rome. The Rome of Horace, Juvenal, and Virgil symbolizes for
Dryden superlative models of wit, satire, and heroic poetry. 118 *sacred
Unction:* the anointing with sacred oil that forever consecrates Shadwell as
king of dullness. 119 *Priest:* Flecknoe was a Roman Catholic priest. 120
sinister: left. Dryden burlesques the pageantry of coronation. *Ball:* a globe
surmounted by a cross, symbolizing the sovereignty of the king as God's
vicegerent on earth. 122 *Love's Kingdom:* play by Flecknoe. 126 *Poppies:*
from which opium is derived; hence symbol of dullness that induces sleep.
129 *Owls:* to Virgil, Chaucer, Shakespeare, and Dryden, not an auspicious
bird—"prophete . . . of wo and of myschaunce" (Chaucer, *Legend of Good
Women*, l. 2249) as well as death; ill-boding (*Aeneid*, IV, 462, and XII, 864–
65); symbol of stupidity masked as grave wisdom and of all who hate the light
(of wit and reason); symbolic of the Jews who "value darkness more than
light" (*Bestiary*).

So *Romulus*, 'tis sung, by *Tyber's Brook*,   130
Presage of Sway from twice six Vultures took.
Th' admiring throng loud acclamations make,
And Omens of his future Empire take.
The *Syre* then shook the honours of his head,
And from his brows damps of oblivion shed   135
Full on the filial dullness: long he stood,
Repelling from his Breast the raging God;
At length burst out in this prophetick mood:
    Heavens bless my Son, from *Ireland* let him reign
To farr *Barbadoes* on the Western main;   140
Of his Dominion may no end be known,
And greater than his Father's be his Throne.
Beyond loves Kingdom let him stretch his Pen;
He paus'd, and all the people cry'd *Amen*.
Then thus, continu'd he, my Son advance   145
Still in new Impudence, new Ignorance.
Success let others teach, learn thou from me
Pangs without birth, and fruitless Industry.
Let *Virtuoso's* in five years be Writ;
Yet not one thought accuse thy toyl of wit.   150
Let gentle *George* in triumph tread the Stage,
Make *Dorimant* betray, and *Loveit* rage;
Let *Cully*, *Cockwood*, *Fopling*, charm the Pit,
And in their folly shew the Writers wit.
Yet still thy fools shall stand in thy defence,   155
And justifie their Author's want of sense.
Let 'em be all by thy own model made
Of dullness, and desire no foreign aid:
That they to future ages may be known,
Not Copies drawn, but Issue of thy own.   160
Nay let thy men of wit too be the same,
All full of thee, and differing but in name;
But let no alien *S—dl—y* interpose
To lard with wit thy hungry *Epsom* prose.
And when false flowers of *Rhetorick* thou would'st cull,   165
Trust Nature, do not labour to be dull;
But write thy best, and top; and in each line,
Sir *Formal's* oratory will be thine.
Sir *Formal*, though unsought, attends thy quill,
And does thy *Northern Dedications* fill.   170

130 *Romulus:* legendary founder of Rome.   151 *George* [Etherege]: Restoration writer of comedies in which the following characters appear.   163, 164 *S*[e]*dl*[e]*y*, *Epsom:* Charles Sedley, from whom Shadwell borrowed in *Epsom Wells*.   168 *Sir Formal* [Trifle]: a character in Shadwell's *The Virtuoso*.   170 *Northern Dedications:* to the Duke of Newcastle and members of his family in the "north country."

Nor let false friends seduce thy mind to fame,
By arrogating *Johnson's* Hostile name.
Let Father *Fleckno* fire thy mind with praise,
And Uncle *Ogleby* thy envy raise.
Thou art my blood, where *Johnson* has no part;   175
What share have we in Nature or in Art?
Where did his wit on learning fix a brand,
And rail at Arts he did not understand?
Where made he love in Prince *Nicander's* vein,
Or swept the dust in *Psyche's* humble strain?   180
Where sold he Bargains, Whip-stitch, kiss my Arse,
Promis'd a Play and dwindled to a Farce?
When did his Muse from *Fletcher* scenes purloin,
As thou whole *Eth'ridg* dost transfuse to thine?
But so transfus'd as Oyl on Waters flow,   185
His always floats above, thine sinks below.
This is thy Province, this thy wondrous way,
New Humours to invent for each new Play:
This is that boasted Byas of thy mind,
By which one way, to dullness, 'tis inclin'd.   190
Which makes thy writings lean on one side still,
And in all changes that way bends thy will.
Nor let thy mountain belly make pretence
Of likeness; thine's a tympany of sense.
A Tun of Man in thy Large bulk is writ,   195
But sure thou'rt but a Kilderkin of wit.
Like mine thy gentle numbers feebly creep,
Thy Tragick Muse gives smiles, thy Comick sleep.
With whate'er gall thou sett'st thy self to write,
Thy inoffensive Satyrs never bite.   200
In thy fellonious heart, though Venom lies,
It does but touch thy *Irish* pen, and dyes.
Thy Genius calls thee not to purchase fame
In keen Iambicks, but mild Anagram:
Leave writing Plays, and chuse for thy command   205
Some peacefull Province in Acrostick Land.

---

172 *arrogating . . . name:* Shadwell pretended to be a literary disciple of Ben Jonson. 174 *Ogleby:* see l. 102 and note. 179 *Nicander's vein:* Nicander's stilted addresses to Psyche, *Psyche*, Act I. 181 *sold he Bargains:* i.e., where he entrapped people into asking innocent questions so as to give an unexpected and coarse answer, such as *Whip-stitch* (presto), *kiss my Arse*. Dryden gives samples of the supposedly comic idiom of Sir Samuel Hearty, a character in *The Virtuoso*. 194 *tympany:* a distension of the abdomen; hence, because it produces flatulence, a synonym for bombast, turgidity. 201-02 *venom . . . dyes:* Since St. Patrick drove the snakes out of Ireland, Irish satire has no venomous bite. Flecknoe, an Irishman, adopting Shadwell as his son, transfers his inability to satirize with venomous effect to Shadwell.

There thou maist wings display and Altars raise,
And torture one poor word Ten thousand ways.
Or if thou would'st thy diff'rent talents suit,
Set thy own Songs, and sing them to thy lute.   210
He said, but his last words were scarcely heard,
For *Bruce* and *Longvil* had a *Trap* prepar'd,
And down they sent the yet declaiming Bard.
Sinking he left his Drugget robe behind,
Born upwards by a subterranean wind.   215
The Mantle fell to the young Prophet's part,
With double portion of his Father's Art.

Epilogue

Spoked by Mrs. Ellen, *when she was to be carried off dead by the Bearers*

To the   Hold, are you mad? you damn'd confounded Dog,
Bearer.   I am to rise, and speak the Epilogue.

To the   I come, kind Gentlemen, strange news to tell ye,
Audience.   I am the Ghost of poor departed *Nelly.*
                   Sweet Ladies, be not frighted, I'le be civil,   5
                   I'm what I was, a little harmless Devil.
                   For after death, we Sprights, have just such Natures,
                   We had for all the World, when humane Creatures;
                   And therefore I that was an Actress here,
                   Play all my Tricks in Hell, a Goblin there.   10
                   Gallants, look to't, you say there are no Sprights;
                   But I'le come dance about your Beds at nights.
                   And faith you'l be in a sweet kind of taking,
                   When I surprise you between sleep and waking.

---

207 *wings . . . Altars:* See Herbert, "Easter Wings" and note. 211 *He said:* characteristic formula of the classical heroic style, here signifying the mock heroic. 212 *Bruce and Longvil:* characters in *The Virtuoso* who cut short *Sir Formal's* (l. 168) speechmaking in Act III by springing the trapdoor. 216–17 *Mantle . . . Art:* Ironic, as Elisha received "a double portion" of his father Elijah's spirit because he saw him translated by a chariot of fire and a whirlwind into heaven. See 2 Kings 2:9–15.

EPILOGUE. Mrs. Ellen is the famous actress Nell Gwyn, who plays the role of the Emperor Maximin's daughter, Princess Valeria (l. 30). She has just killed herself in an attempt to save the life of Porphyrus, whom she loves. According to Scott and Saintsbury, Mrs. Gwyn's delivery of the Epilogue persuaded Charles II to carry her off as his mistress; she remained one of his favourite and most diverting companions to the end of his life. His dying request was, "Let not poor Nelly starve." She was famous for her wildness and spirit and is reported to have quieted the mob at Oxford with, "Pray, good people, be civil; I am the Protestant whore." (D.N.B.) The crowd cheered.

To tell you true, I walk because I dye   15
Out of my Calling in a Tragedy.
O Poet, damn'd dull Poet, who could prove
So sensless! to make *Nelly* dye for Love,
Nay, what's yet worse, to kill me in the prime
Of *Easter*-Term, in Tart and Cheese-cake time!   20
I'le fit the Fopp; for I'le not one word say
T'excuse his godly out of fashion Play.
A Play which if you dare but twice sit out,
You'l all be slander'd, and be thought devout.
But, farewel Gentlemen, make haste to me,   25
I'm sure e're long to have your company.
As for my Epitaph when I am gone,
I'le trust no Poet, but will write my own.

Here Nelly *lies, who, though she liv'd a Slater'n,*
Yet dy'd a Princess, acting in S. Cathar'n.   30

[from *Tyrannick Love*]

To the MEMORY of Mr. OLDHAM

Farewel, too little and too lately known,
Whom I began to think and call my own;
For sure our Souls were near ally'd; and thine
Cast in the same Poetick mould with mine.
One common Note on either Lyre did strike,   5
And Knaves and Fools we both abhorr'd alike:
To the same Goal did both our Studies drive,
The last set out the soonest did arrive.
Thus *Nisus* fell upon the slippery place,
While his young Friend perform'd and won the Race.   10
O early ripe! to thy abundant store
What could advancing Age have added more?
It might (what Nature never gives the young)
Have taught the numbers of thy native Tongue.

---

15 *dye:* (pun) to expire; to subside lifeless after sexual climax. 16 *Tragedy:* her usual roles, and her best, were comic. 21 *I'le . . . Fopp:* I will punish the fool. 30 *S. Cather'n:* St. Catherine, a major character, is marytred in the play by being beheaded (offstage) after refusing the amorous advances of the Emperor Maximin and converting the Empress Berenice to Christianity.

TO THE MEMORY. John Oldham (1653–83) was a savage political satirist for the Whigs whose career was cut short by smallpox. 9 *Nisus:* see Virgil, *Aeneid* V, 286–339, for the story of how he fell during a race and allowed his friend, Euryalus, to win the prize. 14 *numbers:* polished versification.

But Satyr needs not those, and Wit will shine   15
Through the harsh cadence of a rugged line.
A noble Error, and but seldom made,
When Poets are by too much force betray'd.
Thy generous fruits, though gather'd ere their prime ⎫
Still shew'd a quickness; and maturing time   ⎬   20
But mellows what we write to the dull sweets of Rime. ⎭
Once more, hail and farewel; farewel thou young,
But ah too short, *Marcellus* of our Tongue;
Thy Brows with Ivy, and with Laurels bound;
But Fate and gloomy Night encompass thee around.   25

A Song for St. CECILIA's Day, 1687

I

From Harmony, from heav'nly Harmony
   This universal Frame began.
  When Nature underneath a heap
    Of jarring Atomes lay,
   And cou'd not heave her Head,   5
The tuneful Voice was heard from high,
    Arise ye more than dead.
Then cold, and hot, and moist, and dry,
In order to their stations leap,
   And MUSICK's pow'r obey.   10
From Harmony, from heav'nly Harmony
   This universal Frame began:
   From Harmony to Harmony
Through all the compass of the Notes it ran,
The Diapason closing full in Man.   15

---

23 *Marcellus:* See Virgil, *Aeneid* VI, 860–66. Marcellus, Augustus Caesar's
nephew, was adopted by him and chosen to be his successor, but he died at the
age of twenty and was lamented by the whole nation. In this allusion Dryden
reveals clearly the shift from the prophetic role of the poet (Milton's) to that of
"imperial" rule characteristic of the Augustan poets. Cf. Milton's attitude
toward Edward King and the office of the poet in "Lycidas."

A SONG.   St. Cecilia, legendary inventor of the pipe organ, is the patron of
musicians and of music, especially church music.   1–2 *From . . . began:* the
traditional platonic idea of the creation as a harmony of the warring opposites
brought about by divine love, here symbolized by music. Cf. Milton, "At a
Solemn Musick." See Boethius, *Consolation of Philosophy* IV, meter 6.   8 *cold
. . . dry:* properties of the traditional elements—earth, fire, water, and air.
15 *Diapason:* (multiple meanings) the entire compass of creation thought of as
a musical instrument; harmony throughout the whole scale of creation (cf.
Herbert, "Man," ll. 7, 13–15 and notes); the musical scale, octave; and the
principal foundation stop of a pipe organ.

II

What Passion cannot MUSICK raise and quell!
    When *Jubal* struck the corded Shell,
His list'ning Brethren stood around
And wond'ring, on their Faces fell
To worship that Celestial Sound.   20
Less than a God they thought there cou'd not dwell
    Within the hollow of that Shell
    That spoke so sweetly and so well.
What Passion cannot MUSICK raise and quell!

III

    The TRUMPETS loud Clangor   25
       Excites us to Arms
    With shrill Notes of Anger
       And mortal Alarms.
    The double double double beat
       Of the thundring DRUM   30
    Cryes, heark the Foes come;
Charge, Charge, 'tis too late to retreat.

IV

    The soft complaining FLUTE
    In dying Notes discovers
    The Woes of hopeless Lovers,   35
Whose Dirge is whisper'd by the warbling LUTE.

V

    Sharp VIOLINS proclaim
    Their jealous Pangs, and Desperation,
    Fury, frantick Indignation,
    Depth of Pains, and height of Passion,   40
       For the fair, disdainful Dame.

VI

    But oh! what Art can teach
    What human Voice can reach
    The sacred ORGANS praise?
    Notes inspiring holy Love,   45
    Notes that wing their heav'nly ways
       To mend the Choires above.

---

17 *Jubal:* ". . . father of all such as handle the harp and organ" (Gen. 4:21).

VII

Orpheus cou'd lead the savage race;
And Trees unrooted left their place;
   Sequacious of the Lyre: 50
But bright *CECILIA* rais'd the wonder high'r;
When to her ORGAN, vocal Breath was giv'n
An Angel heard, and straight appear'd
   Mistaking Earth for Heaven.

GRAND CHORUS

As from the pow'r of sacred Lays   55
   The Spheres began to move,
And sung the great Creator's praise
   To all the bless'd above;
So when the last and dreadful hour
This crumbling Pageant shall devour,   60
The TRUMPET *shall be heard on high,*
The Dead shall live, the Living die,
And MUSICK *shall untune the Sky.*

The Secular Masque

Enter Janus.

Janus.   *Chronos, Chronos,* mend thy Pace,
               An hundred times the rowling Sun
               Around the Radiant Belt has run
               In his revolving Race.

48 *Orpheus:* See Milton, "L'Allegro," l. 145 and note. 50 *Sequacious:* following. 61 *Trumpet:* the trumpet of Last Judgment. See Matt. 24:31; 1 Cor. 15:52; 1 Thes. 4:16–17; Rev. 8–9.

THE SECULAR MASQUE. *Secular:* celebrated once in an age. Cf. secular games (*ludi saeculares*) of imperial Rome, actually celebrated at irregular periods, in honor of the chief gods and for the prosperity of the empire, instituted in the hope of bringing to an end some period of national danger. Scott suggests that the "Masque" allegorizes the sports of James I, the wars of Charles I, and the licentious loves of Charles II, seemingly the whole course of the history of England in the seventeenth century. The "Masque" was written as an addition to the revival of Fletcher's *The Pilgrim.* 1 *Janus:* God of doors and avenues, represented with two faces, looking inward and outward because he is acquainted with the past and future, custodian of the universe and fastener of all things, whose temple doors are open in time of war, closed in time of peace. He is the god of beginnings—of the first hour of the day and of the first month of the year. (See Ovid, *Fasti,* I, 65–288.) 3 *Radiant Belt:* the "belt" formed by the constellations of the zodiac traversed by the sun once each year.

204

Behold, behold, the Goal in sight,   5
Spread thy Fans, and wing thy flight.

Enter Chronos, *with a Scythe in his hand, and a great Globe on his
Back, which he sets down at his entrance.*

Chronos.   Weary, weary of my weight,
              Let me, let me drop my Freight,
                And leave the World behind.
              I could not bear   10
              Another Year
              The Load of Human-Kind.

Enter Momus *Laughing.*

Momus.   Ha! ha! ha! Ha! ha! ha! well hast thou done,
                To lay down thy Pack,
                And lighten thy Back,   15
              The World was a Fool, e'er since it begun,
              And since neither *Janus*, nor *Chronos*, nor I,
                Can hinder the Crimes,
                Or mend the Bad Times,
              'Tis better to Laugh than to Cry.   20
Cho. of all 3. *'Tis better to Laugh than to Cry.*
Janus.   Since *Momus* comes to laugh below,
              Old Time begin the Show,
              That he may see, in every Scene,
              What Changes in this Age have been,   25
Chronos.   Then Goddess of the Silver Bow begin.

Horns, or Hunting-Musique within.

Enter Diana.

Diana.   With Horns and with Hounds I waken the Day,
              And hye to my Woodland walks away;
              I tuck up my Robe, and am buskin'd soon,

---

7 *Chronos:* Greek name for Saturn, god of time, who revenged himself on his
cannibal father by castrating him with a *scythe* made by his mother from her
own bowels. When he was banished by his son Jupiter, he fled to Italy where
Janus, who was then king, made him his partner. He civilized the people of
Italy with such mildness and beneficial results that his reign was said to be
"golden." He is usually depicted, as here, as an old man with a scythe and a
snake in the form of a hoop, biting its own tail to symbolize the revolution of
time (cf. *revolving Race*). The hilarity of the "Masque" suggests the ironic
possibility of a new and different "golden age." 13 *Momus:* God of raillery,
ridicule, and faultfinding.

And tye to my Forehead a wexing Moon.   30
I course the fleet Stagg, unkennel the Fox,
And chase the wild Goats or'e summets of Rocks,
With shouting and hooting we pierce thro' the Sky;
And Eccho turns Hunter, and doubles the Cry.

Cho. of all. *With shouting and hooting, we pierce through the Skie,*
              And Eccho turns Hunter, and doubles the Cry.   36

Janus.   Then our Age was in it's Prime,
Chronos.   Free from Rage.
Diana.   —————And free from Crime.
Momus.   A very Merry, Dancing, Drinking,
              Laughing, Quaffing, and unthinking Time.   40

Cho. of all. *Then our Age was in it's Prime,*
              Free from Rage, and free from Crime,
              A very Merry, Dancing, Drinking,
              Laughing, Quaffing, and unthinking Time.

              Dance of Diana's *Attendants.*

              Enter Mars.

Mars.   Inspire the Vocal Brass, Inspire;   45
              The World is past its Infant Age:
                  Arms and Honour,
                  Arms and Honour,
              Set the Martial Mind on Fire,
              And kindle Manly Rage.   50
              Mars has lookt the Sky to Red;
              And Peace, the Lazy Good, is fled.
              Plenty, Peace, and Pleasure fly;
                  The Sprightly Green
              In *Woodland*-Walks, no more is seen;   55
              The Sprightly Green, has drunk the *Tyrian* Dye.

Cho. of all. *Plenty, Peace,* &c.
Mars.   Sound the Trumpet, Beat the Drum,
              Through all the World around;
              Sound a Reveille, Sound, Sound,   60
                  The Warrior God is come.

Cho. of all. *Sound the Trumpet,* &c.
Momus.   Thy Sword within the Scabbard keep,
                  And let Mankind agree;
              Better the World were fast asleep,   65
                  Than kept awake by Thee.

30 *wexing:* waxing.   56 *Tyrian Dye:* purple; i.e., the bloodstains of war.

206

	The Fools are only thinner,	
	With all our Cost and Care;	
	But neither side a winner,	
	For Things are as they were.	70
Cho. of all.	*The Fools are only*, &c.	

Enter Venus.

Venus.	Calms appear, when Storms are past;	
	Love will have his Hour at last:	
	Nature is my kindly Care;	
	Mars destroys, and I repair;	75
	Take me, take me, while you may,	
	Venus comes not ev'ry Day.	
Cho. of all.	*Take her, take her*, &c.	
Chronos.	The World was then so light,	
	I scarcely felt the Weight;	80
	Joy rul'd the Day, and Love the Night.	
	But since the Queen of Pleasure left the Ground,	
	I faint, I lag,	
	And feebly drag	
	The pond'rous Orb around.	85
Momus.	All, all, of a piece throughout;	
Pointing to *Diana.*	Thy Chase had a Beast in View;	
to *Mars.*	Thy Wars brought nothing about;	
to *Venus.*	Thy Lovers were all untrue.	
Janus.	'Tis well an Old Age is out,	90
Chro[nos].	And time to begin a New.	
Cho. of all.	*All, all, of a piece throughout;*	
	Thy Chase had a Beast in View;	
	Thy Wars brought nothing about;	
	Thy Lovers were all untrue.	95
	'Tis well an Old Age is out,	
	And time to begin a New.	

Dance of Huntsmen, Nymphs, Warriours and Lovers.

ALEXANDER POPE
1688–1744

The Rape of the Lock

AN HEROIC-COMICAL POEM

Nolueram, Belinda, tuos violare capillos;
Sed juvat, hoc precibus me tribuisse tuis.

[Martial, *Epigrams* XII, 84]

CANTO I

What dire Offense from am'rous Causes springs,
What mighty Contests rise from trivial Things,
I sing—This verse to Caryll, Muse! is due;
This, ev'n Belinda may vouchsafe to view:
Slight is the Subject, but not so the Praise,   5
If She inspire, and He approve my lays.
    Say what strange Motive, Goddess! could compel
A well-bred Lord t' assault a gentle Belle?

THE RAPE OF THE LOCK.   Pope claimed that he first wrote "The Rape" at the suggestion of John Caryll (l. 3) to celebrate an actual incident (Lord Petre did cut off one of Miss Arabella Fermor's locks) and with a private joke to ease tension between the families caused by the breach of propriety. His first version was published anonymously in two cantos in 1712. In 1714 he enlarged it for the authorized edition, using the incident as the fable for a witty, satiric, mock-heroic poem. Pope's literary virtuosity and his brilliant parody of heroic themes, images and situations, diction, and conventions of the *Iliad*, the *Aeneid*, and *Paradise Lost* as he satirizes the follies of society and the pretensions of women who seek to dominate in the wars of the sexes are of far greater significance than possible allusions to a private squabble between persons now known only by obscure references. See *The Rape of the Lock*, ed. Geoffrey Tillotson (London, 1940), pp. 106–24, for an extended account of Pope's mastery of the mock-heroic and the traditions of this genre. Notes specifically derived from this edition are indicated by [T]. For my awareness of the extent of the allusions and their satiric force, I am indebted to Earl Wasserman.

Nolueram . . . tuis: "I was loth, Belinda, to violate your locks; but I am pleased to have granted that much of your prayers." (Adapted from Martial, Tillotson's translation.) Pope leaves out the last two lines of the epigram, which read: "Such wert thou, O Pelops lately shorn, and thus, when thy hair was laid aside, didst thou shine, so that thy spouse saw all the ivory of thy shoulder" (tr. W. C. A. Ker). Thus Polytimus, the man to whom Martial addressed his epigram, having shorn his hair, will emerge more beautiful than before, like Pelops, whose ivory shoulder so revealed made him more radiant. With this allusion Pope suggests that Belinda, having lost her virginal innocence in the "rape" of her hair, may become more beautiful and attractive now that she has been shorn.

CANTO I.   1–3 *What . . . sing:* Pope parodies the opening formula of *Paradise Lost*, I, ll. 1–5; that of the *Aeneid: Arma virumque cano;* and that of the *Iliad:* "Achilles' wrath, to Greece the direful spring / Of woes unnumber'd, heavenly goddess, sing!" (Pope's translation.)

208

Oh say what stranger Cause, yet unexplor'd,
Could make a gentle Belle reject a Lord?   10
In Tasks so bold, can Little Men engage,
And in soft Bosoms dwells such mighty Rage?
   Sol through white Curtains shot a tim'rous Ray,
And op'd those Eyes that must eclipse the Day;
Now Lap-dogs give themselves the rousing Shake,   15
And sleepless Lovers, just at Twelve, awake:
Thrice rung the Bell, the Slipper knock'd the Ground,
And the press'd Watch returned a silver Sound.
Belinda still her downy Pillow press'd,
Her guardian Sylph prolonged the balmy Rest.   20
'Twas He had summon'd to her silent Bed
The Morning-Dream that hover'd o'er her Head.
A Youth more glitt'ring than a Birth-night Beau
(That ev'n in Slumber caus'd her Cheek to glow),
Seem'd to her Ear his winning Lips to lay,   25
And thus in Whispers said, or seem'd to say.
   Fairest of Mortals, thou distinguish'd Care
Of thousand bright Inhabitants of Air!
If e'er one Vision touch'd thy infant Thought,
Of all the Nurse and all the Priest have taught,   30
Of airy Elves by Moonlight Shadows seen,
The silver Token, and the circled Green,
Or Virgins visited by Angel-Pow'rs,
With Golden Crowns and Wreaths of heav'nly Flow'rs,

11 *Little Men:* heroes in epic poems are not *Little.* 14 *Eyes . . . eclipse:*
the old Petrarchan hyperbole. Cf. Shakespeare's Sonnet 130. 17 *Slipper
. . . Ground:* i.e., to summon the maid. 18 *press'd . . . Sound:* the "repeating"
watch, when the pin was *press'd,* sounded the hour and the quarters.
20 *Sylph:* "The Machinery, Madam, is a term invented by the Critics, to
signify that part which the Deities, Angels, or Demons are made to act in a
Poem. . . . These Machines I determin'd to raise on a very new and odd
foundation, the Rosicrucian doctrine of Spirits. . . . According to these
gentlemen, the four Elements are inhabited by Spirits, which they call
Sylphs, Gnomes, Nymphs, and Salamanders. The Gnomes or Demons of
Earth delight in mischief; but the Sylphs, whose habitation is in the
Air, are the best condition'd creatures imaginable. For they say, any mortals
may enjoy the most intimate familiarities with these gentle Spirits, upon condition very easy to all true Adepts, an inviolate preservation of chastity."—
From "To Mrs. Arabella Fermor." Pope playfully accounts for his parody of
the epic convention of the involvement of supernatural agents in human affairs.
The gods often spoke to the hero in dreams. Cf. esp. *Paradise Lost,* V, 28–93,
for the dream that Satan has insinuated into the ear of the sleeping Eve.
23 *Birth-night Beau:* a suitor, particularly at a royal birthday party. 29 *infant:*
literally, incapable of speech. 32 *silver Token:* coin left by *Elves* as evidence
of their visit. *circled Green:* print of the fairy ring in the grass. 33 *Virgins
visited:* as the Virgin Mary and other virgin saints were visited. 34 *heav'nly
Flow'rs:* as in Chaucer, "The Second Nun's Tale," ll. 220–22.

Hear and believe! thy own Importance know,   35
Nor bound thy narrow Views to Things below.
Some secret Truths, from Learned Pride conceal'd,
To Maids alone and Children are reveal'd:
What though no Credit doubting Wits may give?
The Fair and Innocent shall still believe.   40
Know, then, unnumbered Spirits round thee fly,
The light Militia of the lower Sky;
These, though unseen, are ever on the Wing,
Hang o'er the Box, and hover round the Ring.
Think what an Equipage thou hast in air,   45
And view with scorn Two Pages and a Chair.
As now your own, our Beings were of old,
And once inclos'd in Woman's beauteous Mold;
Thence, by a soft Transition, we repair
From earthly Vehicles to these of Air.   50
Think not, when Woman's transient Breath is fled,
That all her Vanities at once are dead;
Succeeding Vanities she still regards,
And though she plays no more, o'erlooks the Cards.
Her Joy in gilded Chariots, when alive,   55
And love of Ombre, after Death survive.
For when the Fair in all their Pride expire,
To their first Elements their Souls retire:
The Sprites of fiery Termagants in Flame
Mount up, and take a Salamander's Name.   60
Soft yielding Minds to Water glide away,
And sip, with Nymphs, their elemental Tea.
The graver Prude sinks downward to a Gnome,
In search of Mischief still on Earth to roam.
The light Coquettes in Sylphs aloft repair,   65
And sport and flutter in the Fields of Air.
    Know farther yet; Whoever fair and chaste
Rejects Mankind, is by some Sylph embrac'd:
For Spirits, freed from mortal Laws, with ease
Assume what Sexes and what Shapes they please.   70
What guards the Purity of melting Maids,
In Courtly Balls, and Midnight Masquerades,

---

44 *Box:* i.e., in the theater. *Ring:* Hyde Park Circus, the fashionable riding and carriage course of London where beauties displayed their charms. 46 *Chair:* sedan chair. 47–48 *As . . . Mold:* with this transition, cf. Dryden, "Epilogue," ll. 4–12. 54 *o'erlooks:* I.e., she is a kibitzer. 55 *Chariots:* carriages. Cf. *Vehicles,* l. 50 and pun. 56 *Ombre:* (from *hombre,* man) pronounced *omber,* a popular three-handed card game of Spanish origin; the name of the challenging player. See Tillotson, Appendix C, for full account of the rules of the game and Belinda's hand. 58 *first:* preponderating. 59 *Termagants:* scolding women. 60 *Salamander's:* See l. 20 and note. 62 *Tea:* pronounced *tay.*

Safe from the treach'rous Friend, the daring Spark,
The Glance by Day, the Whisper in the Dark,
When kind Occasion prompts their warm Desires,   75
When Music softens, and when Dancing fires?
'Tis but their Sylph, the wise Celestials know,
Though Honor is the word with Men below.
  Some Nymphs there are, too conscious of their Face,
For Life predestined to the Gnomes' Embrace.   80
These swell their Prospects and exalt their Pride,
When Offers are disdain'd, and love Denied.
Then gay Ideas crowd the vacant Brain;
While Peers and Dukes, and all their sweeping Train,
And Garters, Stars, and Coronets appear,   85
And in soft Sounds, Your Grace salutes their Ear.
'Tis these that early taint the Female Soul,
Instruct the Eyes of young Coquettes to roll,
Teach Infant-Cheeks a bidden Blush to know,
And little Hearts to flutter at a Beau.   90
  Oft, when the World imagine Women stray,
The Sylphs through mystic Mazes guide their Way,
Through all the giddy Circle they pursue,
And old Impertinence expel by new.
What tender Maid but must a Victim fall   95
To one Man's Treat, but for another's Ball?
When Florio speaks, what Virgin could withstand,
If gentle Damon did not squeeze her Hand?
With varying Vanities, from ev'ry Part,
They shift the moving Toyshop of their Heart;   100
Where Wigs with Wigs, with Sword-knots Sword-knots strive,
Beaux banish Beaux, and Coaches Coaches drive.
This erring mortals Levity may call,
Oh blind to Truth! the Sylphs contrive it all.
  Of these am I, who thy Protection claim,   105
A watchful Sprite, and Ariel is my Name.
Late, as I rang'd the Crystal Wilds of Air,
In the clear Mirror of thy ruling Star
I saw, alas! some dread Event impend,
Ere to the Main this Morning Sun descend,   110
But Heav'n reveals not what, of how, or where:
Warn'd by the Sylph, oh Pious Maid, beware!
This to disclose is all thy Guardian can.
Beware of all, but most beware of Man!

73 *Spark:* a fop.   85 *Garters . . . Coronets:* insignia of orders of honor and
rank, e.g., Knights of the Garter.   86 *Your Grace:* form of address to a
duchess.   89 *bidden Blush:* i.e., rouge.   94 *Impertinence:* a trifle, a folly.   101
Sword-knots: ribbon attached to the hilt of a sword.   109 *dread Event:* Omens
and portents are common in epics.   110 *Main:* the ocean.

He said; when Shock, who thought she slept too long,   115
Leapt up, and wak'd his Mistress with his Tongue.
'Twas then, Belinda! if Report say true,
Thy Eyes first open'd on a Billet-doux;
Wounds, Charms, and Ardors were no sooner read,
But all the Vision vanish'd from thy head.   120
   And now, unveil'd, the Toilet stands display'd,
Each Silver Vase in mystic Order laid.
First, rob'd in White, the Nymph intent adores
With Head uncover'd, the Cosmetic Pow'rs.
A heav'nly Image in the Glass appears,   125
To that she bends, to that her Eyes she rears;
Th' inferior Priestess, at her Altar's side,
Trembling begins the sacred Rites of Pride.
Unnumber'd Treasures ope at once, and here
The various Off'rings of the World appear;   130
From each she nicely culls with curious Toil,
And decks the Goddess with the glitt'ring Spoil.
This Casket India's glowing Gems unlocks,
And all Arabia breathes from yonder Box.
The Tortoise here and Elephant unite,   135
Transform'd to Combs, the speckled, and the white.
Here Files of Pins extend their shining Rows,
Puffs, Powders, Patches, Bibles, Billet-doux.
Now awful Beauty put on all its Arms;
The Fair each moment rises in her Charms,   140
Repairs her Smiles, awakens ev'ry Grace,
And calls forth all the Wonders of her Face;
Sees by Degrees a purer Blush arise,
And keener Lightnings quicken in her Eyes.
The busy Sylphs surround their darling Care,   145
These set the Head, and those divide the Hair,
Some fold the Sleeve, while others plait the Gown;
And Betty's prais'd for Labors not her own.

CANTO II

Not with more Glories, in th' Ethereal Plain,
The Sun first rises o'er the purpled Main,

---

115 *Shock:* Belinda's lap dog. A shock-dog (shag-dog) was a woolly, long-haired lap dog trimmed like a poodle. The hair imagery, with all its sexual suggestiveness, begins here. The lap dog's symbolic value is emphasized by Ariel's assigning himself to guard it (II, 116). 121 *Toilet:* i.e., a vanity table. 125 *Glass:* mirror.   127–28 *Th'inferior . . . Pride:* parody of rites of worship in epics. Cf. *Paradise Lost,* V, 144–208.   135 *Tortoise . . . Elephant:* i.e., shell, ivory.   139. *Arms:* parody of the arming of the epic hero.

Than issuing forth, the Rival of his Beams
Launch'd on the Bosom of the silver Thames.
Fair Nymphs, and well-dress'd Youths around her shone,   5
But ev'ry Eye was fix'd on her alone.
On her white Breast a sparkling Cross she wore,
Which Jews might kiss, and Infidels adore.
Her lively Looks a sprightly Mind disclose,
Quick as her Eyes, and as unfix'd as those: 10
Favors to none, to all she Smiles extends;
Oft she rejects, but never once offends.
Bright as the Sun, her Eyes the Gazers strike,
And, like the Sun, they shine on all alike.
Yet graceful Ease, and Sweetness void of Pride,   15
Might hide her Faults, if Belles had Faults to hide:
If to her share some Female Errors fall,
Look on her Face, and you'll forget 'em all.
   This Nymph, to the Destruction of Mankind,
Nourish'd two Locks which graceful hung behind   20
In equal Curls, and well conspir'd to deck
With shining Ringlets the smooth Iv'ry Neck.
Love in these Labyrinths his Slaves detains,
And mighty Hearts are held in slender Chains.
With hairy Springes we the Birds betray,   25
Slight Lines of Hair surprise the Finny Prey,
Fair Tresses Man's imperial Race insnare,
And Beauty draws us with a single Hair.
   Th' advent'rous Baron the bright Locks admired;
He saw, he wish'd, and to the Prize aspir'd.   30
Resolv'd to win, he meditates the way,
By Force to ravish, or by Fraud betray;
For when Success a Lover's Toil attends,
Few ask, if Fraud or Force attain'd his Ends.
   For this, ere Phoebus rose, he had implor'd   35
Propitious Heav'n, and every Pow'r ador'd,
But chiefly Love—to Love an Altar built,
Of twelve vast French Romances, neatly gilt.
There lay three Garters, half a Pair of Gloves;
And all the Trophies of his former Loves;   40
With tender Billet-doux he lights the Pyre,
And breathes three am'rous Sighs to raise the Fire.

CANTO II. 3 *Rival:* i.e., Belinda, for her eyes are *Bright as the Sun*, l. 13.
4 *Launch'd . . . Thames:* embarked for Hampton Court, a royal palace twelve
miles upriver from London. 20 *Nourish'd:* cherished. 25 *Springes:* snares.
26 *Finny Prey:* i.e., fish. 37 *Altar built:* Epic heroes commonly make sacri-
fices to the gods before undertaking some great action. 39 *Garters:* not the
insignia of honor, as in I, 85, but quite the opposite.

Then prostrate falls, and begs with ardent Eyes
Soon to obtain, and long possess the Prize:
The Pow'rs gave Ear, and granted half his Pray'r,   45
The rest, the Winds dispers'd in empty Air.
  But now secure the painted Vessel glides,
The Sun-beams trembling on the floating Tides,
While melting Music steals upon the Sky,
And soften'd Sounds along the Waters die.   50
Smooth flow the Waves, the Zephyrs gently play,
Belinda smiled, and all the World was gay.
All but the Sylph—with careful Thoughts oppress'd,
Th' impending Woe sat heavy on his Breast.
He summons straight his Denizens of Air;   55
The lucid Squadrons round the Sails repair:
Soft o'er the Shrouds aerial Whispers breathe,
That seem'd but Zephyrs to the Train beneath.
Some to the Sun their Insect-Wings unfold,
Waft on the Breeze, or sink in Clouds of Gold.   60
Transparent Forms, too fine for mortal Sight,
Their fluid Bodies half dissolv'd in Light,
Loose to the Wind their airy Garments flew,
Thin glitt'ring Textures of the filmy Dew,
Dipp'd in the richest Tincture of the Skies,   65
Where Light disports in ever-mingling Dyes,
While ev'ry Beam new transient Colors flings,
Colors that change whene'er they wave their Wings.
Amid the Circle, on the gilded Mast,
Superior by the Head, was Ariel plac'd;   70
His Purple Pinions op'ning to the Sun,
He rais'd his Azure Wand, and thus begun.
  Ye Sylphs and Sylphids, to your Chief give Ear,
Fays, Fairies, Genii, Elves, and Demons hear!
Ye know the Spheres and various Tasks assign'd   75
By Laws Eternal to th' Aerial Kind.
Some in the Fields of purest Ether play,
And bask and whiten in the Blaze of Day.
Some guide the Course of wand'ring Orbs on high,
Or roll the Planets through the boundless Sky.   80

---

45 *granted . . . Pray'r:* Cf. Dryden's translation of the Aeneid, XI, 794–95:
"Appollo heard, and granting half his Pray'r, / Shuffled in Winds the rest,
and toss'd in empty Air" [T].   47 *painted Vessel:* (pun) both the barge on
which Belinda rides and Belinda herself. Cf. *frail China Jar,* l. 106 below and
note.   56 *round . . . repair:* gather around the sails of the barge.   64 *Textures
. . . Dew:* Gossamer, spun by spiders that can sail in the air, was formerly
thought to be a product of sunburned dew [T].   70 *by the Head:* The epic
hero is always taller than his followers by at least a head. Cf. *Paradise Lost,*
I, 589, where Satan, towering "above the rest," marshals his host.

Some less refin'd, beneath the Moon's pale Light
Pursue the Stars that shoot athwart the Night,
Or suck the Mists in grosser Air below,
Or dip their Pinions in the painted Bow,
Or brew fierce Tempests on the wintry Main, 85
Or o'er the Glebe distil the kindly Rain.
Others on Earth o'er human Race preside,
Watch all their Ways, and all their Actions guide:
Of these the Chief the Care of Nations own,
And guard with Arms Divine the British Throne. 90
Our humbler Province is to tend the Fair,
Not a less pleasing, though less glorious Care.
To save the Powder from too rude a Gale,
Nor let th' imprison'd Essences exhale;
To draw fresh Colors from the vernal Flow'rs; 95
To steal from Rainbows e'er they drop in Show'rs
A brighter Wash; to curl their waving Hairs,
Assist their Blushes, and inspire their Airs;
Nay oft, in Dreams, Invention we bestow,
To change a Flounce, or add a Furbelow. 100
This Day, black Omens threat the brightest Fair,
That e'er deserv'd a watchful Spirit's Care;
Some dire Disaster, or by Force, or Slight;
But what, or where, the Fates have wrapp'd in Night.
Whether the Nymph shall break Diana's Law, 105
Or some frail China Jar receive a Flaw;
Or stain her Honor, or her new Brocade;
Forget her Pray'rs, or miss a Masquerade;
Or lose her Heart, or Necklace, at a Ball;
Or whether Heav'n has doomed that Shock must fall. 110
Haste, then, ye Spirits! to your Charge repair:
The flutt'ring Fan be Zephyretta's Care;
The Drops to thee, Brillante, we consign;
And, Momentilla, let the Watch be thine;
Do thou, Crispissa, tend her fav'rite Lock; 115
Ariel himself shall be the Guard of Shock.
To fifty chosen Sylphs, of special Note,

86 *Glebe:* earth, soil. *kindly:* natural and beneficial. 97 *Wash:* a thin coating of color, as in a water-color painting. 103 *Slight:* sleight, trick, artifice. 105 *break Diana's Law:* lose her virginity. 106 *China Jar:* In the sixteenth and seventeenth centuries, as well as in Pope's time, a woman's virtue was traditionally said to be as brittle and breakable as glass or china. Pope associates women with glass and china continually throughout the poem, often with overt sexual suggestion. 113 *Drops:* diamond earrings. 115 *Crispissa:* i.e., one who crisps (curls). The Sylphs' names are appropriate to their duties.

We trust th' important Charge, the Petticoat:
Oft have we known that seven-fold Fence to fail,
Though stiff with Hoops, and arm'd with Ribs of Whale;   120
Form a strong Line about the Silver Bound,
And guard the wide Circumference around.
　　Whatever Spirit, careless of his Charge,
His Post neglects, or leaves the Fair at large,
Shall feel sharp Vengeance soon o'ertake his Sins,   125
Be stopp'd in Vials, or transfix'd with Pins;
Or plung'd in Lakes of bitter Washes lie,
Or wedg'd whole Ages in a Bodkin's Eye:
Gums and Pomatums shall his Flight restrain,
While clogg'd he beats his silken Wings in vain;   130
Or Alum Styptics with contracting Pow'r
Shrink his thin Essence like a rivel'd Flow'r:
Or as Ixion fix'd, the Wretch shall feel
The giddy Motion of the whirling Mill,
In Fumes of burning Chocolate shall glow,   135
And tremble at the Sea that froths below!
　　He spoke; the Spirits from the Sails descend;
Some, Orb in Orb, around the Nymph extend,
Some thrid the mazy Ringlets of her Hair,
Some hang upon the Pendants of her Ear;   140
With beating Hearts the dire Event they wait,
Anxious, and trembling for the Birth of Fate.

CANTO III

Close by those Meads, for ever crown'd with Flow'rs,
Where Thames with Pride surveys his rising Tow'rs,
There stands a Structure of majestic Frame,
Which from the neighb'ring Hampton takes its name.
Here Britain's Statesmen oft the Fall foredoom   5
Of foreign Tyrants, and of Nymphs at home;
Here Thou, Great Anna! whom three Realms obey,
Dost sometimes Counsel take—and sometimes Tea.

118 *Petticoat:* parody of the description of the shield of Achilles (*Iliad*, XVIII, 478–608) and that of Aeneas (*Aeneid*, VIII, 447–53). 127 *bitter Washes:* here, medicinal lotions. 129 *Gums and Pomatums:* perfumed ointments. 132 *rivel'd:* wrinkled. 133 *Ixion:* For attempting to seduce Juno, Ixion was at Jupiter's order bound to an ever turning wheel of fire in Hades. 134 *Mill:* for grinding chocolate. 138 *Orb in Orb:* deployed in concentric circles, like planetary spheres around the sun, whom Belinda rivals (see above, ll. 2–3); also a satiric allusion to Belinda's pride: see *Paradise Lost*, V, 596, where the angels are similarly deployed around God. 139 *thrid:* thread.

CANTO III. 7 *Anna:* Queen Anne, 1702–14. *three Realms:* After union with Scotland (May 1, 1707), Anne was styled Queen of Great Britain, France, and Ireland.

Hither the Heroes and the Nymphs resort,
To taste awhile the Pleasures of a Court; 10
In various Talk th' instructive Hours they pass'd,
Who gave the Ball, or paid the Visit last:
One speaks the Glory of the British Queen,
And one describes a charming Indian Screen;
A third interprets Motions, Looks, and Eyes; 15
At ev'ry word a Reputation dies.
Snuff, or the Fan, supply each Pause of Chat,
With singing, laughing, ogling, and all that.
   Meanwhile declining from the Noon of Day,
The Sun obliquely shoots his burning Ray; 20
The hungry Judges soon the Sentence sign,
And Wretches hang that Jurymen may dine;
The Merchant from th' Exchange returns in Peace,
And the long Labors of the Toilet cease.
Belinda now, whom Thirst of Fame invites, 25
Burns to encounter two advent'rous Knights,
At Ombre singly to decide their doom;
And swells her Breast with Conquests yet to come.
Straight the three Bands prepare in Arms to join,
Each Band the number of the Sacred Nine. 30
Soon as she spreads her Hand, th' Aerial Guard
Descend, and sit on each important Card:
First Ariel perch'd upon a Matadore,
Then each, according to the Rank they bore;
For Sylphs, yet mindful of their ancient Race, 35
Are, as when Women, wond'rous fond of Place.
   Behold, four Kings in Majesty rever'd,
With hoary Whiskers and a forky Beard;
And four fair Queens whose hands sustain a Flow'r,
Th' expressive Emblem of their softer Pow'r; 40
Four Knaves in Garbs succinct, a trusty Band,
Caps on their heads, and Halberds in their hand;
And particolor'd Troops, a shining Train,
Draw forth to Combat on the Velvet Plain.
   The skilful Nymph reviews her Force with Care; 45

---

29 *Arms to join:* mock-heroic reduction of epic single combat to a card game. Cf. the duels between Achilles and Hector, Aeneas and Turnus. Here Belinda's martial valor is like that of Camilla, *Aeneid,* XI. 30 *Sacred Nine:* i.e., the nine cards dealt to each person. 33 *Matadore:* either of the black aces, or *Manillio* (l. 51), some other card designated as a *Matadore* after trump is declared. 36 *Place:* high place. 37–42 *Behold . . . hand:* Pope describes the appearance of the face cards of his time. 41 *succinct:* close-fitting; i.e., short tunics. 44 *Velvet Plain:* i.e., the covering of the card table. Cf. *verdant Field*, l. 52, the "fighting fields" before Troy, and the "dubious Battle on the Plains of Heaven," *Paradise Lost,* II, 104.

Let Spades be trumps! she said, and Trumps they were.
   Now move to war her sable Matadores,
In Show like Leaders of the swarthy Moors.
Spadillio first, unconquerable Lord!
Led off two captive Trumps, and swept the Board.   50
As many more Manillio forc'd to yield,
And marched a Victor from the verdant Field.
Him Basto follow'd, but his Fate more hard
Gain'd but one Trump and one Plebeian Card.
With his broad Saber next, a Chief in years,   55
The hoary Majesty of Spades appears;
Puts forth one manly Leg, to sight reveal'd;
The rest, his many-color'd Robe conceal'd.
The rebel Knave, who dares his Prince engage,
Proves the just Victim of his Royal Rage.   60
E'en mighty Pam, that Kings and Queens o'erthrew,
And mow'd down Armies in the Fights of Lu,
Sad Chance of War! now, destitute of Aid,
Falls undistinguish'd by the Victor Spade!
   Thus far both Armies to Belinda yield;   65
Now to the Baron Fate inclines the Field.
His warlike Amazon her Host invades,
Th' imperial Consort of the Crown of Spades.
The Club's black Tyrant first her Victim died,
Spite of his haughty Mien, and barb'rous Pride: 70
What boots the regal Circle on his Head,
His giant Limbs, in State unwieldy spread?
That long behind he trails his pompous Robe,
And, of all Monarchs, only grasps the Globe?
   The Baron now his Diamonds pours apace;   75
Th' embroidered King who shows but half his Face,
And his refulgent Queen, with Pow'rs combin'd
Of broken Troops an easy Conquest find.
Clubs, Diamonds, Hearts, in wild Disorder seen,
With Throngs promiscuous strow the level Green.   80
Thus when dispers'd a routed Army runs,
Of Asia's Troops, and Afric's Sable Sons,
With like Confusion different Nations fly,
Of various Habit and of various Dye,

---

46 *Let . . . were:* (comic sublime) Cf. Gen. 1:3: "And God said, Let there be Light: and there was light" [T]. 49 *Spadillio:* ace of spades, highest trump. 53 *Basto:* ace of clubs. 61 *Pam:* jack of clubs. In *Lu* (l. 62) it is "wild" (superior to every other card). 74 *Globe:* the "orb," symbol of sovereignty, which only the king of clubs is depicted as holding. 80 *strow:* strew. 81–86 *Thus . . . all:* (epic simile) Epic warfare involves many nations; among others, Asian in the *Iliad*, African in the *Aeneid*. 84 *Habit:* dress.

The pierc'd Battalions dis-united fall,   85
In heaps on heaps; one Fate o'erwhelms them all.
    The Knave of Diamonds tries his wily Arts,
And wins (oh shameful Chance!) the Queen of Hearts.
At this, the Blood the Virgin's Cheek forsook,
A livid Paleness spreads o'er all her Look;   90
She sees, and trembles at th' approaching Ill,
Just in the Jaws of Ruin, and Codille.
And now (as oft in some distemper'd State)
On one nice Trick depends the gen'ral Fate.
An Ace of Hearts steps forth: The King unseen   95
Lurk'd in her Hand, and mourn'd his captive Queen:
He springs to Vengeance with an eager pace,
And falls like Thunder on the prostrate Ace.
The Nymph exulting fills with Shouts the Sky;
The Walls, the Woods, and long Canals reply.   100
Oh thoughtless Mortals! ever blind to Fate,
Too soon dejected, and too soon elate!
Sudden, these Honors shall be snatch'd away,
And curs'd for ever this Victorious Day.
    For lo! the Board with Cups and Spoons is crown'd,   105
The Berries crackle, and the Mill turns round;
On shining Altars of Japan they raise
The silver Lamp; the fiery Spirits blaze.
From silver Spouts the grateful Liquors glide,
While China's Earth receives smoking Tide.   110
At once they gratify their Scent and Taste,
And frequent Cups prolong the rich Repast.
Straight hover round the Fair her Airy Band;
Some, as she sipp'd, the fuming Liquor fann'd,
Some o'er her Lap their careful Plumes display'd,   115
Trembling, and conscious of the rich Brocade.
Coffee (which makes the Politician wise,
And see through all things with his half-shut Eyes),
Sent up in Vapors to the Baron's Brain
New Stratagems, the radiant Lock to gain.   120
Ah cease, rash Youth! desist ere 'tis too late,
Fear the just Gods, and think of Scylla's fate!

---

92 *Codille:* i.e., the final blow of knee (cf. Sp. *codillo*) or elbow (cf. Sp. *codo*) given to the *Ombre* (challenger) if he loses the game. 95 *King:* of hearts, which in *Ombre* beats the Baron's *Ace.* 105–12 *For . . . Repast:* Cf. epic banquets in *Aeneid,* I, 701–08, and *Paradise Lost,* V, 331–49, where Eve "on the board / Heaps with unsparing hand" the abundance of the Garden. 106 *Berries crackle:* Coffee beans crackle when they are roasted. *Mill:* coffee grinder. 107 *shining . . . Japan:* lacquered tables. 110 *China's Earth:* china teapot and cups. Also a comic allusion to the libations poured on the earth in the *Iliad* and *Aeneid.* 116 *Brocade:* Cf. II, 105–07.

Chang'd to a Bird, and sent to flit in Air,
She dearly pays for Nisus' injured Hair!
    But when to Mischief Mortals bend their Will,   125
How soon they find fit Instruments of Ill!
Just then, Clarissa drew with tempting Grace
A two-edg'd Weapon from her shining Case;
So Ladies in Romance assist their Knight,
Present the Spear, and arm him for the Fight.   130
He takes the Gift with rev'rence, and extends
The little Engine on his Fingers' Ends;
This just behind Belinda's Neck he spread,
As o'er the fragrant Steams she bends her Head.
Swift to the Lock a thousand Sprites repair,   135
A thousand Wings, by turns, blow back the Hair;
And thrice they twitch'd the Diamond in her Ear;
Thrice she looked back, and thrice the Foe drew near.
Just in that instant, anxious Ariel sought
The close Recesses of the Virgin's Thought;   140
As on the Nosegay in her Breast reclin'd,
He watched th' Ideas rising in her Mind,
Sudden he view'd, in spite of all her Art,
An Earthly Lover lurking at her Heart.
Amaz'd, confus'd, he found his Pow'r expir'd,   145
Resign'd to Fate, and with a Sigh retir'd.
    The Peer now spreads the glitt'ring Forfex wide,
T' enclose the Lock; now joins it, to divide.
E'en then, before the fatal Engine clos'd,
A wretched Sylph too fondly interpos'd;   150
Fate urged the Shears, and cut the Sylph in twain
(But Airy Substance soon unites again),
The meeting Points the sacred Hair dissever
From the fair Head, for ever, and for ever!
    Then flash'd the living Lightning from her Eyes,   155
And screams of Horror rend th' affrighted Skies.

122–24 *Scylla's . . . hair:* Scylla, daughter of King Nisus of Megara, betrayed her father's city by cutting off his purple lock (if he lost that, he lost his kingdom) and giving it to King Minos of Crete, whom she loved and who was beseiging Megara. Rejected by Minos and transformed by the gods into the bird Ciris ("I cut") for her treachery, she is continually pursued by her father, who was transformed into an osprey. See Ovid, *Met.*, VIII, 1–151. 132 *Engine:* (pun and parody) usually means a war-engine, especially a battering ram; also, a subtle artifice. 144–45 *Earthly . . . expir'd:* Cf. I, 20 and note, and especially I, 67–68. Belinda is not exactly ravished unwillingly. 147 *Forfex:* Latin term, hence "heroic," for the domestic scissors. 152 *But . . . again:* Cf. "The griding sword with discontinuous wound / Pass'd through him [Satan], but th'Eternal substance clos'd / Not long divisible (*Paradise Lost*, VI, 329–31).

220

Not louder Shrieks to pitying Heav'n are cast,
When Husbands, or when Lap-dogs breathe their last;
Or when rich China Vessels fall'n from high,
In glitt'ring Dust and painted Fragments lie!   160
    Let Wreaths of Triumph now my Temples twine
(The Victor cried) the glorious Prize is mine!
While Fish in Streams, or Birds delight in Air,
Or in a Coach and Six the British Fair,
As long as *Atalantis* shall be read,   165
Or the small Pillow grace a Lady's Bed,
While Visits shall be paid on solemn Days,
When num'rous Wax-lights in bright Order blaze,
While Nymphs take Treats, or Assignations give,
So long my Honor, Name, and Praise shall live!   170
What Time would spare, from Steel receives its Date,
And Monuments, like Men, submit to Fate!
Steel could the Labor of the Gods destroy,
And strike to Dust th' Imperial Tow'rs of Troy;
Steel could the Works of mortal Pride confound,   175
And hew Triumphal Arches to the ground.
What wonder then, fair Nymph! thy hairs should feel,
The conqu'ring Force of unresisted Steel?

CANTO IV

But anxious Cares the pensive Nymph oppress'd,
And secret Passions labor'd in her Breast.
Not youthful Kings in Battle seiz'd alive,
Not scornful Virgins who their Charms survive,
Not ardent Lovers robb'd of all their Bliss,   5
Not ancient Ladies when refus'd a Kiss,
Not Tyrants fierce that unrepenting die,
Not Cynthia when her Manteau's pinn'd awry,
E'er felt such Rage, Resentment, and Despair,

159–60 *China . . . lie:* Cf. II, 106 and note. 165 *Atalantis: Secret Memoirs and Manners of several Persons of Quality of Both Sexes.* From the New Atalantis . . . by [Mary Manley], London, 1709, a volume of scandalous gossip of the contemporary world of fashion. 166 *small Pillow:* supposedly used to hide a dildo, a scandalous instrument of female prurience. 168 *Wax-lights:* carried by the fashionable lady's attendants on her *Visits*, i.e., formal calls, an often satirized extravagance and display of idleness. 171 *Date:* conclusion, end. 177–78 *What . . . Steel:* Cf: Agenor's speculations that even the insatiable Achilles is mortal: "Yet sure he too is mortal; he may feel / (Like all the sons of earth) the force of steel" (*Iliad*, XXI, 672–73 in Pope's translation) [T].

CANTO IV. 8 *Cynthia . . . awry:* Diana, goddess of chastity, enraged because Actaeon saw her naked body when she was bathing, caused his death. A *manteau* is a cloak.

As Thou, sad Virgin! for thy ravish'd Hair.   10
    For, that sad moment, when the Sylphs withdrew
And Ariel weeping from Belinda flew,
Umbriel, a dusky, melancholy Sprite,
As ever sullied the fair face of Light,
Down to the Central Earth, his proper Scene,   15
Repaired to search the gloomy Cave of Spleen.
    Swift on his sooty Pinions flits the Gnome,
And in a Vapor reached the dismal Dome.
No cheerful Breeze this sullen Region knows,
The dreaded East is all the Wind that blows.   20
Here, in a Grotto, shelter'd close from Air,
And screen'd in Shades from Day's detested Glare,
She sighs for ever on her pensive Bed,
Pain at her Side, and Megrim at her Head.
    Two Handmaids wait the Throne: alike in Place,   25
But diff'ring far in Figure and in Face.
Here stood Ill-nature like an ancient Maid,
Her wrinkled Form in Black and White array'd;
With store of Pray'rs, for Mornings, Nights, and Noons,
Her Hand is fill'd; her Bosom with Lampoons.   30
    There Affectation, with a sickly Mien,
Shows in her Cheek the Roses of Eighteen,
Practic'd to lisp, and hang the Head aside,
Faints into Airs, and languishes with Pride;
On the rich Quilt sinks with becoming Woe,   35
Wrapp'd in a Gown, for Sickness, and for Show.
The Fair-ones feel such Maladies as these,
When each new Night-Dress gives a new Disease.
    A constant Vapor o'er the Palace flies;
Strange Phantoms rising as the Mists arise;   40
Dreadful, as Hermit's Dreams in haunted Shades,
Or bright, as Visions of expiring Maids.
Now glaring Fiends, and Snakes on rolling Spires,
Pale specters, gaping tombs, and purple fires:
Now Lakes of liquid Gold, Elysian Scenes,   45
And crystal Domes, and Angels in Machines.

---

11 *Sylphs withdrew:* Cf. the return of the angel guard in *Paradise Lost,* X,
17–21, after the Fall.   15–16 *Down . . . Spleen:* The descent to the underworld
is an epic convention. The *Cave of Spleen* is a parody of the Hell of the *Aeneid,*
VI, 268–94, where Aeneas in the Mourning Fields (ll. 440–76) sees the shade of
the still unforgiving Dido. The Spleen was a fashionable neurotic condition
that supposedly produced in the hypochondriac hallucinations like those below,
ll. 49–54.   17 *Gnome:* spirit of mischief; cf. I, 20 above and note.   18 *Vapor:*
(pun) a condition much the same as spleen.   20 *East:* the east wind supposedly
encouraged spleen.   24 *Megrim:* migraine.   30 *Lampoons:* malicious personal
satires. Lines 45–46 allude satirically to the scenic effects and stage devices
of opera and pantomime.

Unnumber'd Throngs on every side are seen,
Of Bodies chang'd to various Forms by Spleen.
Here living Tea-pots stand, one Arm held out,
One bent; the Handle this, and that the Spout: 50
A Pipkin there, like Homer's Tripod walks;
Here sighs a Jar, and there a Goose-pie talks;
Men prove with Child, as pow'rful Fancy works,
And Maids turn'd Bottles, call aloud for Corks.
   Safe pass'd the Gnome through this fantastic Band,   55
A branch of healing Spleenwort in his Hand.
Then thus addressed the Pow'r: Hail, wayward Queen!
Who rule the Sex to Fifty from Fifteen,
Parent of Vapors and of Female Wit,
Who give th' Hysteric, or Poetic fit,   60
On various Tempers act by various ways,
Make some take Physic, others scribble Plays;
Who cause the Proud their visits to delay,
And send the Godly in a Pet, to pray.
A Nymph there is, that all thy Pow'r disdains,   65
And thousands more in equal Mirth maintains.
But oh! if e'er thy Gnome could spoil a Grace,
Or raise a Pimple on a beauteous Face,
Like Citron-Waters Matrons' Cheeks inflame,
Or change Complexions at a losing Game;   70
If e'er with airy Horns I planted Heads,
Or rumpled Petticoats, or Tumbled beds,
Or caused Suspicion when no Soul was rude,
Or discomposed the Head-dress of a Prude
Or e'er to costive Lap-Dog gave Disease   75
Which not the Tears of brightest Eyes could ease:
Hear me, and touch Belinda with Chagrin;
That single Act gives half the World the Spleen.
   The Goddess with a discontented Air
Seems to reject him, though she grants his pray'r.   80
A wondrous Bag with both her Hands she binds,

51 *Homer's Tripod:* far different from Vulcan's tripods, which "instinct with spirit roll'd . . . self-moved" and which Thetis saw on Mt. Olympus when she came to persuade Vulcan to make the Shield of Achilles. See *Iliad*, XVIII, 372–79. 52 *Goose-pie talks:* ". . . a real fact, a Lady of distinction imagined herself in this condition" [Pope]. 54 *Maids turn'd Bottles:* i.e., unmarried and frustrated women turned into glass *bottles*. Cf. II, 106 above and note. 56 *Spleenwort:* a fern considered to be a specific for the spleen, but here a parody of the magical golden bough that allowed Aeneas safe passage through the underworld. See *Aeneid*, VI, 136–48. 71 *airy Horns:* i.e., the invisible horns of the cuckold.

Like that where once Ulysses held the Winds;
There she collects the Force of Female Lungs,
Sighs, Sobs, and Passions, and the War of Tongues.
A Vial next she fills with fainting Fears,   85
Soft Sorrows, melting Griefs, and flowing Tears.
The Gnome rejoicing bears her Gifts away,
Spreads his black Wings, and slowly mounts to Day.
   Sunk in Thalestris' arms the Nymph he found,
Her Eyes dejected and her Hair unbound.   90
Full o'er their heads the swelling Bag he rent,
And all the Furies issu'd at the Vent.
Belinda burns with more than mortal Ire,
And fierce Thalestris fans the rising Fire.
O wretched Maid! she spread her Hands, and cried   95
(While Hampton's echoes, wretched Maid! replied),
Was it for this you took such constant Care
The Bodkin, Comb, and Essence to prepare?
For this your Locks in Paper-Durance bound,
For this with tort'ring Irons wreathed around?   100
For this with Fillets strain'd your tender Head,
And bravely bore the double Loads of Lead?
Gods! shall the Ravisher display your Hair,
While the Fops envy, and the Ladies stare!
Honor forbid! at whose unrival'd Shrine   105
Ease, Pleasure, Virtue, All, our Sex resign.
Methinks already I your Tears survey,
Already hear the horrid things they say,
Already see you a degraded Toast,
And all your Honor in a Whisper lost!   110
How shall I, then, your helpless Fame defend?
'Twill then be Infamy to seem your Friend!
And shall this Prize, th' inestimable Prize,
Expos'd through Crystal to the gazing Eyes,
And heighten'd by the Diamond's circling Rays,   115
On that Rapacious Hand for ever blaze?
Sooner shall Grass in Hyde-Park Circus grow,

---

82 *Ulysses . . . Winds:* Aeolus gave Ulysses a bag containing the winds so he
could have a safe and speedy passage home. When the bag was opened by his
undisciplined sailors, Ulysses' ship was overwhelmed by storms and driven
back just as he was about to arrive home. See *Odyssey,* X, 18–27.   89 *Thalestris:*
Queen of the Amazons, famous for her "Brave and Manly Spirit" [T].   99 *in
Paper-Durance:* i.e., curl papers, said to have been fastened with strips of lead
(cf. *Irons,* ll. 100, 102). Parody of heroic incarceration.   101 *Fillets:* head
bands worn by priestesses.   109 *degraded Toast:* a woman whose health is
drunk with a leer.   113–16 *And . . . blaze:* i.e., the lock made into a ring,
ornamented with diamonds. See l. 138.   117 *Hyde-Park Circus:* famous for its
dust and dirt. See I, 44 above and note.

224

And Wits take Lodgings in the Sound of Bow;
Sooner let Earth, Air, Sea, to Chaos fall,
Men, Monkeys, Lap-dogs, Parrots, perish all!   120
    She said; then raging to Sir Plume repairs,
And bids her Beau demand the precious Hairs:
(Sir Plume of amber Snuff-box justly vain,
And the nice Conduct of a clouded Cane)
With earnest Eyes, and round unthinking Face,   125
He first the Snuff-box open'd, then the Case,
And thus broke out—My Lord, why, what the Devil?
Z——ds! damn the Lock! 'fore Gad, you must be civil!
Plague on 't! 'tis past a Jest—nay prithee, Pox!
Give her the Hair—he spoke, and rapped his Box.   130
    It grieves me much (replied the Peer again)
Who speaks so well should ever speak in vain.
But by this Lock, this sacred Lock I swear
(Which never more shall join its parted Hair;
Which never more its Honors shall renew,   135
Clipp'd from the lovely Head where late it grew),
That while my Nostrils draw the vital Air,
This Hand, which won it, shall for ever wear.
He spoke, and speaking, in proud Triumph spread
The long-contended Honors of her Head.   140
    But Umbriel, hateful Gnome! forbears not so;
He breaks the Vial whence the Sorrows flow.
Then see! the Nymph in beauteous Grief appears,
Her Eyes half-languishing, half-drown'd in Tears;
On her heav'd Bosom hung her drooping Head,   145
Which, with a Sigh, she raised; and thus she said:
    Forever curs'd be this detested Day,
Which snatch'd my best, my fav'rite Curl away!
Happy! ah ten times happy, had I been,
If Hampton Court these Eyes had never seen!   150
Yet am not I the first mistaken Maid,
By love of Courts to num'rous Ills betray'd.
Oh had I rather un-admired remain'd
In some lone Isle, or distant Northern Land;
Where the gilt Chariot never marks the Way,   155
Where none learn Ombre, none e'er taste Bohea!

---

118 *Bow:* bell of the church of St. Mary le Bow. Those born *in the Sound of Bow* are Cockneys, not polite *Wits.* 121 *Sir Plume:* a parody of the epic emissary whose language and dress are a model of decorum and civility. Cf. Hermes (*Iliad,* XXIV, 339–48), with wand and winged sandals, who guides Priam through the Greek lines when he goes to Achilles to beg for the return of Hector's body. 124 *Conduct:* precise manner of carrying. *clouded:* elegantly variegated in color. 156 *Bohea:* black tea; rhymes with *Way.*

There kept my Charms conceal'd from mortal Eye,
Like Roses that in Deserts bloom and die.
What mov'd my Mind with youthful Lords to roam?
O had I stayed, and said my Pray'rs at home!   160
'Twas this, the morning Omens seem'd to tell,
Thrice from my trembling hand the Patch-box fell;
The tott'ring China shook without a wind,
Nay, Poll sat mute, and Shock was most unkind!
A Sylph too warned me of the Threats of Fate,   165
In mystic Visions, now believed too late!
See the poor Remnants of these slighted Hairs!
My hands shall rend what ev'n thy Rapine spares:
These, in two sable Ringlets taught to break,
Once gave new Beauties to the snowy Neck;   170
The Sister-Lock now sits uncouth, alone,
And in its Fellow's Fate foresees its own;
Uncurl'd it hangs, the fatal Shears demands,
And tempts once more thy sacrilegious Hands.
O hadst thou, Cruel! been content to seize   175
Hairs less in sight, or any Hairs but these!

CANTO V

She said: the pitying Audience melt in Tears.
But Fate and Jove had stopp'd the Baron's Ears.
In vain Thalestris with Reproach assails,
For who can move when fair Belinda fails?
Not half so fix'd the Trojan could remain,   5
While Anna begg'd and Dido raged in vain.
Then grave Clarissa graceful waved her Fan;
Silence ensu'd, and thus the Nymph began.
    Say, why are Beauties prais'd and honor'd most,
The wise Man's Passion, and the vain Man's Toast?   10
Why deck'd with all that Land and Sea afford,

158 *Roses . . . die:* Cf. Waller's "Go, Lovely Rose," ll. 8–10. If the rose had
"sprung / In deserts," it would have "uncommended died." 176 *Hairs . . .
sight:* i.e. her merkin, false hairpiece for the female pudendum.

CANTO V. 5–6 *Not . . . vain:* In the *Aeneid*, IV, Aeneas leaves Carthage deaf
to Anna's pleas that he remain, made on behalf of her sister Dido. When Dido
later commits suicide out of revenge and remorse, Iris cuts a lock of her hair to
release her from life and as an offering to Dis, but Belinda is no Dido.   7
Clarissa: "The clear, bright one," introduced, according to Pope, "to open more
clearly the moral of the poem." Cf. "clarify": to brighten, exalt, make pure,
and to clear the mind from ignorance.   9–34 *Say . . . Soul:* not really a
parody, but a witty adaptation of Sarpedon's speech to Glaucus before he leads
the assault on the Greek fortifications (*Iliad*, XII, 371–96 in Pope's translation),
which intensifies the parody of the subsequent "battle" and underscores
Belinda's lack of magnanimity.

226

Why Angels call'd, and Angel-like ador'd?
Why round our Coaches crowd the white-glov'd Beaus,
Why bows the Side-box from its inmost Rows?
How vain are all these Glories, all our Pains,   15
Unless good Sense preserve what Beauty gains;
That Men may say, when we the Front-box grace,
Behold the first in Virtue, as in Face!
Oh! if to dance all night, and dress all day,
Charm'd the Small-pox, or chas'd old Age away;   20
Who would not scorn what Housewife's Cares produce,
Or who would learn one earthly Thing of Use?
To patch, nay ogle, might become a Saint,
Nor could it sure be such a Sin to paint.
But since, alas! frail Beauty must decay,   25
Curl'd or uncurl'd, since Locks will turn to gray,
Since painted, or not painted, all shall fade,
And she who scorns a Man, must die a Maid;
What then remains but well our Pow'r to use,
And keep good Humor still whate'er we lose?   30
And trust me, Dear! good Humor can prevail,
When Airs, and Flights, and Screams, and Scolding fail.
Beauties in vain their pretty Eyes may roll;
Charms strike the Sight, but Merit wins the Soul.
   So spoke the Dame, but no Applause ensu'd;   35
Belinda frowned, Thalestris call'd her Prude.
To Arms, to Arms! the fierce Virago cries,
And swift as Lightning to the Combat flies.
All side in Parties, and begin th' Attack;
Fans clap, Silks rustle, and tough Whalebones crack;   40
Heroes' and Heroines' Shouts confus'dly rise,
And bass, and treble Voices strike the Skies.
No common weapons in their hands are found,
Like Gods they fight, nor dread a mortal Wound.
   So when bold Homer makes the Gods engage,   45
And heav'nly Breasts with human Passions rage;
'Gainst Pallas, Mars; Latona, Hermes arms;
And all Olympus rings with loud Alarms:
Jove's Thunder roars, Heav'n trembles all around,
Blue Neptune storms, the bellowing Deeps resound;   50

14, 17 *Side-box, Front-box:* theater boxes. 23 *To patch:* to wear decorative
patches on the face. 30 *good Humor:* magnanimity, which allows one to
lose gracefully in order to win generously. Cf. "Epistle to a Lady," ll. 263–64.
37 *Virago:* an Amazon, female warrior. 45 *So . . . engage:* Cf. *Iliad,* XX,
43–102, where Jupiter "fired their [the gods'] heavenly breasts with rage" [Pope's
tr.]. Cf. Chaucer's treatment of the mock-heroic battle in "The Nun's Priest's
Tale," see above p. 21, ll. 555–81.

Earth shakes her nodding Tow'rs, the Ground gives way,
And the pale Ghosts start at the Flash of Day!
  Triumphant Umbriel on a Sconce's Height
Clapp'd his glad Wings, and sat to view the Fight:
Propp'd on the Bodkin Spears, the Sprites survey   55
The growing Combat, or assist the Fray.
  While through the Press enrag'd Thalestris flies,
And scatters Deaths around from both her Eyes,
A Beau and Witling perished in the Throng,
One died in Metaphor, and one in Song.   60
O cruel Nymph! a living Death I bear,
Cried Dapperwit, and sunk beside his Chair.
A mournful Glance Sir Fopling upwards cast,
Those Eyes are made so killing—was his last.
Thus on Mæander's flow'ry Margin lies   65
Th' expiring Swan, and as he sings he dies.
  When bold Sir Plume had drawn Clarissa down,
Chloe stepp'd in, and kill'd him with a Frown;
She smil'd to see the doughty Hero slain,
But at her Smile, the Beau revived again.   70
  Now Jove suspends his golden Scales in Air,
Weighs the Men's Wits against the Lady's Hair;
The doubtful Beam long nods from side to side;
At length the Wits mount up, the Hairs subside.
  See fierce Belinda on the Baron flies,   75
With more than usual Lightning in her Eyes;
Nor fear'd the Chief th' unequal Fight to try,
Who sought no more than on his Foe to die.
But this bold Lord with manly Strength indu'd,
She with one Finger and a Thumb subdu'd: 80
Just where the Breath of Life his Nostrils drew,
A Charge of Snuff the wily Virgin threw;
The Gnomes direct, to ev'ry Atom just,
The pungent Grains of titillating Dust.
Sudden, with starting Tears each Eye o'erflows,   85

---

58 *scatters Deaths:* Cf. Wyatt, "And if an eye may save or slay" and note.
62 *Dapperwit:* a fop in Wycherley's comedy *Love in a Wood*.   63 *Sir Fopling*
[Flutter]: principal character in Etherege's comedy *The Man of Mode*.   64
Those . . . killing: from a song in the popular opera *Camilla* by Buononcini.
65–66 *Thus . . . dies:* as the swan ("who living had no voice") in Ovid's
Heroides (VII) dies while singing the lament of "Dido to Aeneas" from the
shallows of the river Meander.   71 *Scales:* symbol of divine justice; cf. *Iliad*,
VIII, 69–72, where the destinies of the Greeks and the Trojans are weighed;
XXII, 209, those of Hector and Achilles; *Aeneid*, XII, 725–27, those of Aeneas
and Turnus; and *Paradise Lost*, IV, 997–1004, that of Satan.   78 *to die:* (pun
and parody) the heroic way to die is to fall lifeless on top of the foe; to
subside lifeless after sexual climax.

228

And the high Dome re-echoes to his Nose.
  Now meet thy Fate, incens'd Belinda cried,
And drew a deadly Bodkin from her Side.
(The same, his ancient Personage to deck,
Her great great Grandsire wore about his Neck   90
In three Seal-Rings; which after, melted down,
Form'd a vast Buckle for his Widow's Gown:
Her infant Grandame's Whistle next it grew,
The Bells she jingled, and the Whistle blew;
Then in a Bodkin grac'd her Mother's Hairs,   95
Which long she wore, and now Belinda wears).
  Boast not my Fall (he cried) insulting Foe!
Thou by some other shalt be laid as low.
Nor think, to die dejects my lofty Mind;
All that I dread is leaving you behind!   100
Rather than so, ah let me still survive,
And burn in Cupid's flames—but burn alive.
  Restore the Lock! she cries; and all around
Restore the Lock! the vaulted Roofs rebound.
Not fierce Othello in so loud a Strain   105
Roar'd for the Handkerchief that caus'd his Pain.
But see how oft Ambitious Aims are cross'd,
And Chiefs contend 'till all the Prize is lost!
The Lock, obtained with Guilt, and kept with Pain,
In ev'ry place is sought, but sought in vain: 110
With such a Prize no Mortal must be bless'd,
So Heav'n decrees! with Heav'n who can contest?
  Some thought it mounted to the Lunar Sphere,
Since all things lost on Earth are treasur'd there.
There Heroes' Wits are kept in pond'rous Vases,   115
And Beaus' in Snuff-boxes and Tweezer-cases.
There broken Vows, and Death-bed Alms are found,
And Lovers' Hearts with Ends of Riband bound,
The Courtier's Promises, and Sick Man's Pray'rs,
The Smiles of Harlots, and the Tears of Heirs,   120
Cages for Gnats, and Chains to yoke a Flea,

---

86 *Nose:* (double entendre) Cf. Shakespeare, *Antony and Cleopatra*, I, ii, 60–63. The sneeze is also orgasmic. 88–96 *Bodkin . . . wears:* parody of the genealogy of the epic weapon. Cf. *Iliad*, X, 266–71. 99 *to die:* Cf. l. 78 and note. 105–06 *Othello . . . Handkerchief:* See *Othello*, IV, i, esp. ll. 38–46. 115–22 *Wits . . . Casuistry:* epic catalogue of the most inconsequential, trivial, and utterly untrustworthy protestations, objects, and intellectual endeavors known to man. Pope notes that this is an allusion to *Orlando Furioso*, XXXIV (stanzas 68–75) where Astolfo journeys to the moon to recover Orlando's lost wits. Cf. also the "Paradise of Fools" (*Paradise Lost*, III, 444–97), which Milton says is the true repository ("not in the . . . moon") of "all things vain."

Dried Butterflies, and Tomes of Casuistry.
   But trust the Muse—she saw it upward rise,
Though mark'd by none but quick, Poetic Eyes:
(So Rome's great Founder to the Heav'ns withdrew,   125
To Proculus alone confess'd in view).
A sudden Star, it shot through liquid Air,
And drew behind a radiant Trail of Hair.
Not Berenice's Locks first rose so bright,
The Heav'ns bespangling with dishevel'd Light.   130
The Sylphs behold it kindling as it flies,
And pleas'd pursue its Progress through the Skies.
   This the Beau-monde shall from the Mall survey,
And hail with Music its propitious Ray.
This the blest Lover shall for Venus take,   135
And send up Vows from Rosamonda's Lake.
This Partridge soon shall view in cloudless Skies,
When next he looks through Galileo's Eyes;
And hence th' Egregious Wizard shall foredoom
The fate of Louis, and the fall of Rome.   140
   Then cease, bright Nymph! to mourn thy ravish'd Hair,

---

122 *Tomes of Casuistry:* wordy, evasive, sophistical books dealing with special problems of conscience. 125–26 *So . . . view:* According to Livy (I, xvi) Romulus was translated to heaven during a thunderstorm. Thanks to the plan of Proculus, who claimed that Romulus appeared exclusively to him to authenticate this explanation for his sudden disappearance, the uneasy populace was placated and cheered with the prophecy of Rome's greatness. So likewise Pope can (ironically) placate and cheer society with his exclusive knowledge of the lock's translation and future influence. 127 *liquid:* clear, shining. 129 *Berenice's Locks:* In Catullus' poem (Loeb, LXVI, tr. F. W. Cornish), the Lock of Berenice tells how she [the lock] was "un-willingly" parted from Berenice, who had vowed that she would sacrifice her cherished lock as an offering for her husband's safe return from war, and how she was translated to heaven and made into a constellation by Venus to honor Berenice's pure, loving devotion to her husband. She commands brides who "reverence marriage in chaste wedlock" to offer gifts to her before they yield their bodies to their husbands. The significance of this allusion is that girls who weep in their "virgin bowers" "lament not truly"; Berenice, weeping for her absent husband does so truly, which the willing and joyful sacrifice of the lock proves. Hence Belinda, hypocritical and selfish, has yet to learn the magnanimity of a Sarpedon-Clarissa and the true meaning of love and chastity that Berenice's sacrifice exemplifies. 130 *dishevel'd:* Berenice's lock was translated "wet with tears," but Belinda' lock makes its passage disarranged, torn apart. 131 *kindling:* growing bright. 133 *Beau-monde:* world of fashion. *Mall:* walk in St. James's Park. 136 *Rosamonda's Lake:* lake in St. James's Park, frequently a place of passion for both innocent and carnal lovers. 137 *Partridge:* a London astrologer, almanac maker, and ridiculous quack who annually predicted the downfall of the Pope and Louis XIV (l. 140). He was satirized in the Bickerstaff papers by Swift who, to Partridge's dismay, predicted and, on the date established, duly announced his death. 138 *Galileo's Eyes:* telescope. 139 *Egregious:* uncommon, extraordinary, but here ironic, in a condemnatory sense. Belinda's stellified lock, thus interpreted by the fops, the promiscuous, and the quacks, is assuredly ambiguous.

Which adds new Glory to the shining Sphere!
Not all the Tresses that fair Head can boast,
Shall draw such Envy as the Lock you lost.
For, after all the Murders of your Eye,   145
When, after Millions slain, yourself shall die;
When those fair Suns shall set, as set they must,
And all those Tresses shall be laid in Dust;
This Lock, the Muse shall consecrate to Fame,
And 'midst the Stars inscribe Belinda's Name.   150

from EPISTLES TO SEVERAL PERSONS

Epistle II

TO A LADY

Of the Characters of Women

Nothing so true as what you once let fall,
"Most Women have no Characters at all."
Matter too soft a lasting mark to bear,
And best distinguish'd by black, brown, or fair.
   How many Pictures of one Nymph we view,   5
All how unlike each other, all how true!
Arcadia's Countess here, in ermin'd Pride,
Is there, Pastora by a fountain side;
Here Fannia, leering on her own good man,
And there a naked Leda with a Swan.   10

145–48 *Murders . . . Dust:* completion of the Petrarchan hyperboles of the
Eye and *Lock* as images of light in this transitory world and reiteration of the
theme *Ars longa, vita brevis est*, already old with the Elizabethan sonneteers.
Cf. Spenser, *Amoretti*, Sonnet 75.

EPISTLE II. Completed in 1733 and first published in 1735, this "Moral
Essay" lacked the portraits of *Philomedé* (ll. 69–86), *Atossa* (ll. 115–50), *Chloe*
(ll. 157–80), and that of the *Queen* [Caroline] (ll. 181–98), which were included
in the 1744 edition. These and the other portraits probably glance at real
persons, but Pope insisted, probably with tongue in cheek, that he uses "no
living examples or real names." Modern conjectures as to their identities con-
tribute little to the literary value of the satire. The poem is derived from Juvenal's
sixth satire on women, but Pope is primarily concerned with subtle psychological portraits of various kinds of fashionable women, delighting in how
"contrarieties run through them all."

TO A LADY. Martha Blount, Pope's devoted friend and companion. 5–14
Pictures . . . divine: costumes and poses in which a fashionable lady could be
painted. The poem may be considered a kind of portrait gallery. 3 *Pastora:*
i.e., a shepherdess. 9 *Fannia:* i.e., a "modest" wife in a double portrait,
leering presumably because she is a dissolute adulteress as was the Roman
Fannia who saved the life of Marius. See Plutarch's "Life of Marius," XXXVIII.
10 *Leda:* mother of Helen, seduced by Zeus in the form of a swan; i.e., a
prurient pose sanctified by art and mythology.

Let then the Fair one beautifully cry,
In Magdalen's loose hair and lifted eye,
Or, dress'd in smiles of sweet Cecilia shine,
With simp'ring Angels, Palms, and Harps divine;
Whether the Charmer sinner it, or saint it,   15
If Folly grow romantic, I must paint it.
    Come then, the colours and the ground prepare!
Dip in the rainbow, trick her off in air;
Choose a firm Cloud, before it fall, and in it
Catch, ere she change, the Cynthia of this minute.   20
    Rufa, whose eye quick-glancing o'er the Park,
Attracts each light gay meteor of a Spark,
Agrees as ill with Rufa studying Locke
As Sappho's diamonds with her dirty smock;
Or Sappho at her toilet's greasy task,   25
With Sappho fragrant at an ev'ning Mask:
So morning insects that in muck begun
Shine, buzz, and fly-blow in the setting sun.
    How soft is Silia! fearful to offend,
The Frail one's advocate, the Weak one's friend: 30
To her Calista prov'd her conduct nice,
And good Simplicius asks of her advice.
Sudden, she storms! she raves! You tip the wink,
But spare your censure; Silia does not drink:
All eyes may see from what the change arose,   35
All eyes may see—a Pimple on her nose.
    Papillia, wedded to her am'rous spark,
Sighs for the shades—"How charming is a Park!"
A Park is purchas'd, but the Fair he sees
All bath'd in tears—"Oh, odious, odious Trees!"   40

11 *cry:* but not with the penitence and humility of Mary Magdalen, the reformed harlot and disciple of Christ, who is usually depicted in Western art with red, flowing hair and upraised weeping eyes. 13 *Cecilia:* St. Cecilia, patroness of music. Cf. Dryden, "A Song for St. Cecilia's Day." 17 *ground:* the basis for a picture; the general tone of color (primer) spread over the surface of canvas, intended either to show through the overlaid color or to relieve it. 20 *Cynthia:* i.e., changeable woman, since the moon (Cynthia) never rests in one phase; ironic in that Cynthia (Diana) is also the goddess of chastity. 21 *Rufa:* i.e., redhead. 23 *Locke:* John Locke, author of *An Essay Concerning Human Understanding* (1690), a difficult book, not for scatterbrains. 24 *Sappho:* a seventh-century B.C. Lesbian poetess, famous for her passionate love poetry; here, any unkempt, *greasy* poetess with perverse inclinations. 28 *fly-blow:* deposit eggs, taint. 29 *Silia:* "contrarieties in the soft-natured" [Pope]. The significance of the name is unknown. 31 *Calista:* promiscuous heroine of Rowe's *The Fair Penitent* (1703); also as Callisto (fairest), one of the nymphs of Artemis. She was seduced by Zeus, became the mother of Arcas, and was transformed into a bear by Artemis for violating the law of chastity; hence, a self-excusing wanton. 32 *Simplicius:* i.e., a simple-minded fool. 33 *tip the wink:* (slang) give a wink. 37 *Papillia:* i.e., butterfly.

Ladies, like variegated tulips, show;
'Tis to their changes half their charms we owe;
Fine by defect, and delicately weak,
Their happy spots the nice admirer take.
'Twas thus Calypso once each heart alarm'd,   45
Aw'd without virtue, without beauty charm'd;
Her tongue bewitch'd as oddly as her eyes,
Less Wit than Mimic, more a Wit than wise;
Strange graces still, and stranger flights she had,
Was just not ugly, and was just not mad;   50
Yet ne'er so sure our passion to create,
As when she touch'd the brink of all we hate.
   Narcissa's nature, tolerably mild,
To make a wash, would hardly stew a child;
Has ev'n been prov'd to grant a lover's pray'r,   55
And paid a Tradesman once to make him stare;
Gave alms at Easter, in a Christian trim,
And made a Widow happy, for a whim.
Why then declare Good-nature is her scorn,
When 'tis by that alone she can be borne?   60
Why pique all mortals, yet affect a name?
A fool to Pleasure, yet a slave to Fame:
Now deep in Taylor and the Book of Martyrs,
Now drinking citron with his Grace and Chartres:
Now Conscience chills her, and now Passion burns;   65
And Atheism and Religion take their turns;
A very Heathen in the carnal part,
Yet still a sad, good Christian at her heart.
   See Sin in State, majestically drunk;
Proud as a Peeress, prouder as a Punk;   70
Chaste to her Husband, frank to all beside,
A teeming Mistress, but a barren Bride.
What then? let Blood and Body bear the fault,
Her Head's untouch'd, that noble Seat of Thought:
Such this day's doctrine—in another fit   75
She sins with Poets through pure Love of Wit.
What has not fir'd her bosom or her brain?
Cæsar and Tall-boy, Charles and Charlemagne.

---

45 *Calypso:* i.e., the hider, so named because by her enticing wiles she hid
Odysseus from the world and his destiny; hence, any bewitching wanton who
beguiles men from duty and public responsibility.   53 *Narcissa:* i.e., the self-
lover.   54 *wash:* astringent lotion.   55 *grant . . . pray'r:* as Narcissus never
did.   63 *Taylor . . . Martyrs:* i.e., absorbed in reading Jeremy Taylor's
Holy Living and Dying (1650-51) and John Foxe's *Book of Martyrs* (1563).
64 *citron:* brandy flavored with citron.   *his Grace:* any duke.   *Chartres:* any
gambler, debauchee, and swindler like Francis Chartres, the most notorious
of his time.   69-86 *Sin . . . Dunce:* contrarieties in the "lewd and vicious"
[Pope].   78 *Tall-boy:* stock booby.   *Charles:* name of a stock servant.

As Helluo, late Dictator of the feast,
The Nose of Hautgout, and the Tip of Taste,   80
Critiqu'd your wine, and analyz'd your meat,
Yet on plain Pudding deign'd at home to eat;
So Philomedé, lect'ring all mankind
On the soft Passion, and the Taste refin'd,
Th' Address, the Delicacy—stoops at once,   85
And makes her hearty meal upon a Dunce.
    Flavia's a Wit, has too much sense to Pray;
To Toast our wants and wishes, is her way;
Nor asks of God, but of her Stars, to give
The mighty blessing, "while we live, to live."   90
Then all for Death, that Opiate of the soul!
Lucretia's dagger, Rosamonda's bowl.
Say, what can cause such impotence of mind?
A Spark too fickle, or a Spouse too kind.
Wise Wretch! with Pleasures too refin'd to please;   95
With too much Spirit to be e'er at ease;
With too much Quickness ever to be taught;
With too much Thinking to have common Thought:
You purchase Pain with all that Joy can give,
And die of nothing but a Rage to live.   100
    Turn then from Wits; and look on Simo's Mate,
No Ass so meek, no Ass so obstinate.
Or her, that owns her Faults, but never mends,
Because she's honest, and the best of Friends.
Or her, whose life the Church and Scandal share,   105
Forever in a Passion, or a Pray'r.
Or her, who laughs at Hell, but (like her Grace)
Cries, "Ah! how charming, if there's no such place!"
Or who in sweet vicissitude appears
Of Mirth and Opium, Ratafie and Tears,   110
The daily Anodyne, and nightly Draught,
To kill those foes to Fair ones, Time and Thought.

---

79 *Helluo:* glutton. 80 *Hautgout:* anything with a strong scent; hence a gross, over-ripe sensibility. 83 *Philomedé:* from the Greek *philomeidês*, standard Homeric epithet for Aphrodite, meaning "laughter loving"; or *philomêdês*, Hesiod's epithet for her (*Theogony*, l. 200), meaning "genital lover." 86 *meal:* double entendre. 87–100 *Flavia's . . . live:* "contrarieties in the witty and refined" [Pope]. 87 *Flavia:* i.e., any blonde. 92 *Lucretia:* Lucretia, ravished by Tarquin, stabbed herself with a dagger to preserve her chastity. *Rosamonda's bowl:* Fair Rosamund, concubine to Henry II, after whom the pond in St. James's Park was named (see "Rape of the Lock," V, 136), was, according to legend, forced by Queen Elinor to take poison. 101–14 *look . . . Wit:* contrarieties in the stupid and silly. 101 *Simo:* "Snub Nose," the old father in Terence's *Andrian* who worries about his son's marriage. 110 *Ratafie:* a liqueur made from black currants, bitter almonds, and cherry or peach stones.

Woman and Fool are two hard things to hit;
For true No-meaning puzzles more than Wit.
    But what are these to great Atossa's mind?   115
Scarce once herself, by turns all Womankind!
Who, with herself, or others, from her birth
Finds all her life one warfare upon earth:
Shines in exposing Knaves, and painting Fools,
Yet is whate'er she hates and ridicules.   120
No Thought advances, but her Eddy Brain
Whisks it about, and down it goes again.
Full sixty years the World has been her Trade,
The wisest Fool much Time has ever made.
From loveless youth to unrespected age,   125
No Passion gratified except her Rage.
So much the Fury still outran the Wit,
The Pleasure miss'd her, and the Scandal hit.
Who breaks with her, provokes Revenge from Hell,
But he's a bolder man who dares be well.   130
Her ev'ry turn with Violence pursu'd,
No more a storm her Hate than Gratitude:
To that each Passion turns, or soon or late;
Love, if it makes her yield, must make her hate:
Superiors? death! and Equals? what a curse!   135
But an Inferior not dependent? worse.
Offend her, and she knows not to forgive;
Oblige her, and she'll hate you while you live:
But die, and she'll adore you—Then the Bust
And Temple rise—then fall again to dust.   140
Last night, her Lord was all that's good and great;
A Knave this morning, and his Will a Cheat.
Strange! by the Means defeated of the Ends,
By Spirit robb'd of Pow'r, by Warmth of Friends,
By Wealth of Follow'rs! without one distress,   145
Sick of herself through very selfishness!
Atossa, curs'd with ev'ry granted pray'r,
Childless with all her Children, wants an Heir.
To Heirs unknown descends th' unguarded store,
Or wanders, Heav'n-directed, to the Poor.   150
    Pictures like these, dear Madam, to design,
Asks no firm hand, and no unerring line;

---

115 *Atossa:* a Persian queen, daughter of Cyrus and wife successively of her brother, Cambyses—a mad, intolerant ruler—and of Darius—wise and constructive but the loser at Marathon—by whom she became the mother of Xerxes, another violent ruler, who was murdered; hence a violent, despotic, eccentric, quarrelsome great lady. 130 *well:* with her; i.e., in her good graces. 139–40 *Bust, Temple:* monuments for the departed.

Some wand'ring touches, some reflected light,
Some flying stroke alone can hit 'em right:
For how should equal Colours do the knack?   155
Chameleons who can paint in white and black?
    "Yet Chloe sure was form'd without a spot"—
Nature in her then err'd not, but forgot.
"With ev'ry pleasing, ev'ry prudent part,
Say, what can Chloe want?"—She wants a Heart.   160
She speaks, behaves, and acts just as she ought;
But never, never, reach'd one gen'rous Thought.
Virtue she finds too painful an endeavour,
Content to dwell in Decencies forever.
So very reasonable, so unmov'd,   165
As never yet to love, or to be lov'd.
She, while her Lover pants upon her breast,
Can mark the figures on an Indian chest;
And when she sees her Friend in deep despair,
Observes how much a Chintz exceeds Mohair.   170
Forbid it Heav'n, a Favour or a Debt
She e'er should cancel—but she may forget.
Safe is your Secret still in Chloe's ear;
But none of Chloe's shall you ever hear.
Of all her Dears she never slander'd one,   175
But cares not if a thousand are undone.
Would Chloe know if you're alive or dead?
She bids her Footman put it in her head.
Chloe is prudent—Would you too be wise?
Then never break your heart when Chloe dies.   180
    One certain Portrait may (I grant) be seen,
Which Heav'n has varnish'd out, and made a Queen;
The same forever! and describ'd by all
With Truth and Goodness, as with Crown and Ball.
Poets heap Virtues, Painters Gems at will,   185
And show their zeal, and hide their want of skill.
'Tis well—but, Artists! who can paint or write,
To draw the Naked is your true delight.
That Robe of Quality so struts and swells,

155 *equal:* i.e., uniform. 157 *Chloe:* "Green," title of Demeter (Ceres),
goddess of the young green crops (See Aristophanes, *Lysistrata*, l. 835),
inconsolable mother of Kore (Proserpina), and initiator of brides and grooms
into the secrets of the marriage bed; but here infertile, calloused, indifferent—no mother-goddess. Also the name of the heroine of the pastoral Greek
romance *Daphnis and Chloe*, but again here no tender, sentimental heroine;
also, in Horace and Martial, a name for a party girl or courtesan, which here
she is, but without enjoying herself. 164 *Decencies:* stylized proprieties.
182 *varnished out:* i.e., given a fair, external appearance (by glossing over
defects). *Queen:* Queen Caroline.

None see what Parts of Nature it conceals: 190
Th' exactest traits of Body or of Mind,
We owe to models of an humble kind.
If Queensberry to strip there's no compelling,
'Tis from a Handmaid we must take a Helen.
From Peer or Bishop 'tis no easy thing   195
To draw the man who loves his God, or King:
Alas! I copy (or my draught would fail)
From honest Mah'met, or plain Parson Hale.
    But grant, in Public Men sometimes are shown,
A Woman's seen in Private life alone: 200
Our bolder Talents in full light display'd;
Your virtues open fairest in the shade.
Bred to disguise, in Public 'tis you hide;
There, none distinguish 'twixt your Shame or Pride,
Weakness or Delicacy; all so nice,   205
That each may seem a Virtue, or a Vice.
    In Men, we various Ruling Passions find;
In Women, two almost divide the kind;
Those, only fix'd, they first or last obey,
The Love of Pleasure, and the Love of Sway.   210
    That, Nature gives; and where the lesson taught
Is but to please, can Pleasure seem a fault?
Experience, this; by Man's Oppression curst,
They seek the second not to lose the first.
    Men, some to Bus'ness, some to Pleasure take;   215
But ev'ry Woman is at heart a Rake:
Men, some to Quiet, some to public Strife;
But ev'ry Lady would be Queen for life.
    Yet mark the fate of a whole Sex of Queens!
Pow'r all their end, but Beauty all the means: 220
In Youth they conquer, with so wild a rage,
As leaves them scarce a Subject in their Age:
For foreign glory, foreign joy, they roam;
No thought of Peace or Happiness at home.
But Wisdom's Triumph is well-tim'd Retreat,   225
As hard a science to the Fair as Great!
Beauties, like Tyrants, old and friendless grown,
Yet hate Repose, and dread to be alone,
Worn out in public, weary ev'ry eye,

193 *Queensberry:* Catherine Hyde, Duchess of Queensberry, universally celebrated as the most beautiful woman of the time. Since she was a great lady, she would not deign to pose in the nude. 197 *draught:* preliminary sketch. 198 *Mah'met:* servant to George I [Pope]. *Parson Hale:* clergyman, physiologist, and friend of Pope. 214 *second . . . first:* i.e., *Sway* so as not to lose *Pleasure.* 219 *Queens:* with pun on queans, i.e., whores.

Nor leave one sigh behind them when they die.   230
   Pleasures the sex, as children Birds, pursue,
Still out of reach, yet never out of view;
Sure, if they catch, to spoil the Toy at most,
To covet flying, and regret when lost:
At last, to follies Youth could scarce defend,   235
It grows their Age's prudence to pretend;
Asham'd to own they gave delight before,
Reduc'd to feign it, when they give no more:
As Hags hold Sabbaths, less for joy than spite,
So these their merry, miserable Night;   240
Still round and round the Ghosts of Beauty glide,
And haunt the places where their Honour died.
   See how the World its Veterans rewards!
A Youth of frolics, an old Age of Cards;
Fair to no purpose, artful to no end,   245
Young without Lovers, old without a Friend;
A Fop their Passion, but their Prize a Sot;
Alive, ridiculous, and dead, forgot!
   Ah! Friend! to dazzle let the Vain design;
To raise the Thought and touch the Heart, be thine!   250
That Charm shall grow, while what fatigues the Ring,
Flaunts and goes down, an unregarded thing:
So when the Sun's broad beam has tir'd the sight,
All mild ascends the Moon's more sober light,
Serene in Virgin Modesty she shines,   255
And unobserv'd the glaring Orb declines.
   Oh! blest with Temper, whose unclouded ray
Can make to-morrow cheerful as to-day;
She, who can love a Sister's charms, or hear
Sighs for a Daughter with unwounded ear;   260
She, who ne'er answers till a Husband cools,
Or, if she rules him, never shows she rules;
Charms by accepting, by submitting sways,
Yet has her humour most, when she obeys;
Let Fops or Fortune fly which way they will;   265
Disdains all loss of Tickets, or Codille;
Spleen, Vapours, or Smallpox, above them all,
And Mistress of herself, though China fall.

---

239 *Hags hold Sabbaths:* i.e., witches' sabbaths, midnight orgies under the leadership of Satan. 240 *Night:* set night for formal visiting. 251 *Ring:* See "Rape of the Lock", I, 44 and note; IV, 117 and note. 254 *Moon:* Cf. l. 20 above and note. 263–64 *Charms . . . obeys:* Cf. "Rape of the Lock," V, 29–30. Cf. Prov. 31:10–31 for parallel description of a "virtuous woman." 266 *Tickets:* i.e., lottery tickets. *Codille:* Cf. "Rape of the Lock," III, 92. 267 *Spleen:* Cf. "Rape of the Lock," IV, 15–54. 268 *China:* (pun) Cf. "Rape of the Lock," III, 159–60.

And yet, believe me, good as well as ill,
Woman's at best a Contradiction still.   270
Heav'n, when it strives to polish all it can
Its last best work, but forms a softer Man;
Picks from each sex, to make the Fav'rite blest,
Your love of Pleasure, our desire of Rest:
Blends, in exception to all gen'ral rules,   275
Your Taste of Follies, with our Scorn of Fools:
Reserve with Frankness, Art with Truth allied,
Courage with Softness, Modesty with Pride;
Fix'd Principles, with Fancy ever new;
Shakes all together, and produces—You.   280
   Be this a Woman's Fame: with this unblest,
Toasts live a scorn, and Queens may die a jest.
This Phœbus promis'd (I forget the year)
When those blue eyes first open'd on the sphere;
Ascendant Phœbus watch'd that hour with care,   285
Averted half your Parents' simple Pray'r;
And gave you Beauty, but denied the Pelf
That buys your sex a Tyrant o'er itself.
The gen'rous God, who Wit and Gold refines,
And ripens Spirits as he ripens Mines,   290
Kept Dross for Duchesses, the world shall know it,
To you gave Sense, Good-humour, and a Poet.

269–80 *And . . . You:* the "estimable woman with the best kinds of contrarieties" [Pope]. Cf. Milton's oxymorons in his account of unfallen Adam and Eve [The Garden], p. 159, ll. 84 ff. and notes.   289 *gen'rous God:* Phoebus Apollo, god of the sun (gold), healing, and poetry, *ripens* and *refines* the wits of poets as well (supposedly) as the gold in the mines.

WILLIAM BLAKE
1757–1827

from POETICAL SKETCHES

Mad Song

The wild winds weep,
  And the night is a-cold;
Come hither, Sleep,
  And my griefs unfold:
But lo! the morning peeps   5
Over the eastern steeps,
And the rustling beds of dawn
The earth do scorn.

Lo! to the vault
  Of pavèd heaven,   10
With sorrow fraught
  My notes are driven:
They strike the ear of night,
Make weep the eyes of day;
They make mad the roaring winds,   15
And with tempests play.

Like a fiend in a cloud,
  With howling woe
After night I do croud,
  And with night will go;   20
I turn my back to the east,
From whence comforts have increas'd;
For light doth seize my brain
With frantic pain.

from SONGS OF INNOCENCE

The Lamb

Little Lamb, who made thee?
Dost thou know who made thee?
Gave thee life and bid thee feed,

MAD SONG. 19 *croud:* play on my fiddle. Cf. *notes*, l. 12. (The croud is an ancient Welsh and Irish instrument, the earliest known member of the viol class.) See *OED*, *Crowd*, v₂. It can also mean hasten on.

By the stream and o'er the mead;
Gave thee clothing of delight,   5
Softest clothing, wooly, bright;
Gave thee such a tender voice,
Making all the vales rejoice?
    Little Lamb who made thee?
    Dost thou know who made thee?   10

    Little Lamb, I'll tell thee,
    Little Lamb, I'll tell thee:
He is callèd by thy name,
For he calls himself a Lamb.
He is meek, and he is mild;   15
He became a little child.
I a child, and thou a lamb,
We are callèd by his name.
    Little Lamb, God bless thee!
    Little Lamb, God bless thee!   20

The Divine Image

To Mercy, Pity, Peace, and Love
All pray in their distress:
And to these virtues of delight
Return their thankfulness.

For Mercy, Pity, Peace, and Love   5
Is God, our father dear:
And Mercy, Pity, Peace, and Love
Is Man, his child and care.

For Mercy has a human heart,
Pity, a human face,   10
And Love, the human form divine,
And Peace, the human dress.

Then every man of every clime,
That prays in his distress,
Prays to the human form divine,   15
Love, Mercy, Pity, Peace.

And all must love the human form,
In heathen, turk, or jew;
Where Mercy, Love, and Pity dwell.
There God is dwelling too.   20

Night

The sun descending in the west,
The evening star does shine;
The birds are silent in their nest,
And I must seek for mine.
The moon, like a flower,   5
In heaven's high bower,
With silent delight
Sits and smiles on the night.

Farewell green fields and happy groves,
Where flocks have took delight: 10
Where lambs have nibbled, silent moves
The feet of angels bright:
Unseen they pour blessing,
And joy without ceasing,
On each bud and blossom,   15
And each sleeping bosom.

They look in every thoughtless nest,
Where birds are cover'd warm:
They visit caves of every beast,
To keep them all from harm.   20
If they see any weeping
That should have been sleeping,
They pour sleep on their head
And sit down by their bed.

When wolves and tigers howl for prey,   25
They pitying stand and weep,
Seeking to drive their thirst away,
And keep them from the sheep.
But if they rush dreadful,
The angels, most heedful,   30
Receive each mild spirit,
New worlds to inherit.

And there the lion's ruddy eyes
Shall flow with tears of gold,
And pitying the tender cries,   35
And walking round the fold,

NIGHT. 33–40 *lion's . . . day:* Cf. Isa., 11:6–7 where the wolf, leopard, and young lion "shall lie down with the kid."

Saying "Wrath, by his meekness,
And, by his health, sickness
Is driven away
From our immortal day.   40

"And now beside thee, bleating lamb,
I can lie down and sleep;
Or think on him who bore thy name,
Graze after thee and weep.
For, wash'd in life's river,   45
My bright mane for ever
Shall shine like the gold
As I guard o'er the fold."

Infant Joy

"I have no name:
I am but two days old."
    What shall I call thee?
"I happy am,
Joy is my name."   5
    Sweet joy befall thee!

Pretty joy!
Sweet joy, but two days old.
    Sweet joy I call thee:
Thou dost smile,   10
I sing the while,
    Sweet joy befall thee!

from SONGS OF EXPERIENCE

Infant Sorrow

My mother groan'd! my father wept.
Into the dangerous world I leapt:
Helpless, naked, piping loud:
Like a fiend hid in a cloud.

Struggling in my father's hands,   5
Striving against my swadling bands,
Bound and weary I thought best
To sulk upon my mother's breast.

45 *wash'd:* Cf. the apocalyptic vision in Rev. 7:14–17 of the saints redeemed
from the violence and grief of this world.

The Sick Rose

O Rose, thou art sick!
The invisible worm,
That flies in the night
In the howling storm,

Has found out thy bed   5
Of crimson joy;
And his dark secret love
Does thy life destroy.

Ah Sun-flower!

Ah Sun-flower! weary of time,
Who countest the steps of the Sun;
Seeking after that sweet golden clime
Where the traveller's journey is done;

Where the Youth pined away with desire,   5
And the pale Virgin shrouded in snow,
Arise from their graves, and aspire
Where my Sun-flower wishes to go.

The Clod and the Pebble

"Love seeketh not Itself to please,
   Nor for itself hath any care,
But for another gives its ease,
   And builds a Heaven in Hell's despair."   *Clod*

So sung a little Clod of Clay,   5
   Trodden with the cattle's feet,
But a Pebble of the brook   *Pebble*
   Warbled out these metres meet:

"Love seeketh only Self to please,
   To bind another to Its delight,   10
Joys in another's loss of ease,
   And builds a Hell in Heaven's despite."

AH SUN-FLOWER! 7 *aspire:* both rise up as an exhalation, like fire, and
seek with longing.

The Tyger

Tyger! Tyger! burning bright
In the forests of the night:
What immortal hand or eye,
Could frame thy fearful symmetry?

In what distant deeps or skies   5
Burnt the fire of thine eyes?
On what wings dare he aspire?
What the hand dare seize the fire?

And what shoulder, and what art,
Could twist the sinews of thy heart?   10
And when thy heart began to beat,
What dread hand? and what dread feet?

What the hammer? what the chain?
In what furnace was thy brain?
What the anvil? what dread grasp   15
Dare its deadly terrors clasp?

When the stars threw down their spears,
And water'd heaven with their tears,
Did he smile his work to see?
Did he who made the Lamb make thee?   20

Tyger! Tyger! burning bright
In the forests of the night:
What immortal hand or eye,
Dare frame thy fearful symmetry?

THE TYGER. *Tyger:* apocalyptic symbol of creative wrath, which, forged on the anvil of inspiration out of both "innocence" and "experience," cleanses by producing pity and fear.   2 *forests:* mythological realm of human wandering in the world of corrupting materialism.   6 *eyes:* the visionary eyes of the artist. 7 *aspire:* soar. 8 *hand . . . fire:* The Creator as blacksmith is Promethean. 17–18 *When . . . tears:* allusion to the capitulation of the angels (i.e., *stars*, passive reason) at the creation of the *Tyger*, the wrath of righteousness, which through destruction creates a new order. Cf. also Job, 38:7. 24 *Dare:* Cf. *Could*, l. 4. Nerve and will, implied in *Dare*, are required to prompt the action needed to resolve the paradox of the *Tyger* and the *Lamb* issuing from the hand of the same Creator.

London

I wander thro' each charter'd street,
Near where the charter'd Thames does flow,
And mark in every face I meet
Marks of weakness, marks of woe.

In every cry of every Man,   5
In every Infant's cry of fear,
In every voice, in every ban,
The mind-forg'd manacles I hear.

How the Chimney-sweeper's cry
Every black'ning Church appalls;   10
And the hapless Soldier's sigh
Runs in blood down Palace walls.

But most thro' midnight streets I hear
How the youthful Harlot's curse
Blasts the new-born Infant's tear,   15
And blights with plagues the Marriage hearse.

The Human Abstract

Pity would be no more
If we did not make somebody Poor;
And Mercy no more could be
If all were as happy as we.

And mutual fear brings peace,   personal desire
Till the selfish loves increase;   5
Then Cruelty knits a snare,
And spreads his baits with care.

LONDON   1 *charter'd:* hired, invested with privileges; i.e., corrupted by
materialism. 7 *ban:* proclamation, prohibition. 8 *mind-forg'd manacles:*
restrictions imposed by materialistic reason that stultify, enclose, and prohibit
natural joy, producing only wretchedness. 10 *appalls:* literally, causes to
grow pale: weakens, dismays. 14 *Harlot's curse:* cry of love perverted,
diseased, and destroyed by being bought and sold. 15 *Blasts:* shrivels,
destroys. 16 *Marriage hearse:* (oxymoron) The marriage bed is productive
of life, the hearse of disease and death.

THE HUMAN ABSTRACT. *Abstract:* summary, epitome. The poem is a paradigm of the way presumed "virtues" are derived (abstracted) from their evil
opposites. Cf. the true virtues in "The Divine Image."

He sits down with holy fears,
And waters the ground with tears;   10
Then Humility takes its root
Underneath his foot.

Soon spreads the dismal shade
Of Mystery over his head;
And the Catterpiller and Fly   15
Feed on the Mystery.

And it bears the fruit of Deceit,
Ruddy and sweet to eat;
And the Raven his nest has made
In its thickest shade.   20

The Gods of the earth and sea
Sought through Nature to find this Tree;
But their search was all in vain:
There grows one in the Human Brain.

from MILTON

And did those feet in ancient time
    Walk upon England's mountains green?
And was the holy Lamb of God
    On England's pleasant pastures seen?

And did the Countenance Divine   5
    Shine forth upon our clouded hills?
And was Jerusalem builded here
    Among these dark Satanic Mills?

14 [Tree of] *Mystery:* established religion.   15 *Catterpiller and Fly:* priests
Cf. "As the catterpiller chooses the fairest leaves to lay her eggs on, so the
priest lays his curse on the fairest joys" ("Proverbs of Hell," in *The Marriage
of Heaven and Hell*).

MILTON.   The conclusion of the preface to the prophetic poem "Milton."
It is Blake's apocalyptic manifesto against the artifices of traditional art and
poetry based on Greek and Latin models and an appeal for art of pure imagination based on prophetic inspiration and for a redeemed society.   8 *Mills:*
allusion to Blake's mythological world. The *Mills* are on a strand of a lake,
"black and deadly," formed from the "tears and sighs and death-sweat" of the
victims of false religion.

Bring me my Bow of burning gold!
  Bring me my Arrows of desire!   10
Bring me my Spear! O clouds, unfold!
  Bring me my Chariot of fire!

I will not cease from Mental Fight,
  Nor shall my Sword sleep in my hand,
Till we have built Jerusalem   15
  In England's green and pleasant Land.

15 *Jerusalem:* i.e., the New Jerusalem, the Bride of Christ, where the saved will walk in the light of the Lamb, after the destruction of the fallen world defiled with the abominations of the flesh. See Rev. 21.

WILLIAM WORDSWORTH
1770–1850

Lines Composed a Few Miles Above Tintern Abbey

Five years have past; five summers, with the length
Of five long winters! and again I hear
These waters, rolling from their mountain-springs
With a soft inland murmur.—Once again
Do I behold these steep and lofty cliffs,   5
That on a wild secluded scene impress
Thoughts of more deep seclusion; and connect
The landscape with the quiet of the sky.
The day is come when I again repose
Here, under this dark sycamore, and view   10
These plots of cottage-ground, these orchard-tufts,
Which at this season, with their unripe fruits,
Are clad in one green hue, and lose themselves
'Mid groves and copses. Once again I see
These hedge-rows, hardly hedge-rows, little lines   15
Of sportive wood run wild: these pastoral farms,
Green to the very door; and wreaths of smoke
Sent up, in silence, from among the trees!
With some uncertain notice, as might seem
Of vagrant dwellers in the houseless woods,   20
Or of some Hermit's cave, where by his fire
The Hermit sits alone.
                         These beauteous forms,
Through a long absence, have not been to me
As is a landscape to a blind man's eye:
But oft, in lonely rooms, and 'mid the din   25
Of towns and cities, I have owed to them
In hours of weariness, sensations sweet,
Felt in the blood, and felt along the heart;
And passing even into my purer mind,
With tranquil restoration:—feelings too   30
Of unremembered pleasure: such, perhaps,
As have no slight or trivial influence
On that best portion of a good man's life,
His little, nameless, unremembered acts
Of kindness and of love. Nor less, I trust,   35

LINES.   The ruins of Tintern Abbey are in Monmouthshire on the banks of
the Wye, a river in western England and eastern Wales. Wordsworth first saw
the abbey in 1793.   27 *sensations:* physiological impressions that produce
perception; feeling and idea.

To them I may have owed another gift,
Of aspect more sublime; that blessed mood,
In which the burthen of the mystery,
In which the heavy and the weary weight
Of all this unintelligible world,   40
Is lightened:—that serene and blessed mood,
In which the affections gently lead us on,—
Until, the breath of this corporeal frame
And even the motion of our human blood
Almost suspended, we are laid asleep   45
In body, and become a living soul:
While with an eye made quiet by the power
Of harmony, and the deep power of joy,
We see into the life of things.
                               If this
Be but a vain belief, yet, oh! how oft—   50
In darkness and amid the many shapes
Of joyless daylight; when the fretful stir
Unprofitable, and the fever of the world,
Have hung upon the beatings of my heart—
How oft, in spirit, have I turned to thee,   55
O sylvan Wye! thou wanderer through the woods,
How often has my spirit turned to thee!
   And now, with gleams of half-extinguished thought,
With many recognitions dim and faint,
And somewhat of a sad perplexity,   60
The picture of the mind revives again:
While here I stand, not only with the sense
Of present pleasure, but with pleasing thoughts
That in this moment there is life and food
For future years. And so I dare to hope,   65
Though changed, no doubt, from what I was when first
I came among these hills; when like a roe
I bounded o'er the mountains, by the sides
Of the deep rivers, and the lonely streams,
Wherever nature led: more like a man   70
Flying from something that he dreads, than one
Who sought the thing he loved. For nature then
(The coarser pleasures of my boyish days,

61–62 *picture . . . stand:* the initial stages of the Wordsworthian pattern of
poetic creation following joyful sight: Recollection and "wise passiveness";
Re-creation; Consolation, which through "primal sympathy" produces union
of all men with each other. "Lines" is an account of the "organic" process
by which the poem is created, which Wordsworth considered parallel to the
development of man himself through the three ages: Boyhood (irrational and
purely expressive), Adolescence (troubled and fearful, ll. 65–83), and Manhood
(ll. 83–111).

And their glad animal movements all gone by)
To me was all in all.—I cannot paint   75
What then I was. The sounding cataract
Haunted me like a passion: the tall rock,
The mountain, and the deep and gloomy wood,
Their colors and their forms, were then to me
An appetite; a feeling and a love,   80
That had no need of a remoter charm,
By thought supplied, nor any interest
Unborrowed from the eye.—That time is past,
And all its aching joys are now no more,
And all its dizzy raptures. Not for this   85
Faint I, nor mourn nor murmur; other gifts
Have followed; for such loss, I would believe,
Abundant recompense. For I have learned
To look on nature, not as in the hour
Of thoughtless youth; but hearing oftentimes   90
The still, sad music of humanity,
Nor harsh nor grating, though of ample power
To chasten and subdue. And I have felt
A presence that disturbs me with the joy
Of elevated thoughts; a sense sublime   95
Of something far more deeply interfused,
Whose dwelling is the light of setting suns,
And the round ocean and the living air,
And the blue sky, and in the mind of man:
A motion and a spirit, that impels   100
All thinking things, all objects of all thought,
And rolls through all things. Therefore am I still
A lover of the meadows and the woods,
And mountains; and of all that we behold
From this green earth; of all the mighty world   105
Of eye, and ear,—both what they half create,
And what perceive; well pleased to recognize
In nature and the language of the sense
The anchor of my purest thoughts, the nurse,
The guide, the guardian of my heart, and soul   110
Of all my moral being.
                Nor perchance,
If I were not thus taught, should I the more
Suffer my genial spirits to decay:
For thou art with me here upon the banks
Of this fair river; thou my dearest Friend,   115

114 *genial:* enlivening and creative.   115 *Friend:* Wordsworth's sister, Dorothy.

My dear, dear Friend; and in thy voice I catch
The language of my former heart, and read
My former pleasures in the shooting lights
Of thy wild eyes. Oh! yet a little while
May I behold in thee what I was once, 120
My dear, dear Sister! and this prayer I make,
Knowing that Nature never did betray
The heart that loved her; 'tis her privilege,
Through all the years of this our life, to lead
From joy to joy: for she can so inform 125
The mind that is within us, so impress
With quietness and beauty, and so feed
With lofty thoughts, that neither evil tongues,
Rash judgments, nor the sneers of selfish men,
Nor greetings where no kindness is, nor all 130
The dreary intercourse of daily life,
Shall e'er prevail against us, or disturb
Our cheerful faith, that all which we behold
Is full of blessings. Therefore let the moon
Shine on thee in thy solitary walk; 135
And let the misty mountain-winds be free
To blow against thee: and, in after years,
When these wild ecstasies shall be matured
Into a sober pleasure; when thy mind
Shall be a mansion for all lovely forms, 140
Thy memory be as a dwelling-place
For all sweet sounds and harmonies; oh! then,
If solitude, or fear, or pain, or grief,
Should be thy portion, with what healing thoughts
Of tender joy wilt thou remember me, 145
And these my exhortations! Nor, perchance—
If I should be where I no more can hear
Thy voice, nor catch from thy wild eyes these gleams
Of past existence—wilt thou then forget
That on the banks of this delightful stream 150
We stood together; and that I, so long
A worshipper of Nature, hither came
Unwearied in that service: rather say
With warmer love—oh! with far deeper zeal
Of holier love. Nor wilt thou then forget, 155
That after many wanderings, many years
Of absence, these steep woods and lofty cliffs,
And this green pastoral landscape, were to me
More dear, both for themselves and for thy sake!

252

She dwelt among the untrodden ways

She dwelt among the untrodden ways
  Beside the springs of Dove,
A Maid whom there were none to praise
  And very few to love:

A violet by a mossy stone   5
  Half hidden from the eye!
—Fair as a star, when only one
  Is shining in the sky.

She lived unknown, and few could know
  When Lucy ceased to be;   10
But she is in her grave, and, oh,
  The difference to me!

A slumber did my spirit seal

A slumber did my spirit seal;
  I had no human fears:
She seemed a thing that could not feel
  The touch of earthly years.

No motion has she now, no force;   5
  She neither hears nor sees;
Rolled round in earth's diurnal course,
  With rocks, and stones, and trees.

It is a beauteous evening, calm and free

It is a beauteous evening, calm and free,
The holy time is quiet as a Nun
Breathless with adoration; the broad sun
Is sinking down in its tranquillity;
The gentleness of heaven broods o'er the Sea: 5
Listen! the mighty Being is awake,

A SLUMBER. 7 *diurnal:* daily.

IT IS A BEAUTEOUS. Composed near Calais, 1802. 9 *Child:* Wordsworth's
natural daughter, Caroline (born December, 1792), by his French sweetheart,
Annette Vallon.

And doth with his eternal motion make
A sound like thunder—everlastingly.
Dear Child! dear Girl! that walkest with me here,
If thou appear untouched by solemn thought,   10
Thy nature is not therefore less divine:
Thou liest in Abraham's bosom all the year;
And worship'st at the Temple's inner shrine,
God being with thee when we know it not.

The world is too much with us

The world is too much with us; late and soon,
Getting and spending, we lay waste our powers:
Little we see in Nature that is ours;
We have given our hearts away, a sordid boon!
This Sea that bares her bosom to the moon;   5
The winds that will be howling at all hours,
And are up-gathered now like sleeping flowers;
For this, for everything, we are out of tune,
It moves us not.—Great God! I'd rather be
A Pagan suckled in a creed outworn;   10
So might I, standing on this pleasant lea,
Have glimpses that would make me less forlorn;
Have sight of Proteus rising from the sea;
Or hear old Triton blow his wreathed horn.

Composed upon Westminster Bridge

SEPTEMBER 3, 1802

Earth has not anything to show more fair:
Dull would he be of soul who could pass by
A sight so touching in its majesty:
This City now doth, like a garment, wear
The beauty of the morning; silent, bare,   5
Ships, towers, domes, theatres, and temples lie
Open unto the fields, and to the sky;
All bright and glittering in the smokeless air.
Never did sun more beautifully steep

---

12 *Abraham's bosom:* God's grace and protection. Cf. Luke 16:22–23.

THE WORLD. 13 *Proteus:* sea god, "The Old Man of the Sea," who herds the seals and can assume different shapes to avoid being questioned. See *Odyssey*, IV, 384–87. 14 *Triton:* son of Poseidon, who rouses or calms the sea by blowing on his conch-shell horn.

In his first splendor, valley, rock, or hill;   10
Ne'er saw I, never felt, a calm so deep!
The river glideth at his own sweet will:
Dear God! the very houses seem asleep;
And all that mighty heart is lying still!

September, 1802

NEAR DOVER

Inland, within a hollow vale, I stood;
And saw, while sea was calm and air was clear,
The coast of France—the coast of France how near!
Drawn almost into frightful neighborhood.
I shrunk; for verily the barrier flood   5
Was like a lake, or river bright and fair,
A span of waters; yet what power is there!
What mightiness for evil and for good!
Even so doth God protect us if we be
Virtuous and wise. Winds blow, and waters roll,   10
Strength to the brave, and Power, and Deity;
Yet in themselves are nothing! One decree
Spake laws to *them*, and said that by the soul
Only, the Nations shall be great and free.

London, 1802

Milton! thou shouldst be living at this hour:
England hath need of thee: she is a fen
Of stagnant waters: altar, sword, and pen,
Fireside, the heroic wealth of hall and bower,
Have forfeited their ancient English dower   5
Of inward happiness. We are selfish men;
Oh! raise us up, return to us again;
And give us manners, virtue, freedom, power.
Thy soul was like a Star, and dwelt apart;
Thou hadst a voice whose sound was like the sea: 10
Pure as the naked heavens, majestic, free,
So didst thou travel on life's common way,
In cheerful godliness; and yet thy heart
The lowliest duties on herself did lay.

Surprised by Joy—impatient as the Wind

Surprised by joy—impatient as the Wind
I turned to share the transport—Oh! with whom
But Thee, deep buried in the silent tomb,
That spot which no vicissitude can find?
Love, faithful love, recalled thee to my mind—   5
But how could I forget thee? Through what power,
Even for the least division of an hour,
Have I been so beguiled as to be blind
To my most grievous loss!—That thought's return
Was the worst pang that sorrow ever bore,   10
Save one, one only, when I stood forlorn,
Knowing my heart's best treasure was no more;
That neither present time nor years unborn
Could to my sight that heavenly sight restore.

The Solitary Reaper

Behold her, single in the field,
Yon solitary Highland Lass!
Reaping and singing by herself;
Stop here, or gently pass!
Alone she cuts and binds the grain,   5
And sings a melancholy strain;
O listen! for the Vale profound
Is overflowing with the sound.

No Nightingale did ever chaunt
More welcome notes to weary bands   10
Of travellers in some shady haunt,
Among Arabian sands:
A voice so thrilling ne'er was heard
In spring-time from the Cuckoo-bird,
Breaking the silence of the seas   15
Among the farthest Hebrides.

Will no one tell me what she sings?—
Perhaps the plaintive numbers flow
For old, unhappy, far-off things,
And battles long ago: 20

SURPRISED BY JOY. 3 *Thee:* Wordsworth's daughter Catherine, who died
June 4, 1812, aged four years. The poem was written in 1815.

SOLITARY REAPER. 1 *Behold her:* Wordsworth did not see the *Highland Lass*
himself but read of her in a friend's account of his tour of Scotland. 17 *Will
. . . sings:* i.e., because her song is in Erse (Gaelic).

Or is it some more humble lay,
Familiar matter of to-day?
Some natural sorrow, loss, or pain,
That has been, and may be again?

Whate'er the theme, the Maiden sang   25
As if her song could have no ending;
I saw her singing at her work,
And o'er the sickle bending;—
I listened, motionless and still;
And, as I mounted up the hill,   30
The music in my heart I bore,
Long after it was heard no more.

Stepping Westward

"What, you are stepping westward?"—*"Yea."*
—'T would be a *wildish* destiny,
If we, who thus together roam
In a strange Land, and far from home,
Were in this place the guests of Chance: 5
Yet who would stop, or fear to advance,
Though home or shelter he had none,
With such a sky to lead him on?

The dewy ground was dark and cold;
Behind, all gloomy to behold;   10
And stepping westward seemed to be
A kind of *heavenly* destiny:
I liked the greeting; 'twas a sound
Of something without place or bound;
And seemed to give me spiritual right   15
To travel through that region bright.

The voice was soft, and she who spake
Was walking by her native lake:
The salutation had to me
The very sound of courtesy: 20
Its power was felt; and while my eye
Was fixed upon the glowing Sky,
The echo of the voice enwrought
A human sweetness with the thought

STEPPING WESTWARD. 1 *What . . . westward:* the greeting that a young woman, a stranger, gave to Wordsworth when he and his sister Dorothy were walking by the shore of Loch Ketterine, Scotland, in 1803. The poem was written in 1805.

Of travelling through the world that lay   25
Before me in my endless way.

My Heart Leaps Up

My heart leaps up when I behold
  A rainbow in the sky:
So was it when my life began;
So is it now I am a man;
So be it when I shall grow old,   5
  Or let me die!
The Child is father of the Man;
And I could wish my days to be
Bound each to each by natural piety.

Ode

INTIMATIONS OF IMMORTALITY FROM RECOLLECTIONS OF
EARLY CHILDHOOD

Pauló majora canamus.

The Child is father of the Man;
And I could wish my days to be
Bound each to each by natural piety.

MY HEART LEAPS UP. 9 *natural piety:* the natural filial obligation of the grown *Man*, remembering his childhood, for his "Father"-Child. The rainbow is the symbol of the covenant between the *Child* and the *Man*. Cf. Gen. 9:9–17.

ODE. Composed 1802–04. *Pauló majora canamus:* "Let us sing a somewhat loftier strain"; from the opening line of Virgil's Fourth ("Messianic") Eclogue, in which he predicts from the birth of a certain child a new golden age of Saturn. This was the original epigraph to the poem; *The Child is father of the Man* was substituted in subsequent editions. The golden age and the covenant of the rainbow, the "Shepherd-boy" and the elegiac tone (Wordsworth printed this poem under the general heading of "Epitaphs and Elegiac Pieces") strongly suggest that this poem has more than accidental affinities with the pastoral tradition of Virgil and Milton, here revised and newly sustained. The "death" that the surviving poet (here, ironically, the "elder" and lesser one) records is his own (i.e., the death of the boy he once was) because the "Man" perceives that *the glory* and *the gleam* that only the boy-poet (*Mighty Prophet! Seer blest!*—l. 114) could see has *die[d] away* (l. 75). The pathetic fallacy is, ironically, that all nature rejoices for the *Shepherd-boy* but not for the speaker, who is unable to respond and for whom nature refuses to weep. The question of faith is the traditional one: whether or not the survivor can find the will and strength to continue in the vocation of the poet. The consolation is felt in the paradox of the "primal sympathy," which comes out of the experience of "human suffering" (cf. "Lycidas," ll. 176–81 and notes); the proof of the apotheosis is seen in the image of the *new-born Day* and *setting sun* (ll. 194–96; cf. "Lycidas," ll. 168–71 and notes) and that of the *flower* (l. 202), seen now under the covenant of the rainbow.

I

There was a time when meadow, grove, and stream,
The earth, and every common sight,
     To me did seem
     Apparelled in celestial light,
The glory and the freshness of a dream.   5
It is not now as it hath been of yore;—
     Turn whereso'er I may,
       By night or day,
The things which I have seen I now can see no more.

II

     The Rainbow comes and goes,   10
     And lovely is the Rose,
     The Moon doth with delight
Look round her when the heavens are bare;
     Waters on a starry night
     Are beautiful and fair;   15
     The sunshine is a glorious birth;
     But yet I know, where'er I go,
That there hath past away a glory from the earth.

III

Now, while the birds thus sing a joyous song,
  And while the young lambs bound   20
     As to the tabor's sound,
To me alone there came a thought of grief:
A timely utterance gave that thought relief,
     And I again am strong:
The cataracts blow their trumpets from the steep;   25
No more shall grief of mine the season wrong;
I hear the Echoes through the mountains throng,
The Winds come to me from the fields of sleep,
     And all the earth is gay;
       Land and sea   30
     Give themselves up to jollity,
     And with the heart of May
     Doth every Beast keep holiday;—
     Thou Child of Joy,
Shout round me, let me hear thy shouts, thou happy
     Shepherd-boy!   35

21 *tabor:* a small tambourine-like drum, used to accompany a pipe and to beat time for dancers.

IV

Ye blessèd Creatures, I have heard the call
   Ye to each other make; I see
The heavens laugh with you in your jubilee;
   My heart is at your festival,
     My head hath its coronal,   40
The fulness of your bliss, I feel—I feel it all.
       Oh evil day! if I were sullen
       While Earth herself is adorning,
         This sweet May-morning,
       And the Children are culling   45
         On every side,
       In a thousand valleys far and wide,
       Fresh flowers; while the sun shines warm,
And the Babe leaps up on his Mother's arm:—
       I hear, I hear, with joy I hear!   50
       —But there's a Tree, of many, one,
A single Field which I have looked upon,
Both of them speak of something that is gone:
       The Pansy at my feet
       Doth the same tale repeat: 55
Whither is fled the visionary gleam?
Where is it now, the glory and the dream?

V

Our birth is but a sleep and a forgetting:
The Soul that rises with us, our life's Star,
       Hath had elsewhere its setting,   60
         And cometh from afar:
       Not in entire forgetfulness,
       And not in utter nakedness,
But trailing clouds of glory do we come
       From God, who is our home: 65
Heaven lies about us in our infancy!
Shades of the prison-house begin to close
       Upon the growing Boy,
But He beholds the light, and whence it flows,
       He sees it in his joy;   70

---

40 *coronal:* wreath of wild flowers to celebrate the joys of May.   45 *culling:* selecting and gathering.   58–61 *Our . . . afar:* the myth of preexistence, which Wordsworth was careful to note was not an article of belief but a means of explaining the "dream-like vividness which invests objects of sight in childhood," and its subsequent loss and compensation in man's life. Cf. Vaughan's "The Retreat."

The Youth, who daily farther from the east
    Must travel, still is Nature's Priest,
    And by the vision splendid
    Is on his way attended;
At length the Man perceives it die away,   75
And fade into the light of common day.

VI

Earth fills her lap with pleasures of her own;
Yearnings she hath in her own natural kind,
And, even with something of a Mother's mind,
    And no unworthy aim,   80
    The homely Nurse doth all she can
To make her Foster-child, her Inmate Man,
    Forget the glories he hath known,
And that imperial palace whence he came.

VII

Behold the Child among his new-born blisses,   85
A six years' Darling of a pigmy size!
See, where 'mid work of his own hand he lies,
Fretted by sallies of his mother's kisses,
With light upon him from his father's eyes!
See, at his feet, some little plan or chart,   90
Some fragment from his dream of human life,
Shaped by himself with newly-learned art;
    A wedding or a festival,
    A mourning or a funeral;
      And this hath now his heart,   95
    And unto this he frames his song:
      Then will he fit his tongue
To dialogues of business, love, or strife;
    But it will not be long
    Ere this be thrown aside,   100
    And with new joy and pride
The little Actor cons another part;
Filling from time to time his 'humorous stage'

---

88 *Fretted:* adorned.   *sallies:* outbursts.   102 *cons:* studies and memorizes.
103 *humorous stage:* (from a sonnet by Daniel in the dedication of Musophilis)
drama exhibiting various peculiar inclinations and individual temperaments
of men according to the old psychology based on the four humors. Cf.
Chaucer's "The Nun's Priest's Tale," l. 105 and note.

With all the Persons, down to palsied Age,
That Life brings with her in her equipage;   105
  As if his whole vocation
  Were endless imitation.

VIII

Thou, whose exterior semblance doth belie
  Thy Soul's immensity;
Thou best Philosopher, who yet dost keep   110
Thy heritage, thou Eye among the blind,
That, deaf and silent, read'st the eternal deep,
Haunted forever by the eternal mind,—
  Mighty Prophet! Seer blest!
  On whom those truths do rest,   115
Which we are toiling all our lives to find,
In darkness lost, the darkness of the grave;
Thou, over whom thy Immortality
Broods like the Day, a Master o'er a Slave,
A Presence which is not to be put by;   120
Thou little Child, yet glorious in the might
Of heaven-born freedom on thy being's height,
Why with such earnest pains dost thou provoke
The years to bring the inevitable yoke,
Thus blindly with thy blessedness at strife?   125
Full soon thy Soul shall have her earthly freight,
And custom lie upon thee with a weight,
Heavy as frost, and deep almost as life!

IX

  O joy! that in our embers
  Is something that doth live,   130
  That Nature yet remembers
  What was so fugitive!
The thought of our past years in me doth breed
Perpetual benediction: not indeed
For that which is most worthy to be blest;   135
Delight and liberty, the simple creed
Of Childhood, whether busy or at rest,
With new-fledged hope still fluttering in his breast:—
  Not for these I raise
  The song of thanks and praise;   140
  But for those obstinate questionings
  Of sense and outward things,
  Fallings from us, vanishings;
  Blank misgivings of a Creature

Moving about in worlds not realized,   145
High instincts before which our mortal Nature
Did tremble like a guilty Thing surprised:
      But for those first affections,
      Those shadowy recollections,
    Which, be they what they may,   150
Are yet the fountain light of all our day,
Are yet a master light of all our seeing;
    Uphold us, cherish, and have power to make
Our noisy years seem moments in the being
Of the eternal Silence: truths that wake,   155
      To perish never;
Which neither listlessness, nor mad endeavor,
      Nor Man nor Boy,
Nor all that is at enmity with joy,
Can utterly abolish or destroy!   160
      Hence in a season of calm weather
      Though inland far we be,
Our Souls have sight of that immortal sea
      Which brought us hither,
      Can in a moment travel thither,   165
And see the Children sport upon the shore,
And hear the mighty waters rolling evermore.

X

Then sing, ye Birds, sing, sing a joyous song!
      And let the young Lambs bound
      As to the tabor's sound!   170
We in thought will join your throng,
      Ye that pipe and ye that play,
      Ye that through your hearts to-day
      Feel the gladness of the May!
What though the radiance which was once so bright   175
Be now for ever taken from my sight,
    Though nothing can bring back the hour
Of splendor in the grass, of glory in the flower;
      We will grieve not, rather find
      Strength in what remains behind;   180
      In the primal sympathy
      Which having been must ever be;
      In the soothing thoughts that spring
      Out of human suffering;
      In the faith that looks through death,   185
In years that bring the philosophic mind.

181 *primal sympathy:* the capacity to understand and feel the bond of union
between man and child that enables the poet, through his imagination, to
possess once more the lost "splendor."

XI

And O, ye Fountains, Meadows, Hills, and Groves,
Forbode not any severing of our loves!
Yet in my heart of hearts I feel your might;
I only have relinquished one delight   190
To live beneath your more habitual sway.
I love the Brooks which down their channels fret,
Even more than when I tripped lightly as they;
The innocent brightness of a new-born Day
        Is lovely yet;   195
The Clouds that gather round the setting sun
Do take a sober coloring from an eye
That hath kept watch o'er man's mortality;
Another race hath been, and other palms are won.
Thanks to the human heart by which we live,   200
Thanks to its tenderness, its joys, and fears,
To me the meanest flower that blows can give
Thoughts that do often lie too deep for tears.

from THE PRELUDE

OR GROWTH OF A POET'S MIND
AN AUTOBIOGRAPHICAL POEM

[*Fair seed-time had my soul*]

  Fair seed-time had my soul, and I grew up
Fostered alike by beauty and by fear:
Much favored in my birth-place, and no less
In that beloved Vale to which erelong
We were transplanted—there were we let loose   5
For sports of wider range. Ere I had told
Ten birth-days, when among the mountain slopes
Frost, and the breath of frosty wind, had snapped
The last autumnal crocus, 'twas my joy
With store of springes o'er my shoulder hung   10
To range the open heights where woodcocks run
Along the smooth green turf. Through half the night,
Scudding away from snare to snare, I plied
That anxious visitation;—moon and stars

192 *fret:* ripple.

THE PRELUDE. Written between 1798 and 1805, and after much revision published in 1850; some parts had already appeared as independent poems.

FAIR SEED TIME. 10 *springes:* snares.

Were shining o'er my head. I was alone,   15
And seemed to be a trouble to the peace
That dwelt among them. Sometimes it befell
In these night wanderings, that a strong desire
O'erpowered my better reason, and the bird
Which was the captive of another's toil   20
Became my prey; and when the deed was done
I heard among the solitary hills
Low breathings coming after me, and sounds
Of undistinguishable motion, steps
Almost as silent as the turf they trod.   25

   Nor less when spring had warmed the cultured Vale,
Moved we as plunderers where the mother-bird
Had in high places built her lodge; though mean
Our object and inglorious, yet the end
Was not ignoble. Oh! when I have hung   30
Above the raven's nest, by knots of grass
And half-inch fissures in the slippery rock
But ill sustained, almost (so it seemed)
Suspended by the blast that blew amain,
Shouldering the naked crag, oh, at that time   35
While on the perilous ridge I hung alone,
With what strange utterance did the loud dry wind
Blow through my ear! the sky seemed not a sky
Of earth—and with what motion moved the clouds!

.   .   .

   One summer evening (led by her) I found   40
A little boat tied to a willow tree
Within a rocky cave, its usual home.
Straight I unloosed her chain, and stepping in
Pushed from the shore. It was an act of stealth
And troubled pleasure, nor without the voice   45
Of mountain-echoes did my boat move on;
Leaving behind her still, on either side,
Small circles glittering idly in the moon,
Until they melted all into one track
Of sparkling light. But now, like one who rows,   50
Proud of his skill, to reach a chosen point
With an unswerving line, I fixed my view
Upon the summit of a craggy ridge,
The horizon's utmost boundary; far above
Was nothing but the stars and the gray sky.   55
She was an elfin pinnace; lustily

I dipped my oars into the silent lake,
And, as I rose upon the stroke, my boat
Went heaving through the water like a swan;
When, from behind that craggy steep till then   60
The horizon's bound, a huge peak, black and huge,
As if with voluntary power instinct
Upreared its head. I struck and struck again,
And growing still in stature the grim shape
Towered up between me and the stars, and still,   65
For so it seemed, with purpose of its own
And measured motion like a living thing,
Strode after me. With trembling oars I turned,
And through the silent water stole my way
Back to the covert of the willow tree;   70
There in her mooring-place I left my bark,—
And through the meadows homeward went, in grave
And serious mood; but after I had seen
That spectacle, for many days, my brain
Worked with a dim and undetermined sense   75
Of unknown modes of being; o'er my thoughts
There hung a darkness, call it solitude
Or blank desertion. No familiar shapes
Remained, no pleasant images of trees,
Of sea or sky, no colors of green fields;   80
But huge and mighty forms, that do not live
Like living men, moved slowly through the mind
By day, and were a trouble to my dreams.

                    .   .   .

    And in the frosty season, when the sun
Was set, and visible for many a mile   85
The cottage windows blazed through twilight gloom,
I heeded not their summons: happy time
It was indeed for all of us—for me
It was a time of rapture! Clear and loud
The village clock tolled six,—I wheeled about,   90
Proud and exulting like an untired horse
That cares not for his home. All shod with steel,
We hissed along the polished ice in games
Confederate, imitative of the chase
And woodland pleasures,—the resounding horn,   95
The pack loud chiming, and the hunted hare.
So through the darkness and the cold we flew,
And not a voice was idle; with the din
Smitten, the precipices rang aloud;

The leafless trees and every icy crag   100
Tinkled like iron; while far distant hills
Into the tumult sent an alien sound
Of melancholy not unnoticed, while the stars
Eastward were sparkling clear, and in the west
The orange sky of evening died away.   105
Not seldom from the uproar I retired
Into a silent bay, or sportively
Glanced sideway, leaving the tumultuous throng,
To cut across the reflex of a star
That fled, and, flying still before me, gleamed   110
Upon the glassy plain; and oftentimes,
When we had given our bodies to the wind,
And all the shadowy banks on either side
Came sweeping through the darkness, spinning still
The rapid line of motion, then at once   115
Have I, reclining back upon my heels,
Stopped short; yet still the solitary cliffs
Wheeled by me—even as if the earth had rolled
With visible motion her diurnal round!
Behind me did they stretch in solemn train,   120
Feebler and feebler, and I stood and watched
Till all was tranquil as a dreamless sleep.

   Ye Presences of Nature in the sky
And on the earth! Ye Visions of the hills!
And Souls of lonely places! can I think   125
A vulgar hope was yours when ye employed
Such ministry, when ye through many a year
Haunting me thus among my boyish sports
On caves and trees, upon the woods and hills,
Impressed upon all forms the characters   130
Of danger or desire; and thus did make
The surface of the universal earth
With triumph and delight, with hope and fear,
Work like a sea?

                    [Book I. *Introduction—Childhood and School-Time*,
                              ll. 301–39; 357–400; 425–75]

109 *reflex:* reflection.   119 *diurnal:* daily.

[*A strong shock*]

A strong shock
Was given to old opinions; all men's minds
Had felt its power, and mine was both let loose,
Let loose and goaded. After what hath been
Already said of patriotic love,   5
Suffice it here to add, that, somewhat stern
In temperament, withal a happy man,
And therefore bold to look on painful things,
Free likewise of the world, and thence more bold,
I summoned my best skill, and toiled, intent   10
To anatomize the frame of social life;
Yea, the whole body of society
Searched to its heart. Share with me, Friend! the wish
That some dramatic tale, endued with shapes
Livelier, and flinging out less guarded words   15
Than suit the work we fashion, might set forth
What then I learned, or think I learned, of truth,
And the errors into which I fell, betrayed
By present objects, and by reasonings false
From their beginnings, inasmuch as drawn   20
Out of a heart that had been turned aside
From Nature's way by outward accidents,
And which was thus confounded, more and more
Misguided, and misguiding. So I fared,
Dragging all precepts, judgments, maxims, creeds,   25
Like culprits to the bar; calling the mind,
Suspiciously, to establish in plain day
Her titles and her honors; now believing,
Now disbelieving; endlessly perplexed
With impulse, motive, right and wrong, the ground   30
Of obligation, what the rule and whence
The sanction; till, demanding formal *proof*,
And seeking it in everything, I lost
All feeling of conviction, and, in fine,
Sick, wearied out with contrarieties,   35
Yielded up moral questions in despair.

.   .   .

A STRONG SHOCK.   Wordsworth spent the years 1791–92 in France, sympathetically watching the progress of the French Revolution and was on the point of volunteering as a leader of the Girondins when he was recalled home. He was strongly attracted to the rationalistic theories of French politics. Although shocked by England's declaration of war against France in 1793, he gradually became disillusioned with the ideals and accomplishments of the Revolution. Bewildered and bitterly depressed, he experienced a severe crisis of mind and spirit.

Then it was—
Thanks to the bounteous Giver of all good!—
That the belovèd Sister in whose sight
Those days were passed, now speaking in a voice   40
Of sudden admonition—like a brook
That did but *cross* a lonely road, and now
Is seen, heard, felt, and caught at every turn,
Companion never lost through many a league—
Maintained for me a saving intercourse   45
With my true self; for, though bedimmed and changed
Much, as it seemed, I was no further changed
Than as a clouded and a waning moon:
She whispered still that brightness would return,
She, in the midst of all, preserved me still   50
A Poet, made me seek beneath that name,
And that alone, my office upon earth;
And, lastly, as hereafter will be shown,
If willing audience fail not, Nature's self,
By all varieties of human love   55
Assisted, led me back through opening day
To those sweet counsels between head and heart
Whence grew that genuine knowledge, fraught with peace,
Which, through the later sinkings of this cause,
Hath still upheld me, and upholds me now.   60

[Book XI. *France* (*Concluded*), ll. 270–305; 333–57.]

[*In one of those excursions*]

In one of those excursions (may they ne'er
Fade from remembrance!) through the Northern tracts
Of Cambria ranging with a youthful friend,
I left Bethgelert's huts at couching-time,
And westward took my way, to see the sun   5
Rise from the top of Snowdon. To the door
Of a rude cottage at the mountain's base
We came, and roused the shepherd who attends
The adventurous stranger's steps, a trusty guide;
Then, cheered by short refreshment, sallied forth.   10

---

52 *office:* duties and responsibilities, public and private. Cf. the "office" of the poet in Blake, "From Milton"; in Dryden, "To the Memory of Mr. Oldham"; in Milton, "Lycidas"; and in Jonson, "To Shakespeare."

IN ONE. 3 *Cambria:* Wales.   6 *Snowdon:* highest point (3,560 ft.) in Wales.

It was a close, warm, breezeless summer night,
Wan, dull, and glaring, with a dripping fog
Low-hung and thick that covered all the sky;
But, undiscouraged, we began to climb
The mountain-side. The mist soon girt us round,   15
And, after ordinary travellers' talk
With our conductor, pensively we sank
Each into commerce with his private thoughts:
Thus did we breast the ascent, and by myself
Was nothing either seen or heard that checked   20
Those musings or diverted, save that once
The shepherd's lurcher, who, among the crags,
Had to his joy unearthed a hedgehog, teased
His coiled-up prey with barkings turbulent.
This small adventure, for even such it seemed   25
In that wild place and at the dead of night,
Being over and forgotten, on we wound
In silence as before. With forehead bent
Earthward, as if in opposition set
Against an enemy, I panted up   30
With eager pace, and no less eager thoughts.
Thus might we wear a midnight hour away,
Ascending at loose distance each from each,
And I, as chanced, the foremost of the band;
When at my feet the ground appeared to brighten,   35
And with a step or two seemed brighter still;
Nor was time given to ask or learn the cause,
For instantly a light upon the turf
Fell like a flash, and lo! as I looked up,
The Moon hung naked in a firmament   40
Of azure without cloud, and at my feet
Rested a silent sea of hoary mist.
A hundred hills their dusky backs upheaved
All over this still ocean; and beyond,
Far, far beyond, the solid vapors stretched,   45
In headlands, tongues, and promontory shapes,
Into the main Atlantic, that appeared
To dwindle, and give up his majesty,
Usurped upon far as the sight could reach.
Not so the ethereal vault; encroachment none   50
Was there, nor loss; only the inferior stars
Had disappeared, or shed a fainter light
In the clear presence of the full-orbed Moon,

22 *lurcher:* a cross between a sheep dog and a greyhound, valued because it hunts by both scent and sight.

Who, from her sovereign elevation, gazed
Upon the billowy ocean, as it lay   55
All meek and silent, save that through a rift—
Not distant from the shore whereon we stood,
A fixed, abysmal, gloomy, breathing-place—
Mounted the roar of waters, torrents, streams
Innumerable, roaring with one voice!   60
Heard over earth and sea, and, in that hour,
For so it seemed, felt by the starry heavens.
   When into air had partially dissolved
That vision, given to spirits of the night
And three chance human wanderers, in calm thought   65
Reflected, it appeared to me the type
Of a majestic intellect, its acts
And its possessions, what it has and craves,
What in itself it is, and would become.
There I beheld the emblem of a mind   70
That feeds upon infinity, that broods
Over the dark abyss, intent to hear
Its voices issuing forth to silent light
In one continuous stream; a mind sustained
By recognitions of transcendent power,   75
In sense conducting to ideal form,
In soul of more than mortal privilege.
One function, above all, of such a mind
Had Nature shadowed there, by putting forth,
'Mid circumstances awful and sublime,   80
That mutual domination which she loves
To exert upon the face of outward things,
So molded, joined, abstracted, so endowed
With interchangeable supremacy,
That men, least sensitive, see, hear, perceive,   85
And cannot choose but feel. The power, which all
Acknowledge when thus moved, which Nature thus
To bodily sense exhibits, is the express
Resemblance of that glorious faculty
That higher minds bear with them as their own.   90
This is the very spirit in which they deal
With the whole compass of the universe:
They from their native selves can send abroad
Kindred mutations; for themselves create
A like existence; and, whene'er it dawns   95
Created for them, catch it, or are caught
By its inevitable mastery,
Like angels stopped upon the wing by sound
Of harmony from Heaven's remotest spheres.

Them the enduring and the transient both   100
Serve to exalt; they build up greatest things
From least suggestions; ever on the watch,
Willing to work and to be wrought upon,
They need not extraordinary calls
To rouse them; in a world of life they live,   105
By sensible impressions not enthralled,
But by their quickening impulse made more prompt
To hold fit converse with the spiritual world,
And with the generations of mankind
Spread over time, past, present, and to come,   110
Age after age, till Time shall be no more.
Such minds are truly from the Deity,
For they are Powers; and hence the highest bliss
That flesh can know is theirs—the consciousness
Of Whom they are, habitually infused   115
Through every image and through every thought,
And all affections by communion raised
From earth to heaven, from human to divine;
Hence endless occupation for the soul,
Whether discursive or intuitive;   120
Hence cheerfulness for acts of daily life,
Emotions which best foresight need not fear,
Most worthy then of trust when most intense.
Hence, amid ills that vex and wrongs that crush
Our hearts—if here the words of Holy Writ   125
May with fit reverence be applied—that peace
Which passeth understanding, that repose
In moral judgments which from this pure source
Must come, or will by man be sought in vain.

[Book XIV. *Conclusion*, ll. 1–129.]

SAMUEL TAYLOR COLERIDGE
1792–1834

The Rime of the Ancient Mariner

IN SEVEN PARTS

ARGUMENT

How a Ship, having first sailed to the Equator, was driven by Storms to the cold Country towards the South Pole; how the Ancient Mariner cruelly and in contempt of the laws of hospitality killed a Seabird and how he was followed by many and strange Judgements: and in what manner he came back to his own Country.

PART I

An ancient Mariner meeteth three Gallants bidden to a wedding-feast, and detaineth one.

It is an ancient Mariner,
And he stoppeth one of three.
"By thy long gray beard and glittering eye,
Now wherefore stopp'st thou me?

"The Bridegroom's doors are opened wide,   5
And I am next of kin;
The guests are met, the feast is set:
May'st hear the merry din."

He holds him with his skinny hand,
"There was a ship," quoth he.   10
"Hold off! unhand me, gray-beard loon!"
Eftsoons his hand dropped he.

The Wedding-Guest is spellbound by the eye of the old seafaring man, and constrained to hear his tale.

He holds him with his glittering eye—
The Wedding-Guest stood still,
And listens like a three years' child: 15
The Mariner hath his will.

THE ANCIENT MARINER. This poem was Coleridge's major contribution to the *Lyrical Ballads*, which he and Wordsworth published jointly in 1798. In 1817 he added the marginal gloss. The ballad form and language (often archaic and "nonpoetic") sharply separate this poem from the taste and conventions of the previous century. The ballad form, however, complements the poem's medieval dream-vision of man's pilgrimage from sin through purgatory to redemption, a journey via the imagination from the world of the familiar, to that of the mysterious, the spiritual, and the supernatural, and back again to the familiar, now forever and terrifyingly changed by the voyage.

12 *Eftsoons:* at once.

The Wedding-Guest sat on a stone:
He cannot choose but hear;
And thus spake on that ancient man,
The bright-eyed Mariner.   20

The ship was cheered, the harbor cleared,
Merrily did we drop
Below the kirk, below the hill,
Below the lighthouse top.

The Mariner tells how the ship sailed southward with a good wind and fair weather, till it reached the Line.

The sun came up upon the left,   25
Out of the sea came he!
And he shone bright, and on the right
Went down into the sea.

Higher and higher every day,
Till over the mast at noon—   30
The Wedding-Guest here beat his breast,
For he heard the loud bassoon.

The Wedding-Guest heareth the bridal music; but the Mariner continueth his tale.

The bride hath paced into the hall,
Red as a rose is she;
Nodding their heads before her goes   35
The merry minstrelsy.

The Wedding-Guest he beat his breast,
Yet he cannot choose but hear;
And thus spake on that ancient man,
The bright-eyed Mariner.   40

The ship driven by a storm toward the south pole.

And now the Storm-blast came, and he
Was tyrannous and strong:
He struck with his o'ertaking wings,
And chased us south along.

With sloping masts and dipping prow,   45
As who pursued with yell and blow
Still treads the shadow of his foe,
And forward bends his head,
The ship drove fast, loud roared the blast,
And southward aye we fled.   50

And now there came both mist and snow,
And it grew wondrous cold:
And ice, mast-high, came floating by,
As green as emerald.

23 *kirk:* church.

The land of ice,
and of fearful
sounds where no
living thing was to
be seen.

And through the drifts the snowy clifts   55
Did send a dismal sheen:
Nor shapes of men nor beasts we ken—
The ice was all between.

The ice was here, the ice was there,
The ice was all around: 60
It cracked and growled, and roared and howled,
Like noises in a swound!

Till a great sea-bird,
called the Albatross,
came through the
snow-fog, and was
received with great
joy and hospitality.

At length did cross an Albatross,
Thorough the fog it came;
As if it had been a Christian soul,   65
We hailed it in God's name.

It ate the food it ne'er had eat,
And round and round it flew.
The ice did split with a thunder-fit;
The helmsman steered us through!   70

And lo! the Alba-
tross proveth a bird
of good omen, and
followeth the ship
as it returned north-
ward through fog
and floating ice.

And a good south wind sprung up behind;
The Albatross did follow,
And every day, for food or play,
Came to the mariner's hollo!

In mist or cloud, on mast or shroud,   75
It perched for vespers nine;
Whiles all the night, through fog-smoke white,
Glimmered the white moon-shine.

The ancient Mariner
inhospitably killeth
the pious bird of
good omen.

"God save thee, ancient Mariner!
From the fiends, that plague thee thus!—   80
Why look'st thou so?"—With my cross-bow
I shot the Albatross!

PART II

The Sun now rose, upon the right:
Out of the sea came he,
Still hid in mist, and on the left   85
Went down into the sea.

---

55 *clifts:* cliffs.   62 *swound:* swoon.   64 *Thorough:* (disyllabic) through.
76 *vespers:* the sixth canonical hour; service of evening worship.   83 *right:*
The ship is now sailing north; cf. l. 25.

And the good south wind still blew behind,
But no sweet bird did follow,
Nor any day for food or play
Came to the mariner's hollo!   90

His shipmates cry
out against the an-
cient Mariner, for
killing the bird of
good luck.

And I had done a hellish thing,
And it would work 'em woe:
For all averred, I had killed the bird
That made the breeze to blow.
Ah wretch! said they, the bird to slay,   95
That made the breeze to blow!

But when the fog
cleared off, they
justify the same,
and thus make
themselves accom-
plices in the crime.

Nor dim nor red, like God's own head,
The glorious Sun uprist:
Then all averred, I had killed the bird
That brought the fog and mist.   100
'Twas right, said they, such birds to slay,
That bring the fog and mist.

The fair breeze con-
tinues; the ship
enters the Pacific
Ocean, and sails
northward, even till
it reaches the Line.

The fair breeze blew, the white foam flew,
The furrow followed free;
We were the first that ever burst   105
Into that silent sea.

The ship hath been
suddenly becalmed.

Down dropt the breeze, the sails dropt down,
'Twas sad as sad could be;
And we did speak only to break
The silence of the sea!   110

All in a hot and copper sky,
The bloody Sun, at noon,
Right up above the mast did stand,
No bigger than the Moon.

Day after day, day after day,   115
We stuck, nor breath nor motion;
As idle as a painted ship
Upon a painted ocean.

And the Albatross
begins to be avenged.

Water, water, every where,
And all the boards did shrink;   120
Water, water, every where,
Nor any drop to drink.

The very deep did rot: O Christ!
That ever this should be!
Yea, slimy things did crawl with legs 125
Upon the slimy sea.

About, about, in reel and rout
The death-fires danced at night;
The water, like a witch's oils,
Burnt green, and blue and white. 130

And some in dreams assured were
Of the Spirit that plagued us so;
Nine fathom deep he had followed us
From the land of mist and snow.

And every tongue, through utter drought, 135
Was withered at the root;
We could not speak, no more than if
We had been choked with soot.

Ah! well a-day! what evil looks
Had I from old and young! 140
Instead of the cross, the Albatross
About my neck was hung.

PART III

There passed a weary time. Each throat
Was parched, and glazed each eye.
A weary time! a weary time! 145
How glazed each weary eye,
When looking westward, I beheld
A something in the sky.

At first it seemed a little speck,
And then it seemed a mist; 150
It moved and moved, and took at last
A certain shape, I wist.

A speck, a mist, a shape, I wist!
And still it neared and neared:
As if it dodged a water-sprite, 155
It plunged and tacked and veered.

A Spirit had followed them; one of the invisible inhabitants of this planet, neither departed souls nor angels; concerning whom the learned Jew, Josephus, and the Platonic Constantinopolitan, Michael Psellus, may be consulted. They are very numerous, and there is no climate or element without one or more.

The shipmates, in their sore distress, would fain throw the whole guilt on the ancient Mariner: in sign whereof they hang the dead sea-bird round his neck.

The ancient Mariner beholdeth a sign in the element afar off.

127 *reel and rout:* whirling and violently dashing movements. 128 *death-fires:* St. Elmo's fire, which when seen on the rigging—like the will-o'-the-wisp seen in the churchyard—often is said to portend disaster. 152 *wist:* knew.

At its nearer ap-
proach, it seemeth
him to be a ship;
and at a dear ran-
som he freeth his
speech from the
bonds of thirst.

With throats unslaked, with black lips baked,
We could nor laugh nor wail;
Through utter drought all dumb we stood!
I bit my arm, I sucked the blood,   160
And cried, A sail! a sail!

With throats unslacked, with black lips baked,
Agape they heard me call:

A flash of joy;

Gramercy! they for joy did grin,
And all at once their breath drew in,   165
As they were drinking all.

And horror follows.
For can it be a ship
that comes onward
without wind or
tide?

See! see! (I cried) she tacks no more!
Hither to work us weal;
Without a breeze, without a tide,
She steadies with upright keel!   170

The western wave was all aflame,
The day was well nigh done!
Almost upon the western wave
Rested the broad bright Sun;
When that strange shape drove suddenly   175
Betwixt us and the Sun.

It seemeth him but
the skeleton of a
ship.

And straight the Sun was flecked with bars,
(Heaven's Mother send us grace!)
As if through a dungeon-grate he peered
With broad and burning face.   180

Alas! (thought I, and my heart beat loud)
How fast she nears and nears!
Are those sails that glance in the Sun,
Like restless gossameres?

And its ribs are seen
as bars on the face
of the setting Sun.
The Specter-Woman
and her Death-mate,
and no other on
board the skeleton-
ship.

Are those her ribs through which the Sun   185
Did peer, as through a grate?
And is that Woman all her crew?
Is that a Death? and are there two?
Is Death that woman's mate?

Her lips were red, her looks were free,   190

Like vessel, like
crew!

Her locks were yellow as gold:
Her skin was as white as leprosy,
The Nightmare Life-in-Death was she,
Who thicks man's blood with cold.

164 *Gramercy:* i.e., great thanks. 168 *weal:* success and happiness. 184
gossameres: spiderwebs that float in the breeze. Cf. "Rape of the Lock," II,
64 and note. 188 *a Death:* a skeleton.

278

The naked hulk alongside came, 195
And the twain were casting dice;
"The game is done! I've won, I've won!"
Quoth she, and whistles thrice.

No twilight within the courts of the Sun.

The Sun's rim dips; the stars rush out:
At one stride comes the dark; 200
With far-heard whisper, o'er the sea,
Off shot the specter-bark.

At the rising of the Moon,

We listened and looked sideways up!
Fear at my heart, as at a cup,
My life-blood seemed to sip! 205
The stars were dim, and thick the night,
The steersman's face by his lamp gleamed white;
From the sails the dew did drip—
Till clomb above the eastern bar
The horned Moon, with one bright star 210
Within the nether tip.

One after one, by the star-dogged Moon,
Too quick for groan or sigh,
Each turned his face with a ghastly pang,
And cursed me with his eye. 215

His shipmates drop down dead.

Four times fifty living men
(And I heard nor sigh nor groan),
With heavy thump, a lifeless lump,
They dropped down one by one.

But Life-in-Death begins her work on the ancient Mariner.

The souls did from their bodies fly,— 220
They fled to bliss or woe!
And every soul, it passed me by,
Like the whizz of my cross-bow!

PART IV

The Wedding-Guest feareth that a spirit is talking to him.

"I fear thee, ancient Mariner!
I fear thy skinny hand! 225
And thou art long, and lank, and brown,
As is the ribbed sea-sand.

209 *clomb:* climbed.   212 *star-dogged Moon:* another omen of evil.

"I fear thee and thy glittering eye,
And thy skinny hand, so brown."—

But the ancient
Mariner assureth
him of his bodily
life, and proceedeth
to relate his horrible
penance.

Fear not, fear not, thou Wedding-Guest!   230
This body dropt not down.

Alone, alone, all, all alone,
Alone on a wide wide sea!
And never a saint took pity on
My soul in agony.   235

He despiseth the
creatures of the
calm,

The many men, so beautiful!
And they all dead did lie:
And a thousand thousand slimy things
Lived on; and so did I.

And envieth that
they should live,
and so many lie
dead.

I looked upon the rotting sea,   240
And drew my eyes away;
I looked upon the rotting deck,
And there the dead men lay.

I looked to heaven, and tried to pray;
But or ever a prayer had gusht,   245
A wicked whisper came, and made
My heart as dry as dust.

I closed my lids, and kept them close,
And the balls like pulses beat;
For the sky and the sea, and the sea and the
          sky,   250
Lay like a load on my weary eye,
And the dead were at my feet.

But the curse liveth
for him in the eye
of the dead men.

The cold sweat melted from their limbs,
Nor rot nor reek did they:
The look with which they looked on me   255
Had never passed away.

An orphan's curse would drag to hell
A spirit from on high;
But oh! more horrible than that
Is the curse in a dead man's eye!   260
Seven days, seven nights, I saw that curse,
And yet I could not die.

280

The moving Moon went up the sky,
And nowhere did abide:
Softly she was going up,   265
And a star or two beside—

In his loneliness and fixedness he yearneth towards the journeying Moon, and the stars that still sojourn, yet still move onward; and every where the blue sky belongs to them, and is their appointed rest, and their native country and their own natural homes, which they enter unannounced, as lords that are certainly expected and yet there is a silent joy at their arrival.

Her beams bemocked the sultry main,
Like April hoar-frost spread;
But where the ship's huge shadow lay,
The charmed water burnt alway   270
A still and awful red.

By the light of the Moon he beholdeth God's creatures of the great calm.

Beyond the shadow of the ship,
I watched the water-snakes:
They moved in tracks of shining white,
And when they reared, the elfish light   275
Fell off in hoary flakes.

Within the shadow of the ship
I watched their rich attire:
Blue, glossy green, and velvet black,
They coiled and swam; and every track   280
Was a flash of golden fire.

Their beauty and their happiness.

O happy living things! no tongue
Their beauty might declare:
A spring of love gushed from my heart,

He blesseth them in his heart.

And I blessed them unaware: 285
Sure my kind saint took pity on me,
And I blessed them unaware.

The spell begins to break.

The selfsame moment I could pray;
And from my neck so free
The Albatross fell off, and sank   290
Like lead into the sea.

275 *elfish:* bewitched.

PART V

Oh sleep! it is a gentle thing,
Beloved from pole to pole!
To Mary Queen the praise be given!
She sent the gentle sleep from Heaven,   295
That slid into my soul.

By grace of the holy
Mother, the ancient
Mariner is refreshed
with rain.

The silly buckets on the deck,
That had so long remained,
I dreamt that they were filled with dew;
And when I awoke, it rained.   300

My lips were wet, my throat was cold,
My garments all were dank;
Sure I had drunken in my dreams,
And still my body drank.

I moved, and could not feel my limbs: 305
I was so light—almost
I thought that I had died in sleep,
And was a blessed ghost.

He heareth sounds
and seeth strange
sights and commo-
tions in the sky and
the element.

And soon I heard a roaring wind:
It did not come anear;   310
But with its sound it shook the sails,
That were so thin and sere.

The upper air burst into life!
And a hundred fire-flags sheen,
To and fro they were hurried about!   315
And to and fro, and in and out,
The wan stars danced between.

And the coming wind did roar more loud,
And the sails did sigh like sedge;
And the rain poured down from one black
          cloud;   320
The Moon was at its edge.

The thick black cloud was cleft, and still
The Moon was at its side:
Like waters shot from some high crag,
The lightning fell with never a jag,   325
A river steep and wide.

297 *silly:* plain, simple. 314 *fire-flags:* bright meteor flames; perhaps the
Aurora Australis, the Southern (Polar) Lights, which also flame up and move
violently. Cf. also l. 128. 325 *jag:* zig-zag.

282

The loud wind never reached the ship,
Yet now the ship moved on!
Beneath the lightning and the Moon
The dead men gave a groan.   330

They groaned, they stirred, they all uprose,
Nor spake, nor moved their eyes;
It had been strange, even in a dream,
To have seen those dead men rise.

The helmsman steered, the ship moved on;   335
Yet never a breeze up blew;
The mariners all 'gan work the ropes,
Where they were wont to do;
They raised their limbs like lifeless tools—
We were a ghastly crew.   340

The body of my brother's son
Stood by me, knee to knee:
The body and I pulled at one rope,
But he said nought to me.

"I fear thee, ancient Mariner!"   345
Be calm, thou Wedding-Guest!
'Twas not those souls that fled in pain,
Which to their corses came again,
But a troop of spirits blest:

For when it dawned—they dropped their
          arms,   350
And clustered round the mast;
Sweet sounds rose slowly through their mouths,
And from their bodies passed.

Around, around, flew each sweet sound,
Then darted to the Sun;   355
Slowly the sounds come back again,
Now mixed, now one by one.

348 *corses:* corpses.

Sometimes a-dropping from the sky
I heard the sky-lark sing;
Sometimes all little birds that are,   360
How they seemed to fill the sea and air
With their sweet jargoning!

And now 'twas like all instruments,
Now like a lonely flute;
And now it is an angel's song,   365
That makes the heavens be mute.

It ceased; yet still the sails made on
A pleasant noise till noon,
A noise like of a hidden brook
In the leafy month of June,   370
That to the sleeping woods all night
Singeth a quiet tune.

Till noon we quietly sailed on,
Yet never a breeze did breathe:
Slowly and smoothly went the ship,   375
Moved onward from beneath.

The lonesome Spirit from the south-pole carries on the ship as far as the Line, in obedience to the angelic troop, but still requireth vengeance.

Under the keel nine fathom deep,
From the land of mist and snow,
The spirit slid: and it was he
That made the ship to go.   380
The sails at noon left off their tune,
And the ship stood still also.

The Sun, right up above the mast,
Had fixed her to the ocean:
But in a minute she 'gan stir,   385
With a short uneasy motion—
Backwards and forwards half her length,
With a short uneasy motion.

Then like a pawing horse let go,
She made a sudden bound: 390
It flung the blood into my head,
And I fell down in a swound.

362 *jargoning:* twittering.

The Polar Spirit's
fellow-demons, the
invisible inhabitants
of the element, take
part in his wrong;
and two of them
relate, one to the
other, that penance
long and heavy for
the ancient Mariner
hath been accorded
to the Polar Spirit,
who returneth south-
ward.

How long in that same fit I lay,
I have not to declare;
But ere my living life returned,   395
I heard, and in my soul discerned
Two voices in the air.

"Is it he?" quoth one, "Is this the man?
By him who died on cross,
With his cruel bow he laid full low   400
The harmless Albatross.

"The spirit who bideth by himself
In the land of mist and snow,
He loved the bird that loved the man
Who shot him with his bow."   405

The other was a softer voice,
As soft as honey-dew:
Quoth he, "The man hath penance done,
And penance more will do."

PART VI

First Voice

But tell me, tell me! speak again   410
Thy soft response renewing—
What makes that ship drive on so fast?
What is the ocean doing?

Second Voice

Still as a slave before his lord,
The ocean hath no blast;   415
His great bright eye most silently
Up to the Moon is cast—

If he may know which way to go;
For she guides him smooth or grim.
See, brother, see! how graciously   420
She looketh down on him.

The Mariner hath
been cast into a
trance; for the an-
gelic power causeth   *First Voice*
the vessel to drive
northward faster
than human life   But why drives on that ship so fast,
could endure.   Without or wave or wind?

407 *honey-dew:* sugary secretion from leaves, appearing as small glistening
drops, like dew; when abundant and dripping on the ground, it has been called
manna; here, exotic food that inspires the imagination and induces the spirit of
love and compassion.

Second Voice

The air is cut away before,
And closes from behind.   425

Fly, brother, fly! more high, more high!
Or we shall be belated:
For slow and slow that ship will go,
When the Mariner's trance is abated.

*The supernatural
motion is retarded;
the Mariner awakes,
and his penance
begins a new.*

I woke, and we were sailing on   430
As in a gentle weather:
'Twas night, calm night, the moon was high;
The dead men stood together.

All stood together on the deck,
For a charnel-dungeon fitter: 435
All fixed on me their stony eyes,
That in the Moon did glitter.

The pang, the curse, with which they died,
Had never passed away:
I could not draw my eyes from theirs,   440
Nor turn them up to pray.

*The curse is finally
expiated.*

And now this spell was snapt: once more
I viewed the ocean green,
And looked far forth, yet little saw
Of what had else been seen—   445

Like one, that on a lonesome road
Doth walk in fear and dread,
And having once turned round walks on,
And turns no more his head;
Because he knows, a frightful fiend   450
Doth close behind him tread.

But soon there breathed a wind on me,
Nor sound nor motion made:
Its path was not upon the sea,
In ripple or in shade.   455

It raised my hair, it fanned my cheek
Like a meadow-gale of spring—
It mingled strangely with my fears,
Yet it felt like a welcoming.

435 *charnel-dungeon:* a depository for bones dug up to make room in over-
populated graveyards for the newly dead.

Swiftly, swiftly flew the ship,   460
Yet she sailed softly too:
Sweetly, sweetly blew the breeze—
On me alone it blew.

And the ancient
Mariner beholdeth
his native country.

Oh! dream of joy! is this indeed
The light-house top I see?   465
Is this the hill? is this the kirk?
Is this mine own countree?

We drifted o'er the harbor-bar,
And I with sobs did pray—
O let me be awake, my God!   470
Or let me sleep alway.

The harbor-bay was clear as glass,
So smoothly it was strewn!
And on the bay the moonlight lay,
And the shadow of the Moon.   475

The rock shone bright, the kirk no less,
That stands above the rock:
The moonlight steeped in silentness
The steady weathercock.

And the bay was white with silent light,   480
Till, rising from the same,

The angelic spirits
leave the dead
bodies.

Full many shapes, that shadows were,
In crimson colors came.

And appear in their
own forms of light.

A little distance from the prow
Those crimson shadows were: 485
I turned my eyes upon the deck—
Oh, Christ! what saw I there!

Each corse lay flat, lifeless and flat,
And, by the holy rood!
A man all light, a seraph-man,   490
On every corse there stood.

This seraph-band, each waved his hand:
It was a heavenly sight!
They stood as signals to the land,
Each one a lovely light;   495

489 *rood:* crucifix. 490 *seraph:* a "flaming" angel, not a demon, of the highest order, traditionally associated with light and fire.

This seraph-band, each waved his hand,
No voice did they impart—
No voice; but oh! the silence sank
Like music on my heart.

But soon I heard the dash of oars,   500
I heard the Pilot's cheer;
My head was turned perforce away,
And I saw a boat appear.

The Pilot and the Pilot's boy,
I heard them coming fast: 505
Dear Lord in Heaven! it was a joy
The dead men could not blast.

I saw a third—I heard his voice:
It is the Hermit good!
He singeth loud his godly hymns   510
That he makes in the wood.
He'll shrieve my soul, he'll wash away
The Albatross's blood.

PART VII

The Hermit of
the Wood.

This Hermit good lives in that wood
Which slopes down to the sea.   515
How loudly his sweet voice he rears!
He loves to talk with marineres
That come from a far countree.

He kneels at morn, and noon, and eve—
He hath a cushion plump: 520
It is the moss that wholly hides
The rotted old oak-stump.

The skiff-boat neared: I heard them talk.
"Why, this is strange, I trow!
Where are those lights so many and fair,   525
That signal made but now?"

Approacheth the
ship with wonder.

"Strange, by my faith!" the Hermit said—
"And they answered not our cheer!
The planks looked warped! and see those sails,
How thin they are and sere!   530
I never saw aught like to them,
Unless perchance it were

512 *shrieve:* hear confession, impose penance, and grant absolution.

"Brown skeletons of leaves that lag
My forest-brook along;
When the ivy-tod is heavy with snow,   535
And the owlet whoops to the wolf below,
That eats the she-wolf's young."

"Dear Lord! it hath a fiendish look—
(The Pilot made reply)
I am a-feared"—"Push on, push on!"   540
Said the Hermit cheerily.

The boat came closer to the ship,
But I nor spake nor stirred;
The boat came close beneath the ship,
And straight a sound was heard.   545

The ship suddenly sinketh.

Under the water it rumbled on,
Still louder and more dread:
It reached the ship, it split the bay;
The ship went down like lead.

The ancient Mariner is saved in the Pilot's boat.

Stunned by that loud and dreadful sound,   550
Which sky and ocean smote,
Like one that hath been seven days drowned,
My body lay afloat;
But swift as dreams, myself I found
Within the Pilot's boat.   555

Upon the whirl, where sank the ship,
The boat spun round and round;
And all was still, save that the hill
Was telling of the sound.

I moved my lips—the Pilot shrieked,   560
And fell down in a fit;
The holy Hermit raised his eyes,
And prayed where he did sit.

I took the oars: the Pilot's boy,
Who now doth crazy go,   565
Laughed loud and long, and all the while
His eyes went to and fro.
"Ha! ha!" quoth he, "full plain I see,
The Devil knows how to row."

535 *tod:* bush.

And now, all in my own countree,   570
I stood on the firm land!
The Hermit stepped forth from the boat,
And scarcely he could stand.

The ancient Mariner
earnestly entreateth
the Hermit to
shrieve him; and
the penance of life
falls on him.

"O shrieve me, shrieve me, holy man!"
The Hermit crossed his brow,   575
"Say quick," quoth he, "I bid thee say—
What manner of man art thou?"

Forthwith this frame of mine was wrenched
With a woeful agony,
Which forced me to begin my tale;   580
And then it left me free.

And ever and anon
throughout his fu-
ture life an agony
constraineth him
to travel from land
to land;

Since then, at an uncertain hour,
That agony returns;
And till my ghastly tale is told,
This heart within me burns.   585

I pass, like night, from land to land;
I have strange power of speech;
That moment that his face I see,
I know the man that must hear me:
To him my tale I teach.   590

What loud uproar bursts from that door!
The wedding-guests are there;
But in the garden-bower the bride
And bride-maids singing are:
And hark the little vesper bell,   595
Which biddeth me to prayer!

O Wedding-Guest! this soul hath been
Alone on a wide wide sea:
So lonely 'twas, that God himself
Scarce seemed there to be.   600

O sweeter than the marriage-feast,
'Tis sweeter far to me,
To walk together to the kirk
With a goodly company!—

575 *crossed:* made the sign of the cross.

To walk together to the kirk, 605
And all together pray,
While each to his great Father bends,
Old men, and babes, and loving friends,
And youths and maidens gay!

And to teach, by
his own example,
love and reverence
to all things that
God made and
loveth.

Farewell, farewell! but this I tell 610
To thee, thou Wedding-Guest!
He prayeth well, who loveth well
Both man and bird and beast.

He prayeth best, who loveth best
All things both great and small; 615
For the dear God who loveth us,
He made and loveth all.

The Mariner, whose eye is bright,
Whose beard with age is hoar,
Is gone: and now the Wedding-Guest 620
Turned from the bridegroom's door.

He went like one that hath been stunned,
And is of sense forlorn:
A sadder and a wiser man,
He rose the morrow morn. 625

Frost at Midnight

The Frost performs its secret ministry,
Unhelped by any wind. The owlet's cry
Came loud—and hark, again! loud as before.
The inmates of my cottage, all at rest,
Have left me to that solitude, which suits 5
Abstruser musings: save that at my side
My cradled infant slumbers peacefully.
'Tis calm indeed! so calm, that it disturbs
And vexes meditation with its strange
And extreme silentness. Sea, hill, and wood, 10
This populous village! Sea, and hill, and wood,
With all the numberless goings-on of life,
Inaudible as dreams! the thin blue flame
Lies on my low-burnt fire, and quivers not;

FROST AT MIDNIGHT. Coleridge called this poem a "conversation poem."
7 *infant:* Coleridge's son, Hartley.

Only that film, which fluttered on the grate,   15
Still flutters there, the sole unquiet thing.
Methinks, its motion in this hush of nature
Gives it dim sympathies with me who live,
Making it a companionable form,
Whose puny flaps and freaks the idling Spirit   20
By its own moods interprets, everywhere
Echo or mirror seeking of itself,
And makes a toy of Thought.

           But O! how oft,
How oft, at school, with most believing mind,
Presageful, have I gazed upon the bars,   25
To watch that fluttering *stranger!* and as oft
With unclosed lids, already had I dreamt
Of my sweet birth-place, and the old church-tower,
Whose bells, the poor man's only music, rang
From morn to evening, all the hot Fair-day,   30
So sweetly, that they stirred and haunted me
With a wild pleasure, falling on mine ear
Most like articulate sounds of things to come!
So gazèd I, till the soothing things, I dreamt,
Lulled me to sleep, and sleep prolonged my dreams!   35
And so I brooded all the following morn,
Awed by the stern preceptor's face, mine eye
Fixed with mock study on my swimming book:
Save if the door half opened, and I snatched
A hasty glance, and still my heart leaped up,   40
For still I hoped to see the *stranger's* face,
Townsman, or aunt, or sister more beloved,
My play-mate when we both were clothed alike!

    Dear babe, that sleepest cradled by my side,
Whose gentle breathings, heard in this deep calm,   45
Fill up the interspersèd vacancies
And momentary pauses of the thought!
My babe so beautiful! it thrills my heart
With tender gladness, thus to look at thee,
And think that thou shalt learn far other lore,   50
And in far other scenes! For I was reared

15 *film:* "In all parts of the kingdom these films are called *strangers* and supposed to portend the arrival of some absent friend" [Coleridge]. 20 *freaks:* sudden, prankish changes. 37 *stern preceptor:* the Rev. James Boyer, Headmaster of the Grammar School, Christ's Hospital, whose severe and rigorous criticism of his schoolboy compositions Coleridge valued greatly. See *Biographia Literaria,* Ch. I. 43 *play-mate:* his sister Ann.

In the great city, pent 'mid cloisters dim,
And saw nought lovely but the sky and stars.
But thou, my babe! shalt wander like a breeze
By lakes and sandy shores, beneath the crags   55
Of ancient mountain, and beneath the clouds,
Which image in their bulk both lakes and shores
And mountain crags: so shalt thou see and hear
The lovely shapes and sounds intelligible
Of that eternal language, which thy God   60
Utters, who from eternity doth teach
Himself in all, and all things in himself.
Great universal Teacher! he shall mould
Thy spirit, and by giving make it ask.

    Therefore all seasons shall be sweet to thee,   65
Whether the summer clothe the general earth
With greenness, or the redbreast sit and sing
Betwixt the tufts of snow on the bare branch
Of mossy apple-tree, while the nigh thatch
Smokes in the sun-thaw; whether the eave-drops fall   70
Heard only in the trances of the blast,
Or if the secret ministry of frost
Shall hang them up in silent icicles,
Quietly shining to the quiet Moon.

Work Without Hope

LINES COMPOSED 21ST FEBRUARY 1825

All Nature seems at work. Slugs leave their lair—
The bees are stirring—birds are on the wing—
And Winter slumbering in the open air,
Wears on his smiling face a dream of Spring!
And I the while, the sole unbusy thing,   5
Nor honey make, nor pair, nor build, nor sing.

WORK WITHOUT HOPE. 1 *Nature:* Cf. Chaucer, "The General Prologue,"
l. 11. 7 *amaranths:* imaginary flowers that when plucked do not fade; here
symbolic of poetry. *blow:* bloom. 8 *nectar:* drink of the gods, reputed to
have life-giving properties, and to impart divine bloom, beauty, and vigor, thus
preserving all who touch it from decay and corruption; here symbolic of poetic
inspiration.

Yet well I ken the banks where amaranths blow,
Have traced the fount whence streams of nectar flow.
Bloom, O ye amaranths! bloom for whom ye may,
For me ye bloom not! Glide, rich streams, away!   10
With lips unbrightened, wreathless brow, I stroll:
And would you learn the spells that drowse my soul?
Work without Hope draws nectar in a sieve,
And Hope without an object cannot live.

LORD BYRON
(GEORGE NOEL GORDON)
1788–1824

She walks in Beauty

I

She walks in Beauty, like the night
    Of cloudless climes and starry skies;
And all that's best of dark and bright
    Meet in her aspect and her eyes:
Thus mellow'd to that tender light   5
    Which Heaven to gaudy day denies.

II

One shade the more, one ray the less,
    Had half impair'd the nameless grace
Which waves in every raven tress,
    Or softly lightens o'er her face;   10
Where thoughts serenely sweet express
    How pure, how dear their dwelling-place.

III

And on that cheek, and o'er that brow,
    So soft, so calm, yet eloquent,
The smiles that win, the tints that glow,   15
    But tell of days in goodness spent,
A mind at peace with all below,
    A heart whose love is innocent!

So we'll go no more a-roving

I

So we'll go no more a-roving
    So late into the night,
Though the heart be still as loving,
    And the moon be still as bright.

SHE WALKS IN BEAUTY. From a collection of lyrics called *Hebrew Melodies*, written to be set to music based on traditional Jewish tunes.

SO WE'LL GO NO MORE. Written in Lent of 1817, after the revelry and dissipation of Carnival (literally, "O Flesh, farewell") in Venice, and included in a letter to Byron's friend and brother-poet Thomas Moore.

II

For the sword outwears its sheath,   5
    And the soul wears out the breast,
And the heart must pause to breathe,
    And love itself have rest.

III

Though the night was made for loving,
    And the day returns too soon,   10
Yet we'll go no more a-roving
    By the light of the moon.

from DON JUAN

['*Tis Sweet*]

CXXII

—'Tis sweet to hear
At midnight on the blue and moonlit deep
The song and oar of Adria's gondolier,
    By distance mellow'd, o'er the waters sweep;
'Tis sweet to see the evening star appear;   5
    'Tis sweet to listen as the night-winds creep
From leaf to leaf; 'tis sweet to view on high
The rainbow, based on ocean, span the sky.

CXXIII

'Tis sweet to hear the watch-dog's honest bark
    Bay deep-mouth'd welcome as we draw near home;   10
'Tis sweet to know there is an eye will mark
    Our coming, and look brighter when we come;

DON JUAN. A comic poem, mock-heroic in style, modeled not on the classical epic but on Italian seriocomic romances of Pulci (*Morgatne Maggiore*, 1480) and Ariosto (*Orlando Furioso*, 1516), as well as on Cervantes, Rabelais, Fielding, and Sterne; *Don Juan* (pronounced Don Joó-un) satirizes not the sexual prowess and escapades of the legendary libertine and champion seducer but the hypocrisy and humbug of society and the cunning wiles of the ladies who invariably seduce the innocent and complaisant hero. Episodic and genially digressive, the poem allows Byron to comment satirically and sympathetically, ironically and enthusiastically, on every aspect of his varied, rich, and complex view of life. The joke is always present in the serious and sentimental, and it is constantly heard in the comic rhymes and rhythms of the *ottava rima* in which the poem is written.

'TIS SWEET. Don Juan, a sixteen-year-old schoolboy, has fallen in love with and been seduced by Donna Julia, a married lady of twenty-three (chosen by his mother as a good and safe companion) on the "sixth of June" at "half-past six—perhaps still nearer seven . . . ." Byron as narrator comments on the event with appropriately ironic *post coitum tristitia*. 3 *Adria:* Venice.

'Tis sweet to be awaken'd by the lark,
　Or lull'd by falling waters; sweet the hum
Of bees, the voice of girls, the song of birds,　　　　15
The lisp of children, and their earliest words.

CXXIV

Sweet is the vintage, when the showering grapes
　In Bacchanal profusion reel to earth,
Purple and gushing: sweet are our escapes
　From civic revelry to rural mirth;　　　　20
Sweet to the miser are his glittering heaps,
　Sweet to the father is his first-born's birth,
Sweet is revenge—especially to women,
Pillage to soldiers, prize-money to seamen.

CXXV

Sweet is a legacy, and passing sweet　　　　25
　The unexpected death of some old lady
Or gentleman of seventy years complete,
　Who've made "us youth" wait too—too long already,
For an estate, or cash, or country-seat,
　Still breaking, but with stamina so steady,　　　　30
That all the Israelites are fit to mob its
Next owner for their double-damn'd post-obits.

CXXVI

'Tis sweet to win, no matter how, one's laurels,
　By blood or ink; 'tis sweet to put an end
To strife; 'tis sometimes sweet to have our quarrels,　　　　35
　Particularly with a tiresome friend:
Sweet is old wine in bottles, ale in barrels;
　Dear is the helpless creature we defend
Against the world; and dear the schoolboy spot
We ne'er forgot, though there we are forgot.　　　　40

CXXVII

But sweeter still than this, than these, than all,
　Is first and passionate Love—it stands alone,
Like Adam's recollection of his fall;

---

24 *prize-money:* money from the sale of a captured ship divided among the victorious officers and crew.　31 *Israelites:* i.e., money lenders.　32 *post-obit:* bond given to a lender to secure a sum of money on the death of a third person from whom the borrower has expectations. The loans so guaranteed were notorious for their exorbitant rates of interest, hence *double-damn'd.*

The Tree of Knowledge has been pluck'd—all's known—
And Life yields nothing further to recall   45
   Worthy of this ambrosial sin, so shown,
No doubt in fable, as the unforgiven
Fire which Prometheus filch'd for us from Heaven.

[From *Canto I*]

[*Juan and Haidée*]

CLXXIV

And thus a moon roll'd on, and fair Haidée
   Paid daily visits to her boy, and took
Such plentiful precautions, that still he
   Remain'd unknown within his craggy nook;
At last her father's prows put out to sea,   5
   For certain merchantmen upon the look,
Not as of yore to carry off an Io,
But three Ragusan vessels, bound for Scio.

CLXXV

Then came her freedom, for she had no mother,
   So that, her father being at sea, she was   10
Free as a married woman, or such other
   Female, as where she likes may freely pass,
Without even the encumbrance of a brother,
   The freest she that ever gazed on glass:
I speak of Christian lands in this comparison,   15
Where wives, at least, are seldom kept in garrison.

48 *Prometheus:* Titan who stole fire from heaven for mankind, thus incurring the relentless wrath of Zeus and daily torture.

JUAN AND HAIDÉE. The sole survivor of a shipwreck, Juan is cast ashore unconscious on "one of the wild and smaller Cyclades" (in the Aegean), inhabited only by Lambro, a widowed slaver, pirate, and smuggler; his household and crew; Haidée, his beautiful seventeen-year-old daughter; and Zoe, her maid. The two girls rescue Juan, hide him in a cave, and nurse him until Lambro sails off on a piratical expedition.   7 *Io:* (pronounced ī′ō) rhymes comically with *Scio*. According to Ovid (*Met.* I, 568–746) and Greek legend, Io, daughter of King Inachus of Argos, was beloved by Zeus, changed by him into a white cow, and pursued to Egypt by a gadfly sent by Hera. According to Herodotus (I, 1), Phoenician sailors abducted Io from Argos, carrying her to Egypt; the Greeks retaliated when Jason abducted Medea and refused to pay reparation, saying that they had received none for Io. Hence she is the much pursued, abducted, ravished, beautiful, white, and shining maiden, a valuable prize worth a rich ransom for a pirate slave connoisseur who, Byron remarks later (Canto III, LV), is also illuminated by a "few heroic rays" of the "spirit of old Greece" of Jason and the Argonauts.   8 *Ragusan:* of Ragusa, the Italian name for Dubrovnik, a port city on the Adriatic in southwestern Yugoslavia. *Scio:* isle in the Aegean sea.

CLXXVI

Now she prolong'd her visits and her talk
    (For they must talk), and he had learnt to say
So much as to propose to take a walk,—
    For little had he wander'd since the day   20
On which, like a young flower snapped from the stalk,
    Drooping and dewy on the beach he lay,—
And thus they walk'd out in the afternoon,
And saw the sun set opposite the moon.

CLXXVII

It was a wild and breaker-beaten coast,   25
    With cliffs above, and a broad sandy shore,
Guarded by shoals and rocks as by an host,
    With here and there a creek, whose aspect wore
A better welcome to the tempest-tost;
    And rarely ceased the haughty billow's roar,   30
Save on the dead long summer days, which make
The outstretch'd Ocean glitter like a lake.

CLXXVIII

And the small ripple split upon the beach
    Scarcely o'erpass'd the cream of your champagne,
When o'er the brim the sparkling bumpers reach,   35
    That spring-dew of the spirit! the heart's rain!
Few things surpass old wine; and they may preach
    Who please,—the more because they preach in vain,—
Let us have Wine and Woman, Mirth and Laughter,
Sermons and soda-water the day after.   40

CLXXIX

Man, being reasonable, must get drunk;
    The best of Life is but intoxication:
Glory, the Grape, Love, Gold, in these are sunk
    The hopes of all men, and of every nation;
Without their sap, how branchless were the trunk   45
    Of Life's strange tree, so fruitful on occasion!
But to return,—Get very drunk; and when
You wake with headache, you shall see what then.

27 *host:* large army.

CLXXX

Ring for your valet—bid him quickly bring
  Some hock and soda-water, then you'll know   50
A pleasure worthy Xerxes the great king;
  For not the blest sherbet, sublimed with snow,
Nor the first sparkle of the desert-spring,
  Nor Burgundy in all its sunset glow,
After long travel, Ennui, Love, or Slaughter,   55
Vie with that draught of hock and soda-water.

CLXXXI

The coast—I think it was the coast that I
  Was just describing—Yes, it *was* the coast—   *labored— conscious way of getting to work* [handwritten annotation]
Lay at this period quiet as the sky,
  The sands untumbled, the blue waves untost,
And all was stillness, save the sea-bird's cry,   60
  And dolphin's leap, and little billow crost
By some low rock or shelve, that made it fret
Against the boundary it scarcely wet.

CLXXXII

And forth they wander'd, her sire being gone,   65
  As I have said, upon an expedition;
And mother, brother, guardian, she had none,
  Save Zoe, who, although with due precision
She waited on her lady with the Sun,
  Thought daily service was her only mission,   70
Bringing warm water, wreathing her long tresses,
And asking now and then for cast-off dresses.

CLXXXIII

It was the cooling hour, just when the rounded
  Red sun sinks down behind the azure hill,
Which then seems as if the whole earth it bounded,   75
  Circling all Nature, hush'd, and dim, and still,
With the far mountain-crescent half surrounded
  On one side, and the deep sea calm and chill
Upon the other, and the rosy sky,
With one star sparkling through it like an eye.   80

62 *crost:* crossed.   63 *fret:* ripple.

CLXXXIV

And thus they wander'd forth, and hand in hand,
    Over the shining pebbles and the shells,
Glided along the smooth and harden'd sand,
    And in the worn and wild receptacles
Work'd by the storms, yet work'd as it were plann'd,   85
    In hollow halls, with sparry roofs and cells,
They turn'd to rest; and, each clasp'd by an arm,
Yielded to the deep Twilight's purple charm.

CLXXXV

They look'd up to the sky, whose floating glow
    Spread like a rosy Ocean, vast and bright;   90
They gazed upon the glittering sea below,
    Whence the broad Moon rose circling into sight;
They heard the wave's splash, and the wind so low,
    And saw each other's dark eyes darting light
Into each other—and, beholding this,   95
Their lips drew near, and clung into a kiss;

CLXXXVI

A long, long kiss, a kiss of Youth, and Love,
    And beauty, all concentrating like rays
Into one focus, kindled from above;
    Such kisses as belong to early days,   100
Where Heart, and Soul, and Sense, in concert move,
    And the blood's lava, and the pulse a blaze,
Each kiss a heart-quake,—for a kiss's strength,
I think, it must be reckon'd by its length.

CLXXXVII

By length I mean duration; theirs endured   105
    Heaven knows how long—no doubt they never reckon'd;
And if they had, they could not have secured
    The sum of their sensations to a second:
They had not spoken; but they felt allured,
    As if their souls and lips each other beckon'd,   110
Which, being join'd, like swarming bees they clung—
Their hearts the flowers from whence the honey sprung.

CLXXXVIII

They were alone, but not alone as they
    Who shut in chambers think it loneliness;
The silent ocean, and the starlight bay,   115
    The twilight glow, which momently grew less,

The voiceless sands, and dropping caves, that lay
  Around them, made them to each other press,
As if there were no life beneath the sky
Save theirs, and that their life could never die.   120

CLXXXIX

They fear'd no eyes nor ears on that lone beach,
  They felt no terrors from the night; they were
All in all to each other: though their speech
  Was broken words, they *thought* a language there,—
And all the burning tongues the Passions teach   125
  Found in one sigh the best interpreter
Of Nature's oracle—first love,—that all
Which Eve has left her daughters since her fall.

CXC

Haidée spoke not of scruples, ask'd no vows,
  Nor offer'd any; she had never heard   130
Of plight and promises to be a spouse,
  Or perils by a loving maid incurr'd;
She was all which pure Ignorance allows,
  And flew to her young mate like a young bird;
And, never having dreamt of falsehood, she   135
Had not one word to say of constancy.

CXCI

She loved, and was beloved—she adored,
  And she was worshipp'd; after Nature's fashion,
Their intense souls, into each other pour'd,
  If souls could die, had perish'd in that passion,—   140
But by degrees their senses were restored,
  Again to be o'ercome, again to dash on;
And, beating 'gainst *his* bosom, Haidée's heart
Felt as if never more to beat apart.

CXCII

Alas! they were so young, so beautiful,   145
  So lonely, loving, helpless, and the hour
Was that in which the Heart is always full,
  And, having o'er itself no further power,
Prompts deeds Eternity can not annul,
  But pays off moments in an endless shower   150
Of hell-fire—all prepared for people giving
Pleasure or pain to one another living.

CXCIII

Alas! for Juan and Haidée! they were
   So loving and so lovely—till then never,
Excepting our first parents, such a pair   155
   Had run the risk of being damn'd for ever;
And Haidée, being devout as well as fair,
   Had, doubtless, heard about the Stygian river,
And Hell and Purgatory—but forgot
Just in the very crisis she should not.   160

CXCIV

They look upon each other, and their eyes
   Gleam in the moonlight; and her white arm clasps
Round Juan's head, and his around hers lies
   Half buried in the tresses which it grasps;
She sits upon his knee, and drinks his sighs,   165
   He hers, until they end in broken gasps;
And thus they form a group that's quite antique,
Half naked, loving, natural, and Greek.

CXCV

And when those deep and burning moments pass'd,
   And Juan sunk to sleep within her arms,   170
She slept not, but all tenderly, though fast,
   Sustain'd his head upon her bosom's charms;
And now and then her eye to Heaven is cast,
   And then on the pale cheek her breast now warms,
Pillow'd on her o'erflowing heart, which pants   175
With all it granted, and with all it grants.

CXCVI

An infant when it gazes on a light,
   A child the moment when it drains the breast,
A devotee when soars the Host in sight,
   An Arab with a stranger for a guest,   180
A sailor when the prize has struck in fight,
   A miser filling his most hoarded chest,
Feel rapture; but not such true joy are reaping
As they who watch o'er what they love while sleeping.

---

158 *Stygian river:* the Styx, which flows around the lower world, whose
waters were used as a symbol in the most binding oaths of the gods.   179
soars . . . sight: The Elevation of the Host is the most solemn and ecstatic
moment of the Mass.   181 *struck:* lowered his colors in surrender.

CXCVII

For there it lies so tranquil, so beloved,   185
    All that it hath of Life with us is living;
So gentle, stirless, helpless, and unmoved,
    And all unconscious of the joy 'tis giving;
All it hath felt, inflicted, pass'd, and proved,
    Hush'd into depths beyond the watcher's diving: 190
There lies the thing we love with all its errors
And all its charms, like Death without its terrors.

CXCVIII

The Lady watch'd her lover—and that hour
    Of Love's, and Night's, and Ocean's solitude,
O'erflow'd her soul with their united power;   195
    Amidst the barren sand and rocks so rude
She and her wave-worn love had made their bower,
    Where nought upon their passion could intrude,
And all the stars that crowded the blue space
Saw nothing happier than her glowing face.   200

CXCIX

Alas! the love of Women! it is known
    To be a lovely and a fearful thing;
For all of theirs upon that die is thrown,
    And if 'tis lost, Life hath no more to bring
To them but mockeries of the past alone,   205
    And their revenge is as the tiger's spring,
Deadly, and quick, and crushing; yet, as real
Torture is theirs, what they inflict they feel.

CC

They are right; for Man, to man so oft unjust,
    Is always so to Women: one sole bond   210
Awaits them, treachery is all their trust;
    Taught to conceal, their bursting hearts despond
Over their idol, till some wealthier lust
    Buys them in marriage—and what rests beyond?
A thankless husband, next a faithless lover,   215
Then dressing, nursing, praying, and all's over.

CCI

Some take a lover, some take drams or prayers,
    Some mind their household, others dissipation,
Some run away, and but exchange their cares,

217 *dram:* a drink of spirits (e.g., brandy) taken at a gulp.

Losing the advantage of a virtuous station;   220
Few changes e'er can better their affairs,
    Theirs being an unnatural situation,
From the dull palace to the dirty hovel:
Some play the devil, and then write a novel.

CCII

Haidée was Nature's bride, and knew not this;   225
    Haidée was Passion's child, born where the sun
Showers triple light, and scorches even the kiss
    Of his gazelle-eyed daughters; she was one
Made but to love, to feel that she was his
    Who was her chosen: what was said or done   230
Elsewhere was nothing.—She had nought to fear,
Hope, care, nor love beyond,—her heart beat *here*.

CCIII

And oh! that quickening of the heart, that beat!
    How much it costs us! yet each rising throb
Is in its cause as its effect so sweet,   235
    That Wisdom, ever on the watch to rob
Joy of its alchemy, and to repeat
    Fine truths; even Conscience, too, has a tough job
To make us understand each good old maxim,
So good—I wonder Castlereagh don't tax 'em.   240

CCIV

And now 'twas done—on the lone shore were plighted
    Their hearts; the stars, their nuptial torches, shed
Beauty upon the beautiful they lighted:
    Ocean their witness, and the cave their bed,
By their own feelings hallow'd and united,   245
    Their priest was Solitude, and they were wed:
And they were happy, for to their young eyes
Each was an angel, and earth Paradise.

[From *Canto II*]

224 *write a novel:* as Lady Caroline Lamb did when Byron threw her over as
his mistress.   240 [Viscount] *Castlereagh:* Robert Stewart, Foreign Secretary,
whose support of a tax program in peacetime to reduce the public debt was
opposed by the Whigs, Byron's party.

PERCY BYSSHE SHELLEY
1792–1822

Ozymandias

I met a traveler from an antique land
Who said: Two vast and trunkless legs of stone
Stand in the desert. Near them, on the sand,
Half sunk, a shattered visage lies, whose frown,
And wrinkled lip, and sneer of cold command,   5
Tell that its sculptor well those passions read
Which yet survive, stamped on these lifeless things,
The hand that mocked them and the heart that fed;
And on the pedestal these words appear:
"My name is Ozymandias, king of kings: 10
Look on my works, ye Mighty, and despair!"
Nothing beside remains. Round the decay
Of that colossal wreck, boundless and bare
The lone and level sands stretch far away.

England in 1819

An old, mad, blind, despised, and dying king,—
Princes, the dregs of their dull race, who flow
Through public scorn—mud from a muddy spring;
Rulers, who neither see, nor feel, nor know,
But leech-like to their fainting country cling,   5
Till they drop, blind in blood, without a blow;
A people starved and stabbed in the untilled field,—
An army, which liberticide and prey
Makes as a two-edged sword to all who wield;

OZYMANDIAS. In the *Bibliothēke Historikē* (I, 47) Diodorus Siculus (*c.* 40 B.C.) describes the thousand-ton colossus of Ozymandias, "the largest of any in Egypt" (Rameses II of Egypt): it is carved from a single block of unblemished stone, on which is enscribed, "King of Kings am I, Osymandias. If anyone would know how great I am and where I lie, let him surpass one of my works" (tr. C. H. Oldfather). The statue, now battered, still exists at Thebes. If Shelley was referring to it, his use of the statue is figuratively, rather than archeologically, correct. 7 *survive:* i.e., the depicted passions. 8 *hand . . . fed:* the *hand* of the sculptor that *mocked* (i.e., both depicted and ridiculed) the passions that were *fed* by the *heart* of the king.

ENGLAND IN 1819. 1 *king:* George III (1738–1820), for many years insane, and always capable of bigotry, bitter animus, and coldness whenever he felt his prerogatives were encroached upon. 7 *people starved:* After the Napoleonic wars, there was a severe economic depression in England. The working class suffered greatly from lack of food and from brutal economic and political restrictions.

Golden and sanguine laws which tempt and slay;   10
Religion Christless, Godless—a book sealed;
A Senate,—Time's worst statute unrepealed,—
Are graves, from which a glorious Phantom may
Burst, to illumine our tempestuous day.

Ode to the West Wind

I

O wild West Wind, thou breath of Autumn's being,
Thou, from whose unseen presence the leaves dead
Are driven, like ghosts from an enchanter fleeing,

Yellow, and black, and pale, and hectic red,
Pestilence-stricken multitudes: O thou,   5
Who chariotest to their dark wintry bed

The wingéd seeds, where they lie cold and low,
Each like a corpse within its grave, until
Thine azure sister of the Spring shall blow

Her clarion o'er the dreaming earth, and fill   10
(Driving sweet buds like flocks to feed in air)
With living hues and odors plain and hill:

Wild Spirit, which art moving everywhere;
Destroyer and preserver; hear, oh hear!

II

Thou on whose stream, 'mid the steep sky's commotion,   15
Loose clouds like earth's decaying leaves are shed,
Shook from the tangled boughs of Heaven and Ocean,

Angels of rain and lightning: there are spread
On the blue surface of thine airy surge,
Like the bright hair uplifted from the head   20

---

10 *Golden . . . laws:* laws passed through bribery and imposed with bloodshed. 12 *Time's . . . unrepealed:* the Test Act, which imposed political
disabilities on Roman Catholics. Shelley began his career as a political
propagandist for Catholic Emancipation in Ireland. 13 *Phantom:* freedom
personified.

ODE TO THE WEST WIND. 1 *breath:* the quickening, animating power, the
soul (cf. Gen. 2:7); also that which kindles, burns (cf. Job 41:21); also vapor,
exhalation. 9 *sister:* Zephyrus (usually masculine), the West Wind, harbinger
of spring. See Chaucer, "The General Prologue," l. 5.

Of some fierce Maenad, even from the dim verge
Of the horizon to the zenith's height
The locks of the approaching storm. Thou dirge

Of the dying year, to which this closing night
Will be the dome of a vast sepulcher,   25
Vaulted with all thy congregated might

Of vapors, from whose solid atmosphere
Black rain, and fire, and hail will burst: Oh hear!

III

Thou who didst waken from his summer dreams
The blue Mediterranean, where he lay,   30
Lulled by the coil of his crystálline streams,

Beside a pumice isle in Baiae's bay,
And saw in sleep old palaces and towers
Quivering within the wave's intenser day,

All overgrown with azure moss and flowers   35
So sweet, the sense faints picturing them! Thou
For whose path the Atlantic's level powers

Cleave themselves into chasms, while far below
The sea-blooms and the oozy woods which wear
The sapless foliage of the ocean, know   40

Thy voice, and suddenly grow gray with fear,
And tremble and despoil themselves: Oh hear!

IV

If I were a dead leaf thou mightest bear;
If I were a swift cloud to fly with thee;
A wave to pant beneath thy power, and share   45

The impulse of thy strength, only less free
Than thou, O uncontrollable! If even
I were as in my boyhood, and could be
The comrade of thy wanderings over heaven,

21 *Maenad:* literally, "madwoman"; the frenzied, possessed votary of Dionysus, the suffering god of vegetation who dies and comes to life again in the spring. His rites are associated with violent ecstasy and mysticism.   31 *coil:* stir, turmoil, tumult.   32 *Baiae's bay:* eleven miles west of Naples.   39–42 *sea-blooms . . . themselves:* The vegetation at the bottom of the sea "sympathizes with that of the land in the changes of seasons, and is consequently influenced by the winds which announce it" [Shelley].

308

As then, when to outstrip thy skyey speed   50
Scarce seemed a vision, I would ne'er have striven

As thus with thee in prayer in my sore need.
Oh! lift me as a wave, a leaf, a cloud!
I fall upon the thorns of life! I bleed!

A heavy weight of hours has chained and bowed   55
One too like thee: tameless, and swift, and proud.

                         v

Make me thy lyre, even as the forest is:
What if my leaves are falling like its own!
The tumult of thy mighty harmonies

Will take from both a deep, autumnal tone,   60
Sweet though in sadness. Be thou, spirit fierce,
My spirit! Be thou me, impetuous one!

Drive my dead thoughts over the universe
Like withered leaves to quicken a new birth;
And, by the incantation of this verse,   65

Scatter, as from an unextinguished hearth
Ashes and sparks, my words among mankind!
Be through my lips to unawakened earth

The trumpet of a prophecy! O Wind,
If Winter comes, can Spring be far behind?   70

                   This is the Day

                [DEMOGORGON'S SONG]

This is the Day, which down the void Abysm
At the Earth-born's spell yawns for Heaven's despotism,
    And Conquest is dragged captive through the deep;
Love, from its awful throne of patient power
In the wise heart, from the last giddy hour   5
    Of dread endurance, from the slippery, steep,
And narrow verge of crag-like agony, springs
And folds over the world its healing wings.
Gentleness, Virtue, Wisdom, and Endurance,—

---

57 *lyre:* i.e., an Aeolian lyre, a wind harp, a characteristic romantic metaphor
(found also in Wordsworth and Coleridge) for the poet who responds with
harmony to the mysterious winds of inspiration and imagination.

These are the seals of that most firm assurance   10
   Which bars the pit over Destruction's strength;
And if, with infirm hand, Eternity,
Mother of many acts and hours, should free
   The serpent that would clasp her with his length,
These are the spells by which to re-assume   15
An empire o'er the disentangled Doom.

To suffer woes which Hope thinks infinite;
To forgive wrongs darker than death or night;
   To defy Power, which seems omnipotent;
To love, and bear; to hope till Hope creates   20
From its own wreck the thing it contemplates:
   Neither to change, nor falter, nor repent;
This, like thy glory, Titan, is to be
Good, great and joyous, beautiful and free;
This is alone Life, Joy, Empire, and Victory.   25

                [*Prometheus Unbound*, IV]

Adonais

AN ELEGY ON THE DEATH OF JOHN KEATS, AUTHOR OF
ENDYMION, HYPERION, ETC.

'Αστὴρ πρὶν μὲν ἔλαμπες ἐνὶ ζώοισιν ἑῶος.
Νῦν δὲ θανὼν λάμπεις ἕσπερος ἐν φθιμένοις.
                PLATO.

I

I weep for Adonais—he is dead!
O, weep for Adonais! though our tears
Thaw not the frost which binds so dear a head!

THIS IS THE DAY.   14 *serpent:* of Doom, which must be disentangled.

ADONAIS.   A pastoral elegy that makes deliberate use of many of the conventions, themes, and attitudes of the classical and English pastoral elegies,
but with a difference. Cf. Spenser, "November," from *The Shepheardes
Calender* and notes; Milton, "Lycidas" and notes; Wordsworth, "Ode" and
notes. For an extended discussion of the themes and traditions of Adonais, see
Earl Wasserman, " 'Adonais': Progressive Revelation as a Poetic Mode,"
ELH (1954), 274–326. *Plato:* a Greek epigram that Shelley prefixed to the
poem as the epigraph and that he translates:
        Thou wert the morning star among the living,
           Ere thy fair light had fled—
        Now, having died, thou art as Hesperus, giving
           New splendor to the dead.
The reference to Venus—Lucifer as the morning star, Hesperus or Vesper as
the evening—indicates the centrality of the star image, its hidden identity and
different aspects.
   1 *Adonais:* allusion to the Greek vegetation god, Adonis, beloved of Venus,
whose ritual death was celebrated in a pastoral elegy by Bion; also to the
Hebrew word *Adon* (God), the plural form of which is *Adonai*.

And thou, sad Hour, selected from all years
To mourn our loss, rouse thy obscure compeers,   5
And teach them thine own sorrow, say: with me
Died Adonais; till the Future dares
Forget the Past, his fate and fame shall be
An echo and a light unto eternity!

II

Where wert thou, mighty Mother, when he lay,   10
When thy Son lay, pierced by the shaft which flies
In darkness? where was lorn Urania
When Adonais died? With veiled eyes,
'Mid listening Echoes, in her Paradise
She sate, while one, with soft enamored breath,   15
Rekindled all the fading melodies,
With which, like flowers that mock the corse beneath,
He had adorned and hid the coming bulk of death.

III

O, weep for Adonais—he is dead!
Wake, melancholy Mother, wake and weep!   20
Yet wherefore? Quench within their burning bed
Thy fiery tears, and let thy loud heart keep
Like his, a mute and uncomplaining sleep;
For he is gone, where all things wise and fair
Descend;—oh, dream not that the amorous Deep   25
Will yet restore him to the vital air;
Death feeds on his mute voice, and laughs at our despair.

IV

Most musical of mourners, weep again!
Lament anew, Urania!—He died,
Who was the Sire of an immortal strain,   30

---

10 *mighty Mother:* Urania (l. 12), the Heavenly Muse (of Astronomy), the highest source of poetic inspiration and traditional muse of cosmological epics; also the Uranian Aphrodite or Heavenly Venus, personifying divine love, mother of all goodness, truth, and love; and by poetic conversion from the passionate, unsatisfied lover of Adonis, the mother of Adonais. 10–13 *Where . . . died:* conventional question concerning the absence of protecting deities. Cf. "Lycidas," l. 50. 29 *He:* Milton.

Blind, old, and lonely, when his country's pride,
The priest, the slave, and the liberticide,
Trampled and mocked with many a loathed rite
Of lust and blood; he went, unterrified,
Into the gulf of death; but his clear Sprite   35
Yet reigns o'er earth; the third among the sons of light.

                                V

Most musical of mourners, weep anew!
Not all to that bright station dared to climb;
And happier they their happiness who knew,
Whose tapers yet burn through that night of time   40
In which suns perished; others more sublime,
Struck by the envious wrath of man or God,
Have sunk, extinct in their refulgent prime;
And some yet live, treading the thorny road,
Which leads, through toil and hate, to Fame's serene abode.   45

                                VI

But now, thy youngest, dearest one, has perished,
The nursling of thy widowhood, who grew,
Like a pale flower by some sad maiden cherished,
And fed with true love tears, instead of dew;
Most musical of mourners, weep anew!   50
Thy extreme hope, the loveliest and the last,
The bloom, whose petals nipt before they blew,
Died on the promise of the fruit, is waste;
The broken lily lies—the storm is overpast.

                                VII

To that high Capital, where kingly Death   55
Keeps his pale court in beauty and decay,
He came; and bought, with price of purest breath,
A grave among the eternal.—Come away!
Haste, while the vault of blue Italian day
Is yet his fitting charnel-roof! while still   60
He lies, as if in dewy sleep he lay;
Awake him not! surely he takes his fill
Of deep and liquid rest, forgetful of all ill.

35 *Sprite:* spirit.   36 *third . . . light:* in Shelley's estimation, the third ranking
epic poet after Homer and Dante.   52 *blew:* bloomed.   55 *Capital:* Rome,
where Keats died and was buried.

VIII

He will awake no more, oh, never more!—
Within the twilight chamber spreads apace,   65
The shadow of white Death, and at the door
Invisible Corruption waits to trace
His extreme way to her dim dwelling-place;
The eternal Hunger sits, but pity and awe
Soothe her pale rage, nor dares she to deface   70
So fair a prey, till darkness, and the law
Of change, shall o'er his sleep the mortal curtain draw.

IX

O, weep for Adonais!—The quick Dreams,
The passion-wingèd Ministers of thought,
Who were his flocks, whom near the living streams   75
Of his young spirit he fed, and whom he taught
The love which was its music, wander not,—
Wander no more, from kindling brain to brain,
But droop there, whence they sprung; and mourn their lot
Round the cold heart, where, after their sweet pain,   80
They ne'er will gather strength, or find a home again.

X

And one with trembling hands clasps his cold head,
And fans him with her moonlight wings, and cries;
"Our love, our hope, our sorrow, is not dead;
See, on the silken fringe of his faint eyes,   85
Like dew upon a sleeping flower, there lies
A tear some Dream has loosened from his brain."
Lost Angel of a ruined Paradise!
She knew not 'twas her own; as with no stain
She faded, like a cloud which had outwept its rain.   90

XI

One from a lucid urn of starry dew
Washed his light limbs as if embalming them;
Another clipt her profuse locks, and threw
The wreath upon him, like an anadem,
Which frozen tears instead of pearls begem;   95
Another in her willful grief would break

68 *extreme:* severe to the outermost limit. 73 *quick:* live and passionate.
73 ff. *Dreams, Splendor, Desires and Adorations, Echo, Spring, etc.:* com-
bination of the conventions of the pastoral life recollected, the procession of
mourners, and the mourning of all nature (the pathetic fallacy). Cf. "Lycidas,"
ll. 25–49 and notes. 94 *anadem:* garland.

Her bow and wingéd reeds, as if to stem
A greater loss with one which was more weak;
And dull the barbéd fire against his frozen cheek.

XII

Another Splendor on his mouth alit,   100
That mouth, whence it was wont to draw the breath
Which gave it strength to pierce the guarded wit,
And pass into the panting heart beneath
With lightning and with music: the damp death
Quenched its caress upon his icy lips;   105
And, as a dying meteor stains a wreath
Of moonlight vapor, which the cold night clips,
It flushed through his pale limbs, and past to its eclipse.

XIII

And others came . . . Desires and Adorations,
Wingéd Persuasions and veiled Destinies,   110
Splendors, and Glooms, and glimmering Incarnations
Of hopes and fears, and twilight Phantasies;
And Sorrow, with her family of Sighs,
And Pleasure, blind with tears, led by the gleam
Of her own dying smile instead of eyes,   115
Came in slow pomp;—the moving pomp might seem
Like pageantry of mist on an autumnal stream.

XIV

All he had loved, and molded into thought,
From shape, and hue, and odor, and sweet sound,
Lamented Adonais. Morning sought   120
Her eastern watchtower, and her hair unbound,
Wet with the tears which should adorn the ground,
Dimmed the aërial eyes that kindle day;
Afar the melancholy thunder moaned,
Pale Ocean in unquiet slumber lay,   125
And the wild winds flew round, sobbing in their dismay.

XV

Lost Echo sits amid the voiceless mountains,
And feeds her grief with his remembered lay,

---

102 *guarded wit:* the habit-bound and fearful minds.   107 *clips:* embraces.
116 *pomp:* solemn procession.|127 *Echo:* a once-chattering nymph whom Juno
made into a mimic capable only of brief speech and who later pined away to
a disembodied voice because of her unrequited love for the disdainful Narcissus
(l. 133); she is silent now as she never was in myth or fact.   See Ovid, *Met.,*
III, 359–401.   128 *lay:* song.

And will no more reply to winds or fountains,
Or amorous birds perched on the young green spray,   130
Or herdsman's horn, or bell at closing day;
Since she can mimic not his lips, more dear
Than those for whose disdain she pined away
Into a shadow of all sounds:—a drear
Murmur, between their songs, is all the woodmen hear.   135

                                XVI

Grief made the young Spring wild, and she threw down
Her kindling buds, as if she Autumn were,
Or they dead leaves; since her delight is flown,
For whom should she have waked the sullen year?
To Phoebus was not Hyacinth so dear,   140
Nor to himself Narcissus, as to both
Thou Adonais: wan they stand and sere
Amid the faint companions of their youth,
With dew all turned to tears; odor, to sighing ruth.

                                XVII

Thy spirit's sister, the lorn nightingale   145
Mourns not her mate with such melodious pain;
Not so the eagle, who like thee could scale
Heaven, and could nourish in the sun's domain
Her mighty youth with morning, doth complain,
Soaring and screaming round her empty nest,   150
As Albion wails for thee: the curse of Cain
Light on his head who pierced thy innocent breast,
And scared the angel soul that was its earthly guest!

140 *Phoebus . . . Hyacinth:* Hyacinth, beloved of Phoebus Apollo, was accidentally killed retrieving the discus Apollo had thrown. To preserve their friendship, Apollo caused him to be reborn as a crimson flower (see Ovid, *Met.,* X, 162–219). Cf. "Lycidas," l. 106.   141 *Narcissus:* That he might know the pangs of unrequited love, Narcissus was condemned by Nemesis to fall passionately in love with his reflected image; he languished and died but was transformed into a flower (see Ovid, *Met.,* III, 346–510).   144 *ruth:* sorrow, compassion.   147 *eagle:* according to the *Bestiary,* the eagle renews its youth, singes away its old plumage, and "evaporates the fog of his eyes" by flying directly into the circle of the sun. Cf. also Isaiah 40:31.   151 *Albion:* England. *curse of Cain:* For killing Abel, Cain was cursed to be a "fugitive and a vagabond" and denied the "strength" that the ground he tilled should yield to him. He was marked on the forehead to prevent other men from killing him. See Gen. 4:9–15.   152 *his head:* of John Wilson Croker, author of the anonymous attack on Keats's *Endymion* in the *Quarterly Review* (April, 1818), thought erroneously by Shelley and others to have been instrumental in Keats's death. Keats himself knew that *Endymion* was not very good. He died of tuberculosis, not of a broken heart.

XVIII

Ah woe is me! Winter is come and gone,
But grief returns with the revolving year;   155
The airs and streams renew their joyous tone;
The ants, the bees, the swallows reappear;
Fresh leaves and flowers deck the dead Seasons' bier;
The amorous birds now pair in every brake,
And build their mossy homes in field and brere;   160
And the green lizard, and the golden snake,
Like unimprisoned flames, out of their trance awake.

XIX

Through wood and stream and field and hill and Ocean
A quickening life from the Earth's heart has burst
As it has ever done, with change and motion,   165
From the great morning of the world when first
God dawned on Chaos; in its stream immersed,
The lamps of Heaven flash with a softer light;
All baser things pant with life's sacred thirst;
Diffuse themselves; and spend in love's delight,   170
The beauty and the joy of their renewèd might.

XX

The leprous corpse, touched by this spirit tender,
Exhales itself in flowers of gentle breath;
Like incarnations of the stars, when splendor
Is changed to fragrance, they illumine death   175
And mock the merry worm that wakes beneath;
Nought we know, dies. Shall that alone which knows
Be as a sword consumed before the sheath
By sightless lightning?—th' intense atom glows
A moment, then is quenched in a most cold repose.   180

XXI

Alas! that all we loved of him should be,
But for our grief, as if it had not been,
And grief itself be mortal! Woe is me!
Whence are we, and why are we? of what scene
The actors or spectators? Great and mean   185

---

159 *brake:* thicket. 160 *brere:* briar. 177–79 *Shall . . . lightning:* The
organic world revives, but shall the mind, which alone knows, be destroyed,
as a sword is disintegrated by lightning, before the *sheath* (i.e., the body that
sheathes the mind) is consumed? The traditional questioning of faith. Cf.
"Lycidas," ll. 75–84 and notes.

Meet massed in death, who lends what life must borrow.
As long as skies are blue, and fields are green,
Evening must usher night, night urge the morrow,
Month follow month with woe, and year wake year to sorrow.

XXII

He will awake no more, oh, never more!   190
"Wake thou," cried Misery, "childless Mother, rise
Out of thy sleep, and slake, in thy heart's core,
A wound more fierce than his with tears and sighs."
And all the Dreams that watched Urania's eyes,
And all the Echoes whom their sister's song   195
Had held in holy silence, cried: "Arise!"
Swift as a Thought by the snake Memory stung,
From her ambrosial rest fading Splendor sprung.

XXIII

She rose like an autumnal Night, that springs
Out of the East, and follows wild and drear   200
The golden Day, which, on eternal wings,
Even as a ghost abandoning a bier,
Had left the Earth a corpse. Sorrow and fear
So struck, so roused, so rapt Urania;
So saddened round her like an atmosphere   205
Of stormy mist; so swept her on her way
Even to the mournful place where Adonais lay.

XXIV

Out of her secret Paradise she sped,
Through camps and cities rough with stone, and steel,
And human hearts, which to her aery tread   210
Yielding not, wounded the invisible
Palms of her tender feet where'er they fall:
And barbèd tongues, and thoughts more sharp than they
Rent the soft Form they never could repel,
Whose sacred blood, like the young tears of May,   215
Paved with eternal flowers that undeserving way.

XXV

In the death chamber for a moment Death,
Shamed by the presence of that living Might,
Blushed to annihilation, and the breath
Revisited those lips, and life's pale light   220

186 *lends . . . borrow:* I.e., life is borrowed from death, the great reality.
204 *rapt:* seized violently. 219 *to annihilation:* as if Death had never been.

Flashed through those limbs, so late her dear delight.
"Leave me not wild and drear and comfortless,
As silent lightning leaves the starless night!
Leave me not!" cried Urania: her distress
Roused Death: Death rose and smiled, and met her vain caress.   225

XXVI

"Stay yet awhile! speak to me once again;
Kiss me, so long but as a kiss may live;
And in my heartless breast and burning brain
That word, that kiss shall all thoughts else survive,
With food of saddest memory kept alive,   230
Now thou art dead, as if it were a part
Of thee, my Adonais! I would give
All that I am to be as thou now art!
But I am chained to Time, and cannot thence depart!

XXVII

"O gentle child, beautiful as thou wert,   235
Why didst thou leave the trodden paths of men
Too soon, and with weak hands though mighty heart
Dare the unpastured dragon in his den?
Defenseless as thou wert, oh where was then
Wisdom the mirrored shield, or scorn the spear?   240
Or hadst thou waited the full cycle, when
Thy spirit should have filled its crescent sphere,
The monsters of life's waste had fled from thee like deer.

XXVIII

"The herded wolves, bold only to pursue;
The obscene ravens, clamorous o'er the dead;   245
The vultures to the conqueror's banner true
Who feed where Desolation first has fed,
And whose wings rain contagion;—how they fled,
When like Apollo, from his golden bow,
The Pythian of the age one arrow sped   250

222–61 *Leave . . . night:* Cf. St. Peter's speech in "Lycidas," ll. 113–31.   228
heartless: because her heart was given to Adonais.   238 *unpastured dragon:*
i.e., the reviewer in his cave, no pastoral saint, whom the shepherd boy
(Adonais) should have left to a veteran hero like Perseus. Perseus wisely
attacked the ossifying Medusa by indirection, looking into his resplendent,
mirror-like shield (l. 240) given him by Athena (Wisdom); thus he avoided
her direct gaze, which would have turned him into stone, and was able to cut
off her head with his adamantine sickle.   242 *filled . . . sphere:* as the full
moon "fills" its *crescent sphere.*   250 *Pythian . . . age:* allusion to Byron who,
in his *English Bards and Scotch Reviewers* (1809), had slaughtered the critics as
Apollo had slain the slime-born serpent Python near Delphi.

318

And smiled!—The spoilers tempt no second blow,
They fawn on the proud feet that spurn them lying low.

XXIX

"The sun comes forth, and many reptiles spawn;
He sets, and each ephemeral insect then
Is gathered into death without a dawn,   255
And the immortal stars awake again;
So is it in the world of living men:
A godlike mind soars forth, in its delight
Making earth bare and veiling heaven, and when
It sinks, the swarms that dimmed or shared its light   260
Leave to its kindred lamps the spirit's awful night."

XXX

Thus ceased she: and the mountain shepherds came,
Their garlands sere, their magic mantles rent;
The Pilgrim of Eternity, whose fame
Over his living head like Heaven is bent,   265
An early but enduring monument,
Came, veiling all the lightnings of his song
In sorrow; from her wilds Ierne sent
The sweetest lyrist of her saddest wrong,
And love taught grief to fall like music from his tongue. 270

XXXI

Midst others of less note, came one frail Form,
A phantom among men; companionless
As the last cloud of an expiring storm
Whose thunder is its knell; he, as I guess,
Had gazed on Nature's naked loveliness,   275
Actaeon-like, and now he fled astray
With feeble steps o'er the world's wilderness,
And his own thoughts, along that rugged way,
Pursued, like raging hounds, their father and their prey.

259 *Making earth bare:* as the sun reveals the beauty of the earth but veils the stars. Cf. l. 367 below.   261 *kindred lamps:* other poets like Adonais.   262 *mountain shepherds came:* the procession of personal mourners, contemporary poets, and defenders of liberty (hence *mountain*), not abstractions as in ll. 73 ff.   264 *Pilgrim:* Byron, as self-depicted in *Childe Harold's Pilgrimage*.   268 *Ierne* [Ireland] *sent:* i.e., Thomas Moore, Irish lyric poet, friend and editor of Byron.   271 *one . . . Form:* Shelley himself, *frail* because a poet's mind, by his definition, "in creation is as a fading coal, which some invisible influence, like an inconstant wind, awakens to transitory brightness."   276 *Actaeon-like:* while hunting, Actaeon accidentally saw Diana the chaste in her bath. Incensed, she turned him into a stag lest he boast of what he had seen. His own hounds then pursued him and tore him to pieces. So also Shelley is pursued by his own thoughts after glimpsing the naked beauty of Nature.

XXXII

A pardlike Spirit beautiful and swift—   280
A Love in desolation masked;—a Power
Girt round with weakness;—it can scarce uplift
The weight of the superincumbent hour;
It is a dying lamp, a falling shower,
A breaking billow;—even whilst we speak   285
Is it not broken? On the withering flower
The killing sun smiles brightly: on a cheek
The life can burn in blood, even while the heart may break.

XXXIII

His head was bound with pansies overblown,
And faded violets, white, and pied, and blue;   290
And a light spear topped with a cypress cone,
Round whose rude shaft dark ivy-tresses grew
Yet dripping with the forest's noonday dew,
Vibrated, as the ever-beating heart
Shook the weak hand that grasped it; of that crew   295
He came the last, neglected and apart;
A herd-abandoned deer struck by the hunter's dart.

XXXIV

All stood aloof, and at his partial moan
Smiled through their tears; well knew that gentle band
Who in another's fate now wept his own;   300
As in the accents of an unknown land,
He sung new sorrow; sad Urania scanned
The Stranger's mien, and murmured: "Who art thou?"
He answered not, but with a sudden hand
Made bare his branded and ensanguined brow,   305
Which was like Cain's or Christ's—Oh! that it should be so!

XXXV

What softer voice is hushed over the dead?
Athwart what brow is that dark mantle thrown?
What form leans sadly o'er the white death-bed,

280 *pardlike:* leopard-like.   289 *pansies overblown:* pansies (symbol of thought
—from the French *pensée*) past their bloom.   290 *violets:* heart's ease, a herb
of Venus; also associated with chastity. Greeks wore wreaths of violets to
induce sleep, cure headaches, assuage anger, and comfort the heart.   *Cypress*
(l. 291) is symbolic of mourning, and the *ivy* (l. 292) of poetry. Cf. the flower
imagery in "Lycidas," ll. 1–3, and ll. 139–50 and notes.   295 *crew:* i.e., of
mountain shepherds.   298 *partial:* personal, sympathetic.   300 *wept his own:*
Cf. "Lycidas," ll. 19–22, and the apostolic succession of poets.   305 *branded
and ensanguined:* for Cain's brow, see l. 151 and note; Christ's brow was
bloodied by the crown of thorns (Matt. 27:29).

320

In mockery of monumental stone,   310
The heavy heart heaving without a moan?
If it be He, who, gentlest of the wise,
Taught, soothed, loved, honored the departed one;
Let me not vex, with inharmonious sighs
The silence of that heart's accepted sacrifice.   315

                              XXXVI

Our Adonais has drunk poison—oh!
What deaf and viperous murderer could crown
Life's early cup with such a draught of woe?
The nameless worm would now itself disown:
It felt, yet could escape the magic tone   320
Whose prelude held all envy, hate, and wrong,
But what was howling in one breast alone,
Silent with expectation of the song,
Whose master's hand is cold, whose silver lyre unstrung.

                              XXXVII

Live thou, whose infamy is not thy fame!   325
Live! fear no heavier chastisement from me,
Thou noteless blot on a remembered name!
But be thyself, and know thyself to be!
And ever at thy season be thou free
To spill the venom when thy fangs o'erflow: 330
Remorse and Self-contempt shall cling to thee;
Hot Shame shall burn upon thy secret brow,
And like a beaten hound tremble thou shalt—as now.

                              XXXVIII

Nor let us weep that our delight is fled
Far from these carrion kites that scream below;   335
He wakes or sleeps with the enduring dead;
Thou canst not soar where he is sitting now.—
Dust to the dust! but the pure spirit shall flow
Back to the burning fountain whence it came,
A portion of the Eternal, which must glow   340
Through time and change, unquenchably the same,
Whilst thy cold embers choke the sordid hearth of shame.

310 *mockery:* imitation. 312 *He:* probably Leigh Hunt, friend of both Keats and Shelley. 319 *nameless:* i.e., the anonymous reviewer. 321 *held:* checked, restrained. 334–42 *Nor . . . shame:* the neoplatonic apotheosis of Adonais, who has returned from the material world to the original and spiritual source of life. Cf. "Lycidas," ll. 165–85.

XXXIX

Peace, peace! he is not dead, he doth not sleep—
He hath awakened from the dream of life—
'Tis we, who lost in stormy visions, keep   345
With phantoms an unprofitable strife,
And in mad trance, strike with our spirit's knife
Invulnerable nothings.—*We* decay
Like corpses in a charnel; fear and grief
Convulse us and consume us day by day,   350
And cold hopes swarm like worms within our living clay.

XL

He has outsoared the shadow of our night;
Envy and calumny and hate and pain,
And that unrest which men miscall delight,
Can touch him not and torture not again;   355
From the contagion of the world's slow stain
He is secure, and now can never mourn
A heart grown cold, a head grown gray in vain;
Nor, when the spirit's self has ceased to burn,
With sparkless ashes load an unlamented urn.   360

XLI

He lives, he wakes—'tis Death is dead, not he;
Mourn not for Adonais.—Thou young Dawn,
Turn all thy dew to splendor, for from thee
The spirit thou lamentest is not gone;
Ye caverns and ye forests, cease to moan!   365
Cease ye faint flowers and fountains, and thou Air,
Which like a mourning veil thy scarf hadst thrown
O'er the abandoned Earth, now leave it bare
Even to the joyous stars which smile on its despair!

XLII

He is made one with Nature: there is heard   370
His voice in all her music, from the moan
Of thunder, to the song of night's sweet bird;
He is a presence to be felt and known
In darkness and in light, from herb and stone,
Spreading itself where'er that Power may move   375
Which has withdrawn his being to its own;

343 *Peace . . . dead:* the traditional words of consolation.   344 *dream of life:*
In neoplatonic thought, life in this world of matter is only a shadow, a dream of
the immutable world of pure light.   352 *night:* Night is actually the shadow
cast by the earth, as well as figuratively the Platonic shadow of the truly real.

322

Which wields the world with never-wearied love,
Sustains it from beneath, and kindles it above.

XLIII

He is a portion of the loveliness
Which once he made more lovely: he doth bear   380
His part, while the one Spirit's plastic stress
Sweeps through the dull dense world, compelling there,
All new successions to the forms they wear;
Torturing th' unwilling dross that checks its flight
To its own likeness, as each mass may bear;   385
And bursting in its beauty and its might
From trees and beasts and men into the Heaven's light.

XLIV

The splendors of the firmament of time
May be eclipsed, but are extinguished not;
Like stars to their appointed height they climb,   390
And death is a low mist which cannot blot
The brightness it may veil. When lofty thought
Lifts a young heart above its mortal lair,
And love and life contend in it, for what
Shall be its earthly doom, the dead live there   396
And move like winds of light on dark and stormy air.

XLV

The inheritors of unfulfilled renown
Rose from their thrones, built beyond mortal thought,
Far in the Unapparent. Chatterton
Rose pale, his solemn agony had not   400
Yet faded from him; Sidney, as he fought
And as he fell and as he lived and loved
Sublimely mild, a Spirit without spot,
Arose; and Lucan, by his death approved:
Oblivion as they rose shrank like a thing reproved.   405

XLVI

And many more, whose names on Earth are dark
But whose transmitted effluence cannot die

380–87 *he doth . . . light:* the rediscovery of faith that answers the despairing
question of ll. 177–79 above. 381 *plastic stress:* molding power. 399, 401,
404 [Thomas] *Chatterton* (1752–70), a suicide; [Sir Philip] *Sidney* (1554–86),
killed at the battle of Zutphen; [Marcus Annaeus] *Lucan* (39–65), commanded
by Nero to take his own life. All are poets who died young, aged 17, 32, and
26 respectively; Keats died aged 25. 404 *approved:* justified.

So long as fire outlives the parent spark,
Rose, robed in dazzling immortality.
"Thou art become as one of us," they cry,   410
"It was for thee yon kingless sphere has long
Swung blind in unascended majesty,
Silent alone amid an Heaven of song.
Assume thy wingèd throne, thou Vesper of our throng!"

XLVII

Who mourns for Adonais? oh come forth   415
Fond wretch! and know thyself and him aright.
Clasp with thy panting soul the pendulous Earth;
As from a center, dart thy spirit's light
Beyond all worlds, until its spacious might
Satiate the void circumference: then shrink   420
Even to a point within our day and night;
And keep thy heart light lest it make thee sink
When hope has kindled hope, and lured thee to the brink.

XLVIII

Or go to Rome, which is the sepulcher,
O, not of him, but of our joy: 'tis nought   425
That ages, empires, and religions there
Lie buried in the ravage they have wrought;
For such as he can lend,—they borrow not
Glory from those who made the world their prey;
And he is gathered to the kings of thought   430
Who waged contention with their time's decay,
And of the past are all that cannot pass away.

XLIX

Go thou to Rome,—at once the Paradise,
The grave, the city, and the wilderness;
And where its wrecks like shattered mountains rise,   435
And flowering weeds, and fragrant copses dress
The bones of Desolation's nakedness
Pass, till the Spirit of the spot shall lead
Thy footsteps to a slope of green access
Where, like an infant's smile, over the dead,   440
A light of laughing flowers along the grass is spread;

414 *Vesper:* one phase of Venus, the evening and brightest star. See epigraph
and note.   416 *Fond:* foolish.

324

And gray walls molder round, on which dull Time
Feeds, like slow fire upon a hoary brand;
And one keen pyramid with wedge sublime,
Pavilioning the dust of him who planned   445
This refuge for his memory, doth stand
Like flame transformed to marble; and beneath,
A field is spread, on which a newer band
Have pitched in Heaven's smile their camp of death,
Welcoming him we lose with scarce extinguished breath.   450

LI

Here pause: these graves are all too young as yet
To have outgrown the sorrow which consigned
Its charge to each; and if the seal is set,
Here, on one fountain of a mourning mind,
Break it not thou! too surely shalt thou find   455
Thine own well full, if thou returnest home,
Of tears and gall. From the world's bitter wind
Seek shelter in the shadow of the tomb.
What Adonais is, why fear we to become?

LII

The One remains, the many change and pass;   460
Heaven's light forever shines, Earth's shadows fly;
Life, like a dome of many-colored glass,
Stains the white radiance of Eternity,
Until Death tramples it to fragments.—Die,
If thou wouldst be with that which thou dost seek!   465
Follow where all is fled!—Rome's azure sky,
Flowers, ruins, statues, music, words, are weak
The glory they transfuse with fitting truth to speak.

LIII

Why linger, why turn back, why shrink, my Heart?
Thy hopes are gone before: from all things here   470
They have departed; thou shouldst now depart!
A light is past from the revolving year,

444 *pyramid:* tomb of Gaius Cestius (Roman praetor and tribune in the Augustan Age) in what is now the Protestant Cemetery, where Keats was buried. 448 *newer band:* i.e., the newly buried, since the cemetery had only been recently established. Shelley's infant son, William (l. 451), had been buried there in 1819. 460–64 *The . . . fragments:* An epigrammatic summary of Shelley's platonism.

And man, and woman; and what still is dear
Attracts to crush, repels to make thee wither.
The soft sky smiles,—the low wind whispers near: 475
'Tis Adonais calls! oh, hasten thither,
No more let Life divide what Death can join together.

LIV

That Light whose smile kindles the Universe,
That Beauty in which all things work and move,
That Benediction which the eclipsing Curse   480
Of birth can quench not, that sustaining Love
Which through the web of being blindly wove
By man and beast and earth and air and sea,
Burns bright or dim, as each are mirrors of
The fire for which all thirst; now beams on me,   485
Consuming the last clouds of cold mortality.

LV

The breath whose might I have invoked in song
Descends on me; my spirit's bark is driven,
Far from the shore, far from the trembling throng
Whose sails were never to the tempest given;   490
The massy earth and spherèd skies are riven!
I am borne darkly, fearfully, afar;
Whilst burning through the inmost veil of Heaven,
The soul of Adonais, like a star,
Beacons from the abode where the Eternal are.   495

485 *thirst:* to return to the "burning fountain," l. 339. Cf. Rev. 7:15–17.
491 *riven:* split asunder.

JOHN KEATS
1795–1821

On First Looking into Chapman's Homer

Much have I travell'd in the realms of gold,
   And many goodly states and kingdoms seen;
   Round many western islands have I been
Which bards in fealty to Apollo hold.
Oft of one wide expanse had I been told   5
   That deep-brow'd Homer ruled as his demesne;
   Yet did I never breathe its pure serene
Till I heard Chapman speak out loud and bold:
Then felt I like some watcher of the skies
   When a new planet swims into his ken;   10
Or like stout Cortez when with eagle eyes
   He star'd at the Pacific—and all his men
Look'd at each other with a wild surmise—
   Silent, upon a peak in Darien.

On the Grasshopper and Cricket

The poetry of earth is never dead:
   When all the birds are faint with the hot sun,
   And hide in cooling trees, a voice will run
From hedge to hedge about the new-mown mead;
That is the Grasshopper's—he takes the lead   5
   In summer luxury—he has never done
   With his delights; for when tired out with fun
He rests at ease beneath some pleasant weed.
The poetry of earth is ceasing never:
   On a lone winter evening, when the frost   10
   Has wrought a silence, from the stove there shrills
The Cricket's song, in warmth increasing ever,
   And seems to one in drowsiness half lost,
      The Grasshopper's among some grassy hills.

ON FIRST LOOKING. 4 *in fealty:* by oath of faithful allegiance. *Apollo:* here, the feudal lord of poetry. 8 [George] Chapman: (1559?–1634) translator of the *Iliad* (1611) and the *Odyssey* (1614–15). 11 *Cortez:* in fact, Balboa. Cortez was the conqueror of Mexico.

On Seeing the Elgin Marbles for the First Time

My spirit is too weak; mortality
  Weighs heavily on me like unwilling sleep,
  And each imagined pinnacle and steep
Of godlike hardship tells me I must die
Like a sick eagle looking at the sky.   5
  Yet 'tis a gentle luxury to weep,
  That I have not the cloudy winds to keep
Fresh for the opening of the morning's eye.
Such dim-conceivèd glories of the brain
  Bring round the heart an indescribable feud;   10
So do these wonders a most dizzy pain,
  That mingles Grecian grandeur with the rude
Wasting of old Time—with a billowy main,
  A sun, a shadow of a magnitude.

On the Sea

It keeps eternal whisperings around
  Desolate shores, and with its mighty swell
  Gluts twice ten thousand caverns, till the spell
Of Hecate leaves their old shadowy sound.
Often 'tis in such gentle temper found,   5
  That scarcely will the very smallest shell
  Be moved for days from where it sometime fell,
When last the winds of heaven were unbound.

ON SEEING THE ELGIN MARBLES. The frieze, a work of Phidias depicting the annual Panathenaic procession honoring Athene, was taken from the *cella* of the Parthenon and acquired by Lord Elgin when envoy to Porte (1799–1803); he later sold the frieze to the British Government. These marbles were the first major examples of Hellenic art seen in England, in contrast to Roman art, and were enormously influential on artists and poets. It was common practice then and now to write a poem in response to a particular painting or statue. See "Ode on a Grecian Urn" and notes and references.

ON THE SEA. 4 *Hecate:* Greek goddess, daughter of the Titans Perses and Asteria; to Hesiod (*Theogeny*, ll. 411–52), honored "above all" by Zeus, for "He gave her splendid gifts, to have a share of the earth and the unfruitful sea. She received honor also in starry heaven." Even after the overthrow of the Titans "she . . . holds privilege both in earth, and in heaven, and in sea" (trans. H. G. Evelyn-White). Hence her later epithet *Diva Triformis*. Later she was called Luna in heaven, Diana on earth, and Proserpina in the underworld and was thought to be queen of ghosts and protectress of enchanters. Both traditions are present here in *spell* (l. 3), which suggests rule as well as magic, and in the suggestions of the underworld in *caverns* (l. 3) and *shadowy* (l. 4).

Oh ye, who have your eye-balls vex'd and tired,
   Feast them upon the wideness of the Sea;   10
     Oh, ye whose ears are dinn'd with uproar rude,
   Or fed too much with cloying melody,—
     Sit ye near some old cavern's mouth, and brood
Until ye start, as if the sea-nymphs quired.

On Sitting Down to Read King Lear Again

O golden tongued Romance, with serene lute!
   Fair-plumèd Syren, Queen of far-away!
   Leave melodizing on this wintry day,
Shut up thine olden pages, and be mute:
Adieu! for, once again, the fierce dispute   5
   Betwixt damnation and impassion'd clay
   Must I burn through; once more humbly assay
The bitter-sweet of this Shakespearian fruit:
Chief Poet! and ye clouds of Albion,
   Begetters of our deep eternal theme!   10
When through the old oak Forest I am gone,
   Let me not wander in a barren dream,
But, when I am consumèd in the fire,
Give me new Phoenix wings to fly at my desire.

When I have fears that I may cease to be

When I have fears that I may cease to be
   Before my pen has glean'd my teeming brain,
Before high-piled books, in charact'ry,
   Hold like rich garners the full-ripen'd grain;
When I behold, upon the night's starr'd face,   5
   Huge cloudy symbols of a high romance,
And think that I may never live to trace
   Their shadows, with the magic hand of chance;
And when I feel, fair creature of an hour!
   That I shall never look upon thee more,   10
Never have relish in the faery power
   Of unreflecting love! then on the shore
Of the wide world I stand alone, and think
Till love and fame to nothingness do sink.

14 *start:* wake up suddenly as if from a dream.   *quired:* sang in chorus.

ON SITTING DOWN TO READ.   14 *Phoenix:* the fabulous bird of Arabia that, after 500 years of life, builds a funeral nest of spices, turns towards the sun, ignites itself, and is consumed; nine days later it arises renewed from its fragrant ashes.

To Spenser

Spenser! a jealous honorer of thine,
    A forester deep in thy midmost trees,
Did, last eve, ask my promise to refine
    Some English, that might strive thine ear to please.
But, Elfin Poet! 'tis impossible   5
    For our inhabitant of wintry earth
To rise, like Phoebus, with a golden quell,
    Fire-winged and make a morning in his mirth.
It is impossible to 'scape from toil
    O' the sudden, and receive thy spiriting: 10
The flower must drink the nature of the soil
    Before it can put forth its blossoming:
Be with me in the summer days, and I
Will for thine honor and his pleasure try.

ODES

Ode to a Nightingale

1

My heart aches, and a drowsy numbness pains
    My sense, as though of hemlock I had drunk,
Or emptied some dull opiate to the drains
    One minute past, and Lethe-wards had sunk:
'Tis not through envy of thy happy lot,   5
    But being too happy in thine happiness,—
        That thou, light-wingèd Dryad of the trees,
        In some melodious plot
Of beechen green, and shadows numberless,
    Singest of summer in full-throated ease.   10

TO SPENSER.   2 *forester:* i.e., another poet, presumably Leigh Hunt.   7 *quell:* probably a variant spelling, for the sake of rhyme, meaning feather, pen, or wing; but as *quell*, possibly also the benign power of poetry to suppress or subdue barbarism.

ODE TO A NIGHTINGALE.   This ode, the "Ode on Melancholy," and the "Ode on a Grecian Urn" were all written in May, 1819. "To fit the naked foot of Poesy," Keats wrote, he employed a set ten-line stanza, a form that he felt combined the virtues of the Petrarchan and Shakespearean sonnet forms without being fettered by the restraining requirements of the "pouncing" rhyme of the former and the "too elegiac" quality of the latter, whose "couplet at the end of it has seldom a pleasing effect" [Letter to George and Georgiana Keats, April 30, 1819].

2 *hemlock:* a powerful sedative and ultimately a poison.   3 *drains:* dregs.   4 *Lethe:* the river in Hades whose water produces forgetfulness.   7 *Dryad:* nymph whose life is associated with that of her own tree.

2

O, for a draught of vintage! that hath been
  Cool'd a long age in the deep-delvèd earth,
Tasting of Flora and the country green,
  Dance, and Provençal song, and sunburnt mirth!
O for a beaker full of the warm South,   15
  Full of the true, the blushful Hippocrene,
    With beaded bubbles winking at the brim,
      And purple-stainèd mouth;
  That I might drink, and leave the world unseen,
    And with thee fade away into the forest dim: 20

3

Fade far away, dissolve, and quite forget
  What thou among the leaves hast never known,
The weariness, the fever, and the fret
  Here, where men sit and hear each other groan;
Where palsy shakes a few, sad, last gray hairs,   25
  Where youth grows pale, and specter-thin, and dies;
    Where but to think is to be full of sorrow
      And leaden-eyed despairs,
  Where Beauty cannot keep her lustrous eyes,
    Or new Love pine at them beyond to-morrow.   30

4

Away! away! for I will fly to thee,
  Not charioted by Bacchus and his pards,
But on the viewless wings of Poesy,
  Though the dull brain perplexes and retards:
Already with thee! tender is the night,   35
  And haply the Queen-Moon is on her throne,
    Cluster'd around by all her starry Fays;
      But here there is no light,
  Save what from heaven is with the breezes blown
    Through verdurous glooms and winding mossy ways.   40

---

13 *Flora:* goddess of flowers.   14 *Provençal song:* love lyrics by twelfth-century troubadours of Provence (southeastern France).   16 *Hippocrene:* fountain sacred to the Muses on Mt. Helicon; poets who drank of it were inspired. 32 *pards:* the chariot of Bacchus (god of wine) was often depicted being drawn by leo*pards.*   33 *viewless:* invisible.   37 *Fays:* fairies.

5

I cannot see what flowers are at my feet,
    Nor what soft incense hangs upon the boughs,
But, in embalmèd darkness, guess each sweet
    Wherewith the seasonable month endows
The grass, the thicket, and the fruit-tree wild;   45
    White hawthorn, and the pastoral eglantine;
        Fast fading violets cover'd up in leaves;
            And mid-May's eldest child,
The coming musk-rose, full of dewy wine,
    The murmurous haunt of flies on summer eves.   50

6

Darkling I listen; and, for many a time
    I have been half in love with easeful Death,
Call'd him soft names in many a musèd rhyme,
    To take into the air my quiet breath;
Now more than ever seems it rich to die,   55
    To cease upon the midnight with no pain,
        While thou art pouring forth thy soul abroad
            In such an ecstasy!
Still wouldst thou sing, and I have ears in vain—
    To thy high requiem become a sod.   60

7

Thou wast not born for death, immortal Bird!
    No hungry generations tread thee down;
The voice I hear this passing night was heard
    In ancient days by emperor and clown:
Perhaps the self-same song that found a path   65
    Through the sad heart of Ruth, when, sick for home,
        She stood in tears amid the alien corn;
            The same that oft-times hath
Charm'd magic casements, opening on the foam
    Of perilous seas, in faery lands forlorn.   70

43 *embalmèd:* filled with sweet odors.   51 *Darkling:* in the dark.   66 *Ruth:*
See the Book of Ruth. Keats's treatment of her is an imaginative interpolation.
67 *corn:* grain field; specifically, in the story of Ruth, barley fields.   70
forlorn: forsaken, abandoned, and hence (l. 71) wretched.

332

8

Forlorn! the very word is like a bell
  To toll me back from thee to my sole self!
Adieu! the fancy cannot cheat so well
  As she is fam'd to do, deceiving elf.
Adieu! adieu! thy plaintive anthem fades   75
  Past the near meadows, over the still stream,
    Up the hill-side; and now 'tis buried deep
      In the next valley-glades:
Was it a vision, or a waking dream?
Fled is that music:—Do I wake or sleep?   80

Ode on Melancholy

1

No, no, go not to Lethe, neither twist
  Wolf's-bane, tight-rooted, for its poisonous wine;
Nor suffer thy pale forehead to be kiss'd
  By nightshade, ruby grape of Proserpine;
Make not your rosary of yew-berries,   5
  Nor let the beetle, nor the death-moth be
    Your mournful Psyche, nor the downy owl
A partner in your sorrow's mysteries;
  For shade to shade will come too drowsily,
    And drown the wakeful anguish of the soul.   10

ODE ON MELANCHOLY. 1 *Lethe:* see above, l. 4 and note. 2 *Wolf's bane:* aconite, also known as monk's-hood, a herb with yellow flowers from whose roots and leaves is produced a highly poisonous narcotic. 4 *nightshade:* deadly nightshade, belladonna (i.e., beautiful lady, so named from Italian women's practice of using it as an eye beautifier and cosmetic), from whose root, leaves, and large shining black berries (hence *grape*) is produced atropine, a poisonous narcotic, chiefly used to dilate the pupil of the eye. *Proserpine:* wife of Pluto, lost daughter of Ceres, and queen of the underworld. 5 *yew-berries:* berries of the European yew, an evergreen with poisonous bark and leaves, traditionally planted in graveyards. 6 *beetle:* i.e., the death-watch beetle, whose ticking sound is thought to be an omen of death. *death-moth:* i.e., the death's-head moth (wing-span four to five inches). The markings on its thorax resemble a human skull, and its appearance is often thought to presage death. 7 *Psyche:* the soul, usually symbolized as a butterfly. *owl:* Its hooting is thought to foretell death. 9 *drowsily:* The poisons referred to above are paralyzing and numbing narcotics whose physiological effects are analogous to the spiritual and esthetic effects of the shades (i.e., ghosts of *Beauty that must die*) of true Melancholy. If the ordinary narcotics were taken, they would prevent the full knowledge of Beauty, Joy, and Pleasure. Hence they are refused.

2

But when the melancholy fit shall fall
   Sudden from heaven like a weeping cloud,
That fosters the droop-headed flowers all,
   And hides the green hill in an April shroud;
Then glut thy sorrow on a morning rose,   15
   Or on the rainbow of the salt sand-wave,
      Or on the wealth of globèd peonies;
Or if thy mistress some rich anger shows,
   Emprison her soft hand, and let her rave,
      And feed deep, deep upon her peerless eyes.   20

3

She dwells with Beauty—Beauty that must die;
   And Joy, whose hand is ever at his lips
Bidding adieu; and aching Pleasure nigh,
   Turning to poison while the bee-mouth sips:
Ay, in the very temple of Delight   25
   Veil'd Melancholy has her sovran shrine,
      Though seen of none save him whose strenuous tongue
Can burst Joy's grape against his palate fine;
His soul shall taste the sadness of her might,
      And be among her cloudy trophies hung.   30

Ode on a Grecian Urn

1

Thou still unravish'd bride of quietness,
   Thou foster-child of silence and slow time,
Sylvan historian, who canst thus express
   A flowery tale more sweetly than our rhyme:
What leaf-fring'd legend haunts about thy shape   5
   Of deities or mortals, or of both,
      In Tempe or the dales of Arcady?
What men or gods are these? What maidens loth?
What mad pursuit? What struggle to escape?
      What pipes and timbrels? What wild ecstasy?   10

---

21 *She:* i.e., Melancholy, not the *mistress*.

ODE ON A GRECIAN URN.   *Urn:* For Keats's use of the visual arts in this poem,
see Ian Jack, *Keats and the Mirror of Art*, Ch. XIII.   7 *Tempe:* a beautiful vale
in Thessaly between Mt. Olympus and Mt. Ossa.   *Arcady:* Arcadia, the legendary home of pastoral romance and idyllic beauty in central Greece. See
Milton, *Arcades*, l. 1 and note.

334

2

Heard melodies are sweet, but those unheard
    Are sweeter; therefore, ye soft pipes, play on;
Not to the sensual ear, but, more endear'd,
    Pipe to the spirit ditties of no tone:
Fair youth, beneath the trees, thou canst not leave   15
    Thy song, nor ever can those trees be bare;
        Bold Lover, never, never canst thou kiss,
Though winning near the goal—yet, do not grieve;
        She cannot fade, though thou hast not thy bliss,
    For ever wilt thou love, and she be fair!   20

3

Ah, happy, happy boughs! that cannot shed
    Your leaves, nor ever bid the Spring adieu;
And, happy melodist, unwearied,
    For ever piping songs for ever new;
More happy love! more happy, happy love!   25
    For ever warm and still to be enjoy'd,
        For ever panting, and for ever young;
All breathing human passion far above,
    That leaves a heart high-sorrowful and cloy'd,
        A burning forehead, and a parching tongue.   30

4

Who are these coming to the sacrifice?
    To what green altar, O mysterious priest,
Lead'st thou that heifer lowing at the skies,
    And all her silken flanks with garlands drest?
What little town by river or sea shore,   35
    Or mountain-built with peaceful citadel,
        Is emptied of this folk, this pious morn?
And, little town, thy streets for evermore
    Will silent be; and not a soul to tell
        Why thou art desolate, can e'er return.   40

35 *little town:* The desolation of the town, which is not depicted on the urn but imaginatively implied, is thought to be derived in part from a sentence in the entry "Hyacinthia" in Lemprière's *Classical Dictionary* (a book Keats knew very well): "During the latter part of the festivity [in honor of Hyacinthus and Apollo], all were eager to be present at the games, and the city was left almost desolate, and without inhabitants."

5

O Attic shape! Fair attitude! with brede
    Of marble men and maidens overwrought,
With forest branches and the trodden weed;
    Thou, silent form, dost tease us out of thought
As doth eternity: Cold Pastoral!   45
    When old age shall this generation waste,
        Thou shalt remain, in midst of other woe
Than ours, a friend to man, to whom thou say'st,
    Beauty is truth, truth beauty,—that is all
        Ye know on earth, and all ye need to know.   50

To Autumn

1

Season of mists and mellow fruitfulness,
    Close bosom-friend of the maturing sun;
Conspiring with him how to load and bless
    With fruit the vines that round the thatch-eaves run;
To bend with apples the moss'd cottage-trees,   5
    And fill all fruit with ripeness to the core;
        To swell the gourd, and plump the hazel shells
    With a sweet kernel; to set budding more,
And still more, later flowers for the bees,
Until they think warm days will never cease,   10
        For Summer has o'er-brimm'd their clammy cells.

2

Who hath not seen thee oft amid thy store?
    Sometimes whoever seeks abroad may find
Thee sitting careless on a granary floor,
    Thy hair soft-lifted by the winnowing wind;   15
Or on a half-reap'd furrow sound asleep,
    Drows'd with the fume of poppies, while thy hook
        Spares the next swath and all its twined flowers:

---

41 *Attic:* i.e., Athenian; hence simple, elegant, pure, and classical. *brede:* embroidery or braid; hence the braid-like design of intertwining figures. 49–50 *Beauty . . . know:* i.e., all man needs to know is *that* when old age and decay *waste* us, the urn is our friend who says to us that in art alone is embodied *Beauty is truth, truth beauty.* Nowhere else can the reality of this comforting truth be found. See Earl Wasserman, *The Finer Tone,* pp. 58–62.

TO AUTUMN.   Written in September, 1819.   17 *hook:* i.e., a reaping hook or sickle.

And sometimes like a gleaner thou dost keep
   Steady thy laden head across a brook;   20
  Or by a cider-press, with patient look,
     Thou watchest the last oozings hours by hours.

3

Where are the songs of Spring? Ay, where are they?
   Think not of them, thou hast thy music too,—
While barred clouds bloom the soft-dying day,   25
  And touch the stubble-plains with rosy hue;
Then in a wailful choir the small gnats mourn
   Among the river sallows, borne aloft
     Or sinking as the light wind lives or dies;
And full-grown lambs loud bleat from hilly bourn;   30
  Hedge-crickets sing; and now with treble soft
  The redbreast whistles from a garden-croft;
    And gathering swallows twitter in the skies.

---

28 *sallows:* willows.   30 *bourn:* region.   32 *croft:* a small, enclosed field.

ALFRED, LORD TENNYSON
1809–1892

The Lotos-Eaters

"Courage!" he said, and pointed toward the land,
"This mounting wave will roll us shoreward soon."
In the afternoon they came unto a land,
In which it seemed always afternoon.
All round the coast the languid air did swoon,   5
Breathing like one that hath a weary dream.
Full-faced above the valley stood the moon;
And like a downward smoke, the slender stream
Along the cliff to fall and pause and fall did seem.

A land of streams! some, like a downward smoke,   10
Slow-dropping veils of thinnest lawn, did go;
And some through wavering lights and shadows broke,
Rolling a slumbrous sheet of foam below.
They saw the gleaming river seaward flow
From the inner land; far off, three mountain-tops,   15
Three silent pinnacles of aged snow,
Stood sunset-flush'd: and, dew'd with showery drops,
Up-clomb the shadowy pine above the woven copse.

The charmed sunset linger'd low adown
In the red West: through mountain clefts the dale   20
Was seen far inland, and the yellow down
Border'd with palm, and many a winding vale
And meadow, set with slender galingale;
A land where all things always seem'd the same!
And round about the keel with faces pale,   25
Dark faces pale against that rosy flame,
The mild-eyed melancholy Lotos-eaters came.

THE LOTOS-EATERS. 1 *he:* Ulysses (Odysseus), King of Ithaca (an island kingdom, facing west, and "farthest out to sea"—in Homer's words—"a rough land, but a fit nurse for men") and hero of the Trojan wars. In Book IX of the *Odyssey*, the epic story of his ten-year voyage home, Ulysses' second stop was at the land of the Lotos-eaters. Those of his men who "browsed" on the lotos wanted only to stay and "to forget they had a home to return to." 23 *galingale:* a plant of the genus *Cyperus;* a ginger-like stimulant is produced from its aromatic root.

Branches they bore of that enchanted stem,
Laden with flower and fruit, whereof they gave
To each, but whoso did receive of them,   30
And taste, to him the gushing of the wave
Far far away did seem to mourn and rave
On alien shores; and if his fellow spake,
His voice was thin, as voices from the grave;
And deep-asleep he seem'd, yet all awake,   35
And music in his ears his beating heart did make.

They sat them down upon the yellow sand,
Between the sun and moon upon the shore;
And sweet it was to dream of Fatherland,
Of child, and wife, and slave; but evermore   40
Most weary seem'd the sea, weary the oar,
Weary the wandering fields of barren foam.
Then some one said, "We will return no more";
And all at once they sang, "Our island home
Is far beyond the wave; we will no longer roam."   45

CHORIC SONG

1

There is sweet music here that softer falls
Than petals from blown roses on the grass,
Or night-dews on still waters between walls
Of shadowy granite, in a gleaming pass;
Music that gentlier on the spirit lies,   50
Than tir'd eyelids upon tir'd eyes;
Music that brings sweet sleep down from the blissful skies.
Here are cool mosses deep,
And through the moss the ivies creep,
And in the stream the long-leaved flowers weep,   55
And from the craggy ledge the poppy hangs in sleep.

2

Why are we weigh'd upon with heaviness,
And utterly consumed with sharp distress,
While all things else have rest from weariness?
All things have rest: why should we toil alone,   60
We only toil, who are the first of things,
And make perpetual moan,
Still from one sorrow to another thrown:
Nor ever fold our wings,
And cease from wanderings,   65

Nor steep our brows in slumber's holy balm;
Nor hearken what the inner spirit sings,
"There is no joy but calm!"
Why should we only toil, the roof and crown of things?

3

Lo! in the middle of the wood,   70
The folded leaf is woo'd from out the bud
With winds upon the branch, and there
Grows green and broad, and takes no care,
Sun-steep'd at noon, and in the moon
Nightly dew-fed; and turning yellow   75
Falls, and floats adown the air.
Lo! sweeten'd with the summer light,
The full-juiced apple, waxing over-mellow,
Drops in a silent autumn night.
All its allotted length of days   80
The flower ripens in its place,
Ripens and fades, and falls, and hath no toil,
Fast-rooted in the fruitful soil.

4

Hateful is the dark-blue sky,
Vaulted o'er the dark-blue sea.   85
Death is the end of life; ah, why
Should life all labor be?
Let us alone. Time driveth onward fast,
And in a little while our lips are dumb.
Let us alone. What is it that will last?   90
All things are taken from us, and become
Portions and parcels of the dreadful Past.
Let us alone. What pleasure can we have
To war with evil? Is there any peace
In ever climbing up the climbing wave?   95
All things have rest, and ripen toward the grave
In silence—ripen, fall, and cease:
Give us long rest or death, dark death, or dreamful ease.

5

How sweet it were, hearing the downward stream,
With half-shut eyes ever to seem   100
Falling asleep in a half-dream!

69 *roof:* i.e., the loftiest part.

To dream and dream, like yonder amber light,
Which will not leave the myrrh-bush on the height;
To hear each other's whisper'd speech;
Eating the Lotos day by day, 105
To watch the crisping ripples on the beach,
And tender curving lines of creamy spray;
To lend our hearts and spirits wholly
To the influence of mild-minded melancholy;
To muse and brood and live again in memory, 110
With those old faces of our infancy
Heap'd over with a mound of grass,
Two handfuls of white dust, shut in an urn of brass!

6

Dear is the memory of our wedded lives,
And dear the last embraces of our wives 115
And their warm tears: but all hath suffer'd change;
For surely now our household hearths are cold:
Our sons inherit us: our looks are strange:
And we should come like ghosts to trouble joy.
Or else the island princes over-bold 120
Have eat our substance, and the minstrel sings
Before them of the ten years' war in Troy,
And our great deeds, as half-forgotten things,
Is there confusion in the little isle?
Let what is broken so remain. 125
The Gods are hard to reconcile:
'Tis hard to settle order once again.
There *is* confusion worse than death,
Trouble on trouble, pain on pain,
Long labor unto aged breath, 130
Sore task to hearts worn out by many wars
And eyes grown dim with gazing on the pilot-stars.

7

But, propt on beds of amaranth and moly,
How sweet (while warm airs lull us, blowing lowly)
With half-dropt eyelid still, 135
Beneath a heaven dark and holy,
To watch the long bright river drawing slowly
His waters from the purple hill—

121 *eat:* eaten, devoured. *substance:* goods. 133 *amaranth:* an imaginary unfading flower. *moly:* the black-rooted herb with a white flower that Hermes gave to Ulysses as protection from Circe's black magic and poison, which would have made him forget his native land.

To hear the dewy echoes calling
From cave to cave through the thick-twined vine—   140
To watch the emerald-color'd water falling
Through many a woven acanthus-wreath divine!
Only to hear and see the far-off sparkling brine,
Only to hear were sweet, stretch'd out beneath the pine.

                                8
The Lotos blooms below the barren peak: 145
The Lotos blows by every winding creek:
All day the wind breathes low with mellower tone:
Through every hollow cave and alley lone
Round and round the spicy downs the yellow Lotos-dust is blown.
We have had enough of action, and of motion we,   150
Roll'd to starboard, roll'd to larboard, when the surge was seething
        free,
Where the wallowing monster spouted his foam-fountains in the sea.
Let us swear an oath, and keep it with an equal mind,
In the hollow Lotos-land to live and lie reclined
On the hills like Gods together, careless of mankind.   155
For they lie beside their nectar, and the bolts are hurl'd
Far below them in the valleys, and the clouds are lightly curl'd
Round their golden houses, girdled with the gleaming world:
Where they smile in secret, looking over wasted lands,
Blight and famine, plague and earthquake, roaring deeps and fiery
        sands,   160
Clanging fights, and flaming towns, and sinking ships, and praying
        hands.
But they smile, they find a music centred in a doleful song
Steaming up, a lamentation and an ancient tale of wrong,
Like a tale of little meaning though the words are strong;
Chanted from an ill-used race of men that cleave the soil,   165
Sow the seed, and reap the harvest with enduring toil,
Storing yearly little dues of wheat, and wine and oil;
Till they perish and they suffer—some, 'tis whisper'd—down in hell
Suffer endless anguish, others in Elysian valleys dwell,
Resting weary limbs at last on beds of asphodel.   170
Surely, surely, slumber is more sweet than toil, the shore
Than labor in the deep mid-ocean, wind and wave and oar;
Oh rest ye, brother mariners, we will not wander more.

142 *acanthus:* a plant cultivated for its beautiful, pointed foliage; also the
conventionalized foliage used in Corinthian capitals: hence the appropriate
leaves for ornate, luxurious wreaths.

Ulysses

It little profits that an idle king,
By this still hearth, among these barren crags,
Match'd with an aged wife, I mete and dole
Unequal laws unto a savage race,
That hoard, and sleep, and feed, and know not me. 5
I cannot rest from travel: I will drink
Life to the lees: all times I have enjoy'd
Greatly, have suffer'd greatly, both with those
That loved me, and alone; on shore, and when
Through scudding drifts the rainy Hyades 10
Vext the dim sea: I am become a name;
For always roaming with a hungry heart
Much have I seen and known; cities of men
And manners, climates, councils, governments,
Myself not least, but honor'd of them all; 15
And drunk delight of battle with my peers,
Far on the ringing plains of windy Troy.
I am a part of all that I have met;
Yet all experience is an arch wherethrough
Gleams that untravel'd world, whose margin fades 20
For ever and for ever when I move.
How dull it is to pause, to make an end,
To rust unburnish'd, not to shine in use!
As though to breathe were life! Life piled on life
Were all too little, and of one to me 25
Little remains; but every hour is saved
From that eternal silence, something more,
A bringer of new things; and vile it were
For some three suns to store and hoard myself,
And this gray spirit yearning in desire 30
To follow knowledge, like a sinking star,
Beyond the utmost bound of human thought.
    This is my son, mine own Telemachus,
To whom I leave the scepter and the isle—

ULYSSES. Although not derived from the action of Homer's *Odyssey* but
from Dante's account of Ulysses (*Inferno*, XXVI), this poem can be
read as a counter-poem to "The Lotos-Eaters." Here, in Dante's words, the
"hunger" of Ulysses' "restless mind" drives him in his old age *away* from
Ithaca to "learn the vice and valour of mankind." 3 *wife:* Penelope, harassed
wife of Ulysses, famous for her devotion to her husband and her ingenuity in
putting off suitors during her husband's twenty-year absence. *mete:* measure
out precisely, as with scales. *dole:* distribute previously measured small
portions. 10 *Hyades:* seven stars that were supposed to indicate rainy weather
when they rose with the sun.

Well-loved of me, discerning to fulfil   35
This labor, by slow prudence to make mild
A rugged people, and through soft degrees
Subdue them to the useful and the good.
Most blameless is he, centred in the sphere
Of common duties, decent not to fail   40
In offices of tenderness, and pay
Meet adoration to my household gods,
When I am gone. He works his work, I mine.
    There lies the port: the vessel puffs her sail:
There gloom the dark broad seas. My mariners,   45
Souls that have toil'd, and wrought, and thought with me—
That ever with a frolic welcome took
The thunder and the sunshine, and opposed
Free hearts, free foreheads—you and I are old;
Old age hath yet his honor and his toil.   50
Death closes all: but something ere the end,
Some work of noble note, may yet be done,
Not unbecoming men that strove with Gods.
The lights begin to twinkle from the rocks:
The long day wanes: the slow moon climbs: the deep   55
Moans round with many voices. Come, my friends,
'Tis not too late to seek a newer world.
Push off, and sitting well in order smite
The sounding furrows; for my purpose holds
To sail beyond the sunset, and the baths   60
Of all the western stars, until I die.
It may be that the gulfs will wash us down:
It may be we shall touch the Happy Isles,
And see the great Achilles, whom we knew.
Though much is taken, much abides; and though   65
We are not now that strength which in old days
Moved earth and heaven, that which we are, we are;—
One equal temper of heroic hearts,
Made weak by time and fate, but strong in will
To strive, to seek, to find, and not to yield.   70

60 *baths:* the seas into which the stars descend.   62 *gulfs:* chasm beyond the
Strait of Gibraltar that was believed to lead to Hades. In Dante, a typhoon
blowing off the Mount of Purgatory caused a waterspout that engulfed
Ulysses' ship.   63 *Happy Isles:* the special abode of true heroes, supposed to
be west of Gibraltar.   64 *Achilles:* the slayer of Hector and greatest of the
Greek heroes in the Trojan war, whose wrath is the subject of the *Iliad.* He was
slain by Paris, who mortally wounded him with an arrow in his heel in the last
year of the seige.

Tithonus

The woods decay, the woods decay and fall,
The vapors weep their burthen to the ground;
Man comes and tills the field and lies beneath,
And after many a summer dies the swan.
Me only cruel immortality   5
Consumes; I wither slowly in thine arms,
Here at the quiet limit of the world,
A white-haired shadow roaming like a dream
The ever-silent spaces of the East,
Far-folded mists, and gleaming halls of morn.   10

Alas! for this gray shadow, once a man—
So glorious in his beauty and thy choice,
Who madest him thy chosen, that he seemed
To his great heart none other than a God!
I asked thee, "Give me immortality."   15
Then didst thou grant mine asking with a smile,
Like wealthy men who care not how they give.
But thy strong Hours indignant worked their wills,
And beat me down and marred and wasted me,
And though they could not end me, left me maimed   20
To dwell in presence of immortal youth,
Immortal age beside immortal youth,
And all I was, in ashes. Can thy love,
Thy beauty, make amends, though even now,
Close over us, the silver star, thy guide,   25
Shines in those tremulous eyes that fill with tears
To hear me? Let me go: take back thy gift:
Why should a man desire in any way
To vary from the kindly race of men,
Or pass beyond the goal of ordinance   30
Where all should pause, as is most meet for all?

A soft air fans the cloud apart; there comes
A glimpse of that dark world where I was born.
Once more the old mysterious glimmer steals
From thy pure brows, and from thy shoulders pure,   35

TITHONUS. Eos (Aurora), goddess of the dawn, overwhelmed by his *glorious . . . beauty* (l. 12), fell in love with Tithonus (brother of Priam, King of Troy), and by him was the mother of Memnon. (See Milton, "Il Penseroso," l. 18 and note.) She successfully begged Zeus to make Tithonus immortal but neglected to obtain for him the eternal youth that the gods enjoyed. He thus shriveled away until he became little more than a voice. The gods, taking pity on him, transformed him into a grasshopper. 25 *star:* morning star.

And bosom beating with a heart renewed.
Thy cheek begins to redden through the gloom,
Thy sweet eyes brighten slowly close to mine,
Ere yet they blind the stars, and the wild team
Which love thee, yearning for thy yoke, arise,   40
And shake the darkness from their loosened manes,
And beat the twilight into flakes of fire.

Lo! ever thus thou growest beautiful
In silence, then before thine answer given
Departest, and thy tears are on my cheek.   45

Why wilt thou ever scare me with thy tears,
And make me tremble lest a saying learnt,
In days far-off, on that dark earth, be true?
"The Gods themselves cannot recall their gifts."

Ay me! ay me! with what another heart   50
In days far-off, and with what other eyes
I used to watch—if I be he that watched—
The lucid outline forming round thee; saw
The dim curls kindle into sunny rings;
Changed with thy mystic change, and felt my blood   55
Glow with the glow that slowly crimsoned all
Thy presence and thy portals, while I lay,
Mouth, forehead, eyelids, growing dewy-warm
With kisses balmier than half-opening buds
Of April, and could hear the lips that kissed   60
Whispering I knew not what of wild and sweet,
Like that strange song I heard Apollo sing,
While Ilion like a mist rose into towers.

Yet hold me not for ever in thine East:
How can my nature longer mix with thine?   65
Coldly thy rosy shadows bathe me, cold
Are all thy lights, and cold my wrinkled feet
Upon thy glimmering thresholds, when the steam
Floats up from those dim fields about the homes
Of happy men that have the power to die,   70
And grassy barrows of the happier dead.
Release me, and restore me to the ground;

---

39 *team:* of horses that draw the chariot of the dawn.   63 *towers:* According
to myth, the walls of Troy (Ilion) rose to the music of Apollo.

Thou seëst all things, thou wilt see my grave:
Thou wilt renew thy beauty morn by morn;
I earth in earth forget these empty courts,   75
And thee returning on thy silver wheels.

Break, Break, Break

Break, break, break,
    On thy cold gray stones, O Sea!
And I would that my tongue could utter
    The thoughts that arise in me.

O well for the fisherman's boy,   5
    That he shouts with his sister at play!
O well for the sailor lad,
    That he sings in his boat on the bay!

And the stately ships go on
    To their haven under the hill;   10
But O for the touch of a vanished hand,
    And the sound of a voice that is still!

Break, break, break,
    At the foot of thy crags, O Sea!
But the tender grace of a day that is dead   15
    Will never come back to me.

from THE PRINCESS

The Splendor Falls on Castle Walls

The splendor falls on castle walls
    And snowy summits old in story;
The long light shakes across the lakes,
    And the wild cataract leaps in glory.
Blow, bugle, blow, set the wild echoes flying,   5
Blow, bugle; answer, echoes, dying, dying, dying.

O hark, O hear! how thin and clear,
    And thinner, clearer, farther going!
O sweet and far from cliff and scar
    The horns of Elfland faintly blowing!   10
Blow, let us hear the purple glens replying:
Blow, bugle; answer, echoes, dying, dying, dying.

O love, they die in yon rich sky,
  They faint on hill or field or river;
Our echoes roll from soul to soul,   15
  And grow for ever and for ever.
Blow, bugle, blow, set the wild echoes flying,
And answer, echoes, answer, dying, dying, dying.

Tears, idle tears

Tears, idle tears, I know not what they mean,
Tears from the depth of some divine despair
Rise in the heart, and gather to the eyes,
In looking on the happy autumn-fields,
And thinking of the days that are no more.   5

Fresh as the first beam glittering on a sail,
That brings our friends up from the underworld,
Sad as the last which reddens over one
That sinks with all we love below the verge;
So sad, so fresh, the days that are no more.   10

Ah, sad and strange as in dark summer dawns
The earliest pipe of half-awakened birds
To dying ears, when unto dying eyes
The casement slowly grows a glimmering square;
So sad, so strange, the days that are no more.   15

Dear as remember'd kisses after death,
And sweet as those by hopeless fancy feign'd
On lips that are for others; deep as love,
Deep as first love, and wild with all regret;
O Death in Life, the days that are no more.   20

Now sleeps the crimson petal

Now sleeps the crimson petal, now the white;
Nor waves the cypress in the palace walk;
Nor winks the gold fin in the porphyry font:
The fire-fly wakens: waken thou with me.

NOW SLEEPS.   From "The Princess." Princess Ida, a feminist who has founded
a college exclusively for women, has refused not only the passion of love but
also the hand of the Prince, who here lies desperately wounded before her. As
she nurses him, she abandons her sexless life when in his delirium he embraces
her. Later in the night, his fever gone, he hears her reading this poem to herself
as she warms to the task of being a whole woman.

Now droops the milkwhite peacock like a ghost,   5
And like a ghost she glimmers on to me.

Now lies the Earth all Danaë to the stars,
And all thy heart lies open unto me.

Now slides the silent meteor on, and leaves
A shining furrow, as thy thoughts in me.   10

Now folds the lily all her sweetness up,
And slips into the bosom of the lake:
So fold thyself, my dearest, thou, and slip
Into my bosom and be lost in me.

from IN MEMORIAM A. H. H.

.   .   .

II

Old yew, which graspest at the stones
    That name the under-lying dead,
    Thy fibers net the dreamless head;
Thy roots are wrapt about the bones.

The seasons bring the flower again,   5
    And bring the firstling to the flock;
    And in the dusk of thee, the clock
Beats out the little lives of men.

O not for thee the glow, the bloom,
    Who changest not in any gale,   10
    Nor branding summer suns avail
To touch thy thousand years of gloom:

---

7 *Danaë:* Imprisoned in a tower by her father to prevent her from bearing the child that oracles had foretold would kill him, Danaë was visited by Zeus in a shower of gold (hence *stars*) and thus became the mother of the hero Perseus, slayer of Medusa and rescuer and husband of Andromeda.

IN MEMORIAM. Addressed to the memory of Arthur Henry Hallam (b. London, 1811; d. Vienna, 1833), Tennyson's closest friend, whom he first met at Trinity College, Cambridge, in 1828. Both were elected to the Apostles, a group of dedicated, able, politically liberal undergraduates who were also early and enthusiastic admirers of Wordsworth, Coleridge, Shelley, and Keats. The profound influence of the personality and enthusiasms of Hallam persisted all of Tennyson's life. At the time of his death, Hallam was engaged to Tennyson's sister, Emily.

And gazing on thee, sullen tree,
  Sick for thy stubborn hardihood,
  I seem to fail from out my blood,   15
And grow incorporate into thee.

III

O Sorrow, cruel fellowship,
  O Priestess in the vaults of Death,
  O sweet and bitter in a breath,
What whispers from thy lying lip?   20

'The stars,' she whispers, 'blindly run;
  A web is wov'n across the sky;
  From out waste places comes a cry,
And murmurs from the dying sun:

'And all the phantom, Nature, stands—   25
  With all the music in her tone,
  A hollow echo of my own,—
A hollow form with empty hands.'

And shall I take a thing so blind,
  Embrace her as my natural good;   30
  Or crush her, like a vice of blood,
Upon the threshold of the mind?

.   .   .

VI

One writes, that 'other friends remain,'
  That 'loss is common to the race'—
  And common is the commonplace,   35
And vacant chaff well meant for grain.

That loss is common would not make
  My own less bitter, rather more.
  Too common! Never morning wore
To evening, but some heart did break.   40

O father, wheresoe'er thou be,
  That pledgest now thy gallant son;
  A shot, ere half thy draught be done,
Hath stilled the life that beat from thee.

O mother, praying God will save 45
   Thy sailor,—while thy head is bowed,
   His heavy-shotted hammock-shroud
Drops in his vast and wandering grave.

.   .   .

VII

Dark house, by which once more I stand
   Here in the long unlovely street, 50
   Doors, where my heart was used to beat
So quickly, waiting for a hand,

A hand that can be clasp'd no more—
   Behold me, for I cannot sleep,
   And like a guilty thing I creep 55
At earliest morning to the door.

He is not here; but far away
   The noise of life begins again,
   And ghastly thro' the drizzling rain
On the bald street breaks the blank day. 60

.   .   .

XI

Calm is the morn without a sound,
   Calm as to suit a calmer grief,
   And only through the faded leaf
The chestnut pattering to the ground;

Calm and deep peace on this high wold, 65
   And on these dews that drench the furze,
   And all the silvery gossamers
That twinkle into green and gold;

Calm and still light on yon great plain
   That sweeps with all its autumn bowers, 70
   And crowded farms and lessening towers,
To mingle with the bounding main;

49–50 *Dark . . . street:* Hallam's father's house on Wimpole Street, London.

Calm and deep peace in this wide air,
   These leaves that redden to the fall;
   And in my heart, if calm at all,   75
If any calm, a calm despair;

Calm on the seas, and silver sleep,
   And waves that sway themselves in rest,
   And dead calm in that noble breast
Which heaves but with the heaving deep.   80

.   .   .

XXXIV

My own dim life should teach me this,
   That life shall live for evermore,
   Else earth is darkness at the core,
And dust and ashes all that is;

This round of green, this orb of flame,   85
   Fantastic beauty; such as lurks
   In some wild Poet, when he works
Without a conscience or an aim.

What then were God to such as I?
   'Twere hardly worth my while to choose   90
   Of things all mortal, or to use
A little patience ere I die;

'Twere best at once to sink to peace,
   Like birds the charming serpent draws,
   To drop head-foremost in the jaws   95
Of vacant darkness and to cease.

.   .   .

XLIII

If Sleep and Death be truly one,
   And every spirit's folded bloom
   Thro' all its intervital gloom
In some long trance should slumber on;   100

---

80 *Which . . . deep:* Hallam's body is being brought home by ship.   99 *inter-vital:* between two lives; i.e., the intermediate state of death between natural life and the supernatural one of the resurrection.

Unconscious of the sliding hour,
   Bare of the body, might it last,
   And silent traces of the past
Be all the colour of the flower:

So then were nothing lost to man;   105
   So that still garden of the souls
   In many a figured leaf enrolls
The total world since life began;

And love will last as pure and whole
   As when he loved me here in Time,   110
   And at the spiritual prime
Rewaken with the dawning soul.

.   .   .

LIV

Oh yet we trust that somehow good
   Will be the final goal of ill,
   To pangs of nature, sins of will,   115
Defects of doubt, and taints of blood:

That nothing walks with aimless feet;
   That not one life shall be destroy'd,
   Or cast as rubbish to the void,
When God hath made the pile complete;   120

That not a worm is cloven in vain;
   That not a moth with vain desire
   Is shrivel'd in a fruitless fire,
Or but subserves another's gain.

Behold, we know not anything;   125
   I can but trust that good shall fall
   At last—far off—at last, to all,
And every winter change to spring.

So runs my dream: but what am I!
   An infant crying in the night: 130
   An infant crying for the light:
And with no language but a cry.

LV

The wish, that of the living whole
   No life may fail beyond the grave,

Derives it not from what we have   135
The likest God within the soul?

Are God and Nature then at strife,
    That Nature lends such evil dreams?
    So careful of the type she seems,
So careless of the single life;   140

That I, considering everywhere
    Her secret meaning in her deeds,
    And finding that of fifty seeds
She often brings but one to bear;

I falter where I firmly trod,   145
    And falling with my weight of cares
    Upon the great world's altar-stairs
That slope thro' darkness up to God;

I stretch lame hands of faith, and grope,
    And gather dust and chaff, and call   150
    To what I feel is Lord of all,
And faintly trust the larger hope.

LVI

'So careful of the type?' but no.
    From scarped cliff and quarried stone
    She cries, 'A thousand types are gone: 155
I care for nothing, all shall go.

'Thou makest thine appeal to me:
    I bring to life, I bring to death:
    The spirit does but mean the breath:
I know no more.' And he, shall he,   160

Man, her last work, who seem'd so fair,
    Such splendid purpose in his eyes,
    Who roll'd the psalm to wintry skies,
Who built him fanes of fruitless prayer,

Who trusted God was love indeed   165
    And love Creation's final law—
    Though Nature, red in tooth and claw
With ravine, shriek'd against his creed—

---

139 *type:* a main division of the animal or vegetable kingdom in which all members possess the same characteristic form, structure, and particulars. 154 *scarped:* steeply cut; i.e., a cliff cut away perpendicularly so that the strata of embedded fossils are exposed. 164 *fanes:* ancient temples. 168 *ravine:* violent, voracious gluttony.

Who loved, who suffer'd countless ills,
   Who battled for the True, the Just,   170
   Be blown about the desert dust,
Or seal'd within the iron hills?

No more? A monster then, a dream,
   A discord. Dragons of the prime,
   That tare each other in their slime,   175
Were mellow music match'd with him.

O life as futile, then, as frail!
   O for thy voice to soothe and bless!
   What hope of answer, or redress?
Behind the veil, behind the veil.   180

      ·   ·   ·

LXXXIII

Dip down upon the northern shore,
   O sweet new-year delaying long;
   Thou doest expectant Nature wrong;
Delaying long, delay no more.

What stays thee from the clouded noons,   185
   Thy sweetness from its proper place?
   Can trouble live with April days,
Or sadness in the summer moons?

Bring orchis, bring the foxglove spire,
   The little speedwell's darling blue,   190
   Deep tulips dash'd with fiery dew,
Laburnums, dropping-wells of fire.

O thou, new-year, delaying long,
   Delayest the sorrow in my blood,
   That longs to burst a frozen bud,   195
And flood a fresher throat with song.

      ·   ·   ·

CVI

Ring out, wild bells, to the wild sky,
   The flying cloud, the frosty light:

---

174 *Dragons . . . prime:* prehistoric monsters. 175 *tare:* tore. 192 *Laburnums . . . fire:* The golden blossoms dropping down on the ground make a pool of fire. Cf. Milton, "Lycidas," ll. 134–51.

The year is dying in the night;
Ring out, wild bells, and let him die.   200

Ring out the old, ring in the new,
   Ring, happy bells, across the snow:
   The year is going, let him go;
Ring out the false, ring in the true.

Ring out the grief that saps the mind,   205
   For those that here we see no more;
   Ring out the feud of rich and poor,
Ring in redress to all mankind.

Ring out a slowly dying cause,
   And ancient forms of party strife;   210
   Ring in the nobler modes of life,
With sweeter manners, purer laws.

Ring out the want, the care, the sin,
   The faithless coldness of the times;
   Ring out, ring out my mournful rhymes,   215
But ring the fuller minstrel in.

Ring out false pride in place and blood,
   The civic slander and the spite;
   Ring in the love of truth and right,
Ring in the common love of good.   220

Ring out old shapes of foul disease,
   Ring out the narrowing lust of gold;
   Ring out the thousand wars of old,
Ring in the thousand years of peace.

Ring in the valiant man and free,   225
   The larger heart, the kindlier hand;
   Ring out the darkness of the land,
Ring in the Christ that is to be.

.   .   .

CXV

Now fades the last long streak of snow,
Now burgeons every maze of quick   230

230 *quick:* a live fence, i.e., hawthorn hedgerow.

356

About the flowering squares, and thick
By ashen roots the violets blow.

Now rings the woodland loud and long,
   The distance takes a lovelier hue,
   And drown'd in yonder living blue   235
The lark becomes a sightless song.

Now dance the lights on lawn and lea,
   The flocks are whiter down the vale,
   And milkier every milky sail
On winding stream or distant sea;   240

Where now the seamew pipes, or dives
   In yonder greening gleam, and fly
   The happy birds, that change their sky
To build and brood; that live their lives

From land to land; and in my breast   245
   Spring wakens too; and my regret
   Becomes an April violet,
And buds and blossoms like the rest.

CXVI

Is it, then, regret for buried time
   That keenlier in sweet April wakes,   250
   And meets the year, and gives and takes
The colors of the crescent prime?

Not all: the songs, the stirring air,
   The life re-orient out of dust,
   Cry thro' the sense to hearten trust   255
In that which made the world so fair.

Not all regret: the face will shine
   Upon me, while I muse alone;
   And that dear voice, I once have known,
Still speak to me of me and mine: 260

231 *flowering squares:* garden plots. 236 *sightless:* invisible. 242 *greening gleam:* i.e., the sea. 252 *crescent prime:* increasing, growing spring.

Yet less of sorrow lives in me
    For days of happy commune dead;
    Less yearning for the friendship fled,
Than some strong bond which is to be.

CXVII

O days and hours, your work is this,   265
    To hold me from my proper place,
    A little while from his embrace,
For fuller gain of after bliss:

That out of distance might ensue
    Desire of nearness doubly sweet;   270
    And unto meeting, when we meet,
Delight a hundredfold accrue,

For every grain of sand that runs,
    And every span of shade that steals,
    And every kiss of toothed wheels,   275
And all the courses of the suns.

CXVIII

Contemplate all this work of Time,
    The giant laboring in his youth;
    Nor dream of human love and truth,
As dying Nature's earth and lime;   280

But trust that those we call the dead
    Are breathers of an ampler day
    For ever nobler ends. They say,
The solid earth whereon we tread

In tracts of fluent heat began,   285
    And grew to seeming-random forms,
    The seeming prey of cyclic storms,
Till at the last arose the man;

Who throve and branch'd from clime to clime,
    The herald of a higher race,   290
    And of himself in higher place,
If so he type this work of time

---

273 *sand that runs:* i.e., as in an hourglass. 274 *span . . . steals:* shadows increasing as the day closes. 275 *kiss . . . wheels:* meshing of cog-wheels in clocks. 277 *Contemplate:* the accent in Tennyson's time was commonly on the second syllable. 285 *tracts:* periods. 292 *type:* typify.

358

Within himself, from more to more;
 Or, crown'd with attributes of woe
 Like glories, move his course, and show   295
That life is not as idle ore,

But iron dug from central gloom,
 And heated hot with burning fears,
 And dipt in baths of hissing tears,
And batter'd with the shocks of doom   300

To shape and use. Arise and fly
 The reeling Faun, the sensual feast;
 Move upward, working out the beast,
And let the ape and tiger die.

. . .

CXXIII

There rolls the deep where grew the tree.   305
 O earth, what changes hast thou seen!
 There where the long street roars, hath been
The stillness of the central sea.

The hills are shadows, and they flow
 From form to form, and nothing stands;   310
 They melt like mist, the solid lands,
Like clouds they shape themselves and go.

But in my spirit will I dwell,
 And dream my dream, and hold it true;
 For tho' my lips may breathe adieu,   315
I cannot think the thing farewell.

CXXIX

Dear friend, far off, my lost desire,
 So far, so near in woe and weal;
 O loved the most, when most I feel
There is a lower and a higher;   320

Known and unknown, human, divine;
 Sweet human hand and lips and eye;
 Dear heavenly friend that canst not die,
Mine, mine, for ever, ever mine;

Strange friend, past, present, and to be;   325
   Loved deeplier, darklier understood;
   Behold, I dream a dream of good,
And mingle all the world with thee.

CXXX

Thy voice is on the rolling air;
   I hear thee where the waters run;   330
   Thou standest in the rising sun,
And in the setting thou art fair.

What art thou then? I cannot guess;
   But tho' I seem in star and flower
   To feel thee some diffusive power,   335
I do not therefore love thee less:

My love involves the love before;
   My love is vaster passion now;
   Tho' mix'd with God and Nature thou,
I seem to love thee more and more.   340

Far off thou art, but ever nigh;
   I have thee still, and I rejoice;
   I prosper, circled with thy voice;
I shall not lose thee tho' I die.

The Eagle

FRAGMENT

He clasps the crag with crooked hands;
Close to the sun in lonely lands,
Ringed with the azure world, he stands.

The wrinkled sea beneath him crawls;
He watches from his mountain walls,   5
And like a thunderbolt he falls.

In the Valley of Cauteretz

All along the valley, stream that flashest white,
Deepening thy voice with the deepening of the night,
All along the valley, where thy waters flow,
I walk'd with one I loved two and thirty years ago.
All along the valley, while I walk'd to-day,   5
The two and thirty years were a mist that rolls away;
For all along the valley, down thy rocky bed,
Thy living voice to me was as the voice of the dead,
And all along the valley, by rock and cave and tree,
The voice of the dead was a living voice to me.   10

Frater Ave Atque Vale

Row us out from Desenzano, to your Sirmione row!
So they row'd, and there we landed—'O venusta Sirmio!'
There to me thro' all the groves of olive in the summer glow,
There beneath the Roman ruin where the purple flowers grow,
Came that 'Ave atque Vale' of the Poet's hopeless woe,   5
Tenderest of Roman poets nineteen-hundred years ago,
'Frater Ave atque Vale'—as we wander'd to and fro
Gazing at the Lydian laughter of the Garda Lake below
Sweet Catullus's all-but-island, olive-silvery Sirmio!

IN THE VALLEY. In August of 1830, Tennyson and Hallam went to the Pyrenees to bring money and secret messages from English sympathizers to the Spanish insurrectionists then attempting to overthrow King Ferdinand. The revolution failed, but Tennyson's memories of mountain landscapes did not.

FRATER AVE ATQUE VALE (Brother, Hail and Farewell). 1 *Desenzano:* a town on Lake Garda near Sirmione, a peninsula on the lake, where Catullus had a favorite retreat. 2 *O venusta Sirmio:* O lovely Sirmione (Catullus, XXXI). 5 *Ave atque Vale:* Catullus thus laments his dead brother in CI, l. 10. 7 *Frater:* Brother. Tennyson had recently lost his brother, Charles, to whom he was devoted. 8 *Lydian:* Catullus, XXXI, l. 13. In Latin poetry, the Etruscans (who had settlements in this region) were traditionally thought to be of Lydian origin.

ROBERT BROWNING
1812–1889

Love Among the Ruins

1

Where the quiet-colored end of evening smiles
    Miles and miles
On the solitary pastures where our sheep
    Half-asleep
Tinkle homeward through the twilight, stray or stop   5
    ·As they crop—
Was the site once of a city great and gay
    (So they say),
Of our country's very capital, its prince
    Ages since   10
Held his court in, gathered councils, wielding far
    Peace or war.

2

Now,—the country does not even boast a tree
    As you see,
To distinguish slopes of verdure, certain rills   15
    From the hills
Intersect and give a name to (else they run
    Into one),
Where the domed and daring palace shot its spires
    Up like fires   20
O'er the hundred-gated circuit of a wall
    Bounding all,
Made of marble, men might march on nor be prest,
    Twelve abreast.

3

And such plenty and perfection, see, of grass   25
    Never was!
Such a carpet as, this summer-time, o'erspreads
    And embeds
Every vestige of the city, guessed alone,
    Stock or stone—   30
Where a multitude of men breathed joy and woe
    Long ago;

Lust of glory pricked their hearts up, dread of shame
    Struck them tame;
And that glory and that shame alike, the gold   35
    Bought and sold.

4

Now,—the single little turret that remains
    On the plains,
By the caper overrooted, by the gourd
    Overscored,   40
While the patching houseleek's head of blossom winks
    Through the chinks—
Marks the basement whence a tower in ancient time
    Sprang sublime,
And a burning ring all round, the chariots traced   45
    As they raced,
And the monarch and his minions and his dames
    Viewed the games.

5

And I know, while thus the quiet-colored eve
    Smiles to leave   50
To their folding, all our many-tinkling fleece
    In such peace,
And the slopes and rills in undistinguished gray
    Melt away—
That a girl with eager eyes and yellow hair   55
    Waits me there
In the turret whence the charioteers caught soul
    For the goal,
When the king looked, where she looks now, breathless, dumb
    Till I come.   60

6

But he looked upon the city, every side,
    Far and wide,
All the mountains topped with temples, all the glades'
    Colonnades,

LOVE AMONG THE RUINS. 39 *caper:* a low shrub whose buds are used as condiments; it commonly grows in Mediterranean countries on old walls, in fissures of rocks, or among rubbish. 41 *patching:* forming patches. *houseleek:* a succulent herb with pink flowers that commonly grows on top of walls and houses; when growing on a rooftop it was considered a safeguard against lightning. These fresh, homely, domestic herbs, still flourishing, are contrasted with the wreckage of imperial splendor.

All the causeys, bridges, aqueducts,—and then,   65
    All the men!
When I do come, she will speak not, she will stand,
    Either hand
On my shoulder, give her eyes the first embrace
    Of my face,   70
Ere we rush, ere we extinguish sight and speech
    Each on each.

7

In one year they sent a million fighters forth
    South and North,
And they built their gods a brazen pillar high   75
    As the sky,
Yet reserved a thousand chariots in full force—
    Gold, of course.
Oh heart! oh blood that freezes, blood that burns!
    Earth's returns   80
For whole centuries of folly, noise and sin!
    Shut them in,
With their triumphs and their glories and the rest!
    Love is best.

from MEN AND WOMEN

The Bishop Orders His Tomb at Saint Praxed's Church

ROME, 15—

Vanity, saith the preacher, vanity!
Draw round my bed: is Anselm keeping back?
Nephews—sons mine . . . ah God, I know not! Well—
She, men would have to be your mother once,
Old Gandolf envied me, so fair she was!   5

---

65 *causeys:* raised cobblestone roadways; also raised sidewalks.

THE BISHOP.   *Saint Praxed:* St. Praxedes was a second-century virgin martyr, venerated in Rome on July 21. The fourth-century church dedicated to her and her sister, St. Pudentiana, was rebuilt in 817–24, and their bones and those of other martyrs were at this time translated to it from the catacombs. Browning was familiar with this ornate church.

1 *Vanity . . . vanity:* "Vanity of vanities, saith the Preacher, vanity of vanities; all is vanity." Eccl. 1:2.   3 *Nephews:* actually sons, but so called for the sake of propriety, as the Bishop was required to be celibate and had vowed to be chaste.

What's done is done, and she is dead beside,
Dead long ago, and I am Bishop since,
And as she died so must we die ourselves,
And thence ye may perceive the world's a dream.
Life, how and what is it? As here I lie   10
In this state-chamber, dying by degrees,
Hours and long hours in the dead night, I ask
"Do I live, am I dead?" Peace, peace seems all.
Saint Praxed's ever was the church for peace;
And so, about this tomb of mine. I fought   15
With tooth and nail to save my niche, ye know:
—Old Gandolf cozened me, despite my care;
Shrewd was that snatch from out the corner South
He graced his carrion with, God curse the same!
Yet still my niche is not so cramped but thence   20
One sees the pulpit o' the epistle-side,
And somewhat of the choir, those silent seats,
And up into the aery dome where live
The angels, and a sunbeam's sure to lurk:
And I shall fill my slab of basalt there,   25
And 'neath my tabernacle take my rest,
With those nine columns round me, two and two,
The odd one at my feet where Anselm stands:
Peach-blossom marble all, the rare, the ripe
As fresh-poured red wine of a mighty pulse.   30
—Old Gandolf with his paltry onion-stone,
Put me where I may look at him! True peach,
Rosy and flawless: how I earned the prize!
Draw close: that conflagration of my church
—What then? So much was saved if aught were missed!   35
My sons, ye would not be my death? Go dig
The white-grape vineyard where the oil-press stood,
Drop water gently till the surface sink,
And if ye find . . . Ah God, I know not, I! . . .
Bedded in store of rotten fig leaves soft,   40
And corded up in a tight olive-frail,
Some lump, ah God, of *lapis lazuli*,
Big as a Jew's head cut off at the nape,
Blue as a vein o'er the Madonna's breast . . .
Sons, all have I bequeathed you, villas, all,   45

17 *cozened:* cheated.   21 *epistle-side:* the right side when one faces the altar,
the side from which the Epistle is read during the Mass.   25 *Basalt:* black
marble.   26 *tabernacle:* an arched canopy over a tomb.   30 *pulse:* i.e., vitality,
as of blood pulsating.   31 *onion-stone:* an inferior, greenish marble that peels
off in layers like an onion.   41 *olive-frail:* olive basket made of rushes.   42
lapis lazuli: a semiprecious bright blue stone.

That brave Frascati villa with its bath,
So, let the blue lump poise between my knees,
Like God the Father's globe on both his hands
Ye worship in the Jesu Church so gay,
For Gandolf shall not choose but see and burst!   50
Swift as a weaver's shuttle fleet our years:
Man goeth to the grave, and where is he?
Did I say basalt for my slab, sons? Black—
'Twas ever antique-black I meant! How else
Shall ye contrast my frieze to come beneath?   55
The bas-relief in bronze ye promised me,
Those Pans and Nymphs ye wot of, and perchance
Some tripod, thyrsus, with a vase or so,
The Savior at his sermon on the mount,
Saint Praxed in a glory, and one Pan   60
Ready to twitch the Nymph's last garment off,
And Moses with the tables . . . but I know
Ye mark me not! What do they whisper thee,
Child of my bowels, Anselm? Ah, ye hope
To revel down my villas while I gasp   65
Bricked o'er with beggar's moldy travertine
Which Gandolf from his tomb-top chuckles at!
Nay, boys, ye love me—all of jasper, then!
'Tis jasper ye stand pledged to, lest I grieve
My bath must needs be left behind, alas!   70
One block, pure green as a pistachio-nut,
There's plenty jasper somewhere in the world—
And have I not Saint Praxed's ear to pray

46 *Frascati:* a wealthy suburb of Rome famous for its opulent villas.   48
globe: symbol of God's sovereignty and power over the world.   49 *Jesu:* the
Jesuit church in Rome.   51 *Swift . . . years:* Cf. Job 7:6, "My days are swifter
than a weaver's shuttle, and are spent without hope."   58 *tripod, thyrsus:* pagan
objects carved in relief: the tripod was the bronze, three-legged altar sacred
to the Pythian Apollo at Delphi, seated upon which in the innermost sanctuary the priestess gave her oracular responses; the thyrsus was the emblem of
Dionysius (Bacchus), a staff tipped with a pine cone and wound with ivy and
vine branches and carried in his riotous festivals. Both are incongruously
contrasted with Christian images and symbols.   59 *Savior . . . mount:* See
Matt. 5.   60 *glory:* luminous glow combining the halo around the head and
the radiant light around the body that expresses the most exalted state of
divinity, usually the exclusive attribute of God. The Bishop exaggerates St.
Praxedes' status.   61 *Nymph:* in contrast to the action of St. Praxedes, who
was martyred under Marcus Antonius for protecting and hiding Christians.
62 *travertine:* literally, "stone of Tibur"; a soft, easily worked, straw-colored
rock that hardens when exposed to the Italian climate and is very durable.
Ironically, the exterior of St. Peter's, no *beggar's* basilica, is made of it.
68 *jasper:* in Biblical usage, a green, translucent precious stone capable of
sustaining a very high polish.

Horses for ye, and brown Greek manuscripts,
And mistresses with great smooth marbly limbs?   75
—That's if ye carve my epitaph aright,
Choice Latin, picked phrase, Tully's every word,
No gaudy ware like Gandolf's second line—
Tully, my masters? Ulpian serves his need!
And then how I shall lie through centuries,   80
And hear the blessed mutter of the mass,
And see God made and eaten all day long,
And feel the steady candle-flame, and taste
Good strong thick stupefying incense-smoke!
For as I lie here, hours of the dead night,   85
Dying in state and by such slow degrees,
I fold my arms as if they clasped a crook,
And stretch my feet forth straight as stone can point,
And let the bedclothes, for a mortcloth, drop
Into great laps and folds of sculptor's-work: 90
And as yon tapers dwindle, and strange thoughts
Grow, with a certain humming in my ears,
About the life before I lived this life,
And this life too, popes, cardinals and priests,
Saint Praxed at his sermon on the mount,   95
Your tall pale mother with her talking eyes,
And new-found agate urns as fresh as day,
And marble's language, Latin pure, discreet,
—Aha, ELUCESCEBAT quoth our friend?
No Tully, said I, Ulpian at the best!   100
Evil and brief hath been my pilgrimage.
All *lapis*, all, sons! Else I give the Pope
My villas! Will ye ever eat my heart?
Ever your eyes were as a lizard's quick,
They glitter like your mother's for my soul,   105
Or ye would heighten my impoverished frieze,
Piece out its starved design, and fill my vase

---

74 *manuscripts:* In the sixteenth century, ancient Greek manuscripts were
greatly prized by genuine as well as by pseudo-humanist scholars. 77 *Tully:*
Marcus Tullius Cicero (106–43 B.C.), Roman statesman and most famous
orator, purist, and stylist of them all. 79 *Ulpian:* Domitius Ulpianus (d. A.D.
228), a famous Roman jurist, but neither purist nor stylist. 82 *God. . . eaten:*
The doctrine of transubstantiation affirms that in the Mass the elements do
in fact become the Body and Blood of Christ, which is then *eaten* by the
communicants. 87 *crook:* The crosier, symbolic of the bishop's office, is
shaped like a sheephook. 89 *mortcloth:* funeral pall. 95 *Saint . . . mount:*
The Bishop's mind wanders; he confuses St. Praxedes, a female saint, with
Christ. 99 *Elucescebat:* "He shone forth." Cicero would have written
elucebat.

With grapes, and add a visor and a term,
And to the tripod ye would tie a lynx
That in his struggle throws the thyrsus down,   110
To comfort me on my entablature
Whereon I am to lie till I must ask
"Do I live, am I dead?" There, leave me, there!
For ye have stabbed me with ingratitude
To death—ye wish it—God, ye wish it! Stone—   115
Gritstone, a-crumble! Clammy squares which sweat
As if the corpse they keep were oozing through—
And no more *lapis* to delight the world!
Well go! I bless ye. Fewer tapers there,
But in a row: and, going, turn your backs   120
—Ay, like departing altar-ministrants,
And leave me in my church, the church for peace,
That I may watch at leisure if he leers—
Old Gandolf—at me, from his onion-stone,
As still he envied me, so fair she was!   125

Fra Lippo Lippi

I am poor brother Lippo, by your leave!
You need not clap your torches to my face.

---

108 *visor:* i.e., a classical *persona*, the mask worn by Greek and Roman actors; also perhaps an ornamental helmet with a lavishly decorated visor, symbolic of hidden thought.   *term:* a bust of the upper part of the human body terminating in a plain block of rectangular form and used as a pillar, baluster, or detached ornament for a niche. Unrelated classical, free-floating objects such as these are often found in Renaissance friezes.   116 *Gritstone:* a coarse sandstone.

FRA LIPPO LIPPI.   According to Vasari (*Lives of the . . . Painters . . .*, trans. De Vere, III, 79–88), writing in 1550, Fra Filippo Lippi was born in Florence (*c.* 1406), orphaned at two, brought up by his aunt, entered the Convent of the Carmine there at the age of eight where he was a poor scholar but a superb caricaturist, and while still very young painted so many pictures worthy of praise "that it was a miracle." Confident of his ability, he left the monastery at seventeen for a life of painting and pleasure (he was of a very amorous disposition, a "friend of gay spirits, and . . . ever lived a joyous life") under the patronage of Cosimo de Medici, who once locked him up to compel him to finish a painting (but as in the poem, he escaped for a two-day fling). While painting the panel for the high altar for the Nuns of Saint Margherita, he fell violently in love with Lucrezia Buti, a novice at the convent, and persuaded the nuns to let him paint her portrait as the Virgin, later abducting her (she bore him a son who also became a famous painter). His painting of the *Coronation of the Virgin* (which Browning knew) is also supposed to be a portrait of his wife (their marriage was recognized by Pope Pius II in 1461). Lippi's painting is naturalistic, realistic (showing to others "how great is the value of invention and of knowing how to express emotions in pictures"), rich in color and contemporary scenes, as opposed to the stiff allegory and piety of conventional ecclesiastical painting. Browning recognized his affinity with Lippi and practiced in his own poetry the same rich, naturalistic esthetic, realistic idiom, and concern for contemporary situations and people.

Zooks, what's to blame? you think you see a monk!
What, 'tis past midnight, and you go the rounds,
And here you catch me at an alley's end   5
Where sportive ladies leave their doors ajar?
The Carmine's my cloister: hunt it up,
Do,—harry out, if you must show your zeal,
Whatever rat, there, haps on his wrong hole,
And nip each softling of a wee white mouse,   10
Weke, weke, that's crept to keep him company!
Aha, you know your betters! Then, you'll take
Your hand away that's fiddling on my throat,
And please to know me likewise. Who am I?
Why, one, sir, who is lodging with a friend   15
Three streets off—he's a certain . . . how d'ye call?
Master—a . . . Cosimo of the Medici,
I' the house that caps the corner. Boh! you were best!
Remember and tell me, the day you're hanged,
How you affected such a gullet's-gripe!   20
But you, sir, it concerns you that your knaves
Pick up a manner nor discredit you:
Zooks, are we pilchards, that they sweep the streets
And count fair prize what comes into their net?
He's Judas to a tittle, that man is!   25
Just such a face! Why, sir, you make amends.
Lord, I'm not angry! Bid your hangdogs go
Drink out this quarter-florin to the health
Of the munificent House that harbors me
(And many more beside, lads! more beside!)   30
And all's come square again. I'd like his face—
His, elbowing on his comrade in the door
With the pike and lantern,—for the slave that holds
John Baptist's head a-dangle by the hair
With one hand ("Look you, now," as who should say)   35
And his weapon in the other, yet unwiped!
It's not your chance to have a bit of chalk,
A wood-coal or the like? or you should see!

3 *Zooks:* a mild oath; literally, God's hooks. 17 *Cosimo:* Florentine
banker (1389–1464), influential statesman, patron of the arts, and then head of
the Medici family. 23 *Pilchards:* a small, common, herring-like fish. 25
Judas . . . tittle: Judas (the betrayer of Christ) to the minutest particle. 28
quarter-florin: a small Florentine coin; the English florin is so named because it
was first struck in Florence in the thirteenth century and stamped with a lily
(*flore*). 34 *John Baptist's head:* The head of John the Baptist, who was executed
by Herod at the instigation of his wife Herodias and her daughter, was carried
by a servant from prison and placed in a platter. See Mark 6:17–28. 38 *wood-
coal:* charcoal. Vasari recounts that Lippi, held captive by the Moors for
eighteen months, obtained his release from slavery by drawing with a piece of
charcoal on a white wall a picture of his master in full Moorish costume.

Yes, I'm the painter, since you style me so.
What, brother Lippo's doings, up and down,   40
You know them and they take you? like enough!
I saw the proper twinkle in your eye—
'Tell you, I liked your looks at very first.
Let's sit and set things straight now, hip to haunch.
Here's spring come, and the nights one makes up bands   45
To roam the town and sing out carnival,
And I've been three weeks shut within my mew,
A-painting for the great man, saints and saints
And saints again. I could not paint all night—
Ouf! I leaned out of window for fresh air.   50
There came a hurry of feet and little feet,
A sweep of lute-strings, laughs, and whifts of song,—
Flower o' the broom,
Take away love, and our earth is a tomb !
Flower o' the quince,   55
I let Lisa go, and what good in life since?
Flower o' the thyme—and so on. Round they went.
Scarce had they turned the corner when a titter
Like the skipping of rabbits by moonlight—three slim shapes,
And a face that looked up . . . zooks, sir, flesh and blood,   60
That's all I'm made of! Into shreds it went,
Curtain and counterpane and coverlet,
All the bed furniture—a dozen knots,
There was a ladder! Down I let myself,
Hands and feet, scrambling somehow, and so dropped,   65
And after them. I came up with the fun
Hard by Saint Laurence, hail fellow, well met—
Flower o' the rose,
If I've been merry, what matter who knows?
And so as I was stealing back again   70
To get to bed and have a bit of sleep
Ere I rise up tomorrow and go work
On Jerome knocking at his poor old breast
With his great round stone to subdue the flesh,
You snap me of the sudden. Ah, I see!   75
Though your eye twinkles still, you shake your head—
Mine's shaved—a monk, you say—the sting's in that!
If Master Cosimo announced himself,
Mum's the word naturally; but a monk!

47 *mew:* cage. 53 *broom: Cytsius*, a hardy leguminous shrub with yellow
flowers, native to the Mediterranean countries. 73 *Jerome:* one of the Four
Doctors of the Church (A.D. 340–420), translator of the Bible (the Vulgate)
and famous for resistance in the desert to lurid temptations.

Come, what am I a beast for? tell us, now!   80
I was a baby when my mother died
And father died and left me in the street.
I starved there, God knows how, a year or two
On fig skins, melon parings, rinds and shucks,
Refuse and rubbish. One fine frosty day,   85
My stomach being empty as your hat,
The wind doubled me up and down I went.
Old Aunt Lapaccia trussed me with one hand,
(Its fellow was a stinger as I knew)
And so along the wall, over the bridge,   90
By the straight cut to the convent. Six words there,
While I stood munching my first bread that month:
"So, boy, you're minded," quoth the good fat father,
Wiping his own mouth, 'twas refection time—
"To quit this very miserable world?   95
Will you renounce" . . . "the mouthful of bread?" thought I;
By no means! Brief, they made a monk of me;
I did renounce the world, its pride and greed,
Palace, farm, villa, shop, and banking house,
Trash, such as these poor devils of Medici   100
Have given their hearts to—all at eight years old.
Well, sir, I found in time, you may be sure,
'Twas not for nothing—the good bellyful,
The warm serge and the rope that goes all round,
And day-long blessèd idleness beside!   105
"Let's see what the urchin's fit for"—that came next.
Not overmuch their way, I must confess.
Such a to-do! They tried me with their books;
Lord, they'd have taught me Latin in pure waste!
Flower o' the clove,   110
All the Latin I construe is "amo," I love !
But, mind you, when a boy starves in the streets
Eight years together, as my fortune was,
Watching folk's faces to know who will fling
The bit of half-stripped grape bunch he desires,   115
And who will curse or kick him for his pains—
Which gentleman processional and fine,
Holding a candle to the Sacrament,
Will wink and let him lift a plate and catch
The droppings of the wax to sell again,   120
Or holla for the Eight and have him whipped—
How say I?—nay, which dog bites, which lets drop

121 *Eight:* the Magistrates of Florence.

His bone from the heap of offal in the street—
Why, soul and sense of him grow sharp alike,
He learns the look of things, and none the less   125
For admonition from the hunger pinch.
I had a store of such remarks, be sure,
Which, after I found leisure, turned to use.
I drew men's faces on my copy books,
Scrawled them within the antiphonary's marge,   130
Joined legs and arms to the long music notes,
Found eyes and nose and chin for A's and B's,
And made a string of pictures of the world
Betwixt the ins and outs of verb and noun,
On the wall, the bench, the door. The monks looked black.   135
"Nay," quoth the Prior, "turn him out, d' ye say?
In no wise. Lose a crow and catch a lark.
What if at last we get our man of parts,
We Carmelites, like those Camaldolese
And Preaching Friars, to do our church up fine   140
And put the front on it that ought to be!"
And hereupon he bade me daub away.
Thank you! my head being crammed, the walls a blank,
Never was such prompt disemburdening.
First, every sort of monk, the black and white,   145
I drew them, fat and lean; then, folk at church,
From good old gossips waiting to confess
Their cribs of barrel droppings, candle ends—
To the breathless fellow at the altar foot,
Fresh from his murder, safe and sitting there   150
With the little children round him in a row
Of admiration, half for his beard and half
For that white anger of his victim's son
Shaking a fist at him with one fierce arm,
Signing himself with the other because of Christ   155
(Whose sad face on the cross sees only this
After the passion of a thousand years)
Till some poor girl, her apron o'er her head,

130 *antiphonary:* music book carried by choirboys.   139 *Carmelites:* a mendicant order of friars; according to early rule they were to abstain from meat
and to observe a strict fast from September 14 to Easter (but cf. l. 93).
Camaldolese: a fraternity of monks, early distinguished for the severity of their
fasting, asceticism, silence, and penance.   140 *Preaching Friars:* the Dominicans,
in England known as the Black Friars, a mendicant order founded in 1216,
whose rule also enjoined fasting, poverty, chastity, and silence. Each of these
orders was constantly competing with its rivals to have its churches decorated in
the most splendid fashion for the greater glory of God and of the order.   148
cribs: thefts.

(Which the intense eyes looked through) came at eve
On tiptoe, said a word, dropped in a loaf,   160
Her pair of earrings and a bunch of flowers
(The brute took growling), prayed, and so was gone.
I painted all, then cried " 'Tis ask and have;
Choose, for more's ready!"—laid the ladder flat,
And showed my covered bit of cloister-wall.   165
The monks closed in a circle and praised loud
Till checked, taught what to see and not to see,
Being simple bodies,—"That's the very man!
Look at the boy who stoops to pat the dog!
That woman's like the Prior's niece who comes   170
To care about his asthma: it's the life!"
But there my triumph's straw-fire flared and funked;
Their betters took their turn to see and say:
The Prior and the learned pulled a face
And stopped all that in no time. "How? what's here?   175
Quite from the mark of painting, bless us all!
Faces, arms, legs, and bodies like the true
As much as pea and pea! it's devil's-game!
Your business is not to catch men with show,
With homage to the perishable clay,   180
But lift them over it, ignore it all,
Make them forget there's such a thing as flesh.
Your business is to paint the souls of men—
Man's soul, and it's a fire, smoke . . . no, it's not . . .
It's vapor done up like a new-born babe—   185
(In that shape when you die it leaves your mouth)
It's . . . well, what matters talking, it's the soul!
Give us no more of body than shows soul!
Here's Giotto with his Saint a-praising God,
That sets us praising,—why not stop with him?   190
Why put all thoughts of praise out of our head
With wonder at lines, colors, and what not?
Paint the soul, never mind the legs and arms!
Rub all out, try at it a second time.
Oh, that white smallish female with the breasts,   195
She's just my niece . . . Herodias, I would say,—

172 *funked:* smoked, i.e., went out.   189 *Giotto:* the great Florentine painter,
sculptor, and architect (1266–1337).   196 *Herodias:* See l. 34 and note, but it
was her daughter Salome who so pleased Herod by her "dexterity" [Vasari]
and voluptuous dancing that he swore to grant her anything she requested.
Herodias then made her ask for "in a charger the head of John the Baptist."
Vasari says that the *Feast of Herod* is part of a larger work for the Chapel of
the High Altar in the parish church of Prato, and the whole is the most
excellent of all of Lippi's paintings because of the grandeur of the figures and
the expression of the faces.

Who went and danced and got men's heads cut off!
Have it all out!" Now, is this sense, I ask?
A fine way to paint soul, by painting body
So ill, the eye can't stop there, must go further   200
And can't fare worse! Thus, yellow does for white
When what you put for yellow's simply black,
And any sort of meaning looks intense
When all beside itself means and looks naught.
Why can't a painter lift each foot in turn,   205
Left foot and right foot, go a double step,
Make his flesh liker and his soul more like,
Both in their order? Take the prettiest face,
The Prior's niece . . . patron-saint—is it so pretty
You can't discover if it means hope, fear,   210
Sorrow or joy? won't beauty go with these?
Suppose I've made her eyes all right and blue,
Can't I take breath and try to add life's flash,
And then add soul and heighten them three-fold?
Or say there's beauty with no soul at all—   215
(I never saw it—put the case the same—)
If you get simple beauty and naught else,
You get about the best thing God invents:
That's somewhat: and you'll find the soul you have missed,
Within yourself, when you return him thanks.   220
"Rub all out!" Well, well, there's my life, in short,
And so the thing has gone on ever since.
I'm grown a man no doubt, I've broken bounds:
You should not take a fellow eight years old
And make him swear to never kiss the girls.   225
I'm my own master, paint now as I please—
Having a friend, you see, in the Corner-house!
Lord, it's fast holding by the rings in front—
Those great rings serve more purposes than just
To plant a flag in, or tie up a horse!   230
And yet the old schooling sticks, the old grave eyes
Are peeping o'er my shoulder as I work,
The heads shake still—"It's art's decline, my son!
You're not of the true painters, great and old;
Brother Angelico's the man, you'll find;   235
Brother Lorenzo stands his single peer:

228 *rings:* iron rings on the front of the palace, symbols for those who hung on
to them of the protection and patronage of Cosimo de Medici. 235–36
Angelico . . . Lorenzo: Fra Angelico (1387–1455), unfairly criticized by Lippi,
and Lorenzo Monaco (1370–1425), famous painters in the pious tradition
against which Lippi is rebelling.

Fag on at flesh, you'll never make the third!"
Flower o' the pine,
You keep your mistr . . . manners, and I'll stick to mine!
I'm not the third, then; bless us, they must know!   240
Don't you think they're the likeliest to know,
They with their Latin? So, I swallow my rage,
Clench my teeth, suck my lips in tight, and paint
To please them—sometimes do and sometimes don't;
For, doing most, there's pretty sure to come   245
A turn, some warm eve finds me at my saints—
A laugh, a cry, the business of the world
(*Flower o' the peach,*
Death for us all, and his own life for each!)—
And my whole soul revolves, the cup runs over,   250
The world and life's too big to pass for a dream,
And I do these wild things in sheer despite,
And play the fooleries you catch me at,
In pure rage! The old mill-horse, out at grass
After hard years, throws up his stiff heels so,   255
Although the miller does not preach to him
The only good of grass is to make chaff.
What would men have? Do they like grass or no—
May they or mayn't they? All I want's the thing
Settled forever one way. As it is,   260
You tell too many lies and hurt yourself;
You don't like what you only like too much,
You do like what, if given you at your word,
You find abundantly detestable.
For me, I think I speak as I was taught;   265
I always see the garden and God there
A-making man's wife; and, my lesson learned—
The value and significance of flesh—
I can't unlearn ten minutes afterwards.

    You understand me; I'm a beast, I know.   270
But see, now—why, I see as certainly
As that the morning-star's about to shine,
What will hap some day. We've a youngster here
Comes to our convent, studies what I do,
Slouches and stares and lets no atom drop.   275
His name is Guidi—he'll not mind the monks—
They call him Hulking Tom, he lets them talk;
He picks my practice up—he'll paint apace,
I hope so—though I never live so long,

276 *Guidi:* Tommaso Guidi, commonly known as Masaccio, who was in reality
Lippi's teacher. Lippi did have pupils, however; among them was Botticelli.

I know what's sure to follow. You be judge!   280
You speak no Latin more than I, belike;
However, you're my man, you've seen the world—
The beauty and the wonder and the power,
The shapes of things, their colors, lights and shades,
Changes, surprises—and God made it all!   285
—For what? Do you feel thankful, aye or no,
For this fair town's face, yonder river's line,
The mountain round it and the sky above,
Much more the figures of man, woman, child,
These are the frame to? What's it all about?   290
To be passed over, despised? or dwelt upon,
Wondered at? Oh, this last of course!—you say.
But why not do as well as say—paint these
Just as they are, careless what comes of it?
God's works—paint any one, and count it crime   295
To let a truth slip. Don't object, "His works
Are here already; nature is complete:
Suppose you reproduce her—which you can't—
There's no advantage! you must beat her, then."
For, don't you mark? we're made so that we love   300
First when we see them painted, things we have passed
Perhaps a hundred times nor cared to see;
And so they are better, painted—better to us,
Which is the same thing. Art was given for that;
God uses us to help each other so,   305
Lending our minds out. Have you noticed, now,
Your cullion's hanging face? A bit of chalk,
And trust me but you should, though! How much more,
If I drew higher things with the same truth!
That were to take the Prior's pulpit-place,   310
Interpret God to all of you! Oh, oh,
It makes me mad to see what men shall do
And we in our graves! This world's no blot for us,
Nor blank; it means intensely, and means good:
To find its meaning is my meat and drink.   315
"Aye, but you don't so instigate to prayer!"
Strikes in the Prior; "when your meaning's plain
It does not say to folk—remember matins,
Or, mind you fast next Friday!" Why, for this
What need of art at all? A skull and bones,   320
Two bits of stick nailed crosswise, or, what's best,
A bell to chime the hour with, does as well.

307 *cullion:* a base, mean wretch.

I painted a Saint Laurence six months since
At Prato, splashed the fresco in fine style;
"How looks my painting, now the scaffold's down?"   325
I ask a brother. "Hugely," he returns—
"Already not one phiz of your three slaves
Who turn the Deacon off his toasted side,
But's scratched and prodded to our heart's content,
The pious people have so eased their own   330
With coming to say prayers there in a rage;
We get on fast to see the bricks beneath.
Expect another job this time next year,
For pity and religion grow i' the crowd—
Your painting serves its purpose!" Hang the fools!   335

—That is—you'll not mistake an idle word
Spoke in a huff by a poor monk, God wot,
Tasting the air this spicy night which turns
The unaccustomed head like Chianti wine!
Oh, the Church knows! don't misreport me, now   340
It's natural a poor monk out of bounds
Should have his apt word to excuse himself;
And hearken how I plot to make amends.
I have bethought me: I shall paint a piece
. . . There's for you! Give me six months, then go, see   345
Something in Sant' Ambrogio's! Bless the nuns!
They want a cast o' my office. I shall paint
God in the midst, Madonna and her babe,
Ringed by a bowery, flowery angel brood,
Lilies and vestments and white faces, sweet   350
As puff on puff of grated orris-root
When ladies crowd to Church at midsummer.
And then i' the front, of course a saint or two—
Saint John, because he saves the Florentines,
Saint Ambrose, who puts down in black and white   355
The convent's friends and gives them a long day,
And Job, I must have him there past mistake,
The man of Uz (and Us without the z,
Painters who need his patience). Well, all these

323 *Saint Laurence:* martyred in 258 by being roasted on a gridiron.   324
Prato: a town near Florence where Lippi executed many of his most famous
paintings.   327 *phiz:* face.   346 *Ambrogio:* St. Ambrose, made Bishop of
Milan in 374 and, along with St. Augustine and St. Jerome, one of the great
Doctors of the Church. It was for St. Ambrose's Convent in Florence that
Lippi painted the *Coronation of the Virgin*, here sketched out.   351 *orris-root:*
the root of *Iris Florentina* from which, because of its agreeable smell, were
made both tooth- and hair-powders.   354 *Saint John:* patron saint of Florence.

Secured at their devotion, up shall come   360
Out of a corner when you least expect,
As one by a dark stair into a great light,
Music and talking, who but Lippo! I!—
Mazed, motionless, and moonstruck—I'm the man!
Back I shrink—what is this I see and hear?   365
I, caught up with my monk's-things by mistake,
My old serge gown and rope that goes all round,
I, in this presence, this pure company!
Where's a hole, where's a corner for escape?
Then steps a sweet angelic slip of a thing   370
Forward, puts out a soft palm—"Not so fast!"
—Addresses the celestial presence, "nay—
He made you and devised you, after all,
Though he's none of you! Could Saint John there draw—
His camel-hair make up a painting-brush?   375
We come to brother Lippo for all that,
Iste perfecit opus!" So, all smile—
I shuffle sideways with my blushing face
Under the cover of a hundred wings
Thrown like a spread of kirtles when you're gay   380
And play hot cockles, all the doors being shut,
Till, wholly unexpected, in there pops
The hothead husband! Thus I scuttle off
To some safe bench behind, not letting go
The palm of her, the little lily thing   385
That spoke the good word for me in the nick,
Like the Prior's niece . . . Saint Lucy, I would say.
And so all's saved for me, and for the church
A pretty picture gained. Go, six months hence!
Your hand, sir, and good-by: no lights, no lights!   390
The street's hushed, and I know my own way back,
Don't fear me! There's the grey beginning. Zooks!

---

361 *corner:* the right-hand corner of the picture in which Lippi himself
appears.   375 *camel-hair:* "And John was clothed with camel's hair, and with
a girdle of skins about his loins; and he did eat locusts and wild honey" (Mark
1:6); i.e., the harsh coat and severe life of the ascetic, in contrast to the fine
camel-hair brush and generous life of the man who experiences richly this
world, limits the creative imagination.   377 *Iste perfecit opus:* "This man made
this work."   380 *kirtles:* petticoats or skirts.   381 *hot cockles:* an amorous
game in which one kneels and, covering his eyes, lays his head in the lap of
another and guesses who pats him. Vasari says Lippi spent "extraordinary sums
on the pleasures of love, in which he continued to take delight right up to the
end of his life."   387 *niece:* Cf. ll. 195–96.   *Saint Lucy:* Cf. Donne, "A Nocturnall," ll. 1–2 and note.

378

Never the Time and the Place

Never the time and the place
  And the loved one all together!
This path—how soft to pace!
  This May—what magic weather!
Where is the loved one's face? 5
In a dream that loved one's face meets mine,
  But the house is narrow, the place is bleak
Where, outside, rain and wind combine
  With a furtive ear, if I strive to speak,
With a hostile eye at my flushing cheek, 10
With a malice that marks each word, each sign!
O enemy sly and serpentine,
  Uncoil thee from the waking man!
    Do I hold the Past
    Thus firm and fast 15
  Yet doubt if the Future hold I can?
  This path so soft to pace shall lead
  Through the magic of May to herself indeed!
  Or narrow if needs the house must be,
  Outside are the storms and strangers; we— 20
  Oh, close, safe, warm sleep I and she,—I and she!

from ASOLANDO

Dubiety

I will be happy if but for once;
  Only help me, autumn weather,
Me and my cares to screen, ensconce
  In luxury's sofa-lap of leather!

Sleep? Nay, comfort—with just a cloud 5
  Suffusing day too clear and bright;
Eve's essence, the single drop allowed
  To sully, like milk, noon's water-white.

Let gauziness shade, not shroud—adjust,
  Dim and not deaden—somehow sheathe 10
Aught sharp in the rough world's busy thrust,
  If it reach me through dreaming's vapor wreath.

Be life so, all things ever the same!
  For, what has disarmed the world? Outside,
Quiet and peace; inside, nor blame   15
  Nor want, nor wish whate'er betide.

What is it like that has happened before?
  A dream? No dream, more real by much.
A vision? But fanciful days of yore
  Brought many; mere musing seems not such.   20

Perhaps but a memory, after all!
  —Of what came once when a woman leant
To feel for my brow where her kiss might fall.
  Truth ever, truth only the excellent!

MATTHEW ARNOLD
1822–1888

To Marguerite

Yes! in the sea of life enisl'd,
With echoing straits between us thrown,
Dotting the shoreless watery wild,
We mortal millions live *alone*.
The islands feel the enclasping flow,   5
And then their endless bounds they know.

But when the moon their hollows lights,
And they are swept by balms of spring,
And in their glens, on starry nights,
The nightingales divinely sing;   10
And lovely notes, from shore to shore,
Across the sounds and channels pour—

Oh then a longing like despair
Is to their farthest caverns sent;
For surely once, they feel, we were   15
Parts of a single continent!
Now round us spreads the watery plain—
Oh might our marges meet again!

Who order'd, that their longing's fire
Should be, as soon as kindled, cool'd?   20
Who renders vain their deep desire?—
A God, a God their severance ruled!
And bade betwixt their shores to be
The unplumb'd, salt, estranging sea.

Memorial Verses

APRIL, 1850

Goethe in Weimar sleeps, and Greece,
Long since, saw Byron's struggle cease.
But one such death remained to come;
The last poetic voice is dumb—
We stand today by Wordsworth's tomb.   5

MEMORIAL VERSES. Wordsworth died at Rydal Mount on April 23, 1850.
1 *Goethe:* great German poet, novelist, dramatist, and scientist (1749–1832);
he died at Weimar. *Greece:* Byron died at Missolonghi, Greece, in 1824,
while on an expedition to help Greek patriots fight against the Turks.

When Byron's eyes were shut in death,
We bowed our head and held our breath.
He taught us little; but our soul
Had *felt* him like the thunder's roll.
With shivering heart the strife we saw   10
Of passion with eternal law;
And yet with reverential awe
We watched the fount of fiery life
Which served for that Titanic strife.

When Goethe's death was told, we said: 15
Sunk, then, is Europe's sagest head.
Physician of the iron age,
Goethe has done his pilgrimage.
He took the suffering human race,
He read each wound, each weakness clear;   20
And struck his finger on the place,
And said: *Thou ailest here, and here!*
He looked on Europe's dying hour
Of fitful dream and feverish power;
His eye plunged down the weltering strife,   25
The turmoil of expiring life—
He said: *The end is everywhere;*
Art still has truth, take refuge there!
And he was happy, if to know
Causes of things, and far below   30
His feet to see the lurid flow
Of terror, and insane distress,
And headlong fate, be happiness.

---

8 *little:* because his poetry had "no critical effort behind it" and hence would
not endure. In his essay on Byron, Arnold agreed with Goethe's estimate
that although Byron had a splendid personality and possessed "the greatest
talent of our century" he failed because "the moment he reflects he is a child."
17 *iron age:* 1789–1832, the age of revolution and war in politics, poetry, and
thought.   23 *dying hour:* the pre-Napoleonic, nonindustrial world of dogma,
royal rule, and hierarchical absolutism. In "On the Study of Celtic Literature"
[VI], Arnold wrote: "But when Goethe came, Europe had lost her basis of
spiritual life; she had to find it again; Goethe's task was,—the inevitable task
for the modern poet henceforth is,—as it was for the Greek poet in the days of
Pericles, not to preach a sublime sermon on a traditional text like Dante, not
to exhibit all the kingdoms of human life like Shakespeare, but to interpret
human life afresh, and to supply a new spiritual basis to it."   29–33 *And . . .*
happiness: an allusion to Virgil, *Georgics*, II, ll. 490–94: "Blessed is he who has
been able to win knowledge of the causes of things, and has cast beneath his
feet all fear and unyielding Fate, and the howls of hungry Acheron!" (trans.
Fairclough). These lines apply to Goethe. But Virgil continues, "Happy, too,
is he who knows the woodland gods, Pan and old Silvanus and the sister
nymphs," lines that describe Wordsworth's genius and career.

And Wordsworth!—Ah, pale ghosts, rejoice!
For never has such soothing voice 35
Been to your shadowy world conveyed,
Since erst, at morn, some wandering shade
Heard the clear song of Orpheus come
Through Hades, and the mournful gloom.
Wordsworth has gone from us—and ye, 40
Ah, may ye feel his voice as we!
He too upon a wintry clime
Had fallen—on this iron time
Of doubts, disputes, distractions, fears.
He found us when the age had bound 45
Our souls in its benumbing round;
He spoke, and loosed our heart in tears.
He laid us as we lay at birth
On the cool flowery lap of earth,
Smiles broke from us and we had ease; 50
The hills were round us, and the breeze
Went o'er the sun-lit fields again;
Our foreheads felt the wind and rain.
Our youth returned; for there was shed
On spirits that had long been dead, 55
Spirits dried up and closely furled,
The freshness of the early world.

Ah! since dark days still bring to light
Man's prudence and man's fiery might,
Time may restore us in his course 60
Goethe's sage mind and Byron's force;
But where will Europe's latter hour
Again find Wordsworth's healing power?
Others will teach us how to dare,
And against fear our breast to steel; 65
Others will strengthen us to bear—
But who, ah! who, will make us feel?
The cloud of mortal destiny,
Others will front it fearlessly—
But who, like him, will put it by? 70

Keep fresh the grass upon his grave
O Rotha, with thy living wave!
Sing him thy best! for few or none
Hears thy voice right, now he is gone.

38 *clear song:* the vivifying song Orpheus sang to Pluto, god of the under-world and the dead, which so entranced the latter that he released Orpheus' wife, Eurydice. Cf. Milton, "L'Allegro," l. 145 and note. 72 *Rotha:* stream near the churchyard at Grasmere where Wordsworth is buried.

The Scholar Gipsy

Go, for they call you, shepherd, from the hill;
  Go, shepherd, and untie the wattled cotes!
    No longer leave thy wistful flock unfed,
  Nor let thy bawling fellows rack their throats,
    Nor the cropp'd herbage shoot another head.   5
      But when the fields are still,
  And the tired men and dogs all gone to rest,
    And only the white sheep are sometimes seen
    Cross and recross the strips of moon-blanch'd green,
      Come, shepherd, and again begin the quest!   10

Here, where the reaper was at work of late—
  In this high field's dark corner, where he leaves
    His coat, his basket, and his earthen cruse,
  And in the sun all morning binds the sheaves,
    Then here, at noon, comes back his stores to use—   15
      Here will I sit and wait,
  While to my ear from uplands far away
    The bleating of the folded flocks is borne;
    With distant cries of reapers in the corn—
      All the live murmur of a summer's day.   20

Screen'd is this nook o'er the high, half-reap'd field,
  And here till sun-down, shepherd! will I be.
    Through the thick corn the scarlet poppies peep,
  And round green roots and yellowing stalks I see

THE SCHOLAR GIPSY.   The poem was originally prefaced with the following condensed version of a passage in Joseph Glanvill's *Vanity of Dogmatizing*, 1661:
"There was very lately a lad in the University of Oxford, who was by his poverty forced to leave his studies there; and at last to join himself to a company of vagabond gipsies. Among these extravagant people, by the insinuating subtilty of his carriage, he quickly got so much of their love and esteem as that they discovered to him their mystery. After he had been a pretty while well exercised in the trade, there chanced to ride by a couple of scholars, who had formerly been of his acquaintance. They quickly spied out their old friend among the gipsies; and he gave them an account of the necessity which drove him to that kind of life, and told them that the people he went with were not such impostors as they were taken for, but that they had a traditional kind of learning among them, and could do wonders by the power of the imagination, their fancy binding that of others: that himself had learned much of their art, and when he had compassed the whole secret, he intended, he said, to leave their company, and give the world an account of what he had learned."

  1 *they:* i.e., the sheep.   2 *wattled cotes:* sheepfolds made of interwoven rods and twigs.   4 *rack:* strain.   10 *quest:* search for the Scholar Gipsy and his secret. See l. 63.   13 *cruse:* water pot or jar.   18 *folded:* penned up.   19 *corn:* i.e., wheat.

Pale pink convolvulus in tendrils creep;   25
    And air-swept lindens yield
Their scent, and rustle down their perfum'd showers
    Of bloom on the bent grass where I am laid,
    And bower me from the August sun with shade;
        And the eye travels down to Oxford's towers.   30

And near me on the grass lies Glanvil's book—
    Come, let me read the oft-read tale again!
    The story of that Oxford scholar poor
    Of pregnant parts and quick inventive brain,
        Who, tir'd of knocking at preferment's door,   35
        One summer morn forsook
His friends, and went to learn the gipsy lore,
    And roam'd the world with that wild brotherhood,
    And came, as most men deem'd, to little good,
        But came to Oxford and his friends no more.   40

But once, years after, in the country lanes,
    Two scholars, whom at college erst he knew,
    Met him, and of his way of life inquir'd.
Whereat he answer'd, that the gipsy crew,
        His mates, had arts to rule as they desir'd   45
        The workings of men's brains,
And they can bind them to what thoughts they will.
    "And I," he said, "the secret of their art,
    When fully learn'd, will to the world impart;
        But it needs heaven-sent moments for this skill."   50

This said, he left them, and return'd no more.—
    But rumors hung about the countryside,
    That the lost Scholar long was seen to stray,
Seen by rare glimpses, pensive and tongue-tied,
        In hat of antique shape, and cloak of gray,   55
        The same the gipsies wore.
Shepherds had met him on the Hurst in spring,
    At some lone alehouse in the Berkshire moors,
    On the warm ingle-bench, the smock-frock'd boors
        Had found him seated at their entering,   60

---

25 *convolvulus:* bindweed, morning-glory. 28 *bent grass:* a kind of stiff grass, such as grows on commons. 29 *bower:* enclose. 30 *Oxford's towers:* all the proper names, unless otherwise noted, are of places around Oxford. 35 *preferment's door:* advancement through ecclesiastical appointment. 46 *arts:* i.e., of hypnotism. 58 *Berkshire:* county adjacent to Oxfordshire. 59 *ingle-bench:* a bench in a nook by a fireplace. *boors:* rustic farmhands.

But, mid their drink and clatter, he would fly.
  And I myself seem half to know thy looks,
    And put the shepherds, wanderer! on thy trace;
  And boys who in lone wheatfields scare the rooks
    I ask if thou hast pass'd their quiet place;   65
      Or in my boat I lie
  Moor'd to the cool bank in the summer-heats,
    Mid wide grass meadows which the sunshine fills,
    And watch the warm, green-muffled Cumner hills,
      And wonder if thou haunt'st their shy retreats.   70

For most, I know, thou lov'st retired ground!
  Thee, at the ferry, Oxford riders blithe,
    Returning home on summer-nights, have met
  Crossing the stripling Thames at Bab-lock-hithe,
    Trailing in the cool stream thy fingers wet,   75
      As the punt's rope chops round;
  And leaning backwards in a pensive dream,
    And fostering in thy lap a heap of flowers
    Pluck'd in shy fields and distant Wychwood bowers,
      And thine eyes resting on the moonlit stream.   80

And then they land, and thou art seen no more!—
  Maidens who from the distant hamlets come
    To dance around the Fyfield elm in May,
  Oft through the darkening fields have seen thee roam,
    Or cross a stile into the public way.   85
      Oft thou hast given them store
  Of flowers—the frail-leaf'd, white anemone,
    Dark bluebells drench'd with dews of summer eves,
    And purple orchises with spotted leaves—
      But none hath words she can report of thee.   90

And, above Godstow Bridge, when hay-time's here
  In June, and many a scythe in sunshine flames,
    Men who through those wide fields of breezy grass
  Where black-wing'd swallows haunt the glittering Thames,
    To bathe in the abandon'd lasher pass,   95
      Have often pass'd thee near

---

76 *punt's . . . round:* As the rope that pulls the punt (a small, flatbottomed boat used at the ferry crossing) suddenly shifts with the wind and current. Early editions read: *As the slow punt swings round.* 78 *fostering:* cherishing, caressing. *Godstow Bridge:* a short distance above a lock confining the water of the Thames north of Oxford. 95 *lasher:* both the slack water collected above a weir or lock and the violent water that "lashes" through the overflow opening of the weir into a dangerous pool below.

Sitting upon the river bank o'ergrown;
   Mark'd thy outlandish garb, thy figure spare,
    Thy dark vague eyes, and soft abstracted air—
      But, when they came from bathing, thou wast gone.   100

At some lone homestead in the Cumner hills,
   Where at her open door the housewife darns,
    Thou hast been seen, or hanging on a gate
   To watch the threshers in the mossy barns.
      Children, who early range these slopes and late   105
       For cresses from the rills,
   Have known thee eying, all an April day,
    The springing pastures and the feeding kine;
    And mark'd thee, when the stars come out and shine,
      Through the long dewy grass move slow away.   110

In autumn, on the skirts of Bagley wood—
   Where most the gipsies by the turf-edg'd way
    Pitch their smoked tents, and every bush you see
   With scarlet patches tagg'd and shreds of gray,
      Above the forest-ground called Thessaly—   115
       The blackbird picking food
   Sees thee, nor stops his meal, nor fears at all;
    So often has he known thee past him stray,
    Rapt, twirling in thy hand a wither'd spray,
      And waiting for the spark from heaven to fall.   120

And once, in winter, on the causeway chill
   Where home through flooded fields foot-travellers go,
    Have I not pass'd thee on the wooden bridge
   Wrapt in thy cloak and battling with the snow,
      Thy face tow'rd Hinksey and its wintry ridge?   125
       And thou hast climb'd the hill,
   And gain'd the white brow of the Cumner range;
    Turn'd once to watch, while thick the snow-flakes fall,
    The line of festal light in Christ-Church hall—
      Then sought thy straw in some sequester'd grange.   130

---

108 *springing:* sprouting, growing; also, flowing with water from springs. 115 *Thessaly:* also the region in northeastern Greece bounded on the north by the Aegean Sea and by Mount Olympus, legendary home of the gods; in mythology regarded as preeminently the country of magicians; hence an appropriate spot for the Scholar Gipsy to be seen. 129 *Christ-Church hall:* the dining hall of Christ Church College at Oxford. 130 *grange:* farmhouse with granary and barns.

But what—I dream! Two hundred years are flown
  Since first thy story ran through Oxford halls,
    And the grave Glanvil did the tale inscribe
  That thou wert wander'd from the studious walls
    To learn strange arts, and join a gipsy tribe;   135
      And thou from earth art gone
  Long since, and in some quiet churchyard laid—
    Some country nook, where o'er thy unknown grave
    Tall grasses and white flowering nettles wave,
      Under a dark, red-fruited yew-tree's shade.   140

—No, no, thou hast not felt the lapse of hours!
  For what wears out the life of mortal men?
    'Tis that from change to change their being rolls;
  'Tis that repeated shocks, again, again,
    Exhaust the energy of strongest souls   145
      And numb the elastic powers.
  Till having us'd our nerves with bliss and teen,
    And tir'd upon a thousand schemes our wit,
    To the just-pausing Genius we remit
      Our worn-out life, and are—what we have been.   150

Thou hast not liv'd, why shouldst thou perish, so?
  Thou hadst *one* aim, *one* business, *one* desire;
    Else wert thou long since number'd with the dead!
  Else hadst thou spent, like other men, thy fire!
    The generations of thy peers are fled,   155
      And we ourselves shall go;
  But thou possessest an immortal lot,
    And we imagine thee exempt from age
    And living as thou liv'st on Glanvil's page,
      Because thou hadst—what we, alas! have not.   160

For early didst thou leave the world, with powers
  Fresh, undiverted to the world without,
    Firm to their mark, not spent on other things;
  Free from the sick fatigue, the languid doubt,
    Which much to have tried, in much been baffled, brings.   165
      O life unlike to ours!
  Who fluctuate idly without term or scope,
    Of whom each strives, nor knows for what he strives,
    And each half lives a hundred different lives;
      Who wait like thee, but not, like thee, in hope.   170

147 *us'd:* exhausted. *teen:* grief, vexation. 149 *just-pausing Genius:* perhaps
the life-giving spirit of the universe that pauses at a man's death to receive
back the life it had given him.

Thou waitest for the spark from heaven! and we,
  Light half-believers of our casual creeds,
    Who never deeply felt, nor clearly will'd,
  Whose insight never has borne fruit in deeds,
    Whose vague resolves never have been fulfill'd;   175
      For whom each year we see
Breeds new beginnings, disappointments new;
  Who hesitate and falter life away,
  And lose to-morrow the ground won to-day—
    Ah! do not we, wanderer! await it too?   180

Yes, we await it!—but it still delays,
  And then we suffer! and amongst us one,
    Who most has suffer'd, takes dejectedly
  His seat upon the intellectual throne;
    And all his store of sad experience he   185
      Lays bare of wretched days;
Tells us his misery's birth and growth and signs,
  And how the dying spark of hope was fed,
  And how the breast was sooth'd, and how the head,
    And all his hourly varied anodynes.   190

This for our wisest! and we others pine,
  And wish the long unhappy dream would end,
    And waive all claim to bliss, and try to bear;
  With close-lipp'd patience for our only friend,
    Sad patience, too near neighbor to despair—   195
      But none has hope like thine!
Thou through the fields and through the woods dost stray,
  Roaming the country side, a truant boy,
  Nursing thy project in unclouded joy,
    And every doubt long blown by time away.   200

O born in days when wits were fresh and clear,
  And life ran gaily as the sparkling Thames;
    Before this strange disease of modern life,
  With its sick hurry, its divided aims,
    Its heads o'ertax'd, its palsied hearts, was rife—   205
      Fly hence, our contact fear!

---

182 *one:* probably Tennyson, whose *In Memoriam* was published in 1850, or
possibly Goethe. Arnold, however, had a low opinion of Tennyson's intellect,
even though "intellectual throne" is from Tennyson's "Palace of Art," l. 216.
190 *anodynes:* soothing pain-killers, not healing drugs.

Still fly, plunge deeper in the bowering wood!
    Averse, as Dido did with gesture stern
    From her false friend's approach in Hades turn,
        Wave us away, and keep thy solitude.   210

Still nursing the unconquerable hope,
    Still clutching the inviolable shade,
      With a free onward impulse brushing through,
    By night, the silver'd branches of the glade—
        Far on the forest-skirts, where none pursue,   215
          On some mild pastoral slope
Emerge, and resting on the moonlit pales
    Freshen thy flowers, as in former years
    With dew, or listen with enchanted ears,
        From the dark dingles, to the nightingales!   220

But fly our paths, our feverish contact fly!
    For strong the infection of our mental strife,
      Which, though it gives no bliss, yet spoils for rest;
    And we should win thee from thy own fair life,
        Like us distracted, and like us unblest.   225
          Soon, soon thy cheer would die,
Thy hopes grow timorous, and unfix'd thy powers,
    And thy clear aims be cross and shifting made;
    And then thy glad perennial youth would fade,
        Fade, and grow old at last, and die like ours.   230

Then fly our greetings, fly our speech and smiles!
    —As some grave Tyrian trader, from the sea,
    Descried at sunrise an emerging prow
Lifting the cool-hair'd creepers stealthily,
      The fringes of a southward-facing brow   235
        Among the Aegean isles;

208 *Dido:* Dido committed suicide after Aeneas deserted her; when he later encountered her shade in the Mourning Fields of Hades (*Aeneid*, VI, ll. 440–76), she spurned his attentions, still grimly unforgiving.   211 *hope:* Cf. l. 120. 217 *pales:* boundary fences. 220 *dingles:* deep, narrow valleys. 232 *Tyrian:* Phoenician (from Tyre). The Phoenicians were the earliest traders in the Mediterranean and hence can be likened to the Scholar Gipsy in his gravity and old-fashioned ways.   233 *prow:* of the rival *Grecian coaster* (l. 237).

And saw the merry Grecian coaster come,
   Freighted with amber grapes, and Chian wine,
   Green, bursting figs, and tunnies steep'd in brine—
    And knew the intruders on his ancient home,   240

The young light-hearted masters of the waves—
   And snatch'd his rudder, and shook out more sail;
   And day and night held on indignantly
O'er the blue Midland waters with the gale,
   Betwixt the Syrtes and soft Sicily,   245
    To where the Atlantic raves
Outside the western straits; and unbent sails
   There, where down cloudy cliffs, through sheets of foam,
   Shy traffickers, the dark Iberians come;
    And on the beach undid his corded bales.   250

Dover Beach

The sea is calm to-night.
The tide is full, the moon lies fair
Upon the Straits;—on the French coast, the light
Gleams and is gone; the cliffs of England stand,
Glimmering and vast, out in the tranquil bay.   5
Come to the window, sweet is the night air!
Only, from the long line of spray
Where the ebb meets the moon-blanch'd land,
Listen! you hear the grating roar
Of pebbles which the waves suck back, and fling,   10
At their return, up the high strand,
Begin, and cease, and then again begin,
With tremulous cadence slow, and bring
The eternal note of sadness in.

---

238 *Chian:* of Chios, an Aegean island (see l. 236), inhabited by Greeks.
239 *tunnies:* tuna fish, an important food-fish systematically fished from the
days of the Phoenicians to the present. 241 *masters:* i.e., the Greeks, exuberant like the ordinary Oxford undergraduates. 245 *Syrtes:* Syrtis Major and
Minor, sand banks off the coast of North Africa. 247 *western straits:*
Gibraltar. 249 *Iberians:* Dark (like the gypsies) inhabitants of Spain and
Portugal.

DOVER BEACH. 9–11 *grating . . . strand:* perhaps an allusion to *King Lear*,
IV, vi, 20–22, where Edgar describes the height of the cliffs at Dover: "The
murmuring surge, / That on th'unnumbered idle pebble chafes / Cannot be
heard so high."

Sophocles long ago   15
Heard it on the Aegean, and it brought
Into his mind the turbid ebb and flow
Of human misery; we
Find also in the sound a thought,
Hearing it by this distant northern sea.   20

The Sea of Faith
Was once, too, at the full, and round earth's shore
Lay like the folds of a bright girdle furl'd.
But now I only hear
Its melancholy, long, withdrawing roar,   25
Retreating, to the breath
Of the night-wind, down the vast edges drear
And naked shingles of the world.

Ah, love, let us be true
To one another! for the world, which seems   30
To lie before us like a land of dreams,
So various, so beautiful, so new,

---

15 *Sophocles:* See *Antigone*, ll. 583 ff. (Ode II), where the Chorus speaks of
God's vengeance on the doomed house of Oedipus:

> Where once the anger of heaven has struck, that house is shaken
> Forever: damnation rises behind each child
> Like a wave cresting out of the black northeast,
> When the long darkness under sea roars up
> And bursts drumming death upon the windwhipped sand.
>   (Trans. Fitts and Fitzgerald)

Cf. also *Oedipus at Colonnus*, epode of 3rd stasimon (Choral Poem, sc. v),
which also describes the fate of Oedipus:

> Think of some shore in the north
> Concussive waves make stream
> This way and that in gales of winter:
> It is like that with him:
> The wild wrack breaking over him
> From head to foot, and coming on forever.
>   (Trans. Fitzgerald)

17 *ebb and flow:* but there is no tide in the Mediterranean Sea. 23 *bright
girdle:* an image from the classical Greek and early medieval concept of the
ocean as a river that girdles the circumference of a flat earth. See the description
of Achilles' shield in the *Iliad*, XVIII: "He made on it the great strength of the
Ocean River / which ran around the uttermost rim of the shield's strong structure" (ll. 606–07, trans. Lattimore). This simile suggests accurately how the old
faith supported by the old astronomy had been radically altered if not ruined
by the new science. 28 *shingles:* an onomatopoetic word, usually singular, for
the coarse, waterworn gravel and debris on beaches, so named from the "singing" noise made by walking on it. Cf. "singing sands." *Shingle* also means
"waist." Cf. *girdle*, l. 23.

Hath really neither joy, nor love, nor light,
Nor certitude, nor peace, nor help for pain;
And we are here as on a darkling plain   35
Swept with confused alarms of struggle and flight,
Where ignorant armies clash by night.

---

35 *darkling:* dark, obscure.   35–37 *plain . . . night:* The source of this figure
is Thucydides, *History of the Peloponnesian War*, VII, Ch. 44, in which he
describes the defeat of the Athenians (who in the whole course of the war were
not *true* / *To one another*) in the night battle of Epipolae (see Kenneth Allott,
The Poems of Matthew Arnold, p. 243):

"By this time the Athenians were getting into a state of great confusion and
perplexity . . . in a battle by night . . . how could anyone know anything
clearly? For though there was a bright moon, they could only see one another,
as it is natural to do in moonlight—seeing before them the vision of a person
but mistrusting their recognition of their own friends . . . . For the front lines
were already all in confusion . . . and the two sides were difficult to distinguish
by reason of the outcries. The Syracusans . . . were cheering; . . . the Athenians . . . were constantly calling out the demand for the watchword . . . .
That which put the Athenians at the greatest disadvantage . . . was the singing
of the paean; for the song of both armies was very similar and caused perplexity . . . . And so finally, when once they had been thrown into confusion,
coming into collision with their own comrades in many different parts of the
army, friends with friends and citizens with fellow-citizens, they not only became panic-stricken but came to blows with one another . . . ."

(Trans. C. Forster Smith)

The allusions in the poem to these works of Shakespeare, Sophocles, and
Thucydides, all of which deal with the hubris and selfishness of men and
nations and the tragic disasters that necessarily ensue, with the destruction of
the most intimate of human relationships, as well as with religious doubt,
underscore the primacy of true love between palpable human beings, which
though frail is the best and only hope there is. Apparently Arnold wrote this
poem shortly after his marriage on June 10, 1851 (see Allott, pp. 239–40).

WALT WHITMAN
1819–1892

Give me the splendid silent sun

1

Give me the splendid silent sun with all his beams full-dazzling,
Give me juicy autumnal fruit ripe and red from the orchard,
Give me a field where the unmow'd grass grows,
Give me an arbor, give me the trellis'd grape,
Give me fresh corn and wheat, give me serene-moving animals
    teaching content,   5
Give me nights perfectly quiet as on high plateaus west of the
    Mississippi, and I looking up at the stars,
Give me odorous at sunrise a garden of beautiful flowers where I
    can walk undisturb'd.
Give me for marriage a sweet-breath'd woman of whom I should
    never tire,
Give me a perfect child, give me away aside from the noise of the
    world a rural domestic life,
Give me to warble spontaneous songs recluse by myself, for my own
    ears only,   10
Give me solitude, give me Nature, give me again O nature your
    primal sanities!

These demanding to have them (tired with ceaseless excitement, and
    rack'd by the war-strife),
These to procure incessantly asking, rising in cries from my heart,
While yet incessantly asking still I adhere to my city,
Day upon day and year upon year O city, walking your streets, 15
Where you hold me enchain'd a certain time refusing to give me up,
Yet giving to make me glutted, enrich'd of soul, you give me forever
    faces;
(O I see what I sought to escape, confronting, reversing my cries,
I see my own soul trampling down what it ask'd for).

2

Keep your splendid silent sun,   20
Keep your woods, O Nature, and the quiet places by the woods,
Keep your fields of clover and timothy, and your corn-fields and
    orchards,
Keep the blossoming buckwheat fields where the Ninth-month bees
    hum;

GIVE ME THE SPLENDID. 12 *war-strife:* i.e., of the Civil War. 23 *Ninth-month bees:* September bees.

Give me faces and streets—give me these phantoms incessant and endless along the trottoirs!

Give me interminable eyes—give me women—give me comrades and lovers by the thousand!   25

Let me see new ones every day—let me hold new ones by the hand every day!

Give me such shows—give me the streets of Manhattan!

Give me Broadway, with the soldiers marching—give me the sound of the trumpets and drums!

(The soldiers in companies or regiments—some starting away, flush'd and reckless,

Some, their time up, returning with thinn'd ranks, young, yet very old, worn, marching, noticing nothing);   30

Give me the shores and wharves heavy-fring'd with black ships!

O such for me! O an intense life, full to repletion and varied!

The life of the theatre, bar-room, huge hotel, for me!

The saloon of the steamer! the crowded excursion for me! the torchlight procession!

The dense brigade bound for the war, with high piled military wagons following;   35

People, endless, streaming, with strong voices, passions, pageants,

Manhattan streets with their powerful throbs, with beating drums as now,

The endless and noisy chorus, the rustle and clank of muskets (even the sight of the wounded),

Manhattan crowds, with their turbulent musical chorus!

Manhattan faces and eyes forever for me.   40

Cavalry Crossing a Ford

A line in long array where they wind betwixt green islands,

They take a serpentine course, their arms flash in the sun—hark to the musical clank,

Behold the silvery river, in it the splashing horses loitering stop to drink,

Behold the brown-faced men, each group, each person a picture, the negligent rest on the saddles,

Some emerge on the opposite bank, others are just entering the ford—while,   5

Scarlet and blue and snowy white,

The guidon flags flutter gayly in the wind.

---

24 *trottoirs:* sidewalks.   30 *time:* term of enlistment.   35 *dense:* i.e., with its full complement.   Cf. *thinn'd ranks,* l. 30.

By the bivouac's fitful flame

By the bivouac's fitful flame,
A procession winding around me, solemn and sweet and slow—but
    first I note,
The tents of the sleeping army, the fields' and woods' dim outline,
The darkness lit by spots of kindled fire, the silence,
Like a phantom far or near an occasional figure moving,   5
The shrubs and trees, (as I lift my eyes they seem to be stealthily
    watching me,)
While wind in procession thoughts, O tender and wondrous
    thoughts,
Of life and death, of home and the past and loved, and of those that
    are far away;
A solemn and slow procession there as I sit on the ground,
By the bivouac's fitful flame.   10

As toilsome I wander'd Virginia's woods

As toilsome I wander'd Virginia's woods,
To the music of rustling leaves kick'd by my feet, (for 'twas autumn,)
I mark'd at the foot of a tree the grave of a soldier;
Mortally wounded he and buried on the retreat, (easily all could I
    understand,)
The halt of a mid-day hour, when up! no time to lose—yet this sign
    left,   5
On a tablet scrawl'd and nail'd on the tree by the grave,
Bold, cautious, true, and my loving comrade.

Long, long I muse, then on my way go wandering,
Many a changeful season to follow, and many a scene of life,
Yet at times through changeful season and scene, abrupt, alone,
    or in the crowded street,   10
Comes before me the unknown soldier's grave, comes the inscription
    rude in Virginia's woods,
Bold, cautious, true, and my loving comrade.

When lilacs last in the door-yard bloom'd

1

When lilacs last in the door-yard bloom'd,
And the great star early droop'd in the western sky in the night,
I mourn'd, and yet shall mourn with ever-returning spring.

Ever-returning spring, trinity sure to me you bring,
Lilac blooming perennial and drooping star in the west,　　　　5
And thought of him I love.

2

O powerful western fallen star!
O shades of night—O moody, tearful night!
O great star disappear'd—O the black murk that hides the star!
O cruel hands that hold me powerless—O helpless soul of me!　10
O harsh surrounding cloud that will not free my soul.

3

In the dooryard fronting an old farm-house near the white-wash'd
　　　palings,
Stands the lilac-bush tall-growing with heart-shaped leaves of rich
　　　green,
With many a pointed blossom rising delicate, with the perfume
　　　strong I love,
With every leaf a miracle—and from this bush in the dooryard,　15
With delicate color'd blossoms and heart-shaped leaves of rich
　　　green,
A sprig with its flower I break.

4

In the swamp in secluded recesses,
A shy and hidden bird is warbling a song.

Solitary the thrush,　　　　　　　　　　　　　　　　　　　　　　20
The hermit withdrawn to himself, avoiding the settlements,
Sings by himself a song.

Song of the bleeding throat,
Death's outlet song of life (for well dear brother I know,
If thou wast not granted to sing thou would'st surely die).　　25

5

Over the breast of the spring, the land, amid cities,
Amid lanes and through old woods, where lately the violets peep'd
　　　from the ground, spotting the gray debris,
Amid the grass in the fields each side of the lanes, passing the
　　　endless grass,

WHEN LILACS LAST. 6 *him:* Abraham Lincoln, assassinated April 14, 1865.
Lincoln's body was taken to Springfield, Illinois, for burial. See ll. 26 ff.
12 *palings:* fence pickets.

Passing the yellow-spear'd wheat, every grain from its shroud in the
      dark-brown fields uprisen,
Passing the apple-tree blows of white and pink in the
      orchards,   30
Carrying a corpse to where it shall rest in the grave,
Night and day journeys a coffin.

6

Coffin that passes through lanes and streets,
Through day and night with the great cloud darkening the land,
With the pomp of the inloop'd flags with the cities draped in
      black,   35
With the show of the States themselves as of crape-veil'd women
      standing,
With processions long and winding and the flambeaus of the night,
With the countless torches lit, with the silent sea of faces and the
      unbared heads,
With the waiting depot, the arriving coffin, and the sombre faces,
With dirges through the night, with the thousand voices rising
      strong and solemn,   40
With all the mournful voices of the dirges pour'd around the coffin,
The dim-lit churches and the shuddering organs—where amid these
      you journey,
With the tolling tolling bells' perpetual clang,
Here, coffin that slowly passes,
I give you my sprig of lilac.   45

7

(Nor for you, for one alone,
Blossoms and branches green to coffins all I bring,
For fresh as the morning, thus would I chant a song for you
      O sane and sacred death.

All over bouquets of roses,
O death, I cover you over with roses and early lilies,   50
But mostly and now the lilac that blooms the first,
Copious I break, I break the sprigs from the bushes,
With loaded arms I come, pouring for you,
For you and the coffins all of you O death.)

8

O western orb sailing the heaven,   55
Now I know what you must have meant as a month since I walk'd,
As I walk'd in silence the transparent shadowy night,

30 *blows:* blossoms.   37 *flambeaus:* torches.

As I saw you had something to tell as you bent to me night after
    night,
As you droop'd from the sky low down as if to my side (while the
    other stars all look'd on),
As we wander'd together the solemn night (for something I know
    not what kept me from sleep),   60
As the night advanced, and I saw on the rim of the west how full
    you were of woe,
As I stood on the rising ground in the breeze in the cool transparent
    night,
As I watch'd where you pass'd and was lost in the netherward black
    of the night,
As my soul in its trouble dissatisfied sank, as where you sad orb,
Concluded, dropt in the night, and was gone.   65

9

Sing on there in the swamp,
O singer bashful and tender, I hear your notes, I hear your call,
I hear, I come presently, I understand you,
But a moment I linger, for the lustrous star has detain'd me,
The star my departing comrade holds and detains me.   70

10

O how shall I warble myself for the dead one there I loved?
And how shall I deck my song for the large sweet soul that has gone?
And what shall my perfume be for the grave of him I love?

Sea-winds blown from east and west,
Blown from the Eastern sea and blown from the Western sea,
    till there on the prairies meeting,   75
These and with these and the breath of my chant,
I'll perfume the grave of him I love.

11

O what shall I hang on the chamber walls?
And what shall the pictures be that I hang on the walls,
To adorn the burial-house of him I love?   80

Pictures of growing spring and farms and homes,
With the Fourth-month eve at sundown, and the gray smoke lucid
    and bright,
With floods of the yellow gold of the gorgeous, indolent, sinking
    sun, burning, expanding the air,

---

63 *netherward:* utter darkness (of the underworld).

With the fresh sweet herbage under foot, and the pale green leaves
    of the trees prolific,
In the distance the flowing glaze, the breast of the river, with a
    wind-dapple here and there,   85
With ranging hills on the banks, with many a line against the sky,
    and shadows,
And the city at hand with dwellings so dense, and stacks of
    chimneys,
And all the scenes of life and the workshops, and the workmen
    homeward returning.

12

Lo, body and soul—this land,
My own Manhattan with spires, and the sparkling and hurrying
    tides, and the ships,   90
The varied and ample land, the South and the North in the light,
    Ohio's shores and flashing Missouri,
And ever the far-spreading prairies cover'd with grass and corn.

Lo, the most excellent sun so calm and haughty,
The violet and purple morn with just-felt breezes,
The gentle soft-born measureless light,   95
The miracle spreading bathing all, the fulfill'd noon,
The coming eve delicious, the welcome night and the stars,
Over my cities shining all, enveloping man and land.

13

Sing on, sing on you gray-brown bird,
Sing from the swamps, the recesses, pour your chant from the
    bushes,   100
Limitless out of the dusk, out of the cedars and pines.

Sing on dearest brother, warble your reedy song,
Loud human song, with voice of uttermost woe.

O liquid and free and tender!
O wild and loose to my soul—O wondrous singer!   105
You only I hear—yet the star holds me (but will soon depart),
Yet the lilac with mastering odor holds me.

14

Now while I sat in the day and look'd forth,
In the close of the day with its light and the fields of spring, and the
    farmers preparing their crops,
In the large unconscious scenery of my land with its lakes and
    forests,   110

In the heavenly aerial beauty (after the perturb'd winds and the
      storms),
Under the arching heavens of the afternoon swift passing, and the
      voices of children and women,
The many-moving sea-tides, and I saw the ships how they sail'd,
And the summer approaching with richness, and the fields all busy
      with labor,
And the infinite separate houses, how they all went on, each with its
      meals and minutia of daily usages,   115
And the streets how their throbbings throbb'd, and the cities
      pent—lo, then and there,
Falling upon them all and among them all, enveloping me with the
      rest,
Appear'd the cloud, appear'd the long black trail,
And I knew death, its thought, and the sacred knowledge of death.

Then with the knowledge of death as walking one side of me,   120
And the thought of death close-walking the other side of me,
And I in the middle as with companions, and as holding the hands
      of companions,
I fled forth to the hiding receiving night that talks not,
Down to the shores of the water, the path by the swamp in the
      dimness,
To the solemn shadowy cedars and ghostly pines so still.   125

And the singer so shy to the rest receiv'd me,
The gray-brown bird I know receiv'd us comrades three,
And he sang the carol of death, and a verse for him I love.

From deep secluded recesses,
From the fragrant cedars and the ghostly pines so still,   130
Came the carol of the bird.
And the charm of the carol rapt me,
As I held as if by their hands my comrades in the night,
And the voice of my spirit tallied the song of the bird.

Come lovely and soothing death,   135
Undulate round the world, serenely arriving, arriving,
In the day, in the night, to all, to each,
Sooner or later delicate death.

Prais'd be the fathomless universe,
For life and joy, and for objects and knowledge curious,   140
And for love, sweet love—but praise! praise! praise!
For the sure-enwinding arms of cool-enfolding death.

134 *tallied:* corresponded, agreed with. (Cf. a notched tally stick, the two halves
matching each other).

Dark mother always gliding near with soft feet,
Have none chanted for thee a chant of fullest welcome?
Then I chant it for thee, I glorify thee above all,   145
I bring thee a song that when thou must indeed come, come
          unfalteringly.

Approach strong deliveress,
When it is so, when thou hast taken them I joyously sing the dead,
Lost in the loving floating ocean of thee,
Laved in the flood of thy bliss O death.   150

From me to thee glad serenades,
Dances for thee I propose saluting thee, adornments and feastings for
          thee,
And the sights of the open landscape and the high-spread sky are
          fitting,
And life and the fields, and the huge and thoughtful night.

The night in silence under many a star,   155
The ocean shore and the husky whispering wave whose voice I know,
And the soul turning to thee O vast and well-veil'd death,
And the body gratefully nestling close to thee.

Over the tree-tops I float thee a song,
Over the rising and sinking waves, over the myriad fields and the
          prairies wide,   160
Over the dense-pack'd cities all and the teeming wharves and ways,
I float this carol with joy, with joy to thee O death.

15

To the tally of my soul,
Loud and strong kept up the gray-brown bird,
With pure deliberate notes spreading filling the night.   165

Loud in the pines and cedars dim,
Clear in the freshness moist and the swamp-perfume,
And I with my comrades there in the night.

While my sight that was bound in my eyes unclosed,
As to long panoramas of visions.   170

163 *tally:* corresponding account. Cf. ll. 134, 187, 200.   198 *retrievements:*
things recovered or restored.

And I saw askant the armies,
I saw as in noiseless dreams hundreds of battle-flags,
Borne through the smoke of the battles and pierc'd with missiles I
    saw them,
And carried hither and yon through the smoke, and torn and
    bloody,
And at last but a few shreds left on the staffs (and all in
    silence),   175
And the staffs all splinter'd and broken.

I saw battle-corpses, myriads of them,
And the white skeletons of young men, I saw them,
I saw the debris and debris of all the slain soldiers of the war,
But I saw they were not as was thought,   180
They themselves were fully at rest, they suffer'd not,
The living remain'd and suffer'd, the mother suffer'd,
And the wife and the child and the musing comrade suffer'd,
And the armies that remain'd suffer'd.

16

Passing the visions, passing the night,   185
Passing, unloosing the hold of my comrades' hands,
Passing the song of the hermit bird and the tallying song of my soul,
Victorious song, death's outlet song, yet varying ever-altering song,
As low and wailing, yet clear the notes, rising and falling, flooding
    the night,
Sadly sinking and fainting, as warning and warning, and yet again
    bursting with joy,   190
Covering the earth and filling the spread of the heaven,
As that powerful psalm in the night I heard from recesses,
Passing, I leave thee lilac with heart-shaped leaves,
I leave thee there in the door-yard, blooming, returning with spring.

I cease from my song for thee,   195
From my gaze on thee in the west, fronting the west, communing
    with thee,
O comrade lustrous with silver face in the night.

Yet each to keep and all, retrievements out of the night,
The song, the wondrous chant of the gray-brown bird,
And the tallying chant, the echo arous'd in my soul,   200
With the lustrous and drooping star with the countenance full of
    woe,
With the holders holding my hand nearing the call of the bird,

Comrades mine and I in the midst, and their memory ever to keep,
     for the dead I loved so well,
For the sweetest, wisest soul of all my days and lands—and this for
     his dear sake,
Lilac and star and bird twined with the chant of my soul,   205
There in the fragrant pines and the cedars dusk and dim.

When the full-grown poet came

When the full-grown poet came,
Out spake pleased Nature (the round impassive globe, with all its
     shows of day and night,) saying, *He is mine;*
But out spake too the Soul of man, proud, jealous and unreconciled,
     Nay, he is mine alone;
—Then the full-grown poet stood between the two, and took each
     by the hand;
And to-day and ever so stands, as blender, uniter, tightly holding
     hands,   5
Which he will never release until he reconciles the two,
And wholly and joyously blends them.

Good-bye my Fancy!

Good-bye my Fancy!
Farewell dear mate, dear love!
I'm going away, I know not where,
Or to what fortune, or whether I may ever see you again,
So Good-bye my Fancy.   5

Now for my last—let me look back a moment;
The slower fainter ticking of the clock is in me,
Exit, nightfall, and soon the heart-thud stopping.

Long have we lived, joy'd, caress'd together;
Delightful!—now separation—Good-bye my Fancy.   10

Yet let me not be too hasty,
Long indeed have we lived, slept, filter'd, become really blended into
     one;
Then if we die we die together, (yes, we'll remain one,)

GOOD-BYE MY FANCY!   *Fancy:* poetic imagination, creative spirit.

If we go anywhere we'll go together to meet what happens,
May-be we'll be better off and blither, and learn something,   15
May-be it is yourself now really ushering me to the true songs, (who
    knows?)
May-be it is you the mortal knob really undoing, turning—so now
    finally,
Good-bye—and hail! my Fancy.

18 *Good-bye—and hail:* Cf. Tennyson, "Frater Ave Atque Vale."

EMILY DICKINSON
1830–1886

18

The Gentian weaves her fringes—
The Maple's loom is red—
My departing blossoms
    Obviate parade.

A brief, but patient illness—   5
An hour to prepare,
And one below, this morning
Is where the angels are—
It was a short procession,
The Bobolink was there—   10
An aged Bee addressed us—
And then we knelt in prayer—
We trust that she was willing—
We ask that we may be.
Summer—Sister—Seraph!   15
Let us go with thee!

In the name of the Bee—
And of the Butterfly—
And of the Breeze—Amen!

187

How many times these low feet staggered—
Only the soldered mouth can tell—
Try—can you stir the awful rivet—
Try—can you lift the hasps of steel!

Stroke the cool forehead—hot so often—   5
Lift—if you care—the listless hair—
Handle the adamantine fingers
Never a thimble—more—shall wear—

The text of these poems, based on the "earliest fair copy," is that established by Thomas H. Johnson. The capitalization and punctuation are those of the poet herself, and although strange to modern eyes they reveal more accurately the intonation of the lines than could modern and conventional punctuation. For authentic variations in lines, words, and punctuation—and there are many —see the Johnson edition.

187.   7 *adamantine:* rigid, immovable.

Buzz the dull flies—on the chamber window—
Brave—shines the sun through the freckled pane—   10
Fearless—the cobweb swings from the ceiling—
Indolent Housewife—in Daisies—lain!

214

I taste a liquor never brewed—
From Tankards scooped in Pearl—
Not all the Frankfort Berries
Yield such an Alcohol!

Inebriate of Air—am I—   5
And Debauchee of Dew—
Reeling—thro endless summer days—
From inns of Molten Blue—

When "Landlords" turn the drunken Bee
Out of the Foxglove's door—   10
When Butterflies—renounce their "drams"—
I shall but drink the more!

Till Seraphs swing their snowy Hats—
And Saints—to windows run—
To see the little Tippler   15
From Manzanilla come!

303

The Soul selects her own Society—
Then—shuts the Door—
To her divine Majority—
Present no more—

Unmoved—she notes the Chariots—pausing—   5
At her low Gate—
Unmoved—an Emperor be kneeling
Upon her Mat—

214. 3 *Frankfort Berries:* i.e., the Sylvaner, Riesling, and Traminer grapes grown near Frankfort on Main, Germany, from which is produced the Stein-wein. 11 *dram:* a drink of spirits taken at a single gulp. 13 *Seraphs:* angels of the highest order, usually associated with the purifying power of fire. Note the oxymoron when combined with *snowy Hats.* 16 *Manzanilla:* a town near Seville, Spain, from which is named a sherry wine of unusually dry, light character. Perhaps also associated with Manzanillo, a port city in southeastern Cuba connected with the New England rum and molasses trade. An authentic variant for line 16 reads: *Leaning against the—Sun—*

I've known her—from an ample nation—
Choose One—   10
Then—close the Valves of her attention—
Like Stone—

328

A Bird came down the Walk—
He did not know I saw—
He bit an Angleworm in halves   *earthworm—used*
And ate the fellow, raw,   *for fishing*

And then he drank a Dew   *refreshing, gently falling*
From a convenient Grass—   *pure, (moisture)*   5
And then hopped sidewise to the Wall   *small*
To let a Beetle pass—   *drops*

He glanced with rapid eyes   *swift, quick (also water rapids)*
That hurried all around—
They looked like frightened Beads, I thought—   10
He stirred his Velvet Head

Like one in danger, Cautious,
I offered him a Crumb
And he unrolled his feathers   15
And rowed him softer home— } *Comparison to*
                                                    boat rowing
Than Oars divide the Ocean,)
Too silver for a seam—
Or Butterflies, off Banks of Noon
Leap, plashless as they swim.   20
          puddle or
          splash

341

After great pain, a formal feeling comes—
The Nerves sit ceremonious, like Tombs—
The stiff Heart questions was it He, that bore,
And Yesterday, or Centuries before?

328. 20 *plashless:* without a splash.
341. 3 *He:* presumably Jesus Christ.

The Feet, mechanical, go round— 5
Of Ground, or Air, or Ought—
A Wooden way
Regardless grown,
A Quartz contentment, like a stone—

This is the Hour of Lead— 10
Remembered, if outlived,
As Freezing persons, recollect the Snow—
First—Chill—then Stupor—then the letting go—

384

No Rack can torture me—
My Soul—at Liberty—
Behind this mortal Bone
There knits a bolder One—

You Cannot prick with saw— 5
Nor pierce with Cimitar—
Two Bodies—therefore be—
Bind One—The Other fly—

The Eagle of his Nest
No easier divest— 10
And gain the Sky
Than mayest Thou—

Except Thyself may be
Thine Enemy—
Captivity is Consciousness— 15
So's Liberty.

448

This was a Poet—It is That
Distills amazing sense
From ordinary Meanings—
And Attar so immense

From the familiar species 5
That perished by the Door—
We wonder it was not Ourselves
Arrested it—before—

Of Pictures, the Discloser—
The Poet—it is He—   10
Entitles Us—by Contrast—
To ceaseless Poverty—

Of Portion—so unconscious—
The Robbing—could not harm—
Himself—to Him—a Fortune—   15
Exterior—to Time—

501

This World is not Conclusion.
A Species stands beyond—
Invisible, as Music—
But positive, as Sound—
It beckons, and it baffles—   5
Philosophy—dont know—
And through a Riddle, at the last—
Sagacity, must go—
To guess it, puzzles scholars—
To gain it, Men have borne   10
Contempt of Generations
And Crucifixion, shown—
Faith slips—and laughs, and rallies—
Blushes, if any see—
Plucks at a twig of Evidence—   15
And asks a Vane, the way—
Much Gesture, from the Pulpit—
Strong Hallelujahs roll—
Narcotics cannot still the Tooth
That nibbles at the soul—   20

510

It was not Death, for I stood up,
And all the Dead, lie down—
It was not Night, for all the Bells
Put out their Tongues, for Noon.

510.   4 *Tongues:* the clappers of the bells.

It was not Frost, for on my Flesh   5
I felt Siroccos—crawl—
Nor Fire—for just my Marble feet
Could keep a Chancel, cool—

And yet, it tasted, like them all,
The Figures I have seen   10
Set orderly, for Burial,
Reminded me, of mine—

As if my life were shaven,
And fitted to a frame,
And could not breathe without a key,   15
And 'twas like Midnight, some—

When everything that ticked—has stopped—
And Space stares all around—
Or Grisly frosts—first Autumn morns,
Repeal the Beating Ground—   20

But, most, like Chaos—Stopless—cool—
Without a Chance, or Spar—
Or even a Report of Land—
To justify—Despair.

511

If you were coming in the Fall,
I'd brush the Summer by
With half a smile, and half a spurn,
As Housewives do, a Fly.

If I could see you in a year,   5
I'd wind the months in balls—
And put them each in separate Drawers,
For fear the numbers fuse—

---

6 *Siroccos:* hot, dust-laden desert winds from Africa.   8 *Chancel:* the choir
and sanctuary of a church.   13 *shaven:* term from cabinet-making; i.e., wood
delicately planed to fit tightly and exactly.   15 *key:* i.e., that unlocks the tightly
closed cabinet (or coffin) to allow air in.   20 *Repeal . . . Ground:* stop the
beating heart of the earth (body).   22 *Spar:* floating wreckage to which the
shipwrecked sailor can cling. Cf. St. Paul's account of his shipwreck (Acts,
27:33–44) where all were saved through faith.

511. 6 *balls:* i.e., of yarn.

If only Centuries, delayed,
I'd count them on my Hand,   10
Subtracting, till my fingers dropped
Into Van Dieman's Land.

If certain, when this life was out—
That your's and mine, should be—
I'd toss it yonder, like a Rind,   15
And take Eternity—

But, now, uncertain of the length
Of this, that is between,
It goads me, like the Goblin Bee—
That will not state—it's sting.   20

524

Departed—to the Judgment—
A Mighty Afternoon—
Great Clouds—like Ushers—leaning—
Creation—looking on—

The Flesh—Surrendered—Cancelled—   5
The Bodiless—begun—
Two Worlds—like Audiences—disperse—
And leave the Soul—alone—

I asked no other thing—
No other—was denied—
I offered Being—for it—
The Mighty Merchant sneered—

Brazil? He twirled a Button—   5
Without a glance my way—
"But—Madam—is there nothing else—
That We can show—Today?"

---

12 *Van Dieman's Land:* Tasmania, an island south of Australia, then used
as an auxiliary penal colony; hence a dreadful place at the bottom of the
world. (Today it is considered an idyllic place.)   14 *your's:* yours.   20 *it's:* its.

412

712

Because I could not stop for Death—
He kindly stopped for me—
The Carriage held but just Ourselves—
And Immortality.

We slowly drove—He knew no haste   5
And I had put away
My labor and my leisure too,
For His Civility— *politeness, courtesy*

We passed the School, where Children strove *youth & freedom*
At Recess—in the Ring—   10
We passed the Fields of Gazing Grain— *maturity*
We passed the Setting Sun— *dusk or later life*

Or rather—He passed Us—
The Dews drew quivering and chill— *flesh gray*
For only Gossamer, my Gown— *protect not*
My Tippet—only Tulle— *long scarf / death*   15

We paused before a House that seemed
A Swelling of the Ground—
The Roof was scarcely visible— *death & maybe hell*
The Cornice—in the Ground—   20

Since then—'tis Centuries—and yet *long time*
Feels shorter than the Day— *reluctance to die, dread*
I first surmised the Horses Heads
Were toward Eternity— *immortality / death*

hearse / carriage of death

passing by / life

the grave

realized

976

Death is a Dialogue between
The Spirit and the Dust.
"Dissolve" says Death—The Spirit "Sir
I have another Trust["]—

Death doubts it—Argues from the Ground—   5
The Spirit turns away
Just laying off for evidence
An Overcoat of Clay.

712. 16 *Tippet:* a short cape covering only the neck and shoulders. *Tulle:* a fine, silken net, usually used for women's veils: both terms are significant as much for consonance as for meaning.

1068

Further in Summer than the Birds
Pathetic from the Grass
A minor Nation celebrates
It's unobtrusive Mass.

No Ordinance be seen   5
So gradual the Grace
A pensive Custom it becomes
Enlarging Loneliness.

Antiquest felt at Noon
When August burning low   10
Arise this spectral Canticle
Repose to typify

Remit as yet no Grace
No Furrow on the Glow
Yet a Druidic Difference   15
Enhances Nature now

1078

The Bustle in a House
The Morning after Death
Is solemnest of industries
Enacted upon Earth—

The Sweeping up the Heart   5
And putting Love away
We shall not want to use again
Until Eternity.

1129

Tell all the Truth but tell it slant—
Success in Circuit lies
Too bright for our infirm Delight
The Truth's superb surprise   [*no stanza break*]

1068.   4 *It's:* its.   5 *Ordinance:* established rite, i.e., a sacrament.   6
gradual: unobtrusive, by easy degrees; also suggests the antiphon sung during
the passage of the missal (after the reading of the Epistle) to the Gospel side
of the altar during the Mass.   *Grace:* thanksgiving; also, power to practice
virtues and bear afflictions with patience.   9 *Antiquest:* i.e., the superlative of
antique.

As Lightning to the Children eased   5
With explanation kind
The Truth must dazzle gradually
Or every man be blind—

1291

Until the Desert knows
That Water grows
His Sands suffice
But let him once suspect
That Caspian Fact   5
Sahara dies

Utmost is relative—
Have not or Have
Adjacent sums
Enough—the first Abode   10
On the familiar Road
Galloped in Dreams—

1422

Summer has two Beginnings—
Beginning once in June—
Beginning in October
Affectingly again—

Without, perhaps, the Riot   5
But graphicer for Grace—
As finer is a going
Than a remaining Face—

Departing then—forever—
Forever—until May—   10
Forever is deciduous—
Except to those who die—

1291. 5 *Caspian Fact:* The Caspian Sea is a salt lake with no outlet, the largest inland body of water in the world, about 85 feet below sea level.

1463

A Route of Evanescence
With a revolving Wheel—
A Resonance of Emerald—
A Rush of Cochineal—
And every Blossom on the Bush   5
Adjusts it's tumbled Head—
The mail from Tunis, probably,
An easy Morning's Ride—

1463. A kind of riddle poem, describing a hummingbird. 1 *Route:*
figuratively the *route* of the bird-postman from flower to flower. Cf. l. 7.   4
Cochineal: a rare, expensive, brilliant crimson dye made from the dried bodies
of the insect *Coccus cacti*. Cf. the coloration of the ruby-throated hummingbird.
6 *it's:* its.   7 *Tunis:* far-away city in Africa, near the site of ancient Carthage,
and one of the Barbary states whose pirates warred against the United States
in 1801–05 and 1812–15: hence an exotic, wild, dangerous, and fanciful place,
as remote and different from Amherst, Massachusetts, as possible.

GERARD MANLEY HOPKINS
1844–1889

God's Grandeur

The world is charged with the grandeur of God.
  It will flame out, like shining from shook foil;
  It gathers to a greatness, like the ooze of oil
Crushed. Why do men then now not reck his rod?
Generations have trod, have trod, have trod;   5
  And all is seared with trade; bleared, smeared with toil;
  And wears man's smudge and shares man's smell: the soil
Is bare now, nor can foot feel, being shod.

And for all this, nature is never spent;
  There lives the dearest freshness deep down things;   10
And though the last lights off the black West went
  Oh, morning, at the brown brink eastward, springs—
Because the Holy Ghost over the bent
  World broods with warm breast and with ah! bright wings.

Spring

Nothing is so beautiful as spring—
  When weeds, in wheels, shoot long and lovely and lush;
  Thrush's eggs look little low heavens, and thrush
Through the echoing timber does so rinse and wring
The ear, it strikes like lightnings to hear him sing;   5
  The glassy peartree leaves and blooms, they brush
  The descending blue; that blue is all in a rush
With richness; the racing lambs too have fair their fling.

GOD'S GRANDEUR. 2 *shook foil:* a sheet of gold foil when shaken flashes dazzling light in many directions from its broken, multifaceted surface. The image also implies thunder. 3 *gathers . . . greatness:* oil when combined with water naturally welling up from great depths in swamps and tar pits forms a great concentrated mass that glistens with iridescent colors. *ooze:* oil crushed from rock, vegetable, or flesh collects slowly in large globules. 4 *rod:* symbol of law and authority seen in the sublimity of creation.

SPRING. Cf. Cardinal Newman's famous sermon "The Second Spring" (1857, in *A Newman Treasury*, ed. Harrold, p. 210), in which he draws an analogy between the youthful human heart when it "puts forth its first leaves, and opens and rejoices in its spring-tide" and the rejuvenated year. Cf. also Chaucer, "The General Prologue," ll. 1–18 and notes. 2 *wheels:* i.e., extending tendrils and vines in a circular fashion. Cf. bindweed or morning glory. 4 *rinse:* to cleanse, purify by overflowing.

416

GERARD MANLEY HOPKINS 417

What is all this juice and all this joy?
    A strain of the earth's sweet being in the beginning   10
In Eden garden.—Have, get, before it cloy,
    Before it cloud, Christ, lord, and sour with sinning,
Innocent mind and Mayday in girl and boy,
    Most, O maid's child, thy choice and worthy the winning.

The Windhover

TO CHRIST OUR LORD

I caught this morning morning's minion, king-
    dom of daylight's dauphin, dapple-dawn-drawn Falcon, in his
        riding
Of the rolling level underneath him steady air, and striding
High there, how he rung upon the rein of a wimpling wing
In his ecstasy! then off, off forth on swing,   5
    As a skate's heel sweeps smooth on a bow-bend: the hurl
        and gliding
Rebuffed the big wind. My heart in hiding
Stirred for a bird,—the achieve of, the mastery of the thing!

Brute beauty and valour and act, oh, air, pride, plume, here
    Buckle! AND the fire that breaks from thee then, a billion   10
Times told lovelier, more dangerous, O my chevalier!

11, 12 *it:* The antecedent is line 10. *Christ, lord:* both vocatives. 14 *child:* Christ.

THE WINDHOVER. *Windhover:* the kestrel, a small European bird of prey related to the falcon, noted for its habit of hovering in the air against the wind.

1 *minion:* beloved favorite, but without the usual pejorative connotation of fawning sycophant. The consonance of *minion* with *morning* is as significant as its meaning. 2 *dauphin:* the crown prince and heir of the King of France. Through its etymological association with "dolphin," the word is also suggestive of the resurrection and salvation, of which the dolphin is the traditional Christian symbol. 4 *rung . . . rein:* image derived from both falconry and horsemanship; "to ring" means that the bird rises in a spiral; also, to guide a horse by a long rein in a large circle. *wimpling:* undulating, folding. 6 *bow-bend:* a curve like that of a tensely bent bow (note what Hopkins called the "instress" and the "inscape"). 8 *achieve:* verb form used as a noun, i.e., *achieve*(ment), to give the noun the strength and intensity of action. 10 *Buckle:* both to gather together and fasten on (a belt, burden, or responsibility), and also to collapse, when released from the tension of *bow-bend* and *rung,* as the windhover seems to do when it plummets on its prey. Both usages suggest submission and self-sacrifice. *And:* i.e., at this moment in the ecstasy of the bird's flight it becomes symbolic of the sacrificial descent of Christ. *fire:* the windhover's breast does in fact appear red at the moment of its descent. 11 *told:* counted. *chevalier:* Cf. *dauphin;* the ideal chivalric, self-sacrificing hero, like Bayard (*Chevalier sans peur et sans reproche*): hence, ultimately, Christ.

No wonder of it: shéer plód makes plough down sillion
Shine, and blue-bleak embers, ah my dear,
Fall, gall themselves, and gash gold-vermilion.

Pied Beauty

Glory be to God for dappled things—
  For skies of couple-colour as a brinded cow;
    For rose-moles all in stipple upon trout that swim;
Fresh-firecoal chestnut-falls; finches' wings;
    Landscape plotted and pieced—fold, fallow, and plough;   5
      And áll trádes, their gear and tackle and trim.

All things counter, original, spare, strange;
  Whatever is fickle, freckled (who knows how?)
    With swift, slow; sweet, sour; adazzle, dim;
He fathers-forth whose beauty is past change: 10
      Praise him.

Spring and Fall:

TO A YOUNG CHILD

Márgarét, are you gríeving
Over Goldengrove unleaving?
Leáves, líke the things of man, you
With your fresh thoughts care for, can you?
Áh! ás the heart grows older   5
It will come to such sights colder
By and by, nor spare a sigh

12 *plod:* functions as verb and noun (*plod*ding); the laborious trudge of the serf-ploughman, the antithesis of the winged grace of the chevalier. *sillion:* obsolete form of selion: a ridge or narrow strip of land of indeterminate size (usually less than an acre) between two furrows formed when an open field is divided into strips for individual cultivation. 13 *Shine:* even the plough, like the plummeting bird, shines when scoured by the earth in sacrificial toil. Cf. Virgil, *Georgics,* I, l. 46: ". . . and the [plough] share glisten when rubbed by the furrow." 14 *gall . . . vermilion:* i.e., the blackened embers of a dying fire collapse in a shower of red and gold sparks, exposing its humble but beautiful death-wounds, which are analogous to those of Christ on the cross.

PIED BEAUTY. *Pied:* parti-colored, spotted. Cf. *dappled* (l. 1), *couple-colour* (l. 2). 2 *brinded:* brindled (branded): variegated dark spots or streaks on a tawny background. 3 *rose-moles . . . stipple:* rose-colored spots (stipple) on the white belly of the trout. 4 *chestnut-falls:* chestnuts stripped of their husks after being roasted. 5 *plotted and pieced:* divided into different rectangular forms. *fold, fallow, plough:* three kinds of fields—enclosed pasture; ploughed field left unseeded for the season; field ploughed and fitted for a crop—each with a distinctive color. 6 *trim:* both equipment as ornament and the neat, balanced appearance of the *gear* and *tackle* of a well-ordered ship fit for the high seas. 7 *counter:* contrary. *spare:* rare.

Though worlds of wanwood leafmeal lie;
And yet you will weep and know why.
Now no matter, child, the name: 10
Sórrow's spríngs áre the same.
Nor mouth had, no nor mind, expressed
What heart heard of, ghost guessed:
It ís the blight man was born for,
It is Margaret you mourn for.   15

(*Carrion Comfort*)

Not, I'll not, carrion comfort, Despair, not feast on thee;
Not untwist—slack they may be—these last strands of man
In me ór, most weary, cry *I can no more*. I can;
Can something, hope, wish day come, not choose not to be.
But ah, but O thou terrible, why wouldst thou rude on me   5
Thy wring-world right foot rock? lay a lionlimb against me?
    scan
With darksome devouring eyes my bruisèd bones? and fan,
O in turns of tempest, me heaped there; me frantic to avoid
    thee and flee?

  Why? That my chaff might fly; my grain lie, sheer and clear.
Nay in all that toil, that coil, since (seems) I kissed the rod,   10
Hand rather, my heart lo! lapped strength, stole joy, would
    laugh, chéer.
Cheer whom though? the hero whose heaven-handling flung
    me, fóot tród
Me? or me that fought him? O which one? is it each one?
    That night, that year
Of now done darkness I wretch lay wrestling with
    (my God!) my God.

SPRING AND FALL. 8 *wanwood:* woods that are dark, gloomy, and also pale and sorrowful. *leafmeal:* leaves ground or broken into a coarse dust. 13 *ghost guessed:* known intuitively by the living spirit; also anticipatory of the nature of the spirit of the dead.

(CARRION COMFORT). 1 *carrion comfort:* i.e., Despair, the "unforgivable sin" because it proposes to limit God's love and power to forgive, a perverse form of pride that would command me, despairing, to feed on my dead, sin-slain flesh. 5–6 *why . . . rock:* why do you roughly wrench me backwards and forwards [not lull, as if rocking a cradle] with your world-twisting foot? 6 *lionlimb:* Cf. Biblical imagery where God usually delivers the faithful from the lion that breaks bones (Isa. 38:13) and devours (Dan. 6:27). 7 *fan:* the winnowing fan that blows the chaff from the heaped grain. 10 *coil:* tumult. *since . . . rod:* because [it seems] I submitted to authority. 11 *lapped:* licked up. 12 *hero:* Christ. 14 *wrestling:* Cf., however, Gen. 32:24–30 where Jacob wrestled successfully with the Angel of God and preserved his life.

No worst, there is none

No worst, there is none. Pitched past pitch of grief,
More pangs will, schooled at forepangs, wilder wring.
Comforter, where, where is your comforting?
Mary, mother of us, where is your relief?

My cries heave, herds-long; huddle in a main, a chief   5
Woe, world-sorrow; on an age-old anvil wince and sing—
Then lull, then leave off. Fury had shrieked 'No ling-
ering! Let me be fell: force I must be brief.'

O the mind, mind has mountains; cliffs of fall
Frightful, sheer, no-man-fathomed. Hold them cheap   10
May who ne'er hung there. Nor does long our small
Durance deal with that steep or deep. Here! creep,
Wretch, under a comfort serves in a whirlwind: all
Life death does end and each day dies with sleep.

To seem the stranger lies my lot

To seem the stranger lies my lot, my life
Among strangers. Father and mother dear,
Brothers and sisters are in Christ not near
And he my peace my parting, sword and strife.
    England, whose honour O all my heart woos, wife   5
To my creating thought, would neither hear
Me, were I pleading, plead nor do I: I wear-
y of idle a being but by where wars are rife.

    I am in Ireland now; now I am at a thírd
Remove. Not but in all removes I can   10
Kind love both give and get. Only what word
Wisest my heart breeds dark heaven's baffling ban
Bars or hell's spell thwarts. This to hoard unheard,
Heard unheeded, leaves me a lonely began.

NO WORST, THERE IS NONE. 1 *Pitched:* hurled; also transfixed, pierced; also fixed intensity, key-note of the cry of grief. *pitch:* with extreme depth (as well as height) and distance as well as tonality (position on the musical scale). 2 *forepangs:* pangs already suffered. 5 *herds-long:* like the *cries* of whole herds of frightened sheep. 8 *fell:* fierce, savage, cruel; literally (when applied to the raven) "eager for slain." *force:* perforce. 13 *comfort serves:* such comfort as avails.

TO SEEM THE STRANGER. 2–3 *Father . . . near:* after his conversion to Roman Catholicism, Hopkins felt—and probably was—cut off from his family both in affection and religious communion. 4 *he:* Christ.

I wake and feel the fell of dark, not day

I wake and feel the fell of dark, not day.
What hours, O what black hoürs we have spent
This night! what sights you, heart, saw; ways you went!
And more must, in yet longer light's delay.
    With witness I speak this. But where I say   5
Hours I mean years, mean life. And my lament
Is cries countless, cries like dead letters sent
To dearest him that lives alas! away.

    I am gall, I am heartburn. God's most deep decree
Bitter would have me taste: my taste was me;   10
Bones built in me, flesh filled, blood brimmed the curse.
    Selfyeast of spirit a dull dough sours. I see
The lost are like this, and their scourge to be
As I am mine, their sweating selves; but worse.

That Nature Is a Heraclitean Fire and of the Comfort of the Resurrection

Cloud-puffball, torn tufts, tossed pillows ⁱ flaunt forth, then
    chevy on an air-
built thoroughfare: heaven-roysterers, in gay-gangs ⁱ they
    throng; they glitter in marches.
Down roughcast, down dazzling whitewash, wherever an elm
    arches,
Shivelights and shadowtackle in long ⁱ lashes lace, ⁱ lance, and
    pair.

I WAKE AND FEEL.   1 *fell:* the rough, hairy hide of an animal (Satanic?), the grim, fierce, oppressive descent of darkness, and mountain, the savage "cliffs of fall / Frightfull" (cf. "No worst, there is none," ll. 9–10) of spiritual darkness.   7 *dead letters:* undeliverable letters returned to the writer or destroyed by the authorities.   10 *Bitter:* modifies *decree* and is also the object of *taste.* 14 *but worse:* i.e., as I am my own scourge, my condition is like that of the damned in Hell who too are their own scourges, but my condition is worse because my ultimate hell is yet to come, although now theirs is *worse* because they are damned.

THAT NATURE IS.   *Heraclitean Fire:* Heraclitus (c. 535–475 B.C.), a major pre-Socratic Greek philosopher, taught that the universe is in a state of ceaseless flux and that its basic principle is fire, which is being transformed into water, earth, air, and then back to fire again in a balanced, harmonious action.

1 *chevy:* to chase or hunt about from place to place.   4 *Shivelights:* thin slivers of light.   *shadowtackle:* delicate tracery of shadows like that of a full-rigged ship's tackle.

Delightfully the bright wind boisterous | ropes, wrestles, beats
    earth bare   5
Of yestertempest's creases; | in pool and rut peel parches
Squandering ooze to squeezed | dough, crust, dust; stanches,
    starches
Squadroned masks and manmarks | treadmire toil there
Footfretted in it. Million-fuelèd, | nature's bonfire burns on.
But quench her bonniest, dearest | to her, her clearest-selvèd
    spark   10
Man, how fast his firedint, | his mark on mind, is gone!
Both are in an unfathomable, all is in an enormous dark
Drowned. O pity and indig | nation! Manshape, that shone
Sheer off, disseveral, a star, | death blots black out; nor mark
                Is any of him at all so stark   15
But vastness blurs and time | beats level. Enough! the
    Resurrection,
A heart's clarion! Away grief's grasping, | joyless days,
    dejection.
                Across my foundering deck shone
A beacon, an eternal beam. | Flesh fade, and mortal trash
Fall to the residuary worm; | world's wildfire, leave but ash: 20
                In a flash, at a trumpet's crash,
I am all at once what Christ is, | since he was what I am, and
This Jack, joke, poor potsherd, | patch, matchwood, immortal
    diamond,
                Is immortal diamond.

6–7 *in . . . ooze:* (the wind) dries up the *ooze* spreading (*Squandering*) in the
pools and upon the rutty surface (*peel*) of the earth. 7 *stanches, starches:*
dries, checks the flow of, and stiffens into. 8 *Squadroned masks:* fixed,
ranked, set expressions (the faces of men). *treadmire:* i.e., mire that functions
as a treadmill. 9 *Footfretted:* foot-chafed, foot-roughened. 11 *firedint:* the
dent or mark of fire. 14 *disseveral:* separate and aloof. 20 *residuary worm:*
the grave worm that is heir to the mortal remains of man, the *mortal trash.*
23 *Jack:* any common fellow. *potsherd:* fragment of a broken pot.

Thou art indeed just, Lord

*Justus quidem tu es, Domine, si disputem tecum: verumtamen
justa loquar ad te: Quare via impiorum prosperatur? &c.*

Thou art indeed just, Lord, if I contend
With thee; but, sir, so what I plead is just.
Why do sinners' ways prosper? and why must
Disappointment all I endeavour end?
    Wert thou my enemy, O thou my friend,   5
How wouldst thou worse, I wonder, than thou dost
Defeat, thwart me? Oh, the sots and thralls of lust
Do in spare hours more thrive than I that spend,
Sir, life upon thy cause. See, banks and brakes
Now, leavèd how thick! lacèd they are again   10
With fretty chervil, look, and fresh wind shakes
Them; birds build—but not I build; no, but strain,
Time's eunuch, and not breed one work that wakes.
Mine, O thou lord of life, send my roots rain.

THOU ART INDEED JUST. *Justus . . . prosperatur? &c.:* the Vulgate version
of Jeremias 12:1: "Thou indeed, O Lord, art just, if I plead with thee, but yet
I will speak what is just to thee: Why doth the way of the wicked prosper:
Why is it well with all them that transgress, and do wickedly?" (Douay version) The whole of the rest of the chapter on the "broken covenant" completes
the context. With regard to the writing of poetry, cf. Coleridge, "Work Without
Hope." 2 *sir:* i.e., God, treated politely as if He were a puzzling and somewhat
hostile friend. 11 *fretty:* pattern of interlacing lines. *chervil:* a garden herb.
13 *wakes:* i.e., one that lives and rejoices. 14 *Mine:* i.e., my roots.

THOMAS HARDY
1840–1928

Neutral Tones

We stood by a pond that winter day,
And the sun was white, as though chidden of God,
And a few leaves lay on the starving sod;
    —They had fallen from an ash, and were gray.

Your eyes on me were as eyes that rove   5
Over tedious riddles of years ago;
And some words played between us to and fro
    On which lost the more by our love.

The smile on your mouth was the deadest thing
Alive enough to have strength to die;   10
And a grin of bitterness swept thereby
    Like an ominous bird a-wing. . . .

Since then, keen lessons that love deceives,
And wrings with wrong, have shaped to me
Your face, and the God-curst sun, and a tree,   15
    And a pond edged with grayish leaves.

The Impercipient

AT A CATHEDRAL SERVICE

That with this bright believing band
    I have no claim to be,
That faiths by which my comrades stand
    Seem fantasies to me,
And mirage-mists their Shining Land,   5
    Is a strange destiny.

Why thus my soul should be consigned
    To infelicity,
Why always I must feel as blind
    To sights my brethren see,   10
Why joys they've found I cannot find,
    Abides a mystery.

NEUTRAL TONES. 2 *chidden:* reproved, scolded.

Since heart of mine knows not that ease
    Which they know; since it be
That He who breathes All's Well to these   15
    Breathes no All's-Well to me,
My lack might move their sympathies
    And Christian charity!

I am like a gazer who should mark
    An inland company   20
Standing upfingered, with, "Hark! hark!
    The glorious distant sea!"
And feel, "Alas, 'tis but yon dark
    And wind-swept pine to me!"

Yet I would bear my shortcomings   25
    With meet tranquillity,
But for the charge that blessed things
    I'd liefer not have be.
O, doth a bird deprived of wings
    Go earth-bound wilfully!   30

.   .   .

Enough. As yet disquiet clings
    About us. Rest shall we.

Drummer Hodge

I

They throw in Drummer Hodge, to rest
    Uncoffined—just as found:
His landmark is a kopje-crest
    That breaks the veldt around;
And foreign constellations west   5
    Each night above his mound.

THE IMPERCIPIENT.   26 *meet:* proper.   28 *liefer:* rather.

DRUMMER HODGE.   In the British Army, the duty of the drummer, often just a boy, was to beat time for all military exercises. The poem is a lament for a young soldier killed in the Boer War (1899–1902).   3 *kopje:* Afrikaans (South African Dutch) word for a small hill.   4 *veldt:* thinly forested land; grass country.   5 *foreign constellations:* the stars and constellations of the southern hemisphere, not visible in the northern hemisphere; hence *strange* (l. 12) to English eyes.

II

Young Hodge the Drummer never knew—
    Fresh from his Wessex home—
The meaning of the broad Karoo,
    The Bush, the dusty loam,   10
And why uprose to nightly view
    Strange stars amid the gloam.

III

Yet portion of that unknown plain
    Will Hodge for ever be;
His homely Northern breast and brain   15
    Grow to some Southern tree,
And strange-eyed constellations reign
    His stars eternally.

The Subalterns

I

"Poor wanderer," said the leaden sky,
    "I fain would lighten thee,
But there are laws in force on high
    Which say it must not be."

II

—"I would not freeze thee, shorn one," cried   5
    The North, "knew I but how
To warm my breath, to slack my stride;
    But I am ruled as thou."

III

—"To-morrow I attack thee, wight,"
    Said Sickness. "Yet I swear   10
I bear thy little ark no spite
    But am bid enter there."

IV

—"Come hither, Son," I heard Death say;
    "I did not will a grave
Should end thy pilgrimage to-day,   15
    But I, too, am a slave!"

---

9 *Karoo:* immense, barren table-land in South Africa, hard as rock in the dry seasons.   10 *Bush:* British colonial word for a wide, uncultivated tract of land covered with scrub and brushwood.

THE SUBALTERNS. *Subalterns:* Junior officers, i.e., subordinates.   2 *fain:* gladly.   9 *wight:* a neutral term, meaning originally any moving thing or creature, whether man, woman, child, or animal.   11 *ark:* i.e., body.

V

We smiled upon each other then,
    And life to me had less
Of that fell look it wore ere when
      They owned their passiveness.   20

To an Unborn Pauper Child

I

Breathe not, hid Heart: cease silently,
And though thy birth-hour beckons thee,
    Sleep the long sleep:
    The Doomsters heap
Travails and teens around us here,   5
And Time-wraiths turn our songsingings to fear.

II

Hark, how the peoples surge and sigh,
And laughters fail, and greetings die:
    Hopes dwindle; yea,
    Faiths waste away,   10
Affections and enthusiasms numb;
Thou canst not mend these things if thou dost come.

III

Had I the ear of wombèd souls
Ere their terrestrial chart unrolls,
    And thou wert free   15
    To cease, or be,
Then would I tell thee all I know,
And put it to thee: Wilt thou take Life so?

IV

Vain vow! No hint of mine may hence
To theeward fly: to thy locked sense   20
    Explain none can
    Life's pending plan:
Thou wilt thy ignorant entry make
Though skies spout fire and blood and nations quake.

---

19 *fell:* remorseless, savage.

   TO AN UNBORN PAUPER CHILD. 5 *teens:* sorrows, troubles. 6 *wraiths:* specters.

V

Fain would I, dear, find some shut plot   25
Of earth's wide wold for thee, where not
        One tear, one qualm,
        Should break the calm.
But I am weak as thou and bare;
No man can change the common lot to rare.   30

VI

Must come and bide. And such are we—
Unreasoning, sanguine, visionary—
        That I can hope
        Health, love, friends, scope
In full for thee; can dream thou wilt find   35
Joys seldom yet attained by humankind!

The Darkling Thrush

I leant upon a coppice gate
    When Frost was specter-gray,
And Winter's dregs made desolate
    The weakening eye of day.
The tangled bine-stems scored the sky   5
    Like strings of broken lyres,
And all mankind that haunted nigh
    Had sought their household fires.

The land's sharp features seemed to be
    The Century's corpse outleant,   10
His crypt the cloudy canopy,
    The wind his death-lament.
The ancient pulse of germ and birth
    Was shrunken hard and dry,
And every spirit upon earth   15
    Seemed fervorless as I.

At once a voice arose among
    The bleak twigs overhead
In a full-hearted evensong
    Of joy illimited;   20

THE DARKLING THRUSH.   1 *coppice gate:* gate leading into a wood or thicket.
5 *bine-stems:* stems of a climbing plant or shrub.   *scored:* marked with notches
or deep scratches.   9 *sharp:* the facial features of the dead seem sharper,
harder than in life.   10 *outleant:* i.e., laid out; also, with *sharp*, made lean and
gaunt. The poem is dated December 31, 1900, the last day of the nineteenth
century.   13 *pulse:* both seed and rhythmic beat of vital life.   *germ:* seed or
bud.

An aged thrush, frail, gaunt, and small,
    In blast-beruffled plume,
Had chosen thus to fling his soul
    Upon the growing gloom.

So little cause for carollings   25
    Of such ecstatic sound
Was written on terrestrial things
    Afar or nigh around,
That I could think there trembled through
    His happy good-night air   30
Some blessed Hope, whereof he knew
    And I was unaware.

Channel Firing

(APRIL, 1919)

That night your great guns, unawares,
Shook all our coffins as we lay,
And broke the chancel window-squares,
We thought it was the Judgment-day

And sat upright. While drearisome   5
Arose the howl of wakened hounds:
The mouse let fall the altar-crumb,
The worms drew back into the mounds,

The glebe cow drooled. Till God called, "No;
It's gunnery practice out at sea   10
Just as before you went below;
The world is as it used to be:

"All nations striving strong to make
Red war yet redder. Mad as hatters
They do no more for Christés sake   15
Than you who are helpless in such matters.

CHANNEL FIRING. Gunnery practice in the English Channel during the
naval arms race between England and Germany just prior to the outbreak of
World War I.

3 *chancel:* choir and sanctuary of a church. 7 *altar-crumb:* the liturgically
non-existent fragment of the broken sacramental bread. 8 *mounds:* i.e.,
graves in the churchyard. 9 *glebe cow:* cow assigned to a clergyman as part
of his benefice and grazing on land forming part of the endowment of the parish
church. 15 *Christés:* the medieval spelling combined with modern collo-
quialisms suggests the timelessness of these events.

"That this is not the judgment-hour
For some of them's a blessed thing,
For if it were they'd have to scour
Hell's floor for so much threatening. . . .   20

"Ha, ha. It will be warmer when
I blow the trumpet (if indeed
I ever do; for you are men,
And rest eternal sorely need)."

So down we lay again. "I wonder,   25
Will the world ever saner be,"
Said one, "than when He sent us under
In our indifferent century!"

And many a skeleton shook his head.
"Instead of preaching forty year,"   30
My neighbour Parson Thirdly said,
"I wish I had stuck to pipes and beer."

Again the guns disturbed the hour,
Roaring their readiness to avenge,
As far inland as Stourton Tower,   35
And Camelot, and starlit Stonehenge.

22 *trumpet:* i.e., of the Last Judgment: see I Cor. 15:52 and Rev. 8–9.   35
Stourton Tower: "King Alfred's Tower," an eighteenth-century tower in
Stourhead Park, Wiltshire, near Penselwood, where King Alfred the Great
(849–99) triumphantly rallied the men of Wessex in May of 878 after he had
been hiding for months in the fens at Athelney. It commemorates his decisive
victory three days later over King Guthrum and the Danes at Edington. One
of the stipulations Alfred required for the surrender of the Danes was that
Guthrum be baptised in the Christian faith. He was, and Alfred was his god-
father. Cf. l. 15.   36 *Camelot:* mythic home of King Arthur, the chivalric
Christian hero of English legend, said by Malory to be at Winchester and by
others to be at Queens Camel or at South Cadbury, Somersetshire.   *Stonehenge:* prehistoric, circular monument with a midsummer sunrise orientation,
consisting of a ditch, a bank, and circles of huge standing stones on the
Salisbury Plain, built during the Stone and Bronze ages in three periods (*c.*
1900 B.C., 1600 B.C., and 1500 B.C.), the last stage perhaps by people of
Mycenaean origin for burial and ceremonial purposes. In Hardy's time (see
Ch. LVIII, *Tess of the D'Urbervilles*) it was popularly associated with the
pagan Druids, sun-worship, and human sacrifice with which the so-called
"Altar" and "Slaughter" stones were identified, romantic suppositions un-
supported by recent archeological investigations. These three places suggest
the lost heroic, Christian, and historic past; the legendary past; and the
mysterious pagan past; and comment ironically on modern civilized ferocity.

The Convergence of the Twain

(LINES ON THE LOSS OF THE "TITANIC")

I

In a solitude of the sea
Deep from human vanity,
And the Pride of Life that planned her, stilly couches she.

II

Steel chambers, late the pyres
Of her salamandrine fires,   5
Cold currents thrid, and turn to rhythmic tidal lyres.

III

Over the mirrors meant
To glass the opulent
The sea-worm crawls—grotesque, slimed, dumb, indifferent.

IV

Jewels in joy designed   10
To ravish the sensuous mind
Lie lightless, all their sparkles bleared and black and blind.

V

Dim moon-eyed fishes near
Gaze at the gilded gear
And query: "What does this vaingloriousness down here?" . . . 15

VI

Well: while was fashioning
This creature of cleaving wing,
The Immanent Will that stirs and urges everything

THE CONVERGENCE OF THE TWAIN. *Titanic:* the White Star liner *Titanic,* the largest and most luxurious liner of its time, considered unsinkable, sank on her westward maiden voyage after hitting an iceberg at high speed off the Grand Banks, Newfoundland, on the night of April 14–15, 1912. There were 1,513 casualties, including many wealthy socialites. The catastrophe shocked the whole world. 4 *Steel chambers:* furnaces and boilers. 5 *salamandrine:* The salamander is supposed to be able to live in fire unharmed; hence these fires were thought incapable of ever being harmed, i.e., put out. 6 *thrid:* thread.

VII

Prepared a sinister mate
For her—so gaily great—
A Shape of Ice, for the time far and dissociate.

20

VIII

And as the smart ship grew
In stature, grace, and hue,
In shadowy silent distance grew the Iceberg too.

IX

Alien they seemed to be:
No mortal eye could see
The intimate welding of their later history,

25

X

Or sign that they were bent
By paths coincident
On being anon twin halves of one august event,

30

XI

Till the Spinner of the Years
Said "Now!" And each one hears,
And consummation comes, and jars two hemispheres.

The Going

Veteris vestigia flammae

Why did you give no hint that night
That quickly after the morrow's dawn,
And calmly, as if indifferent quite,
You would close your term here, up and be gone
    Where I could not follow
    With wing of swallow
To gain one glimpse of you ever anon!

5

THE GOING. *Veteris vestigia flammae:* The sub-title for *Poems of 1912–13*, from Virgil, *Aeneid*, IV, 23: *Agnosco veteris vestigia flammae*—I recognize the traces of the old fire—Dido's confession to her sister Anna that despite her vows to remain faithful to her dead husband, Sychaeus, she has fallen passionately in love with Aeneas. Dido's tragic love for Aeneas (for whom she killed herself when he abandoned her) in Virgil's account seems deeper and more intense than for Sychaeus. "The Going" and "The Voice" were written shortly after the death on November 27, 1912, of Hardy's first wife, Emma, from whom he had

Never to bid good-bye,
Or lip me the softest call,
Or utter a wish for a word, while I   10
Saw morning harden upon the wall,
        Unmoved, unknowing
        That your great going
Had place that moment, and altered all.

Why do you make me leave the house   15
And think for a breath it is you I see
At the end of the alley of bending boughs
Where so often at dusk you used to be;
        Till in darkening dankness
        The yawning blankness   20
Of the perspective sickens me!

        You were she who abode
        By those red-veined rocks far West,
You were the swan-necked one who rode
Along the beetling Beeny Crest,   25
        And, reining nigh me,
        Would muse and eye me,
While Life unrolled us its very best.

Why, then, latterly did we not speak,
Did we not think of those days long dead,   30
And ere your vanishing strive to seek
That time's renewal? We might have said,
        "In this bright spring weather
        We'll visit together
Those places that once we visited."   35

        Well, well! All's past amend,
        Unchangeable. It must go.
I seem but a dead man held on end
To sink down soon. . . . O you could not know
        That such swift fleeing   40
        No soul foreseeing—
Not even I—would undo me so!

---

been quietly but painfully estranged for many years. In ironic contrast with
Dido's, Hardy's love for his wife, now remembered with overwhelming feeling
of his former affection as well as with remorse, was seemingly more strong and
tender after her death than when she lived and continued to be so even though
he remarried in 1914. The phrase from the *Aeneid* intensifies the characteristic
irony of Hardy's personal experience and invests it with a universal poignancy.
25 *Beeny Crest:* cliff on the northwest coast of Cornwall, near St. Juliot, where
he first met his wife.   28 *Life . . . best:* i.e., the joy of their days of courtship.

The Voice

Woman much missed, how you call to me, call to me,
Saying that now you are not as you were
When you had changed from the one who was all to me,
But as at first, when our day was fair.

Can it be you that I hear? Let me view you, then,   5
Standing as when I drew near to the town
Where you would wait for me: yes, as I knew you then,
Even to the original air-blue gown!

Or is it only the breeze, in its listlessness
Travelling across the wet mead to me here,   10
You being ever dissolved to wan wistlessness,
Heard no more again far or near?

Thus I; faltering forward,
Leaves around me falling,
Wind oozing thin through the thorn from norward,   15
And the woman calling.

The Oxen

Christmas Eve, and twelve of the clock.
"Now they are all on their knees,"
An elder said as we sat in a flock
By the embers in hearthside ease.

We pictured the meek mild creatures where   5
They dwelt in their strawy pen,
Nor did it occur to one of us there
To doubt they were kneeling then.

So fair a fancy few would weave
In these years! Yet, I feel,   10
If someone said on Christmas Eve,
"Come; see the oxen kneel

THE VOICE. 11 *wistlessness:* state of being inattentive, unobservant: the direct opposite of being eagerly and yearningly expectant.

THE OXEN. 2 *Now . . . knees:* the persistent Christmas legend that at Christmas Eve the usual course of nature is overturned and the cattle kneel and speak in honor of the Saviour. It was, however, thought dangerous if not fatal to overhear them.

"In the lonely barton by yonder coomb
    Our childhood used to know,"
I should go with him in the gloom,   15
    Hoping it might be so.

In Time of "The Breaking of Nations"

I

Only a man harrowing clods
    In a slow silent walk
With an old horse that stumbles and nods
    Half asleep as they stalk.

II

Only thin smoke without flame   5
    From the heaps of couch-grass;
Yet this will go onward the same
    Though Dynasties pass.

III

Yonder a maid and her wight
    Come whispering by: 10
War's annals will fade into night
    Ere their story die.

"I was the midmost"

I was the midmost of my world
    When first I frisked me free,
For though within its circuit gleamed
    But a small company,
And I was immature, they seemed   5
    To bend their looks on me.

---

13 *barton:* farmyard.   *coomb:* a bowl-shaped valley enclosed by steep cliffs
on all sides but one.

IN TIME. *"The Breaking of Nations":* Cf. Jeremiah 51:20, where God's
severe judgment is laid on Babylon: "Thou art my battle axe and weapons of
war: for with thee will I break in pieces the nations, and with thee will I destroy
kingdoms." In verses 21–23, Jeremiah prophesies that God will "break in
pieces" "horse and rider," "old and young," "the young man and the maid,"
"the shepherd and his flock," "the husbandman and his yoke of oxen," and
"captains and rulers." The allusion greatly intensifies the compassion of Hardy's
prophecy, for only the "captains and rulers," i.e., the *Dynasties*, will pass. The
poem was written in 1915 during World War I.   6 *couch-grass:* a tough,
creeping grass with long root-stocks that chokes out grain crops and is difficult
to eradicate. In the U.S. it is called quack grass.

436

She was the midmost of my world
    When I went further forth,
And hence it was that, whether I turned
    To south, east, west, or north, 10
Beams of an all-day Polestar burned
    From that new axe of earth.

Where now is midmost in my world?
    I trace it not at all:
No midmost shows it here, or there, 15
    When wistful voices call
"We are fain! We are fain!" from everywhere
    On Earth's bewildering ball!

Intra Sepulchrum

What curious things we said,
What curious things we did
Up there in the world we walked till dead,
    Our kith and kin amid!

How we played at love, 5
    And its wildness, weakness, woe;
Yes, played thereat far more than enough
    As it turned out, I trow!

Played at believing in gods
    And observing the ordinances, 10
I for your sake in impossible codes
    Right ready to acquiesce.

Thinking our lives unique,
    Quite quainter than usual kinds,
We held that we could not abide a week 15
    The tether of typic minds.

—Yet people who day by day
    Pass by and look at us
From over the wall in a casual way
    Are of this unconscious. 20

"I WAS THE MIDMOST." 12 *axe:* axis. 17 *fain:* content.

INTRA. *Intra Sepulchrum:* within the tomb. 8 *trow:* suppose.

And feel, if anything,
That none can be buried here
Removed from commonest fashioning,
Or lending note to a bier:

No twain who in heart-heaves proved   25
Themselves at all adept,
Who more than many laughed and loved
Who more than many wept,

Or were as sprites or elves
Into blind matter hurled,   30
Or ever could have been to themselves
The centre of the world.

A Second Attempt

Thirty years after
I began again
An old-time passion:
And it seemed as fresh as when
The first day ventured on: 5
When mutely I would waft her
In Love's past fashion
Dreams much dwelt upon,
Dreams I wished she knew.

I went the course through,   10
From Love's fresh-found sensation—
Remembered still so well—
To worn words charged anew,
That left no more to tell:
Thence to hot hopes and fears,   15
And thence to consummation,
And thence to sober years,
Markless, and mellow-hued.

Firm the whole fabric stood,
Or seemed to stand, and sound   20
As it had stood before.
But nothing backward climbs,
And when I looked around
As at the former times,
There was Life—pale and hoar   25
And slow it said to me,
"Twice-over cannot be!"

24 *note:* distinction.

The Missed Train

How I was caught
Hieing home, after days of allure,
And forced to an inn—small, obscure—
    At the junction, gloom-fraught.

How civil my face   5
To get them to chamber me there—
A roof I had scorned, scarce aware
    That it stood at the place.

And how all the night
I had dreams of the unwitting cause   10
Of my lodgment. How lonely I was;
    How consoled by her sprite!

Thus onetime to me . . .
Dim wastes of dead years bar away
Then from now. But such happenings to-day   15
    Fall to lovers, may be!

Years, years as shoaled seas,
Truly, stretch now between! Less and less
Shrink the visions then vast in me.—Yes,
    Then in me: Now in these.   20

THE MISSED TRAIN. 14 *bar away:* separate. 17 *shoaled seas:* shallow,
because stretched out; treacherous, because filled with shoals that wreck ships;
collected into a multitude, like a shoal or school of fish. (Consonance is as
expressive here as verbal meaning.)

A. E. HOUSMAN
1859–1936

from A SHROPSHIRE LAD

1887

From Clee to heaven the beacon burns,
    The shires have seen it plain,
From north and south the sign returns
    And beacons burn again.

Look left, look right, the hills are bright,   5
    The dales are light between,
Because 'tis fifty years to-night
    That God has saved the Queen.

Now, when the flame they watch not towers
    About the soil they trod,   10
Lads, we'll remember friends of ours
    Who shared the work with God.

To skies that knit their heartstrings right,
    To fields that bred them brave,
The saviours come not home to-night: 15
    Themselves they could not save.

It dawns in Asia, tombstones show
    And Shropshire names are read;
And the Nile spills his overflow
    Beside the Severn's dead.   20

We pledge in peace by farm and town
    The Queen they served in war,
And fire the beacons up and down
    The land they perished for.

'God save the Queen' we living sing,   25
    From height to height 'tis heard;
And with the rest your voices ring,
    Lads of the Fifty-third.

1887.　1 *Clee:* Clee Hill (elevation 1,749 ft.) or Brown Clee Hill (elevation 1,790 ft.), west of the Severn River in Shropshire.　8 *Queen:* Queen Victoria (1819–1901), whose Golden Jubilee was celebrated in 1887.

440

Oh, God will save her, fear you not:
   Be you the men you've been,
Get you the sons your fathers got,
   And God will save the Queen.   30

To an Athlete Dying Young

The time you won your town the race
We chaired you through the market-place;
Man and boy stood cheering by,
And home we brought you shoulder-high.

To-day, the road all runners come,   5
Shoulder-high we bring you home,
And set you at your threshold down,
Townsman of a stiller town.

Smart lad, to slip betimes away
From fields where glory does not stay   10
And early though the laurel grows
It withers quicker than the rose.

Eyes the shady night has shut
Cannot see the record cut,
And silence sounds no worse than cheers   15
After earth has stopped the ears:

Now you will not swell the rout
Of lads that wore their honours out,
Runners whom renown outran
And the name died before the man.   20

So set, before its echoes fade,
The fleet foot on the sill of shade,
And hold to the low lintel up
The still-defended challenge-cup.

And round that early-laurelled head   25
Will flock to gaze the strengthless dead,
And find unwithered on its curls
The garland briefer than a girl's.

TO AN ATHLETE. 2 *chaired:* carried.

Is my team ploughing

'Is my team ploughing,
 That I was used to drive
And hear the harness jingle
 When I was man alive?'

Ay, the horses trample,   5
 The harness jingles now;
No change though you lie under
 The land you used to plough.

'Is football playing
 Along the river shore,   10
With lads to chase the leather,
 No I stand up no more?'

Ay, the ball is flying,
 The lads play heart and soul;
The goal stands up, the keeper   15
 Stands up to keep the goal.

'Is my girl happy,
 That I thought hard to leave,
And has she tired of weeping
 As she lies down at eve?'   20

Ay, she lies down lightly,
 She lies not down to weep:
Your girl is well contented.
 Be still, my lad, and sleep.

'Is my friend hearty,   25
 Now I am thin and pine,
And has he found to sleep in
 A better bed than mine?'

Yes, lad, I lie easy,
 I lie as lads would choose;   30
I cheer a dead man's sweetheart,
 Never ask me whose.

On Wenlock Edge the wood's in trouble

On Wenlock Edge the wood's in trouble;
   His forest fleece the Wrekin heaves;
The gale, it plies the saplings double,
   And thick on Severn snow the leaves.

'Twould blow like this through holt and hanger   5
   When Uricon the city stood:
'Tis the old wind in the old anger,
   But then it threshed another wood.

Then, 'twas before my time, the Roman
   At yonder heaving hill would stare: 10
The blood that warms an English yeoman,
   The thoughts that hurt him, they were there.

There, like the wind through woods in riot,
   Through him the gale of life blew high;
The tree of man was never quiet: 15
   Then 'twas the Roman, now 'tis I.

The gale, it plies the sapplings double,
   It blows so hard, 'twill soon be gone:
To-day the Roman and his trouble
   Are ashes under Uricon.   20

Terence, this is stupid stuff

'Terence, this is stupid stuff:
You eat your victuals fast enough;
There can't be much amiss, 'tis clear,
To see the rate you drink your beer.
But oh, good Lord, the verse you make,   5
It gives a chap the belly-ache.

ON WENLOCK EDGE. 1 *Wenlock Edge:* a sharp ridge in Shropshire. The Severn River flows around its northeast end. 2 *Wrekin:* a rocky hill on the other side of the river, north of Wenlock Edge, near Wroxeter, a village on the Severn just below Shrewsbury; site of a hill-fort in early Roman times. The landscape encompasses both sides of the river looking southeast from *Uricon* to Wenlock Edge and due east to the Wrekin. 5 *holt:* woodland and wooded hill. 6 *Uricon:* Uriconium, walled town in Roman Britain on the site of modern Wroxeter, built *c.* A.D. 80. The basilica was burned finally *c.* 300, and the town appears to have "decayed to annihilation" (*Oxford Classical Dictionary*).

TERENCE. *Terence:* the name by which Housman refers to himself.

The cow, the old cow, she is dead;
It sleeps well, the horned head:
We poor lads, 'tis our turn now
To hear such tunes as killed the cow.   10
Pretty friendship 'tis to rhyme
Your friends to death before their time
Moping melancholy mad:
Come, pipe a tune to dance to, lad.'

Why, if 'tis dancing you would be,   15
There's brisker pipes than poetry.
Say, for what were hop-yards meant,
Or why was Burton built on Trent?
Oh many a peer of England brews
Livelier liquor than the Muse,   20
And malt does more than Milton can
To justify God's ways to man.
Ale, man, ale's the stuff to drink
For fellows whom it hurts to think:
Look into the pewter pot   25
To see the world as the world's not.
And faith, 'tis pleasant till 'tis past:
The mischief is that 'twill not last.
Oh I have been to Ludlow fair
And left my necktie God knows where,   30
And carried half-way home, or near,
Pints and quarts of Ludlow beer:
Then the world seemed none so bad,
And I myself a sterling lad;
And down in lovely muck I've lain,   35
Happy till I woke again.
Then I saw the morning sky:
Heighho, the tale was all a lie;
The world, it was the old world yet,
I was I, my things were wet,   40
And nothing now remained to do
But begin the game anew.

---

17 *hop-yards:* enclosed gardens or fields where hops (whose cones give the bitter flavor to beer) are carefully cultivated and trained to grow on strings hung from wires strung from 10-foot poles; they represent a considerable investment. 18 *Burton:* Burton-on-Trent, one of the most famous of English brewing towns. 19 *peer:* i.e., beer magnates raised to the peerage (satiric). 22 *To . . . man:* Adapted from *Paradise Lost*, I, 26. 29 *Ludlow:* a market town in Shropshire.

Therefore, since the world has still
Much good, but much less good than ill,
And while the sun and moon endure   45
Luck's a chance, but trouble's sure,
I'd face it as a wise man would,
And train for ill and not for good.
'Tis true, the stuff I bring for sale
Is not so brisk a brew as ale: 50
Out of a stem that scored the hand
I wrung it in a weary land.
But take it: if the smack is sour,
The better for the embittered hour;
It should do good to heart and head   55
When your soul is in my soul's stead;
And I will friend you, if I may,
In the dark and cloudy day.

    There was a king reigned in the East:
There, when kings will sit to feast,   60
They get their fill before they think
With poisoned meat and poisoned drink.
He gathered all that springs to birth
From the many-venomed earth;
First a little, thence to more,   65
He sampled all her killing store;
And easy, smiling, seasoned sound,
Sate the king when healths went round.
They put arsenic in his meat
And stared aghast to watch him eat;   70
They poured strychnine in his cup
And shook to see him drink it up:
They shook, they stared as white's their shirt:
Them it was their poison hurt.
—I tell the tale that I heard told.   75
Mithridates, he died old.

51 *scored:* cut.   76 *Mithridates:* (IV, The Great): (132–63 B.C.) King of Pontus (northeast of Asia Minor, adjoining the Black Sea), bitter enemy of Rome and famous for his intellect, courage, hardiness, capacity for eating and drinking, cruelty, distrust of everyone (he murdered his mother, wife, sons, and concubines, among others), and knowledge of medicine. He protected himself against poisoning by daily doses of poisons and antidotes (one of which bears his name) so effectively that when about to be captured by the Romans he found that no poison would kill him and had to request a slave to stab him to death.

from LAST POEMS

Tell me not here, it needs not saying

Tell me not here, it needs not saying,
    What tune the enchantress plays
In aftermaths of soft September
    Or under blanching mays,
For she and I were long acquainted   5
    And I knew all her ways.

On russet floors, by waters idle,
    The pine lets fall its cone;
The cuckoo shouts all day at nothing
    In leafy dells alone;   10
And traveller's joy beguiles in autumn
    Hearts that have lost their own.

On acres of the seeded grasses
    The changing burnish heaves;
Or marshalled under moons of harvest   15
    Stand still all night the sheaves;
Or beeches strip in storms for winter
    And stain the wind with leaves.

Possess, as I possessed a season,
    The countries I resign,   20
Where over elmy plains the highway
    Would mount the hills and shine,
And full of shade the pillared forest
    Would murmur and be mine.

For nature, heartless, witless nature,   25
    Will neither care nor know
What stranger's feet may find the meadow
    And trespass there and go,
Nor ask amid the dews of morning
    If they are mine or no.   30

TELL ME NOT.   4 *blanching mays:* whitening hawthorns.

446

Diffugere Nives

HORACE. ODES IV. 7.

The snows are fled away, leaves on the shaws
    And grasses in the mead renew their birth,
The river to the river-bed withdraws,
    And altered is the fashion of the earth.

The Nymphs and Graces three put off their fear   5
    And unapparelled in the woodland play.
The swift hour and the brief prime of the year
    Say to the soul, *Thou wast not born for aye.*

Thaw follows frost; hard on the heel of spring
    Treads summer sure to die, for hard on hers   10
Comes autumn with his apples scattering;
    Then back to wintertide, when nothing stirs.

But oh, whate'er the sky-led seasons mar,
    Moon upon moon rebuilds it with her beams;
Come *we* where Tullus and where Ancus are   15
    And good Aeneas, we are dust and dreams.

Torquatus, if the gods in heaven shall add
    The morrow to the day, what tongue has told?
Feast then thy heart, for what the heart has had
    The fingers of no heir will ever hold.   20

When thou descendest once the shades among,
    The stern assize and equal judgment o'er,
Not thy long lineage nor thy golden tongue,
    No, nor thy righteousness, shall friend thee more.

DIFFUGERE NIVES. *Diffugere Nives:* Opening words of Horace's ode. This translation and Milton's translation of Horace's fifth Ode (see above, p. 131) are said by classicists to be the finest existing translations of Latin poetry, for the English expresses perfectly—precisely and completely—the tone and meaning of the Latin.
1 *shaws:* woods. 15 *Tullus . . . Ancus:* Tullus (Hostilius) and Ancus (Martius), legendary third and fourth kings of Rome after Romulus, founder and first king of the city. 16 *Aeneas:* son of Anchises and Venus, hero of Virgil's *Aeneid*, and, after the fall of Troy, legendary leader of the Trojan remnant to Italy where eventually the future Roman state was established. 17 *Torquatus:* a friend of Horace's.

Night holds Hippolytus the pure of stain,   25
    Diana steads him nothing, he must stay;
And Theseus leaves Pirithous in the chain
    The love of comrades cannot take away.

Ho, everyone that thirsteth

Ho, everyone that thirsteth
    And hath the price to give,
Come to the stolen waters,
    Drink and your soul shall live.

Come to the stolen waters,   5
    And leap the guarded pale,
And pull the flower in season
    Before desire shall fail.

It shall not last for ever,
    No more than earth and skies;   10
But he that drinks in season
    Shall live before he dies.

June suns, you cannot store them
    To warm the winter's cold,
The lad that hopes for heaven   15
    Shall fill his mouth with mould.

25 *Hippolytus:* son of Theseus (legendary king of Athens and hero extraordinary) and Hippolita (Queen of the Amazons), a huntsman and a man of perfect purity of life; he refused the amorous advances of Phaedra, Theseus' wife, who, repulsed and angered, hanged herself after denouncing her step-son as her seducer. Theseus banished Hippolytus and invoked the vengeance of Poseidon, who sent a sea monster that so frightened Hippolytus' horses that he was thrown from his chariot and dragged to his death. Although Virgil relates (*Aeneid* VII, 766–77) that through Diana's love and Aesculapius' skill he was restored to life and conveyed to Italy to live with the nymph Egeria in her grove for the rest of his life, other legends (which Horace uses) affirm that Diana for all her concern was unable to save him. 27 *Theseus leaves Pirithous:* One of the exploits of Theseus was to descend into Hades with his heroic friend Pirithous to rescue Persephone; both were imprisoned there until rescued by Heracles, but Pirithous was wrenched from the hand of Theseus and chained to a rock.

HO, EVERYONE THAT THIRSTETH. Cf. Isa. 55:1: "Ho, every one that thirsteth, come ye to the waters, and that hath no money; come ye, buy, and eat; yea, come, buy wine and milk without money and without price."

448

Crossing alone the nighted ferry

Crossing alone the nighted ferry
  With the one coin for fee,
Whom, on the wharf of Lethe waiting,
  Count you to find? Not me.

The brisk fond lackey to fetch and carry,   5
  The true, sick-hearted slave,
Expect him not in the just city
  And free land of the grave.

CROSSING ALONE. 2 *coin:* In Greek mythology, Charon, the squalid old man who ferried the dead across the Styx to Hades, received as his fee an obol from each passenger. This coin was placed in the mouth of the dead man when he was buried to pay for his passage. 3 *Lethe:* to the Latin poets the "river of oblivion" in Hades; the souls after their release from Tartarus drank of it to forget their previous existence, whatever they had seen, heard, or done. Hence the speaker, jeering at the insolent masters of this world, the *you* (l. 4) says that even though he might have been a *lackey* in life, in the *just city* he will have happily forgotten how to be a *slave*.

EDWIN ARLINGTON ROBINSON
1869–1935

The Gift of God

Blessed with a joy that only she
Of all alive shall ever know,
She wears a proud humility
For what it was that willed it so,—
That her degree should be so great   5
Among the favored of the Lord
That she may scarcely bear the weight
Of her bewildering reward.

As one apart, immune, alone,
Or featured for the shining ones,   10
And like to none that she has known
Of other women's other sons—
The firm fruition of her need,
He shines anointed; and he blurs
Her vision, till it seems indeed   15
A sacrilege to call him hers.

She fears a little for so much
Of what is best, and hardly dares
To think of him as one to touch
With aches, indignities, and cares;   20
She sees him rather at the goal,
Still shining; and her dream foretells
The proper shining of a soul
Where nothing ordinary dwells.

Perchance a canvass of the town   25
Would find him far from flags and shouts,
And leave him only the renown
Of many smiles and many doubts;
Perchance the crude and common tongue
Would havoc strangely with his worth;   30
But she, with innocence unwrung,
Would read his name around the earth.

THE GIFT OF GOD.   See Luke 1:46–55, 2:25–35, and 2:40–52.

450

And others, knowing how this youth
Would shine, if love could make him great,
When caught and tortured for the truth   35
Would only writhe and hesitate;
While she, arranging for his days
What centuries could not fulfill,
Transmutes him with her faith and praise,
And has him shining where she will.   40

She crowns him with her gratefulness,
And says again that life is good;
And should the gift of God be less
In him than in her motherhood,
His fame, though vague, will not be small,   45
As upward through her dream he fares,
Half clouded with a crimson fall
Of roses thrown on marble stairs.

Eros Turannos

She fears him, and will always ask
    What fated her to choose him;
She meets in his engaging mask
    All reasons to refuse him;
But what she meets and what she fears   5
Are less than are the downward years,
Drawn slowly to the foamless weirs
    Of age, were she to lose him.

Between a blurred sagacity
    That once had power to sound him,   10
And Love, that will not let him be
    The Judas that she found him,
Her pride assuages her almost,
As if it were alone the cost.—
He sees that he will not be lost,   15
    And waits and looks around him.

A sense of ocean and old trees
    Envelops and allures him;
Tradition, touching all he sees,
    Beguiles and reassures him;   20

EROS TURANNOS. *Eros Turannos:* i.e., Eros (love) the Tyrant.

And all her doubts of what he says
Are dimmed with what she knows of days—
Till even prejudice delays
   And fades, and she secures him.

The falling leaf inaugurates   25
   The reign of her confusion:
The pounding wave reverberates
   The dirge of her illusion;
And home, where passion lived and died,
Becomes a place where she can hide,   30
While all the town and harbor side
   Vibrate with her seclusion.

We tell you, tapping on our brows,
   The story as it should be,—
As if the story of a house   35
   Were told, or ever could be;
We'll have no kindly veil between
Her visions and those we have seen,—
As if we guessed what hers have been,
   Or what they are or would be.   40

Meanwhile we do no harm; for they
   That with a god have striven,
Not hearing much of what we say,
   Take what the god has given;
Though like waves breaking it may be,   45
Or like a changed familiar tree,
Or like a stairway to the sea
   Where down the blind are driven.

The Story of the Ashes and the Flame

No matter why, nor whence, nor when she came,
There was her place. No matter what men said,
No matter what she was; living or dead,
Faithful or not, he loved her all the same.
The story was as old as human shame,   5
But ever since that lonely night she fled,
With books to blind him, he had only read
The story of the ashes and the flame.

There she was always coming pretty soon
To fool him back, with penitent scared eyes   10
That had in them the laughter of the moon
For baffled lovers, and to make him think—
Before she gave him time enough to wink—
Her kisses were the keys to Paradise.

The Clerks

I did not think that I should find them there
When I came back again; but there they stood,
As in the days they dreamed of when young blood
Was in their cheeks and women called them fair.
Be sure, they met me with an ancient air,—   5
And yes, there was a shop-worn brotherhood
About them; but the men were just as good,
And just as human as they ever were.

And you that ache so much to be sublime,
And you that feed yourselves with your descent,   10
What comes of all your visions and your fears?
Poets and kings are but the clerks of Time,
Tiering the same dull webs of discontent,
Clipping the same sad alnage of the years.

Reuben Bright

[handwritten marginalia: speaker concerned about man and wanted listener to get facts right]

Because he was a butcher and thereby
Did earn an honest living (and did right),
I would not have you think that Reuben Bright   *[handwritten: determining]*
Was any more a brute than you or I)   *[handwritten: Speaker — poet too]*
[handwritten: Occupation of determining fate] For when they told him that his wife must die,   5
He stared at them, and shook with grief and fright,
And cried like a great baby half that night,
And made the women cry to see him cry.

THE CLERKS. 13 *Tiering:* piling up, arranging in ranks or tiers. 14 *Clipping:* snipping off as well as marking. *alnage:* the official inspection and measurement of woolen cloth by the ell for purposes of laying import duties on it, and affixing lead seals to it to attest to its value (*OED*). The metaphor of *Clipping . . . alnage* suggests dreary stock-taking, methodical snipping-off of the seals, and marking or noting the *sad* value of the *years*, which are woven in a continuous strip on the loom of *Time*, then rolled up and stored like bolts of cloth.

And after she was dead, and he had paid
The singers and the sexton and the rest,   10
He packed a lot of things that she had made
Most mournfully away in an old chest
Of hers, and put some chopped-up cedar boughs
In with them, and tore down the slaughter-house.

[handwritten marginal notes: could be / crumbling / symbol of life; this note impor tant / doesn't want / power to kill; evidson]

George Crabbe

Give him the darkest inch your shelf allows,
Hide him in lonely garrets, if you will,—
But his hard, human pulse is throbbing still
With the sure strength that fearless truth endows.
In spite of all fine science disavows,   5
Of his plain excellence and stubborn skill
There yet remains what fashion cannot kill,
Though years have thinned the laurel from his brows.

Whether or not we read him, we can feel
From time to time the vigor of his name   10
Against us like a finger for the shame
And emptiness of what our souls reveal
In books that are as altars where we kneel
To consecrate the flicker, not the flame.

The Torrent

I found a torrent falling in a glen
Where the sun's light shone silvered and leaf-split;
The boom, the foam, and the mad flash of it
All made a magic symphony; but when
I thought upon the coming of hard men   5
To cut those patriarchal trees away,
And turn to gold the silver of that spray,
I shuddered. Yet a gladness now and then

REUBEN BRIGHT.   13 *cedar boughs:* i.e., as a preservative.

GEORGE CRABBE.   *Crabbe:* (1754–1832) English poet, chiefly famous for
The Village, a satiric depiction of village life that depends for effect primarily
upon grim realism and remorseless fidelity to fact. A physician and clergyman,
born and raised in desperate poverty, Crabbe knew at first hand what he
depicted.

454

Did wake me to myself till I was glad
In earnest, and was welcoming the time   10
For screaming saws to sound above the chime
Of idle waters, and for me to know
The jealous visionings that I had had
Were steps to the great place where trees and torrents go.

Uncle Ananias

description of an old storyteller

His words were magic and his heart was true,
   And everywhere he wandered he was blessed.
Out of all ancient men my childhood knew
   I choose him and I mark him for the best.
Of all authoritative liars, too,   *official liar* 5
   I crown him loveliest.   *storyteller*

children look upon old people in a worship god-like way

How fondly I remember the delight
   That always glorified him in the spring;
The joyous courage and the benedight
   Profusion of his faith in everything!   10
He was a good old man, and it was right
   That he should have his fling.

And often, underneath the apple-trees,
   When we surprised him in the summer time,
With what superb magnificence and ease   15
   He sinned enough to make the day sublime!
And if he liked us there about his knees,
   Truly it was no crime.

All summer long we loved him for the same
   Perennial inspiration of his lies;   20
And when the russet wealth of autumn came,
   There flew but fairer visions to our eyes—
Multiple, tropical, winged with a feathery flame
   Like birds of paradise.

So to the sheltered end of many a year   25
   He charmed the seasons out with pageantry
Wearing upon his forehead, with no fear,
   The laurel of approved iniquity.
And every child who knew him, far or near,
   Did love him faithfully.   30

UNCLE ANANIAS. 5 *liars:* Cf. Acts. 5:1–10. The Biblical Ananias lied, "not
. . . unto men, but unto God." 9 *benedight:* blessed.

Leonora

They have made for Leonora this low dwelling in the ground,
And with cedar they have woven the four walls round.
Like a little dryad hiding she'll be wrapped all in green,
Better kept and longer valued than by ways that would have been.

They will come with many roses in the early afternoon,   5
They will come with pinks and lilies and with Leonora soon;
And as long as beauty's garments over beauty's limbs are thrown,
There'll be lilies that are liars, and the rose will have its own.

There will be a wondrous quiet in the house that they have made,
And to-night will be a darkness in the place where she'll be
        laid;   10
But the builders, looking forward into time, could only see
Darker nights for Leonora than to-night shall ever be.

For a Dead Lady

No more with overflowing light
Shall fill the eyes that now are faded,
Nor shall another's fringe with night
Their woman-hidden world as they did.
No more shall quiver down the days   5
The flowing wonder of her ways,
Whereof no language may requite
The shifting and the many-shaded.

The grace, divine, definitive,
Clings only as a faint forestalling;   10
The laugh that love could not forgive
Is hushed, and answers to no calling;
The forehead and the little ears
Have gone where Saturn keeps the years;
The breast where roses could not live   15
Has done with rising and with falling.

The beauty, shattered by the laws
That have creation in their keeping,
No longer trembles at applause,

LEONORA.   3 *dryad:* a wood nymph whose life is associated with that of her own tree. When the tree dies, she dies.

Or over children that are sleeping;   20
And we who delve in beauty's lore
Know all that we have known before
Of what inexorable cause
Makes Time so vicious in his reaping.

The Dark Hills

Dark hills at evening in the west,
Where sunset hovers like a sound
Of golden horns that sang to rest
Old bones of warriors under ground,
Far now from all the bannered ways   5
Where flash the legions of the sun,
You fade—as if the last of days
Were fading, and all wars were done.

Mr. Flood's Party

abb·decline, withered, worsen

Old Eben Flood, climbing alone one night
Over the hill between the town below
abandon And the forsaken upland hermitage *secluded dwelling*
That held as much as he should ever know
On earth again of home, paused warily.   5
The road was his with not a native near;
And Eben, having leisure, said aloud,
For no man else in Tilbury Town to hear:

Mellow mood   "Well, Mr. Flood, we have the harvest moon
Again, and we may not have many more;   10
The bird is on the wing, the poet says,
And you and I have said it here before.
Drink to the bird." He raised up to the light
The jug that he had gone so far to fill,
And answered huskily: "Well, Mr. Flood,   15   *exhortation to*
Since you propose it, I believe I will." *(old so find lover now)*
                                                    carpe-
Bird is on the wing   *diem*

MR. FLOOD'S PARTY.   8 *Tilbury Town:* fictional town in which many of
Robinson's characters lived, loved, hated, and died.   11 *bird . . . poet:* See
Edward Fitzgerald, *Rubáiyát of Omar Khayyám*, stanza vii: "The Bird of Time
has but a little way / To flutter—and the Bird is on the Wing."

Alone, as if enduring to the end
A valiant armor of scarred hopes outworn,
He stood there in the middle of the road
Like Roland's ghost winding a silent horn.
Below him, in the town among the trees,   20
Where friends of other days had honored him,
A phantom salutation of the dead
Rang thinly till old Eben's eyes were dim.

Then, as a mother lays her sleeping child   25
Down tenderly, fearing it may awake,
He set the jug down slowly at his feet
With trembling care, knowing that most things break;
And only when assured that on firm earth
It stood, as the uncertain lives of men   30
Assuredly did not, he paced away,
And with his hand extended paused again:

"Well, Mr. Flood, we have not met like this
In a long time; and many a change has come
To both of us, I fear, since last it was   35
We had a drop together. Welcome home!"
Convivially returning with himself,
Again he raised the jug up to the light;
And with an acquiescent quaver said:
"Well, Mr. Flood, if you insist, I might.   40

"Only a very little, Mr. Flood—
For auld lang syne. No more, sir; that will do."
So, for the time, apparently it did,
And Eben evidently thought so too;
For soon amid the silver loneliness   45
Of night he lifted up his voice and sang,
Secure, with only two moons listening,
Until the whole harmonious landscape rang—

---

20 *Roland:* See *Song of Roland*, laisse 133: Roland, most famous of Charlemagne's knights, blows his horn Olifant to warn Charlemagne thirty leagues
away that the rear guard at the Pass of Roncesvalles (in the Pyrenees) has been
betrayed and overwhelmed by the Saracens of Spain, and to urge him to
return to give them Christian burial and the honors proper for fallen heroes.
Like Eben, he winds the horn not out of fear but for reasons of valor, honor,
and self-respect.

458

Pessimistic
Bleak

"For auld lang syne." The weary throat gave out,
The last word wavered, and the song was done.   50
He raised again the jug regretfully
And shook his head, and was again alone.
There was not much that was ahead of him,
And there was nothing in the town below—
Where strangers would have shut the many doors   55
That many friends had opened long ago.

Vain Gratuities

Never was there a man much uglier
In eyes of other women, or more grim:
"The Lord has filled her chalice to the brim
So let us pray she's a philosopher,"
They said; and there was more they said of her—   5
Deeming it, after twenty years with him,
No wonder that she kept her figure slim
And always made you think of lavender.

But she, demure as ever, and as fair,
Almost, as they remembered her before   10
She found him, would have laughed had she been there;
And all they said would have been heard no more
Than foam that washes on an island shore
Where there are none to listen or to care.

The Sheaves

Where long the shadows of the wind had rolled,
Green wheat was yielding to the change assigned;
And as by some vast magic undivined
The world was turning slowly into gold.
Like nothing that was ever bought or sold   5
It waited there, the body and the mind;
And with a mighty meaning of a kind
That tells the more the more it is not told.

---

50 *song was done:* Roland, the last survivor, mortally wounded from the prodigious effort of blowing the horn (which burst his temples), staggers from the
battlefield up the hill toward Spain to die alone beneath a pine tree, facing the
enemy to show "That he has died a conqueror at the last." In like manner,
Eben, somewhat the worse for wear from *winding* his horn, will stagger to his
forsaken upland hermitage (l. 3). Heroism takes many forms.

So in a land where all days are not fair,
Fair days went on till on another day   10
A thousand golden sheaves were lying there,
Shining and still, but not for long to stay—
As if a thousand girls with golden hair
Might rise from where they slept and go away.

WILLIAM BUTLER YEATS
1865–1939

The Lake Isle of Innisfree

I will arise and go now, and go to Innisfree,
And a small cabin build there, of clay and wattles made:
Nine bean-rows will I have there, a hive for the honeybee,
And live alone in the bee-loud glade.

And I shall have some peace there, for peace comes dropping
     slow,   5
Dropping from the veils of the morning to where the cricket sings;
There midnight's all a glimmer, and noon a purple glow,
And evening full of the linnet's wings.

I will arise and go now, for always night and day
I hear lake water lapping with low sounds by the shore;   10
While I stand on the roadway, or on the pavements grey,
I hear it in the deep heart's core.

The Song of Wandering Aengus   *[handwritten: Angus Og, Irish god of love & beauty]*

I went out to the hazel wood,
Because a *fire* was in my head,
And cut and peeled a hazel wand,
And hooked a berry to a thread;
And when *white* moths were on the wing,   5
And moth-like *stars* were *flickering* out,
I dropped the berry in a stream
And caught a little *silver* trout.

[handwritten left margin: superstitious, time to fish. Best time?]

INNISFREE. 2 *wattles:* interwoven twigs.

WANDERING AENGUS. *Aengus:* Angus Og, the Irish god of love and beauty, sometimes called the Irish Adonis. Yeats said that the poem was suggested to him by a Greek folksong and by the Irish folk belief in spirits that may assume the shape of a comely girl doing something ordinary like picking nuts and then disappear as if swallowed up by the earth (see *Variorum,* p. 806). One of the famous stories about Angus Og is his long search for the swan-maiden Caer, who had first appeared to him in a dream.

3 *hazel wand:* In Irish mythology the hazel is the tree of knowledge; hazel wands were carried by heralds as a badge of office and were used also to protect cattle from fairy bewitchment and as divining rods.

[handwritten: forked branch or stick used to discover water, minerals etc.]

When I had laid it on the floor
I went to blow the fire aflame,   10
But something rustled on the floor,
And some one called me by my name:
It had become a glimmering girl
With apple blossom in her hair
Who called me by my name and ran   15
And faded through the brightening air.

Though I am old with wandering
Through hollow lands and hilly lands,
I will find out where she has gone,
And kiss her lips and take her hands;   20
And walk among long dappled grass,
And pluck till time and times are done
The silver apples of the moon,
The golden apples of the sun.

No Second Troy

Why should I blame her that she filled my days
With misery, or that she would of late
Have taught to ignorant men most violent ways,
Or hurled the little streets upon the great,
Had they but courage equal to desire?   5
What could have made her peaceful with a mind
That nobleness made simple as a fire,
With beauty like a tightened bow, a kind
That is not natural in an age like this,
Being high and solitary and most stern?   10
Why, what could she have done, being what she is?
Was there another Troy for her to burn?

NO SECOND TROY. 1 *she:* Maud Gonne, a beautiful actress whom Yeats
loved intensely and who alone deserved, he wrote in his *Autobiographies*, the
Virgilian commendation "She walks like a goddess." She was also famous as a
fervent Irish nationalist who urged the people to win their independence
through violence. 12 *Troy:* Helen, the most beautiful woman in the world,
caused the burning of the first Troy.

462

The Magi

Now as at all times I can see in the mind's eye,
In their stiff, painted clothes, the pale unsatisfied ones
Appear and disappear in the blue depth of the sky
With all their ancient faces like rain-beaten stones,
And all their helms of silver hovering side by side,   5
And all their eyes still fixed, hoping to find once more,
Being by Calvary's turbulence unsatisfied,
The uncontrollable mystery on the bestial floor.

The Wild Swans at Coole

The trees are in their autumn beauty,
The woodland paths are dry,
Under the October twilight the water
Mirrors a still sky;
Upon the brimming water among the stones   5
Are nine-and-fifty swans.

The nineteenth autumn has come upon me
Since I first made my count;
I saw, before I had well finished,
All suddenly mount   10
And scatter wheeling in great broken rings
Upon their clamorous wings.

I have looked upon those brilliant creatures,
And now my heart is sore.
All's changed since I, hearing at twilight,   15
The first time on this shore,
The bell-beat of their wings above my head,
Trod with a lighter tread.

THE MAGI. *Magi:* members of the learned and priestly caste in ancient Persia, official custodians of the sacred rites, interpreters of dreams, intimate with supernatural arts, and distinguished by peculiarities of dress and insignia; in Christian tradition, the "three wise men"—the "Three Kings"—who came from the East to worship the new-born Christ.

8 *uncontrollable . . . floor:* The Incarnation is a *mystery* because of the paradox of the loving, gratuitous condescension of God becoming man, of the Son of the King of Kings being born in the lowest place of the low, and of the first witnesses of the event being beasts, not men. It is *uncontrollable* because once manifested, it irrevocably changed history, and its consequences were seemingly out of the control even of God, who now had to submit to the erratic and violent responses of men who could not comprehend the mystery of light shining in darkness (John 1:5). Cf. Hardy, "The Oxen," p. 434; Eliot, "Journey of the Magi," p. 517; and below, "The Second Coming" and notes.

THE WILD SWANS AT COOLE. Coole [Park], the home of Lady Augusta Gregory in Galway, where Yeats was often a guest.

Unwearied still, lover by lover,
They paddle in the cold   20
Companionable streams or climb the air;
Their hearts have not grown old;
Passion or conquest, wander where they will,
Attend upon them still.

But now they drift on the still water,   25
Mysterious, beautiful;
Among what rushes will they build,
By what lake's edge or pool
Delight men's eyes when I awake some day
To find they have flown away?   30

An Irish Airman Foresees His Death

I know that I shall meet my fate
Somewhere among the clouds above;
Those that I fight I do not hate,
Those that I guard I do not love;
My country is Kiltartan Cross,   5
My countrymen Kiltartan's poor,
No likely end could bring them loss
Or leave them happier than before.
Nor law, nor duty bade me fight,
Nor public men, nor cheering crowds,   10
A lonely impulse of delight
Drove to this tumult in the clouds;
I balanced all, brought all to mind,
The years to come seemed waste of breath,
A waste of breath the years behind   15
In balance with this life, this death.

The Dawn

I would be ignorant as the dawn
That has looked down
On that old queen measuring a town
With the pin of a brooch,

AN IRISH AIRMAN.   Major Robert Gregory, distinguished painter and the
only son of Lady Gregory, Yeats's great patroness and friend. He was killed
in action in Italy in January, 1918. Ireland was anything but a fervent ally of
Great Britain during World War I.   5 *Kiltartan:* a village near Coole Park,
County Galway.

THE DAWN.   3–4 *On . . . brooch:* The arms of the city of Armagh (Ireland)
are said to depict the brooch and breast pin of one of the deities of Celtic
folklore.

464

Or on the withered men that saw   5
From their pedantic Babylon
The careless planets in their courses,
The stars fade out where the moon comes,
And took their tablets and did sums;
I would be ignorant as the dawn   10
That merely stood, rocking the glittering coach
Above the cloudy shoulders of the horses;
I would be—for no knowledge is worth a straw—
Ignorant and wanton as the dawn.

The Fisherman

Although I can see him still,
The freckled man who goes
To a grey place on a hill
In grey Connemara clothes
At dawn to cast his flies,   5
It's long since I began
To call up to the eyes
This wise and simple man.
All day I'd looked in the face
What I had hoped 'twould be   10
To write for my own race
And the reality;
The living men that I hate,
The dead man that I loved,
The craven man in his seat,   15
The insolent unreproved,
And no knave brought to book
Who has won a drunken cheer,
The witty man and his joke
Aimed at the commonest ear,   20

---

6 *pedantic Babylon:* The wise men of Babylon were famous for their knowledge of astronomy and astrology. Yeats refers to their achievement as "the Babylonian mathematical starlight," in his system a cycle of history that ended with the birth of Helen. See "Leda and the Swan" and note. 11 *coach:* Cf. Tennyson, "Tithonus," l. 39.

THE FISHERMAN. 4 *Connemara:* a region in County Galway, plain, mountainous, heroic, retaining the ancient folkways; hence to Yeats the natural home of the ideal listener to his poetry. 13 *men:* here and following Yeats refers to Irish men of letters whom he knew; in particular, John Millington Synge (*the dead man,* l. 14).

The clever man who cries
The catch-cries of the clown,
The beating down of the wise
And great Art beaten down.

Maybe a twelvemonth since   25
Suddenly I began,
In scorn of this audience,
Imagining a man,
And his sun-freckled face,
And grey Connemara cloth,   30
Climbing up to a place
Where stone is dark under froth,
And the down-turn of his wrist
When the flies drop in the stream;
A man who does not exist,   35
A man who is but a dream;
And cried, 'Before I am old
I shall have written him one
Poem maybe as cold
And passionate as the dawn.'   40

Easter, 1916

I have met them at close of day
Coming with vivid faces
From counter or desk among grey
Eighteenth-century houses.
I have passed with a nod of the head   5
Or polite meaningless words,
Or have lingered awhile and said
Polite meaningless words,
And thought before I had done
Of a mocking tale or a gibe   10
To please a companion
Around the fire at the club,
Being certain that they and I
But lived where motley is worn:
All changed, changed utterly: 15
A terrible beauty is born.

EASTER, 1916. The "Easter Rising," an armed insurrection instigated by extreme Irish nationalists, took place on Easter Monday, 1916. It was forcibly put down by the English. Fifteen of the leaders, including the four named in the poem, were executed. The poem is not a celebration of the historical event or of Yeats's political sympathies—he was opposed to revolutions—but of an imaginative, surprised awareness of the transformation in the tragedy of the ordinary into *terrible beauty*.

That woman's days were spent
In ignorant good-will,
Her nights in argument
Until her voice grew shrill.   20
What voice more sweet than hers
When, young and beautiful,
She rode to harriers?
This man had kept a school
And rode our wingèd horse;   25
This other his helper and friend
Was coming into his force;
He might have won fame in the end,
So sensitive his nature seemed,
So daring and sweet his thought.   30
This other man I had dreamed
A drunken, vainglorious lout.
He had done most bitter wrong
To some who are near my heart,
Yet I number him in the song;   35
He, too, has resigned his part
In the casual comedy;
He, too, has been changed in his turn,
Transformed utterly:
A terrible beauty is born.   40

Hearts with one purpose alone
Through summer and winter seem
Enchanted to a stone
To trouble the living stream.
The horse that comes from the road,   45
The rider, the birds that range
From cloud to tumbling cloud,
Minute by minute they change;
A shadow of cloud on the stream
Changes minute by minute;   50
A horse-hoof slides on the brim,
And a horse plashes within it;
The long-legged moor-hens dive,
And hens to moor-cocks call;
Minute by minute they live: 55
The stone's in the midst of all.

17 *That woman:* Countess Markiewicz, famous for her beauty and superlative
horsemanship.   24 *This man:* Patrick Pearse, poet and ardent supporter of the
Gaelic language movement.   26 *This other:* Thomas MacDonagh, a writer.
31 *This other man:* John MacBride, husband of Maud Gonne.

Too long a sacrifice
Can make a stone of the heart.
O when may it suffice?
That is Heaven's part, our part   60
To murmur name upon name,
As a mother names her child
When sleep at last has come
On limbs that had run wild.
What is it but nightfall?   65
No, no, not night but death;
Was it needless death after all?
For England may keep faith
For all that is done and said.
We know their dream; enough   70
To know they dreamed and are dead;
And what if excess of love
Bewildered them till they died?
I write it out in a verse—
MacDonagh and MacBride   75
And Connolly and Pearse
Now and in time to be,
Wherever green is worn,
Are changed, changed utterly:
A terrible beauty is born.   80

September 25, 1916 ?

The Second Coming

spiral of flight

Turning and turning in the widening gyre
The falcon cannot hear the falconer;
Things fall apart; the centre cannot hold;
Mere anarchy is loosed upon the world,

THE SECOND COMING. This poem expresses Yeat's prophetic awareness of the flying apart of the western civilization that he knew and of the frightening anarchy in the coming of a new cycle of history or *gyre* (which Yeats pronounced with a hard *g*). The birth of Christ ended the cycle of Greco-Roman civilization begun by Leda's union with the swan, which in turn had ended "the Babylonian mathematical starlight," and now, *twenty centuries later,* a new and ominous, perhaps irrational and terrible *gyre* was about to begin. Yeats combines the traditional prophecy of Revelation and the linking of the Incarnation with Last Judgment with his own belief that the Great Year, which began with the birth of Christ, was coming to an end, at which time all the old values of beauty and civilization would be dreadfully changed. The Second Nativity is as mysterious as the First, but terrible—not joyful—in its regenerative portent.

1 *gyre:* literally, the ever-widening spiral of the falcon's flight.

468

Baptism)

The blood-dimmed tide is loosed, and everywhere   5
The ceremony of innocence is drowned;
The best lack all conviction, while the worst
Are full of passionate intensity.

Surely some revelation is at hand;
Surely the Second Coming is at hand.   10
The Second Coming! Hardly are those words out
When a vast image out of *Spiritus Mundi*   *World Spirit*
Troubles my sight: somewhere in sands of the desert
A shape with lion body and the head of a man,
A gaze blank and pitiless as the sun,   15
Is moving its slow thighs, while all about it
Reel shadows of the indignant desert birds.
The darkness drops again; but now I know
That twenty centuries of stony sleep
Were vexed to nightmare by a rocking cradle *Christ's*   20
And what rough beast, its hour come round at last,
Slouches towards Bethlehem to be born?

Second Coming

Sailing to Byzantium

I

That is no country for old men. The young
In one another's arms, birds in the trees
—Those dying generations—at their song,
The salmon-falls, the mackerel-crowded seas,
Fish, flesh, or fowl, commend all summer long   5
Whatever is begotten, born, and dies.
Caught in that sensual music all neglect
Monuments of unageing intellect.

6 *ceremony of innocence:* i.e., ritual, religious, and esthetic; and social custom, for only in custom and ceremony "Are innocence and beauty born" ("A Prayer for My Daughter," l. 78). 12 *Spiritus Mundi:* World Spirit with which all individual souls are connected; it is also the Great Memory, the universal subconscious in which is preserved the remembered past of the human race, the treasure hoard from which the poet may draw his images and symbols. 14 *A shape . . . man:* a sphinx-like creature, both man and beast. Christ, on the other hand, was both man and God. 20 *cradle:* i.e., of the infant Christ.

SAILING TO BYZANTIUM. *Byzantium:* (modern Istanbul) ancient capital and holy city of Eastern Christendom, famous for its mosaics, its two-dimensional, symbolic, non-naturalistic art, and for the subtlety of its intellectual life; here primarily symbolic of an ideal and eternal world in which all aspects of life are unified. There the artist "spoke to the multitude and the few alike" [Yeats].

1 *That:* the ordinary, natural, sensuous, temporal world perceived largely through sexual experience.

II

An aged man is but a paltry thing,
A tattered coat upon a stick, unless   10
Soul clap its hands and sing, and louder sing
For every tatter in its mortal dress,
Nor is there singing school but studying
Monuments of its own magnificence;
And therefore I have sailed the seas and come   15
To the holy city of Byzantium.

III

O sages standing in God's holy fire
As in the gold mosaic of a wall,
Come from the holy fire, perne in a gyre,
And be the singing-masters of my soul.   20
Consume my heart away; sick with desire
And fastened to a dying animal
It knows not what it is; and gather me
Into the artifice of eternity.

IV

Once out of nature I shall never take   25
My bodily form from any natural thing,
But such a form as Grecian goldsmiths make
Of hammered gold and gold enamelling
To keep a drowsy Emperor awake;
Or set upon a golden bough to sing   30
To lords and ladies of Byzantium
Of what is past, or passing, or to come.

17–18 *sages . . . wall:* like the mosaic figures on the walls of the Church of
Hagia Sophia (Holy Wisdom) in Byzantium.   19 *perne . . . gyre:* A *perne*
is a spool formed by the interpenetration of two whirling cones or *gyres.*
The speaker asks that the sages whirl down from the "holy fire" so that their
spinning motion is perfectly conjoined with that of his soul, completing the
spool or bobbin on which the thread of his regenerated life and that of age-
less art may now be wound. The falcon's *gyre* (in l. 1 of "The Second
Coming") moves in the opposite direction so that "things fall apart."   27
Grecian goldsmiths: Yeats wrote, "I have read somewhere that in the Emperor's
palace at Byzantium was a tree made of gold and silver, and artificial birds
that sang." Later, in 1937, Yeats said in addition that he used the golden tree
and the artificial bird "as a symbol of the intellectual joy of eternity" (see
Curtis Bradford, "Yeats's Byzantium Poems: A Study of Their Development,"
PMLA, LXXV [March, 1960], p. 111).

Leda and the Swan

A sudden blow: the great wings beating still
Above the staggering girl, her thighs caressed
By the dark webs, her nape caught in his bill,
He holds her helpless breast upon his breast.

How can those terrified vague fingers push   5
The feathered glory from her loosening thighs?
And how can body, laid in that white rush,
But feel the strange heart beating where it lies?

A shudder in the loins engenders there
The broken wall, the burning roof and tower   10
And Agamemnon dead.
                              Being so caught up,
So mastered by the brute blood of the air,
Did she put on his knowledge with his power
Before the indifferent beak could let her drop?

Among School Children

I

I walk through the long schoolroom questioning;
A kind old nun in a white hood replies;
The children learn to cipher and to sing,
To study reading-books and histories,
To cut and sew, be neat in everything   5
In the best modern way—the children's eyes
In momentary wonder stare upon
A sixty-year-old smiling public man.

LEDA AND THE SWAN.   In Greek mythology, Leda, a mortal, was beloved by
Zeus, who visited her in the form of a swan. Among their progeny were Helen,
wife of Menelaus, and Clytemnestra, wife of Agamemnon. Helen's abduction
by Paris caused the war that burned Troy. Clytemnestra, in revenge for the
sacrifice of Iphigenia, murdered Agamemnon when he returned victorious from
the burning of Troy. Yeats considered Zeus's visit to Leda a kind of "annunciation" that began Greek civilization.

II

I dream of a Ledaean body, bent
Above a sinking fire, a tale that she   10
Told of a harsh reproof, or trivial event
That changed some childish day to tragedy—
Told, and it seemed that our two natures blent
Into a sphere from youthful sympathy,
Or else, to alter Plato's parable,   15
Into the yolk and white of the one shell.

III

And thinking of that fit of grief or rage
I look upon one child or t'other there
And wonder if she stood so at that age—
For even daughters of the swan can share   20
Something of every paddler's heritage—
And had that colour upon cheek or hair,
And thereupon my heart is driven wild:
She stands before me as a living child.

IV

Her present image floats into the mind—   25
Did Quattrocento finger fashion it
Hollow of cheek as though it drank the wind
And took a mess of shadows for its meat?
And I though never of Ledaean kind
Had pretty plumage once—enough of that,   30
Better to smile on all that smile, and show
There is a comfortable kind of old scarecrow.

AMONG SCHOOL CHILDREN. 9 *Ledaean:* i.e., like Helen of Troy, daughter of Leda and the Swan; a reference to Maud Gonne, whom Yeats loved. See above, "No Second Troy." 15 *Plato's parable:* In the *Symposium,* love is explained by the parable that human beings were once spherical but were later divided into halves; hence each half longs to be reunited with its original half and is unsatisfied until this union is consummated. 16 *shell:* a metaphor of unity that is also an allusion to the egg from which Helen was said to have been born. 26 *Quattrocento:* fifteenth-century Italian painters, especially Botticelli (1444–1510), who in his "Nativity" (which Yeats had seen in the National Gallery) was able to paint the image of "intellectual beauty," "the victory of the soul" (see Yeats, *A Vision,* pp. 292–93). Cf. Browning, "Fra Lippo Lippi," l. 276 and note. 32 *scarecrow:* Cf. "Sailing to Byzantium," l. 10.

472

V

What youthful mother, a shape upon her lap
Honey of generation had betrayed,
And that must sleep, shriek, struggle to escape   35
As recollection or the drug decide,
Would think her son, did she but see that shape
With sixty or more winters on its head,
A compensation for the pang of his birth,
Or the uncertainty of his setting forth?   40

VI

Plato thought nature but a spume that plays
Upon a ghostly paradigm of things;
Solider Aristotle played the taws
Upon the bottom of a king of kings;
World-famous golden-thighed Pythagoras   45
Fingered upon a fiddle-stick or strings
What a star sang and careless Muses heard:
Old clothes upon old sticks to scare a bird.

VII

Both nuns and mothers worship images,
But those the candles light are not as those   50
That animate a mother's reveries,
But keep a marble or a bronze repose.

33–34 *shape . . . betrayed:* The child is betrayed by *Honey of generation*, i.e., the pleasure that the soul experiences in coming into being and the drug that destroys the memory of "pre-natal freedom" (*Variorum*, p. 828); also, in general, sexual pleasure of the mother in begetting the child.   41–42 *Plato . . . things:* For Plato, nature is appearance (*spume*) blown about on the spiritual model (*ghostly paradigm*) of the true reality that lies beyond this world. 43 *Solider Aristotle:* Aristotle believed that form and matter were not wholly separable, and hence nature did have a solid reality.   *played the taws:* Aristotle, tutor of Alexander (*king of kings*), thrashed the royal bottom of his pupil with a tough leather strap (*taws*).   45–47 *Pythagoras . . . heard:* Pythagoras (born *c.* 580 B.C.), celebrated Greek philosopher, astronomer, esoteric religious teacher who believed in the transmigration of souls, and devotee of Apollo (his name means "mouthpiece of Delphi"), whose "thigh was seen to be of gold" (Diogenes Laertius, VIII, 11), discovered the numerical relation between the length of strings and the notes they produced. Using this discovery as the single primordial principle to explain the nature of the world, he thought of the universe essentially in terms of harmony and proportion, in which each *star* had its note that it *sang* and thus contributed to the harmony of the spheres. 48 *Old . . . bird:* a contemptuous summing up of the *blear-eyed wisdom* (l. 60) of the three philosophers.   49 *Both . . . images:* Nuns worship before *images* of saints and mothers before the idealized images of their children, which are in turn *Presences* of *heavenly glory*.

And yet they too break hearts—O Presences
That passion, piety or affection knows,
And that all heavenly glory symbolise—   55
O self-born mockers of man's enterprise;

VIII

Labour is blossoming or dancing where
The body is not bruised to pleasure soul,
Nor beauty born out of its own despair,
Nor blear-eyed wisdom out of midnight oil.   60
O chestnut-tree, great-rooted blossomer,
Are you the leaf, the blossom or the bole?
O body swayed to music, O brightening glance,
How can we know the dancer from the dance?

Coole and Ballylee, 1931

Under my window-ledge the waters race,
Otters below and moor-hens on the top,
Run for a mile undimmed in Heaven's face
Then darkening through "dark" Raftery's "cellar" drop,
Run underground, rise in a rocky place   5
In Coole demesne, and there to finish up
Spread to a lake and drop into a hole.
What's water but the generated soul?

Upon the border of that lake's a wood
Now all dry sticks under a wintry sun,   10
And in a copse of beeches there I stood,
For Nature's pulled her tragic buskin on

---

56 *self-born mockers:* I.e., though the *images, Presences,* are born of themselves and fashioned by man, they mock man because he can never achieve
the ideal they represent.   57 *Labour:* the ideal activity of body and soul united
in common effort, in contrast to *man's enterprise* (l. 56).   61 *chestnut-tree:* In
blossom the tree symbolizes the "Unity of Being," in which beauty is inseparable from the organic process that created it.   62 *bole:* trunk.

COOLE AND BALLYLEE.   Cf. "The Wild Swans at Coole."   *Ballylee:* After
1917, Yeats often lived at Thoor Ballylee, an ancient Norman tower he had
purchased from the estate of Lady Gregory at Coole Park. The same river
flows by both the Tower and the Park.

4 *dark:* i.e., blind.   *Raftery:* a famous nineteenth-century Irish poet who
refers in his poetry to this underground channel.   6 *demesne:* i.e., park.

474

And all the rant's a mirror of my mood:
At sudden thunder of the mounting swan
I turned about and looked where branches break   15
The glittering reaches of the flooded lake.

Another emblem there! That stormy white
But seems a concentration of the sky;
And, like the soul, it sails into the sight
And in the morning's gone, no man knows why;   20
And is so lovely that it sets to right
What knowledge or its lack had set awry,
So arrogantly pure, a child might think
It can be murdered with a spot of ink.

Sound of a stick upon the floor, a sound   25
From somebody that toils from chair to chair;
Beloved books that famous hands have bound,
Old marble heads, old pictures everywhere;
Great rooms where travelled men and children found
Content or joy; a last inheritor   30
Where none has reigned that lacked a name and fame
Or out of folly into folly came.

A spot whereon the founders lived and died
Seemed once more dear than life; ancestral trees,
Or gardens rich in memory glorified   35
Marriages, alliances and families,
And every bride's ambition satisfied.
Where fashion or mere fantasy decrees
Man shifts about—all that great glory spent—
Like some poor Arab tribesman and his tent.   40

We were the last romantics—chose for theme
Traditional sanctity and loveliness;
Whatever's written in what poets name
The book of the people; whatever most can bless
The mind of man or elevate a rhyme;   45
But all is changed, that high horse riderless,
Though mounted in that saddle Homer rode
Where the swan drifts upon a darkening flood.

25 *Sound . . . stick:* i.e., of Lady Gregory, who could then walk only with the aid of a cane. She died the year following the writing of the poem. Yeats here commemorates in particular the aristocratic ideals of art, ceremony, and reverence that Lady Gregory, *a last inheritor,* upheld all her life.

Byzantium

The unpurged images of day recede;
The Emperor's drunken soldiery are abed;
Night resonance recedes, night-walkers' song
After great cathedral gong;
A starlit or a moonlit dome disdains   5
All that man is,
All mere complexities,
The fury and the mire of human veins.

Before me floats an image, man or shade,
Shade more than man, more image than a shade;   10
For Hades' bobbin bound in mummy-cloth
May unwind the winding path;
A mouth that has no moisture and no breath
Breathless mouths may summon;
I hail the superhuman;   15
I call it death-in-life and life-in-death.

Miracle, bird or golden handiwork,
More miracle than bird or handiwork,
Planted on the star-lit golden bough,
Can like the cocks of Hades crow,   20
Or, by the moon embittered, scorn aloud
In glory of changeless metal
Common bird or petal
And all complexities of mire or blood.

BYZANTIUM.   Having come to the "holy city" of Byzantium, the poet (and
all other human beings who have been freed from the "dying animal" of the
body and are now "out of nature") begins the process of purgation, the flaming,
tormenting act of creation that alone produces the inviolable work of art, free
from the imperfections (*fury and the mire*) of nature.   The poem is an account of
the ecstasy of creation, of purgation through annihilation.

5 *dome:* like the dome of Hagia Sophia, the pure image that disdains the
unpurged life.   9 *image:* a pure image of the perfected soul, as it exists solely
in the poet's imagination.   11 *Hades' bobbin:* the spool (*perne*) of the realm
of the dead, onto which the experience of life (*winding path*) can be transferred
(i.e., unwound), and the soul, thus divested of its imprisoning *mummy-cloth*
acquired in life, can be prepared for purified existence.   13 *A mouth:* i.e., of
the inspired, now-purged poet who may only at this time summon images of
the purged dead.   17 *bird:* i.e., the miracle of art purged of the *fury* and *mire*
of nature, the bird of *hammered gold* of "Sailing to Byzantium."   19 *golden
bough:* i.e., of purged art; also an allusion to the "golden bough" consecrated
to Prosperpine, Queen of Hades, which allows Aeneas safe passage through the
underworld so that he may hear the prophecy and see the vision of the future
(see *Aeneid*, VI, ll. 136–48).   20 *cocks of Hades:* heralds of rebirth that crow
one age in and another out.

476

At midnight on the Emperor's pavement flit   25
Flames that no faggot feeds, nor steel has lit,
Nor storm disturbs, flames begotten of flame,
Where blood-begotten spirits come
And all complexities of fury leave,
Dying into a dance,   30
An agony of trance,
An agony of flame that cannot singe a sleeve.

Astraddle on the dolphin's mire and blood,
Spirit after spirit! The smithies break the flood,
The golden smithies of the Emperor!   35
Marbles of the dancing floor
Break bitter furies of complexity,
Those images that yet
Fresh images beget,
That dolphin-torn, that gong-tormented sea.   40

Lapis Lazuli

(FOR HARRY CLIFTON)

I have heard that hysterical women say
They are sick of the palette and fiddle-bow,
Of poets that are always gay,
For everybody knows or else should know
That if nothing drastic is done   5
Aeroplane and Zeppelin will come out,
Pitch like King Billy bomb-balls in
Until the town lie beaten flat.

---

6 *Flames:* the purging flames of the imagination, which release the artist from
the constraints and frailties of nature (*complexities of mire or blood* and of *fury*).
33 *dolphin:* traditional symbol of the resurrection and salvation and protector
of poets (see "Lycidas," l. 164). The purged spirits, cleansed by the flames and
transformed by the hammering of the *golden smithies of the Emperor*, are
transported on the backs of dolphins through time (*gong*) and life (*sea*) to the
eternity of art and the "Unity of Being" on the *dancing floor* (cf. "Among
School Children," ll. 63–64).

LAPIS LAZULI. The Chinese carving described in ll. 37–50, owned by Yeats,
is used as the perfect image of the tragic euphoria of great art whose function
is to sustain man, who can never live in the timeless world of art but only in
the world of nature and disaster. Cf. Keats, "Ode on a Grecian Urn."

7 *King Billy:* William III, the only English king to subdue Ireland. His army
destroyed much of Limerick by bombardment in the unsuccessful siege during
the Jacobite War, and his *bomb-balls* were made famous in popular ballad.

All perform their tragic play,
There struts Hamlet, there is Lear,   10
That's Ophelia, that Cordelia;
Yet they, should the last scene be there,
The great stage curtain about to drop,
If worthy their prominent part in the play,
Do not break up their lines to weep.   15
They know that Hamlet and Lear are gay;
Gaiety transfiguring all that dread.
All men have aimed at, found and lost;
Black out; Heaven blazing into the head:
Tragedy wrought to its uttermost.   20
Though Hamlet rambles and Lear rages,
And all the drop-scenes drop at once
Upon a hundred thousand stages,
It cannot grow by an inch or an ounce.

On their own feet they came, or on shipboard,   25
Camel-back, horse-back, ass-back, mule-back,
Old civilisations put to the sword.
Then they and their wisdom went to rack:
No handiwork of Callimachus,
Who handled marble as if it were bronze,   30
Made draperies that seemed to rise
When sea-wind swept the corner, stands;
His long lamp-chimney shaped like the stem
Of a slender palm, stood but a day;
All things fall and are built again,   35
And those that build them again are gay.

Two Chinamen, behind them a third,
Are carved in lapis lazuli,
Over them flies a long-legged bird,
A symbol of longevity;   40
The third, doubtless a serving-man,
Carries a musical instrument.

---

19 *Black out:* (theatrical term) turn the stage into a black void so that all that individual men *have aimed at, found and lost*—the grief and disaster in which everyone shares—can be imaged in the light of *Heaven blazing into the head*, as when the tragedy of Lear is *wrought to its uttermost:* the completed image of Lear, ecstatic, *gay*, transcendent, holding the dead Cordelia in his arms in the ultimate scene.   22 *drop-scenes:* stage sets dropped from the flys, the space above the stage and proscenium.   29 *Callimachus:* fifth-century B.C. Athenian sculptor, designer, and an artist of elaborate, polished, technical skill. None of his works survives, including the golden chandelier in the Erechtheum, Athens (cf. l. 33).

Every discoloration of the stone,
Every accidental crack or dent,
Seems a water-course or an avalanche,   45
Or lofty slope where it still snows
Though doubtless plum or cherry-branch
Sweetens the little half-way house
Those Chinamen climb towards, and I
Delight to imagine them seated there;   50
There, on the mountain and the sky,
On all the tragic scene they stare.
One asks for mournful melodies;
Accomplished fingers begin to play.
Their eyes mid many wrinkles, their eyes,   55
Their ancient, glittering eyes, are gay.

The Circus Animals' Desertion

I

I sought a theme and sought for it in vain,
I sought it daily for six weeks or so.
Maybe at last, being but a broken man,
I must be satisfied with my heart, although
Winter and summer till old age began   5
My circus animals were all on show,
Those stilted boys, that burnished chariot,
Lion and woman and the Lord knows what.

II

What can I but enumerate old themes?
First that sea-rider Oisin led by the nose   10
Through three enchanted islands, allegorical dreams,
Vain gaiety, vain battle, vain repose,
Themes of the embittered heart, or so it seems,
That might adorn old songs or courtly shows;
But what cared I that set him on to ride,   15
I, starved for the bosom of his faery bride?

THE CIRCUS ANIMALS' DESERTION. *Circus Animals:* symbols and images
Yeats used in his poetry, which he here reviews from early to last. 7 *stilted
. . . chariot:* heroes and artifices of his early poetry dealing with Cuchulain
and Irish mythology. 8 *Lion and woman:* perhaps an allusion to the sphinx-
like figure in "The Second Coming" and to other beast symbols. 10 *Oisin:*
The Wandering of Oisin and Other Poems, 1889.

And then a counter-truth filled out its play,
The Countess Cathleen was the name I gave it;
She, pity-crazed, had given her soul away,
But masterful Heaven had intervened to save it.   20
I thought my dear must her own soul destroy,
So did fanaticism and hate enslave it,
And this brought forth a dream and soon enough
This dream itself had all my thought and love.

And when the Fool and Blind Man stole the bread   25
Cuchulain fought the ungovernable sea;
Heart-mysteries there, and yet when all is said
It was the dream itself enchanted me:
Character isolated by a deed
To engross the present and dominate memory.   30
Players and painted stage took all my love,
And not those things that they were emblems of.

III

Those masterful images because complete
Grew in pure mind, but out of what began?
A mound of refuse or the sweepings of a street,   35
Old kettles, old bottles, and a broken can,
Old iron, old bones, old rags, that raving slut
Who keeps the till. Now that my ladder's gone,
I must lie down where all the ladders start,
In the foul rag-and-bone shop of the heart.   40

21 *my dear:* Maud Gonne.

ROBERT FROST
1875–1963

The Pasture

I'm going out to clean the pasture spring;
I'll only stop to rake the leaves away
(And wait to watch the water clear, I may):
I sha'n't be gone long.—You come too.

I'm going out to collect the little calf   5
That's standing by the mother. It's so young
It totters when she licks it with her tongue.
I sha'n't be gone long.—You come too.

After Apple-Picking

My long two-pointed ladder's sticking through a tree
Toward heaven still,
And there's a barrel that I didn't fill
Beside it, and there may be two or three
Apples I didn't pick upon some bough.   5
But I am done with apple-picking now.
Essence of winter sleep is on the night,
The scent of apples: I am drowsing off.
I cannot rub the strangeness from my sight
I got from looking through a pane of glass   10
I skimmed this morning from the drinking trough
And held against the world of hoary grass.
It melted, and I let it fall and break.
But I was well
Upon my way to sleep before it fell,   15
And I could tell
What form my dreaming was about to take.
Magnified apples appear and disappear,
Stem end and blossom end,
And every fleck of russet showing clear.   20
My instep arch not only keeps the ache,
It keeps the pressure of a ladder-round.
I feel the ladder sway as the boughs bend.
And I keep hearing from the cellar bin
The rumbling sound   25
Of load on load of apples coming in.

For I have had too much
Of apple-picking: I am overtired
Of the great harvest I myself desired.
There were ten thousand thousand fruit to touch,   30
Cherish in hand, lift down, and not let fall.
For all
That struck the earth,
No matter if not bruised or spiked with stubble,
Went surely to the cider-apple heap   35
As of no worth.
One can see what will trouble
This sleep of mine, whatever sleep it is.
Were he not gone,
The woodchuck could say whether it's like his   40
Long sleep, as I describe its coming on,
Or just some human sleep.

The Road Not Taken

Two roads diverged in a yellow wood,
And sorry I could not travel both
And be one traveler, long I stood
And looked down one as far as I could
To where it bent in the undergrowth;   5

Then took the other, as just as fair,
And having perhaps the better claim,
Because it was grassy and wanted wear;
Though as for that the passing there
Had worn them really about the same,   10

And both that morning equally lay
In leaves no step had trodden black.
Oh, I kept the first for another day!
Yet knowing how way leads on to way,
I doubted if I should ever come back.   15

I shall be telling this with a sigh
Somewhere ages and ages hence:
Two roads diverged in a wood, and I—
I took the one less traveled by,
And that has made all the difference.   20

482

Meeting and Passing

As I went down the hill along the wall
There was a gate I had leaned at for the view
And had just turned from when I first saw you
As you came up the hill. We met. But all
We did that day was mingle great and small   5
Footprints in summer dust as if we drew
The figure of our being less than two
But more than one as yet. Your parasol
Pointed the decimal off with one deep thrust.
And all the time we talked you seemed to see   10
Something down there to smile at in the dust.
(Oh, it was without prejudice to me!)
Afterward I went past what you had passed
Before we met and you what I had passed.

The Oven Bird

There is a singer everyone has heard,
Loud, a mid-summer and a mid-wood bird,
Who makes the solid tree trunks sound again.
He says that leaves are old and that for flowers
Mid-summer is to spring as one to ten.   5
He says the early petal-fall is past
When pear and cherry bloom went down in showers
On sunny days a moment overcast;
And comes that other fall we name the fall.
He says the highway dust is over all.   10
The bird would cease and be as other birds
But that he knows in singing not to sing.
The question that he frames in all but words
Is what to make of a diminished thing.

Birches

When I see birches bend to left and right
Across the lines of straighter darker trees,
I like to think some boy's been swinging them.
But swinging doesn't bend them down to stay
As ice-storms do. Often you must have seen them   5
Loaded with ice a sunny winter morning
After a rain. They click upon themselves

As the breeze rises, and turn many-colored
As the stir cracks and crazes their enamel.
Soon the sun's warmth makes them shed crystal shells   10
Shattering and avalanching on the snow-crust—
Such heaps of broken glass to sweep away
You'd think the inner dome of heaven had fallen.
They are dragged to the withered bracken by the load,
And they seem not to break; though once they are bowed   15
So low for long, they never right themselves:
You may see their trunks arching in the woods
Years afterwards, trailing their leaves on the ground
Like girls on hands and knees that throw their hair
Before them over their heads to dry in the sun.   20
But I was going to say when Truth broke in
With all her matter-of-fact about the ice-storm
I should prefer to have some boy bend them
As he went out and in to fetch the cows—
Some boy too far from town to learn baseball,   25
Whose only play was what he found himself,
Summer or winter, and could play alone.
One by one he subdued his father's trees
By riding them down over and over again
Until he took the stiffness out of them,   30
And not one but hung limp, not one was left
For him to conquer. He learned all there was
To learn about not launching out too soon
And so not carrying the tree away
Clear to the ground. He always kept his poise   35
To the top branches, climbing carefully
With the same pains you use to fill a cup
Up to the brim, and even above the brim.
Then he flung outward, feet first, with a swish,
Kicking his way down through the air to the ground.   40
So was I once myself a swinger of birches.
And so I dream of going back to be.
It's when I'm weary of considerations,
And life is too much like a pathless wood
Where your face burns and tickles with the cobwebs   45
Broken across it, and one eye is weeping
From a twig's having lashed across it open.
I'd like to get away from earth awhile
And then come back to it and begin over.
May no fate willfully misunderstand me   50
And half grant what I wish and snatch me away
Not to return. Earth's the right place for love:
I don't know where it's likely to go better.

I'd like to go by climbing a birch tree,
And climb black branches up a snow-white trunk   55
Toward heaven, till the tree could bear no more,
But dipped its top and set me down again.
That would be good both going and coming back.
One could do worse than be a swinger of birches.

Fire and Ice

Some say the world will end in fire,
Some say in ice.
From what I've tasted of desire
I hold with those who favor fire.
But if it had to perish twice,   5
I think I know enough of hate
To say that for destruction ice
Is also great
And would suffice.

Dust of Snow

The way a crow
Shook down on me
The dust of snow
From a hemlock tree

Has given my heart   5
A change of mood
And saved some part
Of a day I had rued.

y Nothing Gold Can Stay

Nature's first green is gold,
Her hardest hue to hold.
Her early leaf's a flower;
But only so an hour.
Then leaf subsides to leaf.   5
So Eden sank to grief,
So dawn goes down to day.
Nothing gold can stay.

Stopping by Woods on a Snowy Evening

Whose woods these are I think I know.
His house is in the village though;
He will not see me stopping here
To watch his woods fill up with snow.

My little horse must think it queer   5
To stop without a farmhouse near
Between the woods and frozen lake
The darkest evening of the year.

He gives his harness bells a shake
To ask if there is some mistake.   10
The only other sound's the sweep
Of easy wind and downy flake.

The woods are lovely, dark and deep,
But I have promises to keep,
And miles to go before I sleep,   15
And miles to go before I sleep.

Once by the Pacific

The shattered water made a misty din.
Great waves looked over others coming in,
And thought of doing something to the shore
That water never did to land before.
The clouds were low and hairy in the skies,   5
Like locks blown forward in the gleam of eyes.
You could not tell, and yet it looked as if
The shore was lucky in being backed by cliff,
The cliff in being backed by continent;
It looked as if a night of dark intent   10
Was coming, and not only a night, an age.
Someone had better be prepared for rage.
There would be more than ocean-water broken
Before God's last *Put out the Light* was spoken.

Acquainted with the Night

I have been one acquainted with the night.
I have walked out in rain—and back in rain.
I have outwalked the furthest city light.

I have looked down the saddest city lane.
I have passed by the watchman on his beat   5
And dropped my eyes, unwilling to explain.

I have stood still and stopped the sound of feet
When far away an interrupted cry
Came over houses from another street,

But not to call me back or say good-by;   10
And further still at an unearthly height,
One luminary clock against the sky

Proclaimed the time was neither wrong nor right
I have been one acquainted with the night.

Desert Places

Snow falling and night falling fast, oh, fast
In a field I looked into going past,
And the ground almost covered smooth in snow,
But a few weeds and stubble showing last.

The woods around it have it—it is theirs.   5
All animals are smothered in their lairs.
I am too absent-spirited to count;
The loneliness includes me unawares.

And lonely as it is that loneliness
Will be more lonely ere it will be less—   10
A blanket whiteness of benighted snow
With no expression, nothing to express.

They cannot scare me with their empty spaces
Between stars—on stars where no human race is.
I have it in me so much nearer home   15
To scare myself with my own desert places.

Design

I found a dimpled spider, fat and white,
On a white heal-all, holding up a moth
Like a white piece of rigid satin cloth—
Assorted characters of death and blight

DESIGN. 2 *heal-all:* any of a number of medicinal herbs (*Prunella Vulgaris*, valerian, yarrow), so named because it was supposed to enable one to do without a physician.

Mixed ready to begin the morning right,   5
Like the ingredients of a witches' broth—
A snow-drop spider, a flower like a froth,
And dead wings carried like a paper kite.

What had that flower to do with being white,
The wayside blue and innocent heal-all?   10
What brought the kindred spider to that height,
Then steered the white moth thither in the night?
What but design of darkness to appall?—
If design govern in a thing so small.

The Silken Tent

She is as in a field a silken tent
At midday when a sunny summer breeze
Has dried the dew and all its ropes relent,
So that in guys it gently sways at ease,
And its supporting central cedar pole,   5
That is its pinnacle to heavenward
And signifies the sureness of the soul,
Seems to owe naught to any single cord,
But strictly held by none, is loosely bound
By countless silken ties of love and thought   10
To everything on earth the compass round,
And only by one's going slightly taut
In the capriciousness of summer air
Is of the slightest bondage made aware.

Come in

As I came to the edge of the woods,
Thrush music—hark!
Now if it was dusk outside,
Inside it was dark.

Too dark in the woods for a bird   5
By sleight of wing
To better its perch for the night,
Though it still could sing.

The last of the light of the sun
That had died in the west   10
Still lived for one song more
In a thrush's breast.

Far in the pillared dark
Thrush music went—
Almost like a call to come in   15
To the dark and lament.

But no, I was out for stars:
I would not come in.
I meant not even if asked,
And I hadn't been.   20

The Most of It

He thought he kept the universe alone;
For all the voice in answer he could wake
Was but the mocking echo of his own
From some tree-hidden cliff across the lake.
Some morning from the boulder-broken beach   5
He would cry out on life, that what it wants
Is not its own love back in copy speech,
But counter-love, original response.
And nothing ever came of what he cried
Unless it was the embodiment that crashed   10
In the cliff's talus on the other side,
And then in the far distant water splashed,
But after a time allowed for it to swim,
Instead of proving human when it neared
And someone else additional to him,   15
As a great buck it powerfully appeared,
Pushing the crumpled water up ahead,
And landed pouring like a waterfall,
And stumbled through the rocks with horny tread,
And forced the underbrush—and that was all.   20

The Gift Outright

The land was ours before we were the land's.
She was our land more than a hundred years
Before we were her people. She was ours
In Massachusetts, in Virginia,
But we were England's, still colonials,   5
Possessing what we still were unpossessed by,

THE MOST OF IT.   11 *talus:* rock debris at the base of a cliff.

Possessed by what we now no more possessed.
Something we were withholding made us weak
Until we found out that it was ourselves
We were withholding from our land of living,   10
And forthwith found salvation in surrender.
Such as we were we gave ourselves outright
(The deed of gift was many deeds of war)
To the land vaguely realizing westward,
But still unstoried, artless, unenhanced,   15
Such as she was, such as she would become.

Directive

directing or intended to direct a general order

Back out of all this now too much for us,
(Go) Back in a time made simple by the loss *(Sun, wind & Rain)*
Of detail, burned, dissolved, and broken off *erosion*
Simile (Like) graveyard marble sculpture in the weather,
There is a house that is no more a house   5
Upon a farm that is no more a farm *forgotten*
And in a town that is no more a town.
The road there, if you'll let a guide direct you *something hunted or pursued*
(as in Statue) Who only has at heart your getting lost,
May seem as if it should have been a quarry— *dead Stone excavated*
Massively Solid smaller uniform Great monolithic knees the former town   10
Long since gave up pretense of keeping covered. → *open ghost town*
And there's a story in a book about it:
Besides the wear of iron wagon wheels
The ledges show lines ruled southeast northwest,
The chisel work of an enormous Glacier   15
That braced his feet against the Arctic Pole.
You must not mind a certain coolness from him
Still said to haunt this side of Panther Mountain.
Nor need you mind the serial ordeal *continuos & irregular*   20
Of being watched from forty cellar holes } *40 thieves (Kats) alabala*
As if by eye pairs out of forty firkins,
As for the woods' excitement over you
That sends light rustle rushes to their leaves, *frightned animals*
Charge that to upstart inexperience. → *frightned animals*   25
Where were they all not twenty years ago?
They think too much of having shaded out *shadow*
A few old pecker-fretted apple trees. *lacking substance or reality + int or degree erase or cover obscure*

DIRECTIVE. 22 *firkins:* small wooden casks. 28 *pecker-fretted:* apple trees marked with a design of small holes made by woodpeckers.

Make yourself up a cheering song of how
Someone's road home from work this once was,　　30
Who may be just ahead of you on foot
Or creaking with a buggy load of grain.
The height of the adventure is the height
Of country where two village cultures faded
Into each other. Both of them are lost.　*the cultures*　35
And if you're lost enough to find yourself
By now, pull in your ladder road behind you
And put a sign up CLOSED to all but me.
Then make yourself at home. The only field
Now left's no bigger than a harness gall.　40
First there's the children's house of make believe,
Some shattered dishes underneath a pine,
The playthings in the playhouse of the children.
Weep for what little things could make them glad.
Then for the house that is no more a house,　　45
But only a belilaced cellar hole,
Now slowly closing like a dent in dough.
This was no playhouse but a house in earnest.
Your destination and your destiny's
A brook that was the water of the house,　　50
Cold as a spring as yet so near its source,
Too lofty and original to rage.
(We know the valley streams that when aroused
Will leave their tatters hung on barb and thorn.)
I have kept hidden in the instep arch　　55
Of an old cedar at the waterside
A broken drinking goblet like the Grail
Under a spell so the wrong ones can't find it,
So can't get saved, as Saint Mark says they mustn't.
(I stole the goblet from the children's playhouse.)　　60
Here are your waters and your watering place.
Drink and be whole again beyond confusion.

[marginal annotations, left:] Concentrate / understand / Retrospect / formulate / meanings

[marginal annotations, right near line 40:] nature healin / sore spot over / man's / minds

[marginal annotations, lower left:] find your / meaning from / looking back / at what / you've learned / and use

[marginal annotation, right near line 55:] Parable

---

40 *harness gall:* a sore spot, usually small but painfully obvious, made by rubbing of the harness.　57 *Grail:* The Holy Grail, the cup Christ used at the Last Supper. In the Arthurian story, all who searched for it, except for Sir Galahad, Sir Percival, and Sir Bors, were unworthy of the quest, hence the *wrong ones.*　59 *So . . . mustn't:* See Mark 4:11–12.

WALLACE STEVENS
1879–1955

Sunday Morning

I

Complacencies of the peignoir, and late
Coffee and oranges in a sunny chair,
And the green freedom of a cockatoo
Upon a rug mingle to dissipate
The holy hush of ancient sacrifice.   5
She dreams a little, and she feels the dark
Encroachment of that old catastrophe,
As a calm darkens among water-lights.
The pungent oranges and bright, green wings
Seem things in some procession of the dead,   10
Winding across wide water, without sound.
The day is like wide water, without sound,
Stilled for the passing of her dreaming feet
Over the seas, to silent Palestine,
Dominion of the blood and sepulchre.   15

II

Why should she give her bounty to the dead?
What is divinity if it can come
Only in silent shadows and in dreams?
Shall she not find in comforts of the sun,
In pungent fruit and bright, green wings, or else   20
In any balm or beauty of the earth,
Things to be cherished like the thought of heaven?
Divinity must live within herself:
Passions of rain, or moods in falling snow;
Grievings in loneliness, or unsubdued   25
Elations when the forest blooms; gusty
Emotions on wet roads on autumn nights;
All pleasures and all pains, remembering
The bough of summer and the winter branch.
These are the measures destined for her soul.   30

SUNDAY MORNING.   5 *sacrifice:* i.e., of the Mass.

III

Jove in the clouds had his inhuman birth.
No mother suckled him, no sweet land gave
Large-mannered motion to his mythy mind
He moved among us, as a muttering king,
Magnificent, would move among his hinds,   35
Until our blood, commingling, virginal,
With heaven, brought such requital to desire
The very hinds discerned it, in a star.
Shall our blood fail? Or shall it come to be
The blood of paradise? And shall the earth   40
Seem all of paradise that we shall know?
The sky will be much friendlier then than now,
A part of labor and a part of pain,
And next in glory to enduring love,
Not this dividing and indifferent blue.   45

IV

She says, "I am content when wakened birds,
Before they fly, test the reality
Of misty fields, by their sweet questionings;
But when the birds are gone, and their warm fields
Return no more, where, then, is paradise?"   50
There is not any haunt of prophecy,
Nor any old chimera of the grave,
Neither the golden underground, nor isle
Melodius, where spirits gat them home,
Nor visionary south, nor cloudy palm   55
Remote on heaven's hill, that has endured
As April's green endures; or will endure
Like her remembrance of awakened birds,
Or her desire for June and evening, tipped
By the consummation of the swallow's wings.   60

V

She says, "But in contentment I still feel
The need of some imperishable bliss."
Death is the mother of beauty; hence from her,
Alone, shall come fulfilment to our dreams
And our desires. Although she strews the leaves   65
Of sure obliteration on our paths,
The path sick sorrow took, the many paths
Where triumph rang its brassy phrase, or love
Whispered a little out of tenderness,
She makes the willow shiver in the sun   70

For maidens who were wont to sit and gaze
Upon the grass, relinquished to their feet.
She causes boys to pile new plums and pears
On disregarded plate. The maidens taste
And stray impassioned in the littering leaves.   75

VI

Is there no change of death in paradise?
Does ripe fruit never fall? Or do the boughs
Hang always heavy in that perfect sky,
Unchanging, yet so like our perishing earth,
With rivers like our own that seek for seas   80
They never find, the same receding shores
That never touch with inarticulate pang?
Why set the pear upon those river-banks
Or spice the shores with odors of the plum?
Alas, that they should wear our colors there,   85
The silken weavings of our afternoons,
And pick the strings of our insipid lutes!
Death is the mother of beauty, mystical,
Within whose burning bosom we devise
Our earthly mothers waiting, sleeplessly.   90

VII

Supple and turbulent, a ring of men
Shall chant in orgy on a summer morn
Their boisterous devotion to the sun,
Not as a god, but as a god might be,
Naked among them, like a savage source.   95
Their chant shall be a chant of paradise,
Out of their blood, returning to the sky;
And in their chant shall enter, voice by voice,
The windy lake wherein their lord delights,
The trees, like serafin, and echoing hills,   100
That choir among themselves long afterward.
They shall know well the heavenly fellowship
Of men that perish and of summer morn.
And whence they came and whither they shall go
The dew upon their feet shall manifest.   105

VIII

She hears, upon that water without sound,
A voice that cries, "The tomb in Palestine
Is not the porch of spirits lingering.
It is the grave of Jesus, where he lay."

We live in an old chaos of the sun,   110
Or old dependency of day and night,
Or island solitude, unsponsored, free,
Of that wide water, inescapable.
Deer walk upon our mountains, and the quail
Whistle about us their spontaneous cries;   115
Sweet berries ripen in the wilderness;
And, in the isolation of the sky,
At evening, casual flocks of pigeons make
Ambiguous undulations as they sink,
Downward to darkness, on extended wings.   120

Anecdote of the Jar

I placed a jar in Tennessee,
And round it was, upon a hill.
It made the slovenly wilderness
Surround that hill.

The wilderness rose up to it,   5
And sprawled around, no longer wild.
The jar was round upon the ground
And tall and of a port in air.

It took dominion everywhere.
The jar was gray and bare.   10
It did not give of bird or bush,
Like nothing else in Tennessee.

Peter Quince at the Clavier

I

Just as my fingers on these keys
Make music, so the selfsame sounds
On my spirit make a music, too.

Music is feeling, then, not sound;
And thus it is that what I feel,   5
Here in this room, desiring you,

PETER QUINCE. *Peter Quince:* The carpenter in *A Midsummer-Night's Dream* who is the director of "The most lamentable comedy, and most cruel death of Pyramus and Thisby." The rustic carpenter and his innocent burlesque are adroitly contrasted with the subtlety of the speaker in the poem and the sophistication of his allusions to the story of Susanna. *Clavier:* in general, any keyboard instrument, but here, perhaps a delicate, intimate "well-tempered" instrument, producing a soft sound.

Thinking of your blue-shadowed silk,
Is music. It is like the strain
Waked in the elders by Susanna.

Of a green evening, clear and warm,   10
She bathed in her still garden, while
The red-eyed elders watching, felt

The basses of their beings throb
In witching chords, and their thin blood
Pulse pizzicati of Hosanna.   15

II

In the green water, clear and warm,
Susanna lay.
She searched
The touch of springs,
And found   20
Concealed imaginings.
She sighed,
For so much melody.

Upon the bank, she stood
In the cool   25
Of spent emotions.
She felt, among the leaves,
The dew
Of old devotions.

9 *Susanna:* See *The Apocrypha*, "The History of Susanna." Susanna, righteous daughter of Chelcias, "a very delicate woman and beauteous to behold,"
and just wife of "a great rich man," Joacim, was the victim of the lust of two
appointed judges, "ancients of the people." "Wounded with her love," they
spied upon her when she bathed privily in her garden ("for it was hot"). They
surprised her and gave her the alternatives of either granting their lewd desires
or being defamed. When she had "sighed" over her dilemma, rather than "sin
in the sight of the Lord" she refused to lie with them and "cried out with a
loud voice." They then publicly accused her of having a scandalous affair with
a "young man in the garden." At first convicted of adultery and condemned to
death, Susanna was quickly saved by the prophet Daniel, who examined the
wicked old men separately, eliciting testimony from one that he saw her and the
young man "companying together" under a "mastick" tree and from the other
that they were under a "holm" tree, thus proving them liars. The lascivious
old men, "full of mischievous imagination," who bore false witness, were put
to death, and the "innocent blood" of Susanna was saved. The Biblical narrative emphasizes the slow, luxurious and innocent happiness of Susanna in
her bath in the garden; the shocking surprise of her seizure; the overwhelming
power of the perverse lust of the elders for her; the helplessness of opulent
innocence entrapped by the wiles of wicked sagacity and senile desire; and the
advantages of having a good lawyer. 15 *pizzicati:* literally, pinchings;
plucking of strings.

She walked upon the grass,   30
Still quavering.
The winds were like her maids,
On timid feet,
Fetching her woven scarves,
Yet wavering.   35

A breath upon her hand
Muted the night.
She turned—
A cymbal crashed,
And roaring horns.   40

III

Soon, with a noise like tambourines,
Came her attendant Byzantines.

They wondered why Susanna cried
Against the elders by her side;

And as they whispered, the refrain   45
Was like a willow swept by rain.

Anon, their lamps' uplifted flame
Revealed Susanna and her shame.

And then, the simpering Byzantines
Fled, with a noise like tambourines.   50

IV

Beauty is momentary in the mind—
The fitful tracing of a portal;
But in the flesh it is immortal.

The body dies; the body's beauty lives.
So evenings die, in their green going,   55
A wave, interminably flowing.
So gardens die, their meek breath scenting
The cowl of winter, done repenting.
So maidens die, to the auroral
Celebration of a maiden's choral.   60
Susanna's music touched the bawdy strings
Of those white elders; but, escaping,
Left only Death's ironic scraping.
Now, in its immortality, it plays
On the clear viol of her memory,   65
And makes a constant sacrament of praise.

Thirteen Ways of Looking at a Blackbird

I

Among twenty snowy mountains,
The only moving thing
Was the eye of the blackbird.

II

I was of three minds,
Like a tree   5
In which there are three blackbirds.

III

The blackbird whirled in the autumn winds.
It was a small part of the pantomime.

IV

A man and a woman
Are one.   10
A man and a woman and a blackbird
Are one.

V

I do not know which to prefer,
The beauty of inflections
Or the beauty of innuendoes,   15
The blackbird whistling
Or just after.

VI

Icicles filled the long window
With barbaric glass.
The shadow of the blackbird   20
Crossed it, to and fro.
The mood
Traced in the shadow
An indecipherable cause.

VII

O thin men of Haddam,   25
Why do you imagine golden birds?
Do you not see how the blackbird
Walks around the feet
Of the women about you?

THIRTEEN WAYS. 25 *Haddam:* agricultural town in Connecticut, on the
Connecticut River, symbolic here of the practical, spare sagacity and bare-bone
aesceticism of the old-time New Englander.

VIII

I know noble accents   30
And lucid, inescapable rhythms;
But I know, too,
That the blackbird is involved
In what I know.

IX

When the blackbird flew out of sight,   35
It marked the edge
Of one of many circles.

X

At the sight of blackbirds
Flying in a green light,
Even the bawds of euphony   40
Would cry out sharply.

XI

He rode over Connecticut
In a glass coach.
Once, a fear pierced him,
In that he mistook   45
The shadow of his equipage
For blackbirds.

XII

The river is moving.
The blackbird must be flying.

XIII

It was evening all afternoon.   50
It was snowing
And it was going to snow.
The blackbird sat
In the cedar-limbs.

Sea Surface Full of Clouds

I

In that November off Tehuantepec,
The slopping of the sea grew still one night
And in the morning summer hued the deck

SEA SURFACE. 1 *Tehuantepec:* town in Oaxaca state, in southern Mexico, on the Pacific coast.

And made one think of rosy chocolate
And gilt umbrellas. Paradisal green   5
Gave suavity to the perplexed machine

Of ocean, which like limpid water lay.
Who, then, in that ambrosial latitude
Out of the light evolved the moving blooms,

Who, then, evolved the sea-blooms from the clouds   10
Diffusing balm in that Pacific calm?
C'était mon enfant, mon bijou, mon âme.

The sea-clouds whitened far below the calm
And moved, as blooms move, in the swimming green
And in its watery radiance, while the hue   15

Of heaven in an antique reflection rolled
Round those flotillas. And sometimes the sea
Poured brilliant iris on the glistening blue.

II

In that November off Tehuantepec
The slopping of the sea grew still one night.   20
At breakfast jelly yellow streaked the deck

And made one think of chop-house chocolate
And sham umbrellas. And a sham-like green
Capped summer-seeming on the tense machine

Of ocean, which in sinister flatness lay.   25
Who, then, beheld the rising of the clouds
That strode submerged in that malevolent sheen,

Who saw the mortal massives of the blooms
Of water moving on the water floor?
C'était mon frère du ciel, ma vie, mon or.   30

The gongs rang loudly as the windy booms
Hoo-hooed it in the darkened ocean-blooms.
The gongs grew still. And then blue heaven spread

Its crystalline pendentives on the sea
And the macabre of the water-glooms   35
In an enormous undulation fled.

12 *C'était . . . âme:* It was my child, my jewel, my soul.   30 *C'était . . .
or:* It was my "brother" from heaven, my life, my gold.

III

In that November off Tehuantepec,
The slopping of the sea grew still one night
And a pale silver patterned on the deck

And made one think of porcelain chocolate   40
And pied umbrellas. An uncertain green,
Piano-polished, held the tranced machine

Of ocean, as a prelude holds and holds.
Who, seeing silver petals of white blooms
Unfolding in the water, feeling sure   45

Of the milk within the saltiest spurge, heard, then,
The sea unfolding in the sunken clouds?
Oh! C'était mon extase et mon amour.

So deeply sunken were they that the shrouds,
The shrouding shadows, made the petals black   50
Until the rolling heaven made them blue,

A blue beyond the rainy hyacinth,
And smiting the crevasses of the leaves
Deluged the ocean with a sapphire blue.

IV

In that November off Tehuantepec   55
The night-long slopping of the sea grew still.
A mallow morning dozed upon the deck

And made one think of musky chocolate
And frail umbrellas. A too-fluent green
Suggested malice in the dry machine   60

Of ocean, pondering dank stratagem.
Who then beheld the figures of the clouds
Like blooms secluded in the thick marine?

Like blooms? Like damasks that were shaken off
From the loosed girdles in the spangling must.   65
C'était ma foi, la nonchalance divine.

The nakedness would rise and suddenly turn
Salt masks of beard and mouths of bellowing,
Would—But more suddenly the heaven rolled

---

48 *C'était . . . amour:* It was my ecstasy and my love. 66 *C'était . . . divine:* It was my faith, divine indifference.

Its bluest sea-clouds in the thinking green,   70
And the nakedness became the broadest blooms,
Mile-mallows that a mallow sun cajoled.

V

In that November off Tehuantepec
Night stilled the slopping of the sea. The day
Came, bowing and voluble, upon the deck,   75

Good clown. . . . One thought of Chinese chocolate
And large umbrellas. And a motley green
Followed the drift of the obese machine

Of ocean, perfected in indolence.
What pistache one, ingenious and droll,   80
Beheld the sovereign clouds as jugglery

And the sea as turquoise-turbaned Sambo, neat
At tossing saucers—cloudy-conjuring sea?
C'était mon esprit bâtard, l'ignominie.

The sovereign clouds came clustering. The conch   85
Of loyal conjuration trumped. The wind
Of green blooms turning crisped the motley hue

To clearing opalescence. Then the sea
And heaven rolled as one and from the two
Came fresh transfigurings of freshest blue.   90

The Idea of Order at Key West

She sang beyond the genius of the sea.
The water never formed to mind or voice,
Like a body wholly body, fluttering
Its empty sleeves; and yet its mimic motion
Made constant cry, caused constantly a cry,   5
That was not ours although we understood,
Inhuman, of the veritable ocean.

The sea was not a mask. No more was she.
The song and water were not medleyed sound
Even if what she sang was what she heard,   10
Since what she sang was uttered word by word.
It may be that in all her phrases stirred
The grinding water and the gasping wind;
But it was she and not the sea we heard.

84 *C'était . . . l'ignominie:* It was my bastard spirit [soul], ignominy.

502

For she was the maker of the song she sang.   15
The ever-hooded, tragic-gestured sea
Was merely a place by which she walked to sing.
Whose spirit is this? we said, because we knew
It was the spirit that we sought and knew
That we should ask this often as she sang.   20

If it was only the dark voice of the sea
That rose, or even colored by many waves;
If it was only the outer voice of sky
And cloud, of the sunken coral water-walled,
However clear, it would have been deep air,   25
The heaving speech of air, a summer sound
Repeated in a summer without end
And sound alone. But it was more than that,
More even than her voice, and ours, among
The meaningless plungings of water and the wind,   30
Theatrical distances, bronze shadows heaped
On high horizons, mountainous atmospheres
Of the sky and sea.
                    It was her voice that made
The sky acutest at its vanishing.
She measured to the hour its solitude.   35
She was the single artificer of the world
In which she sang. And when she sang, the sea,
Whatever self it had, became the self
That was her song, for she was the maker. Then we,
As we beheld her striding there alone,   40
Knew that there never was a world for her
Except the one she sang and, singing, made.

Ramon Fernandez, tell me, if you know,
Why, when the singing ended and we turned
Toward the town, tell why the glassy lights,   45
The lights in the fishing boats at anchor there,
As the night descended, tilting in the air,
Mastered the night and portioned out the sea,
Fixing emblazoned zones and fiery poles,
Arranging, deepening, enchanting night.   50

THE IDEA OF ORDER.   43 *Ramon Fernandez:* French critic (1894–1944) and classicist whose *Messages* (1926) argues that every great writer seeks to impose what Stevens here calls *Blessed rage for order* upon his world through the act of creation and assertion of personality.

Oh! Blessed rage for order, pale Ramon,
The maker's rage to order words of the sea,
Words of the fragrant portals, dimly-starred,
And of ourselves and of our origins,
In ghostlier demarcations, keener sounds.   55

Study of Two Pears

I

Opusculum paedagogum.
The pears are not viols,
Nudes or bottles.
They resemble nothing else.

II

They are yellow forms   5
Composed of curves
Bulging toward the base.
They are touched red.

III

They are not flat surfaces
Having curved outlines.   10
They are round
Tapering toward the top.

IV

In the way they are modelled
There are bits of blue.
A hard dry leaf hangs   15
From the stem.

V

The yellow glistens
It glistens with various yellows,
Citrons, oranges and greens
Flowering over the skin.   20

VI

The shadows of the pears
Are blobs on the green cloth.
The pears are not seen
As the observer wills.

A STUDY OF TWO PEARS.   1 *Opusculum paedagogum:* i.e., a little work of
pedagogues.

Of Modern Poetry

The poem of the mind in the act of finding
What will suffice. It has not always had
To find: the scene was set; it repeated what
Was in the script.
                              Then the theatre was changed
To something else. Its past was a souvenir.
It has to be living, to learn the speech of the place.
It has to face the men of the time and to meet
The women of the time. It has to think about war
And it has to find what will suffice. It has
To construct a new stage. It has to be on that stage
And, like an insatiable actor, slowly and
With meditation, speak words that in the ear,
In the delicatest ear of the mind, repeat,
Exactly, that which it wants to hear, at the sound
Of which, an invisible audience listens,
Not to the play, but to itself, expressed
In an emotion as of two people, as of two
Emotions becoming one. The actor is
A metaphysician in the dark, twanging
An instrument, twanging a wiry string that gives
Sounds passing through sudden rightnesses, wholly
Containing the mind, below which it cannot descend,
Beyond which it has no will to rise.
                              It must
Be the finding of a satisfaction, and may
Be of a man skating, a woman dancing, a woman
Combing. The poem of the act of the mind.

The World as Meditation

> J'ai passé trop de temps à travailler mon violon, à
> voyager. Mais l'exercice essentiel du compositeur—
> la méditation—rien ne l'a jamais suspendu en
> moi . . . Je vis un rêve permanent, qui ne s'arrête
> ni nuit ni jour.
>   Georges Enesco

Is it Ulysses that approaches from the east,
The interminable adventurer? The trees are mended.
That winter is washed away. Someone is moving

THE WORLD AS MEDITATION. *J'ai . . . jour:* I have spent too much time
practicing my violin and traveling. But the essential exercise of the composer—
meditation—nothing has ever stopped it in me. I live a permanent dream which
stops neither night nor day. *Enesco:* Rumanian violinist (1881–1955), composer, and teacher. 1 *Ulysses:* see Tennyson, "Ulysses," and notes.

On the horizon and lifting himself up above it.
A form of fire approaches the cretonnes of Penelope,   5
Whose mere savage presence awakens the world in which she
     dwells.

She has composed, so long, a self with which to welcome him,
Companion to his self for her, which she imagined,
Two in a deep-founded sheltering, friend and dear friend.

The trees had been mended, as an essential exercise   10
In an inhuman meditation, larger than her own.
No winds like dogs watched over her at night.

She wanted nothing he could not bring her by coming alone.
She wanted no fetchings. His arms would be her necklace
And her belt, the final fortune of their desire.   15

But was it Ulysses? Or was it only the warmth of the sun
On her pillow? The thought kept beating in her like her heart.
The two kept beating together. It was only day.

It was Ulysses and it was not. Yet they had met,
Friend and dear friend and a planet's encouragement.   20
The barbarous strength within her would never fail.

She would talk a little to herself as she combed her hair,
Repeating his name with its patient syllables,
Never forgetting him that kept coming constantly so near.

T. S. ELIOT
1888–1965

The Love Song of J. Alfred Prufrock

S'io credesse che mia risposta fosse
A persona che mai tornasse al mondo,
Questa fiamma staria senza piu scosse.
Ma perciocche giammai di questo fondo
Non torno vivo alcun, s'i'odo il vero,
Senza tema d'infamia ti rispondo.

Let us go then, you and I,
When the evening is spread out against the sky
Like a patient etherised upon a table;
Let us go, through certain half-deserted streets,
The muttering retreats   5
Of restless nights in one-night cheap hotels
And sawdust restaurants with oyster-shells:
Streets that follow like a tedious argument
Of insidious intent
To lead you to an overwhelming question . . .   10
Oh, do not ask, "What is it?"
Let us go and make our visit.

In the room the women come and go
Talking of Michelangelo.

The yellow fog that rubs its back upon the window-panes,   15
The yellow smoke that rubs its muzzle on the window-panes
Licked its tongue into the corners of the evening,
Lingered upon the pools that stand in drains,
Let fall upon its back the soot that falls from chimneys,
Slipped by the terrace, made a sudden leap,   20

THE LOVE SONG. *S'io credesse . . . rispondo:* From Dante, *Divine Comedy:
Inferno*, XXVII, 61–66: "If I thought my answer were to one who ever / could
return to the world, this flame should / shake no more. / But since none ever
did return alive from this / depth, if what I hear be true, without fear of / infamy
I answer thee." Spoken by Guido da Montrefeltro, hidden in the flame of his
own sin, when asked why he is being punished. He speaks without fear only
because he thinks he is speaking to one of the damned. Although ordinarily
paralyzed with anxiety, Prufrock also speaks to us without fear of what the
world will say because, like Guido, he thinks the "you" of the poem is also, as
he is, damned and cannot return.

14 *Michelangelo:* Renaissance artist, sculptor, architect, poet, and lover
whose incredible creative energy, power, and appetite for life contrast ironically
with the pale, monotonous chit-chat of sterile society women, sophisticated to
near annihilation.

And seeing that it was a soft October night,
Curled once about the house, and fell asleep.

    And indeed there will be time
For the yellow smoke that slides along the street,
Rubbing its back upon the window-panes;   25
There will be time, there will be time
To prepare a face to meet the faces that you meet;
There will be time to murder and create,
And time for all the works and days of hands
That lift and drop a question on your plate;   30
Time for you and time for me,
And time yet for a hundred indecisions,
And for a hundred visions and revisions,
Before the taking of a toast and tea.

    In the room the women come and go   35
Talking of Michelangelo.

    And indeed there will be time
To wonder, "Do I dare?" and, "Do I dare?"
Time to turn back and descend the stair,
With a bald spot in the middle of my hair—   40
[They will say: "How his hair is growing thin!"]
My morning coat, my collar mounting firmly to the chin,
My necktie rich and modest, but asserted by a simple pin—
[They will say: "But how his arms and legs are thin!"]
Do I dare   45
Disturb the universe?
In a minute there is time
For decisions and revisions which a minute will reverse.

    For I have known them all already, known them all:—
Have known the evenings, mornings, afternoons,   50
I have measured out my life with coffee spoons;
I know the voices dying with a dying fall
Beneath the music from a farther room.
    So how should I presume?

---

29 *works and days:* ironic allusion to *Works and Days* by Hesiod (eighth-century B.C. Greek poet), who describes the productive labors and beliefs of his people. 47 *time:* Cf. Marvell, "To His Coy Mistress," ll. 1–20. Unlike the speaker in Marvell's poem, Prufrock has neither the wit to be ironic nor the strength to accept the ruthless fact that he has no time to decide and revise. 52 *dying fall:* Cf. Duke Orsino's speech, *Twelfth Night*, I, i, 1–7. Unlike the Duke, Prufrock does not have the richness of feeling to say of music ("the food of love"), "Give me excess of it."

And I have known the eyes already, known them all—   55
The eyes that fix you in a formulated phrase,
And when I am formulated, sprawling on a pin,
When I am pinned and wriggling on the wall,
Then how should I begin
To spit out all the butt-ends of my days and ways?   60
    And how should I presume?

    And I have known the arms already, known them all—
Arms that are braceleted and white and bare
[But in the lamplight, downed with light brown hair!]
Is it perfume from a dress   65
That makes me so digress?
Arms that lie along a table, or wrap about a shawl.
    And should I then presume?
    And how should I begin?

                    .   .   .

Shall I say, I have gone at dusk through narrow streets   70
And watched the smoke that rises from the pipes
Of lonely men in shirt-sleeves, leaning out of windows? . . .

    I should have been a pair of ragged claws
Scuttling across the floors of silent seas.

                    .   .   .

And the afternoon, the evening, sleeps so peacefully!   75
Smoothed by long fingers,
Asleep . . . tired . . . or it malingers,
Stretched on the floor, here beside you and me.
Should I, after tea and cakes and ices,
Have the strength to force the moment to its crisis?   80
But though I have wept and fasted, wept and prayed,
Though I have seen my head [grown slightly bald] brought in upon
        a platter,
I am no prophet—and here's no great matter;
I have seen the moment of my greatness flicker,
And I have seen the eternal Footman hold my coat, and snicker,
And in short I was afraid.   86

82 *my . . . platter:* like the head of John the Baptist. See Matt. 14:1–11
and Browning, "Fra Lippo Lippi," l. 34 and note.

And would it have been worth it, after all,
After the cups, the marmalade, the tea,
Among the porcelain, among some talk of you and me,
Would it have been worth while,   90
To have bitten off the matter with a smile,
To have squeezed the universe into a ball
To roll it toward some overwhelming question,
To say: "I am Lazarus, come from the dead,
Come back to tell you all, I shall tell you all"—   95
If one, settling a pillow by her head,
    Should say: "That is not what I meant at all.
    That is not it, at all."

And would it have been worth it, after all,
Would it have been worth while,   100
After the sunsets and the dooryards and the sprinkled streets,
After the novels, after the teacups, after the skirts that trail
    along the floor—
And this, and so much more?—
It is impossible to say just what I mean!
But as if a magic lantern threw the nerves in patterns on a screen:
Would it have been worth while   106
If one, settling a pillow or throwing off a shawl,
And turning toward the window, should say:
    "That is not it at all,
    That is not what I meant, at all."   110

          .   .   .

No! I am not Prince Hamlet, nor was meant to be;
Am an attendant lord, one that will do
To swell a progress, start a scene or two,
Advise the prince; no doubt, an easy tool,
Deferential, glad to be of use,   115
Politic, cautious, and meticulous;
Full of high sentence, but a bit obtuse;
At times, indeed, almost ridiculous—
Almost, at times, the Fool.

92 *To . . . ball:* Cf. Marvell, "To His Coy Mistress," ll. 41–42. Prufrock has no "sweetness" to roll up into "one ball," let alone the ecstasy and strength for such an act. 94 *Lazarus . . . dead:* an allusion both to the raising of Lazarus, brother of Mary and Martha, from the dead (John 11:1–44) and to the comforting redemption of the beggar Lazarus (Luke 16:19–25). Prufrock can hope for neither resurrection nor the bliss of salvation; he can only suggest the horrors of being "dead." 105 *magic lantern:* a projector for throwing magnified pictures upon a screen in a darkened room. 113 *swell a progress:* add to the company attending a prince on a formal, ceremonial journey. 117 *Full . . . sentence:* full of moral maxims and old saws, like Polonius in *Hamlet.*

I grow old. . . . I grow old . . .   120
I shall wear the bottoms of my trousers rolled.

Shall I part my hair behind? Do I dare to eat a peach?
I shall wear white flannel trousers, and walk upon the beach.
I have heard the mermaids singing, each to each.

I do not think that they will sing to me.   125

I have seen them riding seaward on the waves
Combing the white hair of the waves blown back
When the wind blows the water white and black.

We have lingered in the chambers of the sea
By sea-girls wreathed with seaweed red and brown   130
Till human voices wake us, and we drown.

La Figlia Che Piange

O quam te memorem virgo . . .

Stand on the highest pavement of the stair—
Lean on a garden urn—
Weave, weave the sunlight in your hair—
Clasp your flowers to you with a pained surprise—
Fling them to the ground and turn   5
With a fugitive resentment in your eyes:
But weave, weave the sunlight in your hair.

So I would have had him leave,
So I would have had her stand and grieve,
So he would have left   10
As the soul leaves the body torn and bruised,
As the mind deserts the body it has used.
I should find
Some way incomparably light and deft,
Some way we both should understand,   15
Simple and faithless as a smile and shake of the hand.

121 *I . . . rolled:* i.e., affect the latest fashion of the young and sophisticated; *rolled* means cuffed, then a foppish novelty. 125 *I . . . me:* since
he is no heroic adventurer, no Ulysses, the mermaids will not waste their
breath on Prufrock.

LA FIGLIA CHE PIANGE. *La Figlia, etc.:* The Girl who is crying. *O quam . . .
virgo:* "By what name shall I call thee, O maiden." Virgil, *Aeneid,* I, 327:
Aeneas' exclamation when he sees Venus (his mother and divine patroness),
disguised as a huntress near Carthage.

She turned away, but with the autumn weather
Compelled my imagination many days,
Many days and many hours:
Her hair over her arms and her arms full of flowers.   20
And I wonder how they should have been together!
I should have lost a gesture and a pose.
Sometimes these cogitations still amaze
The troubled midnight and the noon's repose.

Gerontion

Basic sym dryness
Ends -water)
(opposite)

Thou hast nor youth nor age
But as it were an after dinner sleep
Dreaming of both.

[*Measure for Measure*, III, i]

Here I am, an old man in a dry month,
Being read to by a boy, waiting for the rain.
I was neither at the hot gates
Nor fought in the warm rain
Nor knee deep in the salt marsh, heaving a cutlass,   5
Bitten by flies, fought.
My house is a decayed house,
And the jew squats on the window sill, the owner,

rented
thatch

Spawned in some estaminet of Antwerp,
Blistered in Brussels, patched and peeled in London.   10
The goat coughs at night in the field overhead;
Rocks, moss, stonecrop, iron, merds.
The woman keeps the kitchen, makes tea,
Sneezes at evening, poking the peevish gutter.
                    I an old man,   15
A dull head among windy spaces.

GERONTION. *Gerontion:* in traditional Christian imagery, the "old man" (Romans 6:6–11), Adam, "of the earth, earthy" (I Cor. 15:47) who cannot be saved unless he be crucified with Christ, the "last" Adam, the "quickening spirit" (I Cor. 15:22, 45). *Thou hast nor youth, etc.:* From the Duke's speech of advice and comfort to the condemned Claudio: "Be absolute [perfectly certain] for death," since life is unreal and futile.

2 *rain:* Cf. the "shoures soote" after the "droghte of March" in Chaucer, "The General Prologue," ll. 1–18. Gerontion is no pilgrim. 3–5 *hot gates . . . warm rain . . . salt marsh:* probably references to three tremendous battles that changed history: Thermopylae, Waterloo, Cannae. Gerontion, no hero, has sat apart, refusing to participate in history. 9 *estaminet:* café. 12 *stonecrop:* a low, spreading, moss-like herb with yellow flowers that grows among rocks. *merds:* turds. 14 *gutter:* drain.

a poem of non-commitment. Similar to J. A. Proof.

apology

Signs are taken for wonders. "We would see a sign!"
The word within a word, unable to speak a word,
Swaddled with darkness. In the juvescence of the year
Came Christ the tiger   20

Oyster period ← [In depraved May] dogwood and chestnut, flowering judas,
To be eaten, to be divided, to be drunk
Among whispers; by Mr. Silvero
With caressing hands, at Limoges
Who walked all night in the next room;   25

must be somewhat intelligent By Hakagawa, bowing among the Titians;
Tr twelve By Madame de Tornquist, in the dark room
Shifting the candles; Fräulein von Kulp
Who turned in the hall, one hand on the door.
               Vacant shuttles   30
not having any experience which whatever contrast with life Weave the wind. I have no ghosts,

17 *Signs . . . wonders:* quoted from Lancelot Andrewes, "Nativity Sermon,"
No. XII (1618). *sign:* The Pharisees, "an evil and adulterous generation,"
said to Christ: "Master, we would see a sign from thee," i.e., a miracle to
authenticate his claim to godhead. See Matt. 12:38–39. 18–19 *The . . . darkness:* Cf. ". . . *Verbum infans*, the Word without a word; the eternal Word
not able to speak a word; a wonder sure. And . . . swaddled [the mute,
infant Christ in his *creche*, the authentic *sign*. See Luke 2:12], a wonder too."
Lancelot Andrewes, "Nativity Sermon," No. XII. 19 *juvescence:* i.e., juvenes-
cence, springtime, the season of rejuvenation. 20 *Christ the tiger:* Cf. "I came
not to send peace, but a sword" (Matt. 10:34). Eliot may be alluding to the
Bestiary in which Christ is the "Spiritual Lion of the Tribe of Judah," and also
the "true Panther" from whose mouth issues the sweet smell like "all spice"
when it awakens in its cave three days after eating. See also Blake's "Tyger"
and notes. In India, Bengal, and Malaya, the tiger is thought to be a shape-
shifter, a familiar of magicians and medicine men, and is considered to be very
sensitive to disrespect, ready to avenge insults. If a man kills a tiger without
divine orders, he or a relative will be killed by a tiger. Even when a man-eating
tiger is slain, his spirit must be propitiated. Indian folklore underscores the
Biblical imagery of mystery, divinity in unusual manifestations, terrifying omnip-
otence, and the miraculous resurrection of power thought to be dead. 21
depraved May: i.e., the mysteries of May, of springtime renewal and joy, are
depraved by the lust, indolence, cruelty, and faithlessness of men. Cf. Chaucer,
"The General Prologue," ll. 1–18, and Herrick, "Corinna's Going a Maying."
22–23 *to . . . whispers:* the service of Holy Communion, the breaking and
eating of the bread (Christ's body), and the drinking of the wine (His blood).
23–29 *by . . . door:* perversions of the Sacrament by the secular and godless
behavior of rootless people who have abandoned their national cultures and
traditions: the Italianate Silvero, thinking of his Limoges china; Hakagawa
bowing to the lush, very un-Japanese paintings of Titian; de Tornquist practicing her un-Scandinavian spiritualism, possibly on von Kulp, her timid victim.
30–31 *shuttles . . . wind:* Cf. Job 7:6–7: "My days are swifter than a weaver's
shuttle, and are spent without hope. O remember that my life is wind: mine
eye shall no more see good." Cf. also Browning, "The Bishop Orders His
Tomb," l. 51. 31 *no ghosts:* i.e., no spiritual powers.

An old man in a draughty house
Under a windy knob.

    After such knowledge, what forgiveness? Think now
History has many cunning passages, contrived corridors   35
And issues, deceives with whispering ambitions,
Guides us by vanities. Think now
She gives when our attention is distracted
And what she gives, gives with such supple confusions
That the giving famishes the craving. Gives too late   40
What's not believed in, or if still believed,
In memory only, reconsidered passion. Gives too soon
Into weak hands, what's thought can be dispensed with
Till the refusal propagates a fear. Think
Neither fear nor courage saves us. Unnatural vices   *what issues*
Are fathered by our heroism. Virtues   *important*
Are forced upon us by our impudent crimes.   *is sin?*
These tears are shaken from the wrath-bearing tree.

    The tiger springs in the new year. Us he devours. Think at   *Christ*
      last   *not the*
We have not reached conclusion, when I   *Redemer*
Stiffen in a rented house. Think at last   50
I have not made this show purposelessly
And it is not by any concitation
Of the backward devils.
I would meet you upon this honestly.   55
I that was near your heart was removed therefrom
To lose beauty in terror, terror in inquisition.
I have lost my passion: why should I need to keep it
Since what is kept must be adulterated?   *fatalist*
I have lost my sight, smell, hearing, taste and touch: 60
How should I use them for your closer contact?

    These with a thousand small deliberations
Protract the profit of their chilled delirium,   *old Recollections*
Excite the membrane, when the sense has cooled.   *in old body*
With pungent sauces, multiply variety
In a wilderness of mirrors. What will the spider do,   65
Suspend its operations, will the weevil

33 *knob:* hill.   34 *forgiveness:* i.e., is there forgiveness for those who know, but ignore, the miracle of the Incarnation and Resurrection?   48 *tree:* i.e., the "interdicted tree" of the Knowledge of Good and Evil, Adam's Tree.   53 *concitation:* stirring up.   54 *backward devils:* false religions preceding Christianity.   55 *you:* Christ.

Delay? De Bailhache, Fresca, Mrs. Cammel, whirled
Beyond the circuit of the shuddering Bear
In fractured atoms. Gull against the wind, in the windy straits
Of Belle Isle, or running on the Horn,   71
White feathers in the snow, the Gulf claims,
And an old man driven by the Trades
To a sleepy corner.

                                        Tenants of the house,   75
Thoughts of a <u>dry brain</u> in a <u>dry season.</u>

Sweeney Among the Nightingales

ὤμοι, πέπληγμαι καιρίαν πληγὴν ἔσω.

Apeneck Sweeney spreads his knees
Letting his arms hang down to laugh,
The zebra stripes along his jaw
Swelling to maculate giraffe.

            The circles of the stormy moon   5
            Slide westward toward the River Plate,

68 *De Bailhache . . . Cammel:* random acquaintances among the lost in the
nationless prewar European society. 68–70 *whirled . . . atoms:* Cf. *Measure
for Measure*, III, i, 19–21, 118, 124–26. 69 *Bear:* the constellation *Ursa Major*,
which never sets. *Beyond the . . . Bear* suggests the terrible nothingness of
outer darkness. 70 *Gull:* The *Gull* is drowned in the immensity of the *Gulf*
despite its struggles; Gerontion, who like Prufrock has not the will to struggle,
will also drown without hope of rescue but without the knowledge gained by
endeavor, utterly lost in the narrow confines of a *sleepy corner.* 70–71 *straits
. . . Horn: Belle Isle* is the strait between Newfoundland and Labrador at the
northern entrance of the Gulf of St. Lawrence; Cape *Horn* is the southernmost
tip of South America, which includes the Strait of Magellan, noted for
ferocious weather. The two suggest the northern and southern extremes of
heroic exploration and discovery in which brave men have died. 73 *Trades:*
Trade Winds, steady winds from about 30° north or south of the equator
blowing toward the equator. 74 *sleepy corner:* i.e., the doldrums, those parts
of the ocean in the Atlantic very close to the equator where the trade winds
cease, and an enervating calm prevails, broken only by baffling light winds: a
deliberate contrast with the gales of Belle Isle and the Horn.

SWEENEY. The modern Agamemnon; his name symbolizes the brutal
vulgarity of the modern world, where heroism has been degraded to obscenity.
Epigraph: "Ay me! I am smitten with a mortal blow." Aeschylus, *Agamemnon*,
1343: the death cry of Agamemnon, murdered by his wife, Clytemnestra.
Sweeney suffers the same fate but reveals no heroic affirmation. Cf. Yeats,
"Leda and the Swan" and note.

1–4 *Apeneck, zebra, giraffe:* The animal imagery suggests the brutalizing,
dehumanizing effect of modern culture. 4 *maculate:* i.e., spotted, like a
giraffe, but also stained and defiled. 6 *River Plate:* Rio de La Plata, estuary
of the Paraná and Uruguay rivers between Argentina and Uruguay, suggesting
the enervated "new world" of degraded Latin and Irish violence in contrast
with the heroic "old" of ancient Greece.

Death and the Raven drift above
And Sweeney guards the hornèd gate.

Gloomy Orion and the Dog
Are veiled; and hushed the shrunken seas;   10
The person in the Spanish cape
Tries to sit on Sweeney's knees

Slips and pulls the table cloth
Overturns a coffee-cup,
Reorganized upon the floor   15
She yawns and draws a stocking up;

The silent man in mocha brown
Sprawls at the window-sill and gapes;
The waiter brings in oranges
Bananas figs and hothouse grapes;   20

The silent vertebrate in brown
Contracts and concentrates, withdraws;
Rachel *née* Rabinovitch
Tears at the grapes with murderous paws;

7 *Raven: Corvus*, a southern constellation; also the bird that traditionally anticipates battles and violent death, hovering over the field eager to feed on the slain. 8 *guards:* as the priest-king guards the sacred tree at the shrine of Diana at Nemi. See below l. 37 and note. *hornèd gate:* See *Odyssey*, XIX, 559 –67, and *Aeneid*, VI, 893–97: the gate of horn through which pass the true but ominous dreams. Like the priest at Nemi, Sweeney knows that he may be assassinated, but he guards against it with a laugh, as Agamemnon and the grim priest never did. 9 *Orion, Dog:* brilliant equatorial constellations. *Orion:* the giant hunter who loved Mereope but was shamefully rejected by her father Oenopion; *gloomy* (compared with Sirius he is of lesser magnitude) because unlucky, for when he took her by violence, Oenopion blinded him after Dionysius put him to sleep; he recovered his sight after his eyes were replenished with light when he was led to gaze full on the sun but was later slain by Artemis (Diana, goddess of the moon, "Queen and huntress, chaste and fair!"), some say by mistake at the instigation of Apollo, others by deliberate intent when she caused him to be stung to death by a scorpion after he tried to ravish her; she translated him to the stars where he shines brilliantly on winter nights (chasing without success the seven sisters, the Pleiades) but fades at the appearance of the constellation Scorpius, which is ill-omened, bringing cold, darkness, and evil influences on men. *Dog: Canis Major:* also Sirius, faithful companion of Orion, the Dog star (Alpha in *Canis Major*, brightest star in the heavens). Both constellations are *veiled*, i.e., hidden, to suggest the magnitude of the difference between the tragic stories of mythology and the gross lewdness of Sweeney's death. 11 *person . . . cape:* i.e., a prostitute, neither a chaste patroness of childbirth (like Diana) nor a fierce avenging wife and mother (like Clytemnestra). 17 *silent man:* possibly the fatigued, latter-day Aegisthus, Clytemnestra's lover and accomplice. 20 *hothouse grapes:* not the natural, sweet, and lifegiving grapes of Dionysius, but unnatural (because forced), tasteless, and sterile. 22 *contracts . . . withdraws:* i.e., serpent-like, cf. ll. 1–4 and notes.

She and the lady in the cape 25
Are suspect, thought to be in league;
Therefore the man with heavy eyes
Declines the gambit, shows fatigue,

Leaves the room and reappears
Outside the window, leaning in, 30
Branches of wistaria
Circumscribe a golden grin;

The host with someone indistinct
Converses at the door apart,
The nightingales are singing near 35
The Convent of the Sacred Heart,

And sang within the bloody wood
When Agamemnon cried aloud,
And let their liquid siftings fall
To stain the stiff dishonoured shroud. 40

28 *gambit:* opening move in chess in which the player risks a pawn to launch
an attack. The term once again underscores the absence of chivalric heroism
in the scene. 35 *nightingales:* See above, Sidney, "The Nightingale" and notes.
The myth of Philomela symbolizes the transformation through tragic suffering
of death and violence, lust and brutality, into "inviolable song," a rebirth that
the associations of *The Convent of the Sacred Heart* emphasize, but Sweeney's
pain and death have no spiritual meaning, even though the only bond between
him and Agamemnon is the song of the nightingale. 37 *bloody wood:* reference
to the Wood of Nemi, sacred to Diana (who here was revered chiefly for blessing
men and women with offspring and an easy delivery, see above, *moon, Orion,*
ll. 5, 9), where the priest-king was murdered with a sword by his younger
successor, who had first secretly plucked the magical golden bough (cf. *golden
grin,* l. 32) from the sacred tree in the guarded wood without the knowledge of
his victim: a vegetation and fertility ritual symbolizing birth, death, and rebirth
(see Frazer, *The Golden Bough,* Ch. 1). Agamemnon was not slain in the wood
but in his bath; however, Orestes, his son who slew Clytemnestra to avenge the
murder of his father, was pursued by the Furies, ministers of punishment for
crimes of bloodshed, whose sacred grove was filled with singing nightingales
(see Sophocles, *Oedipus at Colonus,* 17–18) until peace and reconciliation were
eventually accomplished. Orestes is also supposed to have instituted the
worship of Diana at Nemi. In ritual, myth, and legend, death is the way to life,
hope, and the eternity of art; here it means the way only to sterility, squalid
extinction, and an entry on the police blotter, for Sweeney is no priest-king of
fertility rites, no hero, and has no son to avenge him, nor like Orion will he be
stellified in golden armor. 39 *liquid siftings:* both the lovely song of the birds
and their filthy droppings; cf. above, *maculate,* l. 4.

Journey of the Magi

'A cold coming we had of it,
Just the worst time of the year
For a journey, and such a long journey:
The ways deep and the weather sharp,
The very dead of winter.'   5
And the camels galled, sore-footed, refractory,
Lying down in the melted snow.
There were times we regretted
The summer palaces on slopes, the terraces,
And the silken girls bringing sherbet.   10
Then the camel men cursing and grumbling
And running away, and wanting their liquor and women,
And the night-fires going out, and the lack of shelters,
And the cities hostile and the towns unfriendly
And the villages dirty and charging high prices: 15
A hard time we had of it.
At the end we preferred to travel all night,
Sleeping in snatches,
With the voices singing in our ears, saying
That this was all folly.   20

JOURNEY OF THE MAGI. *Magi:* See Matt. 2:1–12, the Gospel for Epiphany (The Manifestation of Christ to the Gentiles); see also the Epistle (Ephesians 3:1–12) where St. Paul writes that he was made a "minister . . . that [he] should preach among the Gentiles the unsearchable riches of Christ; and to make men see what is the fellowship of the mystery, which from the beginning of the world hath been hid in God, who created all things by Jesus Christ." The "mystery" ("which in other ages was not made known unto the sons of men") is that implicit in creation are the hidden "riches" of salvation (seen in part but never wholly measured) manifested by the life of Christ, beginning with the Journey of the Magi, and revealed through the grace of the Spirit to the Apostles, enabling them to preach with certitude and authority. In the persistent unease of the speaker, still disturbed long after the event, Eliot expresses the struggle of all men to comprehend the "mystery" and their sense of alienation from what was once comfortable and familiar because of their confrontation with the Birth. See also Yeats, "The Magi" and notes.

1–5 *A cold . . . winter:* An adaptation of Lancelot Andrewes, "Nativity Sermon," No. XV (1622): "It was no summer progress. A cold coming they had of it at this time of the year, just the worst time of the year to take a journey, and specially a long journey in. The ways deep, the weather sharp, the days short, the sun farthest off . . . 'the very dead of winter'." Andrewes contrasts the way the Magi came "cheerfully and quickly," "enquiring Him out diligently," "worshipping Him devoutly," with the latter-day Christian's hesitation and indolence and his habit of worshipping with his "hat" and not his "head." Eliot, however, concentrates on the consequence, the lifelong shock and puzzlement (not despair) that the "mystery" afterwards produced in a man struggling to believe, for ironically cheerfulness, diligence, and devotion do not necessarily produce the joyful certitude of a St. Paul. Compare the way Gerontion gives up.   10 *sherbet:* Oriental drink of sweetened fruit juice cooled with snow.

518

Then at dawn we came down to a temperate valley,
Wet, below the snow line, smelling of vegetation;
With a running stream and a water-mill beating the darkness,
And three trees on the low sky,
And an old white horse galloped away in the meadow.   25
Then we came to a tavern with vine-leaves over the lintel,
Six hands at an open door dicing for pieces of silver,
And feet kicking the empty wine-skins.
But there was no information, and so we continued
And arrived at evening, not a moment too soon   30
Finding the place; it was (you may say) satisfactory.

All this was a long time ago, I remember,
And I would do it again, but set down
This set down
This: were we led all that way for   35
Birth or Death? There was a Birth, certainly,
We had evidence and no doubt. I had seen birth and death,
But had thought they were different; this Birth was
Hard and bitter agony for us, like Death, our death.
We returned to our places, these Kingdoms,   40
But no longer at ease here, in the old dispensation,
With an alien people clutching their gods.
I should be glad of another death.

21–22 *temperate . . . vegetation:* after the *hard time*, suggestive of the moist, green Garden of Eden, the unfallen creation of Genesis 1.   24 *three trees:* suggestive of the three crosses on Calvary, of the Atonement for the Fall: "And with him they crucify two thieves; the one on the right hand, and the other on the left. And the scripture was fulfilled which saith, And he was numbered with the transgressors" (Mark 15:27–28).   25 *white horse:* suggestive of Last Judgment: "And I saw, and behold a white horse: and he that sat on him had a bow and a crown was given unto him: and he went forth conquering, and to conquer" (Rev. 6:2). See also Rev. 19:11 for the figure "called Faithful and True" ("The Word of God") on a white horse who in righteousness "doth judge and make war."   27 *dicing:* suggestive of the callous response (recorded in all four Gospels) to the Crucifixion: "And they crucified him, and parted his garments, casting lots: that it might be fulfilled which was spoken of the prophet, They parted my garments among them, and for my vesture did they cast lots." The *valley, trees, horse,* and *dicing* are, to the Magi, dimly and disturbingly prophetic of events that the Bible has already clearly reported to the reader but of which the Magi do not know. Dramatic irony underscores the simplicity and mystery of the Incarnation and Epiphany, the glory of the original Creation, and the ominousness of the Second Coming, of the past, present, and future history of the world in the Christian perspective.   28 *empty wine-skins:* suggestive of Matt. 9:17: the old wine-skins are kicked away, for the new wine of the new dispensation will require new wine-skins, i.e., a new mode of appearance, form.   41 *old dispensation:* in contrast with the "new" revelation of God's will, which The Magi know has occurred with the *Birth* but do not fathom.

from FOUR QUARTETS

Τοῦ λόγου δ'ἐόντος ξυνοῦ ζώουσιν οἱ πολλοὶ
ὡς ἰδίαν ἔχοντες φρόνησιν.

I. p. 77. Fragment 2.

ὁδὸς ἄνω κάτω μία καὶ ὡυτή.

I. p. 89. Fragment 60.

—H. Diels, *Die fragmente der Vorsokratiker* (Herakleitos).

The Dry Salvages

I

I do not know much about gods; but I think that the river
Is a strong brown god—sullen, untamed and intractable,
Patient to some degree, at first recognised as a frontier;
Useful, untrustworthy, as a conveyor of commerce;
Then only a problem confronting the builder of bridges.   5
The problem once solved, the brown god is almost forgotten
By the dwellers in cities—ever, however, implacable,
Keeping his seasons and rages, destroyer, reminder
Of what men choose to forget. Unhonoured, unpropitiated
By worshippers of the machine, but waiting, watching and waiting.
His rhythm was present in the nursery bedroom,   11
In the rank ailanthus of the April dooryard,
In the smell of grapes on the autumn table,
And the evening circle in the winter gaslight.

FOUR QUARTETS.   *Epigraphs:* The two fragments from Heraclitus, epigraphs
to the whole of the *Four Quartets*, poetically suggest the themes of all. See
Hopkins, "That Nature is a Heraclitean Fire" and notes. *Fragment 2:* "Therefore it is a duty to follow the common law. But although the Logos ("Word")
is common to all, the majority of people live as though they had an understanding of their own" (trans. Diels). *Fragment 60:* "The way up and the way
down is one and the same" (trans. John Burnet).

THE DRY SALVAGES: ". . . presumably *les trois sauvages*—a small group of
rocks, with a beacon, off the northeastern coast of Cape Ann, Massachusetts.
Salvages is pronounced to rhyme with *assuages*" [Eliot].

1 *river:* the Mississippi, but also the symbol of the interior flux of the life of
man, the course of his personal history, from birth through all the seasons of
his life to death (see ll. 11–14). 11 *nursery bedroom:* Eliot was born in St.
Louis and knew the river of Huck Finn. 12 *ailanthus:* "tree of heaven," a
large East Indian tree (naturalized in the United States) with evil-smelling
greenish flowers, hence *rank*.

The river is within us, the sea is all about us;   15
The sea is the land's edge also, the granite
Into which it reaches, the beaches where it tosses
Its hints of earlier and other creation:
The starfish, the hermit crab, the whale's backbone;
The pools where it offers to our curiosity   20
The more delicate algae and the sea anemone.
It tosses up our losses, the torn seine,
The shattered lobsterpot, the broken oar
And the gear of foreign dead men. The sea has many voices,
Many gods and many voices.
                         The salt is on the briar rose,   25
The fog is in the fir trees.
                         The sea howl
And the sea yelp, are different voices
Often together heard; the whine in the rigging,
The menace and caress of wave that breaks on water,
The distant rote in the granite teeth,   30
And the wailing warning from the approaching headland
Are all sea voices, and the heaving groaner
Rounded homewards, and the seagull:
And under the oppression of the silent fog
The tolling bell   35
Measures time not our time, rung by the unhurried
Ground swell, a time
Older than the time of chronometers, older
Than time counted by anxious worried women
Lying awake, calculating the future,   40
Trying to unweave, unwind, unravel
And piece together the past and the future,
Between midnight and dawn, when the past is all deception,
The future futureless, before the morning watch
When time stops and time is never ending;   45
And the ground swell, that is and was from the beginning,
Clangs
The bell.

15 *sea:* the eternal flux of time, of the history of the world, which swallows up the *river* of every man, making each one the prisoner of time, as the wreckage on the beach testifies.   30 *rote:* the roaring of the surf on the shore. 32 *groaner:* "a whistling buoy" [Eliot].   33 *Rounded:* i.e., by a ship.   35 *tolling bell:* of a bell buoy, rung rhythmically by the *Ground swell:* hence the *tolling* of the sea, i.e., of time.   44 *before . . . watch:* traditionally the darkest hour. Paradoxical allusion to Ps. 130 (*De Profundis* ["Out of the deep have I called unto thee, O Lord"]): 6: "My soul fleeth unto the Lord: before the morning watch, I say, before the morning watch," which prefigures the certitude of eternity in the midst of calamity and danger revealed in the *angelus* at the end of section IV.   46 *that . . . beginning:* variation of the *Gloria Patri:* "As it was in the beginning, is now and ever shall be: world without end."

II

Where is there an end of it, the soundless wailing,
The silent withering of autumn flowers   50
Dropping their petals and remaining motionless;
Where is there an end to the drifting wreckage,
The prayer of the bone on the beach, the unprayable
Prayer at the calamitous annunciation?

There is no end, but addition: the trailing   55
Consequence of further days and hours,
While emotion takes to itself the emotionless
Years of living among the breakage
Of what was believed in as the most reliable—
And therefore the fittest for renunciation.   60

There is the final addition, the failing
Pride or resentment at failing powers,
The unattached devotion which might pass for devotionless,
In a drifting boat with a slow leakage,
The silent listening to the undeniable   65
Clamour of the bell of the last annunciation.

Where is the end of them, the fishermen sailing
Into the wind's tail, where the fog cowers?
We cannot think of a time that is oceanless
Or of an ocean not littered with wastage   70
Or of a future that is not liable
Like the past, to have no destination.

We have to think of them as forever bailing,
Setting and hauling, while the North East lowers
Over shallow banks unchanging and erosionless   75
Or drawing their money, drying sails at dockage;
Not as making a trip that will be unpayable
For a haul that will not bear examination.

53–54 *unprayable . . . annunciation:* the one whose bone is on the beach
was unable to pray when disaster overwhelmed him, for to pray exclusively
for one's personal safety at such *calamitous* moments (*annunciation*) in
time is impossible and irrelevant. Cf. *annunciation,* ll. 66, 84. 66 *last
annunciation:* i.e., death. 74 *setting and hauling:* working the sails to catch
the wind; to sail nearer to the wind. *North East:* off New England, the
fiercest gales are the Northeasters. 76 *dockage:* while tied up at their berths.
78 *haul:* i.e., of fish. A paradoxical allusion to Luke 5:1–10 when Peter and
Andrew, after having "taken nothing," upon the instruction of Jesus caught a
"great multitude of fishes" and thence became "fishers of men" (Matt. 4:19).
Miracles happen only once, and a skeptic fisherman like the unconverted Peter
usually will not risk an unprofitable trip.

There is no end of it, the voiceless wailing,
No end to the withering of withered flowers,   80
To the movement of pain that is painless and motionless,
To the drift of the sea and the drifting wreckage,
The bone's prayer to Death its God. Only the hardly, barely
     prayable
Prayer of the one Annunciation.

    It seems, as one becomes older,   85
That the past has another pattern, and ceases to be a mere
     sequence—
Or even development: the latter a partial fallacy,
Encouraged by superficial notions of evolution,
Which becomes, in the popular mind, a means of disowning the
     past.
The moments of happiness—not the sense of well-being,   90
Fruition, fulfilment, security or affection,
Or even a very good dinner, but the sudden illumination—
We had the experience but missed the meaning,
And approach to the meaning restores the experience
In a different form, beyond any meaning   95
We can assign to happiness. I have said before
That the past experience revived in the meaning
Is not the experience of one life only
But of many generations—not forgetting
Something that is probably quite ineffable: 100
The backward look behind the assurance
Of recorded history, the backward half-look
Over the shoulder, towards the primitive terror.
Now, we come to discover that the moments of agony
(Whether, or not, due to misunderstanding,   105
Having hoped for the wrong things or dreaded the wrong things,
Is not in question) are likewise permanent
With such permanence as time has. We appreciate this better
In the agony of others, nearly experienced,
Involving ourselves, than in our own.   110
For our own past is covered by the currents of action,
But the torment of others remains an experience
Unqualified, unworn by subsequent attrition.
People change, and smile: but the agony abides.

83–84 *barely . . . Annunciation:* the only relevant and truly honest prayer:
"Behold the handmaid of the Lord; be it unto me according to thy word"
(Luke 1:38), the prayer (that she may accept her destiny) of the Blessed Virgin
Mary at the Annunciation by the Angel Gabriel that she was to bear the
Son of God. 100 *ineffable:* too sacred or lofty to utter. 103 *primitive
terror:* Cf. above, *hints of earlier and other creation,* l. 18.

Time the destroyer is time the preserver,   115
Like the river with its cargo of dead Negroes, cows and chicken
    coops,
The bitter apple and the bite in the apple.
And the ragged rock in the restless waters,
Waves wash over it, fogs conceal it;
On a halcyon day it is merely a monument,   120
In navigable weather it is always a seamark
To lay a course by: but in the sombre season
Or the sudden fury, is what it always was.

                                III

I sometimes wonder if that is what Krishna meant—
Among other things—or one way of putting the same thing: 125
That the future is a faded song, a Royal Rose or a lavender spray
Of wistful regret for those who are not yet here to regret,
Pressed between yellow leaves of a book that has never been opened.
And the way up is the way down, the way forward is the way
    back.
You cannot face it steadily, but this thing is sure,   130
That time is no healer: the patient is no longer here.
When the train starts, and the passengers are settled
To fruit, periodicals and business letters
(And those who saw them off have left the platform)
Their faces relax from grief into relief,   135
To the sleepy rhythm of a hundred hours.
Fare forward, travellers! not escaping from the past
Into different lives, or into any future;

115 *Time . . . preserver:* the paradox that within the flux is the still point of
eternity that preserves, so that flux is the way to changelessness.   117 *apple
. . . apple:* of the Tree of Knowledge of Good and Evil which brought
about the Fall, and the ultimate consequence of the *bite:* salvation through
the *felix culpa.*   The consonance of *bitter* and *bite* underscores the paradox of
Time the destroyer and also the *preserver.*   124 *Krishna:* one of the most
attractive incarnations of the Vishnu of Hinduism, the principle of light
penetrating the whole universe. He was the divine charioteer of Arjuna in the
war of the Pandavas against their cousins, the Kurus. Just before the battle,
Arjuna hesitated to fight, because it would mean killing his relatives. In the
Bhagavad-Gita (*The Song of the Blessed,* a book the Hindus regard as the equal
to the *New Testament*), Krishna replies that if Arjuna shows cowardice he
cannot go to heaven; that killing and dying are merely appearances, for the
soul is eternal, and those on the battlefield have always existed and despite
death will continue to exist; that salvation lies in submitting to one's duty free
from all personal desire; that at one's death, one goes to whatever sphere of
thought he was contemplating at the moment of death; and therefore one
should remember Krishna and fight. Cf. also the epigraphs from Heraclitus.
126–28 *future . . . opened:* various metaphors to express the realization that
the future is the repetition of the past, the past of the not yet arrived future, the
persistence of reincarnation and metempsychosis.   129 *And . . . back:* an
adaptation of the second epigraph from Heraclitus.

You are not the same people who left that station
Or who will arrive at any terminus, 140
While the narrowing rails slide together behind you;
And on the deck of the drumming liner
Watching the furrow that widens behind you,
You shall not think "the past is finished"
Or "the future is before us." 145
At nightfall, in the rigging and the aerial,
Is a voice descanting (though not to the ear,
The murmuring shell of time, and not in any language)
"Fare forward, you who think that you are voyaging;
You are not those who saw the harbour 150
Receding, or those who will disembark.
Here between the hither and the farther shore
While time is withdrawn, consider the future
And the past with an equal mind.
At the moment which is not of action or inaction 155
You can receive this: 'on whatever sphere of being
The mind of a man may be intent
At the time of death'—that is the one action
(And the time of death is every moment)
Which shall fructify in the lives of others: 160
And do not think of the fruit of action.
Fare forward.
    O voyagers, O seamen,
You who come to port, and you whose bodies
Will suffer the trial and judgement of the sea,
Or whatever event, this is your real destination." 165
So Krishna, as when he admonished Arjuna
On the field of battle.
    Not fare well,
But fare forward, voyagers.

142 *drumming:* i.e., the rhythmic beat of the screws that propel the liner.
143 *furrow:* i.e., the wake of the ship. *widens:* Cf. narrowing, l. 141. 147
descanting: an ornamental upper voice (the counterpoint above) commenting
upon the lower melody. 148 *murmuring . . . time:* i.e., the conch shell
(which looks like an ear), in which one can supposedly hear the *murmuring*
of the sea, i.e., of *time.* 152 *Here:* i.e., the present, between past and future.
154 *equal mind:* i.e., quiet mind, free from the perturbations of personal
desire and self-interest. 155 *the moment:* i.e., of *sudden illumination* (l. 92).
156–58 *on. . . death:* Krishna's exhortation to Arjuna (see l. 124 and note).
158 *one action:* i.e., at the moment of death, to be remembering Krishna, to be
intent on his teachings—duty, the immortality of the soul, and death as mere
appearance. 160 *fructify:* bear fruit through selfless acts of charity. 161
fruit: consequences in terms of personal interest and advantage, joy and
grief, and perhaps a paradoxical allusion to the *bitter apple,* l. 117, (cf.
Milton, *Paradise Lost,* I, 1–5), which has caused the perpetual vanity and folly
of human endeavor. 168 *fare forward:* i.e., accept one's destiny (cf. ll. 83–84)
and cheerfully do one's duty (cf. ll. 156–58).

IV

Lady, whose shrine stands on the promontory,
Pray for all those who are in ships, those   170
Whose business has to do with fish, and
Those concerned with every lawful traffic
And those who conduct them.

Repeat a prayer also on behalf of
Women who have seen their sons or husbands   175
Setting forth, and not returning:
Figlia del tuo figlio,
Queen of Heaven.

Also pray for those who were in ships, and
Ended their voyage on the sand, in the sea's lips   180
Or in the dark throat which will not reject them
Or wherever cannot reach them the sound of the sea bell's
Perpetual angelus.

V

To communicate with Mars, converse with spirits,
To report the behaviour of the sea monster,   185
Describe the horoscope, haruspicate or scry,
Observe disease in signatures, evoke
Biography from the wrinkles of the palm
And tragedy from fingers; release omens
By sortilege, or tea leaves, riddle the inevitable   190
With playing cards, fiddle with pentagrams

169 *Lady . . . promontory:* Invocation to the Blessed Virgin Mary, *Stella Maris*, to whom the fishermen and their wives pray. The speaker asks three times as in the prayer of the Angelus for Mary to "pray for us sinners, now and at the hour of our death." 177 *Figlia . . . figlio:* "[Virgin Mother,] Daughter of thine own Son"—from the prayer of St. Bernard to the Virgin in Dante, *Paradiso,* XXXIII, when he prays for intercession for Dante that grace may be granted him to see God. 181 *reject:* spew out, cast back. 183 *angelus:* the bell, rung morning, noon, and night, that calls men to the prayer commemorating the Annunciation by which men ". . . have known the incarnation of . . . Jesus Christ" (Collect for the Annunciation). Cf. above ll. 35–48. The Incarnation thus foretold by the *angelus* is the unmoving center in the ceaseless flux of time, a moment of *illumination,* heard here in the clang of the unmoving bell buoy (anchored firmly to one spot) rung by the ceaseless swell of the sea. 184–94 *To . . . dreams:* The *Pastimes,* etc. (l. 195), by which men delude themselves into thinking they know the past, can foresee the future, or escape from time altogether. 186 *haruspicate:* discover the will of the gods by inspecting entrails of sacrificed animals. *scry:* (descry) look into the crystal ball. 190 *sortilege:* drawing lots, sorcery. 191 *pentagram:* in magic, a five-pointed circle, containing mystical figures, with five lobes like those of a star.

Or barbituric acids, or dissect
The recurrent image into pre-conscious terrors—
To explore the womb, or tomb, or dreams; all these are usual
Pastimes and drugs, and features of the press: 195
And always will be, some of them especially
When there is distress of nations and perplexity
Whether on the shores of Asia, or in the Edgware Road.
Men's curiosity searches past and future
And clings to that dimension. But to apprehend   200
The point of intersection of the timeless
With time, is an occupation for the saint—
No occupation either, but something given
And taken, in a lifetime's death in love,
Ardour and selflessness and self-surrender.   205
For most of us, there is only the unattended
Moment, the moment in and out of time,
The distraction fit, lost in a shaft of sunlight,
The wild thyme unseen, or the winter lightning
Or the waterfall, or music heard so deeply   210
That it is not heard at all, but you are the music
While the music lasts. These are only hints and guesses,
Hints followed by guesses; and the rest
Is prayer, observance, discipline, thought and action.
The hint half guessed, the gift half understood, is Incarnation.   215
Here the impossible union
Of spheres of existence is actual,
Here the past and future
Are conquered, and reconciled,
Where action were otherwise movement   220
Of that which is only moved

192 *barbituric acids:* i.e., sleeping pills.   192–93 *dissect . . . terrors:* as in
psychoanalysis. See also l. 194.   198 *Edgware Road:* a dismal street in London,
particularly associated with sad and lonely human histories.   199–215 *Men's
. . . Incarnation:* a recapitulation (as in the last section of a string quartet) of
the themes and images of the preceding sections (or movements).   202 *occupation . . . saint:* in contrast with the *Pastimes* above, ll. 184–94.   205 *self-
surrender:* e.g., as expressed in the Virgin's prayer, ll. 83–84, and the exhortation
of Krishna, ll. 156–58.   207 *moment . . . out:* birth, death.   208 *shaft of
sunlight:* i.e., the *sudden illumination,* l. 92.   209 *thyme unseen:* (note pun)
herb not seen in the field, but suddenly smelled.   *winter lightning:* unexpected,
for lightning seldom occurs in winter. Cf. the traditional imagery of Christ's
Birth (Incarnation) as a sudden blaze of light at the midnight of the year (see
also John 1:5).   210 *waterfall:* heard before seen.   *Thyme, lightning, waterfall,*
and *music* so perceived are all natural "incarnations," analogous to that of
Christ.   214 *prayer . . . action:* Cf. the exhortation of Krishna to Arjuna to
duty, action; and the Heraclitean "duty" to follow the "common law."   215
Incarnation: the miraculous "point of intersection of the timeless / With time
(ll. 201–02).   216 *impossible union:* i.e., of divine and human, timeless and
timeful, unmoving and moving, a union *impossible* to comprehend by reason.
Cf. Yeats, "The Magi," l. 8: "The uncontrollable mystery on the bestial floor."

And has in it no source of movement—
Driven by daemonic, chthonic
Powers. And right action is freedom
From past and future also. 225
For most of us, this is the aim
Never here to be realised;
Who are only undefeated
Because we have gone on trying;
We, content at the last 230
If our temporal reversion nourish
(Not too far from the yew-tree)
The life of significant soil.

from FIVE-FINGER EXERCISES

IV. Lines to Ralph Hodgson Esqre.

How delightful to meet Mr. Hodgson!
          (Everyone wants to know *him*)—
With his musical sound
And his Baskerville Hound
Which, just at a word from his master 5
Will follow you faster and faster
And tear you limb from limb.
How delightful to meet Mr. Hodgson!
Who is worshipped by all waitresses

223 *chthonic:* underworld.   224 *freedom:* in which there is no thought of *the fruit of the action;* see above l. 161.   228–29 *Who . . . trying:* Cf. above, "Gerontion," ll. 70–74: the old man gives up, but the gull attempts the straits. It is one's duty to keep on *trying* and *freedom* (l. 224) to accept the inevitable death. Only thus is there *right action* and no defeat.   231 *reversion:* residue, the body.   232 *yew-tree:* which borders the consecrated ground of the grave-yard.   233 *significant soil:* the patient, abiding dust out of which man came and to which he returns, the source of life and the image of death; the beginning and the completion, immortal mortality.

IV. LINES TO RALPH HODGSON. *Ralph Hodgson:* (1871–1962) English poet of the Georgian period, celebrated almost exclusively for three poems written in 1913: "The Bull" (the dying reminiscences in the "forest beautiful" by an old bull, now "Half the bull he was before," of his life, e.g., how he "Beat his bull and won his cow," before the vultures get him); "Song of Honour" (in the evening song of the "babble-wren and nightingale" the speaker hears the "universal choir" of "The Sons of Light exalt their Sire" to which with eyes "blind with stars" he cries "Amen"); and "Eve" (the seduction of Eve in an orchard as "Titmouse and Jenny Wren" scold the snake and pity "Poor motherless Eve"). The publication of Eliot's "The Waste Land" in 1922–23 effectively put an end to this school of poetry. Modern poetry has little of Georgian rurality.   4 *Baskerville Hound:* Cf. A Conan Doyle, "The Hound of the Baskervilles."

528

(They regard him as something apart)   10
While on his palate fine he presses
The juice of the gooseberry tart.
How delightful to meet Mr. Hodgson!
        (Everyone wants to know *him*).
He has 999 canaries   15
And round his head finches and fairies
In jubilant rapture skim.
How delightful to meet Mr. Hodgson!
        (Everyone wants to meet *him*).

V. Lines for Cuscuscaraway and Mirza Murad Ali Beg

How unpleasant to meet Mr. Eliot!
With his features of clerical cut,
And his brow so grim
And his mouth so prim
And his conversation, so nicely   5
Restricted to What Precisely
And If and Perhaps and But.
How unpleasant to meet Mr. Eliot!
With a bobtail cur
In a coat of fur   10
And a porpentine cat
And a wopsical hat:
How unpleasant to meet Mr. Eliot!
        (Whether his mouth be open or shut).

v. LINES FOR CUSCUSCARAWAY. *Cuscuscaraway:* i.e., *cuscus*, a Moroccan dish made of an African cereal (like millet), plus *caraway*, a spicy seed used in confections and as a carminative. *Mirza . . . Beg:* proper names of Persian and Arabic origin; *Beg* is a Turkish title of rank. Amusing consonance, fanciful rhythms, and Eastern Mediterranean and Muslim connotations are here more significant than literal meaning. 11 *porpentine:* the Shakespearian spelling of "porcupine," which suggests Elizabethan popular notions that "each particular hair" on the cat's back stands on end "Like quills upon the fretful porpentine" (*Hamlet*, I, v, 20) as if it continually saw the Ghost and heard the horror, and that its nature when angered is to dart its "prickles" from its back, making it capable of killing a lion (*OED*). 12 *wopsical:* comically tangled, disordered (a word probably derived from "wasp").

W. H. AUDEN
1907—

Musée des Beaux Arts

About suffering they were never wrong,
The Old Masters: how well they understood
Its human position; how it takes place
While someone else is eating or opening a window or just walking
      dully along;
How, when the aged are reverently, passionately waiting   5
For the miraculous birth, there always must be
Children who did not specially want it to happen, skating
On a pond at the edge of the wood:
They never forgot
That even the dreadful martyrdom must run its course   10
Anyhow in a corner, some untidy spot
Where the dogs go on with their doggy life and the torturer's horse
Scratches its innocent behind on a tree.

In Brueghel's *Icarus*, for instance: how everything turns away
Quite leisurely from the disaster; the ploughman may   15
Have heard the splash, the forsaken cry,
But for him it was not an important failure; the sun shone
As it had to on the white legs disappearing into the green
Water; and the expensive delicate ship that must have seen
Something amazing, a boy falling out of the sky,   20
Had somewhere to get to and sailed calmly on.

MUSÉE DES BEAUX ARTS. I.e., the *Musées Royaux des Beaux Arts* (The Royal Museums of Fine Arts) in Brussels, Belgium. 5–8 *How . . . wood:* Possibly a reference to Brueghel's "The Numbering at Bethlehem (The Census)," at the Royal Museums. 10–13 *martyrdom . . . tree:* similar to Brueghel's "The Massacre of the Innocents," which is, however, at Vienna. 14 *Icarus:* "Landscape with the Fall of Icarus" by Pieter Brueghel the Elder (1525–69) at Brussels. Daedalus, an ingenious and cunning craftsman, imprisoned with his son Icarus in the Labyrinth he had constructed for King Minos of Crete, escaped by fashioning wings for himself and his son that enabled them to fly out. Icarus, overbold and disobedient, flew too close to the sun, so that the wax that held his wings together melted, and he fell to his death into the sea. 17 *important failure:* i.e., in the history of man's efforts to fly.

529

In Memory of W. B. Yeats

(D. JAN. 1939)

1

He disappeared in the dead of winter:
The brooks were frozen, the airports almost deserted,
And snow disfigured the public statues;
The mercury sank in the mouth of the dying day.
O all the instruments agree   5
The day of his death was a dark cold day.

Far from his illness
The wolves ran on through the evergreen forests,
The peasant river was untempted by the fashionable quays;
By mourning tongues   10
The death of the poet was kept from his poems.

But for him it was his last afternoon as himself,
An afternoon of nurses and rumours;
The provinces of his body revolted,
The squares of his mind were empty,   15
Silence invaded the suburbs,
The current of his feeling failed: he became his admirers.

IN MEMORY. Although not strictly speaking a pastoral elegy like Milton's "Lycidas" or an adaptation of the genre like Wordsworth's "Ode" or Shelley's "Adonais," Auden's poem functions in an ironic and elliptical fashion as a traditional pastoral elegy; from time to time it makes use of the old conventions, but without using the traditional *schema*, the pastoral disguises, or classical myths. See notes to Spenser's "November," *The Shepheardes Calender*, p. 41; Milton's "Lycidas," p. 145; Wordsworth's "Ode," p. 257; and Shelley's "Adonais," p. 309.

2–6 *brooks . . . cold day:* not the pathetic fallacy (cf. "Lycidas," l. 37 and note) but the literal facts (which ironically are adequate and telling "responses" but totally ignored by men) of indifferent nature to the momentous death. 8 *wolves:* i.e., do not stop doing what they have always done: harry the sheep and slaughter the innocent and helpless in the northern forests. Cf. "Lycidas," l. 128 and note, and "Adonais," l. 244. 9 *peasant:* Cf. "uncouth swain" in "Lycidas," l. 186. *Wolves* and *peasant* suggest a reference to the pastoral tradition. 10–11 *mourning . . . poems:* i.e., the *mourning tongues* of the poet's *admirers* (l. 17) *kept* the news of his death secret from the *poems* (his "flocks" in the pastoral tradition, and here conceived as having an autonomous existence) so that they do not lament, sicken, and die (cf. "Adonais," ll. 73–81): another avoidance of (but referral to) the pathetic fallacy. 13 *nurses:* Cf. "Lycidas," l. 50, and the traditional question: "Where were ye Nymphs . . .?" The *nurses* are as helpless as the "Nymphs." 14–17 *provinces . . . failed:* the modern metaphor of civil war and the besieged city overwhelmed (Barcelona fell on January 26, two days before the death of Yeats, in the closing days of the Spanish Civil War, 1936–39) rather than those of classical myths that envelop the deaths of Lycidas and Adonais. 17 *he . . . admirers:* Dead, he entered into the lives of the readers (his *admirers*) of his poems and hence continues to live. Cf. the resurrection of Lycidas as the "Genius of the shore" (ll. 183–85) and particularly that of Adonais (ll. 392–96).

Now he is scattered among a hundred cities
And wholly given over to unfamiliar affections;
To find his happiness in another kind of wood   20
And be punished under a foreign code of conscience.
The words of a dead man
Are modified in the guts of the living.

But in the importance and the noise of tomorrow
When the brokers are roaring like beasts on the floor of the
    Bourse,   25
And the poor have the sufferings to which they are fairly
    accustomed,
And each in the cell of himself is almost convinced of his freedom;
A few thousand will think of this day
As one thinks of a day when one did something slightly unusual.

O all the instruments agree   30
The day of his death was a dark cold day.

2

You were silly like us: your gift survived it all;
The parish of rich women, physical decay,
Yourself; mad Ireland hurt you into poetry.
Now Ireland has her madness and her weather still,   35

---

20 *another . . . wood:* i.e., from that of Irish mythology, legend, and history. Cf. also Dante, *Hell,* I: "Midway this way of life we're bound upon, / I woke to find myself in a dark wood / Where the right road was wholly lost and gone" (trans. Sayers), which would suggest that Yeats, like Dante, must descend into a kind of hell (*guts*), be *punished,* purged, before achieving *happiness* in the lives of free men who have learned through his poetry to *praise* (cf. l. 77). 22–23 *words . . . living:* For Milton and Shelley, the words of a poet have a sacred independence, like that of the divine *Logos,* but Auden admits the modern tendency to make the words mean what the reader wants them to mean. See, however, ll. 66 ff., where the reincarnated poet triumphs over the *guts of the living,* and the *words* master the living man. 25 *brokers . . . Bourse:* i.e., the "false shepherds" of the modern world scrambling at the "shearer's feast" in the Paris Bourse (Stock Exchange), fleecing their trusting customers, a corruption that contributed to the fall of France in 1940. Cf. "Lycidas," ll. 115–24, and also "the unpastured dragon," "Adonais," l. 238 and notes. 26–27 *poor . . . freedom:* the "hungry sheep" of the modern world, enslaved and "not fed." Cf. "Lycidas," ll. 125–27 and the savage language and tone. The satiric mode is part of the pastoral tradition. 32–34 *You . . . poetry:* The modern version of the recollection of the shared life as poets. Cf. "Lycidas," ll. 23–36.

For poetry makes nothing happen: it survives
In the valley of its saying where executives
Would never want to tamper; it flows south
From ranches of isolation and the busy griefs,
Raw towns that we believe and die in; it survives,   40
A way of happening, a mouth.

3

Earth, receive an honoured guest;
William Yeats is laid to rest:
Let the Irish vessel lie
Emptied of its poetry.   45

Time that is intolerant
Of the brave and innocent,
And indifferent in a week
To a beautiful physique,

Worships language and forgives   50
Everyone by whom it lives;
Pardons cowardice, conceit,
Lays its honours at their feet.

Time that with this strange excuse
Pardoned Kipling and his views,   55
And will pardon Paul Claudel,
Pardons him for writing well.

36–40 *For poetry . . . survives:* implies the prior questioning of faith in the worth of tending "the homely slighted shepherd's trade" ("Lycidas," l. 119) and recovery of faith, in this resolute affirmation that poetry has an inviolable existence beyond mortality. Cf. "Lycidas," ll. 76–84. 41 *a mouth:* but not the "Blind mouths" ("Lycidas," l. 119), which pervert, distort, and mislead. 42–45 *Earth . . . poetry:* In the change of tone and form, and in the elevation of language, Auden assumes the completion of the traditional procession of mourners, the acceptance of the propriety of death, and proceeds to the consolation. 55 [Rudyard] *Kipling:* (1865–1936) English author and poet, celebrator of the Empire, perhaps unfairly singled out to symbolize a crass and overbearing imperialistic policy. 56 *Paul Claudel:* (1868–1955) French poet, dramatist, and diplomat (Ambassador at Tokyo, Washington, and Brussels), trained in the school of the Symbolists of Rimbaud, but conservative in politics and in Catholic metaphysical views and themes; an inventive and meticulous craftsman using bold imagery and a verse form of his own invention, and a rich stylist possessing lyric fervor.

In the nightmare of the dark
All the dogs of Europe bark,
And the living nations wait,   60
Each sequestered in its hate;

Intellectual disgrace
Stares from every human face,
And the seas of pity lie
Locked and frozen in each eye.   65

Follow, poet, follow right
To the bottom of the night,
With your unconstraining voice
Still persuade us to rejoice;

With the farming of a verse   70
Make a vineyard of the curse,
Sing of human unsuccess
In a rapture of distress;

In the deserts of the heart
Let the healing fountain start,   75
In the prison of his days
Teach the free man how to praise.

Matthew Arnold

His gift knew what he was—a dark disordered city;
Doubt hid it from the father's fond chastising sky;
Where once the mother-farms had glowed protectively,
Stood the haphazard alleys of the neighbour's pity.

58–65 *In. . .eye:* When Yeats died, the Spanish Civil War was coming to a savage, bloody close, leaving a million people dead; World War II would begin on September 1; and the brutal Russo-Finnish War on November 30: a period unparalleled in human history for cruelty, tyrannic oppression, wholesale slaughter, and deliberate genocide. If, in his note to "Lycidas," Milton "foretells the ruin of our corrupted Clergy," Auden foretells a far worse destruction than what the "two-handed engine" of "Lycidas" invokes. 69 *rejoice:* to Yeats in "Lapis Lazuli," poets must always be "gay" and *rejoice* in the tragic euphoria of great art.   70, 71 *farming, vineyard:* pastoral language and imagery in the tradition of Virgil, Spenser, and Milton; in the paradoxes beginning with *Make a vineyard of the curse*, there is a modern analogy of the traditional apotheosis of the lost poet (the providential bringing of good out of evil) that consoles and inspirits the living. Cf. "Lycidas," ll. 165–85, and "Adonais," ll. 343–468 and notes.   75 *healing fountain:* Cf. Rev. 7:17.

MATTHEW ARNOLD.   2 *father's . . . sky:* Thomas Arnold (1795–1842), famous headmaster of Rugby, possessed of "radiant vigour," seemingly impervious to doubt, and staunch advocate of muscular Christianity. See Matthew Arnold's poem, "Rugby Chapel."

534

—Yet would have gladly lived in him and learned his ways,   5
And grown observant like a beggar, and become
Familiar with each square and boulevard and slum,
And found in the disorder a whole world to praise.

But all his homeless reverence, revolted, cried:
"I am my father's forum and he shall be heard,   10
Nothing shall contradict his holy final word,
Nothing." And thrust his gift in prison till it died,

And left him nothing but a jailor's voice and face,
And all rang hollow but the clear denunciation
Of a gregarious optimistic generation   15
That saw itself already in a father's place.

September 1, 1939

I sit in one of the dives
On Fifty-second Street
Uncertain and afraid
As the clever hopes expire
Of a low dishonest decade: 5
Waves of anger and fear
Circulate over the bright
And darkened lands of the earth,
Obsessing our private lives;
The unmentionable odour of death   10
Offends the September night.

Accurate scholarship can
Unearth the whole offence
From Luther until now
That has driven a culture mad,   15

14 *denunciation:* Arnold was a consistent and eloquent critic of the cultural and spiritual poverty of the Victorian *optimistic generation.*

SEPTEMBER. *September 1, 1939* was the date on which Hitler ordered the invasion of Poland, the blitzkrieg that began World War II. See above, "In Memory of W. B. Yeats," ll. 58–65 and note.

14 [Martin] *Luther:* (1483–1536) German priest, reformer, theologian, and translator of the Bible into German, whose genius, inspiration, and fidelity to his vision led to the establishment of a church separate from Rome, the division of Germany into separate realms of Catholic and Protestant power, and ultimately to the ferocious Thirty Years War (1618–48) between the adherents of the two faiths.

Find what occurred at Linz,
What huge imago made
A psychopathic god:
I and the public know
What all schoolchildren learn,   20
Those to whom evil is done
Do evil in return.

Exiled Thucydides knew
All that a speech can say
About Democracy,   25
And what dictators do,
The elderly rubbish they talk
To an apathetic grave;
Analysed all in his book,
The enlightenment driven away,   30
The habit-forming pain,
Mismanagement and grief:
We must suffer them all again.

Into this neutral air
Where blind skyscrapers use   35
Their full height to proclaim
The strength of Collective Man,
Each language pours its vain
Competitive excuse:

16 *Linz:* city on the Danube, capital of upper Austria, near which Adolf Hitler (1889–1945) lived from the age of six to nineteen. He attended the *Realschule* there at the age of eleven. Hitler's career as dictator and Chancellor of Germany was characterized by demonic power and insane brilliance and truly seemed to drive German *culture mad.*   17 *imago:* in psychoanalysis, the infantile, subconscious conception of a parent, or another loved one, which persists in the adult, compelling him, as here, to act in an abnormal fashion. In *Mein Kampf,* Ch. 1, Hitler mentions one person who at this time influenced him profoundly: his professor of history at Linz, Dr. Leopold Poetsch, a fanatical German nationalist.   20 *learn:* i.e., by practical experience on the playground.   21–22 *Those . . . return:* The inversion and reverse of the "golden rule" that bitter experience teaches everybody; ironically few know the "golden rule" since it is seldom practiced.   23 *Thucydides:* (*c.* 460–*c.* 400 B.C.) Greek historian and general, author of the history of the Peloponnesian War between Athens and Sparta, exiled for his failure in 424 B.C. to save Amphipolis, the Athenian stronghold in the northwest, from the brilliant Spartan general Brasidas.   24 *speech:* In his history, Thucydides makes frequent use of the speeches of politicians to reveal the "workings of men's minds and the impact of circumstances"; to show accurately how politics destroyed the advantages the Athenian army and navy had won; and to show how insolent demagogues corrupted *Democracy:* thus to reveal the causes of the eventual catastrophe of 404 B.C., the fall of Athens, and to provide men with a "knowledge of the past as a key to the future, which in all probability will repeat or resemble the past." See l. 33.   34 *neutral:* The United States was officially *neutral* at the outbreak of the second world war.

But who can live for long   40
In an euphoric dream;
Out of the mirror they stare,
Imperialism's face
And the international wrong.

Faces along the bar   45
Cling to their average day:
The lights must never go out,
The music must always play,
All the conventions conspire
To make this fort assume   50
The furniture of home;
Lest we should see where we are,
Lost in a haunted wood,
Children afraid of the night
Who have never been happy or good.   55

The windiest militant trash
Important Persons shout
Is not so crude as our wish:
What mad Nijinsky wrote
About Diaghilev   60
Is true of the normal heart;
For the error bred in the bone
Of each woman and each man
Craves what it cannot have,
Not universal love   65
But to be loved alone.

From the conservative dark
Into the ethical life
The dense commuters come,
Repeating their morning vow;   70
"I *will* be true to the wife,
I'll concentrate more on my work,"
And helpless governors wake
To resume their compulsory game:

41 *euphoric:* feeling an exaggerated and unreasoning sense of well being.
59–60 *What . . . Diaghilev:* Precisely quoted in ll. 65–66 (*Diary*). Vaslav
Nijinsky (1890–1950), legendary Russian ballet dancer and daring chore-
ographer, was the leading dancer in the company that Sergei Diaghilev, its
impresario, presented to Paris in 1909. The latter tried to dominate the
dancer's life. After Nijinsky's marriage in 1913 their relations were finally
broken. Nijinsky's career ended in 1917 when he was diagnosed as insane.

Who can release them now,   75
Who can reach the deaf,
Who can speak for the dumb?

Defenceless under the night
Our world in stupor lies;
Yet, dotted everywhere,   80
Ironic points of light
Flash out wherever the Just
Exchange their messages:
May I, composed like them
Of Eros and of dust,   85
Beleaguered by the same
Negation and despair,
Show an affirming flame.

Contradiction

The *Unknown* Citizen

State knows Him
But yet
Unknown
(man erected by State)

(*To JS*/*07*/*M*/*378*
This Marble Monument
Is Erected by the State)

He was found by the Bureau of Statistics to be
One against whom there was no official complaint,
And all the reports on his conduct agree
That, in the modern sense of an old-fashioned word, he was a
    saint,
For in everything he did he served the Greater Community.   5
Except for the War till the day he retired
He worked in a factory and never got fired,
But satisfied his employers, Fudge Motors Inc.
Yet he wasn't a scab or odd in his views,

Indicates mentality of speaker
Vulgarity of common people

For his Union reports that he paid his dues,   10
(Our report on his Union shows it was sound)
And our Social Psychology workers found
That he was popular with his mates and liked a drink.
The Press are convinced that he bought a paper every day
And that his reactions to advertisements were normal in every
    way.   15
Policies taken out in his name prove that he was fully insured,
And his Health-card shows he was once in hospital but left it
    cured.
Both Producers Research and High-Grade Living declare
He was fully sensible to the advantages of the Instalment Plan
And had everything necessary to the Modern Man,   20
A phonograph, a radio, a car and a frigidaire.

538

(Our) researchers into Public Opinion are content
That he held the proper opinions for the time of year;
When there was peace, he was for peace; when there was war, he
    went.
He was married and added five children to the population,   25
Which our Eugenist says was the right number for a parent of his
    generation,   *no dissent*
And our teachers report that he never interfered with (their)
    education.
Was he free? Was he happy? The question is absurd: *satire or / ironic*
Had anything been wrong, we should certainly have heard. *or would...*

                        SPEAKER

As I walked out one evening

> As I walked out one evening,
>   Walking down Bristol Street,
> The crowds upon the pavement
>   Were fields of harvest wheat.
>
> And down by the brimming river   5
>   I heard a lover sing
> Under an arch of the railway:
>   "Love has no ending.
>
> I'll love you, dear, I'll love you
>   Till China and Africa meet,   10
> And the river jumps over the mountain
>   And the salmon sing in the street.
>
> I'll love you till the ocean
>   Is folded and hung up to dry,
> And the seven stars go squawking   15
>   Like geese about the sky.
>
> The years shall run like rabbits,
>   For in my arms I hold
> The Flower of the Ages,
>   And the first love of the world."   20

AS I WALKED OUT. 8–20 *Love . . . world:* Cf. the standard Petrarchan conceits affirming the eternity of love and in poetry its victory over time, in the sonnets of Sidney, Spenser, and Shakespeare, as well as the hyperboles of traditional ballad heroes and lovers. 15 *seven stars:* the Pleiades, the seven sisters pursued by Orion, weeping for the death of their sisters, the Hyades. Their rising in May is universally celebrated with joy as a sign of the return of good weather and the reopening of navigation; hence they will never squawk. 19 *The . . . Ages:* In traditional love poetry the girl and her beauty are likened to a flower that fades untimely. The only flower that when plucked does not fade is the amaranth, an imaginary flower said to be immortal.

But all the clocks in the city
   Began to whirr and chime:
"O let not Time deceive you,
   You cannot conquer Time.

In the burrows of the Nightmare   25
   Where Justice naked is,
Time watches from the shadow
   And coughs when you would kiss.

In headaches and in worry
   Vaguely life leaks away,   30
And Time will have his fancy
   Tomorrow or today.

Into many a green valley
   Drifts the appalling snow;
Time breaks the threaded dances   35
   And the diver's brilliant bow.

O plunge your hands in water,
   Plunge them in up to the wrist;
Stare, stare in the basin
   And wonder what you've missed.   40

The glacier knocks in the cupboard,
   The desert sighs in the bed,
And the crack in the tea-cup opens
   A lane to the land of the dead.

Where the beggars raffle the banknotes   45
   And the Giant is enchanting to Jack,
And the Lily-white Boy is a Roarer,
   And Jill goes down on her back.

45 *beggars:* Cf. the nursery rhyme, "Hark, hark, / The dogs do bark, / The beggars are coming to town." In Tudor times, according to Trevelyan, the coming of the beggars was a terrifying event. Like the Fool in *Lear* (III, ii), the speaker here suggests that the truth is the reverse of popular song.   46 *Giant . . . Jack:* Cf. the story of "Jack and the Beanstalk."   47 *Lily-white boy:* Cf. "Two, two, the lily-white boys, clothèd all in green-o," from the song "Green Grow the Rushes-O." The traditional literary connotation of *Lily-white* is of purity; in the slang of the late seventeenth to nineteenth centuries, a "lily-white" was a chimney-sweep (*OED*).   *Roarer:* a wild, riotous reveler and bully.   48 *Jill . . . back:* i.e., the innocent maiden of nursery rhymes ("Jack and Jill") turns out to be a whore. This rhyme is said to be derived from a Scandinavian myth accounting for the markings on the moon. The Moon captured two children, Hjuki and Bil, while they were drawing water; now, when the moon is full, they can be seen holding a bucket on a pole between them (*Oxford Dictionary of Nursery Rhymes*). To *Time,* the happy rhymes and myths of childhood are neither chaste nor true.

O look, look in the mirror,
  O look in your distress;   50
Life remains a blessing
  Although you cannot bless.

O stand, stand at the window
  As the tears scald and start;
You shall love your crooked neighbor   55
  With your crooked heart."

It was late, late in the evening,
  The lovers they were gone;
The clocks had ceased their chiming,
  And the deep river ran on.   60

Lullaby

Lay your sleeping head, my love,
Human on my faithless arm;
Time and fevers burn away
Individual beauty from
Thoughtful children, and the grave   5
Proves the child ephemeral:
But in my arms till break of day
Let the living creature lie,
Mortal, guilty, but to me
The entirely beautiful.   10

Soul and body have no bounds:
To lovers as they lie upon
Her tolerant enchanted slope
In their ordinary swoon,
Grave the vision Venus sends   15
Of supernatural sympathy,
Universal love and hope;
While an abstract insight wakes
Among the glaciers and the rocks
The hermit's carnal ecstasy.   20

Certainty, fidelity
On the stroke of midnight pass
Like vibrations of a bell,
And fashionable madmen raise
Their pedantic boring cry: 25

Every farthing of the cost,
All the dreaded cards foretell,
Shall be paid, but from this night
Not a whisper, not a thought,
Not a kiss nor look be lost.   30

Beauty, midnight, vision dies:
Let the winds of dawn that blow
Softly round your dreaming head
Such a day of sweetness show
Eye and knocking heart may bless,   35
Find the mortal world enough;
Noons of dryness see you fed
By the involuntary powers,
Nights of insult let you pass
Watched by every human love.   40

On This Island

Look, stranger, on this island now
The leaping light for your delight discovers,
Stand stable here
And silent be,
That through the channels of the ear   5
May wander like a river
The swaying sound of the sea.

Here at the small field's ending pause
When the chalk wall falls to the foam and its tall ledges
Oppose the pluck   10
And the knock of the tide,
And the shingle scrambles after the sucking surf,
And the gull lodges
A moment on its sheer side.

Far off like floating seeds the ships   15
Diverge on urgent voluntary errands,
And the full view
Indeed may enter
And move in memory as now these clouds do,
That pass the harbour mirror   20
And all the summer through the water saunter.

LOOK, STRANGER. Cf. Arnold's "Dover Beach." 12 *shingle:* coarse,
waterworn gravel on beaches. Cf. "Dover Beach," l. 28 and note.

542

from HORAE CANONICAE

Prime

Simultaneously, as soundlessly,
  Spontaneously, suddenly
As, at the vaunt of the dawn, the kind
  Gates of the body fly open
To its world beyond, the gates of the mind,   5
  The horn gate and the ivory gate,
Swing to, swing shut, instantaneously
  Quell the nocturnal rummage
Of its rebellious fronde, ill-favored,
  Ill-natured and second-rate,   10
Disenfranchised, widowed and orphaned
  By an historical mistake:
Recalled from the shades to be a seeing being,
  From absence to be on display,
Without a name or history I wake   15
  Between my body and the day.

Holy this moment, wholly in the right,
  As, in complete obedience
To the light's laconic outcry, next
  As a sheet, near as a wall,   20
Out there as a mountain's poise of stone,
  The world is present, about,
And I know that I am, here, not alone
  But with a world, and rejoice
Unvexed, for the will has still to claim   25
  This adjacent arm as my own,
The memory to name me, resume
  Its routine of praise and blame,

PRIME. In the Breviary (book of the daily offices and prayers), the prime is
the first canonical hour (first of the daylight hours); it is an office of preparation
for facing the temptations of the day with patience, prayers for preservation
from evil and a renewal of "a right spirit," so that one's heart and body may be
governed "in the ways of [God's] laws and in the works of [His] command-
ments." The irony is that every Christian who accepts the fact of original sin
knows that he will probably endeavor wilfully to forget these admonitions at the
first opportunity. See ll. 35–37.

6 *horn gate . . . gate:* the twin gates of sleep; through those of *horn* come
the true but ominous dreams, through the *ivory*, the pleasant but deceitful.
See *Odyssey*, XIX, 559–67; *Aeneid*, VI, 893–96. 9 *fronde:* a leaf-like com-
bination of stem and foliage as in a fern or palm leaf, suggestive of the waving,
blurred, layered divisions of dreams.

And smiling to me is this instant while
   Still the day is intact, and I   30
The Adam sinless in our beginning,
   Adam still previous to any act.

I draw breath; that is of course to wish
   No matter what, to be wise,
To be different, to die and the cost,   35
   No matter how, is Paradise
Lost of course and myself owing a death:
   The eager ridge, the steady sea,
The flat roofs of the fishing village
   Still asleep in its bunny,   40
Though as fresh and sunny still, are not friends
   But things to hand, this ready flesh
No honest equal but my accomplice now,
   My assassin to be, and my name
Stands for my historical share of care   45
   For a lying self-made city,
Afraid of our living task, the dying
   Which the coming day will ask.

40 *bunny:* a baby's cozy, fleecy sleeping suit.

DYLAN THOMAS
1914–1953

The force that through the green fuse drives the flower

The force that through the green fuse drives the flower
Drives my green age; that blasts the roots of trees
Is my destroyer.
And I am dumb to tell the crooked rose
My youth is bent by the same wintry fever.   5

The force that drives the water through the rocks
Drives my red blood; that dries the mouthing streams
Turns mine to wax.
And I am dumb to mouth unto my veins
How at the mountain spring the same mouth sucks.   10

The hand that whirls the water in the pool
Stirs the quicksand; that ropes the blowing wind
Hauls my shroud sail.
And I am dumb to tell the hanging man
How of my clay is made the hangman's lime.   15

The lips of time leech to the fountain head;
Love drips and gathers, but the fallen blood
Shall calm her sores.
And I am dumb to tell a weather's wind
How time has ticked a heaven round the stars.   20

And I am dumb to tell the lover's tomb
How at my sheet goes the same crooked worm.

THE FORCE THAT. 1 *fuse:* i.e., stalk, but also the tube containing "gun-powder" that leads to and fires the explosive charge so that the *flower* "bursts" into bloom. See *blasts*, l. 2. 4 *dumb:* inarticulate. 7 *mouthing:* i.e., as if gushing out of a mouth. 9 *mouth:* declaim. 12 *ropes:* catches, ties, con-trols. 13 *Hauls . . . sail:* draws in, controls the sail of my mortality so that I sail (haul) close to the wind, i.e., toward the direction from which the wind (death) is blowing. A *shroud* is a winding sheet for the dead; *sheet* (l. 22 and implied by *shroud*) is a rope attached to a lower corner of a sail to extend or move it. The nautical metaphor accurately compels awareness of death. Cf. also the graveside anthem, "In the midst of life we are in death." 15 *hang-man's lime:* Formerly in England those hanged for capital crimes were buried by the hangman in quicklime within the prison walls (non-consecrated ground) and thus consumed, a custom that preyed terribly on popular imagination. Thomas' chemistry is also accurate. 16 *leech:* cling to and suck, as the blood-sucking leech.

Especially when the October wind

Especially when the October wind
With frosty fingers punishes my hair,
Caught by the crabbing sun I walk on fire
And cast a shadow crab upon the land,
By the sea's side, hearing the noise of birds,   5
Hearing the raven cough in winter sticks,
My busy heart who shudders as she talks
Sheds the syllabic blood and drains her words.

Shut, too, in a tower of words, I mark
On the horizon walking like the trees   10
The wordy shapes of women, and the rows
Of the star-gestured children in the park.
Some let me make you of the vowelled beeches,
Some of the oaken voices, from the roots
Of many a thorny shire tell you notes,   15
Some let me make you of the water's speeches.

Behind a pot of ferns the wagging clock
Tells me the hour's word, the neural meaning

ESPECIALLY WHEN. A birthday poem (Thomas was born on October 27)
celebrating the art and life of the poet. 3 *crabbing:* i.e., the low October sun
moving obliquely across the sky, an ominous movement. 4 *shadow crab:*
distorted shadow that skitters sideways like a crab. 7 *shudders:* in fear of
winter and death, ominously foretold by the coughing *raven,* l. 6; note also the
tension between the natural four-stress rhythm in lines 1, 2, 4, and 7 and the
traditional five-stress iambic pentameter used here, which dramatizes the
jarring effect of *cough* and *shudders.* 8 *sheds . . . blood:* speaks with a rhythmic pulse (the syllable is the basis of rhythm). *drains her words:* empties
herself of words—the life-blood of her being, poetry. The metaphors suggest
the pain and passion of the self-sacrificial act of creation and, in the contrast
between fire and frost, light and shadow, the awareness of the compelling need
to write in the face of the inevitable death. 9 *tower:* the necessary, isolating
prison, but one that prevents him from seizing the stuff of life. 11 *wordy
shapes:* mortal women (constantly talking) seen in terms of words. 12 *star-
gestured:* i.e., children whose bright motions and faces make them seem like
stars, innocent and free. 13 *some:* i.e., some poems. *make:* write, create.
you: i.e., readers of his poetry. *of . . . beeches:* i.e., of the rich, speaking stuff
of earthy nature venerated by Druidic bards, which alone seems eternal;
vowelled not only because the bark of beech trees is often carved with words,
but also because the word "book" is generally thought to be derived from
"beech." 14 *oaken voices:* i.e., oak trees singing in the wind. 14–15 *from
. . . notes:* Let me sing (or name) to you the songs that come from the *roots* of
many a hawthorn-hedged shire. 16 *water's speeches:* the songs of brooks and
flowing springs. The *beeches,* oaks, hawthorn *roots,* and brooks all sing the
essential poetry of earth that is "never dead." Cf. Keats, "On the Grasshopper
and Cricket," p. 326, and also Job 14:7–9 where the "tree will sprout again"
and "through the scent of water will bud" while man dies. 18 *neural:* i.e.,
painful awareness of time felt along the dorsal "neural axis," pain caused by
the arrow-like pointer on the dial (*disk*)—a figure also appropriate for a sundial.

546

Flies on the shafted disk, declaims the morning
And tells the windy weather in the cock.   20
Some let me make you of the meadow's signs;
The signal grass that tells me all I know
Breaks with the wormy winter through the eye.
Some let me tell you of the raven's sins.

Especially when the October wind   25
(Some let me make you of autumnal spells,
The spider-tongued, and the loud hill of Wales)
With fists of turnips punishes the land,
Some let me make you of the heartless words.
The heart is drained that, spelling in the scurry   30
Of chemic blood, warned of the coming fury.
By the sea's side hear the dark-vowelled birds.

In the beginning

In the beginning was the three-pointed star,
One smile of light across the empty face;
One bough of bone across the rooting air,
The substance forked that marrowed the first sun;
And, burning ciphers on the round of space,   5
Heaven and hell mixed as they spun.

20 *cock:* i.e., weathercock, suggestive of the winds of death, yet also the bird that revives the heart and miraculously heralds the return of life and light. Cf. Vaughan (a Welsh poet whose poetry Thomas knew), "Cock-Crowing" and notes, p. 178.   30 *spelling:* naming; perhaps casting spells. Cf. *make, tell* (ll. 13, 15).   *scurry:* whirl, race, "hurry and scurry."   31 *chemic blood:* blood wrought up, agitated (as if in an elemental chemical reaction) from passionate awareness of nature, the timefulness of man, and *the coming fury.*

IN THE BEGINNING.   The poem is based on the traditional notion of the simultaneousness of the beginning and the end: that in the original creation is implicit the whole of subsequent events of divine involvement in history, of Alpha and Omega. Three Biblical passages are constantly referred to: Gen. 1:1–28, John 1:1–18; and Rev. 21:1–6. Cf. also Milton, [The Invocation to Light] and notes, pp. 154–56. The poem is organized according to the order of creation in the first six days from darkness to light to solid form and the fulfillment of all *signs* in subsequent events in time.

1 *three-pointed star:* the uncreated Divine creating light in which are implicit physical *light* (l. 2) and matter (*bough of bone*, l. 3), the "star" of Bethlehem (Matt. 2:2, 9), and the Triune form of the New Testament God.   4 *substance forked:* creation conceived as a process of division, or splitting off of forms (e.g. *first sun*) from the one original *substance;* cf. l. 27. Corn is said to "fork" when it sprouts. Implicit also is the image of the Creator as a gardener forking over the soil.   *marrowed:* provided the pith and essence, made fat and lusty.   5 *burning ciphers:* the implicit "lights in the firmament" (Gen. 1:14), since as yet creation has not occurred. (A cipher is zero, the absence of quantity).   6 *Heaven and hell:* implicit, for there was no *hell* until after the revolt of the angels.

In the beginning was the pale signature,
Three-syllabled and starry as the smile,
And after came the imprints on the water,
Stamp of the minted face upon the moon;   10
The blood that touched the crosstree and the grail
Touched the first cloud and left a sign.

In the beginning was the mounting fire
That set alight the weathers from a spark,
A three-eyed, red-eyed spark, blunt as a flower;   15
Life rose and spouted from the rolling seas,
Burst in the roots, pumped from the earth and rock
The secret oils that drive the grass.

In the beginning was the word, the word
That from the solid bases of the light   20
Abstracted all the letters of the void;

---

7 *pale signature:* i.e., the dawn of creation wrought by God the Divine Author; cf. *-syllabled, imprints, stamp,* which imply language and writing. 8 *Three-syllabled:* i.e., Jehōvah, or Elōhīm, or Adōnāy, God. The first is the Christian form given to the tetragrammaton for the "ineffable name"; the other two are names for God that appear in various texts of the Old Testament. Cf. *three-pointed,* l. 1 and note. 9 *after:* i.e., because light was the creation of the first day; the waters were "divided" on the second and "gathered" on the third. *imprints:* both the mark (*signature*) of creation and the "imprints" of Christ's feet when he was "walking on the sea" (Matt. 14:25–28). 10 *minted . . . moon:* the image of the sovereign ruler stamped on the *minted* silver coin; cf. the "man in the moon." 11 *crosstree:* the cross. *grail:* cup that Christ used at the Last Supper. 12 *Touched:* i.e., with the color of blood. *sign:* prophetic of the future grace as well as testifying to the present glory. Cf. Eliot, "Gerontion," ll. 17–19 and notes. 13 *mounting fire:* i.e., the sun, and "lights in the firmament of the heaven" created on the fourth day, which will "be for signs, for seasons, and for days, and years" (Gen. 1:14). Also the animating force of nature; cf. above, "The force that through the green fuse," l. 1 and note. 14 *weathers:* i.e., seasons. 15 *three-eyed:* cf. *three-pointed, Three-syllabled* and notes. *red-eyed:* red, since creation is four days old and more substantial than on the first; and also because in the assumed pun of son-sun is implied the bloody sacrifice on the crosstree. *blunt:* cf. *pointed,* l. 1. 16 *Life . . . seas:* i.e., the creation of fish and fowl on the fifth day. 19 *the word:* i.e., the *Logos* (John 1:1–4), the *word,* the life, and the *light:* Christ, the dramatic Second Person of the Trinity who created "all things," whose "life was the light of men" which "shineth in darkness and the darkness comprehendeth it not." Implicit in this allusion is the creation of man on the sixth day, man who with his words is also a creator, for every poem is an analogy of and participant in the original creation. 20 *bases:* (multiple meanings) dark foundations; the "dust of the ground" out of which man was made; in printing, the bottom or footing of letters; in grammar, the basic form of a word to which suffixes are added. 21 *Abstracted . . . void:* i.e., man created in the "image of God" (*the word*) is the summary and epitome (abstract—cf. above Blake, "The Human Abstract") of all the *letters* that make up the creation (cf. Adam's intuitive knowledge that enabled him to name all living creatures—Gen. 2:19–20), which was made *ex nihilo,* out of nothing, the void.

[handwritten: D. Thomas: loves riddles, poems, cartoons]

And from the cloudy bases of the breath
The word flowed up, translating to the heart
First characters of birth and death.

In the beginning was the secret brain.   25
The brain was celled and soldered in the thought
Before the pitch was forking to a sun;
Before the veins were shaking in their sieve,
Blood shot and scattered to the winds of light
The ribbed original of love.   30

[handwritten: Celebrates victory of nature over death]

And death shall have no dominion

And death shall have no dominion. *[handwritten: Refers to Death having no more dominion over risen Christ]*
[handwritten: No class distinctions] Dead men naked they shall be one
[handwritten: no personal distinctions] With the man in the wind and the west moon; *[handwritten: spring ReBirth]*
When their bones are picked clean and the clean bones gone,
They shall have stars at elbow and foot; *[handwritten: man one with]*
Though they go mad they shall be sane, *[handwritten: death restores mind & body]* *[handwritten: west wind & moon]*
Though they sink through the sea they shall rise again;
[handwritten: image of being in heaven] Though lovers be lost love shall not; *[handwritten: (universal love)]*
And death shall have no dominion.

22–23 *cloudy . . . up:* Cf. "But there went up a mist from the earth, and *watered* the whole face of the ground. And the Lord God formed man of the dust of the ground, and breathed into his nostrils the breath of life; and man became a living soul" (Gen. 2:6–7).   24 *characters . . . death:* i.e., the letters that formed *birth* (intuitive knowledge of creation) and, in man's freedom to fall, his subsequent *death* (the proved, practical knowledge of creation—the gift of life that the Lord takes away).   26 *brain . . . thought:* i.e., the whole thought and purpose, instrument and plan, were inextricably joined by the Divine Artisan before the perfectly executed act of creation.   27 *Before the pitch:* before the black original nothing (like bitumen that wells up from the depths from earth—cf. l. 17), *substance,* divided, sprouted to become light. 29 *Blood:* God's blood, symbolic of divine love, inseparable from the *secret brain.* Cf. *smile,* l. 2, and *blood,* l. 11.   30 *ribbed . . . love:* I.e., love was a part of God's "Body" before the *beginning,* as Eve, derived from Adam's ribs, and their love were implicit in Adam prior to her coming into being.

AND DEATH SHALL HAVE. *And Death . . . dominion:* Cf. "Christ being raised from the dead dieth no more: death hath no more dominion over him" (Romans 6:9), part of the Easter anthem said in place of the *Venite* on Easter Day. While he does not sing a Sunday school anthem of resurrection, Thomas makes use of the traditional imagery to celebrate the victory of nature over death.

3 *man . . . moon:* i.e., the man in the moon and the west wind (Zephirus, the "sweete breeth" of spring) transliterated by death, but resurrected each month and year to inspire the crops.   4 *bones:* Cf. Ezekiel 37, the resurrection of the "dry bones."   7 *sink . . . again:* Cf. Rev. 21:13: "And the sea gave up the dead which were in it."

And death shall have no dominion.
Under the windings of the sea *storms or stormily* [*wrapping*] 10
They lying long shall not die windily; *in vain* *sheet covers dead*
Twisting on racks when sinews give way,
Strapped to a wheel, yet they shall not break; ⎫ *causing*
Faith in their hands shall snap in two, ⎬ *death* 15
And the unicorn evils run them through; ⎭ *spiritual*
Split all ends up they shan't crack;
And death shall have no dominion.

And death shall have no dominion.
No more may gulls cry at their ears *dead men* 20
Or waves break loud on the seashores;
Where blew a flower may a flower no more
Lifts its head to the blows of the rain; *resurrection*
Though they be mad and dead as nails, *Refers to line 6 & examnote*
Heads of the characters hammer through daisies; 25
Break in the sun till the sun breaks down, *bloom til sun goes*
And death shall have no dominion.

maybe spelt human sun of a flower

When all my five and country senses see

When all my five and country senses see,
The fingers will forget green thumbs and mark
How, through the halfmoon's vegetable eye,
Husk of young stars and handfull zodiac,

12 *windily:* i.e., overwhelmed by storms; also, protesting in a bombastic fashion, in vain. 13, 14 *racks, wheel:* instruments of torture. 16 *unicorn:* mythological one-horned monster, paradoxically the symbol of both fierceness and chastity. In legend it was captured by tricking it to run its horn into a tree and seizing it before it could withdraw; the horn was used as an amulet to detect poisoned food. The paradoxes of the unicorn reinforce those of resurrection. 20–23 *gulls, waves, flower:* all mournful images of grief and mortality of the world (for *flower,* cf. Job 14:1–2), which yet contain within them the seeds of resurrection. 22 *blew:* bloomed. 25 *Heads . . . daisies:* the *heads* of the dead (cf. heads of dead door*nails*) will hammer upward head first (counter to custom and expectation) through the daisies. Cf. "The force that through the green fuse," l. 1. 26 *break:* i.e., burst into bloom; cf. *break,* l. 14. The fragile daisy (its name derived from *daeges eage*—day's eye, the sun) will outbloom and outlast the sun, the ultimate symbol of time.

WHEN ALL MY FIVE. 1 *country:* unsophisticated, earthy. 2 *green thumbs:* the gardener's happy symbol of fertility, instinctive gift to promote growth. *mark:* i.e., see (as well as trace) *How . . . Love,* etc. Throughout, all the organs of the senses (*fingers, ears, tongue, nostrils*) *see, watch,* know in a wholly physical fashion. 3 *vegetable eye:* i.e., the *country* eye, like that of a potato, of the *halfmoon,* which observes the inconstant natural world below. 4 *Husk . . . zodiac:* i.e., through the shells (*Husks*) of fresh (*young*) stars—conceivably analogous to an *eye*—and the *handfull* of stars in the ring (*eye*) of the *zodiac,* which, like the moon, influence bodily life and the gardens of men.

Love in the frost is pared and wintered by,5
The whispering ears will watch love drummed away
Down breeze and shell to a discordant beach,
And, lashed to syllables, the lynx tongue cry
That her fond wounds are mended bitterly.
My nostrils see her breath burn like a bush.10

My one and noble heart has witnesses
In all love's countries, that will grope awake;
And when blind sleep drops on the spying senses,
The heart is sensual, though five eyes break.

A Refusal to Mourn the Death, by Fire, of a Child in London

Never until the mankind making
Bird beast and flower
Fathering and all humbling darkness
Tells with silence the last light breaking
And the still hour5
Is come of the sea tumbling in harness

And I must enter again the round
Zion of the water bead
And the synagogue of the ear of corn
Shall I let pray the shadow of a sound10

5 *pared:* i.e., peeled, like a potato; also "paired" and diminished, withered, by the cold. *wintered by:* i.e., sorted, forgotten, like vegetables stored in a root cellar. 6 *drummed:* i.e., as if dismissed with dishonor to the accompaniment of drums; audibly suggestive of desolation and abandonment. 7 *Down breeze:* i.e., thrown to the four winds. [down] *shell:* i.e., to the empty shells (cf. *Husk,* l. 4) on the beach (which clash under wave and foot). *discordant beach:* i.e., to the cacophonous place of wreckage battered by the tides (time). 8 *lashed to syllables:* whipped, hurt, to poetic utterance. *lynx tongue:* sharp-eyed tongue (the lynx is noted for its fabulous eyesight). *cry:* will cry. 9 *her:* i.e., love's. 10 *burn . . . bush:* i.e., and not be consumed. Cf. Exodus 3:2–6. 11 *witnesses:* i.e., the senses. 12 *love's countries:* the realm of sense experience, in which love lives as well as in the heart. *grope:* i.e., struggle to see after being asleep. 14 *is sensual:* is physically passionate, "of the earth, earthy" (not spiritual), and as afflicted with grief and pain as a broken finger. *though . . . break:* even though the five senses fail utterly, depriving the heart of their "sight."

A REFUSAL TO MOURN. 1–10 *Never . . . pray:* i.e., Never until the end of time shall I pray. 3 *darkness:* that which fathers and humbles all creation. 4 *last light:* death, or the end of the world. 7–9 *enter . . . corn:* return to the heavenly hill (*Zion,* hill in Jerusalem and site of the Temple and royal residence of David) of the drop (a microcosmic "hill") of water: i.e., return to the elemental water that renews life; to the congregation (*synagogue*) of an *ear* of wheat (where the kernels are arranged in symmetrical rows), traditional symbol of fertility and quickening power of nature (cf. 1 Cor. 15:37).

Or sow my salt seed
In the least valley of sackcloth to mourn

The majesty and burning of the child's death.
I shall not murder
The mankind of her going with a grave truth   15
Nor blaspheme down the stations of the breath
With any further
Elegy of innocence and youth.

Deep with the first dead lies London's daughter,
Robed in the long friends,   20
The grains beyond age, the dark veins of her mother,
Secret by the unmourning water
Of the riding Thames.
After the first death, there is no other.

Poem in October

heron — uttered of poet himay

It was my thirtieth year to heaven
Woke to my hearing from harbour and neighbour wood
  And the mussel pooled and the heron
        Priested shore
    The morning beckon   5
With water praying and call of sea gull and rook
And the knock of sailing boats on the net webbed wall
        Myself to set foot
        That second
    In the still sleeping town and set forth.   10

11 *salt seed:* tears. 12 *sackcloth:* traditional garment of mourning and penance.   15 *mankind . . . going:* the common fate of mankind represented in her death.   *grave truth:* Cf. Mercutio's pun as he dies—"And you shall find me a grave man" (*Romeo and Juliet*, III, i):—a self-comment on Thomas' own habit of punning.   16 *down . . . breath:* down the full scale (of the voice), sound all the notes (of elegy). Cf. above, Milton, "Lycidas," l. 188: "He touch'd the tender stops of various Quills." *Stations* may also suggest an analogy with the Stations of the Cross, which represent and commemorate the successive incidents in the Passion of Christ and before which the faithful pray and meditate.   19 *first dead:* not only the first inhabitants of London, but the Adam-dead ("as in Adam all die": I Cor. 15:22) of all representative human figures.   20 *long friends:* those *long* dead, *friends* now in their common humanity.   21 *grains:* Cf. *ear of corn,* l. 9.   *veins:* i.e., of renewing water of the earth, the mother of us all.   22 *unmourning water:* Cf. *water bead,* l. 8; *unmourning* because it is the water of life and rejoices always.   23 *riding Thames:* Cf. the *sea tumbling in harness,* l. 6. London's river rides serenely out to the sea of time and eternal sleep above the lost, burned girl "in sure and certain hope of the resurrection" of nature.

POEM IN OCTOBER.   1 *thirtieth year:* Cf. the earlier "birthday poem," "Especially when the October wind."

My birthday began with the water—
Birds and the birds of the winged trees flying my name
Above the farms and the white horses
                    And I rose
                In rainy autumn   15
And walked abroad in a shower of all my days.
High tide and the heron dived when I took the road
                Over the border
                And the gates
Of the town closed as the town awoke.   20

    A springful of larks in a rolling
Cloud and the roadside bushes brimming with whistling
    Blackbirds and the sun of October
                Summery
            On the hill's shoulder,   25
Here were fond climates and sweet singers suddenly
Come in the morning where I wandered and listened
            To the rain wringing
            Wind blow cold
In the wood faraway under me.   30

    Pale rain over the dwindling harbour
And over the sea wet church the size of a snail
    With its horns through mist and the castle
                Brown as owls
            But all the gardens   35
Of spring and summer were blooming in the tall tales
Beyond the border and under the lark full cloud.
            There could I marvel
            My birthday
Away but the weather turned around.   40

    It turned away from the blithe country
And down the other air and the blue altered sky
    Streamed again a wonder of summer
                With apples
            Pears and red currants   45

---

11 *water:* The poet's first name means "Waves of the Sea." In Cymric mythology, Dylan was one of the twin sons of Arianrod; immediately after his birth
he plunged and swam like a fish, and thus was called Dylan Eil Ton, Son of the
Wave. When he was accidentally killed, the waves rose to avenge him, and
they still make a "sullen sound" over his grave. The voice of the tide when
it turns and roars up into the Conway River is called the dying cry of Dylan
(Funk and Wagnalls *Dictionary of Folklore*).

And I saw in the turning so clearly a child's
Forgotten mornings when he walked with his mother
  Through the parables
   Of sun light
And the legends of the green chapels   50

 And the twice told fields of infancy
That his tears burned my cheeks and his heart moved in mine.
  These were the woods the river and sea
   Where a boy
   In the listening   55
Summertime of the dead whispered the truth of his joy
To the trees and the stones and the fish in the tide.
   And the mystery
    Sang alive
Still in the water and singingbirds.   60

 And there could I marvel my birthday
Away but the weather turned around. And the true
  Joy of the long dead child sang burning
   In the sun.
   It was my thirtieth   65
Year to heaven stood there then in the summer noon
Though the town below lay leaved with October blood.
   O may my heart's truth
    Still be sung
On this high hill in a year's turning.   70

Do not go gentle into that good night

Do not go gentle into that good night,
Old age should burn and rave at close of day;
Rage, rage against the dying of the light.

Though wise men at their end know dark is right,
Because their words had forked no lightning they   5
Do not go gentle into that good night.

Good men, the last wave by, crying how bright
Their frail deeds might have danced in a green bay,
Rage, rage against the dying of the light.

46–60 *And I saw, etc.:* Cf. above, Wordsworth, "My Heart Leaps Up."

Wild men who caught and sang the sun in flight, 10
And learn, too late, they grieved it on its way,
Do not go gentle into that good night.

Grave men, near death, who see with blinding sight
Blind eyes could blaze like meteors and be gay,
Rage, rage against the dying of the light. 15

And you, my father, there on the sad height,
Curse, bless, me now with your fierce tears, I pray.
Do not go gentle into that good night.
Rage, rage against the dying of the light.

In my craft or sullen art

In my craft or sullen art
Exercised in the still night
When only the moon rages
And the lovers lie abed
With all their griefs in their arms, 5
I labour by singing light
Not for ambition or bread
Or the strut and the trade of charms
On the ivory stages
But for the common wages 10
Of their most secret heart.

Not for the proud man apart
From the raging moon I write
On these spindrift pages
Nor for the towering dead 15
With their nightingales and psalms
But for the lovers, their arms
Round the griefs of the ages,
Who pay no praise or wages
Nor heed my craft or art. 20

DO NOT GO GENTLE. 14 *gay:* Cf. Yeats, "Lapis Lazuli," p. 477.

Fern Hill

Now as I was young and easy under the apple boughs
About the lilting house and happy as the grass was green,
      The night above the dingle starry,
          Time let me hail and climb
        Golden in the heydays of his eyes,
And honoured among wagons I was prince of the apple towns
And once below a time I lordly had the trees and leaves
          Trail with daisies and barley
      Down the rivers of the windfall light.

And as I was green and carefree, famous among the barns   10
About the happy yard and singing as the farm was home,
        In the sun that is young once only,
          Time let me play and be
        Golden in the mercy of his means,
And green and golden I was huntsman and herdsman, the calves 15
Sang to my horn, the foxes on the hills barked clear and cold,
          And the sabbath rang slowly
        In the pebbles of the holy streams.

All the sun long it was running, it was lovely, the hay
Fields high as the house, the tunes from the chimneys, it was air 20
          And playing, lovely and watery
            And fire green as grass.
          And nightly under the simple stars
As I rode to sleep the owls were bearing the farm away,
All the moon long I heard, blessed among stables, the night-jars 25
          Flying with the ricks, and the horses
           Flashing into the dark.

And then to awake, and the farm, like a wanderer white
With the dew, come back, the cock on his shoulder: it was all
          Shining, it was Adam and maiden,   30
           The sky gathered again
          And the sun grew round that very day. .
So it must have been after the birth of the simple light
In the first, spinning place, the spellbound horses walking warm
          Out of the whinnying green stable   35
           On to the fields of praise.

FERN HILL. Cf. above, Marvell, "The Garden," p. 167; Vaughan, "The Retreat," p. 173; Wordsworth, "Ode," p. 257; and Hopkins, "Spring," p. 416. 3 *dingle:* deep, narrow valley. 25 *night-jars:* the common goat-sucker, a nocturnal insectivorous bird like the whippoorwill.   26 *ricks:* hay stacks.

And honoured among foxes and pheasants by the gay house
Under the new made clouds and happy as the heart was long,
       In the sun born over and over,
             I ran my heedless ways,   40
       My wishes raced through the house high hay
And nothing I cared, at my sky blue trades, that time allows
In all his tuneful turning so few and such morning songs
       Before the children green and golden
             Follow him out of grace,   45

Nothing I cared, in the lamb white days, that time would take me
Up to the swallow thronged loft by the shadow of my hand,
       In the moon that is always rising,
          Nor that riding to sleep
       I should hear him fly with the high fields   50
And wake to the farm forever fled from the childless land.
Oh as I was young and easy in the mercy of his means,
       Time held me green and dying
       Though I sang in my chains like the sea.

ROBERT LOWELL
1917—

Concord

Ten thousand Fords are idle here in search
Of a tradition. Over these dry sticks—
The Minute Man, the Irish Catholics,
The ruined bridge and Walden's fished-out perch—
The belfry of the Unitarian Church   5
Rings out the hanging Jesus. Crucifix,
How can your whited spindling arms transfix
Mammon's unbridled industry, the lurch
For forms to harness Heraclitus' stream!
This Church is Concord—Concord where Thoreau   10
Named all the birds without a gun to probe
Through darkness to the painted man and bow:
The death-dance of King Philip and his scream
Whose echo girdled this imperfect globe.

CONCORD. 5–6 *Unitarian . . . Jesus:* The Unitarians recognize only the
manhood of Jesus, not His Divinity as the Christ, which orthodox tradition
affirms, and believing primarily in the abiding goodness of human nature,
reject the doctrine of Original Sin and that of the Atonement by Christ on the
cross for human greed and disobedience. 8 *Mammon:* personification of
greed for physical riches—e.g., gold—of the natural resources of creation; in
Paradise Lost (I, 679–81), "the least erected Spirit that fell / From Heav'n, for
ev'n in heav'n his looks and thoughts / Were always downward bent," the
devil who first taught men to rifle the bowels of their mother earth for gold.
9 *Heraclitus:* pre-Socratic Greek philosopher who taught that the universe is in
a state of ceaseless flux seen in the figure of the flowing waters of a river: "You
cannot step twice into the same rivers; for fresh waters are ever flowing in upon
you" (frag. 41, 42, trans. Burnet). See above, Hopkins, "That Nature is a
Heraclitean Fire," and Eliot, epigraphs to "The Dry Salvages" and notes.
10 [Henry David] *Thoreau:* (1817–62) author of *Walden* and *The Maine Woods*,
a naturalist and social philosopher who was fascinated by the wilderness and
by the lives, customs, and languages of the primitive Indians. In "Higher Laws"
(*Walden*) Thoreau urges the young man to leave the "gun and fishpole behind"
so that he may better distinguish "the proper objects" of his life. 13 *King
Philip:* (1639–76) Metacomet, chief of the Wampanoag tribe, leader in the
bloody Indian war against the New England Confederation; treacherously
killed by another Indian on August 12, 1676. His head was exhibited on a pole
in Plymouth for a quarter of a century, and his right hand, preserved in rum,
was given to his slayer as a reward. The end of the war in 1678 brought about
the extermination of all traditional tribal life in southern New England, when
many Indian men, women, and children (including Philip's wife and child)
were sold into slavery, and insured the ultimate victory of traditionless,
materialistic, ruthless civilization in which the machine is god, one now appal-
lingly barren to a man brought up to revere the sanctity of colonial Puritan
culture. 14 *echo . . . globe:* Cf. Emerson, "Hymn: Sung at the Completion
of the Concord Monument, April 19, 1836":

Skunk Hour

(FOR ELIZABETH BISHOP)

Nautilus Island's hermit
heiress still lives through winter in her Spartan cottage;
her sheep still graze above the sea.
Her son's a bishop. Her farmer
is first selectman in our village;   5
she's in her dotage.

Thirsting for
the hierarchic privacy
of Queen Victoria's century,
she buys up all   10
the eyesores facing her shore,
and lets them fall.

The season's ill—
we've lost our summer millionaire,
who seemed to leap from an L. L. Bean   15
catalogue. His nine-knot yawl
was auctioned off to lobstermen.
A red fox stain covers Blue Hill.

And now our fairy
decorator brightens his shop for fall;   20
his fishnet's filled with orange cork,
orange, his cobbler's bench and awl;
there is no money in his work,
he'd rather marry.

One dark night,   25
my Tudor Ford climbed the hill's skull;
I watched for love-cars. Lights turned down,
they lay together, hull to hull,
where the graveyard shelves on the town. . . .
My mind's not right.   30

By the rude bridge that arched the flood
     Their flag to April's breeze unfurled,
Here once the embattled farmers stood
     And fired the shot heard round the world.
Emerson's patriotism is plump and fatuous when heard against the *scream* and
the noise of the *Fords*.

SKUNK HOUR. 15 *L. L. Bean:* mail order house noted for camping and
sporting goods.

A car radio bleats,
"Love, O careless Love. . . ." I hear
my ill-spirit sob in each blood cell,
as if my hand were at its throat. . . .
I myself am hell;   35
nobody's here—

only skunks, that search
in the moonlight for a bite to eat.
They march on their soles up Main Street:
white stripes, moonstruck eyes' red fire   40
under the chalk-dry and spar spire
of the Trinitarian Church.

I stand on top
of our back steps and breathe the rich air—
a mother skunk with her column of kittens swills the garbage pail.
She jabs her wedge-head in a cup   46
of sour cream, drops her ostrich tail,
and will not scare.

Man and Wife

Tamed by *Miltown*, we lie on Mother's bed;
the rising sun in war paint dyes us red;
in broad daylight her gilded bed-posts shine,
abandoned, almost Dionysian.

35 *I . . . hell:* Cf. Satan's soliloquy in *Paradise Lost* (IV, 73–78) in which
he admits his guilt, the justice of his punishment, and his unwillingness to
repent:

> Me miserable! Which way shall I flie
> Infinite wrauth, and infinite despaire?
> Which way I flie is Hell; myself am Hell;
> And in the lowest deep a lower deep
> Still threatning to devour me opens wide,
> To which the Hell I suffer seems a Heav'n.

Cf. also Satan's bitter torment and sexual impotence aroused by the sight of
innocent Adam and Eve who:

> Imparadis't in one anothers arms
> The happier Eden, shall enjoy thir fill
> Of bliss on bliss, while I to Hell am thrust,
> Where neither joy nor love, but fierce desire,
> Among our other torments not the least,
> Still unfulfill'd with pain of longing pines (IV, 506–11).

MAN AND WIFE. 1 *Miltown:* proprietary name of a tranquilizer. 4 *Dionysian:* i.e., the *bed-post* looks like a thyrsus, a phallic staff wreathed with ivy and
crowned with a pine cone, carried by the bacchantes when they celebrated their
orgies in honor of Dionysius (Bacchus).

At last the trees are green on Marlborough Street,   5
blossoms on our magnolia ignite
the morning with their murderous five days' white.
All night I've held your hand,
as if you had
a fourth time faced the kingdom of the mad—   10
its hackneyed speech, its homicidal eye—
and dragged me home alive. . . . Oh my *Petite*,
clearest of all God's creatures, still all air and nerve:
you were in your twenties, and I,
once hand on glass   15
and heart in mouth,
outdrank the Rahvs in the heat
of Greenwich Village, fainting at your feet—
too boiled and shy
and poker-faced to make a pass,   20
while the shrill verve
of your invective scorched the traditional South.

Now twelve years later, you turn your back.
Sleepless, you hold
your pillow to your hollows like a child;   25
your old-fashioned tirade—
loving, rapid, merciless—
breaks like the Atlantic Ocean on my head.

"To Speak of Woe That Is in Marriage"

*"It is the future generation that presses into being by means of
these exuberant feelings and supersensible soap bubbles of ours."*

Schopenhauer

"The hot night makes us keep our bedroom windows open.
Our magnolia blossoms. Life begins to happen.
My hopped up husband drops his home disputes,
and hits the streets to cruise for prostitutes,

17 *Rahvs:* i.e., any literary friend, but also presumably Philip Rahv, American
critic, one of the founding editors of the *Partisan Review*, a journal which first
recognized and encouraged some of the most notable new poets of the present
generation, including Lowell.

"TO SPEAK OF WOE." *Epigraph:* Adapted from Ch. XLIV, "The Metaphysics
of the Love of the Sexes," of *The World as Will and Idea* (trans. Haldane and
Kemp), Vol. III, p. 342. The relevant passage reads: "Now, however loudly
persons of lofty and sentimental soul, and especially those who are in love,
may cry out here about the gross realism of my view [i.e., "all love . . . is
rooted in the sexual impulse alone"], they are yet in error. For is not the definite

free-lancing out along the razor's edge.   5
This screwball might kill his wife, then take the pledge.
Oh the monotonous meanness of his lust. . . .
It's the injustice . . . he is so unjust—
whiskey-blind, swaggering home at five.
My only thought is how to keep alive.   10
What makes him tick? Each night now I tie
ten dollars and his car key to my thigh. . . .
Gored by the climacteric of his want,
he stalls above me like an elephant."

Mr. Edwards and the Spider

I saw the spiders marching through the air,
Swimming from tree to tree that mildewed day
    In latter August when the hay
    Came creaking to the barn. But where

---

determination of the individualities of the next generation a much higher and
more worthy end than those exuberant feelings and supersensible soap bubbles
of theirs? Nay, among earthly aims, can there be one which is greater or more
important? . . . For it is the future generation, in its whole individual determination, that presses into existence by means of these efforts and toils."
Schopenhauer repeatedly argues that the sexual impulse is the "will to live";
that the essential matter is not "reciprocation of love, but possession, i.e., the
physical enjoyment"; that "all sex is one-sided"; that "sexual love is compatible
even with the extremest hatred towards its object"; that "faithfulness in marriage is with the man artificial, with the woman . . . natural"; and quotes with
approval the Spanish proverb, "Who marries from love must live in sorrow."

2 *Life . . . happen:* i.e., instinctive nature blindly begins to reassert its power
over death.   6 *take the pledge:* i.e., might sincerely promise not to drink (and
of course get drunk the next day).   8 *unjust:* To Schopenhauer, the woman,
who naturally has a unique instinct to preserve her child, cannot understand
the lunging, instinctive lust of her mate.   11 *I tie . . . thigh:* i.e., to tell him
that I do not want his sexual attentions and to go out and get a prostitute?
13 *Gored:* i.e., the husband, savagely compelled.   *climacteric:* critical period
of change, i.e., from sentimental, romantic, ethereal love to brute "sexual
impulse."   14 *stalls:* thrust himself into a stall or narrow place; comes to a
standstill; delays; shudders before falling.

MR. EDWARDS . . . SPIDER. *Mr. Edwards.* Jonathan Edwards (1703–58),
extraordinary colonial American philosopher, preacher, and theologian, born
in East Windsor, Connecticut (see l. 28), early interested in scientific observation
as well as religion; at the age of eleven he wrote a remarkable discourse, "Of
Insects," on phenomena concerning the flying spider. "Of all Insects," he
begins, "no one is more wonderful than the Spider especially with Respect to
their sagacity and admirable way of working"; and concludes, "We hence see
the exuberant Goodness of the Creator who hath not only Provided for all
Necessities but also for the Pleasure and Recreation of all sorts of Creatures.
. . . Even the . . . most Despicable." The spider is also to Edwards a symbol of
man considered in the strict Calvinist tradition, for "flying is their pleasure and
their Destruction"; i.e., man is at liberty to do what he likes, but his actions

The wind is westerly, 5
Where gnarled November makes the spiders fly
Into the apparitions of the sky,
They purpose nothing but their ease and die
Urgently beating east to sunrise and the sea;

What are we in the hands of the great God? 10
It was in vain you set up thorn and briar
In battle array against the fire
And treason crackling in your blood;
For the wild thorns grow tame
And will do nothing to oppose the flame; 15
Your lacerations tell the losing game
You play against a sickness past your cure.
How will the hands be strong? How will the heart endure?

A very little thing, a little worm,
Or hourglass-blazoned spider, it is said, 20
Can kill a tiger. Will the dead
Hold up his mirror and affirm
To the four winds the smell

---

inevitably lead to his deserved doom. A resolute Calvinist, Edwards defended the strict interpretation of original sin, arguing that man was absolutely selfish, totally depraved by self-interest, and utterly dependent upon divine Grace for salvation. Two of his most memorable sermons were "The Future Punishment of the Wicked Unavoidable and Intolerable" and "Sinners in the Hands of an Angry God"; during the latter, preached at Enfield, Connecticut, on July 8, 1741, his listeners hysterically believed that they were actually suspended over the pit of hell itself. In the two poems concerning Edwards, Lowell makes use of the ideas, words, and phrases of these three works, contrasting terrifying doctrine and imagery with the beautiful, compassionate, gentle nature of this brilliant and truly humble man, who all his life was completely caught up by the sovereign majesty and immediateness of the Being of God. The verse form of "Mr. Edwards" is apparently modeled on Donne's "A Nocturnall upon S. Lucies Day," see above, p. 102.

8 *They . . . die:* Cf. "Insects": ". . . Spiders and all other insects whenever the sun shines Pretty Warm . . . mount up into the air and Expand their wings to the sun and so flying for nothing but their Ease and Comfort they suffer themselves to Go that way that they find they Can Go Withe Greatest Ease And so wheresoever the Wind Pleases" (p. 9). (All references are to *Jonathan Edwards / Representative Selections*, ed. Faust and Johnson.) 9 *beating:* i.e., "Floating and sailing in the air" ("Of Insects"), moving in a zig-zag fashion (tacking against the wind). 10–15 *What . . . flame:* Cf. "Future Punishment": "What then canst thou do in the hands of God? It is vain to set the briars and thorns in battle array against the glowing flames; the points of thorns, though sharp do nothing to withstand the fire" (p. 151). 18 *How . . . endure:* Cf. Ezek. 22:14: "Can thine heart endure, or can thine hands be strong, in the days that I shall deal with thee?"—the text for "Future Punishment." 19–21 *A . . . tiger:* Cf. "Future Punishment": "A very little thing, a little worm or spider, or some such insect is able to kill thee"—the sentence that precedes the quotation noted at l. 10.

And flash of his authority? It's well
If God who holds you to the pit of hell,   25
Much as one holds a spider, will destroy,
Baffle and dissipate your soul. As a small boy

On Windsor Marsh, I saw the spider die
When thrown into the bowels of fierce fire:
   There's no long struggle, no desire   30
     To get up on its feet and fly—
      It stretches out its feet
And dies. This is the sinner's last retreat;
Yes, and no strength exerted on the heat
Then sinews the abolished will, when sick   35
And full of burning, it will whistle on a brick.

But who can plumb the sinking of that soul?
Josiah Hawley, picture yourself cast
   Into a brick-kiln where the blast
     Fans your quick vitals to a coal—   40
      If measured by a glass,
How long would it seem burning! Let there pass
A minute, ten, ten trillion; but the blaze
Is infinite, eternal: this is death,
To die and know it. This is the Black Widow, death.   45

24–26 *It's . . . spider:* Cf. "Sinners"; "O sinner! Consider the fearful
danger you are in: it is a great furnace of wrath, a wide and bottomless pit. . . .
You hang by a slender thread, with the flames of divine wrath flashing
about it, and ready every moment to singe it, and burn it asunder" (p. 165).
28–33 *spider . . . dies:* Cf. "Future Punishment": "You have often seen
a spider . . . when thrown into the midst of a fierce fire and have observed
how immediately it yields to the force of the flames. There is no long
struggle, . . no strength . . . to fly from it; but it immediately stretches forth
itself and yields" (p. 152). 38 *Josiah Hawley:* either Edwards' uncle, who,
overpowered by melancholy and despair during the "Great Awakening" (see
below, "Jonathan Edwards in Western Massachusetts," note l. 62), committed
suicide by cutting his throat, thus putting his soul in extreme jeopardy; or
Edwards' cousin, Major Joseph Hawley, who was the leader in the public
proceedings that concluded with the dismissal of Edwards from his pulpit in
Northampton. In a letter to Hawley marked by extraordinary restraint and
honesty in response to Hawley's conscience-stricken request for his cousin's
frank opinion of his part in the affair, Edwards concludes: "I think the Guilt
that lies on you in the sight of God is distinguishing, and that you may expect
to be distinguished by God's Frown unless there be true Repentance," and
signed it, "Your Kinsman and Friend" (pp. 400–01). 39–45 *brick-kiln . . .
it:* Cf. "Future Punishment": ". . . Imagine yourself to be cast into . . . the
midst of a glowing brick-kiln . . . for a quarter of an hour, full of fire. . . .
And how long would that quarter of an hour seem to you. If it were measured
by a glass [i.e., hourglass], how long would the glass seem to be running. And
after you had endured it for one minute, how overbearing would it be to you to
think that you had it to endure the other fourteen . . . that torment to the full
for twenty-four hours . . . a whole year . . . a thousand years . . . forever and

Jonathan Edwards in Western Massachusetts

Edwards' great millstone and rock
of hope has crumbled, but the square
white houses of his flock
stand in the open air,

out in the cold,   5
like sheep outside the fold.
Hope lives in doubt.
Faith is trying to do without

faith. In western Massachusetts,
I could almost feel the frontier   10
crack and disappear.
Edwards thought the world would end there.

We know how the world will end,
but where is paradise, each day farther
from the Pilgrim's blues for England   15
and the Promised Land.

Was it some country house
that seemed as if it were
Whitehall, if the Lord were there?
so nobly did he live.   20

Gardens designed
that the breath of the flowers in the wind,
or crushed underfoot,
came and went like warbling music?

---

ever! . . . That after millions and millions of ages your torment would be no
nearer to an end, than ever it was; and that you should never be delivered. . . .
This is the death threatened in the law. . . . This is dying. . . . This is to die
sensibly; to die and to know it. . . . This is to lose the soul. . . ." (pp. 146–47).

JONATHAN EDWARDS. See above, "Mr. Edwards and the Spider" and notes.
1 *millstone:* image of damnation. See Rev. 18:21: "And a mighty angel took
up a stone like a great millstone, and cast it into the sea, saying, Thus with
violence shall that great city Babylon be thrown down, and shall be found no
more." In "The End of the Wicked Contemplated by the Righteous," Edwards
uses Rev. 18:20 as his text: "Rejoice over her [i.e., Babylon], thou heaven . . .
for God hath avenged you on her." Cf. also Matt. 18:6, a text used by Edwards
to suggest Hawley's damnation.   1–2 *rock of hope:* image of salvation. Cf.
the "rock of my salvation" in Psalm 89:26. Although as a boy Edwards thought
predestination a "horrible doctrine," as a man he was "fully satisfied" with the
belief in God's justice in "choosing whom he would to eternal life, and re-
jecting whom he pleased; leaving them eternally to perish . . . tormented in
hell" (p. 58).   2 *crumbled:* Today very few accept the fearful doctrine of predestination symbolized by the *millstone* and *rock.*   3 *flock:* i.e., his parish-
ioners in Northampton, Massachusetts, where Edwards was pastor (1727–51).

Bacon's great oak grove   25
he refused to sell,
when he fell,
saying, "Why should I sell my feathers?"

Ah paradise! Edwards,
I would be afraid   30
to meet you there as a shade.
We move in different circles.

As a boy, you built a booth
in a swamp for prayer;
lying on your back,   35
you saw the spiders fly,

basking at their ease,
swimming from tree to tree—
so high, they seemed tacked to the sky.
You knew they would die.   40

Poor country Berkeley at Yale,
you saw the world was soul,
the soul of God! The soul
of Sarah Pierrepont!

25 [Francis] *Bacon:* (1561–1626) English essayist, philosopher, scientist, and judge, who was dismissed from office as Lord Chancellor in 1621 for "corruption and neglect." 32 *circles:* Cf. the various "circles" of damnation and bliss in Dante's *Divine Comedy.* 33–34 *As . . . prayer:* See *Personal Narrative,* p. 57. 39 *so high . . . sky:* Cf. "Of Insects": "I have . . . seen . . . multitudes of little shining webs and glistening Strings of a Great Length at such a height as one would think they were tack'd to the sky by one end were it not they were moving and floating. . . ." (p. 3). 41 *country Berkeley:* While still an undergraduate at Yale College, and apparently without having read Berkeley's philosophy, Edwards, a country boy, produced his own philosophical system, which was remarkably close to Berkeley's idealism. 42–43 *world . . . God:* Edwards wrote: "That which truly is the Substance of all Bodies, is the infinitely exact, and precise, and perfectly stable Idea, in God's mind, together with his stable Will . . ," for the Universe "exists nowhere, but in the Divine Mind" (Dwight, *Life,* p. 669). 44 *Sarah Pierrepont:* his wife, whom he married in 1727. When she was thirteen (and he twenty) he wrote of her: "They say there is a young lady in [New Haven] who is beloved by that Great Being, who made and rules the world, and that there are certain seasons in which this Great Being, in some way or other, comes to her and fills her mind with exceeding sweet delight, and that she hardly cares for anything, except to meditate on him. . . . She is of a wonderful sweetness, calmness and unusual benevolence of mind. . . . She will sometimes go about from place to place, singing sweetly; and seems to be always full of joy and pleasure; and no one knows for what. She loves to be alone, walking in the fields and groves, and seems to have some one invisible always conversing with her" (p. 56).

So filled with delight in the Great Being,   45
she hardly cared for anything—
walking the fields, sweetly singing,
conversing with some one invisible.

Then God's love shone in sun, moon and stars,
on earth, in the waters,   50
in the air, in the loose winds,
which used to greatly fix your mind.

Often she saw you come home from a ride
or a walk, your coat dotted with thoughts
you had pinned there   55
on slips of paper.

You gave
her Pompey, a Negro slave,
and eleven children.
Yet people were spiders   60

in your moment of glory,
at the Great Awakening—"Alas, how many
in this very meeting house are more than likely
to remember my discourse in hell!"

49–52 *Then . . . mind:* In his *Personal Narrative*, Edwards wrote: "And as I
was walking there, and looking up on the sky and clouds, there came to my mind
so sweet a sense of the glorious *majesty* and *grace* of God, that I knew not how
to express. . . . The appearance of every thing was altered; there seemed to
be. . . a calm, sweet cast, or appearance of divine glory, in almost everything;
God's excellency, his wisdom, his purity and love, seemed to appear in everything; in the sun, moon, and stars; in the clouds, and blue sky; in the grass,
flowers, trees; in the water, and all nature" (pp. 60–61).   54–57 *Often . . .
paper:* Edwards habitually wrote down every idea that came to him, pinning
the bits of paper to his coat when he was away from his study. His wife carefully collected and arranged them for him to insure that they would not be lost.
57–59 *You . . . children:* i.e., Edwards was a gentle, loving, generous husband
and father.   60 *spiders:* Cf. "Mr. Edwards and the Spider," ll. 24–27 and
note.   62 *Great Awakening:* an intense religious revival (1734–40) marked by
ecstatic "conversions" that began in Northampton and spread throughout the
whole of the seaboard colonies, an emotional experience that Edwards strongly
encouraged and studied, recording the varieties, phases, and psychological
phenomena of conversion in minute detail in "A Faithful Narrative . . . ."
62–64 *"Alas . . . hell!":* Cf. "Sinners": "But alas! instead of one, how many
is it likely will remember this discourse in hell? . . . And it would be no wonder
if some persons, that now sit here, in some seats of this meetinghouse, in health,
quiet and secure, should be there before tomorrow morning." This kind of
rhetorical question is rare in Edwards' sermons.

The meeting house remembered!   65
You stood on stilts in the air,
but you fell from your parish.
"All rising is by a winding stair."

On my pilgrimage to Northampton,
I found no relic,   70
except the round slice of an oak
you are said to have planted.

It was flesh-colored, new,
and a common piece of kindling,
only fit for burning.   75
You too must have been green once.

White wig and black coat,
all cut from one cloth,
and designed
like your mind!   80

I love you faded,
old, exiled and afraid
to leave your last flock, a dozen
Houssatonic Indian children;

afraid to leave   85
all your writing, writing, writing,
denying the Freedom of the Will.
You were afraid to be president

67 *fell:* Edwards was "publically rejected" by his church and town in 1751 because he insisted upon "supernatural conversion," not simply baptism, as "Qualifications necessary for admission to the privileges of members, in complete standing, in the Visible Church of Christ" ("Farewell Sermon," p. 188). *Fell* ironically connects Edward's fate with the text for "Sinners": "Their foot shall slide in due time" (Deut. 32:35), which he elaborates by showing the liability of all men "to fall of themselves" since God has "set them in slippery places" (Psalm 73:18).   68 "*All . . . stair*": I.e., "All rising to great place is by a winding stair," Bacon, *Essays* (No. 11), "Of Great Place" Cf. above l. 25.   84 *Houssatonic Indian:* Although he received calls from important churches in Scotland and Virginia after his dismissal, Edwards chose to settle in Stockbridge, Massachusetts, to be a missionary to the Indians, defending them as best he could from mercenary depredations by the white settlers.   87 *Freedom . . . Will:* In 1754, Edwards published an important treatise on the Freedom of the Will, making use of all the resources of modern philosophical and psychological speculation, in which he argued that although man has the liberty to do what he wills, his will is passive, wholly subject to powers outside him; but he insisted that although man's actions are necessary and corrupt, he is still responsible for them. The paradox of his *writing* and *denying* and the tone of wonder suggests the question: Did not Edwards ever wonder if his own argument, which he thought true, could be proved necessarily corrupt by his own theory?   88–89 *president of Princeton:* Edwards succeeded his son-in-law, Aaron Burr, as President of the

568

of Princeton, and wrote:
"My deffects are well known;   90
I have a constitution
peculiarly unhappy:

flaccid solids,
vapid, sizzy, scarse fluids,
causing a childish weakness,   ·   95
a low tide of spirits.

I am contemptible,
stiff and dull.

Why should I leave behind
my delight and entertainment,   100
those studies
that have swallowed up my mind?"

Tenth Muse

Tenth Muse, Oh my heart-felt Sloth,
how often now you come to my bed,
thin as a canvas in your white and red
check dresses like a table cloth,
my Dearest, settling like my shroud!   5

Yes, yes, I ought to remember Moses
jogging down on his mule from the Mount
with the old law, the old mistake,
safe in his saddlebags, and chiselled
on the stones we cannot bear or break.   10

College of New Jersey (Princeton) in January of 1758, but died five weeks later
of smallpox, after being vaccinated.   94 *sizzy:* i.e., sizy, glutinous, viscous, a
term used by eighteenth-century doctors to describe unhealthy blood.   97–
98 *I . . . dull:* Cf. "Letter to Trustees": "I have a . . . constitution . . . often
occasioning a kind of childish weakness and contemptibleness of speech,
presence, and demeanor, with a disagreeable dullness and stiffness, much
unfitting me for conversation, but more especially for the government of a
college. . . . My engaging in this business will not well consist with . . . that
course of study, which have long engaged and swallowed up my mind, and been
the chief entertainment and delight of my life" (p. 410. Lowell's ellipses and
rearrangement of syntax and structure, although they distort what Edwards
actually said, accurately suggest Edwards' consciousness of his own unworthi-
ness and sinfulness, for he was the first to affirm that he too was a spider, a
worm in the hands of an Angry God.

TENTH MUSE.   1 *Tenth:* To the Greeks and classical traditionalists, there are
nine muses. *Sloth* is usually classified as one of the seven deadly sins and is
often allegorized by medieval and Renaissance poets as a lazy monk or porter
(see *Macbeth*, II, iii), drunk, sodden with sleep, and lecherous.

Here waiting, here waiting for an answer
from this malignant surf of unopened letters,
always reaching land too late,
as fact and abstraction accumulate,
and the signature fades from the paper—   15

I like to imagine it must have been simpler
in the days of Lot,
or when Greek and Roman picturebook
gods sat combing their golden beards,
each on his private hill or mountain.   20

But I suppose even God was born
too late to trust the old religion—
all those settings out
that never left the ground,
beginning in wisdom, dying in doubt.   25

For the Union Dead

"Relinquunt Omnia Servare Rem Publicam."

The old South Boston Aquarium stands
in a Sahara of snow now. Its broken windows are boarded.
The bronze weathervane cod has lost half its scales.
The airy tanks are dry.

Once my nose crawled like a snail on the glass;   5
my hand tingled
to burst the bubbles
drifting from the noses of the cowed, compliant fish.

My hand draws back. I often sigh still
for the dark downward and vegetating kingdom   10
of the fish and reptile. One morning last March,
I pressed against the new barbed and galvanized

fence on the Boston Common. Behind their cage,
yellow dinosaur steamshovels were grunting
as they cropped up tons of mush and grass   15
to gouge their underworld garage.

FOR THE UNION DEAD. *Epigraph:* "They left everything to serve the state."

Parking spaces luxuriate like civic
sandpiles in the heart of Boston.
A girdle of orange, Puritan-pumpkin colored girders
braces the tingling Statehouse,⁣   20

shaking over the excavations, as it faces Colonel Shaw
and his bell-cheeked Negro infantry
on St. Gaudens' shaking Civil War relief,
propped by a plank splint against the garage's earthquake.

Two months after marching through Boston,   25
half the regiment was dead;
at the dedication,
William James could almost hear the bronze Negroes breathe.

Their monument sticks like a fishbone
in the city's throat.   30
Its Colonel is as lean
as a compass-needle.

He has an angry wrenlike vigilance,
a greyhound's gentle tautness;
he seems to wince at pleasure,   35
and suffocate for privacy.

He is out of bounds now. He rejoices in man's lovely,
peculiar power to choose life and die—
when he leads his black soldiers to death,
he cannot bend his back.   40

On a thousand small town New England greens,
the old white churches hold their air
of sparse, sincere rebellion; frayed flags
quilt the graveyards of the Grand Army of the Republic.

19 *orange:* i.e., the color of red lead, the standard primer paint for structural steel. 21 *Colonel Shaw:* Colonel Robert Gould Shaw, commanding officer of the 54th Massachusetts Infantry, an all-Negro regiment, who had given up his commission in his own regiment at the request of Governor Andrews to participate in an experiment in which "loneliness was certain, ridicule inevitable, and failure probable" (James—see l. 28 and note). 26 *half . . . dead:* In the unsuccessful frontal attack on Fort Wagner, the battery controlling the entrance to the harbor of Charleston, South Carolina, on the night of July 18, 1863, two-thirds of the officers and five-twelfths of the men were shot or bayoneted [James]. 28 *William . . . breathe:* William James (1842–1910), noted American philosopher and psychologist, who gave the oration at the dedication of the monument on May 31, 1897, said: "There on foot go the dark outcasts, so true to nature that one can almost hear them breathing as they march. . . . There on horseback, among them, in his very habit as he lived, sits the blue-eyed child of fortune, upon whose happy youth every divinity had smiled" (*Memories and Studies*, p. 40). 40 *he . . . back:* Shaw, at the head of his regiment, was killed on the parapet of Fort Wagner.

The stone statues of the abstract Union Soldier   45
grow slimmer and younger each year—
wasp-waisted, they doze over muskets
and muse through their sideburns . . .

Shaw's father wanted no monument
except the ditch,   50
where his son's body was thrown
and lost with his "niggers."

The ditch is nearer.
There are no statues for the last war here;
on Boylston Street, a commercial photograph   55
shows Hiroshima boiling

over a Mosler Safe, the "Rock of Ages"
that survived the blast. Space is nearer.
When I crouch to my television set,
the drained faces of Negro school-children rise like balloons. 60

Colonel Shaw
is riding on his bubble,
he waits
for the blessèd break.

The Aquarium is gone. Everywhere,   65
giant finned cars nose forward like fish;
a savage servility
slides by on grease.

45 *The . . . Soldier:* Cf. ". . . and long after the abstract [epitomized] soldier's
monuments have been reared on every village green, we have chosen to take
Robert Shaw and his regiment as the first soldier's monument to be raised to a
particular set of comparatively undistinguished men" (James, p. 40).   49–52
Shaw's . . . niggers: Cf. "His body, half stripped of its clothing, and the
corpses of his dauntless Negroes were flung into one common trench together,
and the sand was shoveled over them, without a stake or stone to signalize
the spot. In death as in life, then, the Fifty-fourth bore witness to the brotherhood of man" (p. 54).   53 *The . . . nearer:* The poet seems to respond to
James's peroration: "What we really need the poet's and orator's help to keep
alive is not, then, the common gregarious courage which Robert Shaw showed
when he marched with you, men of the Seventh Regiment. It is that more
lonely courage which he showed when he dropped his warm commission in
the glorious Second to head your dubious fortunes, Negroes of the Fifty-fourth.
That lonely kind of courage [civic courage . . . to "resist enthroned abuse"]
is the kind of valor to which the monuments of nations should most of all be
reared, for the survival of the fittest has not bred it into the bone of human
beings as it has bred military valor. . . . The deadliest enemies of nations are
not their foreign foes; they always dwell within their borders. And from these
internal enemies civilization is always in need of being saved" (James, pp. 57–
58). Cf. the ominous *savage servility*, l. 67.

INDEX OF AUTHORS, TITLES, AND FIRST LINES

Authors' names are printed in capitals, titles in italic, first lines in roman. When the first line of a poem supplies the title, only a first-line entry is given.

574

575

576

578

B 9
C 0
D 1
E 2
F 3
G 4
H 5
I 6
J 7
8